# PROGRAMMING IN ADA

## Third Edition

### J.G.P. Barnes

Alsys Ltd

ADDISON-WESLEY
PUBLISHING
COMPANY

Wokingham, England · Reading, Massachusetts · Menlo Park, California
New York · Don Mills, Ontario · Amsterdam · Bonn
Sydney · Singapore · Tokyo · Madrid · San Juan

Cover designed by Crayon Design of Henley-on-Thames and printed by The Riverside Printing Co. (Reading) Ltd. The portrait appearing on the cube is of Ada, Countess of Lovelace, who is acknowledged to be the world's first programmer. It is adapted from the line-drawing that appeared on the cover of the previous editions.
Typeset by Quorum Technical Services Ltd, Cheltenham.
Printed and bound in Great Britain by Mackays of Chatham PLC, Chatham, Kent

First printed 1989. Reprinted 1989.


**British Library Cataloguing in Publication Data**
Barnes, J.G.P. (John Gilbert Presslie)
   Programming in ADA — 3rd ed. — (International
computer science series).
   1. Computer systems. Programming languages:
ADA language
   I. Title   II. Series
   005.13'3

   ISBN 0–201–17566–5

**Library of Congress Cataloging in Publication Data**
Barnes, J.G.P. (John Gilbert Presslie)
   Programming in ADA / J.G.P. Barnes — 3rd ed.
      p.    cm. — (International computer science series)
   Includes index.
   ISBN 0–201–17566–5
   1. Ada (Computer program language)   I. Title.   II. Series.
QA76.73.A35B37      1989
005.13'3—dc19                                                    88–31878
                                                                       CIP

# L▯GRAMMING IN ADA
## Third Edition

)9

000

# INTERNATIONAL COMPUTER SCIENCE SERIES

*Consulting editors*     **A D McGettrick**   University of Strathclyde

**J van Leeuwen**   University of Utrecht

## SELECTED TITLES IN THE SERIES

UNIX® is a trademark of AT & T

*To* BARBARA

# Foreword

In May 1979 came the eagerly awaited announcement by the United States High Order Language Working Group, that 'Green is Ada'.

We were all expecting it in our team and were thus not surprised, but the announcement was certainly an enormous pleasure for all of us. At that time we all considered the preliminary version of Ada to be perfect. It may sound strange, considering the amount of revision that was done in the next fifteen months leading to the July 1980 Ada definition. But there is an easy explanation. In order to design anything you must believe in what you design, you must be continually examining the interweaving of all the features. Certainly, many decisions are the result of compromises between conflicting goals, but after rehearsing time and time again the arguments leading to these compromises you end up by integrating them into the basic assumptions of your design. And so it is not surprising that the result should appear to be the perfect answer.

Clearly, further progress can only come by a reappraisal of implicit assumptions underlying certain compromises. Here is the major contradiction in any design work. On the one hand, one can only reach an harmonious integration of several features by immersing oneself into the logic of the existing parts; it is only in this way that one can achieve a perfect combination. On the other hand, this perception of perfection, and the implied acceptance of certain unconscious assumptions, will prevent further progress.

In the design of Ada, John Barnes has certainly shown a unique ability to switch appropriately between acceptance and reappraisal. In May 1979, John was as proud as anyone else in the design team about our achievement. But, even by the early days of June, John was already reflective, giving a sharp, even severe look to the Ada tasking model as if he had had nothing to do with its design. He authored the first Language study note, of a series of two hundred, called 'Problems with tasking'. The note outlined ten major problems perceived in the preliminary Ada tasking facilities. These problems occupied our team for several months in the Ada revision, and satisfactory solutions could then be given to these ten issues in the final Ada version. In my own case it undoubtedly took me much more time to become objective about preliminary Ada and I certainly was initially upset by John's sacrilege. But with time I have learned to value enormously this kind of interaction with John.

*Programming in Ada* is thus written by one of the key members of the Ada language design team, by someone who understands all facets of the design of the language, both in a constructive and in a critical manner. I am confident that – with humour as usual – John's enthusiasms and understanding of the spirit of the language will be passed on to readers of this book.

Versailles
May 1981                                                                Jean D. Ichbiah

# Preface to the Third Edition

The third edition of this book has not been prompted by any specific event but rather a general feeling that sufficient feedback had been received from the growing use of Ada to make a thorough revision worthwhile.

Before deciding upon the revisions I asked a number of those who had been using the book as a teaching text for their suggestions. Their answers were very helpful although inevitably they were not without conflict. At the end of the day the decisions were mine and I apologize if I have not been able to exactly meet everyone's requirements. Perhaps the most important piece of advice was not to spoil the book by unnecessary change. I hope I have at least succeeded in this.

Users of earlier editions might find it helpful to have a brief list of the major changes.

- Chapter 2 has been considerably enlarged. It now gives an overview of almost all of the language except tasking. In particular it contains enough of generics and input–output to enable the reader to write complete programs right from the beginning. This will be helpful to those who wish to experiment with some of the exercises using a compiler.

- A number of existing sections were rather long and have been subdivided and rearranged so that the reader is spared daunting lumps of material without the relief of some exercises. Section 6.2 on array types and aggregates has thus been split and the material on aggregates (which I always find difficult) has been rewritten with, it is hoped, much greater clarity and rationale. Section 11.1 on discriminated records was also long and has been subdivided with the material on default discriminants rearranged to form a new section. The very long Section 14.4 on the select statement has also been subdivided.

- A number of new sections have been added. Section 6.5 discusses arrays of arrays and slices which were barely covered before. Section 10.3 contains material on the costs of the checks which are required to raise the predefined exceptions. Section 13.4 addresses the use of generics for the mathematical library; much of the discussion is around the draft standard for elementary functions which is being discussed by ISO at the time of writing. Section 16.4 adds further material of a general nature; it discusses the composition of large scale programs from individual components with particular regard to the import and export of entities and the rules for compilation and recompilation.

- Significant additional material has also been added on generic subprogram parameters, fixed point types and the model of the main program which were not fully covered before.

- Since writing the previous edition a number of aspects of the language have been clarified by the publication of Ada Issues as explained in more detail in Chapter 1. This third edition has been revised to conform to the current interpretation of the language and references to relevant approved Issues have been inserted where appropriate.

- Finally, the text has been thoroughly scrutinized for ambiguities, obscurities and errors and polished where necessary. Many additional exercises and examples have also been added where they give additional insight into the use of the language.

It is impossible to remember all those who have helped with this edition in various ways. However, I would particularly like to thank Morteza Anvari, Rodney Bown, Don Greenwell, Charlene Hayden, Stuart Handley, Floyd Holliday, Kit Lester, Fred Long, Peter Martin, Charles Mooney, Ruth Rudolph and Stephen Sangwine for their helpful suggestions on the scope of revision. I would also like to thank Angel Alvarez and Vincent Amiot (who translated the second edition into Spanish and French respectively) for their many comments. Then, I must thank my colleague Alun Tlusty-Sheen with whom I have given many Ada courses for numerous comments and suggestions. Thanks are also due to Vittorio Frigo and Ron Pierce for spotting some nasty bugs, to Graham Hodgson for advice on the mathematical library and to Alison Wearing for many detailed suggestions on improvements to the clarity of the text. Next, I must thank my daughter Janet for suggesting a number of the new exercises and examples and especially for spotting that her ageing father got them wrong on a first writing. Finally, I must thank my wife Barbara for her valued efforts in typing much of the text.

I would also like to continue to record the names of those whose copious comments helped with the second edition. They were Angel Alvarez, Randall Barron, Theodore Chaplin, Donald Clarson, Edward Colbert, Ian Mearns, Mike Tedd and Jo Whitfield.

The original intent of this book was as a comprehensive text to teach the Ada language. It has, however, also found much favour as a friendly reference book. Although these uses conflict I hope that this new edition will be found to be a significant improvement for both purposes.

Reading
December 1988                                                J. G. P. Barnes

# Preface to the First Edition

This book is about Ada, the new and powerful programming language originally developed on behalf of the US Department of Defense for use in embedded systems. Typical of such systems are those for process control, missile guidance or even the sequencing of a dishwasher. Historically these systems have been programmed in languages such as JOVIAL, CORAL 66 and RTL/2.

Based on Pascal, Ada is the first practical language to bring together important features such as data abstraction, multitasking, exception handling, encapsulation and generics. Although originally intended for embedded systems, it is a general purpose language and could, in time, supersede FORTRAN and even COBOL. The political and technical forces behind Ada suggest it will become an important language in the 1980s.

My purpose in writing this book is to present an overall description of Ada. Some knowledge of the principles of programming is assumed and an acquaintance with Pascal would be helpful but is not strictly necessary. The book is written in a tutorial style with numerous examples and exercises. I have also tried to explain the rationale behind many of the features of the language because this not only makes the discussion of more interest but also makes the facts easier to remember. Wherever possible I have tried to use examples which do not assume a particular application background; they are mostly drawn from parallels with normal human life or from mathematics which, after all, is the cornerstone of science and engineering. I hope the reader does not find the occasional attempt at humour misplaced; learning a programming language can be dull and any means of easing the burden seems worthwhile.

I would like to take this opportunity to thank those who directly or indirectly have helped me to write this book. First, I must acknowledge the US Department of Defense for permission to use material from the Ada *Language Reference Manual*. Then, I must acknowledge Jean Ichbiah and Robert Firth with whom I have had the pleasure of giving Ada courses in various parts of the world. These courses not only helped me to gain a useful perspective of the language as a whole but also provided the origins of some of the examples. Next, I must thank Andrew McGettrick for a great number of useful comments on the original draft and for spurring me on to completion with many helpful suggestions. I must also thank my

colleagues on the UK Ada Study for their valued comments. Finally, I am
deeply grateful to my wife for her untiring efforts in typing the manuscript;
without her assistance the labour would have been much prolonged.

Reading
April 1981                                              J. G. P. Barnes

# Contents

# Chapter 1
# Introduction

---

---

Ada is a high level programming language originally sponsored by the US Department of Defense for use in the so-called embedded system application area. (An embedded system is one in which the computer is an integral part of a larger system such as a chemical plant, missile or dishwasher.) In this introductory chapter we briefly trace the development of Ada, its place in the overall language scene and the general structure of the remainder of this book.

## 1.1  History

The story of Ada goes back to about 1974 when the United States Department of Defense realized that it was spending far too much on software. It carried out a detailed analysis of how its costs were distributed over the various application areas and discovered that over half of them were directly attributed to embedded systems.

Further analysis was directed towards the programming languages in use in the various areas. It was discovered that COBOL was the universal standard for data processing and FORTRAN was a similar standard for scientific and engineering computation. Although these languages were not modern, the fact that they were uniformly applied in their respective areas meant that unnecessary and expensive duplication was avoided.

The situation with regard to embedded systems was, however, quite different. The number of languages in use was enormous. Not only did each of the three Armed Services have their own favourite high level languages, but they also used many assembly languages as well. Moreover, the high level languages had spawned variants. It seemed that successive contracts had encouraged the development of special versions aimed at

1

different applications. The net result was that a lot of money was being spent on an unnecessary number of compilers. There were also all the additional costs of training and maintenance associated with a lack of standardization.

It was therefore realized that standardization had to be established in the embedded system area if the costs were to be contained. The ultimate goal was, of course, a single language. In the short term a list of interim approved languages was introduced. This consisted of CMS-2Y, CMS-2M, SPL/1, TACPOL, JOVIAL J3, JOVIAL J73 and of course COBOL and FORTRAN for the other areas.

The first step in moving towards the development of a single standard was the writing of a document outlining the requirements. The first version was known as Strawman and was published in early 1975. After receiving comments from various sources it was refined and became Woodenman. A further iteration produced Tinman in June 1976. This was quite a specific document and identified the functionality required of the language.

At this stage many existing languages were evaluated against Tinman, partly to see whether one of them could be used as the ultimate standard and partly to invoke detailed evaluation of the requirements themselves. As one might expect, none of the existing languages proved satisfactory; on the other hand the general impression was gained that a single language based on state-of-the-art concepts could be developed to meet the requirements.

The evaluation classified the existing languages into three categories which can be paraphrased as

| | |
|---|---|
| 'not appropriate' | These languages were obsolete or addressed the wrong area and were not to be considered further. This category included FORTRAN and CORAL 66. |
| 'not inappropriate' | These languages were also unsatisfactory as they stood but had some interesting features which could be looked at for inspiration. This category included RTL/2 and LIS. |
| 'recommended bases' | These were the three languages Pascal, PL/I and Algol 68 and were seen as possible starting points for the design of the final language. |

At this point the requirements document was revised and reorganized to give Ironman. Proposals were then invited from contractors to design a new language starting from one of the recommended bases. Seventeen proposals were received and four were chosen to go ahead in parallel and in competition. The four contractors with their colour codings were CII Honeywell Bull (Green), Intermetrics (Red), Softech (Blue) and SRI International (Yellow). The colour codings were introduced so that the resulting initial designs could be compared anonymously and hopefully therefore without bias.

The initial designs were delivered in early 1978 and many groups all over the world considered their relative merit. The DoD judged that the Green and Red designs showed more promise than Blue and Yellow and so the latter were eliminated.

The development then entered its second phase and the two remaining contractors were given a further year in which to refine their designs. The requirements were also revised in the light of feedback from the initial designs and became the final document Steelman[1].

The final choice of language was made on 2 May 1979 when the Green language developed at CII Honeywell Bull by an international team led by Jean Ichbiah was declared the winner.

The DoD then announced that the new language would be known as Ada in honour of Augusta Ada Byron, Countess of Lovelace (1815–52). Ada, the daughter of Lord Byron, was the assistant and patron of Charles Babbage and worked on his mechanical analytical engine. In a very real sense she was therefore the world's first programmer.

The development of Ada then entered a third phase. The purpose of this was to expose the language to a significant cross section of eventual users in order to allow them to comment on its suitability for their needs. Various courses were given in the USA and Europe and many teams then settled down to carry out their evaluations. Some 80 general reports were written and presented at a conference in Boston in October 1979. The general conclusion was that Ada was good but a few areas needed further refinement. In addition, nearly a thousand shorter technical language issue reports were received. After all these reports had been considered the preliminary Ada design was revised and this resulted in the publication in July 1980 of the first definitive version of the language. It was then proposed to the American National Standards Institute (ANSI) as a standard.

The ANSI standardization process occupied over two years and resulted in a certain number of changes to Ada. Most of these were small but often of subtle significance especially for the compiler writer. The ANSI standard *Language Reference Manual* (*LRM*) was finally published in January 1983 and it is this edition which forms the subject of this book[2].

ANSI then proposed to the International Standards Organization that Ada become an ISO standard. This resulted in the establishment of an ISO working group which performed the required activities. Ada became ISO standard 8652 in 1987. During this process (and since) a large number of technical queries were and continue to be analysed by the so-called Ada Rapporteur Group (ARG) whose recommendations are passed for approval to both the ISO working group and the USDoD Ada Board, a federal advisory committee established to help the Ada Joint Program Office in its deliberations on how to reap the benefits of Ada. These recommendations are known as Ada Issues (AIs) and come in various categories.

The *LRM* is a complex document and it is not surprising that the ARG identified a number of gaps, ambiguities, inconsistencies, and the occasional plain error. Most of these are subtle and concern fine detail that will rarely impact on the average programmer. However, a few are of note, and they are referred to where appropriate as, for example, AI-6. These references have been inserted so that the reader will not be confused by apparent contradictions between the *LRM* and this book. The AIs are in the public domain, and are available through the various national standards bodies, ISO, the Ada Information Clearinghouse and other Ada related organizations.

The ISO working group is, at the time of writing, considering a number of secondary standards relating to Ada. An important one is that relating to mathematical functions and the current draft is thus treated here very much as if it were part of the language standard.

However, it should not be thought that Ada is just another programming language. Ada is about Software Engineering and by analogy with other branches of engineering it can be seen that there are two main problems with the development of software: the need to reuse software components as much as possible and the need to establish disciplined ways of working.

As a language, Ada largely solves the problem of writing reusable software components (or at least through its excellent ability to prescribe interfaces, provides an enabling technology in which reusable software can be written).

Concerning the establishment of a disciplined way of working, it was realized that the language is just one component, although an important one, of the toolkit that every programmer (and his manager) should have available. It was therefore felt that additional benefit would be achieved if a uniform programming environment could also be established. And so, in parallel with the language design, a series of requirements documents for an Ada Programming Support Environment (APSE) were developed. These were entitled Sandman, Pebbleman and finally Stoneman[3]. These documents are less detailed than the corresponding language documents because the state-of-the-art in this area was (and perhaps still is) in its infancy. A number of grandiose attempts to build an APSE were undertaken in the early 1980s. They failed for a number of reasons – the requirements were not well understood and moreover the hardware technology used for the larger projects, which would benefit most from an APSE, started to undergo a transformation from a central machine with dumb terminals to a distributed intelligent environment requiring a rather different approach. The current situation (1988) is that a number of smaller environment systems are now emerging with longer term efforts being focused on the establishment of Public Tool Interfaces which are intended to allow tools to be moved between the different environments. But that is another story outside the scope of this book.

The failure of the early APSEs coupled with the difficulties in ironing out the problems during ANSI standardization plus the sheer effort required to develop good Ada compilers cast gloom on the development of Ada which is thankfully over. Excellent production quality Ada compilers are now available for all major architectures and millions of lines of real Ada applications have been written. It is now clear that Ada is living up to its promise of providing a language which can reduce the cost of both the initial development of software and its later maintenance. Even if Ada is seen as just another programming language, it reaches parts of the software development process that other languages do not reach.

## 1.2   Technical background

The evolution of programming languages has apparently occurred in a
rather *ad hoc* fashion, but with hindsight it is now possible to see three
major advances. Each advance seems to be associated with the introduction of a level of abstraction which removes unnecessary and harmful detail
from the program.

The first advance occurred in the early 1950s with high level
languages such as FORTRAN and Autocode which introduced 'expression
abstraction'. It thus became possible to write statements such as

    X=A+B(I)

so that the use of the machine registers to evaluate the expression was
completely hidden from the programmer. In these early languages the
expression abstraction was not perfect since there were somewhat arbitrary
constraints on the complexity of expressions; subscripts had to take a
particularly simple form for instance. Later languages such as Algol 60
removed such constraints and completed the abstraction.

The second advance concerned 'control abstraction'. The prime
example was Algol 60 which took a remarkable step forward; no language
since then has made such an impact on later developments. The point
about control abstraction is that the flow of control is structured and
individual control points do not have to be named or numbered. Thus we
write

    **if** X=Y **then** P:=Q **else** A:=B

and the compiler generates the gotos and labels which would have to be
explicitly used in languages such as FORTRAN. The imperfection of early
expression abstraction was repeated with control abstraction. In this case
the obvious flaw was the horrid Algol 60 switch which has now been
replaced by the case statement of languages such as Pascal. (The earlier
case clause of Algol 68 had its own problems.)

The third advance which is now occurring is 'data abstraction'. This
means separating the details of the representation of data from the abstract
operations defined upon the data.

Older languages take a very simple view of data types. In all cases
the data is directly described in numerical terms. Thus if the data to be
manipulated is not really numerical (it could be traffic light colours) then
some mapping of the abstract type must be made by the programmer into a
numerical type (usually integer). This mapping is purely in the mind of the
programmer and does not appear in the written program except perhaps as
a comment. It is probably a consequence of this fact that software libraries
have not emerged except in numerical analysis. Numerical algorithms,
such as those for finding eigenvalues of a matrix, are directly concerned
with manipulating numbers and so these languages, whose data values are
numbers, have proved appropriate. The point is that the languages provide
the correct abstract values in this case only. In other cases, libraries are not
successful because there is unlikely to be agreement on the required

mappings. Indeed different situations may best be served by different mappings and these mappings pervade the whole program. A change in mapping usually requires a complete rewrite of the program.

Pascal introduced a certain amount of data abstraction as instanced by the enumeration type. Enumeration types allow us to talk about the traffic light colours in their own terms without our having to know how they are represented in the computer. Moreover, they prevent us from making an important class of programming errors – accidentally mixing traffic lights with other abstract types such as the names of fish. When all such types are described in the program as numerical types, such errors can occur.

Another form of data abstraction concerns visibility. It has long been recognized that the traditional block structure of Algol 60 is not adequate. For example, it is not possible in Algol 60 to write two procedures to operate on some common data and make the procedures accessible without also making the data directly accessible. Many languages have provided control of visibility through separate compilation; this technique is adequate for medium-sized systems but since the separate compilation facility usually depends upon some external system, total control of visibility is not gained. The module of Modula is an example of an appropriate construction.

Another language which made an important contribution to the development of data abstraction is Simula 67 with its concept of class. Many other experimental languages too numerous to mention have also made detailed contributions.

Ada seems to be the first practical language to bring together the various categories of data abstraction. We are probably too close to the current scene to achieve a proper perspective. There are no doubt several imperfections in Ada data abstraction just as FORTRAN expression abstraction and Algol 60 control abstraction were imperfect. However, Ada is an important advance and offers the possibility of writing significant reusable software libraries for areas other than numerical analysis. It should therefore encourage the creation of a software components industry.

## 1.3   Structure and objectives of this book

Learning a programming language is a bit like learning to drive a car. Certain key things have to be learnt before any real progress is possible. Although we need not know how to use the windscreen washer, nevertheless we must at least be able to start the engine, engage gears, steer and brake. So it is with programming languages. We do not need to know all about Ada before we can write useful programs but quite a lot must be learnt. Moreover many virtues of Ada become apparent only when writing large programs just as many virtues of a Rolls-Royce are not apparent if we only use it to drive to the local shop.

This book is not an introduction to programming but an overall description of programming in Ada. It is assumed that the reader will have a significant knowledge of programming in some high level language. A knowledge of Pascal would be helpful but is certainly not necessary.

It should also be noted that this book strives to remain neutral regarding methods of program design and should therefore prove useful whatever techniques are used. However, certain features of Ada naturally align themselves with different design concepts such as Functional Decomposition (based on control flow) and Object Oriented Design (based on data abstraction) and will be mentioned as appropriate.

Chapter 2 gives a brief overview of some Ada concepts and is designed to give the reader a feel of the style and objectives of Ada. The rest of the book is in a tutorial style and introduces topics in a fairly straightforward sequence. By Chapter 7 we will have covered the traditional facilities of small languages such as Pascal. The remaining chapters cover modern and exciting material associated with data abstraction, programming in the large and parallel processing.

Most sections contain exercises. It is important that the reader does most, if not all, of these since they are an integral part of the discussion and later sections often use the results of earlier exercises. Solutions to all the exercises will be found at the end of the book.

Most chapters conclude with a short checklist of key points to be remembered. Although incomplete, these checklists should help to consolidate understanding. Furthermore the reader is encouraged to refer to the syntax in Appendix 4 which is organized to correspond to the order in which the topics are introduced.

This book covers all aspects of Ada but does not explore every pathological situation. Its purpose is to teach the reader the effect of and intended use of the features of Ada. In two areas the discussion is incomplete; these are machine dependent programming and input–output. Machine dependent programming (as its name implies) is so dependent upon the particular implementation that only a brief overview seems appropriate. Input–output, although important, does not introduce new concepts but is rather a mass (mess?) of detail; again a simple overview is presented. Further details of these areas can be found in the *Language Reference Manual* (*LRM*) which is referred to from time to time.

Various appendices are provided in order to make this book reasonably self-contained; they are mostly based upon material drawn from the *Language Reference Manual*. Access to the *LRM*, which is the official definition of Ada, is recommended but should not be absolutely essential.

## 1.4 References

1    Defense Advanced Research Projects Agency (1978). *Department of Defense Requirements for High Order Computer Programming Languages – 'STEELMAN'*. Arlington, Virginia.

2    United States Department of Defense (1983). *Reference Manual for the Ada Programming Language* (ANSI/MIL-STD-1815A). Washington DC.

3    Defense Advanced Research Projects Agency (1980). *Department of Defense Requirements for Ada Programming Support Environments – 'STONEMAN'*. Arlington, Virginia.

# Chapter 2
# Ada Concepts

In this chapter we present a brief overview of some of the goals, concepts and features of Ada. Enough material is also given to enable the reader to create a framework in which the exercises and other fragments of program can be executed if desired, before all the required topics (such as input–output) are discussed in depth.

## 2.1  Key goals

Ada is a large language since it addresses many important issues relevant to the programming of practical systems in the real world. It is, for instance, much larger than Pascal, which, unless extended in some way, is really only suitable for training purposes (for which it was designed) and for small personal programs. Some of the key issues in Ada are

- Readability – it is recognized that professional programs are read much more often than they are written. It is important therefore to avoid an over-terse notation such as in APL which, although allowing a program to be written down quickly, makes it almost impossible to be read except perhaps by the original author soon after it was written.

- Strong typing – this ensures that each object has a clearly defined set of values and prevents confusion between logically distinct concepts. As a consequence many errors are detected by the compiler which in other languages (such as C) would have led to an executable but incorrect program.

9

- Programming in the large – mechanisms for encapsulation, separate compilation and library management are necessary for the writing of portable and maintainable programs of any size.

- Exception handling – it is a fact of life that programs of consequence are rarely perfect. It is necessary to provide a means whereby a program can be constructed in a layered and partitioned way so that the consequences of unanticipated events in one part can be contained.

- Data abstraction – as mentioned earlier, extra portability and maintainability can be obtained if the details of the representation of data can be kept separate from the specifications of the logical operations on the data.

- Tasking – for many applications it is important that the program be conceived as a series of parallel activities rather than just as a single sequence of actions. Building appropriate facilities into a language rather than adding them via calls to an operating system gives better portability and reliability.

- Generic units – in many cases the logic of part of a program is independent of the types of the values being manipulated. A mechanism is therefore necessary for the creation of related pieces of program from a single template. This is particularly useful for the creation of libraries.

## 2.2   Overall structure

One of the most important objectives of Software Engineering is to reuse existing pieces of program so that the effort of detailed new coding is kept to a minimum. The concept of a program library naturally emerges and an important aspect of a programming language is therefore its ability to express how to use the items in this library.

Ada recognizes this situation and introduces the concept of library units. A complete Ada program is conceived as a main program (itself a library unit) which calls upon the services of other library units. These library units can be thought of as forming the outermost lexical layer of the total program.

The main program takes the form of a procedure of an appropriate name. The service library units can be subprograms (procedures or functions) but they are more likely to be packages. A package is a group of related items such as subprograms but may be other entities as well.

Suppose we wish to write a program to print out the square root of some number such as 2.5. We can expect various library units to be available to provide us with a means of computing square roots and producing output. Our job is merely to write a main program to use these services as we wish.

For the sake of argument we will suppose that the square root can be obtained by calling a function in our library whose name is SQRT. In addition we will suppose that our library includes a package called

SIMPLE_IO containing various simple input–output facilities. These facilities might include procedures for reading numbers, printing numbers, printing strings of characters and so on.

Our program might look like

```
with SQRT, SIMPLE_IO;
procedure PRINT_ROOT is
    use SIMPLE_IO;
begin
    PUT(SQRT(2.5));
end PRINT_ROOT;
```

The program is written as a procedure called PRINT_ROOT preceded by a with clause giving the names of the library units which it wishes to use. The body of the procedure contains the single statement

```
PUT(SQRT(2.5));
```

which calls the procedure PUT in the package SIMPLE_IO with a parameter which in turn is the result of calling the function SQRT with the parameter 2.5.

Writing

```
use SIMPLE_IO;
```

gives us immediate access to the facilities in the package SIMPLE_IO. If we had omitted this use clause we would have had to write

```
SIMPLE_IO.PUT(SQRT(2.5));
```

in order to indicate where PUT was to be found.

We can make our program more useful by making it read in the number whose square root we require. It might then become

```
with SQRT, SIMPLE_IO;
procedure PRINT_ROOT is
    use SIMPLE_IO;
    X: FLOAT;
begin
    GET(X);
    PUT(SQRT(X));
end PRINT_ROOT;
```

The overall structure of the procedure is now clearer. Between **is** and **begin** we can write declarations and between **begin** and **end** we write statements. Broadly speaking, declarations introduce the entities we wish to manipulate and statements indicate the sequential actions to be performed.

We have now introduced a variable X of type FLOAT which is a predefined language type. Values of this type are a set of certain floating point numbers and the declaration of X indicates that X can have values only from this set. In our example a value is assigned to X by calling the procedure GET which is also in our package SIMPLE_IO.

Some small-scale details should be noted. The various statements and declarations all terminate with a semicolon; this is unlike some other languages such as Algol and Pascal where semicolons are separators rather than terminators. The program contains various identifiers such as **procedure**, PUT and X. These fall into two categories. A few (63 in fact) such as **procedure** and **is** are used to indicate the structure of the program; they are reserved and can be used for no other purpose. All others, such as PUT and X, can be used for whatever purpose we desire. Some of these, notably FLOAT in our example, have a predefined meaning but we can nevertheless reuse them if we so wish although it might be confusing to do so. For clarity in this book we use lower case bold letters for the reserved identifiers and upper case letters for the others. This is purely a notational convenience; the language rules do not distinguish the two cases except when we consider the manipulation of characters themselves. Note also how the underline character is used to break up long identifiers into meaningful parts.

Finally, observe that the name of the procedure, PRINT_ROOT, is repeated between the final **end** and the terminating semicolon. This is optional but is recommended in order to clarify the overall structure although this is obvious in a small example such as this.

Our program is still very simple; it might be more useful to enable it to cater for a whole series of numbers and print out each answer on a separate line. We could stop the program somewhat arbitrarily by giving it a value of zero.

```
with SQRT, SIMPLE_IO;
procedure PRINT_ROOTS is
    use SIMPLE_IO;
    X: FLOAT;
begin
    PUT("Roots of various numbers");
    NEW_LINE(2);
    loop
        GET(X);
        exit when X = 0.0;
        PUT(" Root of ");
        PUT(X);
        PUT(" is ");
        if X < 0.0 then
            PUT("not calculable");
        else
            PUT(SQRT(X));
        end if;
        NEW_LINE;
    end loop;
    NEW_LINE;
    PUT("Program finished");
    NEW_LINE;
end PRINT_ROOTS;
```

The output has been enhanced by the calls of further procedures NEW_LINE and PUT in the package SIMPLE_IO. A call of NEW_LINE will output the number of new lines specified by the parameter (which is of the predefined type INTEGER); the procedure NEW_LINE has been written in such a way that if no parameter is supplied then a default value of one is assumed. There are also calls of PUT with a string as argument. This is in fact a different procedure from the one which prints the number X. The compiler knows which is which because of the different types of parameters. Having more than one procedure with the same name is known as overloading. Note also the form of the string; this is a situation where the case of the letters does matter.

Various new control structures are also introduced. The statements between **loop** and **end loop** are repeated until the condition X = 0.0 in the **exit** statement is found to be true; when this is so the loop is finished and we immediately carry on after **end loop**. We also check that X is not negative; if it is we output the message 'not calculable' rather than attempting to call SQRT. This is done by the if statement; if the condition between **if** and **then** is true, then the statements between **then** and **else** are executed, otherwise those between **else** and **end if** are executed.

The general bracketing structure should be observed; **loop** is matched by **end loop** and **if** by **end if**. All the control structures of Ada have this closed form rather than the open form of Pascal which can lead to poorly structured and incorrect programs.

We will now consider in outline the possible general form of the function SQRT and the package SIMPLE_IO that we have been using.

The function SQRT will have a structure similar to that of our main program; the major difference will be the existence of parameters.

```
function SQRT(F: FLOAT) return FLOAT is
    R: FLOAT;
begin
    -- compute value of SQRT(F) in R
    return R;
end SQRT;
```

We see here the description of the formal parameters (in this case only one) and the type of the result. The details of the calculation are represented by the comment which starts with a double hyphen. The return statement is the means by which the result of the function is indicated. Note the distinction between a function which returns a result and is called as part of an expression and a procedure which does not have a result and is called as a single statement.

The package SIMPLE_IO will be in two parts: the specification which describes its interface to the outside world, and the body which contains the details of how it is implemented. If it just contained the procedures that we have used, its specification might be

```
package SIMPLE_IO is
    procedure GET(F: out FLOAT);
    procedure PUT(F: in FLOAT);
```

```
    procedure PUT(S: in STRING);
    procedure NEW_LINE(N: in INTEGER:= 1);
end SIMPLE_IO;
```

The parameter of GET is an **out** parameter because the effect of calling GET as in

```
GET(X);
```

is to transmit a value out from the procedure to the actual parameter X. The other parameters are all **in** parameters because the value goes in to the procedures.

Only a part of the procedures occurs in the package specification; this part is known as the procedure specification and just gives enough information to enable the procedures to be called.

We see also the two overloaded specifications of PUT, one with a parameter of type FLOAT and the other with a parameter of type STRING. Finally, note how the default value of 1 for the parameter of NEW_LINE is indicated.

The package body for SIMPLE_IO will contain the full procedure bodies plus any other supporting material needed for their implementation and which is naturally hidden from the outside user. In vague outline it might look like

```
with TEXT_IO;
package body SIMPLE_IO is
    ...
    procedure GET(F: out FLOAT) is
        ...
    begin
        ...
    end GET;
    -- other procedures similarly
end SIMPLE_IO;
```

The with clause shows that the implementation of the procedures in SIMPLE_IO uses the more general package TEXT_IO. It should also be noticed how the full body of GET repeats the procedure specification which was given in the corresponding package specification. (The procedure specification is the bit up to but not including **is**.) Note that the package TEXT_IO really exists whereas SIMPLE_IO is a figment of our imagination made up for the purpose of our example. We will say more about TEXT_IO in Section 2.6.

The example in this section has briefly revealed some of the overall structure and control statements of Ada. One purpose of this section has been to stress that the idea of packages is one of the most important concepts in Ada. A program should be conceived as a number of components which provide services to and receive services from each other. In the next few chapters we will of necessity be dealing with the small-scale features of Ada but in doing so we should not lose sight of the overall structure which we will return to in Chapter 8.

Perhaps this is an appropriate point to mention the special package STANDARD. This is a package which exists in every implementation and contains the declarations of all the predefined identifiers such as FLOAT and INTEGER. We can assume access to STANDARD automatically and do not have to give its name in a with clause. It is discussed in detail in Appendix 2.

---

*Exercise 2.2*

1    In practice it is likely that the function SQRT will not be in the library on its own but in a package along with other mathematical functions. Suppose this package has the identifier SIMPLE_MATHS and other functions are LOG, LN, EXP, SIN and COS. By analogy with the specification of SIMPLE_IO, write the specification of such a package. How would our program PRINT_ROOTS need to be changed?

---

## 2.3 Errors and exceptions

We introduce this topic by considering what would have happened in the example in the previous section if we had not tested for a negative value of X and consequently called SQRT with a negative argument. Assuming that SQRT has itself been written in an appropriate manner then it clearly cannot deliver a value to be used as the parameter of PUT. Instead an exception will be raised. The raising of an exception indicates that something unusual has happened and the normal sequence of execution is broken. In our case the exception might be NUMERIC_ERROR which is a predefined exception declared in the package STANDARD. If we did nothing to cope with this possibility then our program would be terminated and no doubt the Ada Run Time System (that is the non-Ada magic that drives our program from the operating system) will give us a rude message saying that our program has failed and why. We can, however, look out for an exception and take remedial action if it occurs. In fact we could replace the conditional statement

```
if X < 0.0 then
    PUT("not calculable");
else
    PUT(SQRT(X));
end if;
```

by

```
begin
    PUT(SQRT(X));
exception
```

```
    when NUMERIC_ERROR =>
        PUT("not calculable");
end;
```

This fragment of program is an example of a block. If an exception is raised by the sequence of statements between **begin** and **exception**, then control immediately passes to the one or more statements following the handler for that exception and these are obeyed instead. If there were no handler for the exception (it might be another exception such as STORAGE_ERROR) then control passes up the flow hierarchy until we come to an appropriate handler or fall out of the main program which then becomes terminated as we mentioned with a rude message from the Run Time System.

The above example is not a good illustration of the use of exceptions since the event we are guarding against can easily be tested for directly. Nevertheless it does show the general idea of how we can look out for unexpected events and leads us into a brief consideration of errors in general.

There are two underlying causes of errors in software as perceived externally: an incorrect software specification in which a possible sequence of external events has not been taken into consideration and an incorrect implementation of the software specification itself. The first type of error can be allowed for to some extent by exception handlers. The second type leads to an incorrect Ada program.

From the linguistic viewpoint, an Ada program may be incorrect for various reasons. Four categories are recognized according to how they are detected.

- Some errors will be detected by the compiler – these will include simple punctuation mistakes such as leaving out a semicolon or attempting to violate the type rules such as mixing up colours and fish. In these cases the program will not be executed.

- Other errors are detected when the program is executed. An attempt to find the square root of a negative number or divide by zero are examples of such errors. In these cases an exception is raised as we have just seen and we have an opportunity to recover from the situation.

- There are also certain situations where the program breaks the language rules but there is no simple way in which this violation can be detected. For example, a program should not use a variable before a value is assigned to it. If it does then the behaviour is quite unpredictable and the program is said to be erroneous.

- Finally there are situations where, for implementation reasons, the language does not prescribe the order in which things are to be done. For example, the order in which the parameters of a procedure call are evaluated is not defined. If the behaviour of a program does depend on such an order then it is illegal and said to have an incorrect order dependency.

Care must be taken to avoid writing erroneous programs and those with incorrect order dependencies. In practice, if we avoid clever tricks then all will usually be well.

## 2.4 The type model

We have said that one of the key benefits of Ada is its strong typing. This is well illustrated by the enumeration type. Consider

```
declare
    type COLOUR is (RED, AMBER, GREEN);
    type FISH is (COD, HAKE, PLAICE);
    X, Y: COLOUR;
    A, B: FISH;
begin
    X:= RED;        -- ok
    A:= HAKE;       -- ok
    B:= X;          -- illegal
    ...
end;
```

Here we have a block which declares two enumeration types COLOUR and FISH and two variables of each type and then performs various assignments. The declarations of the types gives the allowed values of the types. Thus the variable X can only take one of the three values RED, AMBER or GREEN. The fundamental rule of strong typing is that we cannot assign a value of one type to a variable of a different type. So we cannot mix up colours and fish and thus our (presumably accidental) attempt to assign the value of X to B is illegal and will be detected during compilation.

There are two enumeration types predefined in the package STANDARD. One is

```
type BOOLEAN is (FALSE, TRUE);
```

which plays a fundamental role in control flow. Thus the predefined relational operators such as < produce a result of this type and such a value follows **if** as we saw in the construction

**if** X < 0.0 **then**

in the example of Section 2.2. The other predefined enumeration type is CHARACTER whose values are the ASCII characters; this type naturally plays an important role in input–output. The literal values of this type include the printable characters and these are represented by placing them in single quotes thus 'X' or 'a' or indeed ' ' '.

The other fundamental types are the numeric types. One way or another all other data types are built out of enumeration types and numeric types. The two major classes of numeric types are the integer types and floating point types (there are also fixed point types which are rather obscure and deserve no further mention in this brief overview). All implementations will have the types INTEGER and FLOAT used in Section 2.2. In addition, if the architecture is appropriate, an implementation may have other predefined numeric types, LONG_INTEGER, LONG_FLOAT, SHORT_FLOAT and so on.

One of the problems of numeric types is how to obtain both portability and efficiency in the face of variation in machine architecture. In order to explain how this is done in Ada we have to introduce the perhaps surprising concept of a derived type.

A derived type introduces a new type which is almost identical to an existing type except that it is logically distinct. If we write

```
type LIGHT is new COLOUR;
```

then LIGHT will, like COLOUR, be an enumeration type with literals RED, AMBER and GREEN. However, values of the two types cannot be arbitrarily mixed since they are logically distinct. Nevertheless, in recognition of the close relationship, a value of one type can be converted to the other by explicitly using the destination type name. So we can write

```
declare
    type LIGHT is new COLOUR;
    C: COLOUR;
    L: LIGHT;
begin
    L:= AMBER;           -- the light amber, not the colour
    C:= COLOUR(L);       -- explicit conversion
    ...
end;
```

whereas a direct assignment

```
    C:= L;               -- illegal
```

would violate the strong typing rule and this violation would be detected during compilation.

Returning now to our numeric types, if we write

```
type REAL is new FLOAT;
```

then REAL will have all the operations (+, − etc.) of FLOAT and in general can be considered as equivalent. Now suppose we transfer our program to a different computer on which the predefined type FLOAT is not so accurate and that LONG_FLOAT is necessary. Assuming that our program has been written using REAL rather than FLOAT then replacing our declaration of REAL by

```
type REAL is new LONG_FLOAT;
```

is the only change necessary. We can actually do better than this by directly stating the precision that we require, thus

    **type** REAL **is digits** 7;

will cause REAL to be derived from the smallest predefined type with at least 7 decimal digits of accuracy.

The point of all this is that it is not good practice to use the type FLOAT directly and accordingly we will use our type REAL in examples in future.

A similar approach is possible with integer types but for a number of reasons the predefined type INTEGER has a fundamental place in the language and so we will continue to use it directly. We will say no more about numeric types for the moment except that all the expected operations apply to all integer and floating types.

Ada naturally enables the creation of composite array and record types and these are discussed in Chapters 6 and 11. There are also access types (the Ada name for pointer types) which allow list processing and these are also discussed in Chapter 11. In conclusion we note that the type STRING which we encountered in Section 2.2 is in fact an array type whose components are of the enumeration type CHARACTER.

## 2.5  Generics

At the beginning of Section 2.2 we said that an important objective of Software Engineering is to reuse existing software components. However, the strong typing model of Ada rather gets in the way unless we have some method of writing software components which can be used for various different types. For example, the program to do a sort is largely independent of what it is sorting – all it needs is a rule for comparing the values. Record input–output is another example – the actions are quite independent of the contents of the records.

So we need a means of writing pieces of software which can be parameterized as required for different types. In Ada this is done by the generic mechanism. We can make a package or subprogram generic with respect to one or more parameters which can include types. Such a generic unit provides a template out of which we can create genuine packages and subprograms by so-called instantiation. The full details are quite extensive and will be dealt with in Chapter 13. However, we want to give the reader the immediate ability to do some input–output and the standard packages for this involve the generic mechanism.

The standard package for the input and output of floating point values in text form is generic with respect to the actual floating type. This is because we want a single package to cope with all the possible floating types such as the underlying machine types FLOAT and LONG_FLOAT as well as our own portable type REAL. Its specification is

    **generic**
        **type** NUM **is digits** <>;
    **package** FLOAT_IO **is**

```
    ...
    procedure GET(ITEM: out NUM; ... );
    procedure PUT(ITEM: in NUM; ... );
    ...
end FLOAT_IO;
```

where we have omitted various details relating to the format. The one generic parameter is NUM and the notation **digits** <> indicates that it must be a floating point type and echoes the declaration of REAL using **digits** 10 that we briefly mentioned in the last section.

In order to create an actual package to manipulate values of our type REAL, we write

```
package REAL_IO is new FLOAT_IO(REAL);
```

which creates a package with the name REAL_IO where the formal type NUM has been replaced throughout with our actual type REAL. As a consequence, procedures GET and PUT taking parameters of the type REAL are created and we can then call these as required. But we are straying into the next section.

Another simple area where the Ada generic mechanism is used is for the mathematical library. This library, discussed in detail in Section 13.4, includes a generic package which contains among other things the various familiar elementary functions such as SQRT. Its specification is

```
with MATHEMATICAL_EXCEPTIONS;
generic
    type FLOAT_TYPE is digits <>;
package GENERIC_ELEMENTARY_FUNCTIONS is
    function SQRT(X: FLOAT_TYPE) return FLOAT_TYPE;
    ...    -- and so on
end;
```

Again there is a single generic parameter giving the floating type. In order to call the function SQRT we must first instantiate the generic package much as we did for FLOAT_IO, thus

```
package REAL_MATHS is
                new GENERIC_ELEMENTARY_FUNCTIONS(REAL);
use REAL_MATHS;
```

and we can then write a call of SQRT directly. Note that the use clause for REAL_MATHS avoids us having to write REAL_MATHS.SQRT everywhere.

The reader will have noticed that the generic package commences with a with clause for MATHEMATICAL_EXCEPTIONS. This is another package which contains just the declaration of a single exception, ARGUMENT_ERROR, thus

```
package MATHEMATICAL_EXCEPTIONS is
    ARGUMENT_ERROR: exception;
end MATHEMATICAL_EXCEPTIONS;
```

This exception is raised if the parameter of a function such as SQRT is unacceptable. This contrasts with our hypothetical function SQRT introduced earlier which we assumed raised the predefined exception NUMERIC_ERROR when given a negative parameter. We will see later when we deal with exceptions in detail in Chapter 10 that it is generally better to declare and raise our own exceptions rather than use the predefined ones.

## 2.6 Input–output

The Ada language is defined in such a way that all input and output is performed in terms of other language features. There are no special intrinsic features just for input and output. In fact input–output is just a service required by a program and so is provided by one or more Ada packages. This approach runs the attendant risk that different implementations will provide different packages and program portability will be compromised. In order to avoid this, the *Language Reference Manual* describes certain standard packages that can be expected to be available. Other, more elaborate, packages may be appropriate to special circumstances and the language does not prevent this. Indeed very simple packages such as our purely illustrative SIMPLE_IO may also be appropriate. Full consideration of input and output is deferred until Chapter 15 when we discuss interfaces between our program and the outside world in general. However, we will now briefly describe how to use some of the features so that the reader will be able to run some simple exercises. We will restrict ourselves to the input and output of simple text.

Text input–output is performed through the use of a standard package called TEXT_IO. Unless we specify otherwise all communication will be through two standard files, one for input and one for output and we will assume that (as is likely for most implementations), these are such that input is from the keyboard and output is to the screen. The full details of TEXT_IO cannot be described here but if we restrict ourselves to just a few useful facilities it looks a bit like

```
with IO_EXCEPTIONS;
package TEXT_IO is
    type COUNT is ...     -- an integer type
    ...
    procedure NEW_LINE(SPACING: in COUNT:= 1);
    procedure SET_COL(TO: in COUNT);
    function COL return COUNT;
    ...
    procedure GET(ITEM: out CHARACTER);
    procedure PUT(ITEM: in CHARACTER);
    procedure PUT(ITEM: in STRING);
    ...
    -- the package FLOAT_IO outlined in the previous section
    -- plus a similar package INTEGER_IO
    ...
end TEXT_IO;
```

Note first that this package commences with a with clause for IO_EXCEPTIONS. This is a further package which contains the declaration of a number of different exceptions relating to a variety of things which can go wrong with input–output. For toy programs the most likely to arise is probably DATA_ERROR which would occur for example if we tried to read in a number from the keyboard but then accidentally typed in something which was not a number at all or was in the wrong format.

The next thing to note is the outline declaration of the type COUNT. This is an integer type having similar properties to the type INTEGER and almost inevitably derived from it (just as our type REAL is likely to be derived from FLOAT). The parameter of NEW_LINE is of the type COUNT rather than plain INTEGER although since the parameter will typically be a literal such as 2 (or be omitted so that the default of 1 applies) this will not be particularly evident.

The procedure SET_COL and function COL are useful for tabulation. The character positions along a line of output are numbered starting at 1. So if we write (and assuming **use** TEXT_IO;)

    SET_COL(10);

then the next character output will go at position 10. A call of NEW_LINE naturally sets the current position to 1 so that output commences at the beginning of the line. The function COL returns the current position and so

    SET_COL(COL + 10);

will move the position on by 10 and thereby leave 10 spaces. Note that COL is an example of a function that has no parameters.

A single character can be output by for example

    PUT('A');

and a string of characters by

    PUT("This is a string of characters");

A value of the type REAL can be output in various formats. But first we have to instantiate the package FLOAT_IO mentioned in the previous section and which is declared inside TEXT_IO. Having done that we can call PUT with a single parameter, the value of type REAL to be output, in which case a standard default format is used, or we can add further parameters controlling the format. This is best illustrated by a few examples and we will suppose that our type REAL was declared to have 7 decimal digits as in the example in Section 2.4.

If we do not supply any format parameters then an exponent notation is used with 7 significant digits, 1 before the point and 6 after (the 7 matches the precision given in the declaration of REAL). There is also a leading space or minus sign. The exponent consists of the letter E followed by the exponent sign (+ or −) and then a two-digit decimal exponent. The effect is shown by the following statements with the output given as a comment. For clarity the output is surrounded by quotes and s designates a space; in reality there are no quotes and spaces are spaces.

```
PUT(12.34);           --  "s1.234000E+01"
PUT(-987.65);         --  "-9.876500E+02"
PUT(0.00289);         --  "s2.890000E-03"
```

We can override the default by providing three further parameters which give respectively the number of characters before the point, the number of characters after the point, and the number of characters after E. However, there is still always only one digit before the point. So

```
PUT(12.34, 3, 4, 2);    -- "ss1.2340E+1"
```

If we do not want exponent notation then we simply specify the last parameter as zero and we then get normal decimal notation. So

```
PUT(12.34, 3, 4, 0);    -- "s12.3400"
```

The output of values of type INTEGER follows a similar pattern. First we have to instantiate the generic package inside TEXT_IO which applies to all integer types with the particular type INTEGER thus

```
package INT_IO is new INTEGER_IO(INTEGER);
use INT_IO;
```

and (much as for the type REAL), we can then call PUT with a single parameter, the value of type INTEGER, in which case a standard default field is used, or we can add a further parameter specifying the field. The default field is the smallest which will accommodate all values of the type INTEGER allowing for a leading minus sign. Thus for a 16 bit implementation of INTEGER, the default field is 6. It should be noticed that if we specify a field which is too small then it is expanded as necessary. So

```
PUT(123);        --   "sss123"
PUT(-123);       --   "ss-123"
PUT(123, 4);     --    "s123"
PUT(123, 0);     --     "123"
```

That covers enough output for simple toy programs. The only input likely to be needed is of integer and real values and perhaps single characters. This is easily done by a call of GET with a parameter which must be a variable of the appropriate type just as we wrote GET(X); in the simple program in Section 2.2.

A call of GET with a real or integer parameter will expect us to type in an appropriate number at the keyboard; this must have a decimal point if the parameter is real. It should also be noted that leading blanks (spaces)

and newlines are skipped. A call of GET with a parameter of type
CHARACTER will read the very next character and this can be neatly used
for controlling the flow of an interactive program, thus

```
C: CHARACTER;
...
PUT("Do you want to stop? Answer Y if so. ");
GET(C);
if C = 'Y' then
...
```

That concludes our brief introduction to input–output which has
inevitably been of a rather cookbook nature. Hopefully it has provided
enough to enable the reader to drive such trial examples as desired as well
as giving some further flavour to the nature of Ada.

## 2.7  Running a program

We are now in a position to put together a complete program using the
proper input–output facilities and avoiding the non-portable type FLOAT.
As an example we will rewrite the simple example of Section 2.2 and also
use the standard mathematical library. It becomes

```
with TEXT_IO, GENERIC_ELEMENTARY_FUNCTIONS;
procedure PRINT_ROOTS is
    type REAL is digits 7;
    X: REAL;

    use TEXT_IO;
    package REAL_IO is new FLOAT_IO(REAL);
    use REAL_IO;

    package REAL_MATHS is
                new GENERIC_ELEMENTARY_FUNCTIONS(REAL);
    use REAL_MATHS;

begin
    PUT("Roots of various numbers");
    ...
    ...      -- and so on as before
    ...
end PRINT_ROOTS;
```

To have to write all that introductory stuff just to run a toy program
each time is rather a burden so we will put it in a standard package of our
own and then compile it once so that it is permanently in our program
library and can then be accessed without more ado. We can write

```
with TEXT_IO, GENERIC_ELEMENTARY_FUNCTIONS;
package ETC is
```

```
type REAL is digits 7;

package REAL_IO is new TEXT_IO.FLOAT_IO(REAL);
package INT_IO is new TEXT_IO.INTEGER_IO(INTEGER);

package REAL_MATHS is
            new GENERIC_ELEMENTARY_FUNCTIONS(REAL);
end ETC;
```

and having compiled ETC our typical program can look like

```
with TEXT_IO, ETC;
use TEXT_IO, ETC;
procedure PROGRAM is
    use REAL_IO, INT_IO, REAL_MATHS;    -- as required
    ...
    ...
end PROGRAM;
```

Note that we can put the use clause for the packages mentioned in the with clause immediately after the with clause. The reader will realize that the author had great difficulty in identifying an appropriate and short name for our package ETC and hopes that he is forgiven for the pun on etcetera.

The reader should now be in a position to write complete simple programs. The exercises in this book have been written as fragments rather than complete programs for two reasons: one is that complete programs would take up a lot of space (and actually be rather repetitive) and the other is that Ada is really all about software components anyway.

Unfortunately it is not possible to explain how to call the Ada compiler and manipulate the program library because this depends upon the implementation and so we must leave the reader to find out how to do this last and vital step from the documentation for the implementation concerned.

---

*Exercise 2.7*

1    Write a program to output the ten times table. Make each column of the table 5 characters wide.

2    Write a program to output a table of square roots of numbers from 1 up to some limit specified by the user in response to a suitable question. Print the numbers as integers and the square roots to 5 decimal places in two columns. Use SET_COL to set the second column position so that the program can be easily modified. Note that a value N of type INTEGER can be converted to the corresponding REAL value by writing REAL(N).

## 2.8  Terminology

We conclude this introductory chapter with a few remarks on terminology.
Every subject has its own terminology or jargon and Ada is no exception.
(Indeed in Ada an exception is a kind of error as we have seen!) A full
glossary of terms will be found in Appendix 3.

Terminology will generally be introduced as required but before
starting off with the detailed description of Ada it is convenient to mention
a couple of concepts which will occur from time to time.

The term static refers to things that can be determined at compilation, whereas dynamic refers to things determined during execution.
Thus a static expression is one whose value can be determined by the
compiler such as

$$2 + 3$$

and a static array is one whose bounds are known at compilation time.

Sometimes it is necessary to make a parenthetic remark to the
compiler where the remark is often not a part of the program as such but
more a useful hint. This can be done by means of a construction known as a
pragma. As an example we can indicate that only parts of our program are
to be listed by writing

**pragma** LIST(ON);

and

**pragma** LIST(OFF);

at appropriate places. Another similar example is

**pragma** PAGE;

which indicates that a new page should occur in the listing at this point.

Generally a pragma can appear anywhere that a declaration or
statement can appear, after any semicolon and in some other contexts also.
Sometimes there may be restrictions on the position of a particular
pragma. For fuller details on pragmas see Appendix 1.

# Chapter 3
# Lexical Style

---

---

In the previous chapter, we introduced some concepts of Ada and illustrated the general appearance of Ada programs with some simple examples. However, we have so far only talked around the subject. In this chapter we get down to serious detail.

Regrettably it seems best to start with some rather unexciting but essential material – the detailed construction of things such as identifiers and numbers which make up the text of a program. However, it is no good learning a human language without getting the spelling sorted out. And as far as programming languages are concerned, compilers are usually very unforgiving regarding such corresponding and apparently trivial matters.

We also take the opportunity to introduce the notation used to describe the syntax of Ada language constructs. In general we will not use this syntax notation to introduce concepts but, in some cases, it is the easiest way to be precise. Moreover, if the reader wishes to consult the *LRM* then knowledge of the syntax notation is necessary. For completeness and easy reference the full syntax is given in Appendix 4.

## 3.1 Syntax notation

The syntax of Ada is described using a modified version of Backus-Naur Form or BNF. In this, syntactic categories are represented by lower case names; some of these contain embedded underlines to increase readability. A category is defined in terms of other categories by a sort of equation known as a production. Some categories are atomic and cannot be decomposed further – these are known as terminal symbols. A production consists of the name being defined followed by the special symbol ::= and its defining sequence.

Other symbols used are

[ ]     square brackets enclose optional items,
{ }     braces enclose items which may be omitted, appear once or be repeated many times,
|       a vertical bar separates alternatives.

In some cases the name of a category is prefixed by a word in italics. In such cases the prefix is intended to convey some semantic information and can be treated as a form of comment as far as the context free syntax is concerned. Sometimes a production is presented in a form that shows the recommended layout.

## 3.2   Lexical elements

An Ada program is written as a sequence of lines of text containing the following characters

- the alphabet A–Z
- the digits 0–9
- various other characters " # & ' ( ) * + , – . / : ; < = > _ |
- the space character

The lower case alphabet may be used instead of or in addition to the upper case alphabet, but the two are generally considered the same. (The only exception is where the letters stand for themselves in character strings and character literals.)
Some other special characters such as ! may also be used in strings and literals. Certain of them may be used as alternatives to |, # and " if these are not available. We will not bother with the alternatives and the extra rules associated with them but will stick to the normal characters in this book.
The *LRM* does not prescribe how one proceeds from one line of text to the next. This need not concern us. We can just imagine that we type our Ada program as a series of lines using whatever mechanism the keyboard provides for starting a new line.
A line of Ada text can be thought of as a sequence of groups of characters known as lexical elements. We have already met several forms of lexical elements in Chapter 2. Consider for example

    AGE:= 43;    -- John's age

This consists of five such elements

- the identifier AGE
- the compound symbol :=
- the number 43

- the single symbol ;

- the comment -- John's age

Other classes of lexical element are strings and character literals; they are dealt with in Chapter 6.

Individual lexical elements may not be split by spaces but otherwise spaces may be inserted freely in order to improve the appearance of the program. A most important example of this is the use of indentation to reveal the overall structure. Naturally enough a lexical element must fit on one line.

Particular care should be taken that the following compound delimiters do not contain spaces

| | |
|---|---|
| => | used in aggregates, cases, etc. |
| .. | for ranges |
| ** | exponentiation |
| := | assignment |
| /= | not equals |
| >= | greater than or equals |
| <= | less than or equals |
| << | label bracket |
| >> | the other label bracket |
| <> | the 'box' for arrays and generics |

However, spaces may occur in strings and character literals where they stand for themselves and also in comments.

Note that adjacent identifiers and numbers must be separated from each other by spaces otherwise they would be confused. Thus we must write **end loop** rather than **endloop**.

## 3.3   Identifiers

We met identifiers in the simple examples in Chapter 2. As an example of the use of the syntax notation we now consider the following definition of an identifier.

identifier ::= letter {[underline] letter_or_digit}

letter_or_digit ::= letter | digit

letter ::= upper_case_letter | lower_case_letter

This states that an identifier consists of a letter followed by zero, one or more instances of letter_or_digit optionally preceded by a single underline. A letter_or_digit is, as its name implies, either a letter or a digit. Finally a letter is either an upper_case_letter or a lower_case_letter. As far as this example is concerned the categories underline, digit, upper_case_letter and lower_case_letter are not decomposed further and so are considered to be terminal symbols.

In plain English this merely says that an identifier consists of a letter possibly followed by one or more letters or digits with embedded isolated underlines. Either case of letter can be used. What the syntax does not convey is that the meaning attributed to an identifier does not depend upon the case of the letters. In fact identifiers which differ only in the case of corresponding letters are considered to be the same. But, on the other hand, the underline characters are considered to be significant.

Ada does not impose any limit on the number of characters in an identifier. Moreover all are significant. There may however be a practical limit since an identifier must fit onto a single line and an implementation is likely to impose some maximum line length. Programmers are encouraged to use meaningful names such as TIME_OF_DAY rather than cryptic or meaningless names such as T. Long names may seem tedious when first writing a program but in the course of its lifetime a program is read much more often than it is written and clarity aids subsequent understanding both by the original author and by others who may be called upon to maintain the program. Of course, in short mathematical or abstract subprograms, identifiers such as X and Y may be appropriate.

Identifiers are used to name all the various entities in a program. However, some identifiers are reserved for special syntactic significance and may not be reused. We encountered several of these in Chapter 2 such as **if**, **procedure** and **end**. There are 63 reserved words; they are listed in Appendix 1. For readability they are printed in boldface in this book but that is not important. In program text they could, like all identifiers, be in either case or indeed in a mixture of cases – procedure, PROCEDURE and Procedure are all acceptable. Nevertheless some discipline aids understanding and a useful convention is to use lower case for the reserved words and upper case for all others. But this is a matter of taste.

There are minor exceptions regarding the reserved words **delta**, **digits** and **range**. As will be seen later they are also used as attributes DELTA, DIGITS and RANGE. However, when so used they are always preceded by a prime or single quote character and so there is no confusion.

Some identifiers such as INTEGER and TRUE have a predefined meaning from the package STANDARD. These are not reserved and can be reused although to do so is usually unwise since the program could become very confusing.

---

*Exercise 3.3*

**1**    Which of the following are not legal identifiers and why?

| | | | | | |
|---|---|---|---|---|---|
| (a) | Ada | (d) | UMO164G | (g) | X_ |
| (b) | fish&chips | (e) | TIME__LAG | (h) | tax rate |
| (c) | RATE–OF–FLOW | (f) | 77E2 | (i) | goto |

## 3.4  Numbers

Numbers (or numeric literals to use the proper jargon) take two forms
according to whether they denote an integer (an exact whole number) or a
real (an approximate and not usually whole number). The important
distinguishing feature is that real literals always contain a decimal point
whereas integer literals never do. Ada is strict on mixing up types. It is
illegal to use an integer literal where the context demands a real literal and
vice versa. Thus

    AGE: INTEGER:= 43.0;

and

    WEIGHT: REAL:= 150;

are both illegal. (We are using a type REAL rather than FLOAT for reasons
which were outlined in Section 2.4 and will be fully explained later.)
    The simplest form of integer literal is simply a sequence of decimal
digits. If the literal is very long it may be convenient to split it up into
groups of digits by inserting isolated underlines thus

    123_456_789

In contrast to identifiers such underlines are, of course, of no significance
other than to make the literal easier to read.
    The simplest form of real literal is a sequence of decimal digits
containing a decimal point. Note that there must be at least one digit on
either side of the decimal point. Again, isolated underlines may be inserted
to improve legibility provided they are not adjacent to the decimal point;
thus

    3.14159_26536

    Unlike most languages both integer and real literals can have an
exponent. This takes the form of the letter E (either case) followed by a
signed or unsigned decimal integer. This exponent indicates the power of
ten by which the preceding simple literal is to be multiplied. The exponent
cannot be negative in the case of an integer literal – otherwise it might not
be a whole number. (As a trivial point an exponent of −0 is not allowed for
an integer literal but it is for a real literal.)
    Thus the real literal 98.4 could be written with an exponent in any of
the following ways

    9.84E1     98.4e0     984.0e−1     0.984E+2

Note that 984e−1 would not be allowed.
    Similarly, the integer literal 1900 could also be written as

    19E2     190e+1     1900E+0

but not as 19000e−1 nor as 1900E−0.

The exponent may itself contain underlines if it consists of two or more digits but it is unlikely that the exponent would be so large as to make this necessary. However, the exponent may not itself contain an exponent!

A final facility is the ability to express a literal in a base other than 10. This is done by enclosing the digits between # characters and preceding the result by the base. Thus

    2#111#

is an integer literal of value $4 + 2 + 1 = 7$.

Any base from 2 to 16 inclusive can be used and, of course, base 10 can always be expressed explicitly. For bases above 10 the letters A to F are used to represent the superdigits 10 to 15. Thus

    14#ABC#

equals $10 \times 14^2 + 11 \times 14 + 12 = 2126$.

A based literal can also have an exponent. But note carefully that the exponent gives the power of the base by which the simple literal is to be multiplied and not a power of ten – unless, of course, the base happens to be ten. The exponent itself, like the base, is always expressed in normal decimal notation. Thus

    16#A#E2

equals $10 \times 16^2 = 2560$ and

    2#11#E11

equals $3 \times 2^{11} = 6144$.

A based literal can be real. The distinguishing mark is again the point. (We can hardly say 'decimal point' if we are not using a decimal base! A better term is radix point.) So

    2#101.11#

equals $4 + 1 + \frac{1}{2} + \frac{1}{4} = 5.75$ and

    7#3.0#e−1

equals $\frac{3}{7} = 0.\overset{\cdot}{4}2857\overset{\cdot}{1}$.

The reader may have felt that the possible forms of based literal are unduly elaborate. This is not really so. Based literals are useful – especially for fixed point types since they enable the programmer to represent values in the form in which he or she thinks about them. Obviously bases 2, 8 and 16 will be the most useful. But the notation is applicable to any base and the compiler can compute to any base so why not?

Finally note that a numeric literal cannot be negative. A form such as $-3$ consists of a literal preceded by the unary minus operator.

---

*Exercise 3.4*

1    Which of the following are not legal literals and why? For those that are legal, state whether they are integer or real literals.

    (a)   38.6         (e)   2#1011        (i)   16#FfF#
    (b)   .5           (f)   2.71828_18285   (j)   1_0#1_0#E1_0
    (c)   32e2       (g)   12#ABC#      (k)   27.4e_2
    (d)   32e−2      (h)   E+6         (l)   2#11#e−1

2    What is the value of the following?

    (a)   16#E#E1       (c)   16#F.FF#E+2
    (b)   2#11#E11      (d)   2#1.1111_1111_111#E11

3    How many different ways can you express the following as a numeric literal?

    (a)   the integer 41   (b)   the integer 150

(Forget underlines, distinction between E and e, nonsignificant leading zeros and optional + in an exponent.)

---

## 3.5  Comments

It is important to add appropriate comments to a program to aid its understanding by someone else or yourself at a later date. We met some comments in Chapter 2.

A comment in Ada is written as an arbitrary piece of text following two hyphens (or minus signs – the same thing). Thus

    −− this is a comment

The comment extends to the end of the line. There is no facility in Ada to insert a comment into the middle of a line. Of course, the comment may be the only thing on the line or it may follow some other Ada text. A long comment that needs several lines is merely written as successive comments.

    −− this comment is spread
    −− over
    −− several
    −− lines.

It is important that the leading hyphens are adjacent and are not separated by spaces.

*Exercise 3.5*

1    How many lexical elements are there in each of the following
     lines of text?

    (a)    X:= X+2; -- add two to X
    (b)    -- that was a silly comment
    (c)    ------------------------
    (d)    - - - - - - - - - - - - - -

2    Distinguish

    (a)   **delay** 2.0;
    (b)   **delay**2.0;

## Checklist 3

The case of a letter is immaterial in all contexts except strings and character literals.

Underlines are significant in identifiers but not in numeric literals.

Spaces are not allowed in lexical elements, except in strings, character literals and comments.

The presence or absence of a point distinguishes real and integer literals.

An integer may not have a negative exponent.

Numeric literals cannot be signed.

Nonsignificant leading zeros are allowed in all parts of a numeric literal.

# Chapter 4
# Scalar Types

This chapter lays the foundations for the small-scale aspects of Ada. We start by considering the declaration of objects, the assignment of values to them and the ideas of scope and visibility. We then introduce the important concepts of type, subtype and constraints. As examples of types, the remainder of the chapter discusses the numeric types INTEGER and REAL, enumeration types in general, the type BOOLEAN in particular and the operations on them.

## 4.1 Object declarations and assignments

Values can be stored in objects which are declared to be of a specific type. Objects are either variables, in which case their value may change (or vary) as the program executes, or they may be constants, in which case they keep their same initial value throughout their life.

A variable is introduced into the program by a declaration which consists of the name (that is, the identifier) of the variable followed by a colon and then the name of the type. This can then optionally be followed by the := symbol and an initial value. The declaration terminates with a semicolon. Thus we might write

```
I: INTEGER;
P: INTEGER:= 38;
```

This introduces the variable I of type INTEGER but gives it no particular initial value and then the variable P and gives it the specific initial value of 38.

We can introduce several variables at the same time in one declaration by separating them by commas thus

```
I, J, K: INTEGER;
P, Q, R: INTEGER:= 38;
```

In the second case all of P, Q and R are given the initial value of 38.

If a variable is declared and not given an initial value then great care must be taken not to use the undefined value of the variable until one has been properly given to it. If a program does use the undefined value in an uninitialized variable, its behaviour will be unpredictable; the program is said to be erroneous. As mentioned in Chapter 2, this means that the program is strictly illegal but the compiler and run time system may not be able to tell us.

A common way to give a value to a variable is by using an assignment statement. In this, the identifier of the variable is followed by := and then some expression giving the new value. The statement terminates with a semicolon. Thus

```
I:= 36;
```

and

```
P:= Q+R;
```

are both valid assignment statements and place new values in I and P thereby overwriting their previous values.

Note that := can be followed by any expression provided that it produces a value of the type of the variable being assigned to. We will discuss all the rules about expressions later but it suffices to say at this point that they can consist of variables and constants with operations such as + and round brackets (parentheses) and so on just like an ordinary mathematical expression.

There is a lot of similarity between a declaration containing an initial value and an assignment statement. Both use := before the expression and the expression can be of arbitrary complexity.

An important difference, however, is that although several variables can be declared and given the same initial value together, it is not possible for an assignment statement to give the same value to several variables. This may seem odd but in practice the need to give the same value to several variables usually only arises with initial values anyway.

Perhaps we should remark at this stage that strictly speaking a multiple declaration such as

```
A, B: INTEGER:= E;
```

is really a shorthand for

```
A: INTEGER:= E;
B: INTEGER:= E;
```

This means that in principle the expression E is evaluated for each variable. This is a subtle point and does not usually matter but we will encounter some examples later where the effect is important.

A constant is declared in a similar way to a variable by inserting the reserved word **constant** after the colon. Of course, a constant must be initialized in its declaration otherwise it would be useless. Why? An example might be

PI: **constant** REAL:= 3.14159_26536;

In the case of numeric types, and only numeric types, it is possible to omit the type from the declaration of a constant thus

PI: **constant**:= 3.14159_26536;

It is then technically known as a number declaration and merely provides a name for the number. The distinction between integer and real named numbers is made by the form of the initial value. In this case it is real because of the presence of the decimal point. It is usually good practice to omit the type when declaring numeric constants for reasons which will appear later. We will therefore do so in future examples. But note that the type cannot be omitted in numeric variable declarations even when an initial value is provided.

There is an important distinction between the allowed forms of initial values in constant declarations (with a type) and number declarations (without a type). In the former case the initial value may be any expression and is evaluated when the declaration is encountered at run time, whereas in the latter case it must be a static expression and so is evaluated at compilation time. Full details are deferred until Chapter 12.

---

*Exercise 4.1*

1   Write a declaration of a real variable R giving it an initial value of one.

2   Write appropriate declarations of real constants ZERO and ONE.

3   What is wrong with the following declarations and statements?

   (a)   **var** I: INTEGER;
   (b)   G: **constant**:= 981
   (c)   P, Q: **constant** INTEGER;
   (d)   P:= Q:= 7;
   (e)   MN: **constant** INTEGER:= M*N;
   (f)   2PI: **constant**:= 2.0*PI;

---

## 4.2  Blocks and scopes

Ada carefully distinguishes between declarations which introduce new identifiers and statements which do not. It is clearly only sensible that the declarations which introduce new identifiers should precede the statements which manipulate them. Accordingly, declarations and statements occur in separate places in the program text. The simplest fragment of text which includes declarations and statements is a block.

A block commences with the reserved word **declare**, some declarations, **begin**, some statements and concludes with the reserved word **end** and the terminating semicolon. A trivial example is

```
declare
    I: INTEGER:= 0;    − − declarations here
begin
    I:= I+1;           − − statements here
end;
```

A block is itself an example of a statement and so one of the statements in its body could be another block. This textual nesting of blocks can continue indefinitely.

Since a block is a statement it can be executed like any other statement. When this happens the declarations in its declarative part (the bit between **declare** and **begin**) are elaborated in order and then the statements in the body (between **begin** and **end**) are executed in the usual way. Note the terminology: we elaborate declarations and execute statements. All that the elaboration of a declaration does is make the thing being declared come into existence and then evaluate and assign any initial value to it. When we come to the **end** of the block all the things which were declared in the block automatically cease to exist.

We can now see that the above simple example of a block is rather foolish; it introduces I, adds 1 to it but then loses it before use is made of the resulting value.

Another point to note is that the objects used in an initial value must, of course, exist. They could be declared in the same declarative part but the declarations must precede their use. For example

```
declare
    I: INTEGER:= 0;
    K: INTEGER:= I;
begin
```

is allowed, but

```
declare
    K: INTEGER:= I;
    I: INTEGER:= 0;
begin
```

is generally not. (We will see in a moment that this could have a valid but different meaning.)

This idea of elaborating declarations in order is important; the jargon is 'linear elaboration of declarations'.

Like other block structured languages, Ada also has the idea of hiding. Consider

```
declare
    I, J: INTEGER;
begin
    ...                     -- here I is the outer one
    declare
        I: INTEGER;
    begin
        ...                 -- here I is the inner one
    end;
    ...                     -- here I is the outer one
end;
```

In this, a variable I is declared in an outer block and then redeclared in an inner block. This redeclaration does not cause the outer I to cease to exist but merely makes it temporarily invisible. In the inner block I refers to the new I, but as soon as we leave the inner block, this new I ceases to exist and the outer one again becomes visible.

We distinguish the terms 'scope' and 'visibility'. The scope is the region of text where the entity is potentially visible and it is visible at a given point if its identifier can be used to refer to it at that point. We will now illustrate these terms but a fuller discussion has to be left until Chapter 8.

In the case of a block the scope of a variable (or constant) extends from the start of its declaration until the end of the block. However, it is not visible in its own declaration nor in any inner block after the redeclaration of the same identifier. The regions of scope and visibility are illustrated by the following:

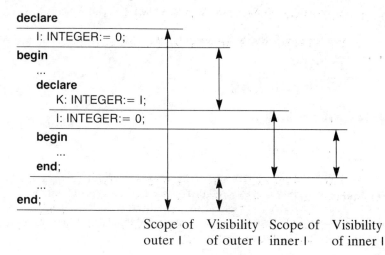

```
declare
    I: INTEGER:= 0;
begin
    ...
    declare
        K: INTEGER:= I;
        I: INTEGER:= 0;
    begin
        ...
    end;
    ...
end;
```

Scope of    Visibility    Scope of    Visibility
outer I     of outer I    inner I     of inner I

The initial value of K refers to the outer I because it precedes the introduction of the inner I.

Thus

```
K: INTEGER:= I;
I: INTEGER:= 0;
```

may or may not be legal – it depends upon its environment.

---

*Exercise 4.2*

**1**   How many errors can you see in the following?

```
declare
    I: INTEGER:= 7;
    J, K: INTEGER
begin
    J:= I+K;
    declare
        P: INTEGER=I;
        I, J: INTEGER;
    begin
        I:= P+Q;
        J:= P−Q;
        K:= I*J;
    end;
    PUT(K);          −− output value of K
end;
```

---

## 4.3  Types

'A type is characterized by a set of values and a set of operations' (*LRM* 3.3).

In the case of the built-in type INTEGER, the set of values is represented by

..., −3, −2, −1, 0, 1, 2, 3, ...

and the operations include

+, −, * and so on.

With two minor exceptions to be discussed later (arrays and tasks) every type has a name which is introduced in a type declaration. (The built-in types such as INTEGER are considered to be declared in the package STANDARD.) Moreover, every type declaration introduces a new type quite distinct from any other type.

The set of values belonging to two distinct types are themselves quite distinct although in some cases the actual lexical form of the values may be identical – which one is meant at any point is determined by the context. The idea of one lexical form representing two or more different things is known as overloading.

Values of one type cannot be assigned to variables of another type. This is the fundamental rule of strong typing. Strong typing, correctly used, is an enormous aid to the rapid development of correct programs since it ensures that many errors are detected at compilation time. (Overused, it can tie one in knots; we will discuss this thought in Chapter 16.)

A type declaration uses a somewhat different syntax to an object declaration in order to emphasize the conceptual difference. It consists of the reserved word **type**, the identifier to be associated with the type, the reserved word **is** and then the definition of the type followed by the terminating semicolon. We can imagine that the package STANDARD contains type declarations such as

    **type** INTEGER **is** ... ;

The type definition between **is** and ; gives in some way the set of values belonging to the type. As a concrete example consider the following

    **type** COLOUR **is** (RED, AMBER, GREEN);

(This is an example of an enumeration type and will be dealt with in more detail in a later section in this chapter.)

This introduces a new type called COLOUR. Moreover, it states that there are only 3 values of this type and they are denoted by the identifiers RED, AMBER and GREEN.

Objects of this type can then be declared in the usual way

    C: COLOUR;

An initial value can be supplied

    C: COLOUR:= RED;

or a constant can be declared

    DEFAULT: **constant** COLOUR:= RED;

We have stated that values of one type cannot be assigned to variables of another type. Therefore one cannot mix colours and integers and so

    I: INTEGER;
    C: COLOUR;
    ...
    I:= C;

is illegal. In older languages it is often necessary to implement concepts such as enumeration types by more primitive types such as integers and give values such as 0, 1 and 2 to variables named RED, AMBER and GREEN. Thus in Algol 60 one could write

```
integer RED, AMBER, GREEN;
RED:= 0; AMBER:= 1; GREEN:= 2;
```

and then use RED, AMBER and GREEN as if they were literal values. Obviously the program would be easier to understand than if the code values 0, 1 and 2 had been used directly. But, on the other hand, the compiler could not detect the accidental assignment of a notional colour to a variable which was, in the mind of the programmer, just an ordinary integer. In Ada, as we have seen, this is detected during compilation, thus making a potentially tricky error quite trivial to discover.

## 4.4  Subtypes

We now introduce subtypes and constraints. A subtype, as its name suggests, characterizes a set of values which is just a subset of the values of some other type known as the base type. The subset is defined by means of a constraint. Constraints take various forms according to the category of the base type. As is usual with subsets, the subset may be the complete set. There is, however, no way of restricting the set of operations of the base type. The subtype takes all the operations; subsetting applies only to the values.

As an example, suppose we wish to manipulate dates; we know that the day of the month must lie in the range 1 .. 31 so we declare a subtype thus

```
subtype DAY_NUMBER is INTEGER range 1 .. 31;
```

We can then declare variables and constants using the subtype identifier in exactly the same way as a type identifier.

```
D: DAY_NUMBER;
```

We are then assured that the variable D can take only integer values from 1 to 31 inclusive. The compiler will insert run-time checks if necessary to ensure that this is so; if a check fails then the CONSTRAINT_ERROR exception is raised.

It is important to realize that a subtype declaration does not introduce a new distinct type. An object such as D is of type INTEGER and so the following is perfectly legal from the syntactic point of view.

```
D: DAY_NUMBER;
I: INTEGER;
...
D:= I;
```

Of course, on execution, the value of I may or may not lie in the range 1 .. 31. If it does, then all is well; if not then CONSTRAINT_ERROR will be raised. Assignment in the other direction

    I:= D;

will, of course, always work.

It is not always necessary to introduce a subtype explicitly in order to impose a constraint. We could equally have written

    D: INTEGER **range** 1 .. 31;

Furthermore a subtype need not impose a constraint. It is perfectly legal to write

    **subtype** DAY_NUMBER **is** INTEGER;

although in this instance it is not of much value.

A subtype (explicit or not) may be defined in terms of a previous subtype

    **subtype** FEB_DAY **is** DAY_NUMBER **range** 1 .. 29;

Any additional constraint must of course satisfy existing constraints

    DAY_NUMBER **range** 0 .. 10

would be incorrect and cause CONSTRAINT_ERROR to be raised.

The above examples have shown constraints with static bounds. This is not necessarily the case; in general the bounds can be given by arbitrary expressions and so the set of values of a subtype need not be static, that is known at compilation time. However, it is an important fact that a type is always static.

In conclusion then, a subtype does not introduce a new type but is merely a shorthand for an existing type with an optional constraint. However, in later chapters we will encounter several contexts in which an explicit constraint is not allowed; a subtype has to be introduced for these cases. We refer to a type or subtype name as a type mark and to the form consisting of a type mark followed by an optional constraint as a subtype indication as shown by the syntax

    type_mark ::= *type*_name | *subtype*_name
    subtype_indication ::= type_mark [constraint]

Thus we can restate the previous remark as saying that there are situations where a type mark has to be used whereas, as we have seen here, the more general subtype indication (which includes a type mark on its own) is allowed in object declarations.

The sensible use of subtypes has two advantages. It can ensure that programming errors are detected earlier by preventing variables from being assigned inappropriate values. It can also increase the execution efficiency of a program. This particularly applies to array subscripts as we shall see later.

We conclude this section by summarizing the assignment statement and the rules of strong typing. Assignment has the form

```
VARIABLE := expression;
```

and the two rules are

- both sides must have the same base type,
- the expression must satisfy any constraints on the variable; if it does not, the assignment does not take place, and CONSTRAINT_ERROR is raised instead.

Note carefully the general principle that type errors (violations of the first rule) are detected during compilation whereas subtype errors (violations of the second rule) are detected during execution by the raising of CONSTRAINT_ERROR. (A clever compiler might give a warning during compilation.)

We have now introduced the basic concepts of types and subtypes. The remaining sections of this chapter illustrate these concepts further by considering in more detail the properties of the simple types of Ada.

---

*Exercise 4.4*

1    Given the following declarations

```
I, J: INTEGER range 1 .. 10;
K  : INTEGER range 1 .. 20;
```

which of the following assignment statements could raise CONSTRAINT_ERROR?

(a)   I:= J;
(b)   K:= J;
(c)   J:= K;

---

## 4.5  Simple numeric types

Perhaps surprisingly a full description of the numeric types of Ada is deferred until much later in this book. The problems of numerical analysis (error estimates and so on) are complex and Ada is correspondingly complex in this area so that it can cope in a reasonably complete way with the needs of the numerical specialist. For our immediate purposes such complexity can be ignored. Accordingly, in this section, we merely consolidate a simple understanding of the two numeric types INTEGER and REAL which we have been using as background for elementary examples. For the everyday programmer these two numeric types will probably suffice.

First a reminder. The type INTEGER is a genuine built-in Ada type. But as mentioned in Section 2.4, the type REAL is not. It has to be declared somewhere in terms of one of the built-in floating point types. The reason for supposing that this has been done concerns portability and will be discussed when the truth about numeric types is revealed in more detail. For the moment, however, we will suppose that REAL is the floating point type. (The author is not deceiving you but in fact encouraging good Ada programming practice.)

As we have seen, a constraint may be imposed on the type INTEGER by using the reserved word **range**. This is then followed by two expressions separated by two dots which, of course, must produce values of integer type. These expressions need not be literal constants. One could have

P: INTEGER **range** 1 .. I+J;

A range can be null as would happen in the above case if I+J turned out to be zero. Null ranges may seem pretty useless but they often automatically occur in limiting cases, and to exclude them would mean taking special action in such cases.

The minimum value of the type INTEGER is given by INTEGER'FIRST and the maximum value by INTEGER'LAST. These are our first examples of attributes. Ada contains various attributes denoted by a single quote followed by an identifier.

The value of INTEGER'FIRST will depend on the implementation but will always be negative. On a two's complement machine it will be −INTEGER'LAST−1 whereas on a one's complement machine it will be −INTEGER'LAST. So on a typical 16 bit two's complement implementation we will have

INTEGER'FIRST = −32768
INTEGER'LAST = +32767

Of course, we should always write INTEGER'LAST rather than +32767 if that is what we logically want. Otherwise program portability could suffer.

Two useful subtypes are

**subtype** NATURAL **is** INTEGER **range** 0 .. INTEGER'LAST;
**subtype** POSITIVE **is** INTEGER **range** 1 .. INTEGER'LAST;

These are so useful that they are declared for us in the package STANDARD. The attributes FIRST and LAST also apply to subtypes so

POSITIVE'FIRST = 1
NATURAL'LAST = INTEGER'LAST

We turn now to a brief consideration of the type REAL. It is possible to apply constraints to the type REAL in order to reduce the range and precision but this takes us into the detail which has been deferred until later. There are also attributes REAL'FIRST and REAL'LAST. It is not really necessary to say any more at this point.

The other predefined operations that can be performed on the types INTEGER and REAL are much as one would expect in a modern programming language. They are summarized below.

+, −    These are either unary operators (that is, taking a single operand) or binary operators taking two operands.

In the case of a unary operator, the operand can be either integer or real; the result will be of the same type. Unary + effectively does nothing. Unary − changes the sign.

In the case of a binary operator, both operands must be integer or both operands must be real; the result will be of the type of the operands. Normal addition or subtraction is performed.

\*    Multiplication; both operands must be integer or both operands must be real; again the result is of the same type.

/    Division; both operands must be integer or both operands must be real; again the result is of the same type. Integer division truncates towards zero.

rem    Remainder; in this case both operands must be integer and the result is an integer. It is the remainder on division.

mod    Modulo; again both operands must be integer and the result is an integer. This is the mathematical modulo operation.

abs    Absolute value; this is a unary operator and the single operand may be integer or real. The result is again of the same type and is the absolute value. That is, if the operand is positive, the result is the same but if it is negative, the result is the corresponding positive value.

\*\*    Exponentiation; this raises the first operand to the power of the second. If the first operand is of integer type, the second must be a positive integer or zero. If the first operand is of real type, the second can be any integer. The result is of the same type as the first operand.

In addition, we can perform the operations =, /=, <, <=, > and >= in order to return a Boolean result TRUE or FALSE. Again both operands must be of the same type. Note the form of the not equals operator /=.

Although the above operations are mostly straightforward a few points are worth noting.

It is a general rule that mixed mode arithmetic is not allowed. One cannot, for example, add an integer value to a real value; both must be of the same type. A change of type from INTEGER to REAL or vice versa can be done by using the desired type name (or indeed subtype name) followed by the expression to be converted in brackets.

So given

```
I: INTEGER:= 3;
R: REAL:= 5.6;
```

we cannot write

```
I+R
```

but we must write

```
REAL(I)+R
```

which uses real addition to give the real value 8.6, or

```
I+INTEGER(R)
```

which uses integer addition to give the integer value 9.

Conversion from real to integer always rounds rather than truncates, thus

```
1.4 becomes 1
1.6 becomes 2
```

but a value midway between two integers, such as 1.5, may be rounded up or down according to the implementation.

There is a subtle distinction between **rem** and **mod**. The **rem** operation produces the remainder corresponding to the integer division operation /. Integer division truncates towards zero; this means that the absolute value of the result is always the same as that obtained by dividing the absolute values of the operands. So

```
  7 /  3  =  2
(−7) /  3  = −2
  7 / (−3) = −2
(−7) / (−3) =  2
```

and the corresponding remainders are

```
  7 rem   3  =  1
(−7) rem   3  = −1
  7 rem (−3) =  1
(−7) rem (−3) = −1
```

The remainder and quotient are always related by

```
(I/J) * J + I rem J = I
```

and it will also be noted that the sign of the remainder is always equal to the sign of the first operand I (the dividend).

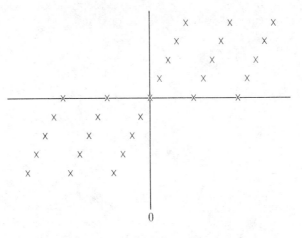

**Figure 4.1**  Behaviour of I **rem** 5 around zero.

However, **rem** is not always satisfactory. If we plot the values of I **rem** J for a fixed value of J (say 5) for both positive and negative values of I we get the pattern shown in Figure 4.1.

As we can see, the pattern is symmetric about zero and consequently changes its incremental behaviour as we pass through zero.

The **mod** operation, on the other hand, does have uniform incremental behaviour as shown in Figure 4.2.

The **mod** operation enables us to do normal modulo arithmetic. For example

$$(A+B) \textbf{ mod } n = (A \textbf{ mod } n + B \textbf{ mod } n) \textbf{ mod } n$$

for all values of A and B both positive and negative. For positive n, A **mod** n is always in the range 0 .. n−1; for negative n, A **mod** n is always in the range n+1 .. 0. Of course, modulo arithmetic is only usually performed with a positive value for n. But the **mod** operator gives consistent and sensible behaviour for negative values of n also.

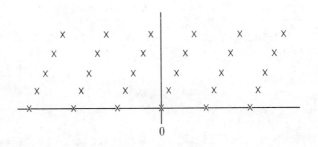

**Figure 4.2**  Behaviour of I **mod** 5 around zero.

We can look upon **mod** as giving the remainder corresponding to division with truncation towards minus infinity. So

```
    7 mod    3 =   1
 (−7) mod    3 =   2
    7 mod (−3) = −2
 (−7) mod (−3) = −1
```

In the case of **mod** the sign of the result is always equal to the sign of the second operand whereas with **rem** it is the sign of the first operand.

The reader may have felt that this discussion has been somewhat protracted. In summary, it is perhaps worth saying that integer division with negative operands is rare. The operators **rem** and **mod** only differ when one or both operands is negative. It will be found that in such cases it is almost always **mod** that is wanted.

Finally some notes on the exponentiation operator ∗∗. For a positive second operand, the operation corresponds to repeated multiplication. So

```
3**4 = 3*3*3*3 = 81
3.0**4 = 3.0*3.0*3.0*3.0 = 81.0
```

The second operand can be 0 and, of course, the result is then always the value one

```
3**0 = 1
3.0**0 = 1.0
0**0 = 1
0.0**0 = 1.0
```

The second operand cannot be negative if the first operand is an integer, as the result might not be a whole number. In fact, the exception CONSTRAINT_ERROR would be raised in such case. But it is allowed for a real first operand and produces the corresponding reciprocal

```
3.0**(−4) = 1.0/81.0 = 0.0123456780123 ...
```

We conclude this section with a brief discussion on combining operators in an expression. As is usual the operators have different precedence levels and the natural precedence can be overruled by the use of brackets. Operators of the same precedence are applied in order from left to right. A subexpression in brackets obviously has to be evaluated before it can be used. But note that the order of evaluation of the two operands of a binary operator is not specified. The precedence levels of the operators we have met so far are shown below in increasing order of precedence

```
= /= < <= > >=
+ −          (binary)
+ −          (unary)
* / mod rem
** abs
```

Thus

| | | |
|---|---|---|
| A/B*C | means | (A/B)*C |
| A+B*C+D | means | A+(B*C)+D |
| A*B+C*D | means | (A*B)+(C*D) |
| A*B**C | means | A*(B**C) |

In general, as stated above, several operations of the same precedence can be applied from left to right and brackets are not necessary. However, the syntax rules forbid multiple instances of the exponentiating operator without brackets. Thus we cannot write

A**B**C

but must explicitly write either

(A**B)**C    or    A**(B**C)

This restriction avoids the risk of accidentally writing the wrong thing. Note however that the well established forms

A−B−C    and    A/B/C

are allowed. The syntax rules similarly prevent the mixed use of **abs** and ** without brackets.

The precedence of unary minus needs care

−A**B    means    −(A**B)    rather than    (−A)**B

as in Algol 68. Also

A**−B and A*−B

are illegal. Brackets are necessary.

Note finally that the precedence of **abs** is, confusingly, not the same as that of unary minus. As a consequence we can write

− **abs** X    but not    **abs** − X

---

*Exercise 4.5*

1    Evaluate the expressions below given the following

        I: INTEGER:= 7;
        J: INTEGER:= −5;
        K: INTEGER:= 3;

| | | | | |
|---|---|---|---|---|
| (a) | I*J*K | (e) | J + 2 **rem** I |
| (b) | I/J*K | (f) | K**K**K |
| (c) | I/J/K | (g) | −J **mod** 3 |
| (d) | J + 2 **mod** I | (h) | −J **rem** 3 |

**2**     Rewrite the following mathematical expressions in Ada. Use
        suitable identifiers of appropriate type.

    (a)  $Mr^2$              – moment of inertia of black hole
    (b)  $b^2 - 4ac$         – discriminant of quadratic
    (c)  $\frac{4}{3}\pi r^3$ – volume of sphere
    (d)  $\dfrac{p\pi a^4}{8l\eta}$  – viscous flowrate through tube

---

## 4.6   Enumeration types

Here are some examples of declarations of enumeration types starting with
COLOUR which we introduced when discussing types in general.

```
type COLOUR is (RED, AMBER, GREEN);
type DAY is (MON, TUE, WED, THU, FRI, SAT, SUN);
type STONE is (AMBER, BERYL, QUARTZ);
type GROOM is (TINKER, TAILOR, SOLDIER, SAILOR,
               RICH_MAN, POOR_MAN, BEGGAR_MAN, THIEF);
type SOLO is (ALONE);
```

This introduces an example of overloading. The literal AMBER can
represent a COLOUR or a STONE. Both meanings of the same name are
visible together and the second declaration does not hide the first whether
they are declared in the same declarative part or one is in an inner
declarative part. We can usually tell which is meant from the context but in
those odd cases when we cannot we can always qualify the literal by placing
it in brackets and preceding it by an appropriate type mark (that is its type
name or a relevant subtype name) and a single quote. Thus

```
COLOUR'(AMBER)
STONE'(AMBER)
```

Examples where this is necessary will occur later.
    Although we can use AMBER as' an enumeration literal in two
distinct enumeration types, we cannot use it as an enumeration literal and
the identifier of a variable at the same time. The declaration of one would
hide the other and they could not both be declared in the same declarative
part. Later we will see that an enumeration literal can be overloaded with a
subprogram.
    There is no upper limit on the number of values in an enumeration
type but there must be at least one. An empty enumeration type is not
allowed.
    Constraints on enumeration types and subtypes are much as for
integers. The constraint has the form

```
range lower_bound_expression .. upper_bound_expression
```

and this indicates the set of values from the lower bound to the upper bound inclusive. So we can write

>**subtype** WEEKDAY **is** DAY **range** MON .. FRI;
>D: WEEKDAY;

or

>D: DAY **range** MON .. FRI;

and then we know that D cannot be SAT or SUN.

If the lower bound is above the upper bound then we get a null range, thus

>**subtype** COLOURLESS **is** COLOUR **range** AMBER .. RED;

Note the curious anomaly that we cannot have a null subtype of a type such as SOLO (since it only has one value).

The attributes FIRST and LAST also apply to enumeration types and subtypes, so

>COLOUR'FIRST = RED
>WEEKDAY'LAST = FRI

There are built-in functional attributes to give the successor or predecessor of an enumeration value. These consist of SUCC or PRED following the type name and a single quote. Thus

>COLOUR'SUCC(AMBER) = GREEN
>STONE'SUCC(AMBER) = BERYL
>DAY'PRED(FRI) = THU

Of course, the thing in brackets can be an arbitrary expression of the appropriate type. If we try to take the predecessor of the first value or the successor of the last then the exception CONSTRAINT_ERROR is raised. In the absence of this exception we have, for any type T and any value X,

>T'SUCC(T'PRED(X)) = X

and vice versa.

Another functional attribute is POS. This gives the position number of the enumeration value, that is the position in the declaration with the first one having a position number of zero. So

>COLOUR'POS(RED) = 0
>COLOUR'POS(AMBER) = 1
>COLOUR'POS(GREEN) = 2

The opposite to POS is VAL. This takes the position number and returns the corresponding enumeration value. So

```
COLOUR'VAL(0) = RED
DAY'VAL(6) = SUN
```

If we give a position value outside the range, as for example

```
SOLO'VAL(1)
```

then CONSTRAINT_ERROR is raised.
Clearly we always have

```
T'VAL(T'POS(X)) = X
```

and vice versa.
We also note that

```
T'SUCC(X) = T'VAL(T'POS(X) + 1)
```

they either both give the same value or both raise an exception.
It should be noted that these four attributes SUCC, PRED, POS and VAL may also be applied to subtypes but are then identical to the same attributes of the corresponding base type.
It is probably rather bad practice to mess about with POS and VAL when it can be avoided. To do so encourages the programmer to think in terms of numbers rather than the enumeration values and hence destroys the abstraction.
Finally the operators =, /=, <, <=, > and >= also apply to enumeration types. The result is defined by the order of the values in the type declaration. So

```
RED < GREEN     is     TRUE
WED >= THU      is     FALSE
```

The same result would be obtained by comparing the position values. So

```
T'POS(X) < T'POS(Y)     and     X < Y
```

are always equivalent (except that X < Y might be ambiguous).

---

*Exercise 4.6*

**1**    Evaluate
   (a)   DAY'SUCC(WEEKDAY'LAST)
   (b)   WEEKDAY'SUCC(WEEKDAY'LAST)
   (c)   STONE'POS(QUARTZ)

**2**    Write suitable declarations of enumeration types for
   (a)   the colours of the rainbow,
   (b)   typical fruits.

**3**    Write an expression that delivers one's predicted bridegroom after eating a portion of pie containing N stones. Use the type GROOM declared at the beginning of this section.

**4**    If the first of the month is in D where D is of type DAY, then write an assignment replacing D by the day of the week of the Nth day of the month.

**5**    Why might X < Y be ambiguous?

---

## 4.7   The Boolean type

The Boolean type is a predefined enumeration type whose declaration can be considered to be

    **type** BOOLEAN **is** (FALSE, TRUE);

Boolean values are used in constructions such as the if statement which we briefly met in Chapter 2. Boolean values are produced by the operators $=$, $/=$, $<$, $<=$, $>$ and $>=$ which have their expected meaning and apply to many types. So we can write constructions such as

```
if TODAY = SUN then
    TOMORROW:= MON;
else
    TOMORROW:= DAY'SUCC(TODAY);
end if;
```

The Boolean type (we capitalize the name in memory of the mathematician Boole) has all the normal properties of an enumeration type, so, for instance

    FALSE < TRUE = TRUE !!
    BOOLEAN'POS(TRUE) = 1

We could even write

    **subtype** ALWAYS **is** BOOLEAN **range** TRUE .. TRUE;

although it would not seem very useful.
    The Boolean type also has other operators which are as follows

**not**    This is a unary operator and changes TRUE to FALSE and vice versa. It has the same precedence as **abs**.

**and**    This is a binary operator. The result is TRUE if both operands are TRUE, and FALSE otherwise.

**or**    This is a binary operator. The result is TRUE if one or other or both operands are TRUE, and FALSE only if they are both FALSE.

**xor**   This is also a binary operator. The result is TRUE if one or other operand but not both are TRUE. (Hence the name – eXclusive OR.) Another way of looking at it is to note that the result is TRUE if and only if the operands are different. (The operator is known as 'not equivalent' in some languages.)

The effects of **and**, **or** and **xor** are summarized in the usual truth tables shown in Figure 4.3.

The precedences of **and**, **or** and **xor** are equal to each other but lower than that of any other operator. In particular they are of lower precedence than the relational operators =, /=, <, <=, > and >=. This is unlike Pascal and as a consequence brackets are not needed in expressions such as

P < Q **and** I = J

However, although the precedences are equal, **and**, **or** and **xor** cannot be mixed up in an expression without using brackets (unlike + and – for instance). So

B **and** C **or** D        is illegal

whereas

I + J – K           is legal

We have to write

B **and** (C **or** D)    or    (B **and** C) **or** D

in order to emphasize which meaning is required.

The reader familiar with other programming languages will remember that **and** and **or** usually have a different precedence. The problem with this is that the programmer often gets confused and writes the wrong thing. It is to prevent this that Ada makes them the same precedence and insists on brackets. Of course, successive applications of the same operator are permitted so

B **and** C **and** D    is legal

and as usual evaluation goes from left to right although, of course, it does not matter in this case since the operator **and** is associative.

| and | F | T |
|-----|---|---|
| F | F | F |
| T | F | T |

| or | F | T |
|----|---|---|
| F | F | T |
| T | T | T |

| xor | F | T |
|-----|---|---|
| F | F | T |
| T | T | F |

**Figure 4.3**   Truth tables for **and**, **or** and **xor**.

Take care with **not**. Its precedence is higher than **and, or** and **xor** as in other languages and so

    **not** A **or** B

means

    (**not** A) **or** B

rather than

    **not** (A **or** B)

which those familiar with logic will remember is the same as

    (**not** A) **and** (**not** B)

Boolean variables and constants can be declared and manipulated in the usual way.

```
DANGER: BOOLEAN;
SIGNAL: COLOUR;
...
DANGER:= SIGNAL = RED;
```

The variable DANGER is then TRUE if the signal is RED. We can then write

```
if DANGER then
    STOP_TRAIN;
end if;
```

Note that we do not have to write

    **if** DANGER = TRUE **then**

although this is perfectly acceptable; it just misses the point that DANGER is already a Boolean and so can be used directly as the condition.

    A worse sin is to write

```
if SIGNAL = RED then
    DANGER:= TRUE;
else
    DANGER:= FALSE;
end if;
```

rather than

```
DANGER:= SIGNAL = RED;
```

The literals TRUE and FALSE could be overloaded by declaring for example

```
type ANSWER is (FALSE, DONT_KNOW, TRUE);
```

but to do so might make the program rather confusing.

Finally, it should be noted that it is often clearer to introduce our own two-valued enumeration type rather than use the type BOOLEAN. Thus instead of

```
WHEELS_OK: BOOLEAN;
...
if WHEELS_OK then
```

it is much better (and safer!) to write

```
type WHEEL_STATE is (UP, DOWN);
WHEEL_POSITION: WHEEL_STATE;
...
if WHEEL_POSITION = UP then
```

since whether the wheels are OK or not depends upon the situation. Being OK for landing is different to being OK for cruising. The enumeration type removes any doubt as to which is meant.

---

*Exercise 4.7*

1   Write declarations of constants T and F having the values TRUE and FALSE.

2   Using T and F from the previous exercise, evaluate

(a)  T and F and T            (d)  (F = F) = (F = F)
(b)  not T or T               (e)  T < T < T < T
(c)  F = F = F = F

3   Evaluate

(A /= B) = (A xor B)

for all combinations of values of Boolean variables A and B.

---

## 4.8   Type classification

At this point we pause to consolidate the material presented in this chapter so far.

The types in Ada can be classified as shown in Figure 4.4.

This chapter has discussed scalar types. In Chapter 6 we will deal with the composite types but access, private and task types will be dealt with much later.

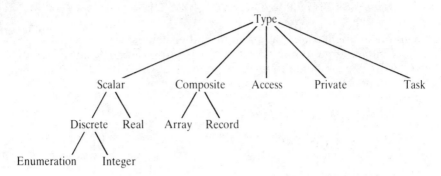

**Figure 4.4**   Classification of types.

The scalar types themselves can be subdivided into real types and discrete types. Our sole example of a real type has been the type REAL – the other real types are discussed in Chapter 12. The other types, INTEGER, BOOLEAN and enumeration types in general are discrete types – the only other kinds of discrete types to be introduced are other integer types, again dealt with in Chapter 12, and character types which are in fact a form of enumeration type and are dealt with in Chapter 6.

The key abstract distinction between the discrete types and the real types is that the former have a clear-cut set of distinct separate (that is, discrete) values. The type REAL, on the other hand, should be thought of as having a continuous set of values – we know in practice that a finite digital computer must implement a real type as actually a set of distinct values but this is an implementation detail, the abstract concept is of a continuous set of values.

The attributes POS, VAL, SUCC and PRED apply to all discrete types (and subtypes) because the operations reflect the discrete nature of the values. We explained their meaning with enumeration types in Section 4.6. In the case of type INTEGER the position number is simply the number itself so

```
INTEGER'POS(N) = N
INTEGER'VAL(N) = N
INTEGER'SUCC(N) = N+1
INTEGER'PRED(N) = N−1
```

The application of these attributes to integers does at first sight seem pretty futile but when we come to the concept of generic units in Chapter 13 we will see that it is convenient to allow them to apply to all discrete types.

The attributes FIRST and LAST however apply to all scalar types and subtypes including real types.

Again we emphasize that POS, VAL, SUCC and PRED for a subtype are identical to the corresponding operations on the base type, whereas in the case of FIRST and LAST this is not so.

Finally we note the difference between a type conversion and a type qualification.

```
REAL(I)            -- conversion
INTEGER ' (I)      -- qualification
```

In the case of a conversion we are changing the type, in the second, we are just stating it (usually to overcome an ambiguity). As a mnemonic aid *q*ualification uses a *q*uote.

In both cases we can use a subtype name and CONSTRAINT_ERROR could consequently arise. Thus

```
POSITIVE(R)
```

would convert the value of the real variable R to integer and then check that it was positive, whereas

```
POSITIVE ' (I)
```

would just check that the value of I was positive. In both cases, of course, the result is the checked value and is then used in an overall expression; these checks cannot just stand alone.

## 4.9   Expression summary

All the operators introduced so far are shown in Table 4.1 grouped by precedence level.

In all the cases of binary operators except for **, the two operands must be of the same type.

We have actually now introduced all the operators of Ada except for one (&) although as we shall see in Chapter 6 there are further possible meanings to be added.

There are also two membership tests which apply to all scalar types (among others). These are **in** and **not in**. They are technically not operators although their precedence is the same as that of the relational operators =, /= and so on. They enable us to test whether a value lies within a specified range (including the end values) or satisfies a constraint implied by a subtype. The first operand is therefore a scalar expression, the second is a range or type mark and the result is, of course, of type Boolean. Examples are

```
I not in 1 .. 10
I in POSITIVE
TODAY in WEEKDAY
```

Note that this is one of the situations where we have to use a type mark rather than a subtype indication. We could not replace the last example by

```
TODAY in DAY range MON .. FRI
```

**Table 4.1** Scalar operators.

| Operator | Operation | Operand(s) | Result |
|---|---|---|---|
| **and** | conjunction | BOOLEAN | BOOLEAN |
| **or** | inclusive or | BOOLEAN | BOOLEAN |
| **xor** | exclusive or | BOOLEAN | BOOLEAN |
| = | equality | any | BOOLEAN |
| /= | inequality | any | BOOLEAN |
| < | less than | scalar | BOOLEAN |
| <= | less than or equals | scalar | BOOLEAN |
| > | greater than | scalar | BOOLEAN |
| >= | greater than or equals | scalar | BOOLEAN |
| + | addition | numeric | same |
| − | subtraction | numeric | same |
| + | identity | numeric | same |
| − | negation | numeric | same |
| * | multiplication | INTEGER | INTEGER |
|  |  | REAL | REAL |
| / | division | INTEGER | INTEGER |
|  |  | REAL | REAL |
| **mod** | modulo | INTEGER | INTEGER |
| **rem** | remainder | INTEGER | INTEGER |
| ** | exponentiation | INTEGER: NATURAL | INTEGER |
|  |  | REAL: INTEGER | REAL |
| **not** | negation | BOOLEAN | BOOLEAN |
| **abs** | absolute value | numeric | same |

although we could write

    TODAY **in** MON .. FRI

Ada seems a bit curious here!

The test **not in** is equivalent to using **in** and then applying **not** to the result, but **not in** is usually more readable. So the first expression above could be written as

    **not** (I **in** 1 .. 10)

where the brackets are necessary.

The reason that **in** and **not in** are not technically operators is explained in Chapter 7 when we deal with subprograms.

There are also two short circuit control forms **and then** and **or else** which like **in** and **not in** are also not technically classed as operators.

The form **and then** is closely related to the operator **and** whereas

**or else** is closely related to the operator **or**. They may occur in expressions and have the same precedence as **and**, **or** and **xor**. The difference lies in the rules regarding the evaluation of their operands.

In the case of **and** and **or**, both operands are always evaluated but the order is not specified. In the case of **and then** and **or else** the left hand operand is always evaluated first and the right hand operand is only evaluated if it is necessary in order to determine the result.

So in

X **and then** Y

X is evaluated first. If X is false, the answer is false whatever the value of Y so Y is not evaluated. If X is true, Y has to be evaluated and the value of Y is the answer.

Similarly in

X **or else** Y

X is evaluated first. If X is true, the answer is true whatever the value of Y so Y is not evaluated. If X is false, Y has to be evaluated and the value of Y is the answer.

The forms **and then** and **or else** should be used in cases where the order of evaluation matters. A common circumstance is where the first condition protects against the evaluation of the second condition in circumstances that could raise an exception.

Suppose we need to test

I/J > K

and we wish to avoid the risk that J is zero. In such a case we could write

J /= 0 **and then** I/J > K

and we would then know that if J is zero there is no risk of an attempt to divide by zero. The observant reader will realize that this is not a very good example because one could usually write I>K*J (assuming J positive) – but even here we could get overflow. Better examples occur with arrays and access types and will be mentioned in due course.

Like **and** and **or**, the forms **and then** and **or else** cannot be mixed without using brackets.

We now summarize the primary components of an expression (that is the things upon which the operators operate) that we have met so far. They are

- identifiers          used for variables, constants, numbers and enumeration literals
- literals             such as 4.6, 2#101#
- type conversions     such as INTEGER(R)

- qualified expressions        such as COLOUR'(AMBER)
- attributes                   such as INTEGER'LAST
- function calls               such as DAY'SUCC(TODAY)

A full consideration of functions and how they are declared and called has to be deferred until later. However, it is worth noting at this point that a function with one parameter is called by following its name by the parameter in brackets. The parameter can be any expression of the appropriate type and could include further function calls. We will assume for the moment that we have available a simple mathematical library containing familiar functions such as

SQRT   square root

LOG    logarithm to base 10

LN     natural logarithm

EXP    exponential function

SIN    sine

COS    cosine

In each case they take a REAL argument and deliver a REAL result.
We are now in a position to write statements such as

```
ROOT:= (−B+SQRT(B**2−4.0*A*C)) / (2.0*A);
SIN2X:= 2.0*SIN(X)*COS(X);
```

Finally a note on errors although this is not the place to deal with them in depth. The reader will have noticed that whenever anything could go wrong we have usually stated that the exception CONSTRAINT_ERROR will be raised. This is a general exception which applies to all sorts of violations of ranges. The only other exception which needs to be mentioned at this point is NUMERIC_ERROR. This will usually be raised if something goes wrong with the evaluation of an arithmetic expression itself before an attempt is made to store the result. An obvious example is an attempt to divide by zero. It might be thought that the distinction between these two exceptions was quite clear. However, consider on the one hand

```
INTEGER'SUCC(INTEGER'LAST)
```

which might be expected to raise CONSTRAINT_ERROR, and on the other hand

```
INTEGER'LAST+1
```

which might be expected to raise NUMERIC_ERROR. In practice, the object code for these two expressions is likely to be the same. As a consequence, AI-387 concludes that CONSTRAINT_ERROR and NUMERIC_ERROR cannot be crisply distinguished and therefore must be considered to be the same exception. (This is our first example of an AI where the language has been concluded not to be quite as it appears from the *LRM*. See Section 1.1.)

As well as exceptions there are erroneous constructs and incorrect order dependencies as mentioned in Chapter 2. The use of a variable before a value has been assigned to it is an important example of an erroneous situation. Two cases which we have encountered so far where the order is not defined are

- The destination variable in an assignment statement may be evaluated before or after the expression to be assigned.
- The order of evaluation of the two operands of a binary operator is not defined.

(In the first case it should be realized that the destination variable could be an array component such as A(I+J) and so the expression I+J has to be evaluated as part of evaluating the destination variable; we will deal with arrays in Chapter 6.) Examples where these orders matter cannot be given until we deal with functions in Chapter 7.

---

*Exercise 4.9*

**1**    Rewrite the following mathematical expressions in Ada.

(a)   $2\pi\sqrt{l/g}$          – period of a pendulum

(b)   $\dfrac{m_0}{\sqrt{1-v^2/c^2}}$          – mass of relativistic particle

(c)   $\sqrt{2\pi n}\,.n^n\,.e^{-n}$  – Stirling's approximation for $n!$ (integral $n$)

**2**    Rewrite **1**(c) replacing $n$ by the real value $x$.

---

## Checklist 4

Declarations and statements are terminated by a semicolon.

Initialization, like assignment uses :=.

Any initial value is evaluated for each object in a declaration.

Elaboration of declarations is linear.

An identifier may not be used in its own declaration.

Each type definition introduces a quite distinct type.

A subtype is not a new type but merely a shorthand for a type with a possible constraint.

A type is always static, a subtype need not be.

No mixed mode arithmetic.

Distinguish **rem** and **mod** for negative operands.

Exponentiation with a negative exponent only applies to real types.

Take care with the precedence of the unary operators.

A scalar type cannot be empty, a subtype can.

POS, VAL, SUCC and PRED on subtypes are the same as on the base type.

FIRST and LAST are different for subtypes.

Qualification uses a quote.

Order of evaluation of binary operands is not defined.

Distinguish **and, or** and **and then, or else**.

# Chapter 5
# Control Structures

This chapter describes the three bracketed sequential control structures of Ada. These are the if statement which we have briefly met before, the case statement and the loop statement. It is now recognized that these three control structures are not only necessary but also sufficient to be able to write programs with a clearly discernible flow of control without recourse to goto statements and labels. However, for pragmatic reasons, Ada does actually contain a goto statement and this is also described in this chapter.

The three control structures exhibit a similar bracketing style. There is an opening reserved word **if, case** or **loop** and this is matched at the end of the structure by the same reserved word preceded by **end**. The whole is, as usual, terminated by a semicolon. So we have

```
if              case            loop
   ...             ...             ...
end if;         end case;       end loop;
```

In the case of the loop statement the word loop can be preceded by an iteration clause commencing with **for** or **while**.

## 5.1   If statements

The simplest form of if statement starts with the reserved word **if** followed by a Boolean expression and the reserved word **then**. This is then followed by a sequence of statements which will be executed if the Boolean expression turns out to be TRUE. The end of the sequence is indicated by the closing **end if**. The Boolean expression can, of course, be of arbitrary complexity and the sequence of statements can be of arbitrary length.

A simple example is

```
if HUNGRY then
    EAT;
end if;
```

In this, HUNGRY is a Boolean variable and EAT is a subprogram describing the details of the eating activity. The statement EAT; merely calls the subprogram (subprograms are dealt with in detail in Chapter 7).

The effect of this if statement is that if variable HUNGRY is TRUE then we call the subprogram EAT and otherwise we do nothing. In either case we then obey the statement following the if statement.

As we have said there could be a long sequence between **then** and **end if**. Thus we might break down the process into more detail

```
if HUNGRY then
    COOK;
    EAT;
    WASH_UP;
end if;
```

Note how we indent the statements to show the flow structure of the program. This is most important since it enables the program to be understood so much more easily. The **end if** should be underneath the corresponding **if** and **then** is best placed on the same line as the **if**.

Sometimes, if the whole statement is very short it can all go on one line.

```
if X < 0.0 then X:= −X; end if;
```

Note that **end if** will always be preceded by a semicolon. This is because the semicolons terminate statements rather than separate them as in Algol and Pascal. Readers familiar with those languages will probably feel initially that the Ada style is irksome. However, it is consistent and makes line by line program editing so much easier.

Often we will want to do alternative actions according to the value of the condition. In this case we add **else** followed by the alternative sequence to be obeyed if the condition is FALSE. We saw an example of this in the last chapter

```
if TODAY = SUN then
    TOMORROW:= MON;
else
    TOMORROW:= DAY'SUCC(TODAY);
end if;
```

Algol 60 and Algol 68 users should note that Ada is not an expression language and so conditional expressions are not allowed. We cannot write something like

```
    TOMORROW:=
        if TODAY = SUN then MON else DAY'SUCC(TODAY) end if;
```

The statements in the sequences after **then** and **else** can be quite arbitrary and so could be further nested if statements. Suppose we have to solve the quadratic equation

$$ax^2 + bx + c = 0$$

The first thing to check is $a$. If $a = 0$ then the equation degenerates into a linear equation with a single root $-c/b$. (Mathematicians will understand that the other root has slipped off to infinity.) If $a$ is not zero then we test the discriminant $b^2 - 4ac$ to see whether the roots are real or complex. We could program this as

```
    if A = 0.0 then
                -- linear case
    else
        if B**2 - 4.0*A*C >= 0.0 then
                -- real roots
        else
                -- complex roots
        end if;
    end if;
```

Observe the repetition of **end if**. This is rather ugly and occurs sufficiently frequently to justify an additional construction. This uses the reserved word **elsif** as follows

```
    if A = 0.0 then
                -- linear case
    elsif B**2 - 4.0*A*C >= 0.0 then
                -- real roots
    else
                -- complex roots
    end if;
```

This construction emphasizes the essentially equal status of the three cases and also the sequential nature of the tests.

The **elsif** part can be repeated an arbitrary number of times and the final **else** part is optional. The behaviour is simply that each condition is evaluated in turn until one that is TRUE is encountered; the corresponding sequence is then obeyed. If none of the conditions turns out to be TRUE then the else part, if any, is taken; if there is no else part then none of the sequences is obeyed.

Note the spelling of **elsif**. It is the only reserved word of Ada that is not an English word (apart from operators such as **xor**). Note also the layout – we align **elsif** and **else** with the **if** and **end if** and all the sequences are indented equally.

As a further example, suppose we are drilling soldiers and they can obey four different orders described by

```
type MOVE is (LEFT, RIGHT, BACK, ON);
```

and that their response to these orders is described by calling subprograms TURN_LEFT, TURN_RIGHT and TURN_BACK or by doing nothing at all respectively. Suppose that the variable ORDER of type MOVE contains the order to be obeyed. We could then write the following

```
if ORDER = LEFT then
    TURN_LEFT;
else
    if ORDER = RIGHT then
        TURN_RIGHT;
    else
        if ORDER = BACK then
            TURN_BACK;
        end if;
    end if;
end if;
```

But it is far clearer and neater to write

```
if ORDER = LEFT then
    TURN_LEFT;
elsif ORDER = RIGHT then
    TURN_RIGHT;
elsif ORDER = BACK then
    TURN_BACK;
end if;
```

This illustrates a situation where there is no **else** part. However, although better than using nested if statements, this is still a bad solution because it obscures the symmetry and mutual exclusion of the four cases ('mutual exclusion' means that by their very nature only one can apply). We have been forced to impose an ordering on the tests which is quite arbitrary and not the essence of the problem. The proper solution is to use the case statement as we shall see in the next section.

Contrast this with the quadratic equation. In that example, the cases were not mutually exclusive and the tests had to be performed in order. If we had tested $b^2 - 4ac$ first then we would have been forced to test $a$ against zero in each alternative.

There is no directly corresponding contraction for **then if** as in Algol 68. Instead the short circuit control form **and then** can often be used.

So, rather than

```
if J > 0 then
    if I/J > K then
        ACTION;
    end if;
end if;
```

we can, as we have seen, write

```
if J > 0 and then I/J > K then
   ACTION;
end if;
```

---

*Exercise 5.1*

1      The variables DAY, MONTH and YEAR contain today's date. They are declared as

```
DAY: INTEGER range 1 .. 31;
MONTH: MONTH_NAME;
YEAR: INTEGER range 1901 .. 2099;
```

where

```
type MONTH_NAME is (JAN, FEB, MAR, APR, MAY, JUN, JUL,
                    AUG, SEP, OCT, NOV, DEC);
```

Write statements to update the variables to contain tomorrow's date. What happens if today is 31 DEC 2099?

2      X and Y are two real variables. Write statements to swap their values, if necessary, to ensure that the larger value is in X. Use a block to declare a temporary variable T.

---

## 5.2   Case statements

A case statement allows us to choose one of several sequences of statements according to the value of an expression. For instance, the example of the drilling soldiers should be written as

```
case ORDER is
   when LEFT => TURN_LEFT;
   when RIGHT => TURN_RIGHT;
   when BACK => TURN_BACK;
   when ON => null;
end case;
```

All possible values of the expression must be provided for in order to guard against accidental omissions. If, as in this example, no action is required for one or more values then the null statement has to be used.

The null statement, written

```
null;
```

does absolutely nothing but its presence indicates that we truly want to do nothing. The sequence of statements here, as in the if statement, must contain at least one statement. (There is no empty statement as in Algol 60.)

It often happens that the same action is desired for several values of the expression. Consider the following

```
case TODAY is
    when MON | TUES | WED | THU  => WORK;
    when FRI                     => WORK; PARTY;
    when SAT | SUN               => null;
end case;
```

This expresses the idea that on Monday to Thursday we go to work. On Friday we also go to work and then go to a party. At the weekend we do nothing. The alternative values are separated by the vertical bar character. Note again the use of a null statement.

If several successive values have the same action then it is more convenient to use a range

```
when MON .. THU => WORK;
```

Sometimes we wish to express the idea of a default action to be taken by all values not explicitly stated; this is provided for by the reserved word **others**. The above example could be rewritten

```
case TODAY is
    when MON .. THU  => WORK;
    when FRI         => WORK; PARTY;
    when others      => null;
end case;
```

It is possible to have ranges as alternatives. In fact this is probably a situation where the clearest explanation of what is allowed is given by the formal syntax*.

```
case_statement ::=
    case expression is
        case_statement_alternative
        {case_statement_alternative}
    end case;
case_statement_alternative ::=
    when choice { | choice} => sequence_of_statements
choice ::= simple_expression | discrete_range | others |
    component_simple_name
discrete_range ::= discrete_subtype_indication | range
subtype_indication ::= type_mark [constraint]
type_mark ::= type_name | subtype_name
range ::= range_attribute | simple_expression .. simple_expression
```

(*In the production for case_statement_alternative, the vertical bar stands for itself and is not a metasymbol.)

We see that **when** is followed by one or more choices separated by vertical bars and that a choice may be a simple expression, a discrete range or **others**. (The syntax shows that a choice may be a component simple name; however this only applies to choices used in a different situation which we have not yet met and so can be ignored for the moment.) A simple expression, of course, just gives a single value – FRI being a trivial example. A discrete range offers several possibilities. It can be the syntactic form range which the syntax tells us can be two simple expressions separated by two dots – MON .. THU is a simple example; a range can also be given by a range attribute which we will meet in the next chapter. A discrete range can also be a subtype indication which as we know is a type mark (a type name or subtype name) followed optionally by an appropriate constraint. In this case the constraint has to be a range constraint which is merely the reserved word **range** followed by the syntactic form range. Examples of discrete ranges are

```
MON .. THU
DAY range MON .. THU
WEEKDAY
WEEKDAY range MON .. THU
```

All these possibilities may seem unnecessary but as we shall see later the form, discrete range, is used in other contexts as well as the case statement. In the case statement there is not usually much point in using the type name since this is known from the context anyway. Similarly, there is not much point in using the subtype name followed by a constraint since the constraint alone will do. However, it might be useful to use a subtype name alone when that exactly corresponds to the range required. So we could rewrite the example as

```
case TODAY is
    when WEEKDAY  => WORK;
                            if TODAY = FRI then
                                PARTY;
                            end if;
    when others      => null;
end case;
```

although this solution feels untidy.

There are various other restrictions that the syntax does not tell us. One is that if we use **others** then it must appear alone and as the last alternative. As stated earlier it covers all values not explicitly covered by the previous alternatives (one is still allowed to write **others** even if there are no other cases to be considered!).

Another very important restriction is that all the choices must be static so that they can be evaluated at compilation time. Thus all expressions in choices must be static – in practice they will usually be literals as in our examples. Similarly, if a choice is simply a subtype such as WEEKDAY then it too must be static.

Finally we return to the point made at the beginning of this section that all possible values of the expression after **case** must be provided for. This usually means all values of the type of the expression. This is certainly the case of a variable declared as of a type without any constraints (as in the case of TODAY). However, if the expression is of a simple form and belongs to a static subtype (that is one whose constraints are static expressions and so can be determined at compilation time) then only values of that subtype need be provided for. In other words if the compiler can tell that only a subset of values is possible then only that subset need and must be covered. The simple forms allowed for the expression are the name of an object of the static subtype or a qualified or converted expression whose type mark is that of the static subtype.

In the case of our example, if TODAY had been of subtype WEEKDAY then we would know that only the values MON .. FRI are possible and so only these can and need be covered. Even if TODAY is not constrained we can still write our expression as a qualified expression WEEKDAY'(TODAY) and then again only MON .. FRI is possible. So we could write

```
case WEEKDAY'(TODAY) is
    when MON .. THU  => WORK;
    when FRI         => WORK; PARTY;
end case;
```

but, of course, if TODAY happens to take a value not in the subtype WEEKDAY (that is, SAT or SUN) then CONSTRAINT_ERROR will be raised. Mere qualification cannot prevent TODAY from being SAT or SUN. So this is not really a solution to our original problem.

As further examples, suppose we had variables

```
I: INTEGER range 1 .. 10;
J: INTEGER range 1 .. N;
```

where N is not static. Then we know that I belongs to a static subtype (albeit anonymous) whereas we cannot say the same about J. If I is used as an expression in a case statement then only the values 1 .. 10 have to be catered for, whereas if J is so used then the full range of values of type INTEGER (INTEGER'FIRST .. INTEGER'LAST) have to be catered for.

The above discussion on the case statement has no doubt given the reader the impression of considerable complexity. It therefore seems wise to summarize the key points which will in practice need to be remembered.

- Every possible value of the expression after **case** must be covered once and once only.

- All values and ranges after **when** must be static.

- If **others** is used it must be last and on its own.

---

*Exercise 5.2*

1    Rewrite Exercise 5.1(**1**) to use a case statement to set the correct
     value in END_OF_MONTH.

2    A vegetable gardener digs in winter, sows seed in spring, tends
     the growing plants in summer and harvests the crop in the autumn
     or fall. Write a case statement to call the appropriate subprogram
     DIG, SOW, TEND or HARVEST according to the month M. Declare
     appropriate subtypes if desired.

3    An improvident man is paid on the first of each month. For the
     first ten days he gorges himself, for the next ten he subsists and
     for the remainder he starves. Call subprograms GORGE, SUBSIST
     and STARVE according to the day D. Assume END_OF_MONTH
     has been set and that D is declared as

          D: INTEGER **range** 1 .. END_OF_MONTH;

---

## 5.3  Loop statements

The simplest form of loop statement is

**loop**
     sequence_of_statements
**end loop**;

The statements of the sequence are then repeated indefinitely unless one
of them terminates the loop by some means. So immortality could be
represented by

**loop**
     WORK;
     EAT;
     SLEEP;
**end loop**;

As a more concrete example consider the problem of computing the
base *e* of natural logarithms from the infinite series

$$e = 1 + 1/1! + 1/2! + 1/3! + 1/4! + \ldots$$

where

$$n! = n \times (n - 1) \times (n - 2) \ldots 3 \times 2 \times 1$$

A possible solution is

```
declare
    E: REAL:= 1.0;
    I: INTEGER:= 0;
    TERM: REAL:= 1.0;
begin
    loop
        I:= I + 1;
        TERM:= TERM / REAL(I);
        E:= E + TERM;
    end loop;
    ...
```

Each time around the loop a new term is computed by dividing the previous term by I. The new term is then added to the sum so far which is accumulated in E. The term number I is an integer because it is logically a counter and so we have to write REAL(I) as the divisor. The series is started by setting values in E, I and TERM which correspond to the first term (that for which I = 0).

The computation then goes on for ever with E becoming a closer and closer approximation to $e$. In practice, because of the finite accuracy of the computer, TERM will become zero and continued computation will be pointless. But in any event we presumably want to stop at some point so that we can do something with our computed result. We can do this with the statement

```
exit;
```

If this is obeyed inside a loop then the loop terminates at once and control passes to the point immediately after end loop.

Suppose we decide to stop after $N$ terms of the series – that is when I = N. We can do this by writing the loop as

```
loop
    if I = N then exit; end if;
    I:= I + 1;
    TERM:= TERM / REAL(I);
    E:= E + TERM;
end loop;
```

The construction

```
if condition then exit; end if;
```

is so common that a special shorthand is provided

```
exit when condition;
```

So we now have

```
loop
    exit when I = N;
    I:= I + 1;
    TERM:= TERM / REAL(I);
    E:= E + TERM;
end loop;
```

Although an exit statement can appear anywhere inside a loop – it could be in the middle or near the end – a special form is provided for the frequent case where we want to test a condition at the start of each iteration. This uses the reserved word **while** and gives the condition for the loop to be continued. So we could write

```
while I /= N loop
    I:= I + 1;
    TERM:= TERM / REAL(I);
    E:= E + TERM;
end loop;
```

The condition is naturally evaluated each time around the loop.

The final form of loop allows for a specific number of iterations with a loop parameter taking in turn all the values of a discrete range. Our example could be recast as

```
for I in 1 .. N loop
    TERM:= TERM / REAL(I);
    E:= E + TERM;
end loop;
```

where I takes the values 1, 2, 3, ... N.

The parameter I is implicitly declared by its appearance in the iteration scheme and does not have to be declared outside. It takes its type from the discrete range and within the loop behaves as a constant so that it cannot be changed except by the loop mechanism itself. When we leave the loop (by whatever means) I ceases to exist (because it was implicitly declared by the loop) and so we cannot read its final value from outside.

We could leave the loop by an exit statement – if we wanted to know the final value we could copy the value of I into a variable declared outside the loop thus

```
if condition_to_exit then
    LAST_I:= I;
    exit;
end if;
```

The values of the discrete range are normally taken in ascending order. Descending order can be specified by writing

```
for I in reverse 1 .. N loop
```

but the range itself is always written in ascending order.

It is not possible to specify a numeric step size of other than 1. This should not be a problem since the vast majority of loops go up by steps of 1 and almost all the rest go down by steps of 1. The very few which do behave otherwise can be explicitly programmed using the while form of loop.

The range can be null (as for instance if N happened to be zero or negative in our example) in which case the sequence of statements will not be obeyed at all. Of course, the range itself is evaluated only once and cannot be changed inside the loop.

Thus

```
N:= 4;
for I in 1 .. N loop
    ...
    N:= 10;
end loop;
```

results in the loop being executed just four times despite the fact that N is changed to ten.

Our examples have all shown the lower bound of the range being 1. This, of course, need not be the case. Both bounds can be arbitrary dynamically evaluated expressions. Furthermore the loop parameter need not be of integer type. It can be of any discrete type, as determined by the discrete range.

We could, for instance, simulate a week's activity by

```
for TODAY in MON .. SUN loop
    case TODAY is
        ...
    end case;
end loop;
```

This implicitly declares TODAY to be of type DAY and obeys the loop with the values MON, TUE, ... SUN in turn.

The other forms of discrete range (using a type or subtype name) are of advantage here. The essence of MON .. SUN is that it embraces all the values of the type DAY. It is therefore better to write the loop using a form of discrete range that conveys the idea of completeness

```
for TODAY in DAY loop
    ...
end loop;
```

And again since we know that we do nothing at weekends anyway we could write

```
for TODAY in DAY range MON .. FRI loop
```

or better

> **for** TODAY **in** WEEKDAY **loop**

It is interesting to note a difference regarding the determination of types in the case statement and for statement. In the case statement, the type of a discrete range after **when** is determined from the type of the expression after **case**. In the for statement, the type of the loop parameter is determined from the type of the discrete range after **in**. The dependency is the other way round.

It is therefore necessary for the type of the discrete range to be unambiguous in the for statement. This is usually the case but if we had two enumeration types with two overloaded literals such as

> **type** PLANET **is** (MERCURY, VENUS, EARTH, MARS, JUPITER,
> SATURN, URANUS, NEPTUNE, PLUTO);
> **type** ROMAN_GOD **is** (JANUS, MARS, JUPITER, JUNO, VESTA,
> VULCAN, SATURN, MERCURY, MINERVA);

then

> **for** X **in** MARS .. SATURN **loop**

would be ambiguous and the compiler would not compile our program. We could resolve the problem by qualifying one of the expressions

> **for** X **in** PLANET'(MARS) .. SATURN **loop**

or (probably better) by using a form of discrete range giving the type explicitly

> **for** X **in** PLANET **range** MARS .. SATURN **loop**

When we have dealt with numerics in more detail we will realize that the range 1 .. 10 is not necessarily of type INTEGER. A general application of our rule that the type must not be ambiguous in a for statement would lead us to have to write

> **for** I **in** INTEGER **range** 1 .. 10 **loop**

However, this would be so tedious in such a common case that there is a special rule which applies to discrete ranges in for statements which says that if both bounds are integer literals then type INTEGER is implied. We can therefore conveniently write

> **for** I **in** 1 .. 10 **loop**

But note carefully that we cannot write

> **for** I **in** −1 .. 10 **loop**

because −1 is not a literal as explained in Section 3.4. This perhaps surprising conclusion is confirmed by AI-148. We will return to this topic in Section 12.1.

Finally we reconsider the exit statement. The simple form encountered earlier always transfers control to immediately after the innermost embracing loop. But of course loops may be nested and sometimes we may wish to exit from a nested construction. As an example suppose we are searching in two dimensions

```
for I in 1 .. N loop
    for J in 1 .. M loop
        -- if values of I and J satisfy
        -- some condition then leave nested loop
    end loop;
end loop;
```

A simple exit statement in the inner loop would merely take us to the end of that loop and we would have to recheck the condition and exit again. This can be avoided by naming the outer loop and using the name in the exit statement thus

```
SEARCH:
for I in 1 .. N loop
    for J in 1 .. M loop
        if condition_OK then
            I_VALUE:= I;
            J_VALUE:= J;
            exit SEARCH;
        end if;
    end loop;
end loop SEARCH;
-- control passes here
```

A loop is named by preceding it with an identifier and colon. (It looks remarkably like a label in other languages but it is not and cannot be 'gone to'.) The identifier must be repeated between the corresponding **end loop** and the semicolon.

The conditional form of exit can also refer to a loop by name

```
exit SEARCH when condition;
```

---

*Exercise 5.3*

1    The statement GET(I); reads the next value from the input file into the integer variable I. Write statements to read and add together a series of numbers. The end of the series is indicated by a dummy negative value.

2    Write statements to determine the power of 2 in the factorization of N. Compute the result in COUNT but do not alter N.

3        Compute

$$g = \sum_{p=1}^{n} \frac{1}{p} - \log n$$

(As $n \to \infty$, $g \to \gamma = 0.577215665...$)

---

## 5.4  Goto statements and labels

Many will be surprised that a modern programming language should contain a goto statement at all. It is now considered to be extremely bad practice to use goto statements because of the resulting difficulty in proving correctness of the program, maintenance and so on. And indeed Ada contains adequate control structures so that it should not normally be necessary to use a goto at all.

So why provide a goto statement? The main reason concerns automatically generated programs. If we try to transliterate (by hand or machine) a program from some other language into Ada then the goto will probably be useful. Another example might be where the program is generated automatically from some high-level specification. Finally there may be cases where the goto is the neatest way – perhaps as a way out of some deeply nested structure – but the alternative of raising an exception (see Chapter 10) could also be considered.

In order to put us off using gotos and labels (and perhaps so that our manager can spot them if we do) the notation for a label is unusual and stands out like a sore thumb. A label is an identifier enclosed in double angled brackets thus

        <<THE_DEVIL>>

and a goto statement takes the expected form of the reserved word **goto** followed by the label identifier and semicolon

        **goto** THE_DEVIL;

A goto statement cannot be used to transfer control into an if, case or loop statement nor between the arms of an if or case statement.

---

*Exercise 5.4*

1        Rewrite the nested loop of Section 5.3 using a label
         <<SEARCH>> rather than naming the outer loop. Why is this
         not such a good solution?

## 5.5  Statement classification

The statements in Ada can be classified as shown in Figure 5.1.

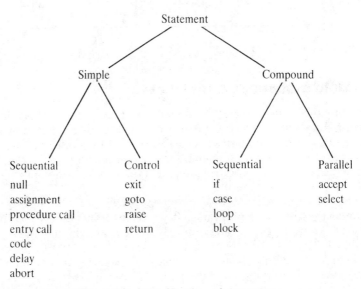

**Figure 5.1**  Classification of statements.

Further detail on the assignment statement is in the next chapter when we discuss composite types. Procedure calls and return statements are discussed in Chapter 7 and the raise statement which is concerned with exceptions is discussed in Chapter 10. The code statement is mentioned in Chapter 15. The remaining statements (entry call, delay, abort, accept and select) concern tasking and are dealt with in Chapter 14.

All statements can have one or more labels. The simple statements cannot be decomposed lexically into other statements whereas the compound statements can be so decomposed and can therefore be nested. Statements are obeyed sequentially unless one of them is a control statement (or an exception is implicitly raised).

## Checklist 5

Statement brackets must match correctly.

Use **elsif** where appropriate.

The choices in a case statement must be static.

All possibilities in a case statement must be catered for.

If **others** is used it must be last and on its own.

The expression after **case** can be qualified in order to reduce the alternatives.

A loop parameter behaves as a constant.

A named loop must have the name at both ends.

Avoid gotos.

Use the recommended layout.

# Chapter 6
# Composite Types

In this chapter we describe the composite types which are arrays and records. We also complete our discussion of enumeration types by introducing characters and strings. At this stage we discuss arrays fairly completely but consider only simple forms of records. The more elaborate discriminated records which include variant records are deferred until Chapter 11.


## 6.1 Arrays

An array is a composite object consisting of a number of components all of the same type (strictly, subtype). An array can be of one, two or more dimensions. A typical array declaration might be

A: **array** (INTEGER **range** 1 .. 6) **of** REAL;

This declares A to be a variable object which has six components, each of which is of type REAL. The individual components are referred to by following the array name with an expression in brackets giving an integer value in the discrete range 1 .. 6. If this expression, known as the index value, has a value outside the range, then the exception CONSTRAINT_ ERROR will be raised. We could set zero in each component of A by writing

```
for I in 1 .. 6 loop
    A(I):= 0.0;
end loop;
```

An array can be of several dimensions, in which case a separate range is given for each dimension. So

AA: **array** (INTEGER **range** 0 .. 2, INTEGER **range** 0 .. 3) **of** REAL;

is an array of 12 components in total, each of which is referred to by two integer index values, the first in the range 0 .. 2 and the second in the range 0 .. 3. Each component of this two-dimensional array could be set to zero by a nested loop thus

```
for I in 0 .. 2 loop
    for J in 0 .. 3 loop
        AA(I, J):= 0.0;
    end loop;
end loop;
```

The discrete ranges do not have to be static: one could have

```
N: INTEGER:= ... ;
B: array (INTEGER range 1 .. N) of BOOLEAN;
```

and the value of N at the point when the declaration of B is elaborated would determine the number of components in B. Of course, the declaration of B might be elaborated many times during the course of a program – it might be inside a loop for example – and each elaboration will give rise to a new life of a new array and the value of N could be different each time. Like other declared objects, the array B ceases to exist once we pass the end of the block containing its declaration. Because of 'linear elaboration of declarations' both N and B could be declared in the same declarative part but the declaration of N would have to precede that of B.

The discrete range in an array index follows similar rules to that in a for statement. An important one is that a range such as 1 .. 6 implies type INTEGER so we could have written

A: **array** (1 .. 6) **of** REAL;

However, an array index could be of any discrete type. We could for example have

HOURS_WORKED: **array** (DAY) **of** REAL;

This array has seven components denoted by HOURS_WORKED (MON), ... HOURS_WORKED(SUN). We could set suitable values in these variables by

```
for D in WEEKDAY loop
    HOURS_WORKED(D):= 8.0;
end loop;
HOURS_WORKED(SAT):= 0.0;
HOURS_WORKED(SUN):= 0.0;
```

If we only wanted to declare the array HOURS_WORKED to have components corresponding to MON .. FRI then we could write

HOURS_WORKED: **array** (DAY **range** MON .. FRI) **of** REAL;

or (better)

HOURS_WORKED: **array** (WEEKDAY) **of** REAL;

Arrays have various attributes relating to their indexes. A'FIRST and A'LAST give the lower and upper bound of the first (or only) index of A. So using our last declaration of HOURS_WORKED

HOURS_WORKED 'FIRST = MON
HOURS_WORKED 'LAST = FRI

A'LENGTH gives the number of values of the first (or only) index.

HOURS_WORKED 'LENGTH = 5

A'RANGE is short for A'FIRST .. A'LAST. So

HOURS_WORKED 'RANGE     is     MON .. FRI

The same attributes can be applied to the various dimensions of a multidimensional array by adding the dimension number in brackets. It has to be a static expression. So, in the case of our two-dimensional array AA we have

AA'FIRST(1)   = 0
AA'FIRST(2)   = 0
AA'LAST(1)    = 2
AA'LAST(2)    = 3
AA'LENGTH(1) = 3
AA'LENGTH(2) = 4

and

AA'RANGE(1)     is 0 .. 2
AA'RANGE(2)     is 0 .. 3

The first dimension is assumed if (1) is omitted. It is perhaps better practice to specifically state (1) for multidimensional arrays and omit it for one-dimensional arrays.

It is always best to use the attributes where possible in order to reflect relationships among entities in a program because it generally means that if the program is modified, the modifications are localized.

The RANGE attribute is particularly useful with loops. Our earlier examples are better written as

```
for I in A'RANGE loop
    A(I):= 0.0;
end loop;

for I in AA'RANGE(1) loop
    for J in AA'RANGE(2) loop
        AA(I, J):= 0.0;
    end loop;
end loop;
```

The RANGE attribute can also be used in a declaration. Thus

```
J: INTEGER range A'RANGE;
```

is equivalent to

```
J: INTEGER range 1 .. 6;
```

If a variable is to be used to index an array as in A(J) it is usually best if the variable has the same constraints as the discrete range in the array declaration. This will usually minimize the run-time checks necessary. It has been found that in such circumstances it is usually the case that the index variable J is assigned less frequently than the array component A(J) is accessed. We will return to this topic in Section 10.3.

The array components we have seen are just variables in the ordinary way. They can therefore be assigned to and used in expressions.

Like other variable objects, arrays can be given an initial value. This will often be denoted by an aggregate which is the literal form for an array value. The simplest form of aggregate consists of a list of expressions giving the values of the components in order, separated by commas and enclosed in brackets. So we could initialize the array A by

```
A: array (1 .. 6) of REAL:= (0.0, 0.0, 0.0, 0.0, 0.0, 0.0);
```

In the case of a multidimensional array the aggregate is written in a nested form

```
AA: array (0 .. 2, 0 .. 3) of REAL:= ((0.0, 0.0, 0.0, 0.0),
                                      (0.0, 0.0, 0.0, 0.0),
                                      (0.0, 0.0, 0.0, 0.0));
```

and this illustrates that the first index is the 'outer' one. Or thinking in terms of rows and columns, the first index is the row number.

An aggregate must be complete. If we initialize any component of an array, we must initialize them all.

The initial values for the individual components need not be literals, they can be any expressions. These expressions are evaluated when the declaration is elaborated but the order of evaluation of the expressions in the aggregate is not specified.

An array can be declared as constant in which case an initial value is mandatory as explained in Section 4.1. Constant arrays are of frequent value as look-up tables. The following array can be used to determine whether a particular day is a working day or not

> WORK_DAY: **constant array** (DAY) **of** BOOLEAN
> := (TRUE, TRUE, TRUE, TRUE, TRUE, FALSE, FALSE);

An interesting example would be an array enabling tomorrow to be determined without worrying about the end of the week.

> TOMORROW: **constant array** (DAY) **of** DAY
> := (TUE, WED, THU, FRI, SAT, SUN, MON);

For any day D, TOMORROW (D) is the following day.

Finally, it should be noted that the array components can be of any type or subtype. Also the dimensions of a multidimensional array can be of different discrete types. An extreme example would be

> STRANGE: **array** (COLOUR, 2 .. 7, WEEKDAY **range** TUE .. THU)
> **of** PLANET **range** MARS .. SATURN;

---

*Exercise 6.1*

**1**    Declare an array F of integers with index running from 0 to N. Write statements to set the components of F equal to the Fibonacci numbers given by

$$F_0 = 0, \; F_1 = 1, \; F_i = F_{i-1} + F_{i-2} \qquad i > 1$$

**2**    Write statements to find the index values I, J of the maximum component of

> A: **array** (1 .. N, 1 .. M) **of** REAL;

**3**    Declare an array DAYS_IN_MONTH giving the number of days in each month. See Exercise 5.1(**1**). Use it to rewrite that example. See also Exercise 5.2(**1**).

**4**    Declare an array YESTERDAY analogous to the example TOMORROW above.

**5**    Declare a constant array BOR such that

> BOR(P, Q) = P **or** Q

**6**    Declare a constant unit matrix UNIT of order 3. A unit matrix is one for which all components are zero except those whose indexes are equal which have value one.

---

## 6.2   Array types

The arrays we introduced in the last section did not have an explicit type name. They were in fact of anonymous type. This is one of the few cases in Ada where an object can be declared without naming the type – another case is with tasks.

Reconsidering the first example in the previous section, we could write

   **type** VECTOR_6 **is array** (1 .. 6) **of** REAL;

and then declare A using the type name in the usual way

   A: VECTOR_6;

An advantage of using a type name is that it enables us to assign whole arrays that have been declared separately. If we also have

   B: VECTOR_6;

then we can write

   B:= A;

which has the effect of

   B(1):= A(1); B(2):= A(2); ... B(6):= A(6);

although the order of assigning the components is not relevant.
   On the other hand if we had written

   C: **array** (1 .. 6) **of** REAL;
   D: **array** (1 .. 6) **of** REAL;

then D:= C; is illegal because C and D are not of the same type. They are of different types both of which are anonymous. The underlying rule is that every type definition introduces a new type and in this case the syntax tells us that an array type definition is the piece of text from **array** up to (but not including) the semicolon.
   Moreover, even if we had written

   C, D: **array** (1 .. 6) **of** REAL;

then D:= C; would still have been illegal. This is because of the rule mentioned in Section 4.1 that such a multiple declaration is only a shorthand for the two declarations above. There are therefore still two distinct type definitions even though they are not explicit.

Whether or not we introduce a type name for particular arrays depends very much on the abstract view of each situation. If we are thinking of the array as a complete object in its own right then we should use a type name. If, on the other hand, we are thinking of the array as merely an indexable conglomerate not related as a whole to other arrays then it should probably be of an anonymous type.

Arrays like TOMORROW and WORK_DAY of the last section are good examples of arrays which are of the anonymous category. To be forced to introduce a type name for such arrays would introduce unnecessary clutter and a possibly false sense of abstraction.

On the other hand if we are manipulating lots of arrays of reals of length 6 then there is a common underlying abstract type and so it should be named.

The model for array types introduced so far is still not satisfactory. It does not allow us to represent an abstract view that embraces the commonality between arrays which have different bounds but are other- wise of the same type. In particular, it would not allow the writing of subprograms which could take an array of arbitrary bounds as an actual parameter. This is generally recognized as a major difficulty with the original design of Pascal. So the concept of an unconstrained array type is introduced in which the constraints for the indexes are not given. Consider

    **type** VECTOR **is array** (INTEGER **range** <>) **of** REAL;

(The compound symbol <> is read as 'box'.)

This says that VECTOR is the name of a type which is a one- dimensional array of REAL components with an INTEGER index. But the lower and upper bounds are not given; **range** <> is meant to convey the notion of information to be added later.

When we declare objects of type VECTOR we must supply the bounds. We can do this in various ways. We can introduce an intermediate subtype and then declare the objects.

    **subtype** VECTOR_5 **is** VECTOR(1 .. 5);
    V: VECTOR_5;

Or we can declare the objects directly

    V: VECTOR(1 .. 5);

In either case the bounds are given by an index constraint which takes the form of a discrete range in brackets. All the usual forms of discrete range can be used.

The index can also be given by a subtype name, thus

    **type** P **is array** (POSITIVE **range** <>) **of** REAL;

in which case the actual bounds of any declared object must lie within the range implied by the index subtype POSITIVE. Note that the index subtype must be given by a type mark and not by a subtype indication; this avoids the horrid double use of **range** which could otherwise occur as in

    **type** NASTY **is array** (INTEGER **range** 1 .. 100 **range** <>) **of** ... ;

We can now see that when we wrote

    **type** VECTOR_6 **is array** (1 .. 6) **of** REAL;

this was really a shorthand for

    **subtype** index **is** INTEGER **range** 1 .. 6;
    **type** anon **is array** (index **range** <>) **of** REAL;
    **subtype** VECTOR_6 **is** anon(1 .. 6);

Another useful array type declaration is

    **type** MATRIX **is array** (INTEGER **range** <>, INTEGER **range** <>)
                                              **of** REAL;

And again we could introduce subtypes thus

    **subtype** MATRIX_3 **is** MATRIX(1 .. 3, 1 .. 3);
    M: MATRIX_3;

or the objects directly

    M: MATRIX(1 .. 3, 1 .. 3);

An important point to notice is that an array type or subtype must give all the bounds or none at all. It would be perfectly legal to introduce an alternative name for MATRIX by

    **subtype** MAT **is** MATRIX;

in which no bounds are given, but we could not have a type or subtype that just gave the bounds for one dimension but not the other.

In all of the cases we have been discussing, the ranges need not have static bounds. The bounds could be any expressions and are evaluated when the index constraint is encountered. We could have

    M: MATRIX(1 .. N, 1 .. N);

and then the upper bounds of M would be the value of N when M is declared. A range could even be null as would happen in the above case if N turned out to be zero. In this case the matrix M would have no components at all.

There is a further way in which the bounds of an array can be supplied but this only applies to constant arrays which like other constants have to be given an initial value. The bounds can then be taken from the initial value if they are not supplied directly. The initial value can be any expression of the appropriate type but will often be an aggregate as shown in the previous section. The form of aggregate shown there consisted of a list of expressions in brackets. Such an aggregate is known as a positional aggregate since the values are given in position order. In the case of a positional aggregate used as an initial value and supplying the bounds, the lower bound is S'FIRST where S is the subtype of the index. The upper bound is deduced from the number of components. (The bounds of positional aggregates in other contexts will be discussed in the next section.)

Suppose we had

```
type W is array (WEEKDAY range <>) of DAY;
NEXT_WORK_DAY: constant W:= (TUE, WED, THU, FRI, MON);
```

then the lower bound of the array is WEEKDAY'FIRST = MON and the upper bound is FRI. It would not have mattered whether we had written DAY or WEEKDAY in the declaration of W because DAY'FIRST and WEEKDAY'FIRST are the same.

Using initial values to supply the bounds needs care. Consider

```
UNIT_2: constant MATRIX:= ((1.0, 0.0), (0.0, 1.0));
```

intended to declare a 2 × 2 unit matrix with UNIT_2(1, 1) = UNIT_2(2, 2) = 1.0 and UNIT_2(1, 2) = UNIT_2(2, 1) = 0.0.

But disaster! We have actually declared an array whose lower bounds are INTEGER'FIRST which is probably −32768 or some such number but is certainly not 1.

If we declared the type MATRIX as

```
type MATRIX is array (POSITIVE range <>, POSITIVE range <>)
                                                  of REAL;
```

then all would have been well since POSITIVE'FIRST = 1.

So array bounds deduced from an initial value may lead to surprises.

We continue by returning to the topic of whole array assignment. In order to perform such assignment it is necessary that the array value and the array being assigned to have the same type and that the components can be matched. This does not mean that the bounds have to be equal but merely that the number of components in corresponding dimensions is the same. In other words so that one array can be slid onto the other, giving rise to the term 'sliding semantics'. So we can write

```
V: VECTOR(1 .. 5);
W: VECTOR(0 .. 4);
...
V:= W;
```

Both V and W are of type VECTOR and both have five components.
It is also valid to have

```
P: MATRIX(0 .. 1, 0 .. 1);
Q: MATRIX(6 .. 7, N .. N+1);
...
P:= Q;
```

Equality and inequality of arrays follow similar sliding rules to assignment. Two arrays may only be compared if they are of the same type. They are equal if corresponding dimensions have the same number of components and the matching components are themselves equal. Note however that if the dimensions of the two arrays are not of the same length then equality will return FALSE whereas an attempt to assign one array to the other will naturally cause CONSTRAINT_ERROR.

Although assignment and equality can only occur if the arrays are of the same type, nevertheless an array value of one type can be converted to another type if the component types and index types are the same. The usual notation for type conversion is used. So if we have

```
type VECTOR is array (INTEGER range <>) of REAL;
type ROW    is array (INTEGER range <>) of REAL;

V: VECTOR(1 .. 5);
R: ROW(0 .. 4);
```

then

```
R:= ROW(V);
```

is valid. In fact, since ROW is an unconstrained type, the bounds of ROW(V) are those of V. The normal assignment rules then apply. However, if the conversion uses a constrained type or subtype then the bounds are those of the type or subtype and the number of components in corresponding dimensions must be the same. Array type conversion is of particular value when subprograms from different libraries are used together as we shall see later.

We conclude this section by observing that the attributes FIRST, LAST, LENGTH and RANGE, as well as applying to array objects, may also be applied to array types and subtypes provided they are constrained (that is, have their bounds given). So

```
VECTOR_6'LENGTH = 6
```

but

```
VECTOR'LENGTH      is illegal
```

---

*Exercise 6.2*

**1**      Declare an array type BBB corresponding to the array BOR of
Exercise 6.1(**5**).

**2**      Declare a two-dimensional array type suitable for declaring
operator tables on values of

              **subtype** RING5 **is** INTEGER **range** 0 .. 4;

Then declare addition and multiplication tables for modulo 5
arithmetic. Use the tables to formulate the expression (A + B) ∗ C
using modulo 5 arithmetic and assign the result to D where A, B, C
and D have been appropriately declared. See Section 4.5.

---

## 6.3  Named array aggregates

There is another form of aggregate known as a named aggregate in which
the component values are preceded by the corresponding index value and
=>. (The symbol => is akin to the ☞ sign encountered in old railway
timetables and used for indicating directions especially on the Paris
Metro.) A simple example would be

      (1 => 0.0, 2 => 0.0, 3 => 0.0, 4 => 0.0, 5 => 0.0, 6 => 0.0)

with the expected extension to several dimensions. The bounds of such an
aggregate are self-evident and so our problem with the unit 2 × 2 matrix of
the previous section could be overcome by writing

      UNIT_2: **constant** MATRIX:= (1 => (1 => 1.0, 2 => 0.0),
                                2 => (1 => 0.0, 2 => 1.0));

     The rules for named aggregates are very similar to the rules for the
alternatives in a case statement.
     Each choice can be given as a series of alternatives each of which can
be a single value or a discrete range. We could therefore rewrite some
previous examples as follows

      A: **array** (1 .. 6) **of** REAL:= (1 .. 6 => 0.0);

      WORK_DAY: **constant array** (DAY) **of** BOOLEAN
                := (MON .. FRI => TRUE, SAT | SUN => FALSE);

     In contrast to a positional aggregate, the index values need not
appear in order. We could equally have written

      (SAT | SUN => FALSE, MON .. FRI => TRUE)

We can also use **others** but then as for the case statement it must be last and on its own.

The use of **others** raises some problems since it must be clear what the totality of values is. It should also be realized that although we have been showing aggregates as initial values, they can be used quite generally in any place where an expression of an array type is required. It is therefore necessary that the context supplies the bounds if **others** is used. One way of supplying the context is by qualifying the aggregate as we did to distinguish between overloaded enumeration literals. In order to do this we must have an appropriate (constrained) type or subtype name. So we introduce

**type** SCHEDULE **is array** (DAY) **of** BOOLEAN;

and can then write an expression such as

SCHEDULE'(MON .. FRI => TRUE, **others** => FALSE)

which could be part of a larger expression or maybe an initial value as we shall see in a moment. (Note that when qualifying an aggregate we do not, as for an expression, need to put it in brackets because it already has brackets.)

Other contexts which supply the bounds will be met in due course when we discuss subprogram parameters and results in Chapter 7 and generic parameters in Chapter 13. These same contexts will also supply the bounds of a positional aggregate; like a named aggregate with **others**, a positional aggregate does not have self-evident bounds.

However, in other contexts such as assignment and as an initial value the bounds are not provided by the context because of the concept of 'sliding semantics' introduced in the previous section. In the case of a positional aggregate in such a context, all is not lost since we recall that the lower bound is taken to be S'FIRST where S is the index subtype and the upper bound is then deduced from the number of components. Of course a named aggregate with **others** cannot use such a rule since the number of components represented by **others** is not known and so such an aggregate is illegal in such a context.

Array aggregates may not mix positional and named notation except that **others** may be used at the end of a positional aggregate. Such a positional aggregate then follows the general rules for a named aggregate with **others**.

Although the context of an assignment or an initial value cannot give the bounds (because of sliding), nevertheless provided the array type is constrained (which it will be unless we are declaring a constant and are going to deduce its bounds from the initial value), the context will tell us the length of the aggregate. So, in the case of a positional aggregate with **others**, taking the lower bound as S'FIRST, we can deduce the upper bound from the length (or in other words the values represented by **others** are taken to follow on from those explicitly given as far as necessary in order to provide the correct length) and so such an aggregate is allowed in a sliding context. However, we cannot do this in the case of a named aggregate with **others** because the whole essence of a named aggregate is that the components are not in order and so such an aggregate is not allowed in a sliding context. There is one exception – a named aggregate with **others** as the only choice is allowed because there can be no ambiguity in that case. So we cannot write

      WORK_DAY: **constant array** (DAY) **of** BOOLEAN
             := (MON .. FRI => TRUE, **others** => FALSE);        –– illegal

but we must instead write

      WORK_DAY: **constant array** (DAY) **of** BOOLEAN
             := (TRUE, TRUE, TRUE, TRUE, TRUE, **others** => FALSE);

or change the context by using qualification and write

      WORK_DAY: **constant** SCHEDULE
             := SCHEDULE ' (MON .. FRI => TRUE, **others** => FALSE);

The rules regarding the bounds of array aggregates seem very difficult and to be one of the most curious aspects of Ada. However, if you are very confused, do not be too worried at this point; we will return to this topic when we summarize a number of aspects of expressions in Section 16.1. Meanwhile, remember than an aggregate can always be qualified if in doubt.

Array aggregates really are rather complicated and we still have a few points to make. The first is that in a named aggregate all the ranges and values before => must be static (as in a case statement) except for one special situation. This is where there is only one alternative consisting of a single choice – it could then be a dynamic range or (unlikely) a single dynamic value. An example might be

      A: **array** (1 .. N) **of** INTEGER:= (1 .. N => 0);

This is valid even if N is zero (or negative) and then gives a null array and a null aggregate. The following example illustrates a general rule that the expression after => is evaluated once for each corresponding index value; of course it usually makes no difference but consider

      A: **array** (1 .. N) **of** INTEGER:= (1 .. N => 1/N);

If N is zero then there are no values and so 1/N is not evaluated and NUMERIC_ERROR cannot occur. The reader will recall from Section 4.1 that a similar multiple evaluation also occurs when several objects are declared and initialized together.

In order to avoid awkward problems with null aggregates, a null choice is only allowed if it is the only choice. Foolish aggregates such as

      (7 .. 6 | 1 .. 0 => 0)

are thus forbidden and there is no question of the lower bound of such an aggregate.

Another point is that although we cannot mix named and positional notation within an aggregate, we can, however, use different forms for the different components and levels of a multidimensional aggregate. So the initial value of our matrix UNIT_2 could also be written as

```
(1 => (1.0, 0.0),    or    ((1 => 1.0, 2 => 0.0),
   2 => (0.0, 1.0))            (1 => 0.0, 2 => 1.0))
```

or even as

```
(1 => (1 => 1.0, 2 => 0.0),
   2 => (    0.0,        1.0))
```

and so on.

Note also that the RANGE attribute stands for a range and therefore can be used as one of the choices in a named aggregate. However, we cannot use the range attribute of an object in its own initial value. Thus

```
A: array (1 .. N) of INTEGER:= (A'RANGE => 0);    -- illegal
```

is not allowed. This is because an object is not visible until the end of its declaration. However, we could write

```
A: array (1 .. N) of INTEGER:= (others => 0);
```

and this is probably better than repeating 1 .. N because it localizes the dependency on N.

A final point is that a positional aggregate cannot contain just one component because otherwise it would be ambiguous. We could not distinguish an aggregate of one component from a scalar value which happened to be in brackets. An aggregate of one component must therefore use the named notation. So instead of

```
A: array (1 .. 1) of INTEGER:= (99);    -- illegal
```

we must write

```
A: array (1 .. 1) of INTEGER:= (1 => 99);
```

or even

```
A: array (N .. N) of INTEGER:= (N => 99);
```

which illustrates the obscure case of an aggregate with a single choice and a single dynamic value being that choice.

The reader will by now have concluded that arrays in Ada are somewhat complicated. That is a fair judgement, but in practice there should be few difficulties. There is always the safeguard that if we do something wrong, the compiler will inevitably tell us. In cases of ambiguity, qualification solves the problems provided we have an appropriate type or subtype name to use. Much of the complexity with aggregates is similar to that in the case statement.

We conclude this section by pointing out that the named aggregate notation can greatly increase program legibility. It is especially valuable in initializing large constant arrays and guards against the accidental misplacement of individual values. Consider

```
type EVENT is (BIRTH, ACCESSION, DEATH);
type MONARCH is (WILLIAM_I, WILLIAM_II, HENRY_I, ... ,
                 VICTORIA, EDWARD_VII, GEORGE_V, ... );
...
ROYAL_EVENTS: constant array (MONARCH, EVENT) of INTEGER

   := (WILLIAM_I    => (1027, 1066, 1087),
       WILLIAM_II   => (1056, 1087, 1100),
       HENRY_I      => (1068, 1100, 1135),
       ...
       VICTORIA     => (1819, 1837, 1901),
       EDWARD_VII   => (1841, 1901, 1910),
       GEORGE_V     => (1865, 1910, 1936),
       ...
                                          );
```

The accidental interchange of two lines of the aggregate causes no problems, whereas if we had just used the positional notation then an error would have been introduced and this might have been tricky to detect.

---

*Exercise 6.3*

1     Rewrite the declaration of the array DAYS_IN_MONTH in Exercise 6.1(**3**) using a named aggregate for an initial value.

2     Declare a constant MATRIX whose bounds are both 1 .. N where N is dynamic and whose components are all zero.

3     Declare a constant MATRIX as in **2** but make it a unit matrix.

4     Declare a constant two-dimensional array which gives the numbers of each atom in a molecule of the various aliphatic alcohols. Declare appropriate enumeration types for both the atoms and the molecules. Consider methanol $CH_3OH$, ethanol $C_2H_5OH$, propanol $C_3H_7OH$ and butanol $C_4H_9OH$.

---

## 6.4   Characters and strings

We now complete our discussion of enumeration types by introducing character types. In the enumeration types seen so far such as

```
type COLOUR is (RED, AMBER, GREEN);
```

the values have been represented by identifiers. It is also possible to have an enumeration type in which some or all of the values are represented by character literals.

A character literal is a further form of lexical element. It consists of a single character within a pair of single quotes. The character must be one of the printable characters or it could be a single space. It must not be a control character such as horizontal tabulate or new line.

This is a situation where there is a distinction between upper and lower case letters. The character literals

    'A', 'a'

are different.

So we could declare an enumeration type

    **type** ROMAN_DIGIT **is** ('I', 'V', 'X', 'L', 'C', 'D', 'M');

and then

    DIG: ROMAN_DIGIT:= 'D';

All the usual properties of enumeration types apply.

    ROMAN_DIGIT'FIRST = 'I'
    ROMAN_DIGIT'SUCC('X') = 'L'
    ROMAN_DIGIT'POS'('M') = 6

    DIG < 'L' = FALSE

There is a predefined enumeration type CHARACTER which is (naturally) a character type. We can think of its declaration as being of the form

    **type** CHARACTER **is** (*nul*, ... , '0', '1', '2', ... , 'A', 'B', 'C', ... ,
                                                    'a', 'b', 'c', ... , *del*);

but for technical reasons which cannot be explained here the literals which are not actual character literals (such as *nul*) are not really identifiers either (which is why they are represented here in italics). It is however possible to refer to them as ASCII.NUL and so on (or under suitable circumstances to be discussed later as simply NUL). This predefined type CHARACTER represents the standard ASCII character set and describes the set of characters normally used for input and output; for its full declaration see Appendix 2. It is unfortunate that the type CHARACTER is hedged around with subtleties but in practice these do not matter.

It should be noted that the introduction of both the type ROMAN_DIGIT and the predefined type CHARACTER results in overloading of some of the literals. An expression such as

    'X' < 'L'

is ambiguous. We do not know whether we are comparing characters of the type ROMAN_DIGIT or CHARACTER. In order to resolve the ambiguity we must qualify one or both literals.

```
CHARACTER'('X') < 'L' = FALSE
ROMAN_DIGIT'('X') < 'L' = TRUE
```

As well as the predefined type CHARACTER there is also the predefined type STRING

**type** STRING **is array** (POSITIVE **range** <>) **of** CHARACTER;

This is a perfectly normal array type and obeys all the rules of the previous section. So we can write

S: STRING (1 .. 7);

to declare an array of range 1 .. 7. In the case of a constant array the bounds can be deduced from the initial value thus

G: **constant** STRING:= ('P', 'I', 'G');

where the initial value takes the form of a normal positional aggregate. The lower bound of G (that is, G'FIRST) is 1 since the index subtype of STRING is POSITIVE and POSITIVE'FIRST is 1.

An alternative notation is provided for a positional aggregate each of whose components is a character literal. This is the string. So we could more conveniently write

G: **constant** STRING:= "PIG";

The string is the last lexical element to be introduced. It consists of a sequence of printable characters and spaces enclosed in double quotes. A double quote may be represented in a string by two double quotes so that

('A', '"', 'B') = "A""B"

The string may also have just one character or may be null. The equivalent aggregates using character literals have to be written in named notation.

```
(1 => 'A') = "A"
(1 .. 0 => 'A') = ""
```

Note how we have to introduce an arbitrary character in the null named form. Ada has some strange quirks!

Another rule about a lexical string is that it must fit onto a single line. Moreover it cannot contain control characters such as SOH. And, of course, as with character literals, the two cases of alphabet are distinct in strings

"PIG" /= "pig"

In Section 6.6 we will see how to overcome the limitations that a string must fit onto a single line and yet cannot contain control characters.

A major use for strings is, of course, for creating text to be output. A simple sequence of characters can be output by a call of the (overloaded) subprogram PUT. Thus

    PUT ("The Countess of Lovelace");

will output the text

    The Countess of Lovelace

onto some appropriate file.

However, the lexical string is not reserved just for use with the built-in type STRING. It can be used to represent an array of any character type. We can write

    **type** ROMAN_NUMBER **is array** (POSITIVE **range** <>) **of**
                                                      ROMAN_DIGIT;

and then

    NINETEEN_EIGHTY_FOUR: **constant** ROMAN_NUMBER :=
                                                 "MCMLXXXIV";

or indeed

    FOUR: **array** (1 .. 2) **of** ROMAN_DIGIT:= "IV";

---

*Exercise 6.4*

1    Declare a constant array ROMAN_TO_INTEGER which can be used for table look-up to convert a ROMAN_DIGIT to its normal integer equivalent (for example, converts 'C' to 100).

2    Given an object R of type ROMAN_NUMBER write statements to compute the equivalent integer value V. It may be assumed that R obeys the normal rules of construction of Roman numbers.

---

## 6.5  Arrays of arrays and slices

The components of an array can be of any type (or subtype) for which we can declare objects. Thus we can declare arrays of any scalar type; we can also declare arrays of arrays. So we can have

    **type** MATRIX_3_6 **is array** (1 .. 3) **of** VECTOR_6;

where, as in Section 6.2

**type** VECTOR_6 **is array** (1 .. 6) **of** REAL;

However, we cannot declare an array of unconstrained arrays (just as we cannot declare an object which is an unconstrained array). So we cannot write

**type** MATRIX_3_N **is array** (1 .. 3) **of** VECTOR;     −− illegal

On the other hand there is nothing to prevent us declaring an unconstrained array of constrained arrays thus

**type** MATRIX_N_6 **is array** (INTEGER **range** <>) **of** VECTOR_6;

It is instructive to compare the practical differences between declaring an array of arrays

AOA: MATRIX_3_6;     or     AOA: MATRIX_N_6(1 .. 3);

and the similar multidimensional array

MDA: MATRIX(1 .. 3, 1 .. 6);

Aggregates for both are completely identical, for example

((1.0, 2.0, 3.0, 4.0, 5.0, 6.0),
 (4.0, 4.0, 4.0, 4.0, 4.0, 4.0),
 (6.0, 5.0, 4.0, 3.0, 2.0, 1.0))

but component access is quite different, thus

AOA(I)(J)
MDA(I, J)

where in the case of AOA the internal structure is naturally revealed. The individual rows of AOA can be manipulated as arrays in their own right but the structure of MDA cannot be decomposed. So we could change the middle row of AOA to zero by

AOA(2):= (1 .. 6 => 0.0);

but a similar technique cannot be applied to MDA.

Arrays of arrays are not restricted to one dimension, we can have a multidimensional array of arrays or an array of multidimensional arrays; the notation extends in an obvious way.

Arrays of strings are revealing. Consider

**type** STRING_ARRAY **is array** (POSITIVE **range** <>,
                                         POSITIVE **range** <>) **of** CHARACTER;

which is an unconstrained two-dimensional array type. We can then declare

>       FARMYARD: **constant** STRING_ARRAY:= ("pig", "cat", "dog",
>                                   "cow", "rat", "ass");

where the bounds are conveniently deduced from the aggregate. But note that we cannot have a ragged array where the individual strings are of different lengths such as

>       ZOO: **constant** STRING_ARRAY:= ("aardvark", "baboon", "camel",
>               "dolphin", "elephant", ..., "zebra");    -- illegal

This is a real nuisance and means we have to pad the strings to be the same length

>       ZOO: **constant** STRING_ARRAY:= ( "aardvark",
>                               "baboon  ",
>                               "camel   ",
>                               "dolphin ",
>                               "elephant",
>                               ...
>                               "zebra   ");

The next problem is that we cannot select an individual one of the strings. We might want to output one and so attempt

>       PUT(FARMYARD(5));

hoping to print the text

>       rat

but this is not allowed since we can only select an individual component of an array which in this case is just one character.

An alternative approach is to use an array of arrays. A problem here is that the component in the array type declaration has to be constrained and so we have to decide on the length of our strings right from the beginning thus

>       **type** STRING_3_ARRAY **is array** (POSITIVE **range** <>) **of**
>                                       STRING(1 .. 3);

and then

>       FARMYARD: **constant** STRING_3_ARRAY:= ("pig", "cat", "dog",
>                                   "cow", "rat", "ass");

With this formulation we can indeed select an individual string as a whole and so the statement PUT(FARMYARD(5)); now works. However, we still cannot declare our ZOO as a ragged array; we will return to this topic in Section 11.2 when another approach will be discussed.

We thus see that arrays of arrays and multidimensional arrays each have their own advantages and disadvantages. Neither is ideal; Ada arrays are rather restrictive and do not offer the flexibility of Algol 68.

A special feature of one-dimensional arrays is the ability to denote a slice of an array object. A slice is written as the name of the object (variable or constant) followed by a discrete range in brackets.

So given

S: STRING(1 .. 10);

then we can write S(3 .. 8) to denote the middle six characters of S. The bounds of the slice are the bounds of the range and not those of the index subtype. We could write

T: **constant** STRING:= S(3 .. 8);

and then T'FIRST = 3, T'LAST = 8.

The bounds of the slice need not be static but can be any expressions. A slice would be null if the range turned out to be null.

The use of slices emphasizes the nature of array assignment. The value of the expression to be assigned is completely evaluated before any components are assigned. No problems arise with overlapping slices. So

S(1 .. 4):= "BARA";
S(4 .. 7):= S(1 .. 4);

results in S(1 .. 7) = "BARBARA". S(4) is only updated after the expression S(1 .. 4) is safely evaluated. There is no risk of setting S(4) to 'B' and then consequently making the expression "BARB" with the final result of

"BARBARB"

The ability to use slices is another consideration in deciding between arrays of arrays and multidimensional arrays. With our second FARMYARD we can write

PETS: STRING_3_ARRAY(1 .. 2):= FARMYARD(2 .. 3);

which uses sliding assignment so that the two components of PETS are "cat" and "dog". Moreover, if we had declared the FARMYARD as a variable rather than a constant then we could also write

FARMYARD(1)(1 .. 2):= "ho";

which turns the "pig" into a "hog"! We can do none of these things with the old FARMYARD.

*Exercise 6.5*

1    Write a single assignment statement to swap the first and second rows of AOA.

2    Declare the second FARMYARD as a variable. Then change the cow into a sow.

3    Assume that R contains a Roman number. Write statements to see if the last digit of the corresponding decimal arabic value is a 4 and change it to a 6 if it is.

## 6.6  One-dimensional array operations

Many of the operators that we met in Chapter 4 may also be applied to one-dimensional arrays.

The Boolean operators **and**, **or**, **xor** and **not** may be applied to one-dimensional Boolean arrays. In the case of the binary operators, the two operands must have the same number of components and be of the same type. The underlying scalar operation is applied component by component and the resulting array is again of the same type. The lower bound of the index of the result is equal to the lower bound of the subtype of the left or only operand.

Consider

```
type BIT_ROW is array (POSITIVE range <>) of BOOLEAN;
A, B: BIT_ROW(1 .. 4);
C, D: array (1 .. 4) of BOOLEAN;
T: constant BOOLEAN:= TRUE;
F: constant BOOLEAN:= FALSE;
```

then we can write

```
A:= (T, T, F, F);
B:= (T, F, T, F);

A:= A and B;
B:= not B;
```

and A now equals (T, F, F, F), and B equals (F, T, F, T). Similarly for **or** and **xor**. But note that C **and** D would not be allowed because they are of different (and anonymous) types because of the rule regarding multiple declarations (Section 4.1). This is clearly a case where it is appropriate to give a name to the array type because we are manipulating the arrays as complete objects.

Note that these operators also use sliding semantics, like assignment as explained in Section 6.2, and so only demand that the types and the number of components are the same. The bounds themselves do not have to be equal. However, if the number of components are not the same then, naturally, CONSTRAINT_ERROR will be raised.

Boolean arrays can be used to represent sets. Consider

```
type PRIMARY is (R, Y, B);
type COLOUR is array (PRIMARY) of BOOLEAN;
C: COLOUR;
```

then there are $8 = 2 \times 2 \times 2$ values that C can take. C is, of course, an array with three components and each of these has value TRUE or FALSE; the three components are

C(R),     C(Y)     and     C(B)

The 8 possible values of the type COLOUR can be represented by suitably named constants as follows

```
WHITE     : constant COLOUR:= (F, F, F);
RED       : constant COLOUR:= (T, F, F);
YELLOW    : constant COLOUR:= (F, T, F);
BLUE      : constant COLOUR:= (F, F, T);
GREEN     : constant COLOUR:= (F, T, T);
PURPLE    : constant COLOUR:= (T, F, T);
ORANGE    : constant COLOUR:= (T, T, F);
BLACK     : constant COLOUR:= (T, T, T);
```

and then we can write expressions such as

RED or YELLOW

which is equal to ORANGE and

not BLACK

which is WHITE.

So the values of our type COLOUR are effectively the set of colours obtained by taking all combinations of the primary colours represented by R, Y, B. The empty set is the value of WHITE and the full set is the value of BLACK. We are using the paint pot mixing colour model rather than light mixing. A value of TRUE for a component means that the primary colour concerned is mixed in our pot. The murky mess we got at school from mixing too many colours together is our black!

The operations or, and and xor may be interpreted as set union, set intersection and symmetric difference. A test for set membership can be made by inspecting the value of the appropriate component of the set. Thus

C(R)

is TRUE if R is in the set represented by C. We cannot use the predefined operation **in** for this. A literal value can be represented using the named aggregate notation, so

(R | Y => T, **others** => F)

has the same value as ORANGE. A more elegant way of doing this will appear in the next chapter.

We now consider the equality and relational operators. The operators = and /= apply to all types anyway and we gave the rules for arrays when we discussed assignment in Section 6.2.

The relational operators <, <=, > and >= may be applied to one-dimensional arrays of a discrete type. (Note discrete.) The result of the comparison is based upon the lexicographic (that is, dictionary) order using the defined order relation for the components. This is best illustrated with strings which we assume for the moment are unambiguously values of the type STRING. The following are all TRUE

```
"CAT" < "DOG"
"CAT" < "CATERPILLAR"
"AZZ" < "B"
""    < "A"
```

The strings are compared component by component until they differ in some position. The string with the lower component is then lower. If one string runs out of components as in CAT versus CATERPILLAR then the shorter one is lower. The null string is lowest of all.

If we assume that we have declared our type ROMAN_NUMBER then

"CCL" < "CCXC"

is ambiguous since we do not know whether we are comparing type STRING or type ROMAN_NUMBER. We must qualify one or both of the strings. This is done in the usual way but a string, unlike the bracketed form of aggregates, has to be placed in brackets otherwise we would get an ugly juxtaposition of a single and double quote. So

```
STRING'("CCL") < "CCXC"          is TRUE
ROMAN_NUMBER'("CCL") < "CCXC"    is FALSE
```

Note that our compiler is too stupid to know about the interpretation of Roman numbers in our minds and has said that 250 < 290 is false. The only thing that matters is the order relation of the characters 'L' and 'X' in the type definition. In the next chapter we will show how we can redefine < so that it works 'properly' for Roman numbers.

Of course, the relational operators also apply to general expressions and not just to literal strings.

```
NINETEEN_EIGHTY_FOUR < "MM"      is TRUE
```

The relational operators can be applied to arrays of any discrete types. So

```
(1, 2, 3) < (2, 3)
(JAN, JAN) < (1 => FEB)
```

The predefined operators <=, > and >= are defined by analogy with <.

We finally introduce a new binary operator & which denotes catenation (or concatenation) of one-dimensional arrays. It has the same precedence as binary plus and minus. The two operands must be of the same type and the result is an array of the same type whose value is obtained by juxtaposing the two operands. The lower bound of the result is, as usual, the lower bound of the left operand.

So

```
"CAT" & "ERPILLAR" = "CATERPILLAR"
```

String catenation can be used to construct a string which is too long to fit on one line

```
"This string goes" &
"on and on"
```

One or both operands of & can also be a single value of the component type. If the left operand is such a single value then the lower bound of the result is the lower bound of the subtype of the array index.

```
"CAT" & 'S' = "CATS"
'S' & "CAT" = "SCAT"
'S' & 'S' = "SS"
```

This is useful for representing the control characters such as CR and LF in strings.

```
"First line" & ASCII.CR & ASCII.LF & "Next line"
```

Of course, it might be neater to declare

```
CRLF: constant STRING:= (ASCII.CR, ASCII.LF);
```

and then write

```
"First line" & CRLF & "Next line"
```

The operation & can be applied to any one-dimensional array type and so we can apply it to our Roman numbers. Consider

```
R: ROMAN_NUMBER(1 .. 5);
S: STRING(1 .. 5);

R:= "CCL" & "IV";
S:= "CCL" & "IV";
```

This is valid. The context tells us that in the first case we apply & to two Roman numbers whereas in the second we apply it to two values of type STRING. There is no ambiguity as in

    B: BOOLEAN:= "CCL" < "IV";

---

*Exercise 6.6*

1   Write the eight possible constants WHITE ... BLACK of the type COLOUR in ascending order as determined by the operator < applied to one-dimensional arrays.

2   Evaluate

    (a)   RED **or** GREEN
    (b)   BLACK **xor** RED
    (c)   **not** GREEN

3   Show that **not** (BLACK **xor** C) = C is true for all values of C.

4   Why did we not write

        (JAN, JAN) < (FEB)

5   Put in ascending order the following values of type STRING: "ABC", "123", "abc", "Abc", "abC", "aBc".

6   Given

        C: CHARACTER;
        S: STRING(5 .. 10);

    What is the lower bound of

    (a)   C & S
    (b)   S & C

---

## 6.7  Records

As stated at the beginning of this chapter we are only going to consider the simplest form of record at this point. A fuller treatment covering variant records and so on is left until Chapter 11.

A record is a composite object consisting of named components which may be of different types. In contrast to arrays, we cannot have anonymous record types – they all have to be named. Consider

```
type MONTH_NAME is (JAN, FEB, MAR, APR, MAY, JUN, JUL,
                    AUG, SEP, OCT, NOV, DEC);

type DATE is
    record
        DAY: INTEGER range 1 .. 31;
        MONTH: MONTH_NAME;
        YEAR: INTEGER;
    end record;
```

This declares the type DATE to be a record containing three named components: DAY, MONTH and YEAR.

We can declare variables and constants of record types in the usual way.

```
D: DATE;
```

declares an object D which is a date. The individual components of D can be denoted by following D with a dot and the component name. Thus we could write

```
D.DAY:= 4;
D.MONTH:= JUL;
D.YEAR:= 1776;
```

in order to assign new values to the individual components.

Records can be manipulated as whole objects. Literal values can be written as aggregates much like arrays; both positional and named forms can be used. So we could write

```
D: DATE:= (4, JUL, 1776);
E: DATE;
```

and then

```
E:= D;
```

or

```
E:= (MONTH => JUL, DAY => 4, YEAR => 1776);
```

The reader will be relieved to know that much of the complexity of array aggregates does not apply to records. This is because the number of components is always known.

In a positional aggregate the components come in order. In a named aggregate they may be in any order. In the particular example shown the use of a named aggregate avoids the necessity to know on which side of the Atlantic the record type was declared.

A named aggregate cannot use a range because the components are not considered to be closely related and the vertical bar can only be used with components which have the same (base) type. The choice **others** can be used but again only when the remaining components are of the same type.

There is one extra possibility for records and that is that the positional and named notations can be mixed in one aggregate. But if this is done then the positional components must come first and in order (without holes) as usual. So in other words we can change to the named notation at any point in the aggregate but must then stick to it. The above date could therefore also be expressed as

```
(4, JUL, YEAR => 1776)
(4, YEAR => 1776, MONTH => JUL)
```

and so on

It is possible to give default expressions for some or all of the components in the type declaration. Thus

```
type COMPLEX is
   record
      RL: REAL:= 0.0;
      IM: REAL:= 0.0;
   end record;
```

or more succinctly

```
type COMPLEX is
   record
      RL, IM: REAL:= 0.0;
   end record;
```

declares a record type containing two components of type REAL and gives a default expression of 0.0 for each. This record type represents a complex number $x + iy$ where RL and IM are the values of $x$ and $y$. The default value is thus $(0, 0)$, the origin of the Argand plane. We can now declare

```
C1: COMPLEX;
C2: COMPLEX:= (1.0, 0.0);
```

The object C1 will now have the values 0.0 for its components by default. In the case of C2 we have overridden the default values. Note that, irritatingly, even if there are default expressions, an aggregate must be complete even if it supplies the same values as the default expressions for some of the components.

In this case both components are the same type and so the following named forms are possible

```
(RL | IM => 1.0)
(others => 1.0)
```

The only operations predefined on record types are = and /= as well as assignment of course. Other operations must be performed at the component level or be explicitly defined by a subprogram as we shall see in the next chapter.

A record type may have any number of components. It may pathologically have none in which case its declaration takes the form

```
type HOLE is
    record
        null;
    end record;
```

The reserved word **null** confirms that we meant to declare a null record type. Null records have their uses but they will not be apparent yet.

The components of a record type can be of any type; they can be other records or arrays. However, if a component is an array then it must be fully constrained (that is, its index must not contain <>) and it must be of a named type and not an anonymous type. And obviously a record cannot contain an instance of itself.

The components cannot be constants but the record as a whole can be. Thus

```
I: constant COMPLEX:= (0.0, 1.0);
```

is allowed and represents the square root of −1.

A more elaborate example of a record is

```
type PERSON is
    record
        BIRTH: DATE;
        NAME: STRING(1 .. 20):= (1 .. 20 => ' ');
    end record;
```

The record PERSON has two components, the first is another record, a DATE, the second an array. The array which is a string of length 20 has a default value of all spaces.

We can now write

```
JOHN: PERSON;
JOHN.BIRTH:= (19, AUG, 1937);
JOHN.NAME(1 .. 4):= "JOHN";
```

and we would then have

```
JOHN = ((19, AUG, 1937), "JOHN              ")
```

The notation is as expected. The aggregates nest and for objects we proceed from left to right using the dot notation to select components of a record and indexes in brackets to select components of an array and ranges in brackets to slice arrays. There is no limit. We could have an array of persons

```
PEOPLE: array (1 .. N) of PERSON;
```

and then have

```
PEOPLE(6).BIRTH.DAY:= 19;
PEOPLE(8).NAME(3):= 'H';
```

and so on.

A final point concerns the evaluation of expressions in a record declaration. An expression in a constraint applied to a component is evaluated when the record type is elaborated. So our type PERSON could have

```
NAME: STRING(1 .. N):= (others => ' ');
```

and the length of the component NAME will be the value of N when the type PERSON is elaborated. Of course, N need not be static and so if the type declaration is in a loop, for example, then each execution of the loop might give rise to a type with a different size component. However, for each elaboration of the record type declaration all objects of the type will have the same component size.

On the other hand, a default expression in a record type is only evaluated when an object of the type is declared and only then if no explicit initial value is provided. Of course, in simple cases, like our type COMPLEX, it makes no difference but it could bring surprises. For example, suppose we write the component NAME as

```
NAME: STRING(1 .. N):= (1 .. N => ' ');
```

then the length of the component NAME is the value of N when the record type is declared whereas when a PERSON is subsequently declared without an initial value, the aggregate will be evaluated using the value of N which then applies. Of course, N may by then be different and so CONSTRAINT_ERROR will be raised. This is rather surprising; we do seem to have strayed into an odd backwater of Ada!

---

*Exercise 6.7*

1    Rewrite the solution to Exercise 6.1(**3**) using a variable D of type DATE rather than three individual variables.

2    Declare three variables C1, C2 and C3 of type COMPLEX. Write one or more statements to assign (a) the sum, (b) the product, of C1 and C2 to C3.

3    Write statements to find the index of the first person of the array PEOPLE born on or after 1 January 1950.

# Checklist 6

Array types can be anonymous, but records cannot.

Aggregates must always be complete.

Distinguish constrained array types from unconstrained array types (those with <>).

Named and positional notations cannot be mixed for array aggregates – they can for records.

An aggregate with **others** must have a context giving its bounds.

A choice in an array aggregate can only be dynamic or null if it is the only choice.

The attributes FIRST, LAST, LENGTH and RANGE apply to array objects and constrained array types and subtypes but not to unconstrained types and subtypes.

For array assignment to be valid, the number of components must be equal for each dimension – not the bounds.

The cases of alphabet are distinct in character literals and strings.

An aggregate with one component must use the named notation. This applies to records as well as to arrays.

A record component cannot be an anonymous array.

A default component expression is only evaluated when an uninitialized object is declared.

# Chapter 7
# Subprograms

---

---

Subprograms are the conventional parameterized unit of programming. In Ada, subprograms fall into two categories: functions and procedures. Functions are called as components of expressions and return a value as part of the expression, whereas procedures are called as statements standing alone.

As we shall see, the actions to be performed when a subprogram is called are described by a subprogram body. Subprogram bodies are declared in the usual way in a declarative part which may for instance be in a block or indeed in another subprogram.

## 7.1 Functions

A function is a form of subprogram that can be called as part of an expression. In Chapter 4 we met examples of calls of functions such as DAY'SUCC, SQRT and so on.

We now consider the form of a function body which describes the statements to be executed when the function is called. For example the body of the function SQRT might have the form

```
function SQRT(X: REAL) return REAL is
    R: REAL;
begin
    -- compute value of SQRT(X) in R
    return R;
end SQRT;
```

All function bodies start with the reserved word **function** and the designator of the function being defined. If the function has parameters the designator is followed by a list of parameter specifications in brackets. If there are several specifications then they are separated by semicolons. Each specification gives the identifiers of one or more parameters followed by a colon and its type or subtype. The parameter list, if any, is then followed by the reserved word **return** and the type or subtype of the result of the function. In the case of both parameters and result, the type or subtype must be given by a type mark and not by a subtype indication. This is an important example of a situation where an explicit constraint is not allowed; the reason will be mentioned later in this chapter.

The part of the body we have described so far is called the function specification. It specifies the function to the outside world in the sense of providing all the information needed to call the function.

After the specification comes **is** and then the body proper which is just like a block – it has a declarative part, **begin**, a sequence of statements, and then **end**. As for a block the declarative part can be empty but there must be at least one statement in the sequence of statements. Between **end** and the terminating semicolon we may repeat the designator of the function. This is optional but, if present, must correctly match the designator after **function**.

It is often necessary or just convenient to give the specification on its own but without the rest of the body. In such a case it is immediately followed by a semicolon thus

```
function SQRT(X: REAL) return REAL;
```

and is then correctly known as a function declaration – although often still carelessly referred to as a specification. The uses of such declarations will be discussed later.

The formal parameters of a function act as local constants whose values are provided by the corresponding actual parameters. When the function is called the declarative part is elaborated in the usual way and then the statements are executed. A return statement is used to indicate the value of the function call and to return control back to the calling expression.

Thus considering our example suppose we had

```
S:= SQRT(T + 0.5);
```

then first T + 0.5 is evaluated and then SQRT is called. Within the body the parameter X behaves as a constant with the initial value given by T + 0.5. It is rather as if we had

```
X: constant REAL:= T + 0.5;
```

The declaration of R is then elaborated. We then obey the sequence of statements and assume they compute the square root of X and assign it to R. The last statement is **return** R; this passes control back to the calling expression with the result of the function being the value of R. This value is then assigned to S.

The expression in a return statement can be of arbitrary complexity and must be of the same type as and satisfy any constraints implied by the type mark given in the function specification. If the constraints are violated then, of course, the exception CONSTRAINT_ERROR is raised.

A function body may have several return statements. The execution of any of them will terminate the function. Thus the function SIGN which takes an integer value and returns +1, 0 or −1 according to whether the parameter is positive, zero or negative could be written as

```
function SIGN(X: INTEGER) return INTEGER is
begin
    if X > 0 then
        return +1;
    elsif X < 0 then
        return −1;
    else
        return 0;
    end if;
end SIGN;
```

So we see that the last lexical statement of the body need not be a return statement since there is one in each branch of the statement. Any attempt to 'run' into the final end will raise the exception PROGRAM_ERROR. This is our first example of a situation giving rise to PROGRAM_ERROR; this exception is generally used for situations which would violate the run time control structure.

It should be noted that each call of a function produces a new instance of any objects declared within it (including parameters of course) and these disappear when we leave the function. It is therefore possible for a function to be called recursively without any problems. So the factorial function could be declared as

```
function FACTORIAL(N: POSITIVE) return POSITIVE is
begin
    if N = 1 then
        return 1;
    else
        return N * FACTORIAL(N−1);
    end if;
end FACTORIAL;
```

If we write

```
F:= FACTORIAL(4);
```

then the function calls itself until, on the fourth call (with the other three calls all partly executed and waiting for the result of the call they did before doing the multiply) we find that N is 1 and the calls then all unwind and all the multiplications are performed.

Note that there is no need to check that the parameter N is positive since the parameter is of subtype POSITIVE. So calling FACTORIAL(−2) will result in CONSTRAINT_ERROR. Of course, FACTORIAL(10_000) could result in the computer running out of space in which case STORAGE_ERROR would be raised. The more moderate call FACTORIAL(20) would undoubtedly cause overflow and thus raise NUMERIC_ERROR (or the equivalent CONSTRAINT_ERROR – see Section 4.9).

A formal parameter may be of any type but the type must have a name. It cannot be an anonymous type such as

```
array (1 .. 6) of REAL
```

In any event no actual parameter (other than an aggregate) could match such a formal parameter even if it were allowed since the actual and formal parameters must have the same type.

A formal parameter can, however, be an unconstrained array type such as

```
type VECTOR is array (INTEGER range <>) of REAL;
```

In such a case the bounds of the formal parameter are taken from those of the actual parameter.

Consider

```
function SUM(A: VECTOR) return REAL is
    RESULT: REAL:= 0.0;
begin
    for I in A'RANGE loop
        RESULT:= RESULT + A(I);
    end loop;
    return RESULT;
end SUM;
```

then we can write

```
V: VECTOR(1 .. 4):= (1.0, 2.0, 3.0, 4.0);
S: REAL;
...
S:= SUM(V);
```

The formal parameter A then takes the bounds of the actual parameter V. So for this call we have

```
A'RANGE    is    1 .. 4
```

and the effect of the loop is to compute the sum of A(1), A(2), A(3) and A(4). The final value of RESULT which is returned and assigned to S is therefore 10.0.

The function SUM can be used to sum the components of a vector with any bounds. Ada thus overcomes one of the problems of original

Pascal which insists that array parameters have static bounds. Of course, an Ada function could have a constrained array type as a formal parameter. However, remember that we cannot apply the constraint in the parameter list using a subtype indication as in

**function** SUM_6(A: VECTOR(1 .. 6)) **return** REAL          —— illegal

but must use the name of a constrained array type such as

**type** VECTOR_6 **is array** (1 .. 6) **of** REAL;

as a type mark as in

**function** SUM_6(A: VECTOR_6) **return** REAL

As another example consider

```
function INNER(A, B: VECTOR) return REAL is
    RESULT: REAL:= 0.0;
begin
    for I in A'RANGE loop
        RESULT:= RESULT + A(I)*B(I);
    end loop;
    return RESULT;
end INNER;
```

This computes the inner product of the two vectors A and B by adding together the sum of the products of corresponding components. This is our first example of a function with more than one parameter. Such a function is called by following the function name by a list of the expressions giving the values of the actual parameters separated by commas and in brackets. The order of evaluation of the actual parameters is not defined.
    So

```
V: VECTOR(1 .. 3):= (1.0, 2.0, 3.0);
W: VECTOR(1 .. 3):= (2.0, 3.0, 4.0);
R: REAL;
...
R:= INNER(V, W);
```

results in R being assigned the value

$$1.0 * 2.0 + 2.0 * 3.0 + 3.0 * 4.0 = 20.0$$

Note that the function INNER is not written well since it does not check that the bounds of A and B are the same. It is not symmetric with respect to A and B since I takes (or tries to take) the values of the range A'RANGE irrespective of B'RANGE. So if the array W had bounds of 0 and 2,

CONSTRAINT_ERROR would be raised on the third time round the loop. If the array W had bounds of 1 and 4 then no exception would be raised but the result might not be what we expected.

It would be nice to ensure the equality of the bounds by placing a constraint on B at the time of call but this cannot be done. The best we can do is simply check the bounds for equality inside the function body and perhaps explicitly raise CONSTRAINT_ERROR if they are not equal.

```
if A'FIRST /= B'FIRST or A'LAST /= B'LAST then
    raise CONSTRAINT_ERROR;
end if;
```

(The use of the raise statement is described in detail in Chapter 10.)

We saw above that a formal parameter can be of an unconstrained array type. In a similar way the result of a function can be an array whose bounds are not known until the function is called. The result type can be an unconstrained array and the bounds are then obtained from the expression in the appropriate return statement.

As an example the following function returns a vector which has the same bounds as the parameter but whose component values are in the reverse order

```
function REV(X: VECTOR) return VECTOR is
    R: VECTOR(X'RANGE);
begin
    for I in X'RANGE loop
        R(I):= X(X'FIRST+X'LAST-I);
    end loop;
    return R;
end REV;
```

The variable R is declared to be of type VECTOR with the same bounds as X. Note how the loop reverses the value. The result takes the bounds of the expression R. Note that we have called the function REV rather than REVERSE; this is because **reverse** is a reserved word.

If a function returns a record or array value then a component can be immediately selected, indexed or sliced as appropriate without assigning the value to a variable. So we could write

```
REV(Y)(I)
```

which denotes the component indexed by I of the array returned by the call of REV.

It should be noted that a parameterless function call, like a parameterless procedure call, has no brackets. There is therefore a possible ambiguity between calling a function with one parameter and indexing the result of a parameterless call; such an ambiguity could be resolved by, for example, renaming the functions as will be described in Chapter 8.

*Exercise 7.1*

**1**    Write a function EVEN which returns TRUE or FALSE according to whether its INTEGER parameter is even or odd.

**2**    Rewrite the factorial function so that the parameter may be positive or zero but not negative. Remember that the value of FACTORIAL(0) is to be 1. Use the subtype NATURAL introduced in Section 4.5.

**3**    Write a function OUTER that forms the outer product of two vectors. The outer product $C$ of two vectors $A$ and $B$ is a matrix such that $C_{ij} = A_i \,.\, B_j$.

**4**    Write a function MAKE_COLOUR which takes an array of values of type PRIMARY and returns the corresponding value of type COLOUR. See Section 6.6. Check that MAKE_COLOUR((R, Y)) = ORANGE.

**5**    Write a function VALUE which takes a parameter of type ROMAN_NUMBER and returns the equivalent integer value. See Exercise 6.4(**2**).

**6**    Write a function MAKE_UNIT that takes a single parameter N and returns a unit $N \times N$ real matrix. Use the function to declare a constant unit $N \times N$ matrix. See Exercise 6.3(**3**).

**7**    Write a function GCD to return the greatest common divisor of two nonnegative integers. Use Euclid's algorithm that

$$\gcd (x, y) = \gcd (y, x \bmod y) \quad y \neq 0$$
$$\gcd (x, 0) = x$$

Write the function using recursion and then rewrite it using a loop statement.

**8**    Rewrite the function INNER to use sliding semantics so that it works providing the arrays have the same length. Raise CONSTRAINT_ERROR (as outlined above) if the arrays do not match.

## 7.2   Operators

In the last section we carefully stated that a function body commenced with the reserved word **function** followed by the designator of the function. In all the examples of the last section the designator was in fact an identifier.

However, it can also be a character string provided that the string is one of the following language operators in double quotes

| and | or | xor | | |
|-----|-----|-----|-----|-----|
| = | < | <= | > | >= |
| + | − | & | abs | not |
| * | / | mod | rem | ** |

In such a case the function defines a new meaning of the operator concerned. As an example we can rewrite the function INNER of the last section as an operator.

```
function "*" (A, B: VECTOR) return REAL is
    RESULT: REAL:= 0.0;
begin
    for I in A'RANGE loop
        RESULT:= RESULT + A(I)*B(I);
    end loop;
    return RESULT;
end "*";
```

We call this new function by the normal syntax of uses of the operator "*". Thus instead of

```
R:= INNER(V, W);
```

we now write

```
R:= V*W;
```

This meaning of "*" is distinguished from the existing meanings of integer and real multiplication by the context provided by the types of the actual parameters V and W and the type required by R.

The giving of several meanings to an operator is another instance of overloading which we have already met with enumeration literals. The rules for the overloading of subprograms in general are discussed later in this chapter. It suffices to say at this point that any ambiguity can usually be resolved by qualification. Overloading of predefined operators is not new. It has existed in most programming languages for the past thirty years. What is new is the ability to define additional overloadings and indeed the use of the term 'overloading' is itself relatively new.

We can now see that the predefined meanings of all operators are as if there were a series of functions with declarations such as

```
function "+" (LEFT, RIGHT: INTEGER) return INTEGER;
function "<" (LEFT, RIGHT: INTEGER) return BOOLEAN;
function "<" (LEFT, RIGHT: BOOLEAN) return BOOLEAN;
```

Moreover, every time we declare a new type, new overloadings of some operators such as "=" and "<" may be created.

Although we can add new meanings to operators we cannot change the syntax of the call. Thus the number of parameters of "*" must always be two and the precedence cannot be changed and so on. The operators "+" and "−" are unusual in that a new definition can have either one parameter or two parameters according to whether it is to be called as a unary or binary operator. Thus the function SUM could be rewritten as

```
function "+" (A: VECTOR) return REAL is
    RESULT: REAL:= 0.0;
begin
    for I in A'RANGE loop
        RESULT:= RESULT + A(I);
    end loop;
    return RESULT;
end "+";
```

and we would then write

```
S:= +V;
```

rather than

```
S:= SUM(V);
```

Function bodies whose designators are operators often contain interesting examples of uses of the operator being overloaded. Thus the body of "*" contains a use of "*" in A(I)*B(I). There is, of course, no ambiguity since the expressions A(I) and B(I) are of type REAL whereas our new overloading is for type VECTOR. Sometimes there is the risk of accidental recursion. This particularly applies if we try to replace an existing meaning rather than add a new one.

Apart from the operator "=" there are no special rules regarding the types of the operands and results of new overloadings. Thus a new overloading of "<" need not return a BOOLEAN result. On the other hand, the operator "=" can only be given new overloadings which return a value of type BOOLEAN and then only under special circumstances which will be described in Chapter 9. Note that "/=" may never be explicitly redeclared – it always takes its meaning from "=".

The membership tests **in** and **not in** and the short circuit forms **and then** and **or else** cannot be given new meanings. That is why we said in Section 4.9 that they were not technically classed as operators.

Finally note that in the case of operators represented by reserved words, the characters in the string can be in either case. Thus a new overloading of **or** can be declared as "or" or "OR" or even "Or".

---

*Exercise 7.2*

**1**     Write a function "<" that operates on two Roman numbers and compares them according to their corresponding numeric values. That is, so that "CCL" <"CCXC". Use the function VALUE of Exercise 7.1(**5**).

**2**    Write functions "+" and "*" to add and multiply two values of type COMPLEX. See Exercise 6.7(**2**).

**3**    Write a function "<" to test whether a value of type PRIMARY is in a set represented by a value of type COLOUR. See Section 6.6.

**4**    Write a function "<=" to test whether one value of type COLOUR is a subset of another.

**5**    Write a function "<" to compare two values of the type DATE of Section 6.7.

---

## 7.3  Procedures

The other form of subprogram is a procedure; a procedure is called as a statement. We have seen many examples of procedure calls where there are no parameters such as WORK; PARTY; ACTION; and so on.

The body of a procedure is very similar to that of a function. The differences are

- a procedure starts with **procedure**,
- its name must be an identifier,
- it does not return a result,
- the parameters may be of three different modes **in**, **out** or **in out**.

The mode of a parameter is indicated by following the colon in the parameter specification by **in** or by **out** or by **in out**. If the mode is omitted then it is taken to be **in**. In the case of functions the only allowed mode is **in**; the examples earlier in this chapter omitted **in** but could have been written for instance, as

> **function** SQRT(X: **in** REAL) **return** REAL;
> **function** "*" (A, B: **in** VECTOR) **return** REAL;

The effect of the three modes is best summarized by quoting the *LRM* (Section 6.2).

|  |  |
|---|---|
| **in** | The formal parameter is a constant and permits only reading of the value of the associated actual parameter. |
| **in out** | The formal parameter is a variable and permits both reading and updating of the value of the associated actual parameter. |
| **out** | The formal parameter is a variable and permits updating of the value of the associated actual parameter. |

As a simple example of the modes **in** and **out** consider

```
procedure ADD(A, B: in INTEGER; C: out INTEGER) is
begin
    C:= A+B;
end ADD;
```

with

```
P, Q: INTEGER;
...
ADD(2+P, 37, Q);
```

On calling ADD, the expressions 2+P and 37 are evaluated (in any order) and assigned to the formals A and B which behave as constants. The value of A+B is then assigned to the formal variable C. On return the value of C is assigned to the variable Q. Thus it is (more or less) as if we had written

```
declare
    A: constant INTEGER:= 2+P;       -- in
    B: constant INTEGER:= 37;        -- in
    C: INTEGER;                      -- out
begin
    C:= A+B;                         -- body
    Q:= C;                           -- out
end;
```

As an example of the mode **in out** consider

```
procedure INCREMENT(X: in out INTEGER) is
begin
    X:= X+1;
end;
```

with

```
I: INTEGER;
...
INCREMENT(I);
```

On calling INCREMENT, the value of I is assigned to the formal variable X. The value of X is then incremented. On return, the final value of X is assigned to the actual parameter I. So it is rather as if we had written

```
declare
    X: INTEGER:= I;
begin
    X:= X+1;
    I:= X;
end;
```

For any scalar type (such as INTEGER) the modes correspond simply to copying the value **in** at the call or **out** upon return or both in the case of **in out**.

If the mode is **in** then the actual parameter may be any expression of the appropriate type or subtype. If the mode is **out** or **in out** then the actual parameter must be a variable. The identity of such a variable is determined when the procedure is called and cannot change during the call.

Suppose we had

```
I: INTEGER;
A: array (1 .. 10) of INTEGER;
procedure SILLY(X: in out INTEGER) is
begin
    I:= I+1;
    X:= X+1;
end;
```

then the statements

```
A(5):= 1;
I:= 5;
SILLY(A(I));
```

result in A(5) becoming 2, I becoming 6, but A(6) is not affected.

If a parameter is a composite type (such as an array or record) then the mechanism of copying, described above, may be used but alternatively an implementation may use a reference mechanism in which the formal parameter provides direct access to the actual parameter. A program which depends on the particular mechanism is erroneous. An example of such a program is given in the exercises at the end of this section. Note that because a formal array parameter takes its bounds from the actual parameter, the bounds are always copied in at the start even in the case of an **out** parameter. Of course, for simplicity, an implementation could always copy in the whole array anyway.

We now discuss the question of constraints on parameters.

In the case of scalar parameters the situation is as expected from the copying model. For an **in** or **in out** parameter any constraint on the formal must be satisfied by the actual at the beginning of the call. Conversely for an **in out** or **out** parameter any constraint on the variable which is the actual parameter must be satisfied by the value of the formal parameter upon return from the subprogram.

In the case of arrays the situation is somewhat different. If the formal parameter is a constrained array type, the bounds of the actual must be identical; it is not enough for the number of components in each dimension to be the same; the parameter mechanism is more rigorous than assignment. If, on the other hand, the formal parameter is an unconstrained array type, then, as we have seen, it takes its bounds from those of the actual. The foregoing applies irrespective of the mode of the array parameter. Similar rules apply to function results; if the result is a constrained array type then the expression in a return statement must have the same bounds. As an aside, one consequence of the parameter and result mechanism being more rigorous than assignment is that array aggregates with **others** are allowed as actual parameters and in return statements. On the other hand, as we saw in Section 6.3, they are not generally allowed in an assignment statement unless qualified.

In the case of the simple records we have discussed so far there are no constraints and so there is nothing to say. The parameter mechanism for other types will be discussed when they are introduced.

We stated above that an actual parameter corresponding to a formal **out** or **in out** parameter must be a variable. This includes the possibility of the actual parameter in turn being a formal parameter of some outer subprogram; but naturally an **out** parameter cannot be an actual parameter to a formal **in out** (or **in**) parameter because otherwise there might (will) be an attempt to read the **out** parameter.

A further possibility is that an actual parameter can also be a type conversion of a variable provided, of course, that the conversion is allowed. As an example, since conversion is allowed between any numeric types, we can write

    R: REAL;
    ...
    INCREMENT(INTEGER(R));

If R initially had the value 2.3, it would be converted to the integer value 2 incremented to give 3 and then on return converted back to 3.0 and assigned to R.

This conversion of **in out** or **out** parameters is particularly useful with arrays. Suppose we write a library of subprograms applying to our type VECTOR and then acquire from someone else some subprograms written to apply to the type ROW of Section 6.2. The types ROW and VECTOR are essentially the same; it just so happened that the authors used different names. Array type conversion allows us to use both sets of subprograms without having to change the type names systematically.

As a final example consider the following

```
procedure QUADRATIC(A, B, C: in REAL; ROOT_1, ROOT_2:
                    out REAL; OK: out BOOLEAN) is
    D: constant REAL:= B**2-4.0*A*C;
begin
    if D<0.0 or A=0.0 then
        OK:= FALSE;
        return;
    end if;
    ROOT_1:= (-B+SQRT(D)) / (2.0*A);
    ROOT_2:= (-B-SQRT(D)) / (2.0*A);
    OK:= TRUE;
end QUADRATIC;
```

The procedure QUADRATIC attempts to solve the equation

$$ax^2 + bx + c = 0$$

If the roots are real they are returned via the parameters ROOT_1 and ROOT_2 and OK is set to TRUE. If the roots are complex (D<0.0) or the equation degenerates (A=0.0) then OK is set to FALSE.

Note the use of the return statement. Since this is a procedure there is no result to be returned and so the word **return** is not followed by an expression. It just updates the **out** or **in out** parameters as necessary and returns control back to where the procedure was called. Note also that unlike a function we can 'run' into the **end**; this is equivalent to obeying **return**.

The reader will note that if OK is set to FALSE then no value is assigned to the **out** parameters ROOT_1 and ROOT_2. The copy rule for scalars then implies that the corresponding actual parameters become undefined. In practice, junk values are presumably assigned to the actual parameters and this could possibly raise CONSTRAINT_ERROR if an actual parameter were constrained. This is probably bad practice and so it might be better to assign safe values such as 0.0 to the roots just in case. (In examples like this, the **out** mechanism does not seem so satisfactory as the simple reference mechanism of Algol 68 or Pascal.)

The procedure could be used in a sequence such as

```
declare
    L, M, N: REAL;
    P, Q: REAL;
    STATUS: BOOLEAN;
begin
    -- sets values into L, M and N
    QUADRATIC(L, M, N, P, Q, STATUS);
    if STATUS then
        -- roots are in P and Q
    else
        -- fails
    end if;
end;
```

This is a good moment to emphasize the point made in Section 4.7 that it is often better to introduce our own two-valued enumeration type rather than use the predefined type BOOLEAN. The above example would be clearer if we had declared

```
type ROOTS is (REAL_ROOTS, COMPLEX_ROOTS);
```

with other appropriate alterations.

We conclude this section by emphasizing that an **out** parameter cannot be treated as a proper variable since it cannot be read. Thus the statements of the above example could not be recast in the form

```
begin
    OK:= D>=0.0 and A/=0.0;
    if not OK then
        return;
```

```
        end if;
        ROOT_1:= ... ;
        ROOT_2:= ... ;
    end QUADRATIC;
```

because the Boolean expression **not** OK attempts to read the **out** parameter OK.

An exception to this rule is that the bounds of an **out** array can be read even though the components cannot. Remember that a formal array always takes its bounds from the actual array. A similar situation applies to discriminants of records which we will meet in Chapter 11.

---

*Exercise 7.3*

1   Write a procedure SWAP to interchange the values of the two real parameters.

2   Rewrite the function REV of Section 7.1 as a procedure with a single parameter. Use it to reverse an array R of type ROW.

3   Why is the following erroneous?

```
    A: VECTOR(1 .. 1);

    procedure P(V: VECTOR) is
    begin
        A(1):= V(1)+V(1);
        A(1):= V(1)+V(1);
    end;
    ...
    A(1):= 1.0;
    P(A);
```

4   Draw up a table showing what modes of formal parameter of an outer procedure are possible as actual parameters of various modes of a call of another procedure.

---

## 7.4  Named and default parameters

The forms of subprogram call we have been using so far have given the actual parameters in positional order. As with aggregates we can also use the named notation in which the formal parameter name is also supplied; the parameters do not then have to be in order.

So we could write

```
QUADRATIC(A => L, B => M, C => N,
                    ROOT_1 => P, ROOT_2 => Q, OK => STATUS);
INCREMENT(X => I);
ADD(C => Q, A => 2+P, B => 37);
```

We could even write

        INCREMENT(X => X);

the scopes do not interfere.
        This notation can also be used with functions

        F:= FACTORIAL(N => 4);
        S:= SQRT(X => T+0.5);
        R:= INNER(B => W, A => V);

The named notation cannot, however, be used with operators called with the usual infixed syntax (such as V*W) because there is clearly no convenient place to put the names of the formal parameters.
        As with record aggregates, the named and positional notations can be mixed and any positional parameters must come first and in their correct order. However, unlike record aggregates, each parameter must be given individually and **others** may not be used. So we could write

        QUADRATIC(L, M, N,
                        ROOT_1 => P, ROOT_2 => Q, OK => STATUS);

The named notation leads into the topic of default parameters. It sometimes happens that one or more **in** parameters usually take the same value on each call; we can given a default expression in the subprogram specification and then omit it from the call.
        Consider the problem of ordering a dry martini in the USA. One is faced with choices described by the following enumeration types

        **type** SPIRIT **is** (GIN, VODKA);
        **type** STYLE **is** (ON_THE_ROCKS, STRAIGHT_UP);
        **type** TRIMMING **is** (OLIVE, TWIST);

The standard default expressions can then be given in a procedure specification thus

        **procedure** DRY_MARTINI(BASE: SPIRIT:= GIN;
                                HOW: STYLE:= ON_THE_ROCKS;
                                PLUS: TRIMMING:= OLIVE);

Typical calls might be

        DRY_MARTINI(HOW => STRAIGHT_UP);
        DRY_MARTINI(VODKA, PLUS => TWIST);
        DRY_MARTINI;
        DRY_MARTINI(GIN, STRAIGHT_UP);

        The first call uses the named notation; we get gin, straight up plus olive. The second call mixes the positional and named notations; as soon as a parameter is omitted the named notation must be used. The third call illustrates that all parameters can be omitted. The final call shows that a parameter can, of course, be supplied even if it happens to take the same value as the default expression; in this case it avoids using the named form for the second parameter.

Note that default expressions can only be given for **in** parameters. They cannot be given for operators but they can be given for functions designated by identifiers. Such a default expression (like a default expression for an initial value in a record type declaration) is only evaluated when required; that is, it is evaluated each time the subprogram is called and no corresponding actual parameter is supplied. Hence the default value need not be the same on each call although it usually will be. Default expressions are widely used in the standard input–output package to provide default formats.

Default expressions illustrate the subtle rule that a parameter specification of the form

```
P, Q: in INTEGER:= E
```

is strictly equivalent to

```
P: in INTEGER:= E;
Q: in INTEGER:= E
```

(The reader will recall a similar rule for object declarations; it also applies to record components.) As a consequence, the default expression is evaluated for each omitted parameter in a call. This does not usually matter but would be significant if the expression E included a function call with side effects.

---

*Exercise 7.4*

1    Write a function ADD which returns the sum of the two integer parameters and takes a default value of 1 for the second parameter. How many different ways can it be called to return N+1 where N is the first actual parameter?

2    Rewrite the specification of DRY_MARTINI to reflect that you prefer VODKA at weekends. Hint: declare a function to return your favourite spirit according to the global variable TODAY.

---

## 7.5  Overloading

We saw in Section 7.2 how new meanings could be given to existing language operators. This overloading applies to subprograms in general.

A subprogram will overload an existing meaning rather than hide it, provided that its specification is sufficiently different. Hiding will occur if the order and base types of the parameters and result (if any) are the same.

A procedure cannot hide a function and vice versa. Note that the names of the parameters, their mode and the presence or absence of default expressions do not matter. Two or more overloaded subprograms may be declared in the same declarative part.

Subprograms and enumeration literals can overload each other. In fact an enumeration literal is formally thought of as a parameterless function with a result of the enumeration type. There are two classes of uses of identifers – the overloadable ones and the non-overloadable ones. At any point an identifier either refers to a single entity of the non-overloadable class or to one or many of the overloadable class. A declaration of one class hides the other class and cannot occur in the same declaration list.

As we have seen, ambiguities arising from overloading can be resolved by qualification. This was necessary when the operator "<" was used with the strings in Section 6.4. As a further example consider the British Channel Islands; the larger three are Guernsey, Jersey and Alderney. There are woollen garments named after each island.

```
type GARMENT is (GUERNSEY, JERSEY, ALDERNEY);
```

and breeds of cattle named after two of them (the Alderney breed became extinct as a consequence of the Second World War).

```
type COW is (GUERNSEY, JERSEY);
```

and we can imagine (just) shops that sell both garments and cows according to

```
procedure SELL(G: GARMENT);
procedure SELL(C: COW);
```

Although

```
SELL(ALDERNEY);
```

is not ambiguous

```
SELL(JERSEY);
```

is, since we cannot tell which subprogram is being called. We must write for example

```
SELL(COW'(JERSEY));
```

We conclude by noting that ambiguities typically arise only when there are several overloadings. In the case here both SELL and JERSEY are overloaded; in the example in Section 6.4 both the operator "<" and the literals 'X' and 'L' were overloaded.

---

**1**　　How else could SELL(JERSEY); be made unambiguous?

---

## 7.6　Declarations, scopes and visibility

We said earlier that it is sometimes necessary or just convenient to give a subprogram specification on its own without the body. The specification is then followed by a semicolon and is known as a subprogram declaration. A complete subprogram, which always includes the full specification, is known as a subprogram body.

Subprogram declarations and bodies must, like other declarations, occur in a declarative part and a subprogram declaration must be followed by the corresponding body in the same declarative part.

An example of where it is necessary to use a subprogram declaration occurs with mutually recursive procedures. Suppose we wish to declare two procedures F and G which call each other. Because of the rule regarding linear elaboration of declarations we cannot write the call of F in the body of G until after F has been declared and vice versa. Clearly this is impossible if we just write the bodies because one must come second. However, we can write

```
procedure F( ... );      -- declaration of F

procedure G( ... ) is    -- body of G
begin
   F( ... );
end G;

procedure F( ... ) is    -- body of F repeats
begin                    -- its specification
   G( ... );
end F;
```

and then all is well.

If the specification is repeated then it must be given in full and the two must be the same. Technically we say that the two specifications must conform. Some slight variation is allowed. A numeric literal can be replaced by another numeric literal with the same value; an identifier can be replaced by a dotted name as described later in this section; the lexical spacing can be different. It is worth noting that the key reason for not allowing subtype indications in parameter specifications is to remove any problem regarding conformance since there is then no question of evaluating constraint expressions twice and possibly having different results because of side effects. No corresponding question arises with default expressions (which are of course written out twice) since they are only evaluated when the subprogram is called.

Another important case, where we have to write a subprogram declaration as well as a body, occurs in the next chapter when we discuss packages. Even if not always necessary, it is sometimes clearer to write subprogram declarations as well as bodies. An example might be in the case where many subprogram bodies occur together. The subprogram declarations could then be placed together at the head of the declarative part in order to act as a summary of the bodies to come.

Subprogram bodies and other declarations must not be mixed up in an arbitrary way. A body cannot, for example, be followed by object, type and number declarations. This ensures that small declarations are not 'lost' in between large bodies. The rules will be given in more detail when we discuss packages in the next chapter.

Since subprograms occur in declarative parts and themselves contain declarative parts they may be textually nested without limit. The normal hiding rules applicable to blocks described in Section 4.2 also apply to declarations in subprograms. (The only complication concerns overloading as discussed in the previous section.) Consider

```
procedure P is
    I: INTEGER:= 0;

    procedure Q is
        K: INTEGER:= I;
        I: INTEGER;
        J: INTEGER;
    begin
        ...
    end Q;
    ...
end P;
```

Just as for the example in Section 4.2, the inner I hides the outer one and so the outer I is not visible inside the procedure Q after the declaration of the inner I.

However, we can always refer to the outer I by the so-called dotted notation, in which it is prefixed by the name of the unit immediately containing its declaration followed by a dot. So within Q we can refer to the outer I as P.I and so, for example, we could initialize J by writing

```
J: INTEGER:= P.I;
```

If the prefix is itself hidden then it can always be written the same way. Thus the inner I could be referred to as P.Q.I.

An object declared in a block cannot usually be referred to in this way since a block does not normally have a name. However, a block can be named in a similar way to a loop as shown in the following

```
OUTER:
declare
    I: INTEGER:= 0;
```

```
begin
   ...
   declare
      K: INTEGER:= I;
      I: INTEGER;
      J: INTEGER:= OUTER.I;
   begin
      ...
   end;
end OUTER;
```

Here the outer block has the identifier OUTER. Unlike subprograms, but like loops, the identifier has to be repeated after the matching **end**. Naming the block enables us to initialize the inner declaration of J with the value of the outer I.

Within a loop it is possible to refer to a hidden loop parameter in the same way. We could even rewrite the example in Section 6.1 of assigning zero to the elements of AA as

```
L:
for I in AA'RANGE(1) loop
   for I in AA'RANGE(2) loop
      AA(L.I, I):= 0.0;
   end loop;
end loop L;
```

although one would be a little crazy to do so!

It should be noted that the dotted form can always be used even if it is not necessary.

This notation can also be applied to operators and character literals. Thus the variable RESULT declared inside "*" can be referred to as "*".RESULT. And equally if "*" were declared inside a block B then it could be referred to as B."*". If it is called with this form of name then the normal function call must be used

```
R:= B."*"(V, W);
```

Indeed, the functional form can always be used as in

```
R:= "*"(V, W);
```

and we could then also use the named notation

```
R:= "*"(A => V, B => W);
```

As we have seen, subprograms can alter global variables and therefore have side effects. (A side effect is one brought about other than via the parameter mechanism.) It is generally considered rather un-desirable to write subprograms, especially functions, which have side effects. However, some side effects are beneficial. Any subprogram which performs input–output has a side effect on the file; a function delivering successive members of a sequence of random numbers only works because of its side effects; if we need to count how many times a function is called then we use a side effect; and so on. However, care must be taken when using functions with side effects that the program is correct since there are various circumstances in which the order of evaluation is not defined.

We conclude this section with a brief discussion of the hierarchy of **exit**, **return** and **goto** and the scopes of block and loop identifiers and labels.

A **return** statement terminates the execution of the immediately embracing subprogram. It can occur inside an inner block or inside a loop in the subprogram and therefore also terminate the loop. On the other hand an **exit** statement terminates the named or immediately embracing loop. It can also occur inside an inner block but cannot occur inside a subprogram declared in the loop and thereby also terminate the subprogram. A **goto** statement can transfer control out of a loop or block but not out of a subprogram.

As far as scope is concerned, identifiers of labels, blocks and loops behave as if they are declared at the end of the declarative part of the immediately embracing subprogram or block (or package or task body). Moreover distinct identifiers must be used for all blocks, loops and labels inside the same subprogram (or package or task body) even if some are in inner blocks. Thus two labels in the same subprogram cannot have the same identifier even if they are inside different inner blocks. This rule reduces the risk of goto statements going to the wrong label particularly when a program is amended.

## Checklist 7

Parameter and result subtypes must be given by a type mark and not a subtype indication.

A function must return a result and should not run into its final **end** although a procedure can.

The order of evaluation of parameters is not defined.

A default parameter expression is only evaluated when the subprogram is called and the corresponding parameter is omitted.

The actual and formal parameters of a constrained array type must have equal bounds.

Scalar parameters are copied. The mechanism for arrays and records is not defined.

Formal parameter specifications are separated by semicolons not commas.

# Chapter 8
# Overall Structure

---

---

The previous chapters have described the small-scale features of Ada in considerable detail. The language presented so far corresponds to the areas addressed by languages of the 1960s and early 1970s, although Ada provides more functionality in those areas. However, we now come to the new areas which broadly speaking correspond to the concepts of data abstraction and programming in the large which were discussed in Chapter 1.

In this chapter we discuss packages (which is what Ada is all about) and the mechanisms for separate compilation. We also say a little more about scope and visibility.

## 8.1  Packages

One of the major problems with the traditional block structured languages, such as Algol and Pascal, is that they do not offer enough control of visibility. For example, suppose we have a stack represented by an array and a variable which indexes the current top element, a procedure PUSH to add an item and a function POP to remove an item. We might write

```
MAX: constant:= 100;
S: array (1 .. MAX) of INTEGER;
TOP: INTEGER range 0 .. MAX;
```

to represent the stack and then declare

```
procedure PUSH(X: INTEGER) is
begin
   TOP:= TOP+1;
```

137

```
      S(TOP):= X;
end PUSH;

function POP return INTEGER is
begin
      TOP:= TOP-1;
      return S(TOP+1);
end POP;
```

In a simple block structured language there is no way in which we can be given access to the subprograms PUSH and POP without also being given direct access to the variables S and TOP. As a consequence we cannot be forced to use the correct protocol and so be prevented from making use of knowledge of how the stack is implemented.

The Ada package overcomes this by allowing us to place a wall around a group of declarations and only permit access to those which we intend to be visible. A package actually comes in two parts: the specification which gives the interface to the outside world, and the body which gives the hidden details.

The above example should be written as

```
package STACK is                          -- specification
      procedure PUSH(X: INTEGER);
      function POP return INTEGER;
end STACK;

package body STACK is                     -- body
      MAX: constant:= 100;
      S: array (1 .. MAX) of INTEGER;
      TOP: INTEGER range 0 .. MAX;

      procedure PUSH(X: INTEGER) is
      begin
            TOP:= TOP+1;
            S(TOP):= X;
      end PUSH;

      function POP return INTEGER is
      begin
            TOP:= TOP-1;
            return S(TOP+1);
      end POP;

begin                                     -- initialization
      TOP:= 0;
end STACK;
```

The package specification (strictly declaration) starts with the reserved word **package**, the identifier of the package and **is**. This is then followed by declarations of the entities which are to be visible. It finishes with **end**, the identifier (optionally) and the terminating semicolon. In the example we just have the declarations of the two subprograms PUSH and POP.

The package body also starts with **package** but this is then followed by **body**, the identifier and **is**. We then have a normal declarative part, **begin**, sequence of statements, **end**, optional identifier and terminating semicolon just as in a block or subprogram body.

In the example the declarative part contains the variables which represent the stack and the bodies of PUSH and POP. The sequence of statements between **begin** and **end** is executed when the package is declared and can be used for initialization. If there is no need for an initialization sequence, the **begin** can be omitted. Indeed in this example we could equally and perhaps more naturally have performed the initialization by writing

```
TOP: INTEGER range 0 .. MAX:= 0;
```

Note that a package is itself declared and so is just one of the items in an outer declarative part (unless it is a library unit which is the outermost layer anyway).

The package illustrates another case where we need distinct subprogram declarations and bodies. Indeed we cannot put a body into a package specification. And moreover, if a package specification contains the specification of a subprogram, then the package body must contain the corresponding subprogram body. We can think of the package specification and body as being just one large declarative part with only some items visible. But, of course, a subprogram body can be declared in a package body without its specification having to be given in the package specification. Such a subprogram would be internal to the package and could only be called from within, either from other subprograms, some of which would presumably be visible, or perhaps from the initialization sequence.

The elaboration of a package body consists simply of the elaboration of the declarations inside it followed by the execution of the initialization sequence if there is one. The package continues to exist until the end of the scope in which it is declared. Entities declared inside the package have the same lifetime as the package itself. Thus the variables S and TOP can be thought of as 'own' variables in the Algol 60 sense; their values are retained between successive calls of PUSH and POP.

Packages may be declared in any declarative part such as that in a block, subprogram or indeed another package. If a package specification is declared inside another package specification then, as for subprograms, the body of one must be declared in the body of the other. But again both specification and body could be in a package body.

Apart from the rule that a package specification cannot contain bodies, it can contain any of the other kinds of declarations we have met.

Now to return to the use of our package. The package itself has a name and the entities in its visible part (the specification) can be thought of as components of the package in some sense. It is entirely natural therefore that, in order to call PUSH, we must also mention STACK. In fact the dotted notation is used. So we could write

```
declare
    package STACK is          -- specification
        ...                   -- and
        ...                   -- body
    end STACK;
begin
    ...
    STACK.PUSH(M);
    ...
    N:= STACK.POP;
    ...
end;
```

Inside the package we would call PUSH as just PUSH, but we could still write STACK.PUSH just as in the last chapter we saw how we could refer to a local variable X of procedure P as P.X. Inside the package we can refer to S or STACK.S, but outside the package MAX, S and TOP are not accessible in any way.

It would in general be painful always to have to write STACK.PUSH to call PUSH from outside. Instead we can write

```
use STACK;
```

as a sort of declaration and we may then refer to PUSH and POP directly. The use clause could follow the declaration of the specification of STACK in the same declarative part or could be in another declarative part where the package is visible. So we could write

```
declare
    use STACK;
begin
    ...
    PUSH(M);
    ...
    N:= POP;
    ...
end;
```

The use clause is like a declaration and similarly has a scope to the end of the block. Outside we would have to revert to the dotted notation. We could have an inner use clause referring to the same package – it would do no harm.

Two or more packages could be declared in the same declarative part. Generally, we could arrange all the specifications together and then all the bodies, or alternatively the corresponding specifications and bodies, could be together. Thus we could have spec A, spec B, body A, body B, or spec A, body A, spec B, body B.

The rules governing the order are simply

- linear elaboration of declarations,

- specification must precede body for same package (or subprogram),

- small items must generally precede big ones.

More precisely, the last rule is that a body can only be followed by other bodies, subprogram and package (and task) specifications (strictly declarations) or indeed use clauses. The general intent of this rule is to prevent small items from being lost among big ones; the use clause is allowed as a 'big' item (as well as a small item) because it is very convenient to follow the declaration of a package by a corresponding use clause in the same declarative part.

Of course, the specification of a package may contain things other than subprograms. Indeed, an important case is where it does not contain subprograms at all but merely a group of related variables, constants and types. In such a case the package needs no body. It does not provide any hiding properties but merely gives commonality of naming. (A body could be provided; its only purpose would be for initialization.)

As an example we could provide a package containing our type DAY and some useful related constants.

```
package DIURNAL is
    type DAY is (MON, TUE, WED, THU, FRI, SAT, SUN);
    subtype WEEKDAY is DAY range MON .. FRI;
    TOMORROW: constant array (DAY) of DAY
            := (TUE, WED, THU, FRI, SAT, SUN, MON);
    NEXT_WORK_DAY: constant array (WEEKDAY) of WEEKDAY
            := (TUE, WED, THU, FRI, MON);
end DIURNAL;
```

A final point. A subprogram cannot be called successfully during the elaboration of a declarative part if its body appears later. This did not prevent the mutual recursion of the procedures F and G in Section 7.6 because in that case the call of F actually only occurred when we executed the sequence of statements of the body of G. But it does prevent the use of a function in an initial value. So

```
function A return INTEGER;
I: INTEGER:= A;
```

is illegal, and would result in PROGRAM_ERROR being raised.

A similar rule applies to subprograms in packages. If we call a subprogram from outside a package but before the package body has been elaborated, then PROGRAM_ERROR will be raised.

*Exercise 8.1*

1    The sequence defined by

$$X_{n+1} = X_n.5^5 \bmod 2^{13}$$

provides a crude source of pseudo random numbers. The initial value $X_0$ should be an odd integer in the range 0 to $2^{13}$.
Write a package RANDOM containing a procedure INIT to initialize the sequence and a function NEXT to deliver the next value in the sequence.

2    Write a package COMPLEX_NUMBERS which makes visible

- the type COMPLEX,
- a constant $I = \sqrt{-1}$ ,
- functions +, −, *, / acting on values of type COMPLEX.

See Exercise 7.2(**2**).

## 8.2   Library units

Many languages in the past have ignored the simple fact that programs are written in pieces, compiled separately and then joined together. Ada recognizes the need for separate compilation and provides two mechanisms – one top down and one bottom up.

The top down mechanism is appropriate for the development of a large coherent program which nevertheless, for various reasons, is broken down into subunits which can be compiled separately. The subunits are compiled after the unit from which they are taken. This mechanism is described in the next section.

The bottom up mechanism is appropriate for the creation of a program library where units are written for general use and consequently are written before the programs that use them. This mechanism will now be discussed in detail.

A library unit may be a subprogram specification or a package specification; the corresponding bodies are called secondary units. These units may be compiled individually or for convenience several could be submitted to the compiler together. Thus we could compile the specification and body of a package together but as we shall see it may be more convenient to compile them individually. As usual a subprogram body alone is sufficient to define the subprogram fully; it is then classed as a library unit rather than a secondary unit.

When a unit is compiled it goes into a program library. There will obviously be several such libraries according to user and project, etc. The creation and manipulation of libraries is outside the scope of this book. Once in the library, a unit can be used by any subsequently compiled unit but the using unit must indicate the dependency by a with clause.

As a simple example suppose we compile the package STACK. This package depends on no other unit and so it needs no with clause. We will compile both specification and body together so the text submitted will be

```
package STACK is
    ...
end STACK;

package body STACK is
    ...
end STACK;
```

As well as producing the object code corresponding to the package, the compiler also places in the program library the information describing the interface that the package presents to the outside world; this is of course the information in the specification.

We now suppose that we write a procedure MAIN which will use the package STACK. Our procedure MAIN is going to be the main program in the usual sense. It will have no parameters and we can imagine that it is called by some magic outside the language itself. The Ada definition does not prescribe that the main program should have the identifier MAIN; it is merely a convention which we are adopting here because it has to be called something.

The text we submit to the compiler could be

```
with STACK;
procedure MAIN is
    use STACK;
    M, N: INTEGER;
begin
    ...
    PUSH(M);
    ...
    N:= POP;
    ...
end MAIN;
```

The with clause goes before the unit so that the dependency of the unit on other units is clear at a glance. A with clause may not be embedded in an inner scope.

On encountering a with clause the compiler retrieves from the program library the information describing the interface presented by the withed unit so that it can check that the unit being compiled uses the interface correctly. Thus if procedure MAIN tried to call PUSH with the wrong number or type of parameters then this will be detected during compilation. This thorough checking between separately compiled units is a major factor in the increased productivity obtained through using Ada.

If a unit is dependent on several other units then they can go in the one with clause, or it might be a convenience to use distinct with clauses.

Thus we could write

      **with** STACK, DIURNAL;
      **procedure** MAIN **is**
         ...

or equally

      **with** STACK;
      **with** DIURNAL;
      **procedure** MAIN **is**
         ...

For convenience we can place a use clause after a with clause. Thus

      **with** STACK; **use** STACK;
      **procedure** MAIN **is**
         ...

and then PUSH and POP are directly visible without more ado. A use clause in such a position can only refer to packages mentioned in the with clause.

Only direct dependencies need be given in a with clause. Thus if package P uses the facilities of package Q which in turn uses the facilities of package R, then, unless P also directly uses R, the with clause for P should mention only Q. The user of Q does not care about R and must not need to know since otherwise the hierarchy of development would be made more complicated.

Another point is that the with clause in front of a package or subprogram declaration will also apply to the body. It can, but need not, be repeated. Of course, the body may have additional dependencies which will need indicating with a with clause anyway. Dependencies which apply only to the body should not be given with the specification since otherwise the independence of the body and the specification would be reduced.

If a package specification and body are compiled separately then the body must be compiled after the specification. We say that the body is dependent on the specification. However, any unit using the package is dependent only on the specification and not the body. If the body is changed in a manner consistent with not changing the specification, any unit using the package will not need recompiling. The ability to compile specification and body separately should simplify program maintenance.

The dependencies between the specification and body of the package STACK and the procedure MAIN are illustrated by the graph in Figure 8.1.

The general rule regarding the order of compilation is simply that a unit must be compiled after all units on which it depends. Consequently, if a unit is changed and recompiled then all dependent units must also be recompiled. Any order of compilation consistent with the dependency rule is acceptable.

There is one package that need not be mentioned in a with clause. This is the package STANDARD which effectively contains the declarations

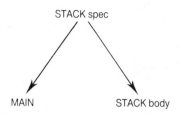

**Figure 8.1**   Dependencies between units.

of all the predefined types such as INTEGER and BOOLEAN and their predefined operations. It also contains an internal package ASCII containing constants defining the control characters such as CR and LF. We now see why the control characters were represented as ASCII.CR etc. in Chapter 6. By writing **use** ASCII; they can, of course, just be referred to as CR. The package STANDARD is described in more detail in Appendix 2.

Finally there are two important rules regarding library units. They must have distinct identifiers; they cannot be overloaded. Moreover they cannot be operators. These rules enable an Ada program library to be implemented quite easily on top of a basic filing system with simple identifiers.

---

*Exercise 8.2*

1    The package D and subprograms P and Q and MAIN have correct
     with clauses as follows

|                     |                 |
|---------------------|-----------------|
| specification of D  | no with clause  |
| body of D           | **with** P, Q;  |
| subprogram P        | no with clause  |
| subprogram Q        | no with clause  |
| subprogram MAIN     | **with** D;     |

     Draw a graph showing the dependencies between the units. How
     many different orders of compilation are possible?

---

## 8.3   Subunits

In this section we introduce a further form of secondary unit known as a subunit. The body of a package, subprogram (or task, see Chapter 14) can be 'taken out' of an immediately embracing library unit or secondary unit and itself compiled separately. The body in the embracing unit is then replaced by a body stub. As an example suppose we remove the bodies of the subprograms PUSH and POP from the package STACK. The body of STACK would then become

```
package body STACK is
    MAX: constant:= 100;
    S: array (1 .. MAX) of INTEGER;
    TOP: INTEGER range 0 .. MAX;
    procedure PUSH(X: INTEGER) is separate;        -- stub
    function POP return INTEGER is separate;       -- stub
begin
    TOP:= 0;
end STACK;
```

The removed units are termed subunits; they may then be compiled separately. They have to be preceded by **separate** followed by the name of the parent unit in brackets. Thus the subunit PUSH becomes

```
separate (STACK)
procedure PUSH(X: INTEGER) is
begin
    TOP:= TOP+1;
    S(TOP):= X;
end PUSH;
```

and similarly for POP.

In the above example the parent unit is (the body of) a library unit. The parent unit could itself be a subunit; in such a case its name must be given in full using the dotted notation starting with the ancestor library unit. Thus if R is a subunit of Q which is a subunit of P which is a library unit, then the text of R must start

```
separate (P.Q)
```

As with library units and for similar reasons, the subunits of a unit must have distinct identifiers. But, of course, this does not prevent subunits of different units having the same identifier. And again subunits cannot be operators.

A subunit is dependent on its parent (and any library units explicitly mentioned) and so must be compiled after them.

Visibility within a subunit is as at the corresponding body stub – it is exactly as if the subunit were plucked out with its environment intact (and indeed the compiler will store the relevant information on compiling the stub and retrieve it on compiling the subunit so that full type checking is maintained). As a consequence any with clause applying to the parent need not be repeated just because the subunit is compiled separately. However, it is possible to give the subunit access to additional library units by preceding it with its own with clauses (and possibly use clauses). Such clauses precede **separate**. So the text of R might commence

```
with X; use X;
separate (P.Q)
...
```

A possible reason for doing this might be if we can then remove any reference to library unit X from the parent P.Q and so reduce the dependencies. This would give us greater freedom with the order of compilation; if X were recompiled for some reason then only R would need recompiling as a consequence and not also Q.

Note that a with clause only refers to library units and never to subunits. Finally observe that several subunits or a mixture of library units, library unit bodies and subunits can be compiled together.

---

*Exercise 8.3*

1    Suppose that the package STACK is written with separate subunits PUSH and POP. Draw a graph showing the dependencies between the five units: procedure MAIN, procedure PUSH, function POP, package specification STACK, package body STACK. How many different orders of compilation are possible?

---

## 8.4  Scope and visibility

We return once more to the topic of scope and visibility. In this section we summarize the major points which will be relevant to the everyday use of Ada. For some of the fine detail, the reader is referred to the *LRM*. It is perhaps worth mentioning that the *LRM* uses the term declarative region in order to explain the visibility and scope rules. Blocks and subprograms are examples of declarative regions and the scope rules associated with them were described in Sections 4.2 and 7.6. We now have to consider the effect of the introduction of packages.

A package specification and body together constitute a single declarative region. Thus if we declare a variable X in the specification then we cannot redeclare X in the body (except of course in an inner region such as a local subprogram).

In the case of a declaration in the visible part of a package, its scope extends from the declaration to the end of the scope of the package itself. Note that if the package is inside the visible part of another package then this means that, applying the rule again, the scope extends to the end of that of the outer package and so on.

In the case of a declaration in a package body (or in the private part of a package – to be described in the next chapter), its scope extends to the end of the package body.

In the case of the simple nesting of blocks and subprograms an entity is visible throughout its scope unless hidden by another declaration. We saw in Section 7.6 how even if it was hidden it could nevertheless in general be referred to by using the dotted notation where the prefixed name is that of the unit embracing the declaration. In essence, writing the name of the embracing unit makes the entity visible.

In the case of an entity declared in a package the same rules apply inside the package. But outside the package it is not visible unless we write the package name or alternatively write a use clause.

The identifiers visible at a given point are those visible before considering any use clauses plus those made visible by use clauses.

The basic rule is that an identifier in a package is made visible by a use clause provided the same identifier is not also in another package with a use clause and also provided that the identifier is not already visible anyway. If these conditions are not met then the identifier is not made visible and we have to continue to use the dotted notation.

A slightly different rule applies if all the identifiers are subprograms or enumeration literals. In this case they all overload each other unless of course their specifications clash (could hide each other) in which case they are not made visible. Thus an identifier made visible by a use clause can never hide another identifier although it may overload it.

The general purpose of these rules is to ensure that adding a use clause cannot invalidate an existing piece of text. We have only given a brief sketch here and the reader is probably confused. In practice there should be no problems since the Ada compiler will, we hope, indicate any ambiguities or other difficulties and things can always be put right by adding a qualifier or using a dotted name.

There are other rules regarding record component names, subprogram parameters and so on which are as expected. For example there is no conflict between an identifier of a record component and another use of the identifier outside the type definition itself. The reason is that although the scopes may overlap, the regions of visibility do not. Consider

```
declare
    type R is
        record
            I: INTEGER;
        end record;
    type S is
        record
            I: INTEGER;
        end record;
    AR: R;
    AS: S;
    I: INTEGER;
begin
    ...
    I:= AR.I+AS.I;    -- legal
    ...
end;
```

The scope of the I in the type R extends from the component declaration until the end of the block. However, its visibility is confined to within the declaration of R except that it is made visible by the use of AR in the selected component. Hence no conflict.

Similar considerations prevent conflict in named aggregates and in named parameters in subprogram calls.

Observe that a use clause can mention several packages and that it may be necessary for a package name to be given as a selected component itself. A use clause does not take effect until the semicolon. Suppose we have nested packages

```
package P1 is
    package P2 is
        ...
    end P2;
    ...
end P1;
```

then outside P1 we could write

```
use P1; use P2;
```

or

```
use P1, P1.P2;
```

but not

```
use P1, P2;
```

We could even write **use** P1.P2; to gain visibility of the entities in P2 but not those in P1 – however, this seems an odd thing to do. Remember, moreover, that a use clause following a with clause can only refer to packages directly mentioned in the with clause.

Earlier we mentioned the existence of the package STANDARD. This contains all the predefined entities but moreover every library unit should be thought of as being declared inside and at the end of STANDARD. This explains why an explicit use clause for STANDARD is not required. Another important consequence is that, provided we do not hide the name STANDARD by redefining it, a library unit P can always be referred to as STANDARD.P. Hence, in the absence of anonymous blocks, loops and overloading, every identifier in the program has a unique name commencing with STANDARD. Thus we could even pedantically refer to the predefined operators in this way

```
FOUR: INTEGER:= STANDARD."+" (2, 2);
```

It is probably good advice not to redefine STANDARD!

## 8.5  Renaming

Certain entities can be renamed. As an example we can write

```
declare
    procedure SPUSH(X: INTEGER) renames STACK.PUSH;
    function SPOP return INTEGER renames STACK.POP;
```

```
begin
    ...
    SPUSH(M);
    ...
    N:= SPOP;
    ...
end;
```

A possible reason for doing this is to resolve ambiguities and yet avoid the use of the full dotted notation. Thus if we had two packages with a procedure PUSH (with an INTEGER parameter) then the use clause would be of no benefit since the full name would still be needed to resolve the ambiguity.

There is also a strong school of thought that use clauses are bad for you. Consider the case of a large program with many library units and suppose that the unit we are in has withed several packages. If we have use clauses for all these packages then it is not clear from which package an arbitrary identifier has been imported. In the absence of use clauses we have to use the full dotted notation and the origin of everything is then obvious. However, it is also commonly accepted that long meaningful identifiers should be generally used. A long meaningful package name followed by the long meaningful name of an entity in the package is often too much. However, we can introduce an abbreviation by renaming such as

V: REAL **renames** AEROPLANE_DATA.CURRENT_VELOCITY;

and then compactly use V in local computation and yet still have the full identification available in the text of the current unit.

As another example suppose we wish to use both the function INNER and the equivalent operator "$*$" of Chapter 7 without declaring two distinct subprograms. We can write

**function** "$*$" (X, Y: VECTOR) **return** REAL **renames** INNER;

or

**function** INNER(X, Y: VECTOR) **return** REAL **renames** "$*$";

according to which we declare first.

Renaming is also useful in the case of library units. Thus we might wish to have two or more overloaded subprograms and yet compile them separately. This cannot be done directly since library units must have distinct names. However, differently named library units could be renamed so that the user sees the required effect. The restriction that a library unit cannot be an operator can similarly be overcome. The same tricks can be done with subunits.

If a subprogram is renamed, the number, base types and modes of the parameters (and result if a function) must be the same. This information can be used to resolve overloadings (as in the example of "$*$") and, of course, this matching occurs during compilation. Rather strangely, any constraints on the parameters or result in the new subprogram are ignored; those on the original still apply.

On the other hand, the presence, absence or value of default parameters do not have to match. Renaming can be used to introduce, change or delete default expressions; the default parameters associated with the new name are those shown in the renaming declaration. Hence renaming cannot be used as a trick to give an operator default values. Similarly, parameter names do not have to match but naturally the new names must be used for named parameters of calls of the new subprogram.

The unification of subprograms and enumeration literals is further illustrated by the fact that an enumeration literal can be renamed as a parameterless function with the appropriate result. For example

```
function TEN return ROMAN_DIGIT renames 'X';
```

Renaming can also be used to partially evaluate the name of an object. Suppose we have an array of records such as the array PEOPLE in Section 6.7 and that we wish to scan the array and print out the dates of birth in numerical form. We could write

```
for I in PEOPLE'RANGE loop
    PUT(PEOPLE(I).BIRTH.DAY); PUT(":");
    PUT(MONTH_NAME'POS(PEOPLE(I).BIRTH.MONTH)+1);
    PUT(":");
    PUT(PEOPLE(I).BIRTH.YEAR);
end loop;
```

It is clearly painful to repeat PEOPLE(I).BIRTH each time. We could declare a variable D of type DATE and copy PEOPLE(I).BIRTH into it, but this would be very wasteful if the record were at all large. A better technique is to use renaming thus

```
for I in PEOPLE'RANGE loop
    declare
        D: DATE renames PEOPLE(I).BIRTH;
    begin
        PUT(D.DAY); PUT(":");
        PUT(MONTH_NAME'POS(D.MONTH)+1);
        PUT(":");
        PUT(D.YEAR);
    end;
end loop;
```

Beware that renaming does not correspond to text substitution – the identity of the object is determined when the renaming occurs. If any variable in the name subsequently changes then the identity of the object does not change. Any constraints implied by the type mark in the renaming declaration are ignored; those of the original object still apply.

Renaming can be applied to objects (variables and constants), components of composite objects (including slices of arrays), exceptions (see Chapter 10), subprograms and packages. In the case of a package it takes the simple form

**package** P **renames** STACK;

Although renaming does not directly apply to types an almost identical effect can be achieved by the use of a subtype

**subtype** S **is** T;

or in order to overcome a lack of standardization even

**subtype** COLOR **is** COLOUR;

Finally note that renaming does not hide the old name nor does it ever introduce a new entity; it just provides another way of referring to an existing entity (that is why new constraints in a renaming declaration are ignored). Renaming can be very useful at times but the indiscriminate use of renaming should be avoided since the aliases introduced make program proving much more difficult.

---

*Exercise 8.5*

1    Declare a renaming of the literal MON of type DAY from the package DIURNAL of Section 8.1.

2    Declare a renaming of DIURNAL.NEXT_WORK_DAY.

3    Declare PETS as a renaming of the relevant part of the second FARMYARD of Section 6.5.

---

## Checklist 8

Variables inside a package exist between calls of subprograms of the package.

A library unit must be compiled after other library units mentioned in its with clause.

A subunit must be compiled after its parent.

A body must be compiled after the corresponding specification.

A package specification and body form a single declarative region.

Do not redefine STANDARD.

Renaming is not text substitution.

# Chapter 9
# Private Types

We have seen how packages enable us to hide internal objects from the user of a package. Private types enable us to hide the details of the construction of a type from a user.

## 9.1   Normal private types

In Exercise 8.1(**2**) we wrote a package COMPLEX_NUMBERS providing a type COMPLEX, a constant I and some operations on the type. The specification of the package was

```
package COMPLEX_NUMBERS is
    type COMPLEX is
        record
            RL, IM: REAL;
        end record;

    I: constant COMPLEX:= (0.0, 1.0);

    function "+" (X: COMPLEX) return COMPLEX;        -- unary +
    function "−" (X: COMPLEX) return COMPLEX;        -- unary −

    function "+" (X, Y: COMPLEX) return COMPLEX;
    function "−" (X, Y: COMPLEX) return COMPLEX;
    function "*" (X, Y: COMPLEX) return COMPLEX;
    function "/" (X, Y: COMPLEX) return COMPLEX;
end;
```

The trouble with this formulation is that the user can make use of the fact that the complex numbers are held in cartesian representation.

Rather than always using the complex operator "+", the user could also write things like

    C.IM:= C.IM + 1.0;

rather than the more abstract

    C:= C + I;

In fact, with the above package, the user has to make use of the representation in order to construct values of the type.

We might wish to prevent use of knowledge of the representation so that we could change the representation to perhaps polar form at a later date and know that the user's program would still be correct. We can do this with a private type. Consider

```
package COMPLEX_NUMBERS is
    type COMPLEX is private;
    I: constant COMPLEX;
    function "+" (X: COMPLEX) return COMPLEX;
    function "−" (X: COMPLEX) return COMPLEX;
    function "+" (X, Y: COMPLEX) return COMPLEX;
    function "−" (X, Y: COMPLEX) return COMPLEX;
    function "*" (X, Y: COMPLEX) return COMPLEX;
    function "/" (X, Y: COMPLEX) return COMPLEX;
    function CONS(R, I: REAL) return COMPLEX;
    function RL_PART(X: COMPLEX) return REAL;
    function IM_PART(X: COMPLEX) return REAL;

private
    type COMPLEX is
        record
            RL, IM: REAL;
        end record;
    I: constant COMPLEX:= (0.0, 1.0);
end;
```

The part of the package specification before the reserved word **private** is the visible part and gives the information available externally to the package. The type COMPLEX is declared to be private. This means that outside the package nothing is known of the details of the type. The only operations available are assignment, = and /= plus those added by the writer of the package as subprograms specified in the visible part.

We may also declare constants of a private type such as I, in the visible part. The initial value cannot be given in the visible part because the details of the type are not yet known. Hence we just state that I is a constant; we call it a deferred constant.

After **private** we have to give the details of types declared as private and give the initial values of corresponding deferred constants.

A private type can be implemented in any way consistent with the operations visible to the user. It can be a record as we have shown; equally it could be an array, an enumeration type and so on; it could even be declared in terms of another private type. In our case it is fairly obvious that the type COMPLEX is naturally implemented as a record; but we could equally have used an array of two components such as

```
type COMPLEX is array (1 .. 2) of REAL;
```

Having declared the details of the private type we can use them and so declare the constants properly and give their initial values.

It should be noted that as well as the functions $+$, $-$, $*$ and $/$ we have also provided CONS to create a complex number from its real and imaginary components and RL_PART and IM_PART to return the components. Some such functions are necessary because the user no longer has direct access to the internal structure of the type. Of course, the fact that CONS, RL_PART and IM_PART correspond to our thinking externally of the complex numbers in cartesian form does not prevent us from implementing them internally in some other form as we shall see in a moment.

The body of the package is as shown in the answer to Exercise 8.1(2) plus the additional functions which are trivial. It is therefore

```
package body COMPLEX_NUMBERS is

    -- unary + -

    function "+" (X, Y: COMPLEX) return COMPLEX is
    begin
        return (X.RL + Y.RL, X.IM + Y.IM);
    end "+";

    -- - * / similarly

    function CONS(R, I: REAL) return COMPLEX is
    begin
        return (R, I);
    end CONS;

    function RL_PART(X: COMPLEX) return REAL is
    begin
        return X.RL;
    end RL_PART;

    -- IM_PART similarly

end COMPLEX_NUMBERS;
```

The package COMPLEX_NUMBERS could be used in a fragment such as

```
declare
    use COMPLEX_NUMBERS;
    C, D: COMPLEX;
    R, S: REAL;
begin
    C:= CONS(1.5, −6.0);
    D:= C + I;                          -- COMPLEX +
    R:= RL_PART(D) + 6.0;               -- REAL +
    ...
end;
```

Outside the package we can declare variables and constants of type COMPLEX in the usual way. Note the use of CONS to create a complex literal. We cannot, of course, do mixed operations between our complex and real numbers. Thus we cannot write

```
C:= 2.0 * C;
```

but instead must write

```
C:= CONS(2.0, 0.0) * C;
```

If this is felt to be tedious we could add further overloadings of the operators to allow mixed operations.

Let us suppose that for some reason we now decide to represent the complex numbers in polar form. The visible part of the package will be unchanged but the private part could now become

```
private
    PI: constant:= 3.14159_26536;
    type COMPLEX is
        record
            R: REAL;
            THETA: REAL range 0.0 .. 2.0*PI;
        end record;
    I: constant COMPLEX:= (1.0, 0.5*PI);
end;
```

Note how the constant PI is for convenience declared in the private part; anything other than a body can be declared in a private part if it suits us – we are not restricted to just declaring the types and constants in full. Things declared in the private part are also available in the body.

The body of our package COMPLEX_NUMBERS will now need completely rewriting. Some functions will become simpler and others will be more intricate. In particular it will be convenient to provide a function to normalize the angle $\theta$ so that it lies in the range 0 to $2\pi$. The details are left for the reader.

However, since the visible part has not been changed the user's program will not need changing; we are assured of this since there is no way in which the user could have written anything depending on the details of the private type. Nevertheless, the user's program will need recompiling because of the general dependency rules explained in Section 8.2. This may seem slightly contradictory but remember that the compiler needs the information in the private part in order to be able to allocate storage for objects of the private type declared in the user's program. If we change the private part the size of the objects could change and then the object code of the user's program would change even though the source was the same.

An interesting point is that rather than declare a deferred constant we could provide a parameterless function

**function** I **return** COMPLEX;

This has the slight advantage that we can change the value returned without changing the package specification and so having to recompile the user's program. Of course in the case of I we are unlikely to need to change the value anyway!

Finally note that between a private type declaration and the later full type declaration, the type is in a curiously half-defined state. Because of this there are severe restrictions on its use; it can only be used to declare deferred constants, other types and subtypes and subprogram specifications (also entries of tasks which we will meet in Chapter 14). It cannot be used to declare variables.

Thus we could write

**type** COMPLEX_ARRAY **is array** (INTEGER **range** <>) **of** COMPLEX;

and then

C: **constant** COMPLEX_ARRAY;

But until the full declaration is given we cannot declare variables of the type COMPLEX or COMPLEX_ARRAY.

However, we can declare the specifications of subprograms with parameters of the types COMPLEX and COMPLEX_ARRAY and can even supply default expressions. Such default expressions can use deferred constants and functions; this is allowed because of course a default expression is only evaluated when a subprogram is called and this cannot occur until the body of the package has been declared and this is bound to be after the full type declaration.

An interesting point with regard to deferred constants is that the syntax

deferred_constant_declaration ::=
                                    identifier_list : **constant** type_mark;

shows that we cannot use an explicit constraint in their type declaration. This avoids the possibility of a constraint producing a different value when it is repeated in the subsequent full constant declaration. Thus the type marks have to conform just as in repeated subprogram specifications (see Section 7.6). In the case of the array C above the full declaration might be

C: **constant** COMPLEX_ARRAY(1 .. 10):= ... ;

or even

C: **constant** COMPLEX_ARRAY:= ... ;

where in the latter case the bounds are taken from the initial value. If we wish to impose a constraint on the visible deferred constant declaration of C then we would have to introduce a subtype. Similar rules apply to discriminated records which we will discuss in Section 11.1.

There are various other subtle points which need not concern the normal user but which are described in the *LRM*. However, the general rule is that you can only use what you know. Outside the package we know only that the type is private; inside the package and after the full type declaration we know all the properties implied by the declaration.

As an example consider the type COMPLEX_ARRAY and the operator "<". (Remember that "<" only applies to arrays if the component type is discrete.) Outside the package we cannot use "<" since we do not know whether or not type COMPLEX is discrete. Inside the package we find that it is not discrete and so still cannot use "<". If it had been discrete we could have used "<" after the full type declaration but of course we still could not use it outside. On the other hand slicing is applicable to all one-dimensional arrays and so can be used both inside and outside the package.

---

*Exercise 9.1*

1    Write additional functions "*" to enable mixed multiplication of real and complex numbers.

2    Rewrite the fragment of user program for complex numbers omitting the use clause.

3    Complete the package RATIONAL_NUMBERS whose visible part is

```
package RATIONAL_NUMBERS is

    type RATIONAL is private;
    function "+" (X: RATIONAL) return RATIONAL; -- unary +
    function "-" (X: RATIONAL) return RATIONAL; -- unary -
    function "+" (X, Y: RATIONAL) return RATIONAL;
    function "-" (X, Y: RATIONAL) return RATIONAL;
    function "*" (X, Y: RATIONAL) return RATIONAL;
    function "/" (X, Y: RATIONAL) return RATIONAL;

    function "/" (X: INTEGER; Y: POSITIVE) return RATIONAL;
```

**function** NUMERATOR(R: RATIONAL) **return** INTEGER;
**function** DENOMINATOR(R: RATIONAL) **return** POSITIVE;

**private**

...

**end**;

A rational number is a number of the form N/D where N is an integer and D is a positive integer. For predefined equality to work it is essential that rational numbers are always reduced by cancelling out common factors. This may be done using the function GCD of Exercise 7.1(**7**). Ensure that an object of type RATIONAL has an appropriate default value of zero.

**4**     Why does

**function** "/" (X: INTEGER; Y: POSITIVE) **return** RATIONAL;

not hide the predefined integer division?

---

## 9.2   Limited private types

The operations available on a private type can be completely restricted to those specified in the visible part of the package. This is done by declaring the type as limited as well as private thus

**type** T **is limited private**;

In such a case assignment and predefined = and /= are not available outside the package. However, the package may define a function "=" if the two parameters are of the same limited type; it must return a value of type BOOLEAN. The operator /= always takes its meaning from = and so cannot be explicitly defined.

An important consequence of the absence of assignment for limited types is that the declaration of an object cannot include an initial value; this in turn implies that a constant cannot be declared outside the defining package. Similarly, a record component of a limited type cannot have a default initial expression. However, remember that the procedure parameter mechanism is not formally assignment and in fact we can declare our own subprograms with limited types as parameters of mode **in** or **in out** outside the defining package and we can even supply default expressions for **in** parameters; parameters of mode **out** are however not allowed for a reason which will become apparent in the next section.

The advantage of making a private type limited is that the package writer has complete control over the objects of the type – the copying of resources can be monitored and so on.

As a simple example consider the following

```
package STACKS is
    type STACK is limited private;
    procedure PUSH(S: in out STACK; X: in INTEGER);
    procedure POP(S: in out STACK; X: out INTEGER);
    function "=" (S, T: STACK) return BOOLEAN;
private
    MAX: constant:= 100;
    type INTEGER_VECTOR is
                            array (INTEGER range <>) of INTEGER;
    type STACK is
        record
            S: INTEGER_VECTOR(1 .. MAX);
            TOP: INTEGER range 0 .. MAX:= 0;
        end record;
end;
```

Each object of type STACK is a record containing an array S and integer TOP. Note that TOP has a default initial value of zero. This ensures that when we declare a stack object, it is correctly initialized to be empty. Note also the introduction of the type INTEGER_VECTOR because a record component may not be an anonymous array.

The body of the package could be

```
package body STACKS is

    procedure PUSH(S: in out STACK; X: in INTEGER) is
    begin
        S.TOP:= S.TOP+1;
        S.S(S.TOP):= X;
    end PUSH;

    procedure POP(S: in out STACK; X: out INTEGER) is
    begin
        X:= S.S(S.TOP);
        S.TOP:= S.TOP−1;
    end POP;

    function "=" (S, T: STACK) return BOOLEAN is
    begin
        if S.TOP /= T.TOP then
            return FALSE;
        end if;
        for I in 1 .. S.TOP loop
            if S.S(I) /= T.S(I) then
                return FALSE;
            end if;
        end loop;
```

```
        return TRUE;
    end "=";

  end STACKS;
```

This example illustrates many points. The parameter S of PUSH has mode **in out** because we need both to read from and to write to the stack. Further note that POP cannot be a function since S has to be **in out** and functions can only have **in** parameters. However, "=" can be a function because we only need to read the values of the two stacks and not to update them.

The function "=" has the interpretation that two stacks are equal only if they have the same number of items and the corresponding items have the same value. It would obviously be quite wrong to compare the whole records because the unused components of the arrays would also be compared. It is because of this that the type STACK has been made limited private rather than just private. If it were just private then we could not redefine "=" to give the correct meaning.

This is a typical example of a data structure where the value of the whole is more than just the sum of the parts; the interpretation of the array S depends on the value of TOP. Cases where there is such a relationship usually need a limited private type.

A minor point is that we are using the identifier S in two ways: as the name of the formal parameter denoting the stack and as the array inside the record. There is no conflict because, although the scopes overlap, the regions of visibility do not as was explained in Section 8.4. Of course, it is rather confusing to the reader and not good practice but it illustrates the freedom of choice of record component names.

The package could be used in a fragment such as

```
declare
    use STACKS;
    ST: STACK;
    EMPTY: STACK;
    ...
begin
    PUSH(ST, N);
    ...
    POP(ST, M);
    ...
    if ST = EMPTY then
        ...
    end if;
    ...
end;
```

Here we have declared two stacks ST and EMPTY. Both are originally empty because their internal component TOP has an initial value of zero. Assuming that we do not manipulate EMPTY then it can be used to see whether the stack ST is empty or not by calling the function "=". This seems a rather dubious way of testing for an empty stack since there is no guarantee that EMPTY has not been manipulated. It would be better if EMPTY were a constant but as mentioned earlier we cannot declare a constant of a limited private type outside the package. We could however declare a constant EMPTY in the visible part of the package. A much better technique for testing the state of a stack would, of course, be to provide a function EMPTY and a corresponding function FULL in the package.

We can write subprograms with limited private types as parameters outside the defining package despite the absence of assignment. As a simple example, the following procedure enables us to determine the top value on the stack without removing it.

```
procedure TOP_OF(S: in out STACK; X: in out INTEGER) is
begin
    POP(S, X);
    PUSH(S, X);
end;
```

The declaration of a function "=" does not have to be confined to the package containing the declaration of the limited type. The only point is that outside the package, we cannot see the structure of the type. Furthermore, a composite type containing one or more components of a limited type is itself considered to be limited and so we could define "=" for such a type. Thus outside the package STACKS we could declare

```
type STACK_ARRAY is array (INTEGER range <>) of STACK;
function "=" (A, B: STACK_ARRAY) return BOOLEAN;
```

where the definition of an appropriate body is left to the reader.

Remember that within the private part (after the full type declaration) and within the body, any private type (limited or not) is treated in terms of how it is represented. Thus within the body of STACKS the type STACK is just a record type and so assignment and things consequential upon assignment (initialization and constants) are allowed. So we could declare a procedure ASSIGN (intended to be used outside the package) as

```
procedure ASSIGN(S: in STACK; T: out STACK) is
begin
    T:= S;
end;
```

The parameter mechanism for a private type is simply that corresponding to how the type is represented. This applies both inside and outside the package. Of course, outside the package, we know nothing of how the type is represented and therefore should make no assumption about the mechanism used.

It is unfortunate that Ada does not separate the ability to permit assignment and redefinition of equality. For instance, it would be reasonable to allow assignment of stacks, but, of course, predefined equality is of no value. Equally in the case of a type such as RATIONAL of Exercise 9.1(2), it would be quite reasonable to allow manipulation – including assignment – of values which were not reduced provided that equality was suitably redefined. We are therefore forced to use a procedural form such as ASSIGN or reduce all values to a canonical form in which component by component equality is satisfactory. In the case of type STACK a suitable form would be one in which all unused elements of the stack had a standard dummy value such as zero.

---

*Exercise 9.2*

1    Rewrite the specification of STACKS to include a constant EMPTY in the visible part.

2    Write functions EMPTY and FULL for STACKS.

3    Rewrite the **function** "=" (S, T: STACK) using slices.

4    Write a suitable body for the function "=" applying to the type STACK_ARRAY. Make it conform to the normal rules for array equality which we mentioned towards the end of Section 6.2.

5    Rewrite ASSIGN for STACKS so that only the meaningful part of the record is copied.

6    Rewrite STACKS so that STACK is a normal private type. Ensure that predefined equality is satisfactory.

---

## 9.3  Resource management

An important example of the use of a limited private type is in providing controlled resource management. Consider the simple human model where each resource has a corresponding unique key. This key is then issued to the user when the resource is allocated and then has to be shown whenever the resource is accessed. So long as there is only one key and copying and stealing are prevented we know that the system is foolproof. A mechanism for handing in keys and reissuing them is usually necessary if resources are not to be permanently locked up. Typical human examples are the use of metal keys with safe deposit boxes, credit cards and so on.
   Now consider the following

```
package KEY_MANAGER is
    type KEY is limited private;
    procedure GET_KEY(K: in out KEY);
    procedure RETURN_KEY(K: in out KEY);
    function VALID(K: KEY) return BOOLEAN;
    ...
    procedure ACTION(K: in KEY; ... );
```

```
    ...
private
    MAX: constant:= 100;                        -- number of keys
    subtype KEY_CODE is INTEGER range 0 .. MAX;
    type KEY is
        record
            CODE: KEY_CODE:= 0;
        end record;
end;


package body KEY_MANAGER is
    FREE: array (KEY_CODE range 1 .. KEY_CODE'LAST) of
                                BOOLEAN:= (others => TRUE);

    function VALID(K: KEY) return BOOLEAN is
    begin
        return K.CODE /= 0;
    end VALID;

    procedure GET_KEY(K: in out KEY) is
    begin
        if K.CODE = 0 then
            for I in FREE'RANGE loop
                if FREE(I) then
                    FREE(I):= FALSE;
                    K.CODE:= I;
                    return;
                end if;
            end loop;
                                -- all keys in use
        end if;
    end GET_KEY;

    procedure RETURN_KEY(K: in out KEY) is
    begin
        if K.CODE /= 0 then
            FREE(K.CODE):= TRUE;
            K.CODE:= 0;
        end if;
    end RETURN_KEY;
    ...

    procedure ACTION(K: in KEY; ... ) is
    begin
        if VALID(K) then
            ...
    end ACTION;

end KEY_MANAGER;
```

The type KEY is represented by a record with a single component CODE. This has a default value of 0 which represents an unused key. Values from 1 .. MAX represent the allocation of the corresponding resource. When we declare a variable of type KEY it automatically takes an internal code value of zero. In order to use the key we must first call the procedure GET_KEY; this allocates the first free key number to the variable. The key may then be used with various procedures such as ACTION which represents a typical request for some access to the resource guarded by the key.

Finally, the key may be relinquished by calling RETURN_KEY. So a typical fragment of user program might be

```
declare
    use KEY_MANAGER;
    MY_KEY: KEY;
begin
    ...
    GET_KEY(MY_KEY);
    ...
    ACTION(MY_KEY, ... );
    ...
    RETURN_KEY(MY_KEY);
    ...
end;
```

A variable of type KEY can be thought of as a container for a key. When initially declared the default value can be thought of as representing that the container is empty; the type KEY has to be a record because only record components can take default initial values. Note how the various possible misuses of keys are overcome.

• If we call GET_KEY with a variable already containing a valid key then no new key is allocated. It is important not to overwrite an old valid key otherwise that key would be lost.

• A call of RETURN_KEY resets the variable to the default state so that the variable cannot be used as a key until a new one is issued by a call of GET_KEY. Note that the user is unable to retain a copy of the key because assignment is not valid since the type KEY is limited.

The function VALID is provided so that the user can see whether a key variable contains the default value or an allocated value. It is obviously useful to call VALID after GET_KEY to ensure that the key manager was able to provide a new key value; note that once all keys are issued, a call of GET_KEY does nothing.

One apparent flaw is that there is no compulsion to call RETURN_KEY before the scope containing the declaration of MY_KEY is left. The key would then be lost. This corresponds to the real life situation of losing a key (although in our model no one else can find it again – it is as if it were thrown into a black hole). To guard against this the key manager might assume (as in life) that a key not used for a certain period of time is no longer in use. Of course, the same key would not be reissued but the resource guarded might be considered reusable; this would involve keeping separate records of keys in use and resources in use and a cross-reference from keys to resources.

---

*Exercise 9.3*

1    Complete the package whose visible part is

```
package BANK is
    subtype MONEY is NATURAL;
    type KEY is limited private;
    procedure OPEN_ACCOUNT(K: in out KEY; M: in MONEY);
        -- open account with initial deposit M
    procedure CLOSE_ACCOUNT(K: in out KEY;
                                        M: out MONEY);
        -- close account and return balance
    procedure DEPOSIT(K: in KEY; M: in MONEY);
        -- deposit amount M
    procedure WITHDRAW(K: in out KEY; M in out MONEY);
        -- withdraw amount M; if account does not contain M
        -- then return what is there and close account
    function STATEMENT(K: KEY) return MONEY;
        -- returns a statement of current balance
    function VALID(K: KEY) return BOOLEAN;
        -- checks the key is valid
private
    ...
```

2    Assuming that your solution to the previous question allowed the bank the use of the deposited money, reformulate the private type to represent a home savings box or safe deposit box where the money is in a box kept by the user.

3    A thief writes the following

```
declare
    use KEY_MANAGER;
    MY_KEY: KEY;
    procedure CHEAT(COPY: in out KEY) is
    begin
        RETURN_KEY(MY_KEY);
        ACTION(COPY, ... );
        ...
    end;
begin
    GET_KEY(MY_KEY);
    CHEAT(MY_KEY);
    ...
end;
```

He attempts to return his key and then use the copy. Why is he thwarted?

**4**    A vandal writes the following

```
declare
    use KEY_MANAGER;
    MY_KEY: KEY;
    procedure DESTROY(K: out KEY) is
    begin
        null;
    end;
begin
    GET_KEY(MY_KEY);
    DESTROY(MY_KEY);
    ...
end;
```

He attempts to destroy the value in his key by calling a procedure which does not update the **out** parameter; he anticipates that the copy back rule will result in a junk value being assigned to the key. Why is he thwarted?

---

## Checklist 9

For predefined equality to be sensible, the values should be in a canonical form.

An unlimited private type can be implemented in terms of another private type provided it is also unlimited.

A limited private type can be implemented in terms of any private type limited or not.

"/=" can never be defined – it always follows from "=".

"=" can be defined outside the package defining the limited private type concerned.

The rules apply transitively to composite types.

# Chapter 10
# Exceptions

---

---

At various times in the preceding chapters we have said that if something goes wrong when the program is executed, then an exception, often CONSTRAINT_ERROR, will be raised. In this chapter we describe the exception mechanism and show how remedial action can be taken when an exception occurs. We also show how we may define and use our own exceptions. Exceptions concerned with interacting tasks are dealt with when we come to Chapter 14.

## 10.1   Handling exceptions

We have seen that if we break various language rules then an exception may be raised when we execute the program.

There are five predefined exceptions (declared in the package STANDARD) of which we have met four so far

| | |
|---|---|
| CONSTRAINT_ERROR | This generally corresponds to something going out of range. |
| NUMERIC_ERROR | This can occur when something goes wrong with arithmetic such as an attempt to divide by zero. However, as explained in Section 4.9, AI-387 concludes that it is not always possible to distinguish this exception from CONSTRAINT_ERROR and recommends that CONSTRAINT_ERROR should always be raised in such circumstances. |
| PROGRAM_ERROR | This will occur if we attempt to violate the control structure in some way such as |

169

running into the **end** of a function or calling a subprogram whose body has not yet been elaborated – see Sections 7.1 and 8.1.

STORAGE_ERROR          This will occur if we run out of storage space as, for example, if we called our recursive function FACTORIAL with a large parameter – see Section 7.1.

The other predefined exception is TASKING_ERROR. This is concerned with tasking and so is dealt with in Chapter 14.

If we anticipate that an exception may occur in a part of our program then we can write an exception handler to deal with it. For example, suppose we write

```
begin
    -- sequence of statements
exception
    when CONSTRAINT_ERROR =>
        -- do something
end;
```

If CONSTRAINT_ERROR is raised while we are executing the sequence of statements between **begin** and **exception** then the flow of control is interrupted and immediately transferred to the sequence of statements following the =>. The clause starting **when** is known as an exception handler.

As a trivial example we could compute TOMORROW from TODAY by writing

```
begin
    TOMORROW:= DAY'SUCC(TODAY);
exception
    when CONSTRAINT_ERROR =>
        TOMORROW:= DAY'FIRST;
end;
```

If TODAY is DAY'LAST (that is, SUN) then when we attempt to evaluate DAY'SUCC(TODAY), the exception CONSTRAINT_ERROR is raised. Control is then transferred to the handler for CONSTRAINT_ERROR and the statement TOMORROW:= DAY'FIRST; is executed. Control then passes to the end of the block.

This is really a bad example. Exceptions should be used for rarely occurring cases or those which are inconvenient to test for at their point of occurrence. By no stretch of the imagination is Sunday a rare day. Over 14% of all days are Sundays. Nor is it difficult to test for the condition at the point of occurrence. So we should really have written

```
if TODAY = DAY'LAST then
    TOMORROW:= DAY'FIRST;
else
    TOMORROW:= DAY'SUCC(TODAY);
end if;
```

However, it is a simple example with which to illustrate the mechanism involved.

Several handlers can be written between **exception** and **end**. Consider

```
begin
    -- sequence of statements
exception
    when NUMERIC_ERROR | CONSTRAINT_ERROR =>
        PUT("Numeric or Constraint error occurred");
        ...
    when STORAGE_ERROR =>
        PUT("Ran out of space");
        ...
    when others =>
        PUT("Something else went wrong");
        ...
end;
```

In this example a message is output according to the exception. Note the similarity to the case statement. Each **when** is followed by one or more exception names separated by vertical bars. As usual we can write **others** but it must be last and on its own; it handles any exception not listed in the previous handlers. Note also that we have a common handler for NUMERIC_ERROR and CONSTRAINT_ERROR in accordance with AI-387.

Exception handlers can appear at the end of a block, subprogram body, package body (or task body) and have access to all entities declared in the unit (called a frame in the *LRM* although we will continue to use the more informal term unit). The examples have shown a degenerate block in which there is no **declare** and declarative part; the block was introduced just for the purpose of providing somewhere to hang the handlers. We could rewrite our bad example to determine tomorrow as a function thus

```
function TOMORROW(TODAY: DAY) return DAY is
begin
    return DAY'SUCC(TODAY);
exception
    when CONSTRAINT_ERROR =>
        return DAY'FIRST;
end TOMORROW;
```

It is important to realize that control can never be returned directly to the unit where the exception was raised. The sequence of statements following => replaces the remainder of the unit containing the handler and thereby completes execution of the unit. Hence a handler for a function must generally contain a return statement in order to provide the 'emergency' result.

In particular, a goto statement cannot transfer control from a unit into one of its handlers or vice versa, or from one handler to another. However, the statements of a handler can otherwise be of arbitrary complexity. They can include blocks, calls of subprograms and so on. A handler of a block could contain a goto statement which transferred control to a label outside the block and it could contain an exit statement if the block were inside a loop.

A handler at the end of a package body applies only to the initialization sequence of the package and not to subprograms in the package. Such subprograms must have individual handlers if they are to deal with exceptions.

We now consider the question of what happens if a unit does not provide a handler for a particular exception. The answer is that the exception is propagated dynamically. This simply means that the unit is terminated and the exception is raised at the point where the unit was invoked. In the case of a block we therefore look for a handler in the unit containing the block.

In the case of a subprogram, the call is terminated and we look for a handler in the unit which called the subprogram. This unwinding process is repeated until either we reach a unit containing a handler for the particular exception or come to the top level. If we find a unit containing a relevant handler then the exception is handled at that point. Alternatively we have reached the main program and have still found no handler – the main program is then abandoned and we can expect the run time environment to provide us with a suitable diagnostic message. (Unhandled exceptions in tasks are dealt with in Chapter 14.)

It is most important to understand that exceptions are propagated dynamically and not statically. That is, an exception not handled by a subprogram is propagated to the unit calling the subprogram and not to the unit containing the declaration of the subprogram – these may or may not be the same.

If the statements in a handler themselves raise an exception then the unit is terminated and the exception propagated to the calling unit; the handler does not loop.

---

*Exercise 10.1*

Note: these are exercises to check your understanding of exceptions. They do not necessarily reflect good Ada programming techniques.

1    Assuming that calling SQRT with a negative parameter and attempting to divide by zero both raise NUMERIC_ERROR, rewrite the procedure QUADRATIC of Section 7.3 without explicitly testing D and A.

2    Rewrite the function FACTORIAL of Section 7.1 so that if it is called with a negative parameter (which would normally raise CONSTRAINT_ERROR) or a large parameter (which would normally raise STORAGE_ERROR or NUMERIC_ERROR alias

CONSTRAINT_ERROR) then a standard result of say −1 is returned. Hint: declare an inner function SLAVE which actually does the work.

---

## 10.2 Declaring and raising exceptions

Relying on the predefined exceptions to detect unusual but anticipated situations is usually bad practice because they do not provide a guarantee that the exception has in fact been raised because of the anticipated situation. Something else may have gone wrong instead.

As an illustration consider the package STACK of Section 8.1. If we call PUSH when the stack is full then the statement TOP:= TOP+1; will raise CONSTRAINT_ERROR and similarly if we call POP when the stack is empty then TOP:= TOP−1; will also raise CONSTRAINT_ERROR. Since PUSH and POP do not themselves have exception handlers, the exception will be propagated to the unit calling them. So we could write

```
declare
    use STACK;
begin
    ...
    PUSH(M);
    ...
    N:= POP;
    ...
exception
    when CONSTRAINT_ERROR =>
        -- stack manipulation incorrect?
end;
```

and misuse of the stack would then result in control being transferred to the handler for CONSTRAINT_ERROR. However, there would be no guarantee that the exception had arisen because of misuse of the stack; something else in the block could have gone wrong.

A better solution is to raise an exception specifically declared to indicate misuse of the stack. Thus the package could be rewritten

```
package STACK is
    ERROR: exception;
    procedure PUSH(X: INTEGER);
    function POP return INTEGER;
end STACK;

package body STACK is
    MAX: constant:= 100;
    S: array (1 .. MAX) of INTEGER;
    TOP: INTEGER range 0 .. MAX;
```

```
        procedure PUSH(X: INTEGER) is
        begin
            if TOP = MAX then
                raise ERROR;
            end if;
            TOP:= TOP+1;
            S(TOP):= X;
        end PUSH;

        function POP return INTEGER is
        begin
            if TOP = 0 then
                raise ERROR;
            end if;
            TOP:= TOP-1;
            return S(TOP+1);
        end POP;

    begin
        TOP:= 0;
    end STACK;
```

An exception is declared in a similar way to a variable and is raised by an explicit raise statement naming the exception. The handling and propagation rules are just as for the predefined exceptions. We can now write

```
    declare
        use STACK;
    begin
        ...
        PUSH(M);
        ...
        N:= POP;
        ...
    exception
        when ERROR =>
            -- stack manipulation incorrect
        when others =>
            -- something else went wrong
    end;
```

We have now successfully separated the handler for misusing the stack from the handler for other exceptions.

Note that if we had not provided a use clause then we would have had to refer to the exception in the handler as STACK.ERROR; the usual dotted notation applies.

What could we expect to do in the handler in the above case? Apart from reporting that the stack manipulation has gone wrong, we might also expect to reset the stack to an acceptable state although we have not provided a convenient means of doing so. A procedure RESET in the package STACK would be useful. A further thing we might do is relinquish any resources that were acquired in the block and might otherwise be inadvertently retained. Suppose for instance that we had also been using the package KEY_MANAGER of Section 9.3. We might then call RETURN_KEY to ensure that a key declared and acquired in the block had been returned. Remember that RETURN_KEY does no harm if called unnecessarily.

We would probably also want to reset the stack and return the key in the case of any other exception as well; so it would be as well to declare a procedure CLEAN_UP to do all the actions required. So our block might look like

```
declare
    use STACK, KEY_MANAGER;
    MY_KEY: KEY;

    procedure CLEAN_UP is
    begin
        RESET;
        RETURN_KEY(MY_KEY);
    end;

begin
    GET_KEY(MY_KEY);
    ...
    PUSH(M);
    ...
    ACTION(MY_KEY, ... );
    ...
    N:= POP;
    ...
    RETURN_KEY(MY_KEY);
exception
    when ERROR =>
        PUT("Stack used incorrectly");
        CLEAN_UP;
    when others =>
        PUT("Something else went wrong");
        CLEAN_UP;
end;
```

We have rather assumed that RESET is a further procedure declared in the package STACK but note that we could write our own procedure externally as follows

```
procedure RESET is
    JUNK: INTEGER;
    use STACK;
```

```
begin
   loop
      JUNK:= POP;
   end loop;
exception
   when ERROR =>
      null;
end RESET;
```

This works by repeatedly calling POP until ERROR is raised. We then know that the stack is empty. The handler needs to do nothing other than prevent the exception from being propagated; so we merely write **null**. This procedure seems a bit like trickery; it would be far better to have a reset procedure in the package.

Sometimes the actions that require to be taken as a consequence of an exception need to be performed on a layered basis. In the above example we returned the key and then reset the stack but it is probably the case that the block as a whole cannot be assumed to have done its job correctly. We can indicate this by raising an exception as the last action of the handler.

```
exception
   when ERROR =>
      PUT("Stack used incorrectly");
      CLEAN_UP;
      raise ANOTHER_ERROR;
   when others =>
      ...
end;
```

The exception ANOTHER_ERROR will then be propagated to the unit containing the block. We could put the statement

**raise** ANOTHER_ERROR;

in the procedure CLEAN_UP.

Sometimes it is convenient to handle an exception and then propagate the same exception. This can be done by just writing

**raise**;

This is particularly useful when we handle several exceptions with the one handler since there is no way in which we can explicitly name the exception which occurred.

So we might have

```
when others =>
   PUT("Something else went wrong");
   CLEAN_UP;
   raise;
end;
```

The current exception will be remembered even if the action of the handler raises and handles its own exceptions such as occurred in our trick procedure RESET. However, note that there is a rule that we can only write **raise**; directly in a handler and not for instance in a procedure called by the handler such as CLEAN_UP.

The stack example illustrates a legitimate use of exceptions. The exception ERROR should rarely, if ever, occur and it would also be inconvenient to test for the condition at each possible point of occurrence. To do that we would presumably have to provide an additional parameter to PUSH of type BOOLEAN and mode **out** to indicate that all was not well, and then test it after each call. In the case of POP we would also have to recast it as a procedure since a function cannot take a parameter of mode **out**.

The package specification would then become

```
package STACK is
    procedure PUSH(X: in INTEGER; B: out BOOLEAN);
    procedure POP(X: out INTEGER; B: out BOOLEAN);
end;
```

and we would have to write

```
declare
    use STACK;
    OK: BOOLEAN;
begin
    ...
    PUSH(M, OK);
    if not OK then ...     end if;
    ...
    POP(N, OK);
    if not OK then ...     end if;
end;
```

It is clear that the use of an exception provides a better structured program.

Note finally that nothing prevents us from explicitly raising one of the predefined exceptions. We recall that in Section 7.1 when discussing the function INNER we stated that probably the best way of coping with parameters whose bounds were unequal was to explicitly raise CONSTRAINT_ERROR.

---

*Exercise 10.2*

1     Rewrite the package RANDOM of Exercise 8.1(**1**) so that it declares and raises an exception BAD if the initial value is not odd.

2     Rewrite your answer to Exercise 10.1(**2**) so that the function FACTORIAL always raises CONSTRAINT_ERROR if the parameter is negative or too large.

3    Declare a function "+" which takes two parameters of type
     VECTOR and returns their sum using sliding semantics by analogy
     with the predefined one-dimensional array operations described in
     Section 6.6. Use type VECTOR from Section 6.2. Raise
     CONSTRAINT_ERROR if the arrays do not match.

4    Are we completely justified in asserting that STACK.ERROR could
     only be raised by the stack going wrong?

## 10.3  Checking and exceptions

In the previous section we came to the conclusion that it was logically
better to check for the stack overflow condition ourselves rather than rely
upon the built-in check associated with the violation of the subtype of TOP.
At first sight the reader may well feel that this would reduce the execution
efficiency of the program. However, this is not necessarily so, assuming a
reasonably intelligent compiler, and this example can be used to illustrate
the advantages of the use of appropriate subtypes.

We will concentrate on the procedure PUSH, similar arguments
apply to the function POP.

First consider the original package STACK of Section 8.1. In that we had

```
...
S: array (1 .. MAX) of INTEGER;
TOP: INTEGER range 0 .. MAX;

procedure PUSH(X: INTEGER) is
begin
    TOP:= TOP+1;
    S(TOP):= X;
end PUSH;
```

If the stack is full (that is TOP = MAX) and we call PUSH then it is the
assignment to TOP that raises CONSTRAINT_ERROR. This is because TOP
has a range constraint. However, the only run-time check that needs to be
compiled is that associated with checking the upper bound of TOP. There is
no need to check for violation of the lower bound since the expression
TOP+1 could not be less than 1 (assuming that the value in TOP is always in
range). Note, moreover, that no checks need be compiled with respect to the
assignment to S(TOP). This is because the value of TOP at this stage must lie
in the range 1 .. MAX (which is the index range of S) – it cannot exceed MAX
because this has just been checked by the previous assignment and it cannot
be less than 1 since 1 has just been added to its previous value which could
not have been less than 0. So just one check needs to be compiled in the
procedure PUSH.

On the other hand, if the variable TOP had not been given a range
constraint but just declared as

```
TOP: INTEGER;
```

then although no checks would have been applied to the assignment to TOP, nevertheless checks would have had to be compiled for the assignment to S(TOP) instead in order to ensure that TOP lay within the index range of S. Two checks would be necessary – one for each end of the index range.

So applying the range constraint to TOP actually reduces the number of checks required. This is typical behaviour given a compiler with a moderate degree of flow analysis. The more you tell the compiler about the properties of the variables (and assuming the constraints on the variables match their usage), the better the object code.

Now consider what happens when we add our own test as in the previous section (and we assume that TOP now has its range constraint)

```
procedure PUSH(X: INTEGER) is
begin
    if TOP = MAX then
        raise ERROR;
    end if;
    TOP:= TOP+1;
    S(TOP):= X;
end PUSH;
```

Clearly we have added a check of our own. However, there is now no need for the compiler to insert the check on the upper bound of TOP in the assignment

```
TOP:= TOP+1;
```

because our own check will have caused control to be transferred away via the raising of the ERROR exception for the one original value of TOP that would have caused trouble. So the net effect of adding our own check is simply to replace a compiler check by our own; the object code is not less efficient.

There are two morals to this tale. The first is that we should tell the compiler the whole truth about our program; the more it knows about the properties of our variables, the more likely it is to be able to keep checks to the appropriate minimum. In fact this is just an extension of the advantage of strong typing discussed in Section 4.3 where we saw how arbitrary run-time errors can be replaced by easily understood compile-time errors.

The second moral is that introducing our own exceptions rather than relying upon the predefined ones need not reduce the efficiency of our program. In fact it is generally considered bad practice to rely upon the predefined exceptions for steering our program and especially bad to raise the predefined exceptions explicitly ourselves. It is all too easy to mask an unexpected genuine error that needs fixing.

It should also be noted that we can always ask the compiler to omit the run-time checks by using the pragma SUPPRESS. This is described in Section 15.5.

Finally, an important warning. Our analysis of when checks can be omitted depends upon all variables satisfying their constraints at all times. Provided checks are not suppressed we can be reasonably assured of this apart from one nasty loophole. This is that we are not obliged to supply initial values in the declarations of variables in the first place. So they can start with a junk value which does not satisfy any constraints and may not even be a value of the base type. If such a variable is read before being updated then our program is erroneous and all our analysis is worthless. It is thus a good idea to initialize all variables unless it is perfectly obvious that updating will occur first.

---

*Exercise 10.3*

**1**    Consider the case of the procedure PUSH with explicit raising of ERROR but suppose that there is no range constraint on TOP.

---

## 10.4    Scope of exceptions

To a large extent exceptions follow the same scope rules as other entities. An exception can hide and be hidden by another declaration; it can be made visible by the dotted notation and so on. An exception can be renamed

> HELP: **exception renames** BANK.ALARM;

Exceptions are, however, different in many ways. We cannot declare arrays of exceptions, and they cannot be components of records, parameters of subprograms and so on. In short, exceptions are not objects and so cannot be manipulated. They are merely tags.

A very important characteristic of exceptions is that they are not created dynamically as a program executes but should be thought of as existing throughout the life of the program. This relates to the way in which exceptions are propagated dynamically up the chain of execution rather than statically up the chain of scope. An exception can be propagated outside its scope although of course it can then only be handled anonymously by **others**. This is illustrated by the following

```
declare
    procedure P is
        X: exception;
    begin
        raise X;
    end P;
begin
    P;
exception
    when others =>
            -- X handled here
end;
```

The procedure P declares and raises the exception X but does not handle it. When we call P, the exception X is propagated to the block calling P where it is handled anonymously.

It is even possible to propagate an exception out of its scope, where it becomes anonymous, and then back in again where it can once more be handled by its proper name. Consider (and this is really a crazy example)

```
declare
    package P is
        procedure F;
        procedure H;
    end P;

    procedure G is
    begin
        P.H;
    exception
        when others =>
            raise;
    end G;

    package body P is
        X: exception;

        procedure F is
        begin
            G;
        exception
            when X =>
                PUT("Got it!");
        end F;

        procedure H is
        begin
            raise X;
        end H;

    end P;

begin
    P.F;
end;
```

The block declares a package P containing procedures F and H and also a procedure G. The block calls F in P which calls G outside P which in turn calls H back in P. The procedure H raises the exception X whose scope is the body of P. The procedure H does not handle X, so it is propagated to G which called H. The procedure G is outside the package P, so the exception X is now outside its scope; nevertheless G handles the exception anonymously and propagates it further by reraising it. G was called by F so

X is now propagated back into the package and so can be handled by F by its proper name.

A further illustration of the nature of exceptions is afforded by a recursive procedure containing an exception declaration. Unlike variables declared in a procedure we do not get a new exception for each recursive call. Each recursive activation refers to the same exception. Consider the following artificial example

```
procedure F(N: INTEGER) is
    X: exception;
begin
    if N = 0 then
        raise X;
    else
        F(N−1);
    end if;
exception
    when X =>
        PUT("Got it");
        raise;
    when others =>
        null;
end F;
```

Suppose we execute F(4); we get recursive calls F(3), F(2), F(1) and finally F(0). When F is called with parameter zero, it raises the exception X, handles it, prints out a confirmatory message and then reraises it. The calling instance of F (which itself had N = 1) receives the exception and again handles it as X and so on. The message is therefore printed out five times in all and the exception is finally propagated anonymously. Observe that if each recursive activation had created a different exception then the message would only be printed out once.

In all the examples we have seen so far exceptions have been raised in statements. An exception can however also be raised in a declaration. Thus

```
N: POSITIVE:= 0;
```

would raise CONSTRAINT_ERROR because the initial value of N does not satisfy the range constraint 1 .. INTEGER ' LAST of the subtype POSITIVE. An exception raised in a declaration is not handled by a handler (if any) of the unit containing the declaration but is immediately propagated up a level. This means that in any handler we are assured that all declarations of the unit were successfully elaborated and so there is no risk of referring to something that does not exist.

Finally, a warning regarding parameters of mode **out** or **in out**. If a subprogram is terminated by an exception then any actual parameter of a scalar type will not have been updated since such updating occurs on a normal return. For an array or record type the parameter mechanism is not so closely specified and the actual parameter may or may not have its original value. A program assuming a particular mechanism is of course erroneous. As an example consider the procedure WITHDRAW of the package BANK in Exercise 9.3(1). It would be incorrect to attempt to take the key away and raise an alarm as in

```
procedure WITHDRAW (K: in out KEY; M: in out MONEY) is
begin
    if VALID (K) then
        if M > amount remaining then
            M:= amount remaining;
            FREE(K.CODE):= TRUE;
            K.CODE:= 0;
            raise ALARM;
        else
            ...
        end if;
    end if;
end WITHDRAW;
```

If the parameter mechanism were implemented by copy then the bank would think that the key were now free but would have left the greedy customer with a copy.

---

*Exercise 10.4*

1    Rewrite the package BANK of Exercise 9.3(1) to declare an exception ALARM and raise it when any illegal banking activity is attempted. Avoid problems with the parameters.

2    Consider the following pathological procedure

```
procedure P is
begin
    P;
exception
    when STORAGE_ERROR =>
        P;
end P;
```

What happens when P is called? To be explicit suppose that there is enough stack space for only $N$ simultaneous recursive calls of P but that on the $N + 1$th call the exception STORAGE_ERROR is raised. How many times will P be called in all and what eventually happens?

---

## Checklist 10

Do not use exceptions unnecessarily.

Use specific user declared exceptions rather than predefined exceptions where relevant.

Ensure that handlers return resources correctly.

Match the constraints on index variables to the arrays concerned.

Beware of uninitialized variables.

Out and in out parameters may not be updated correctly if a procedure is terminated by an exception.

# Chapter 11
# Advanced Types

In this chapter we describe most of the remaining classes of types. These are discriminated record types, access types and derived types. Numeric types, which are explained in terms of derived types, are described in the next chapter and task types are described in Chapter 14.

## 11.1 Discriminated record types

In the record types we have seen so far there was no formal language dependency between the components. Any dependency was purely in the mind of the programmer as for example in the case of the limited private type STACK in Section 9.2 where the interpretation of the array S depended on the value of the integer TOP.

In the case of a discriminated record type, some of the components are known as discriminants and the remaining components can depend upon these. The discriminants, which have to be of a discrete type, can be thought of as parameterizing the type and the syntax reveals this analogy.

As a simple example, suppose we wish to write a package providing various operations on square matrices and that in particular we wish to write a function TRACE which sums the diagonal elements of a square matrix. We could contemplate using the type MATRIX of Section 6.2.

```
type MATRIX is array (INTEGER range <>, INTEGER range <>)
                                              of REAL;
```

but our function would then have to check that the matrix passed as an actual parameter was indeed square. We would have to write something like

```
function TRACE(M: MATRIX) return REAL is
    SUM: REAL:= 0.0;
begin
    if M'FIRST(1) /= M'FIRST(2) or M'LAST(1) /= M'LAST(2) then
        raise NON_SQUARE;
    end if;
    for I in M'RANGE loop
        SUM:= SUM + M(I, I);
    end loop;
    return SUM;
end TRACE;
```

This is somewhat unsatisfactory; we would prefer to use a formulation which ensured that the matrix was always square and had a lower bound of 1. We can do this using a discriminated type. Consider

```
type SQUARE(ORDER: POSITIVE) is
    record
        MAT: MATRIX(1 .. ORDER, 1 .. ORDER);
    end record;
```

This is a record type having two components: the first, ORDER, is a discriminant of the discrete subtype POSITIVE and the second, MAT, is an array whose bounds depend upon the value of ORDER.

Variables of type SQUARE can be declared in the usual way but a value of the discriminant must be given as a constraint thus

```
M: SQUARE(3);
```

The named form can also be used

```
M: SQUARE(ORDER => 3);
```

The value provided as the constraint could be any dynamic expression but once the variable is declared its constraint cannot be changed. An initial value for M could be provided by an aggregate, but, perhaps surprisingly, this must be complete and repeat the constraint which must match, thus

```
M: SQUARE(3):= (3, (1 .. 3 => (1 .. 3 => 0.0)));
```

However, we could not write

```
M: SQUARE(N):= (M.ORDER, (M.MAT'RANGE(1) =>
                              (M.MAT'RANGE(2) => 0.0)));
```

in order to avoid repeating N because of the rule that we cannot refer to an object in its own declaration. However

```
declare
    M: SQUARE(N);
begin
    M:= (M.ORDER, (M.MAT'RANGE(1) =>
                        (M.MAT'RANGE(2) => 0.0)));
```

is perfectly valid. If we attempt to assign a value to M which does not have the correct discriminant value then CONSTRAINT_ERROR will be raised.

Constants can be declared as usual and, like array bounds, the discriminant constraint can be deduced from the initial value.

We can, of course, introduce subtypes

```
subtype SQUARE_3 is SQUARE(3);
M: SQUARE_3;
```

We can now rewrite our function TRACE as follows

```
function TRACE(M: SQUARE) return REAL is
    SUM: REAL:= 0.0;
begin
    for I in M.MAT'RANGE loop
        SUM:= SUM + M.MAT(I, I);
    end loop;
    return SUM;
end TRACE;
```

There is now no way in which a call of TRACE can be supplied with a non-square matrix. Note that the discriminant of the formal parameter is taken from that of the actual parameter in a similar way to the bounds of an array. Discriminants of parameters have much in common with array bounds. For example a discriminant can be read even in the case of an **out** parameter. Again like arrays, the formal parameter could be constrained as in

```
function TRACE_3(M: SQUARE_3) return REAL;
```

but then the actual parameter would have to have a discriminant value of 3; otherwise CONSTRAINT_ERROR would be raised.

The result of a function could be of a discriminated type and, like arrays, the result could be a value whose discriminant is not known until the function is called. Thus we could write a function to return the transpose of a square matrix

```
function TRANSPOSE(M: SQUARE) return SQUARE is
    R: SQUARE(M.ORDER);
begin
    for I in 1 .. M.ORDER loop
        for J in 1 .. M.ORDER loop
```

```
            R.MAT(I, J):= M.MAT(J, I);
        end loop;
      end loop;
      return R;
   end TRANSPOSE;
```

A private type can also have discriminants and it must then be implemented in terms of a record type with corresponding discriminants. A good example is provided by considering the type STACK in Section 9.2. We can overcome the problem that all the stacks had the same maximum length of 100 by making MAX a discriminant. Thus we can write

```
package STACKS is
   type STACK(MAX: NATURAL) is limited private;
   procedure PUSH(S: in out STACK; X: in INTEGER);
   procedure POP(S: in out STACK; X out INTEGER);
   function "=" (S, T: STACK) return BOOLEAN;
private
   type INTEGER_VECTOR is
                        array (INTEGER range <>) of INTEGER;
   type STACK(MAX: NATURAL) is
      record
         S: INTEGER_VECTOR(1 .. MAX);
         TOP: INTEGER:= 0;
      end record;
end;
```

Each variable of type STACK now includes a discriminant component giving the maximum stack size. When we declare a stack we must supply the value thus

```
ST: STACK(100);
```

and as for the type SQUARE the value of the discriminant cannot later be changed. Of course, the discriminant is visible and can be referred to as ST.MAX although the remaining components are private.

The body of the package STACKS remains as before (see Section 9.2). Observe in particular that the function "=" can be used to compare stacks with different values of MAX since it only compares those components of the internal array which are in use.

Although constants of the type STACK cannot be declared outside the defining package (because the type is limited private), we can declare a deferred constant in the visible part. Such a declaration need not supply a value for the discriminant since it will be given in the private part.

This is a good point to mention that discriminants bear a resemblance to subprogram parameters in several respects. The type or subtype of a discriminant must be given by a type mark and not by a subtype indication. This is so that the same simple conformance rules can be used

when a discriminant specification has to be repeated in the case of a private
type with discriminants, as illustrated by the type STACK above.

A conformance problem also arises in the case of deferred constants
with discriminants which are analogous to the deferred array constants
discussed in Section 9.1. Suppose we wish to declare a constant STACK with
a discriminant of 3. We can omit the discriminant in the visible part and
merely write

    C: **constant** STACK;

and then give the discriminant in the private part either as a constraint or
through the mandatory initial value (or both)

    C: **constant** STACK(3):= (3, (1, 2, 3), 3);

However, if we wish to give the discriminant in the visible part then we
must introduce a subtype to do so; we cannot use an explicit constraint in a
subtype indication. Having introduced the subtype then the full constant
declaration must also use it since the type marks must conform. Thus we
can write

    **subtype** STACK_3 **is** STACK(3);
    C: **constant** STACK_3;

and then

    C: **constant** STACK_3:= (3, (1, 2, 3), 3);

in the private part.

It is possible to declare a type with several discriminants. We may
for instance wish to manipulate matrices which although not constrained to
be square nevertheless have both lower bounds of 1. This could be done by

    **type** RECTANGLE(ROWS, COLUMNS: POSITIVE) **is**
        **record**
            MAT: MATRIX(1 .. ROWS, 1 .. COLUMNS);
        **end record**;

and we could then declare

    R: RECTANGLE(2, 3);

or

    R: RECTANGLE(ROWS => 2, COLUMNS => 3);

The usual rules apply: positional values must be given in order, named
ones may be in any order, mixed notation can be used but the positional
ones must come first.

Similarly to multidimensional arrays, a subtype must supply all the constraints or none at all. We could not declare

```
subtype ROW_3 is RECTANGLE(ROWS => 3);
```

in order to get the equivalent of

```
type ROW_3(COLUMNS: POSITIVE) is
    record
        MAT: MATRIX(1 .. 3, 1 .. COLUMNS);
    end record;
```

In the examples we have shown, discriminants have been used in index constraints as the upper bounds of arrays; they can also be used as the lower bounds of arrays. In Section 11.3 we will describe how a discriminant can also be used to introduce a variant part. In these cases a discriminant must be used directly and not as part of a larger expression. So we could not declare

```
type SYMMETRIC_ARRAY(N: POSITIVE) is
    record
        A: VECTOR(-N .. N);              -- illegal
    end record;
```

or

```
type TWO_BY_ONE(N: POSITIVE) is
    record
        A: MATRIX(1 .. N, 1 .. 2*N);     -- illegal
    end record;
```

---

*Exercise 11.1*

1    Suppose that M is an object of the type MATRIX. Write a call of the function TRACE whose parameter is an aggregate of type SQUARE in order to determine the trace of M. What would happen if the two dimensions of M were not equal?

2    Rewrite the specification of STACKS to include a constant EMPTY in the visible part. See also Exercise 9.2(**1**).

3    Write a function FULL for STACKS. See also Exercise 9.2(**2**).

4    Declare a constant SQUARE of order N and initialize it to a unit matrix. Use the function MAKE_UNIT of Exercise 7.1(**6**).

---

## 11.2  Default discriminants

The discriminant types we have encountered so far have been such that once a variable is declared, its discriminant cannot be changed. It is possible, however, to provide a default expression for a discriminant and the situation is then different. A variable can then be declared with or without a discriminant constraint. If one is supplied then that value overrides the default and as before the discriminant cannot be changed. If, on the other hand, a variable is declared without a value for the discriminant, then the value of the default expression is taken but it can then be changed by a complete record assignment.

Suppose we wish to manipulate polynomials of the form

$$P(x) = a_0 + a_1 x + a_2 x^2 + \ldots a_n x^n$$

where $a_n \neq 0$ if $n \neq 0$.

Such a polynomial could be represented by

```
type POLY(N: INDEX) is
    record
        A: INTEGER_VECTOR(0 .. N);
    end record;
```

where

```
subtype INDEX is INTEGER range 0 .. MAX;
```

but then a variable of type POLY would have to be declared with a constraint and would thereafter be a polynomial of that fixed size. This would be most inconvenient because the sizes of the polynomials may be determined as the consequences of elaborate calculations. For example, if we subtract two polynomials which have $n = 3$, then the result will only have $n = 3$ if the coefficients of $x^3$ are different.

However, if we declare

```
type POLYNOMIAL(N: INDEX:= 0) is
    record
        A: INTEGER_VECTOR(0 .. N);
    end record;
```

then we can declare variables

```
P, Q: POLYNOMIAL;
```

which do not have constraints. The initial value of their discriminants would be zero because the default value of N is zero but the discriminants could later be changed by assignment. Note, however, that a discriminant can only be changed by a complete record assignment. So

```
P.N:= 6;
```

would be illegal. This is quite natural since we cannot expect the array P.A to adjust its bounds by magic.

Variables of the type POLYNOMIAL could be declared with constraints

    R: POLYNOMIAL(5);

but R would thereafter be constrained forever to be a polynomial with $n = 5$.

Initial values can be given in declarations in the usual way.

    P: POLYNOMIAL:= (3, (5, 0, 4, 2));

which represents $5 + 4x^2 + 2x^3$. Note that despite the initial value, P is not constrained.

In practice we would make the type POLYNOMIAL a private type so that we could enforce the rule that $a_n \neq 0$. Observe that predefined equality is satisfactory and so we do not have to make it a limited private type. Both the private type declaration and the full type declaration must give the default expression for N.

Note once more the similarity to subprogram parameters; the default expression is only evaluated when required and so need not produce the same value each time. Moreover, the same conformance rules apply when it has to be written out again in the case of a private type.

If we declare functions such as

    **function** "−" (P, Q: POLYNOMIAL) **return** POLYNOMIAL;

then it will be necessary to ensure that the result is normalized so that $a_n$ is not zero. This could be done by the following function

```
function NORMAL(P: POLYNOMIAL) return POLYNOMIAL is
    SIZE: INTEGER:= P.N;
begin
    while SIZE > 0 and P.A(SIZE) = 0 loop
        SIZE:= SIZE−1;
    end loop;
    return (SIZE, P.A(0 .. SIZE));
end NORMAL;
```

This is a further illustration of a function returning a value whose discriminant is not known until it is called. Note the use of the array slice.

If default expressions are supplied then they must be supplied for all discriminants of the type. Moreover, an object must be fully constrained or not at all; we cannot supply constraints for some discriminants and use the defaults for others.

The attribute CONSTRAINED can be applied to an object of a discriminated type and gives a Boolean value indicating whether the object is constrained or not. For any object of types such as SQUARE and STACK which do not have default values for the discriminants this attribute will, of course, be TRUE. But in the case of objects of a type such as POLYNOMIAL which does have a default value, the attribute may be TRUE or FALSE.

```
P'CONSTRAINED = FALSE
R'CONSTRAINED = TRUE
```

We mentioned above that an unconstrained formal parameter will take the value of the discriminant of the actual parameter. In the case of an **out** or **in out** parameter, the formal parameter will be constrained if the actual parameter is constrained (an **in** parameter is constant anyway). Suppose we declare a procedure to truncate a polynomial by removing its highest order term.

```
procedure TRUNCATE (P: in out POLYNOMIAL) is
begin
    P:= (P.N−1, P.A(0 .. P.N−1));
end;
```

Then given

```
Q: POLYNOMIAL;
R: POLYNOMIAL(5);
```

the statement

```
TRUNCATE(Q);
```

will be successful, but

```
TRUNCATE(R);
```

will result in CONSTRAINT_ERROR being raised.

We conclude this section by considering the problem of variable length strings. In Section 6.5 we noted, when declaring the ZOO, that the animals (or rather their names) all had to be the same length. The strong type model of Ada means that the type STRING does not have the flexibility found in cruder languages such as BASIC. However, with a bit of ingenuity, we can build our own flexibility by using discriminated records. There are a number of possibilities such as

```
subtype STRING_SIZE is INTEGER range 0 .. 80;
```

```
type V_STRING(N: STRING_SIZE:= 0) is
    record
        S: STRING(1 .. N);
    end record;
```

The type V_STRING is very similar to the type POLYNOMIAL (the lower bound is different). We have chosen a maximum string size corresponding to a typical page width (or historic punched card).

We can now declare fixed or varying v-strings and make appropriate assignments

```
V: V_STRING:= (5, "Hello");
```

We see that although we no longer have to pad the strings to a fixed length, we now have the burden of specifying the length explicitly. However, we can craftily write

```
function "+" (S: STRING) return V_STRING is
begin
    return (S'LENGTH, S);
end "+";
```

and then

```
type V_STRING_ARRAY is array (POSITIVE range <>) of V_STRING;

ZOO: constant V_STRING_ARRAY
     := (+"aardvark", +"baboon", +"camel", +"dolphin",
         +"elephant", ..., +"zebra");
```

Remember from Section 6.5 that we can declare an array of any type or subtype for which we can declare objects. Since v-strings have default discriminants we can declare unconstrained v-strings and hence arrays of them.

We thus see that we have more or less created a ragged array. However, there is a limit of 80 on our strings and, moreover, the storage space for the maximum size string is likely to be allocated irrespective of the actual string. We will return to the topic of ragged arrays when we discuss access types in Section 11.6.

---

*Exercise 11.2*

1     Declare a POLYNOMIAL representing zero (that is, $0x^0$).

2     Write a function "*" to multiply two polynomials.

3     Write a function "−" to subtract two polynomials. Use the function NORMAL.

4     Rewrite the procedure TRUNCATE to raise TRUNCATE_ERROR if we attempt to truncate a constrained polynomial.

5     What would be the effect of replacing the discriminant of the type POLYNOMIAL by (N: INTEGER:= 0)?

6     Write a function "&" to concatenate two v-strings.

7       Write the converse unary function "+" which takes a V_STRING
        as parameter and returns the corresponding STRING. Use this
        function to output the camel.

---

## 11.3  Variant parts

It is sometimes convenient to have a record type in which part of the
structure is fixed for all objects of the type but the remainder can take one
of several different forms. This can be done using a variant part and the
choice between the alternatives is governed by the value of a discriminant.
    Consider the following

```
type GENDER is (MALE, FEMALE);

type PERSON(SEX: GENDER) is
    record
        BIRTH: DATE;
        case SEX is
            when MALE =>
                BEARDED: BOOLEAN;
            when FEMALE =>
                CHILDREN: INTEGER;
        end case;
    end record;
```

This declares a record type PERSON with a discriminant SEX. The
component BIRTH of type DATE (see Section 6.7) is common to all objects
of the type. However, the remaining components depend upon SEX and
are declared as a variant part. If the value of SEX is MALE then there
is a further component BEARDED whereas if SEX is FEMALE then there is
a component CHILDREN. Only men can have beards and only women
(directly) have children.
    Since no default expression is given for the discriminant all objects
of the type must be constrained. We can therefore declare

```
JOHN: PERSON(MALE);
BARBARA: PERSON(FEMALE);
```

or we can introduce subtypes and so write

```
subtype MAN is PERSON(SEX => MALE);
subtype WOMAN is PERSON(SEX => FEMALE);
JOHN: MAN;
BARBARA: WOMAN;
```

Aggregates take the usual form but, of course, give only the components
for the corresponding alternative in the variant. The value for a

discriminant governing a variant must be static so that the compiler can check the consistency of the aggregate. We can therefore write

```
JOHN:= (MALE, (19, AUG, 1937), FALSE);
BARBARA:= (FEMALE, (13, MAY, 1943), 2);
```

but not

```
S: GENDER:= FEMALE;
BARBARA:= (S, (13, MAY, 1943), 2);
```

because S is not static but a variable.

The components of a variant can be accessed and changed in the usual way. We could write

```
JOHN.BEARDED:= TRUE;
BARBARA.CHILDREN:= BARBARA.CHILDREN+1;
```

but an attempt to access a component of the wrong alternative such as JOHN.CHILDREN would raise CONSTRAINT_ERROR.

Note that although the sex of objects of type PERSON cannot be changed, it need not be known at compilation time. We could have

```
S: GENDER:= ...
CHRIS: PERSON(S);
```

where the sex of CHRIS is not determined until he or she is declared. The rule that a discriminant must be static applies only to aggregates.

The variables of type PERSON are necessarily constrained because the type had no default expression for the discriminant. It is therefore not possible to assign a value which would change the sex; an attempt to do so would raise CONSTRAINT_ERROR. However, as with the type POLYNOMIAL, we could declare a default initial expression for the discriminant and consequently declare unconstrained variables. Such unconstrained variables could then be assigned values with different discriminants but only by a complete record assignment.

We could therefore have

```
type GENDER is (MALE, FEMALE, NEUTER);

type MUTANT(SEX: GENDER:= NEUTER) is
    record
        BIRTH: DATE;
        case SEX is
            when MALE =>
                BEARDED: BOOLEAN;
            when FEMALE =>
                CHILDREN: INTEGER;
            when NEUTER =>
                null;
        end case;
    end record;
```

Note that we have to write **null** as the alternative in the case of NEUTER where we did not want any components. In a similar way to the use of a null statement in a case statement this indicates that we really meant to have no components and did not omit them by accident.

We can now declare

M: MUTANT;

The sex of this unconstrained mutant is neuter by default but can be changed by a whole record assignment.

Note the difference between

M: MUTANT:= (NEUTER, (1, JAN, 1984));

and

N: MUTANT(NEUTER):= (NEUTER, (1, JAN, 1984));

In the first case the mutant is not constrained but just happens to be initially neuter. In the second case the mutant is permanently neuter. This example also illustrates the form of the aggregate when there are no components in the alternative; there are none so we write none – we do not write **null**.

The rules regarding the alternatives closely follow those regarding the case statement described in Section 5.2. Each **when** is followed by one or more choices separated by vertical bars and each choice is either a simple expression or a discrete range. The choice **others** can also be used but must be last and on its own. All values and ranges must be static and all possible values of the discriminant must be covered once and once only. The possible values of the discriminant are those of its static subtype (if there is one) or type. Each alternative can contain several component declarations and as we have seen could also be null.

A record can only contain one variant part and it must follow other components. However, variants can be nested; the component lists in a variant part could themselves contain one variant part but again it must follow other components.

Also observe that it is unfortunately not possible to use the same identifier for components in different alternatives of a variant – all components of a record must have distinct identifiers.

It is perhaps worth emphasizing the rules regarding the changing of discriminants. If an object is declared with a discriminant constraint then it cannot be changed – after all it is a constraint just like a range constraint and so the discriminant must always satisfy the constraint. Because the constraint allows only a single value this naturally means that the discriminant can only take that single value and so cannot be changed.

The other basic consideration is that, for implementation reasons, all objects must have values for discriminant components. Hence, if the type does not provide a default initial expression, the object declaration must and since it is expressed as a constraint the object is then consequently constrained.

There is a restriction on renaming components of a variable of a discriminated type. If the existence of the component depends upon the value of a discriminant then it cannot be renamed if the variable is unconstrained. So we cannot write

    C: INTEGER **renames** M.CHILDREN;

because there is no guarantee that the component M.CHILDREN of the mutant M will continue to exist after the renaming even if it does exist at the moment of renaming. However

    C: INTEGER **renames** BARBARA.CHILDREN;

is valid because BARBARA is a person and cannot change sex.

Note, amazingly, that we can write

    BOBBY: MAN **renames** BARBARA;

because the constraint in the renaming declaration is ignored (see Section 8.5). Barbara has not had a sex change – she is merely in disguise!

We have seen that a discriminant can be used as the bound of an array and also as the expression governing a variant. In a similar way it can also be used as the discriminant constraint of an inner component. We could declare a type representing rational polynomials (that is one polynomial divided by another) by

    **type** RATIONAL_POLYNOMIAL(N, D: INDEX:= 0) **is**
        **record**
            NUM: POLYNOMIAL(N);
            DEN: POLYNOMIAL(D);
        **end record**;

The relationship between constraints on the rational polynomial as a whole and its component polynomials is interesting. If we declare

    R: RATIONAL_POLYNOMIAL(2, 3);

then R is constrained for ever and the components R.NUM and R.DEN are also permanently constrained with constraints 2 and 3 respectively. However

    P: RATIONAL_POLYNOMIAL:= (2, 3, NUM  => (2, (−1, 0, 1)),
                              DEN  => (3, (−1, 0, 0, 1)));

is not constrained. This means that we can assign complete new values to P with different values of N and D. The fact that the components NUM and DEN are declared as constrained does not mean that P.NUM and P.DEN must always have a fixed length but simply that for given N and D they are constrained to have the appropriate length. So we could not write

    P.NUM => (1, (1, 1));

because this would violate the constraint on P.NUM. However, we can write

P:= (1, 2, NUM => (1, (1, 1)), DEN => (2, (1, 1, 1)));

because this changes everything together. Of course we can always make a direct assignment to P.NUM that does not change the current value of its own discriminant.

The original value of P represented $(x^2 - 1)/(x^3 - 1)$ and the final value represents $(x + 1)/(x^2 + x + 1)$ which is, in fact, the same with the common factor $(x - 1)$ cancelled. The reader will note the strong analogy between the type RATIONAL_POLYNOMIAL and the type RATIONAL of Exercise 9.1(**3**). We could write an equivalent function NORMAL to cancel common factors of our rational polynomials and the whole package of operations would then follow.

The remaining possible use of a discriminant is as part of the expression giving a default initial value for one of the other record components (but not another discriminant). Although the discriminant value may not be known until an object is declared, this is not a problem since the default initial expression is, of course, only evaluated when the object is declared and no other initial value is supplied.

However, we cannot use a discriminant for any other purpose. This unfortunately meant that when we declared the type STACK in the previous section we could not continue to apply the constraint to TOP by writing

```
type STACK(MAX: NATURAL) is
    record
        S: INTEGER_VECTOR(1 .. MAX);
        TOP: INTEGER range 0 .. MAX:= 0;    -- illegal
    end record;
```

since the use of MAX in the range constraint is not allowed.

Finally, a discriminant need not be used at all. It could just be treated as one component of a record. This might be particularly relevant when we wish to have a type where some components are private and others are visible. As an interesting and extreme example we can reconsider the type KEY of Section 9.3. We could change this to

```
type KEY(CODE: NATURAL:= 0) is limited private;
```

with

```
type KEY(CODE: NATURAL:= 0) is
    record
        null;
    end record;
```

With this formulation the user can read the code number of his key, but cannot change it. There is, however, a small flaw whose detection and cure is left as an exercise. Note also that we have declared CODE as subtype NATURAL rather than subtype KEY_CODE; this is because KEY_CODE is not visible to the user. Of course we could make KEY_CODE visible but this would make MAX visible as well and we might not want the user to know how many keys there are.

We conclude our discussion of discriminated records by recalling the rule in Section 6.5 that the components of an array can be of any type or subtype for which we can declare objects. So we can declare arrays of type MUTANT and subtypes MAN and WOMAN, but not of type PERSON.

---

*Exercise 11.3*

1    Write a procedure SHAVE which takes an object of type PERSON and removes any beard if the object is male and raises the exception SHAVING_ERROR if the object is female.

2    Write a procedure STERILIZE which takes an object of type MUTANT and ensures that its sex is NEUTER by changing it if necessary and possible and otherwise raises an appropriate exception.

3    Declare a type OBJECT which describes geometrical objects which are either a circle, a square or a rectangle. A circle is characterized by its radius, a square by its side and a rectangle by its length and breadth.

4    Write a function AREA which returns the area of an OBJECT.

5    Rewrite the declaration of the type POLYNOMIAL of Section 11.2 so that the default initial value of a polynomial of degree $n$ represents $x^n$. Hint: declare an auxiliary function returning an appropriate array value.

6    What is the flaw in the suggested new formulation for the type KEY? Hint: remember that the user declares keys explicitly. Show how it can be overcome.

7    Write the specification of a package RATIONAL_POLYNOMIALS. Make the type RATIONAL_POLYNOMIAL private with visible discriminants. The functions should correspond to those of the package RATIONAL_NUMBERS of Exercise 9.1(3).

---

## 11.4  Access types

In the case of the types we have met so far, the name of an object has been bound irretrievably to the object itself, and the lifetime of an object has been from its declaration until control leaves the unit containing the declaration. This is too restrictive for many applications where a more fluid control of the allocation of objects is desired. In Ada this can be done by access types. Objects of an access type, as the name implies, provide access to other objects and these other objects can be allocated in a manner independent of the block structure.

For those familiar with other languages, an access object can be thought of as a reference or pointer. The term reference has been brought into disrepute because of dangling references in Algol 68 and pointer has been brought into disrepute because of anonymous pointers in PL/I. Thus the new term access can be thought of as a polite term for reference or pointer. However, Ada access objects are strongly typed and, as we shall see, there are no dangling reference problems.

One of the simplest uses of an access type is for list processing. Consider

```
type CELL;

type LINK is access CELL;

type CELL is
    record
        VALUE: INTEGER;
        NEXT: LINK;
    end record;

L: LINK;
```

These declarations introduce type LINK which accesses CELL. The variable L can be thought of as a reference variable which can only point at objects of type CELL; these are records with two components, VALUE of type INTEGER and NEXT which is also a LINK and can therefore access (point to or reference) other objects of type CELL. The records can therefore be formed into a linked list. Initially there are no record objects, only the single pointer L which by default takes the value **null** which points nowhere. We could have explicitly given L this default value thus

```
L: LINK:= null;
```

Note the circularity in the definitions of LINK and CELL. Because of this circularity and the rule of linear elaboration it is necessary first to give an incomplete declaration of CELL. Having done this we can declare LINK and then complete the declaration of CELL. Between the incomplete and complete declarations, the type name CELL can only be used in the definition of an access type. Moreover, the incomplete and complete declarations must be in the same list of declarations except for one case which we will mention in the next section.

The accessed objects are created by the execution of an allocator which can (but need not) provide an initial value. An allocator consists of the reserved word **new** followed by either just the type of the new object or a qualified expression providing also the initial value of the object. The result of an allocator is an access value which can then be assigned to a variable of the access type.

So

```
L:= new CELL;
```

**Figure 11.1**   An access object.

creates a record of type CELL and then assigns to L a designation of (reference to or pointer to) the object. We can picture the result as in Figure 11.1. Note that the NEXT component of the record takes the default value **null** whereas the VALUE component is undefined.

The components of the object referred to by L can be accessed using the normal dotted notation. So we could assign 37 to the VALUE component by

    L.VALUE:= 37;

Alternatively we could have provided an initial value with the allocator

    L:= **new** CELL'(37, **null**);

The initial value here takes the form of a qualified aggregate and as usual has to provide values for all the components irrespective of whether some have default initial expressions.

Of course, the allocator could have been used to initialize L when it was declared

    L: LINK:= **new** CELL'(37, **null**);

Distinguish carefully the types LINK and CELL. L is of type LINK which accesses CELL and it is the accessed type which follows **new**.

Suppose we now want to create a further record and link it to our existing record. We can do this by declaring a further variable

    N: LINK;

and then executing

    N:= **new** CELL'(10, L);
    L:= N;

The effect of these three steps is illustrated in Figure 11.2. Note how the assignment statement

    L:= N;

copies the access values (that is, the pointers) and not the objects. If we wanted to copy the objects we could do it component by component.

    L.VALUE:= N.VALUE;
    L.NEXT:= N.NEXT;

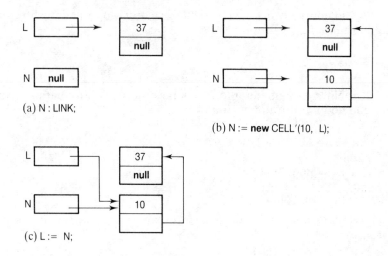

(a) N : LINK;

(b) N := **new** CELL'(10,  L);

(c) L := N;

**Figure 11.2**   Extending a list.

or by using **all**

L.**all**:= N.**all**;

L.**all** refers to the whole object accessed by L. In fact we can think of L.VALUE as short for L.**all**.VALUE. Unlike Pascal, dereferencing is automatic.
Similarly

L = N

will be true if L and N refer to the same object, whereas

L.**all** = N.**all**

will be true if the objects referred to happen to have the same value.
We could declare a constant of an access type but, of course, since it is a constant we must supply an initial value.

C: **constant** LINK:= **new** CELL' (0, **null**);

The fact that C is constant means that it must always refer to the same object. However, the value of the object could itself be changed. So

C.**all**:= L.**all**;

is allowed but

C:= L;

is not.

We did not really need the variable N in order to extend the list since we could simply have written

```
L:= new CELL'(10, L);
```

This statement can be made into a general procedure for creating a new record and adding it to the beginning of a list.

```
procedure ADD_TO_LIST(LIST: in out LINK; V: in INTEGER) is
begin
    LIST:= new CELL'(V, LIST);
end;
```

The new record containing the value 10 can now be added to the list accessed by L by

```
ADD_TO_LIST (L, 10);
```

The parameter passing mechanism for access types is defined to be by copy like that for scalar types. However, in order to prevent an access value from becoming undefined an **out** parameter is always copied in at the start. Remember also that an uninitialized access object takes the specific default value **null**. These two facts prevent undefined access values which could cause a program to go berserk.

The value **null** is useful for determining when a list is empty. The following function returns the sum of the VALUE components of the records in a list.

```
function SUM(LIST: LINK) return INTEGER is
    L: LINK:= LIST;
    S: INTEGER:= 0;
begin
    while L /= null loop
        S:= S+L.VALUE;
        L:= L.NEXT;
    end loop;
    return S;
end SUM;
```

Observe that we have to make a copy of LIST because formal parameters of mode **in** are constants. The variable L is then used to work down the list until we reach the end. The function works even if the list is empty.

A more elaborate data structure is the binary tree. This consists of nodes each of which has a value plus two subtrees one or both of which could be null. Appropriate declarations are

```
type NODE;
type TREE is access NODE;
```

```
type NODE is
  record
    VALUE: REAL;
    LEFT, RIGHT: TREE;
  end record;
```

As an interesting example of the use of trees consider the following procedure SORT which sorts the values in an array into ascending order.

```
procedure SORT(A: in out VECTOR) is
  I: INTEGER;
  BASE: TREE:= null;

  procedure INSERT(T: in out TREE; V: REAL) is
  begin
    if T = null then
      T:= new NODE'(V, null, null);
    else
      if V < T.VALUE then
        INSERT(T.LEFT, V);
      else
        INSERT(T.RIGHT, V);
      end if;
    end if;
  end INSERT;

  procedure OUTPUT(T: TREE) is
  begin
    if T /= null then
      OUTPUT(T.LEFT);
      A(I):= T.VALUE;
      I:= I+1;
      OUTPUT(T.RIGHT);
    end if;
  end OUTPUT;

begin                              -- body of SORT
  for J in A'RANGE loop
    INSERT(BASE, A(J));
  end loop;
  I:= A'FIRST;
  OUTPUT(BASE);
end SORT;
```

The recursive procedure INSERT adds a new node containing the value V to the tree T in such a way that the values in the left subtree of a node are always less than the value at the node and the values in the right subtree are always greater than (or equal to) the value at the node.

The recursive procedure OUTPUT copies the values at all the nodes of the tree into the array A by first outputting the left subtree (which has the smaller values) and then copying the value at the node and finally outputting the right subtree.

The procedure SORT simply builds up the tree by calling INSERT with each of the components of the array in turn and then calls OUTPUT to copy the ordered values back into the array.

The access types we have met so far have referred to records. This will often be the case but an access type can refer to any type, even another access type. So we could have

```
type REF_INT is access INTEGER;
R: REF_INT:= new INTEGER'(46);
```

Note that the value of the integer referred to by R is, perhaps inappropriately, denoted by R.all. So we can write

```
R.all:= 13;
```

to change the value from 46 to 13.

It is most important to understand that all objects referred to by access types must be acquired through an allocator. We cannot write

```
C: CELL;
...
L: LINK:= C;     -- illegal
```

This is to avoid the dangling reference problem of Algol 68 where it was possible to leave the scope of the referenced object while still within that of the referring object thus leaving the latter pointing nowhere.

In Ada, the accessed objects form a collection whose scope is that of the access type. The collection will cease to exist only when the scope is finally left but, of course, by then all the access variables will also have ceased to exist; so no dangling reference problems can arise.

If an object becomes inaccessible because no variables refer to it directly or indirectly then the storage it occupies may be reclaimed so that it can be reused by other objects. An implementation may (but need not) provide a garbage collector to do this.

Alternatively, there is a mechanism whereby a program can indicate that an object is no longer required; if, mistakenly, there are still references to such objects then the program is erroneous. For fuller details the reader is referred to Section 15.6. In this chapter we will assume that a garbage collector tidies up for us when necessary.

A few final points of detail. Allocators illustrate the importance of the rules regarding the number of times and when an expression is evaluated in certain contexts. For example, an expression in an aggregate is evaluated for each index value concerned and so

```
A: array (1 .. 10) of LINK:= (1 .. 10 => new CELL);
```

creates an array of ten components and initializes each of them to access a different new cell. As a further example

```
A, B: LINK:= new CELL;
```

creates two new cells (see Section 4.1), whereas

    A: LINK:= **new** CELL;
    B: LINK:= A;

naturally creates only one. Remember also that default expressions for record components, discriminants and subprogram parameters are re-evaluated each time they are required; if such an expression contains an allocator then a new object will be created each time.

    If an allocator provides an initial value then this can take the form of any qualified expression. So we could have

    L: LINK:= **new** CELL'(N.**all**);

in which case the object is given the same value as the object referred to by N. We could have

    I: INTEGER:= 46;
    R: REF_INT:= **new** INTEGER'(I);

in which case the new object takes the value of I; it does not matter that I is not an access object since only its value concerns us.

    The type accessed could be constrained, so we could have

    **type** REF_POS **is access** POSITIVE;

or equivalently

    **type** REF_POS **is access** INTEGER **range** 1 .. INTEGER'LAST;

    The values of the objects referred to are all constrained to be positive. We can write

    RN: REF_POS:= **new** POSITIVE'(10);

or even

    RN: REF_POS:= **new** INTEGER'(10);

Note that if we wrote **new** POSITIVE'(0) then CONSTRAINT_ERROR would be raised because 0 is not of subtype POSITIVE. However, if we wrote **new** INTEGER'(0) then CONSTRAINT_ERROR is only raised because of the context of the allocator.

    It is important to realize that each declaration of an access type introduces a new collection. Two collections can be of objects of the same type but the access objects must not refer to objects in the wrong collection. So we could have

    **type** REF_INT_A **is access** INTEGER;
    **type** REF_INT_B **is access** INTEGER;
    RA: REF_INT_A:= **new** INTEGER'(10);
    RB: REF_INT_B:= **new** INTEGER'(20);

The objects created by the two allocators are both of the same type but the access values are of different types determined by the context of the allocator and the objects are in different collections.

So, although we can write

    RA.all:= RB.all;

we cannot write

    RA:= RB;            — illegal

---

*Exercise 11.4*

**1**    Write a

            **procedure** APPEND(FIRST: **in out** LINK; SECOND: **in** LINK);

which appends the list SECOND (without copying) to the end of the list FIRST. Take care of any special cases.

**2**    Write a function SIZE which returns the number of nodes in a tree.

**3**    Write a function COPY which makes a complete copy of a tree.

---

## 11.5  Access types and private types

A private type can be implemented as an access type. Consider once more the type STACK and suppose that we wish to impose no maximum stack size other than that imposed by the overall size of the computer. This can be done by representing the stack as a list.

```
package STACKS is
    type STACK is limited private;
    procedure PUSH(S: in out STACK; X: in INTEGER);
    procedure POP(S: in out STACK; X: out INTEGER);
private
    type CELL;
    type STACK is access CELL;
    type CELL is
        record
            VALUE: INTEGER;
            NEXT: STACK;
        end record;
end;
```

```
package body STACKS is

    procedure PUSH(S: in out STACK; X: in INTEGER) is
    begin
        S:= new CELL'(X, S);
    end;

    procedure POP(S: in out STACK; X: out INTEGER) is
    begin
        X:= S.VALUE;
        S:= S.NEXT;
    end;

end STACKS;
```

When the user declares a stack

```
S: STACK;
```

it automatically takes the default initial value **null** which denotes that the stack is empty. If we call POP when the stack is empty then this will result in attempting to evaluate

```
null.VALUE
```

and this will raise CONSTRAINT_ERROR. The only way in which PUSH can fail is by running out of storage; an attempt to evaluate

```
new CELL'(X, S)
```

could raise STORAGE_ERROR.

This formulation of stacks is one in which we have made the type limited private. Predefined equality would merely have tested two stacks to see if they were the same stack rather than if they had the same values, and assignment would, of course, copy only the pointer to the stack rather than the stack itself. The writing of an appropriate function "=" needs some care. We could attempt

```
function "=" (S, T: STACK) return BOOLEAN is
    SS: STACK:= S;
    TT: STACK:= T;
begin
    while SS /= null and TT /= null loop
        SS:= SS.NEXT;
        TT:= TT.NEXT;
        if SS.VALUE /= TT.VALUE then
            return FALSE;
        end if;
```

```
        end loop;
        return SS = TT;         -- TRUE if both null
    end;
```

but this does not work because we have hidden the predefined equality (and hence inequality) which we wish to use inside the body of "=" by the new definition itself. So this function will recurse indefinitely. The solution is to distinguish between the type STACK and its representation in some way. One possibility would be to make the type STACK a record of one component thus

```
    type CELL;
    type LINK is access CELL;
    type CELL is
        record
            VALUE: INTEGER;
            NEXT: LINK;
        end record;
    type STACK is
        record
            LIST: LINK;
        end record;
```

so that we can distinguish between S, the STACK, and S.LIST, its internal representation.

In the previous section we stated that if we had to write an incomplete declaration first because of circularity (as in the type CELL) then there was an exception to the general rule that the complete declaration had to occur in the same list of declarations. The exception is that a private part and the corresponding package body are treated as a single list of declarations as far as this rule is concerned.

Thus, in either of the above formulations the complete declaration of the type CELL could be moved from the private part to the body of the package STACKS. This might be an advantage since it then follows from the dependency rules that a user program would not need recompiling just because the details of the type CELL are changed. In implementation terms it is possible to do this because it is assumed that values of all access types occupy the same space – typically a single word.

Finally, an access type could conversely refer to a private type. So we could have

```
    type REF_STACK is access STACK;
```

The only special point of interest is that if the accessed type is limited private then an allocator cannot provide an initial value since this would be equivalent to assignment and assignment is not allowed for limited types.

*Exercise 11.5*

1    Assuming that the exception ERROR is declared in the
     specification of STACKS, rewrite procedures PUSH and POP so
     that they raise ERROR rather than STORAGE_ERROR and
     CONSTRAINT_ERROR.

2    Rewrite PUSH, POP and "=" to use the formulation

```
type STACK is
  record
     LIST: LINK;
  end record;
```

     Ignore the possibility of exceptions.

3    Complete the package whose visible part is

```
package QUEUES is
  EMPTY: exception;
  type QUEUE is limited private;
  procedure JOIN(Q: in out QUEUE; X: in ITEM);
  procedure REMOVE(Q: in out QUEUE; X: out ITEM);
  function LENGTH(Q: QUEUE) return INTEGER;
private
```

     Items join a queue at one end and are removed from the other so
     that a normal first-come-first-served protocol is enforced. An
     attempt to remove an item from an empty queue raises the
     exception EMPTY. Implement the queue as a singly-linked list but
     maintain pointers to both ends of the list so that scanning of the
     list is avoided. The function LENGTH returns the number of items
     in the queue; again, avoid scanning the list.

## 11.6  Access types and constraints

Access types can also refer to arrays and discriminated record types. In
both cases they can be constrained or not.

     Consider the problem of representing a family tree. We could
declare

```
type PERSON;
type PERSON_NAME is access PERSON;
```

```
type PERSON is
  record
       SEX: GENDER;
       BIRTH: DATE;
       SPOUSE: PERSON_NAME;
       FATHER: PERSON_NAME;
       FIRST_CHILD: PERSON_NAME;
       NEXT_SIBLING: PERSON_NAME;
  end record;
```

This model assumes a monogamous and legitimate system. The children are linked together through the component NEXT_SIBLING and a person's mother is identified as the spouse of the father.

It might however be more useful to use a discriminated type for a person so that different components could exist for the different sexes and more particularly so that appropriate constraints could be applied. Consider

```
type PERSON(SEX: GENDER);
type PERSON_NAME is access PERSON;

type PERSON(SEX: GENDER) is
  record
       BIRTH: DATE;
       FATHER: PERSON_NAME(MALE);
       NEXT_SIBLING: PERSON_NAME;

       case SEX is
          when MALE =>
             WIFE: PERSON_NAME(FEMALE);
          when FEMALE =>
             HUSBAND: PERSON_NAME(MALE);
             FIRST_CHILD: PERSON_NAME;
       end case;

  end record;
```

The incomplete declaration of PERSON also gives the discriminants (and any default initial expressions); these must, of course, conform to those in the subsequent complete declaration. The component FATHER is now constrained always to access a person whose sex is male (or **null** of course). Similarly the components WIFE and HUSBAND are constrained; note that these had to have distinct identifiers and so could not both be SPOUSE. However, the components FIRST_CHILD and NEXT_SIBLING are not constrained and so could access a person of either sex. We have also taken the opportunity to save on storage by making the children belong to the mother only.

When the object of type PERSON is created by an allocator a value must be provided for the discriminant either through an explicit initial value as in

> JANET: PERSON_NAME;
>
> ...
>
> JANET:= **new** PERSON'(FEMALE, (22, FEB, 1967), JOHN, **others** =>
>                                                        **null**);

or by supplying a discriminant constraint thus

> JANET:= **new** PERSON(FEMALE);

Note the subtle distinction whereby a quote is needed in the case of the full initial value but not when we just give the constraint. This is because the first takes the form of a qualified expression whereas the second is just a subtype indication. Note also the use of **others** in the aggregate; this is allowed because the last three components all have the same base type.

We could not write

> JANET:= **new** PERSON;

because the type PERSON does not have a default discriminant. However, we could declare

> **subtype** WOMAN **is** PERSON(FEMALE);

and then

> JANET:= **new** WOMAN;

Such an object cannot later have its discriminant changed. This rule applies even if the discriminant has a default initial expression; objects created by an allocator are in this respect different to objects created by a normal declaration where, the reader will recall, a default initial expression allows unconstrained objects to be declared and later to have their discriminant changed.

On the other hand, we see that despite the absence of a default initial expression for the discriminant, we can nevertheless declare unconstrained objects of type PERSON_NAME; such objects, of course, take the default initial value **null** and so no problem arises. Thus although an allocated object cannot have its discriminant changed, nevertheless an unconstrained access object could refer from time to time to objects with different discriminants.

The reason for not allowing an allocated object to have its discriminant changed is that it could be accessed from several constrained objects such as the components FATHER and it would be difficult to ensure that such constraints were not violated.

For convenience we can define subtypes

> **subtype** MANS_NAME **is** PERSON_NAME(MALE);
> **subtype** WOMANS_NAME **is** PERSON_NAME(FEMALE);

We can now write a procedure to marry two people.

```
procedure MARRY(BRIDE: WOMANS_NAME;
                GROOM: MANS_NAME) is
begin
   if BRIDE.HUSBAND /= null or GROOM.WIFE /= null then
      raise BIGAMY;
   end if;
   BRIDE.HUSBAND:= GROOM;
   GROOM.WIFE:= BRIDE;
end MARRY;
```

The constraints on the parameters are checked when the parameters are passed (remember that access parameters are always implemented by copy). An attempt to marry people of the wrong sex will raise CONSTRAINT_ERROR at the point of call. On the other hand an attempt to marry a nonexistent person will result in CONSTRAINT_ERROR being raised inside the body of the procedure. Remember that although **in** parameters are constants we can change the components of the accessed objects – we are not changing the values of BRIDE and GROOM to access different objects.

A function could return an access value as for example

```
function SPOUSE(P: PERSON_NAME) return PERSON_NAME is
begin
   case P.SEX is
      when MALE =>
         return P.WIFE;
      when FEMALE =>
         return P.HUSBAND;
   end case;
end SPOUSE;
```

The result of such a function call can be directly used as part of a name so we can write

```
SPOUSE(P).BIRTH
```

to give the birthday of the spouse of P. (See the end of Section 7.1.) We could even write

```
SPOUSE(P).BIRTH:= NEWDATE;
```

but this is only possible because the function delivers an access value. It could not be done if the function actually delivered a value of type PERSON rather than PERSON_NAME. However, we cannot write

```
SPOUSE(P):= Q;
```

in an attempt to replace our spouse by someone else, whereas

```
SPOUSE(P).all:= Q.all;
```

is valid and would change all the components of our spouse to be the same as those of Q.

The following function gives birth to a new child. We need the mother, the sex of the child and the date as parameters.

```
function NEW_CHILD(MOTHER: WOMANS_NAME;
                      BOY_OR_GIRL: GENDER; BIRTHDAY: DATE)
               return PERSON_NAME is
   CHILD: PERSON_NAME;
begin
   if MOTHER.HUSBAND = null then
      raise ILLEGITIMATE;
   end if;
   CHILD:= new PERSON(BOY_OR_GIRL);
   CHILD.BIRTH:= BIRTHDAY;
   CHILD.FATHER:= MOTHER.HUSBAND;
   declare
      LAST: PERSON_NAME:= MOTHER.FIRST_CHILD;
   begin
      if LAST = null then
         MOTHER.FIRST_CHILD:= CHILD;
      else
         while LAST.NEXT_SIBLING /= null loop
            LAST:= LAST.NEXT_SIBLING;
         end loop;
         LAST.NEXT_SIBLING:= CHILD;
      end if;
   end;
   return CHILD;
end NEW_CHILD;
```

Observe that a discriminant constraint need not be static – the value of BOY_OR_GIRL is not known until the function is called. As a consequence we cannot give the complete initial value with the allocator because we do not know which components to provide. Hence, we allocate the child with just the value of the discriminant and then separately assign the date of birth and the father. The remaining components take the default value null. We can now write

```
HELEN: PERSON_NAME:=
               NEW_CHILD(BARBARA, FEMALE, (28, SEP, 1969));
```

Access types can also refer to constrained and unconstrained arrays. We could have

```
type REF_MATRIX is access MATRIX;
R: REF_MATRIX;
```

and then obtain new matrices with an allocator thus

```
R:= new MATRIX(1 .. 10, 1 .. 10);
```

Alternatively, the matrix could be initialized

```
R:= new MATRIX'(1 .. 10 => (1 .. 10 => 0.0));
```

but as for discriminated records we could not write just

```
R:= new MATRIX;
```

because all array objects must have bounds. Moreover the bounds cannot be changed. However, R can refer to matrices of different bounds from time to time.

As expected we can create subtypes

```
subtype REF_MATRIX_3 is REF_MATRIX(1 .. 3, 1 .. 3);
R_3: REF_MATRIX_3;
```

and R_3 can then only reference matrices with corresponding bounds. Alternatively we could have written

```
R_3: REF_MATRIX(1 .. 3, 1 .. 3);
```

Using

```
subtype MATRIX_3 is MATRIX(1 .. 3, 1 .. 3);
```

we can then write

```
R_3:= new MATRIX_3;
```

This is allowed because the subtype supplies the array bounds just as we were allowed to write

```
JANET:= new WOMAN;
```

because the subtype WOMAN supplied the discriminant SEX.

This introduces another example of an array aggregate with **others**. Because the subtype MATRIX_3 supplies the array bounds and qualifies the aggregate, we could initialize the new object as follows

```
R_3:= new MATRIX_3'(others => (others => 0.0));
```

The components of an accessed array can be referred to by the usual mechanism, so

```
R(1, 1):= 0.0;
```

would set component (1, 1) of the matrix accessed by R to zero. The whole matrix can be referred to by **all**. So

```
R_3.all:= (1 .. 3 => (1 .. 3 => 0.0));
```

would set all the components of the matrix accessed by R_3 to zero. We can therefore think of R(1, 1) as an abbreviation for R.**all**(1, 1). As with records, dereferencing is automatic. We can also write attributes R'FIRST(1) or alternatively R.**all**'FIRST(1). In the case of a one-dimensional array slicing is also allowed.

We conclude this section by returning to the topic of ragged arrays. By analogy with the type V_STRING of Section 11.2, we can introduce a type A_STRING which uses an access type

     **type** A_STRING **is access** STRING;

and then

```
function "+" (S: STRING) return A_STRING is
begin
    return new STRING'(S);
end "+";
```

and

     **type** A_STRING_ARRAY **is array** (POSITIVE **range** <>) **of** A_STRING;

     ZOO: **constant** A_STRING_ARRAY
       := (+"aardvark", +"baboon", ..., +"very long animal... ", ...,
         +"zebra");

With this formulation there is no limit on the length of the strings. But of course there is the overhead of the access value which is significant if the strings are short.

---

*Exercise 11.6*

1     Write a function to return a person's heir. Follow the normal rules of primogeniture – the heir is the eldest son if there is one and otherwise is the eldest daughter. Return **null** if there is no heir.

2     Write a procedure to divorce a woman. Divorce is only permitted if there are no children.

3     Modify the procedure MARRY in order to prevent incest. A person may not marry their sibling, parent or child.

4     Write functions to return the number of children, the number of siblings, the number of grandchildren and the number of cousins of a person.

---

## 11.7  Derived types

Sometimes it is useful to introduce a new type which is similar in most respects to an existing type but which is nevertheless a distinct type. If T is a type we can write

**type** S **is new** T;

and then S is said to be a derived type and T is the parent type of S.

A derived type belongs to the same class of type as its parent. If T is a record type then S will be a record type and its components will have the same names and so on.

It will be remembered that the key things that distinguish a type are its set of values and its set of operations; we now consider these.

The set of values of a derived type is a copy of the set of values of the parent. An important instance of this is that if the parent type is an access type then the derived type is also an access type and they share the same collection. Note that we say that the set of values is a copy; this reflects that they are truly different types and values of one type cannot be assigned to objects of the other type; however, as we shall see in a moment, conversion between the two types is possible. The notation for literals and aggregates (if any) is the same and any default initial expressions for the type or its components are the same.

The operations applicable to a derived type are as follows. First, it has the same attributes as the parent. Second, unless the parent type, and consequently the derived type, are limited, assignment and predefined equality and inequality are also applicable. Third, a derived type will derive or inherit certain subprograms applicable to the parent type. (We say that a subprogram applies to a type if it has one or more parameters or a result of that type or one of its subtypes.) Such derived subprograms are implicitly declared at the place of the derived type definition but may be later redefined in the same declarative region.

If the parent type is a predefined type then the inherited subprograms are just the predefined subprograms. If the parent type is a user defined type then again there will be some predefined subprograms such as "<" and these will be inherited. If the parent type is itself a derived type then its inherited subprograms will be passed on again.

In addition, if the parent type is declared in the visible part of a package then any applicable subprograms declared in that visible part will also be inherited provided that the derived type is declared after the visible part. Thus the new subprograms only really 'belong' to the type in the sense that they can be derived with it when we reach the end of the visible part; this is quite reasonable since it is at this point that the definition of the type and its operations can be considered to be complete in an abstract sense.

We will now illustrate these rules with some examples. If we have

**type** INTEGER_A **is new** INTEGER;

then INTEGER_A will inherit all the predefined subprograms such as "+", "−" and "abs" as well as attributes such as FIRST and LAST.

If we derive a further type from INTEGER_A then these inherited subprograms are passed on again. However, suppose that INTEGER_A is declared in a package specification and that the specification includes further subprograms, thus

```
package P is
    type INTEGER_A is new INTEGER;
    procedure INCREMENT(I: in out INTEGER_A);
    function "&" (I, J: INTEGER_A) return INTEGER_A;
end;
```

If we now have

```
type INTEGER_B is new INTEGER_A;
```

declared after the end of the specification (either outside the package or in its body) then INTEGER_B will inherit the new subprograms INCREMENT and "&" as well as the predefined ones.

If we do not like one of the inherited subprograms then it can be redefined in the same declarative region. So we could write

```
package Q is
    type INTEGER_X is new INTEGER;
    function "abs" (X: INTEGER_X) return INTEGER_X;
end;
```

in which for some reason we have chosen to replace the predefined operator "abs" by a new version.

If we now write

```
type INTEGER_Y is new INTEGER_X;
```

after the end of the package specification, the new version of "abs" will be inherited rather than the original one.

There are a couple of other minor rules. We cannot derive from a private type until after its full type declaration. Also, if the parent type is itself a derived type declared in the visible part of a package (such as INTEGER_A) then a type derived from it (such as INTEGER_B) cannot be declared inside that visible part. This restriction does not apply if the parent type is not a derived type; but remember that a type so derived from such a parent will inherit just the predefined subprograms and not any new or replaced ones.

Finally, it should be realized that the predefined types are not really a special case since they and the predefined subprograms are considered to be declared in the visible part of the package STANDARD.

Although derived types are distinct, the values can be converted from one to another using the same notation as was used for converting between numeric types. So given

```
type S is new T;
TX: T;
SX: S;
```

we can write

    TX:= T(SX);

or

    SX:= S(TX);

but not

    TX:= SX;    -- illegal

or

    SX:= TX;    -- illegal

If multiple derivations are involved then only the overall conversion is required; the individual steps need not be given. So if we have

```
type SS is new S;
type TT is new T;
SSX: SS;
TTX: TT;
```

then we can laboriously write

    SSX:= SS(S(TX));

and

    TTX:= TT(T(SX));

or merely

    SSX:= SS(TX);

and

    TTX:= TT(SX);

The introduction of derived types extends the possibility of conversion between array types discussed in Section 6.2. In fact, a value of one array type can be converted to another array type if the component types are the same and the index types are the same or convertible to each other.

Having introduced conversion we can now describe the effective specification of a derived subprogram in more detail. It is obtained from that of the parent by simply replacing all instances of the parent base type in the original specification by the new derived type. Subtypes are replaced by equivalent subtypes with corresponding constraints and default initial expressions are converted by adding a type conversion. Any parameters or result of a different type are left unchanged. As an abstract example consider

```
type T is ... ;
subtype S is T range L .. R;

function F(X: T; Y: T:= E; Z: Q) return S;
```

where E is an expression of type T and the type Q is quite unrelated. If we write

```
type TT is new T;
```

then it is as if we had also written

```
subtype SS is TT range TT(L) .. TT(R);
```

and the specification of the derived function F will then be

```
function F(X: TT; Y: TT:= TT(E); Z: Q) return SS;
```

in which we have replaced T by TT, S by SS, added the conversion to the expression E but left the unrelated type Q unchanged. Note that the parameter names are naturally the same.

We can now rewrite the type STACK of Section 11.5 using a derived type as follows

```
type CELL;
type LINK is access CELL;

type CELL is
    record
        VALUE: INTEGER;
        NEXT: LINK;
    end record;

type STACK is new LINK;
```

It is now possible to write the function "=" thus

```
function "=" (S, T: STACK) return BOOLEAN is
    SL: LINK:= LINK(S);
    TL: LINK:= LINK(T);
begin
    -- as the answer to Exercise 11.5(2)
end "=";
```

An advantage of using a derived type rather than making the type STACK into a record of one component is that the procedures PUSH and

POP of Section 11.5 still work and do not have to be modified. This is because the type STACK is still an access type and shares its collection with the type LINK.

Derived types are often used for private types and in fact we have to use a derived type if we want to express the private type as an existing type such as INTEGER.

Another use for derived types is when we want to use the operations of existing types, but wish to avoid the accidental mixing of objects of conceptually different types. Suppose we wish to count apples and oranges. Then we could declare

```
type APPLES is new INTEGER;
type ORANGES is new INTEGER;
NO_OF_APPLES: APPLES;
NO_OF_ORANGES: ORANGES;
```

Since APPLES and ORANGES are derived from the type INTEGER they both inherit "+". So we can write

```
NO_OF_APPLES:= NO_OF_APPLES+1;
```

and

```
NO_OF_ORANGES:= NO_OF_ORANGES+1;
```

but we cannot write

```
NO_OF_APPLES:= NO_OF_ORANGES;
```

If we did want to convert the oranges to apples we would have to write

```
NO_OF_APPLES:= APPLES(NO_OF_ORANGES);
```

In the next chapter we will consider the numeric types in more detail but it is worth mentioning here that strictly speaking a type such as INTEGER has no literals. Literals such as 1 and integer named numbers are of a type known as universal integer and implicit conversion to any integer type occurs if the context so demands. Thus we can use 1 with APPLES and ORANGES because of this implicit conversion and not because the literal is inherited. Enumeration literals on the other hand do properly belong to their type and are inherited; in fact, as mentioned in Section 7.5, enumeration literals behave as parameterless functions and so can be considered to be inherited in the same way as any other applicable subprogram.

Returning to our apples and oranges suppose that we have over-loaded procedures to sell them

```
procedure SELL(N: APPLES);
procedure SELL(N: ORANGES);
```

Then we can write

    SELL(NO_OF_APPLES);

but

    SELL(6);

is ambiguous because we do not know which fruit we are selling. We can resolve the ambiguity by qualification thus

    SELL(APPLES'(6));

When a subprogram is derived a new subprogram is not actually created. A call of the derived subprogram is really a call of the parent subprogram; **in** and **in out** parameters are implicitly converted just before the call; **in out** and **out** parameters or a function result are implicitly converted just after the call.

So

    MY_APPLES + YOUR_APPLES

is effectively

    APPLES(INTEGER(MY_APPLES) + INTEGER(YOUR_APPLES))

Derived types are in some ways an alternative to private types. Derived types have the advantage of inheriting literals but they often have the disadvantage of inheriting too much. For instance, we could derive types LENGTH and AREA from REAL.

    **type** LENGTH **is new** REAL;
    **type** AREA **is new** REAL;

We would then be prevented from mixing lengths and areas but we would also have inherited the ability to multiply two lengths to give a length and to multiply two areas to give an area as well as hosts of irrelevant operations such as exponentiation. Of course, it is possible to redefine these operations to be useful or to raise exceptions but it is often simpler to use private types and just define the operations we need.

As a further example of the use of derived types, reconsider the package BANK of Exercise 9.3(**1**). In that package we declared

    **subtype** MONEY **is** NATURAL;

in order to introduce the meaningful identifier MONEY and also to ensure that monies were never negative. However, being only a subtype, we could still mix up monies and integers by mistake. It would be far better to write

    **type** MONEY **is new** NATURAL;

so that the proper distinction is made.

In the private part shown in the solution we should perhaps similarly have written

    **type** KEY_CODE **is new** INTEGER **range** 0 .. MAX;

The above cases illustrate that we can derive from a subtype using either a type mark or the more general subtype indication. The derived type is then actually anonymous and is derived from the underlying base type. In the case of KEY_CODE it is as if we had written

    **type** anon **is new** INTEGER;
    **subtype** KEY_CODE **is** anon **range** 0 .. MAX;

(where there was no need to write anon(0) .. anon(MAX) because the literal 0 and the named number MAX are of type universal integer and conversion is implicit). So KEY_CODE is not really a type at all but a subtype. The set of values of the new derived type is actually the full set of values of the type INTEGER. The derived operations "+", ">" and so on also work on the full set of values. So given

    K: KEY_CODE;

we can legally write

    K > −2

even though −2 could never be assigned to K. The Boolean expression is, of course, always true.

The reader may have felt that derived types are not very useful because in the examples we have seen there is usually an alternative mechanism open to us – usually involving record types or private types. However, one importance of derived types is that they are crucial to the mechanism for numeric types as we shall see in the next chapter. In truth, derived types are of fundamental importance to the capability to create types; this will become clearer as we proceed.

We finish this chapter by mentioning a curious anomaly concerning the type BOOLEAN which really does not matter so far as the normal user is concerned. If we derive a type from BOOLEAN then the predefined relational operators =, < and so on continue to deliver a result of the predefined type BOOLEAN whereas the logical operators **and**, **or**, **xor** and **not** are inherited normally and deliver a result of the derived type. We cannot go into the reason here other than to say that it is because of the fundamental nature of the type BOOLEAN. However, it does mean that the theorem of Exercise 4.7(**3**) that **xor** and /= are equivalent only applies to the type BOOLEAN and not to a type derived from it.

*Exercise 11.7*

1    Declare a package containing types LENGTH and AREA with appropriate redeclarations of the incorrect operations "*".

## Checklist 11

If a discriminant does not have a default expression then all objects must be constrained.

The discriminant of an unconstrained object can only be changed by a complete record assignment.

Discriminants can only be used as array bounds or to govern variants or as nested discriminants or in default initial expressions for components.

A discriminant in an aggregate and governing a variant must be static.

Any variant must appear last in a component list.

An incomplete declaration can only be used in an access type.

The scope of an accessed object is that of the access type.

If an accessed object has a discriminant then it is always constrained.

Functions returning access values can be used in names.

Access objects have a default initial value of **null**.

An allocator in an aggregate is evaluated for each index value.

An allocator with a complete initial value uses a quote.

# Chapter 12
# Numeric Types

---

---

We now come at last to a more detailed discussion of numeric types. There are two classes of numeric types in Ada: integer types and real types. The real types are further subdivided into floating point types and fixed point types.

There are two problems concerning the representation of numeric types in a computer. First, the range may be restricted and indeed many machines have hardware operations for various ranges so that we can chose our own compromise between range of values and space occupied by values. Second, it may not be possible to represent accurately all the possible values of a type. These difficulties cause problems with program portability because the constraints vary from machine to machine. Ada recognizes these difficulties and provides numeric types in such a way that a recognized minimum set of properties is provided; this enables the programmer to keep portability problems to a minimum.

This chapter starts by discussing integer types because these suffer only from range problems but not from accuracy problems.

## 12.1 Integer types

All implementations of Ada have the predefined type INTEGER. In addition there may be other predefined types such as LONG_INTEGER, SHORT_INTEGER and so on. The range of values of these predefined types will be symmetric about zero except for an extra negative value in two's complement machines (which now seem to dominate over one's complement machines). All predefined integer types have the same predefined operations that were described in Chapter 4 as applicable to the type INTEGER (except that the second operand of "**" is always just type INTEGER).

Thus we might find that on machine A we have types INTEGER and LONG_INTEGER with

range of INTEGER:
    −32768 .. +32767                                                    (i.e. 16 bits)

range of LONG_INTEGER:
    −21474_83648 .. +21474_83647                                        (i.e. 32 bits)

whereas on machine B we might have types SHORT_INTEGER, INTEGER and LONG_INTEGER with

range of SHORT_INTEGER:
    −2048 .. +2047                                                      (i.e. 12 bits)

range of INTEGER:
    −83_88608 .. +83_88607                                              (i.e. 24 bits)

range of LONG_INTEGER:
    −14073_74883_55328 .. +14073_74883_55327                            (i.e. 48 bits)

For most purposes the type INTEGER will suffice on either machine and that is why we have simply used INTEGER in examples in this book so far. However, suppose we have an application where we need to manipulate signed values up to a million. The type INTEGER is inadequate on machine A and to use LONG_INTEGER on machine B would be extravagant. We can overcome our problem by using derived types and writing (for machine A)

**type** MY_INTEGER **is new** LONG_INTEGER;

and then using MY_INTEGER throughout the program. To move the program to machine B we just replace this one declaration by

**type** MY_INTEGER **is new** INTEGER;

However, Ada enables this choice to be made automatically; if we write

**type** MY_INTEGER **is range** −1E6 .. 1E6;

then the implementation will implicitly chose the smallest appropriate type and it will be as if we had written either

**type** MY_INTEGER **is new** LONG_INTEGER **range** −1E6 .. 1E6;

or

**type** MY_INTEGER **is new** INTEGER **range** −1E6 .. 1E6;

So in fact MY_INTEGER will be a subtype of an anonymous type derived from one of the predefined types and so objects of type MY_INTEGER will be constrained to take only the values in the range −1E6 .. 1E6 and not the full range of the anonymous type. Note that the range must have static bounds since the choice of base type is made at compilation time.

If, out of curiosity, we wanted to know the full range we could use MY_INTEGER'BASE'FIRST and MY_INTEGER'BASE'LAST.

The attribute BASE applies to any type or subtype and gives the corresponding base type. It can only be used to form other attributes as in this example. We could even go so far as to ensure that we could use the full range of the predefined type by writing

    **type** X **is range** −1E6 .. 1E6;
    **type** MY_INTEGER **is range** X'BASE'FIRST .. X'BASE'LAST;

This would have the dubious merit of avoiding the constraint checks when values are assigned to objects of type MY_INTEGER and would destroy the very portability we were seeking.

We can convert between one integer type and another by using the normal notation for type conversion. Given

    **type** MY_INTEGER **is range** −1E6 .. 1E6;
    **type** INDEX **is range** 0 .. 10000;
    M: MY_INTEGER;
    I: INDEX;

then we can write

    M:= MY_INTEGER(I);
    I:= INDEX(M);

On machine A a genuine hardware conversion is necessary but on machine B both types will be derived from INTEGER and the conversion will be null.

Note that, as mentioned in the last chapter, we can convert directly between related derived types and do not have to give each individual step. If this were not so we would have to write

    M:= MY_INTEGER(LONG_INTEGER(INTEGER(I)));

on machine A and

    M:= MY_INTEGER(INTEGER(I));

on machine B and our portability would be lost.

The integer literals are considered to belong to a type known as universal integer. The range of this type is at least as large as any of the predefined integer types and it has all the usual operations of an integer type such as +, −, < and =. Integer numbers declared in a number declaration (see Section 4.1) such as

    TEN: **constant**:= 10;

are also of type universal integer. However, there are no universal integer variables and as a consequence most universal integer expressions are static. The initial value in a number declaration has to be a static universal expression. So

    M: **constant**:= 10;
    MM: **constant**:= M∗M;

is allowed since M∗M is a static universal expression. However

    N: **constant** INTEGER:= 10;
    NN: **constant**:= N∗N;

is not allowed since N∗N is not a static expression of type universal integer but merely a static expression of type INTEGER.

It should be noted that certain attributes such as POS in fact deliver a universal integer value, and since POS can take a dynamic argument it follows that certain universal integer expressions may actually be dynamic.

Conversion of integer literals, integer numbers and universal integer attributes to other integer types is automatic and does not require an explicit type conversion. Problems of ambiguity, however, demand that conversion of more general expressions has to be explicit.

The reader may recall that a range such as 1 .. 10 occurring in a for statement or in an array type definition is considered to be of type INTEGER. The full rule is that the bounds must again be integer literals, integer numbers or universal integer attributes but not a more general expression. Note incidentally that specifying that the range is type INTEGER rather than any other integer type means that the predefined type INTEGER does have rather special properties.

We now see why we could not write

    **for** I **in** −1 .. 10 **loop**

in Section 5.3. But we could introduce an integer number for −1 and then use that as the lower bound

    MINUS_ONE: **constant**:= −1;
    ...
    **for** I **in** MINUS_ONE .. 10 **loop**

The use of integer type declarations which reflect the need of the program rather than the arbitrary use of INTEGER and LONG_INTEGER is good practice because it not only encourages portability but also enables us to distinguish between different classes of objects as, for example, when we were counting apples and oranges in the last chapter.

Consideration of separation of classes is the key to deciding whether or not to use numeric constants (of a specific type) or named numbers (of type universal integer). If a literal value is a pure mathematical number then it should be declared as a named number. If, however, it is a value related naturally to just one of the program types then it should be declared as a constant of that type. Thus if we are counting oranges and are checking against a limit of 100 it is better to write

```
MAX_ORANGES: constant ORANGES:= 100;
```

rather than

```
MAX_ORANGES: constant:= 100;
```

so that the accidental mixing of types as in

```
if NO_OF_APPLES = MAX_ORANGES then
```

will be detected by the compiler.

Returning to the question of portability it should be realized that complete portability is not easily obtained. For example, assume

```
type MY_INTEGER is range −1E6 .. +1E6;
I, J: MY_INTEGER;
```

and consider

```
I:= 100000;
J:= I*I;
```

In order to understand the behaviour it is most important to remember that MY_INTEGER is really only a subtype of an anonymous type derived from LONG_INTEGER on machine A or INTEGER on machine B. The derived operations +, −, *, / and so on have the anonymous type as operands and results and the subtype constraint is only relevant when we attempt to assign to J. So J:= I*I; is effectively (on machine A)

```
J:= anon(LONG_INTEGER(I)*LONG_INTEGER(I));
```

and the multiplication is performed with the operation of the type LONG_INTEGER. The result is 1E10 and this is well within the range of LONG_INTEGER. However, when we attempt to assign the result to J we get CONSTRAINT_ERROR.

On machine B on the other hand the type is derived from INTEGER and this time the result of the multiplication is outside the range of INTEGER. So NUMERIC_ERROR is raised by the multiplication itself.

Thus, although the program fails in both cases, the actual exception raised could be different. However, we recall from Section 11.1 that NUMERIC_ERROR and CONSTRAINT_ERROR should be treated as the same and so this example is somewhat irrelevant although it does perhaps illustrate another reason for not distinguishing the two exceptions.

A more interesting case is

```
I:= 100000;
J:= (I*I)/100000;
```

On machine A the intermediate product and final result are computed with no problem and, moreover, the final result lies within the range of J and so no exception is raised. But on machine B we again get NUMERIC_ERROR (alias CONSTRAINT_ERROR).

(The above analysis has ignored the possibility of optimization. The language allows the implementation to use a wider type in order to avoid NUMERIC_ERROR provided that the correct result is obtained. However, the example is certainly valid if machine B did not have a type LONG_INTEGER.)

Finally, we note that the most negative and most positive values supported by the predefined integer types are given by SYSTEM.MIN_INT and SYSTEM.MAX_INT. These are, of course, implementation dependent and are numbers declared in the package SYSTEM which is a predefined library package containing various such implementation dependent constants.

---

*Exercise 12.1*

1    What types on machines A and B are used to represent

        **type** P **is range** 1 .. 1000;
        **type** Q **is range** 0 .. +32768;
        **type** R **is range** −1E14 .. +1E14;

2    Would it make any difference if A and B were one's complement machines with the same number of bits in the representations?

3    Given

        N: INTEGER:= 6;
        P: **constant**:= 3;
        R: MY_INTEGER:= 4;

what is the type of

    (a)    N+P

    (b)    N+R

    (c)    P+R

    (d)    N∗N

    (e)    P∗P

    (f)    R∗R

4    Declare a type LONGEST_INTEGER which is the maximum supported by the implementation.

## 12.2  Real types

Integer types are exact types. Real types, however, are approximate and introduce problems of accuracy which have subtle effects. This book is not a specialized treatise on errors in numerical analysis and so we do not intend to give all the details of how the features of Ada can be used to minimize errors and maximize portability but will concentrate instead on outlining the basic principles.

Real types are subdivided into floating point types and fixed point types. Apart from the details of representation, the key abstract difference is that floating point values have a relative error whereas fixed point values have an absolute error. Concepts common to both floating and fixed point types are dealt with in this section and further details of the individual types are in subsequent sections.

There is a type universal real having similar properties to the type universal integer. Static operations on this type are notionally carried out with infinite accuracy during compilation. The real literals (see Section 3.4) are of type universal real. Real numbers declared in a number declaration such as

PI: **constant**:= 3.14159_26536;

are also of type universal real. (The reader will recall that the difference between an integer literal and a real literal is that a real literal always has a point in it.)

As well as the usual operations on a real type, some mixing of universal real and universal integer operands is also allowed. Specifically, a universal real can be multiplied by a universal integer and vice versa and division is allowed with the first operand being universal real and the second operand being universal integer; in all cases the result is universal real.

So we can write either

TWO_PI: **constant**:= 2*PI;

or

TWO_PI: **constant**:= 2.0*PI;

but not

PI_PLUS_TWO: **constant**:= PI+2;

because mixed addition is not defined. Note that we cannot do an explicit type conversion between universal integer and universal real although we can always convert the former into the latter by multiplying by 1.0.

An important concept is the idea of a model number. When we declare a real type T we demand a certain accuracy. The implementation will, typically, use a greater accuracy just as an implementation of an integer type uses a base type which has a larger range than that requested.

Corresponding to the accuracy requested will be a set of model numbers which are guaranteed to be exactly represented. Because the implemented accuracy will usually be higher, other values will also be represented. Associated with each value will be a model interval. If a value is a model number then the model interval is simply the model number. Otherwise the model interval is the interval consisting of the two model numbers surrounding the value. Special cases arise if a value is greater than the largest model number T'LARGE.

When an operation is performed the bounds of the result are given by the smallest model interval that can arise as a consequence of operating upon any values in the model intervals of the operands.

The relational operators =, > and so on are also defined in terms of model intervals. If the result is the same, whatever values are chosen in the intervals, then its value is clearly not in dispute. If, however, the result depends upon which values in the intervals are chosen then the result is undefined.

Some care is needed in the interpretation of these principles. A key point is that although we may not know where a value lies in a model interval, nevertheless it does have a specific value and should not be treated in a stochastic manner. There is perhaps some philosophical analogy here with Quantum Mechanics – the knowing of the specific value is the collapse of the wave packet! The behaviour of model numbers will be illustrated with examples in the next section and hopefully these remarks will then make more sense.

---

*Exercise 12.2*

1    Given

                TWO: INTEGER:= 2;
                E: **constant**:= 2.71828_18285;
                MAX: **constant**:= 100;

    what is the type of

    (a)    TWO*E
    (b)    TWO*MAX
    (c)    E*MAX
    (d)    TWO*TWO
    (e)    E*E
    (f)    MAX*MAX

2    Given

            N: **constant**:= 100;

    declare a real number R having the same value as N.

---

## 12.3  Floating point types

Our discussion so far has been in terms of a type REAL introduced in Section 2.4. This is not a predefined type but has been used to emphasize that the direct use of the predefined floating point types is not good practice.

In fact, in a similar way to integers, all implementations have a predefined type FLOAT and may also have further predefined types SHORT_FLOAT, LONG_FLOAT and so on with respectively less and more precision. These types all have the predefined operations that were described in Chapter 4 as applicable to the type REAL.

So, as outlined earlier, we can derive our own type directly by

**type** REAL **is new** FLOAT;

or perhaps

**type** REAL **is new** LONG_FLOAT;

according to the implemented precision but just as with the integer types it is better to state the precision required and allow the implementation to choose appropriately.

If we write

**type** REAL **is digits** 7;

then we are asking the implementation to derive REAL from a predefined type with at least 7 decimal digits of precision.

The precise behaviour is defined in terms of our model numbers. Suppose we consider the more general case

**type** REAL **is digits** D;

where D is a positive static integer expression. $D$ is the number of decimal digits required and we first convert this to $B$, the corresponding number of binary digits giving at least the same relative precision. $B$ has to be one more than the least integer greater than $D.\log_2 10$ or in other words

$$B-1 < 1 + (3.3219... \times D) < B$$

The binary precision $B$ determines the model numbers; these are defined to be zero plus all numbers of the form

$$sign.mantissa.2^{exponent}$$

where

$sign$ is $+1$ or $-1$,

$\frac{1}{2} \leq mantissa < 1$,

$-4B \leq exponent \leq +4B$

and the mantissa has exactly $B$ digits after the binary point when expressed in base 2. The range of the exponent, which is an integer, has been chosen to be $\pm 4B$ somewhat arbitrarily after a survey of ranges provided by contemporary architectures.

When we say

**type** REAL **is digits** 7;

we are guaranteed that the model numbers of the predefined floating point type chosen will include the model numbers for decimal precision 7.

As an extreme example suppose we consider

**type** ROUGH **is digits** 1;

Then $D$ is 1 and so $B$ is 5. The model numbers are values where the mantissa can be one of

$$^{16}/_{32},\ ^{17}/_{32},\ \ldots,\ ^{31}/_{32}$$

and the binary exponent lies in $-20\ ..\ 20$.

The model numbers around one are

$$\ldots,\ ^{30}/_{32},\ ^{31}/_{32},\ 1,\ 1^{1}/_{16},\ 1^{2}/_{16},\ 1^{3}/_{16},\ \ldots$$

and the model numbers around zero are

$$\ldots,\ -^{17}/_{32}{\cdot}2^{-20},\ -^{16}/_{32}{\cdot}2^{-20},\ 0,\ +^{16}/_{32}{\cdot}2^{-20},\ +^{17}/_{32}{\cdot}2^{-20},\ \ldots$$

Note the change of absolute accuracy at one and the hole around zero. By the latter we mean the gaps between zero and the smallest model numbers which in this case are 16 times the difference between them and the next model numbers. There is therefore a gross loss of accuracy at zero. These model numbers are illustrated in Figure 12.1.

The largest model numbers are

$$\ldots,\ ^{29}/_{32}{\cdot}2^{20},\ ^{30}/_{32}{\cdot}2^{20},\ ^{31}/_{32}{\cdot}2^{20}$$

or

$$\ldots,\ 950272,\ 983040,\ 1015808$$

(a) around 1       ... X X X X    X    X    X ...

                                           1

(b) around 0       ... X X X X      X      X X X X ...

                                           0

**Figure 12.1**    Model numbers of type ROUGH.

Suppose we write

    R: ROUGH:= 1.05;

then without considering the actual predefined floating point type chosen for R the literal 1.05 will be converted to a number between 1 and $1\frac{1}{16}$ inclusive which are the model numbers surrounding 1.05 but we do not know which. So all we know is that the value of R lies in the model interval $[1, 1\frac{1}{16}]$.

If we compute

    R:= R*R;

then the computed mathematical result must lie between $1^2 = 1$ and $(1\frac{1}{16})^2 = {}^{289}/_{256} = 1{}^{33}/_{256}$. However, $1{}^{33}/_{256}$ is not a model number and so we take the next model number above as the upper bound of the result; this is $1{}^{3}/_{16}$. Hence all we can conclude is that R must now lie in the model interval $[1, 1{}^{3}/_{16}]$. And this is all we know! Type ROUGH indeed.

The result of

    R > 1.0

is not defined since $1 > 1$ is false but $1{}^{3}/_{16} > 1$ is true.

Similarly

    R = 1.0

is not defined since $1 = 1$ is true but $1{}^{3}/_{16} = 1$ is false.

However

    R >= 1.0

is well defined and is true. So, perhaps surprisingly, the operations $=$, $>$ and $>=$ do not always have their expected relationship when applied to floating point types.

The analysis we have just done should be understood to be in terms of predicting the values before executing the program. Of course, when the program actually runs, R has a genuine value and is not undefined in any way. Thus $R > 1.0$ will have the value true or the value false but will not be undefined; what is undefined is that we cannot beforehand, just given the pure Ada and without knowing any extraneous information about the implementation, predict which of true and false will be the value. In particular $R = R$ is always true no matter what operations are performed. Hopefully the remark in the last section about Quantum Mechanics can now be appreciated. It is as if when we run the program we perform an observation on R and it then takes on an eigenvalue; but we cannot push the analogy too far.

The crudity of the type ROUGH in the above example is extreme but illustrates the dangers of errors. The hole around zero is a particular danger – if a result falls in that hole then we say that underflow has occurred and all accuracy will be lost. Our value has gone down a black hole!

In practice we will do rather better because the type ROUGH will undoubtedly be derived from a predefined type with more precision. Suppose that on a particular machine we just have a predefined type FLOAT with D = 7. Then writing

**type** ROUGH **is digits** 1;

is equivalent to

**type** anon **is new** FLOAT;
**subtype** ROUGH **is** anon **digits** 1;

The type ROUGH is therefore really a subtype of the derived type anon and operations on values will be performed with the numbers of the type FLOAT. In order to describe the mechanism more precisely we introduce the concept of safe numbers.

The safe numbers of a type are a superset of the model numbers and have similar computational properties. The safe numbers have the same number of digits $B$ but the exponent range is $\pm E$ where $E$ is at least equal to $4B$. Thus the safe numbers extend the reliable range and allow an implementation to take better advantage of the hardware. Another important difference between model numbers and safe numbers is that the safe numbers of a subtype are those of the base type whereas the model numbers of a subtype are those implied by the accuracy requested in its definition.

As an example, the safe numbers of the type ROUGH are the safe numbers of FLOAT whereas the model numbers of ROUGH are those defined by $D = 1$. The operations apply to the safe numbers and it is these numbers that can be stored in objects of the type ROUGH.

The point of all this is that if we wish to write a portable program then we must stick to the properties of the model numbers, whereas if we wish to get the most out of an implementation then we can exploit the properties of the safe numbers. Note also that an implementation may provide additional numbers to the safe numbers; they cannot be relied upon in the sense that the language does not define their properties other than those implied by the model intervals or safe intervals.

As a minor point we could also impose a range constraint on a floating point subtype or object by for example

R: ROUGH **range** 0.0 .. 100.0;

or

**subtype** POSITIVE_REAL **is** REAL **range** 0.0 .. REAL'LAST;

and so on. If a range is violated then CONSTRAINT_ERROR is raised.

As well as a type REAL, we might declare a more accurate type LONG_REAL perhaps for the more sensitive parts of our calculation

**type** LONG_REAL **is digits** 12;

and then declare variables of the two types

```
R: REAL;
LR: LONG_REAL;
```

as required. Conversion between these follows similar rules to integer types

```
R:= REAL(LR);
LR:= LONG_REAL(R);
```

and we need not concern ourselves with whether REAL and LONG_REAL are derived from the same or different predefined types.

Again in a similar manner to integer types, conversion of real literals, real numbers and universal real attributes to floating types is automatic but more general universal real expressions require explicit conversion.

Various attributes are available and they can be used to help in writing more portable programs. For any type (or subtype) F (predefined or not) they are

| | |
|---|---|
| F'DIGITS | the number of decimal digits, $D$, |
| F'MANTISSA | the corresponding number of binary digits, $B$, |
| F'EMAX | the maximum exponent, $4*F'MANTISSA$, |
| F'SMALL | the smallest possible model number, $2.0**(-F'EMAX-1)$, |
| F'LARGE | the largest positive model number, $2.0**F'EMAX*(1.0-2.0**(-F'MANTISSA))$, |
| F'EPSILON | the difference between 1.0 and the next model number above, $2.0**(1-F'MANTISSA)$. |

In addition there are attributes F'SAFE_EMAX, F'SAFE_SMALL and F'SAFE_LARGE which give the corresponding properties of the safe numbers of the type or subtype.

There are also the usual attributes F'FIRST and F'LAST which need not be model numbers or safe numbers but are the actual extreme values of the type or subtype.

DIGITS, MANTISSA, EMAX and SAFE_EMAX are of type universal integer; SMALL, SAFE_SMALL, LARGE, SAFE_LARGE and EPSILON are of type universal real; FIRST and LAST are of type F.

The attribute BASE can again be used to enable us to find out about the implemented type. So ROUGH'DIGITS=1 and ROUGH'BASE'DIGITS=7.

No more will be said about floating point but it is hoped that the reader will have understood the principles involved. In general one can simply specify the precision required and all will work. But care is sometimes needed and the advice of a professional numerical analyst should be sought when in doubt. For further details the reader should consult the *LRM*.

---

*Exercise 12.3*

1     What is the value of ROUGH'EPSILON?

2     Compute the model interval in which the value of R must lie after

    **type** REAL **is digits** 5;

    P: REAL:= 2.0;
    Q: REAL:= 3.0;
    R: REAL:= (P/Q)*Q;

3     What would be the effect of writing

    P: **constant**:= 2.0;
    Q: **constant**:= 3.0;
    R: REAL:= (P/Q)*Q;
    S: REAL:= REAL((P/Q)*Q);

4     How many model numbers are there of type ROUGH?

5     The function

    ```
    function HYPOTENUSE(X, Y: REAL) return REAL is
    begin
        return SQRT(X**2+Y**2);
    end;
    ```

    suffers from underflow if X and Y are small. Rewrite it to avoid this by testing X and Y against a suitable value and then rescaling if necessary.

6     Explain why $B$ is not just the least integer greater than $D.\log_2 10$ but one more. Use the type ROUGH to illustrate your answer.

7     What is the ratio between the size of the hole around zero and the gap between the next model numbers for a general value of $B$?

8     Rewrite the function INNER of Section 7.1 using a local type LONG_REAL with 14 digits accuracy to perform the calculation in the loop.

---

## 12.4  Fixed point types

Fixed point is normally used only in specialized applications or for doing approximate arithmetic on machines without floating point hardware.

The general principle of derivation from predefined types applies also to fixed point. However, unlike the integer and floating point types, the predefined fixed point types are anonymous and so cannot be used directly but have to be used via a fixed point declaration. Such a declaration specifies an absolute error and also a mandatory range. It takes the form

**type** F **is delta** D **range** L .. R;

In effect this is asking for values in the range L to R with an accuracy of D which must be positive. D, L and R must be real and static. The above declaration is essentially equivalent to

**type** anon **is new** fixed;
**subtype** F **is** anon **range** anon(L) .. anon(R);

where fixed is an appropriate predefined and anonymous fixed point type.

A fixed point type (or subtype) is characterized by two attributes, a positive integer $B$ and a positive real number *small*. $B$ indicates the number of bits required for the number (apart from the sign) and *small* is the absolute precision. The model numbers are therefore zero plus all numbers of the form

*sign.mantissa.small*

where

*sign* is $+1$ or $-1$
$0 < mantissa < 2^B$

The definition

**delta** D **range** L .. R

implies a value of *small* which is the largest power of 2 less than or equal to D and a value of $B$ which is the smallest integer such that L and R are no more than *small* from a model number.

As an example, if we have

**type** T **is delta** 0.1 **range** $-1.0$ .. $+1.0$;

then *small* will be $\frac{1}{16}$ and $B$ will be 4. The model numbers of T are therefore

$$-\tfrac{15}{16}, -\tfrac{14}{16}, \ldots, -\tfrac{1}{16}, 0, +\tfrac{1}{16}, \ldots, +\tfrac{14}{16}, +\tfrac{15}{16}$$

Note carefully that L and R are actually outside the range of model numbers and are both exactly *small* from a model number; the definition just allows this.

If we have a typical 16 bit implementation then there will be a wide choice of predefined types from which T can be derived. The only requirement is that the model numbers of the predefined type include those of T. Assuming therefore that the predefined type will have $B = 15$, then at one extreme *small* could be $2^{-15}$ which would give us a much greater accuracy but the same range whereas at the other extreme *small* could be $\frac{1}{16}$ in which case we would have a much greater range but the same accuracy.

If we assume for the sake of argument that the implementation chooses the predefined type with the greatest accuracy then its model numbers will be

$$ - \frac{2^{15} - 1}{2^{15}} , \quad \dots, \quad - \frac{1}{2^{15}} , \quad 0, \quad + \frac{1}{2^{15}} , \quad \dots, \quad + \frac{2^{15} - 1}{2^{15}} $$

The concept of safe numbers is also defined for fixed point types. The safe numbers of a type are the model numbers of its base type and the safe numbers of a predefined type are just its model numbers. So the safe numbers of T are the model numbers of the chosen predefined type. Similar remarks apply regarding portability as with floating point types. If we just assume the properties of the model numbers then portability is assured but we can also rely upon the safe numbers if we wish to get the best out of a particular implementation.

Returning to the type T, a different implementation might use just eight bits. Moreover, using representation clauses (which will be discussed in more detail in Chapter 15) it is possible to give the compiler more precise instructions. We can say

**for** T'SIZE **use** 5;

which will force the implementation to use the minimum five bits. Of course, it might be ridiculous for a particular architecture and in fact the compiler is allowed to refuse unreasonable representation clauses.

We can also override the rule that *small* is a power of 2 by using a representation clause. Writing

**for** T'SIZE **use** 5;
**for** T'SMALL **use** 0.1;

will result in the model numbers being

$$-1.5, -1.4, \dots, -0.1, 0, +0.1, \dots, +1.4, +1.5$$

In this case the predefined type has to have the same model numbers. This is because we have pinned down the possible implementation so tightly that there is only one *a priori* possible value for the predefined *small* anyway. However, and perhaps surprisingly, AI-341 states that specifying *small* via a representation clause always ensures that the selected predefined type will also have this value of *small*. In other words, any spare bits give extra range and not extra accuracy. This is yet another win for the accountants at the expense of the engineers!

The advantage of using the default standard whereby *small* is a power of 2 is that conversion between fixed point and other numeric types can be based on shifting. The use of other values of *small* will in general mean that conversion requires implicit multiplication and division.

It should be realized that the predefined fixed point types are somewhat ephemeral; they are not so much predefined as made up anonymously on the spot as required. However, an implementation is only formally required to have one anonymous predefined type. In such a case the *small* for the one type would inevitably be a power of 2 and so any attempt to specify a value of *small* which was not a multiple of this value would fail. Hence the sophisticated use of fixed point types is very dependent upon the implementation.

A standard simple example is given by

```
DEL: constant:= 2.0**(-15);
type FRAC is delta DEL range -1.0 .. 1.0;
```

which will be represented as a pure fraction on a 16 bit two's complement machine. Note that it does not really matter whether the upper bound is written as 1.0 or 1.0−DEL; the largest model number will be 1.0−DEL in either case. Moreover, −1.0 is not a model number either; the model numbers are symmetric about zero (AI-147).

A good example of the use of a specified value for *small* is given by a type representing an angle and which uses the whole of a 16 bit word

```
type ANGLE is delta 0.1 range -PI .. PI;
for ANGLE'SMALL use PI*2**(-15);
```

Note that the value given for the representation clause for ANGLE'SMALL must not exceed the value for delta which it overrides.

The arithmetic operations +, −, *, / and **abs** can be applied to fixed point values. Addition and subtraction can only be applied to values of the same type and, of course, return that type. Multiplication and division are allowed between different fixed types but always return values of an infinitely accurate type known as universal fixed. Such a value must be explicitly converted by a type conversion to a particular type before any further operation can be performed. Multiplication and division by type INTEGER are also allowed and these return a value of the fixed point type.

The behaviour of fixed point arithmetic is, like floating point arithmetic, defined in terms of the model numbers. Conversion of real literals and other universal real expressions to fixed point types follows similar rules to the floating types.

So given

```
F, G: FRAC;
```

we can write

```
F:= F+G;
```

but not

```
F:= F*G;              -- illegal
```

but must explicitly state

```
F:= FRAC(F*G);
```

It should be noted that multiplication and division between a fixed point type and a universal real operand is not allowed. Moreover, because multiplication and division are defined between any pair of fixed point types it follows that automatic conversion of a simple universal real operand to match a fixed point operand is not possible because there is not a unique fixed point type to which it can be converted. The net result is that we cannot write

```
F:= FRAC(0.5*F);       -- illegal
```

but must explicitly write

```
F:= FRAC(FRAC(0.5)*F);
```

On the other hand we can write

```
F:= F+0.5;
```

because addition is only allowed between the same fixed point types and so the universal real 0.5 is uniquely converted to type FRAC. Note, moreover, that we can write

```
F:= 2*F;
```

because multiplication is defined between fixed point types and INTEGER (and not other integer types) and so the universal integer 2 is uniquely converted to type INTEGER.

As a more detailed example we return to the package COMPLEX_ NUMBERS of Section 9.1 and consider how we might implement the package body using a polar representation. Any reader who gave thought to the problem will have realized that writing a function to normalize an angle expressed in radians to lie in the range 0 to $2\pi$ using floating point raises problems of accuracy since $2\pi$ is not a model number.

An alternative approach is to use a fixed point type. We can then arrange for $\pi$ to be a model number. Another natural advantage is that fixed point types have uniform absolute error which matches the physical behaviour. The type ANGLE declared above is not quite appropriate because, as we shall see, it will be convenient to allow for angles of up to $2\pi$.

The private part of the package could be

```
private
    PI: constant:= 3.14159_26536;
    type ANGLE is delta 0.1 range −4*PI .. 4*PI;
    for ANGLE'SMALL use PI*2**(−13);
    type COMPLEX is
        record
            R: REAL;
            THETA: ANGLE range −PI .. PI;
        end record;
    I: constant COMPLEX:= (1.0, 0.5*PI);
end;
```

The function for normalizing an angle to lie in the range of the component THETA (which is neater if symmetric about zero) could now be

```
function NORMAL(A: ANGLE) return ANGLE is
begin
    if A >= PI then
        return A − ANGLE(2*PI);
    elsif A < −PI then
        return A + ANGLE(2*PI);
    else
        return A;
    end if;
end NORMAL;
```

Note how we had to use the explicit type conversion in order to convert the universal real expression 2*PI to type ANGLE; remember that automatic conversion of universal real values only applies to single items and not to general expressions. We could alternatively have written

```
    return A − TWO_PI;
```

where TWO_PI is a real number as declared in Section 12.2.

Another interesting point is that the values for THETA that we are using do not include the upper bound of the range +PI; the function NORMAL converts this into the equivalent −PI. Unfortunately, we cannot express the idea of an open bound in Ada although it would be perfectly straightforward to implement the corresponding checks.

The range for the type ANGLE has been chosen so that it will accommodate the sum of any two values of THETA. This includes −2*PI; however, making the lower bound of the range for ANGLE equal to −2*PI is not adequate since there is no guarantee that the lower bound will be a model number − not even on a two's complement implementation. So to be on the safe side we squander a bit on doubling the range.

The various functions in the package body can now be written; we assume that we have access to appropriate trigonometric functions applying to the fixed point type ANGLE and returning results of type REAL. So we might have

```
package body COMPLEX_NUMBERS is
    function NORMAL ...    -- as above
        ...
    function "*" (X, Y: COMPLEX) return COMPLEX is
    begin
        return (X.R * Y.R, NORMAL(X.THETA + Y.THETA));
     end "*";
        ...
    function RL_PART(X: COMPLEX) return REAL is
    begin
        return X.R * COS(X.THETA);
    end RL_PART;
        ...
end COMPLEX_NUMBERS;
```

where we have left the more complicated functions for the enthusiastic reader.

We conclude by noting that the various attributes of a fixed point type or subtype F are as follows

| | |
|---|---|
| F'DELTA | the requested delta, $D$, |
| F'MANTISSA | the number of bits, $B$, |
| F'SMALL | the smallest positive model number, *small*, |
| F'LARGE | the largest positive model number, $(2**F'MANTISSA-1)*F'SMALL$. |

In addition there are attributes F'SAFE_SMALL and F'SAFE_LARGE which give the corresponding properties of the safe numbers. Note that F'SAFE_SMALL = F'BASE'SMALL for fixed point types.

There are also the usual attributes F'FIRST and F'LAST which give the actual upper and lower bounds of the type or subtype and of course need not be model numbers.

DELTA, SMALL, SAFE_SMALL, LARGE and SAFE_LARGE are of type universal real; MANTISSA is of type universal integer; FIRST and LAST are of type F.

---

*Exercise 12.4*

1    Given F of type FRAC compute the model interval of F after

```
F:= 0.1;
```

2    Why could we not have written

```
return A - 2.0*PI;
```

in the function NORMAL in order to avoid the explicit type conversion?

**3** Write the following further function for the package COMPLEX_NUMBERS implemented as in this section

> **function** "**\*\***" (X: COMPLEX; N: INTEGER) **return** COMPLEX;

Remember that if a complex number $z$ is represented in polar form $(r, \theta)$, then

$$z^n \equiv (r, \theta)^n = (r^n, n\theta)$$

**4** An alternative approach to the representation of angles in fixed point would be to hold the values in degrees. Rewrite the private part and the function NORMAL using a canonical range of 0.0 .. 360.0 for THETA. Make the most of a 16 bit word but use a power of 2 for *small*.

---

## Checklist 12

Use implicitly derived types for increased portability.

Beware of overflow in intermediate expressions.

Use named numbers or typed constants as appropriate.

Beware of underflow into the hole around floating point zero.

Beware of the relational operations with real types.

If in doubt consult a numerical analyst.

# Chapter 13
# Generics

There are two major concepts in Ada which are static. These are types and subprograms. By this statement we mean that all types and subprograms are identified before program execution. The static nature of these concepts increases the possibility of proving the correctness of programs as well as simplifying implementation considerations. The idea that types are static will be familiar from other languages. However, many languages (such as Algol, FORTRAN and Pascal) have dynamic procedures (at least as parameters to other procedures) and their absence in Ada comes as a bit of a surprise.

In this chapter we describe the generic mechanism which allows us to overcome the static nature of types and subprograms by a special form of parameterization which can be applied to subprograms and packages. The generic parameters can be types and subprograms as well as values and objects.

## 13.1  Declarations and instantiations

One of the problems with a typed language such as Ada is that all types have to be determined at compilation time. This means naturally that we cannot pass types as run-time parameters. However, we often get the situation that the logic of a piece of program is independent of the types involved and it therefore seems unnecessary to repeat it for all the different types to which we might wish it to apply. A simple example is provided by the procedure SWAP of Exercise 7.3(**1**)

```
procedure SWAP(X, Y: in out REAL) is
    T: REAL;
begin
    T:= X;  X:= Y;  Y:= T;
end;
```

It is clear that the logic is independent of the type of the values being swapped. If we also wanted to swap integers or Booleans we could of course write other procedures but this would be tedious. The generic mechanism allows us to overcome this. We can declare

```
generic
    type ITEM is private;
procedure EXCHANGE(X, Y: in out ITEM);

procedure EXCHANGE(X, Y: in out ITEM) is
    T: ITEM;
begin
    T:= X;  X:= Y;  Y:= T;
end;
```

The subprogram EXCHANGE is a generic subprogram and acts as a kind of template. The subprogram specification is preceded by the generic formal part consisting of the reserved word **generic** followed by a (possibly empty) list of generic formal parameters. The subprogram body is written exactly as normal but note that, in the case of a generic subprogram, we have to give both the body and the specification separately.

The generic procedure cannot be called directly but from it we can create an actual procedure by a mechanism known as generic instantiation. For example, we may write

```
procedure SWAP is new EXCHANGE(REAL);
```

This is a declaration and states that SWAP is to be obtained from the template described by EXCHANGE. Actual generic parameters are provided in a parameter list in the usual way. The actual parameter in this case is the type REAL which corresponds to the formal parameter ITEM. We could also use the named notation

```
procedure SWAP is new EXCHANGE(ITEM => REAL);
```

So we have now created the procedure SWAP acting on type REAL and can henceforth call it in the usual way. We can make further instantiations

```
procedure SWAP is new EXCHANGE(INTEGER);
procedure SWAP is new EXCHANGE(DATE);
```

and so on. We are here creating further overloadings of SWAP which can be distinguished by their parameter types just as if we had laboriously written them out in detail.

Superficially, it may look as if the generic mechanism is merely one of text substitution and indeed in this simple case the behaviour would be the same. However, the important difference relates to the meaning of identifiers in the generic body but which are neither parameters nor local to the body. Such non-local identifiers have meanings appropriate to where the generic body is declared and not to where it is instantiated. If text substitution were used then non-local identifiers would of course take their meaning at the point of instantiation and this could give very surprising results.

As well as generic subprograms we may also have generic packages. A simple example is provided by the package STACK in Section 8.1. The trouble with that package is that it only works on type INTEGER although of course the same logic applies irrespective of the type of the values manipulated. We can also take the opportunity to make MAX a parameter as well so that we are not tied to an arbitrary limit of 100. We write

```
generic
    MAX: POSITIVE;
    type ITEM is private;
package STACK is
    procedure PUSH(X: ITEM);
    function POP return ITEM;
end STACK;

package body STACK is
    S: array (1 .. MAX) of ITEM;
    TOP: INTEGER range 0 .. MAX;
    -- etc. as before but with INTEGER
    -- replaced by ITEM
end STACK;
```

We can now create and use a stack of a particular size and type by instantiating the generic package as in the following

```
declare
    package MY_STACK is new STACK(100, REAL);
    use MY_STACK;
begin
    ...
    PUSH(X);
    ...
    Y:= POP;
    ...
end;
```

The package MY_STACK which results from the instantiation behaves just as a normal directly written out package. The use clause allows us to refer to PUSH and POP directly. If we did a further instantiation

```
package ANOTHER_STACK is new STACK(50, INTEGER);
use ANOTHER_STACK;
```

then PUSH and POP are further overloadings and can be distinguished by the type provided by the context. Of course, if ANOTHER_STACK was also declared with the actual generic parameter being REAL, then we would have to use the dotted notation to distinguish the instances of PUSH and POP despite the use clauses.

Both generic units and generic instantiations may be library units. Thus having put the generic package STACK in the program library an instantiation could itself be separately compiled just on its own thus

```
with STACK;
package BOOLEAN_STACK is new STACK(200, BOOLEAN);
```

If we added an exception ERROR to the package as in Section 10.2 so that the generic package declaration was

```
generic
    MAX: POSITIVE;
    type ITEM is private;
package STACK is
    ERROR: exception;
    procedure PUSH(X: ITEM);
    function POP return ITEM;
end STACK;
```

then each instantiation would give rise to a distinct exception and because exceptions cannot be overloaded we would naturally have to use the dotted notation to distinguish them.

We could, of course, make the exception ERROR common to all instantiations by making it global to the generic package. It and the generic package could perhaps be declared inside a further package

```
package ALL_STACKS is
    ERROR: exception;
    generic
        MAX: POSITIVE;
        type ITEM is private;
    package STACK is
        procedure PUSH(X: ITEM);
        function POP return ITEM;
    end STACK;
end ALL_STACKS;

package body ALL_STACKS is
    package body STACK is
        ...
    end STACK;
end ALL_STACKS;
```

This illustrates the binding of identifiers global to generic units. The meaning of ERROR is determined at the point of the generic declaration irrespective of the meaning at the point of instantiation.

The above examples have illustrated formal parameters which were types and also integers. In fact generic formal parameters can be values and objects much as the parameters applicable to subprograms; they can also be types and subprograms. As we shall see in the following sections, we can express the formal types and subprograms so that we can assume in the generic body that the actual parameters have the properties we require.

In the case of the familiar parameters which also apply to subprograms they can be of mode **in** or **in out** but not **out**. As with subprograms, **in** is taken by default as illustrated by MAX in the example above.

An **in** generic parameter acts as a constant the value of which is provided by the corresponding actual parameter. A default expression is allowed as in the case of parameters of subprograms; such a default expression is evaluated at instantiation if no actual parameter is supplied in the same way that a default expression for a subprogram parameter is evaluated when the subprogram is called if no actual parameter is supplied. Observe that an **in** generic parameter cannot be of a limited type; this is because assignment is not allowed for limited types and the mechanism of giving the value to the parameter is treated as assignment. Note that this is a different mechanism to that used for **in** subprogram parameters where limited types are allowed.

An **in out** parameter, however, acts as a variable renaming the corresponding actual parameter. The actual parameter must therefore be the name of a variable and its identification occurs at the point of instantiation using the same rules as for renaming described in Section 8.5. One such rule is that any constraints on the actual parameter apply to the formal parameter and any constraints implied by the formal type mark are, perhaps surprisingly, completely ignored. Another rule is that if any identifier in the name subsequently changes then the identity of the object referred to by the generic formal parameter does not change. Because of this there is a restriction that the actual parameter cannot be a component of an unconstrained discriminated record if the very existence of the component depends on the value of the discriminant. Thus if M is a MUTANT as in Section 11.3, M.CHILDREN could not be an actual generic parameter because M could have its SEX changed. However, M.BIRTH would be valid. This restriction also applies to renaming itself.

It will now be realized that although the notation **in** and **in out** is identical to subprogram parameters the meaning is somewhat different. Thus there is no question of copying in and out and indeed no such thing as **out** parameters.

Inside the generic body, the formal generic parameters can be used quite freely except for one restriction. This arises because generic parameters (and their attributes) are not considered to be static. There are various places where an expression has to be static such as in the alternatives in a case statement or variant, and in the range in an integer type definition, or the number of digits in a floating point type definition and so on. In all these situations a generic formal parameter cannot be used because the expression would not then be static. A further consequence is

that the type of the expression in a case statement and similarly the type of
the discriminant in a variant may not be a generic formal type.

Our final example in this section illustrates the nesting of generics.
The following generic procedure performs a cyclic interchange of three
values and for amusement is written in terms of the generic procedure
EXCHANGE.

```
generic
    type THING is private;
procedure CAB(A, B, C: in out THING);

procedure CAB(A, B, C: in out THING) is
    procedure SWAP is new EXCHANGE(ITEM => THING);
begin
    SWAP(A, B);
    SWAP(A, C);
end CAB;
```

Although nesting is allowed, it must not be recursive.

---

*Exercise 13.1*

1    Write a generic package declaration based on the package
     STACKS in Section 11.1 so that stacks of arbitrary type may be
     declared. Declare a stack S of length 30 and type BOOLEAN. Use
     named notation.

2    Write a generic package containing both SWAP and CAB.

---

## 13.2  Type parameters

In the previous section we introduced types as generic parameters. The
examples showed the formal parameter taking the form

```
type T is private;
```

In this case, inside the generic subprogram or package, we may assume
that assignment and equality are defined for T. We can assume nothing else
unless we specifically provide other parameters, as we shall see in a
moment. Hence, T behaves in the generic unit much as a private type
outside the package defining it; this analogy explains the notation for the
formal parameter. The corresponding actual parameter must, of course,
provide assignment and equality and so it can be any type except one that is
limited.

A formal generic type parameter can take other forms. It can be

```
type T is limited private;
```

and in this case assignment and equality are not available automatically. The corresponding actual parameter can be any type.

Either of the above forms could have discriminants

**type** T( ... ) **is private**;

and the actual type must then have discriminants with the same types. The formal type must not have default expressions for the discriminants but the actual type can as we shall see later.

The formal parameter could also be one of

**type** T **is** (<>);
**type** T **is range** <>;
**type** T **is digits** <>;
**type** T **is delta** <>;

In the first case the actual parameter must be a discrete type – an enumeration type or integer type. In the other cases the actual parameter must be an integer type, floating point type or fixed point type respectively. Within the generic unit the appropriate predefined operations and attributes are available.

As a simple example consider

```
generic
    type T is (<>);
function NEXT(X: T) return T;

function NEXT(X: T) return T is
begin
    if X=T'LAST then
        return T'FIRST;
    else
        return T'SUCC(X);
    end if;
end NEXT;
```

The formal parameter T requires that the actual parameter must be a discrete type. Since all discrete types have attributes FIRST, LAST and SUCC we can use these attributes in the body in the knowledge that the actual parameter will supply them.

We could now write

**function** TOMORROW **is new** NEXT(DAY);

so that TOMORROW(SUN) = MON.

An actual generic parameter can also be a subtype but an explicit constraint is not allowed; in other words the actual parameter must be just a type mark and not a subtype indication. The formal generic parameter then denotes the subtype. Thus we can have

**function** NEXT_WORK_DAY **is new** NEXT(WEEKDAY);

so that NEXT_WORK_DAY(FRI) = MON. Note how the behaviour depends on the fact that the LAST attribute applies to the subtype and not to the base type so that DAY'LAST is SUN and WEEKDAY'LAST is FRI.

The actual parameter could also be an integer type so we could have

```
subtype DIGIT is INTEGER range 0 .. 9;
function NEXT_DIGIT is new NEXT(DIGIT);
```

and then NEXT_DIGIT(9) = 0.

Now consider the package COMPLEX_NUMBERS of Section 9.1; this could be made generic so that the particular floating point type upon which the type COMPLEX is based can be a parameter. It would then take the form

```
generic
    type REAL is digits <>;
package GENERIC_COMPLEX_NUMBERS is
    type COMPLEX is private;
    -- as before
    I: constant COMPLEX:= (0.0, 1.0);
end;
```

Note that we can use the literals 0.0 and 1.0 because they are of the universal real type which can be converted to whichever type is passed as actual parameter. The package could then be instantiated by for instance

```
package MY_COMPLEX_NUMBERS is
        new GENERIC_COMPLEX_NUMBERS(MY_REAL);
```

A formal generic parameter can also be an array type. The actual parameter must then also be an array type with the same component type and constraints, if any, the same number of dimensions and the same index subtypes. Either both must be unconstrained arrays or both must be constrained arrays. If they are constrained then the index ranges must be the same for corresponding indexes.

It is possible for one generic formal parameter to depend upon a previous formal parameter which is a type. This will often be the case with arrays. As an example consider the simple function SUM in Section 7.1. This added together the elements of a real array with integer index. We can generalize this to add together the elements of any floating point array with any index type.

```
generic
    type INDEX is (<>);
    type FLOATING is digits <>;
    type VEC is array (INDEX range <>) of FLOATING;
function SUM(A: VEC) return FLOATING;

function SUM(A: VEC) return FLOATING is
    RESULT: FLOATING:= 0.0;
```

```
    begin
        for I in A'RANGE loop
            RESULT:= RESULT+A(I);
        end loop;
        return RESULT;
    end SUM;
```

Note that although INDEX is a formal parameter it does not explicitly appear in the generic body; nevertheless it is implicitly used since the loop parameter I is of type INDEX.

We could instantiate this by

**function** SUM_VECTOR **is new** SUM(INTEGER, REAL, VECTOR);

and this will give the function SUM of Section 7.1.

The matching of actual and formal arrays takes place after any formal types have been replaced in the formal array by the corresponding actual types. As an example of matching index subtypes note that if we had

**type** VECTOR **is array** (POSITIVE **range** <>) **of** REAL;

then we would have to use POSITIVE (or an equivalent subtype) as the actual parameter for the INDEX.

The final possibility for formal type parameters is the case of an access type. The formal can be

**type** A **is access** T;

where T may but need not be a previous formal parameter. The actual parameter corresponding to A must then access T. Constraints on the accessed type must also be the same.

Observe that there is no concept of a formal record type. This is because the internal structure of records is somewhat arbitrary and the possibilities for matching would therefore be rare.

As a final example in this section we return to the question of sets. We saw in Section 6.6 how a Boolean array could be used to represent a set. Exercises 7.1(**4**), 7.2(**3**) and 7.2(**4**) also showed how we could write suitable functions to operate upon sets of the type COLOUR. The generic mechanism allows us to write a package to enable the manipulation of sets of an arbitrary type.

Consider

```
generic
    type BASE is (<>);
package SET_OF is
    type SET is private;
    type LIST is array (POSITIVE range <>) of BASE;

    EMPTY, FULL: constant SET;

    function MAKE_SET(X: LIST) return SET;
```

```
function MAKE_SET(X: BASE) return SET;
function DECOMPOSE(X: SET) return LIST;

function "+" (X, Y: SET) return SET;          -- union
function "*" (X, Y: SET) return SET;          -- intersection
function "-" (X, Y: SET) return SET;          -- symmetric difference
function "<" (X: BASE; Y: SET) return BOOLEAN;       -- inclusion
function "<=" (X, Y: SET) return BOOLEAN;      -- contains
function SIZE(X: SET) return NATURAL;          -- no of elements

private
  type SET is array (BASE) of BOOLEAN;

  EMPTY: constant SET:= (SET'RANGE => FALSE);
  FULL: constant SET:= (SET'RANGE => TRUE);
end;
```

The single generic parameter is the base type which must be discrete. The type SET is made private so that the Boolean operations cannot be directly applied (inadvertently or malevolently). Aggregates of the type LIST are used to represent literal sets. The constants EMPTY and FULL denote the empty and full set respectively. The functions MAKE_SET enable the creation of a set from a list of the base values or a single base value. DECOMPOSE turns a set back into a list.

The operators +, * and - represent union, intersection and symmetric difference; they are chosen as more natural than the underlying or, and and xor. The operator < tests to see whether a base value is in a set. The operator <= tests to see whether one set is a subset of another. Finally, the function SIZE returns the number of base values present in a particular set.

In the private part the type SET is declared as a Boolean array indexed by the base type (which is why the base type had to be discrete). The constants EMPTY and FULL are declared as arrays whose elements are all FALSE and all TRUE respectively. The body of the package is left as an exercise.

Turning back to Section 6.6, we can instantiate the package to work on our type PRIMARY by

```
package PRIMARY_SETS is new SET_OF(PRIMARY);
use PRIMARY_SETS;
```

For comparison we could then write

```
subtype COLOUR is SET;
WHITE: COLOUR renames EMPTY;
BLACK: COLOUR renames FULL;
```

and so on.

We can use this example to explore the creation and composition of types. Our attempt to give the type SET the name COLOUR through a subtype is poor. We would really like to pass the name COLOUR in some

way to the generic package as the type to be used. We cannot do this and
retain the private nature of the type. But we can use the derived type
mechanism to create a proper type COLOUR from the type SET

```
type COLOUR is new SET;
```

Recalling the rules for inheriting applicable subprograms from
Section 11.7, we note that the new type COLOUR automatically inherits all
the functions in the specification of SET_OF (strictly the instantiation
PRIMARY_SETS) because they all have the type SET as a parameter or result
type.

However, this is a bit untidy; the constants EMPTY and FULL will not
have been derived and the type LIST will still be as before.

One improvement therefore is to replace the constants EMPTY and
FULL by equivalent parameterless functions so that they will also be derived.
A better approach to the type LIST is to make it and its index type into
further generic parameters. The visible part of the package will then just
consist of the type SET and its applicable subprograms

```
generic
    type BASE is (<>);
    type INDEX is (<>);
    type LIST is array (INDEX range <>) of BASE;
package NICE_SET_OF is
    type SET is private;
    function EMPTY return SET;
    function FULL return SET;
    ...
private
```

We can now write

```
type PRIMARY_LIST is array (POSITIVE range <>) of PRIMARY;
```

```
package PRIMARY_SETS is new NICE_SET_OF(BASE => PRIMARY,
                                        INDEX => POSITIVE,
                                        LIST => PRIMARY_LIST);
```

```
type COLOUR is new PRIMARY_SETS.SET;
```

The type COLOUR now has all the functions we want and the array type has a
name of our choosing. We might still want to rename EMPTY and FULL thus

```
function WHITE return COLOUR renames EMPTY;
```

or we can still declare WHITE as a constant by

```
WHITE: constant COLOUR:= EMPTY;
```

As a general rule it is better to use derived types rather than subtypes
because of the greater type checking provided during compilation; some-

times, however, derived types introduce a need for lots of explicit type conversions which clutter the program, in which case the formal distinction is probably a mistake and one might as well use subtypes.

We conclude by summarizing the general principle regarding the matching of actual to formal generic types which should now be clear. The formal type represents a class of types which have certain common properties and these properties can be assumed in the generic unit. The corresponding actual type must then supply these properties. The matching rules are designed so that this is assured by reference to the parameters only and without considering the details of the generic body. As a consequence the user of the generic unit need not see the body for debugging purposes. This notion of matching guaranteed by the parameters is termed the contract model.

Unfortunately there is an important violation of the contract model in the case of unconstrained types. If we have the basic formal type

**type** T **is private**;

then this can be matched by an unconstrained array type such as VECTOR provided that we do not use T in the generic unit in a way that would require the array to be constrained. The most obvious example is that we must not declare an object of type T.

In a similar way the actual type could be an unconstrained discriminated type provided that T is not used in a way that would require constraints. Thus again we could not declare an unconstrained object of type T; but note that if the actual type has default discriminants then the defaults will be used in the generic body and then we will be able to declare an object. This interpretation is given in AI-37 and contrasts with the apparent statement in the *LRM*.

The attribute CONSTRAINED can be applied to the formal type T and gives a Boolean value indicating whether the actual type is a constrained type or not. Thus considering the types of Section 11.3, T'CONSTRAINED would be TRUE if the actual parameter were MAN but FALSE if the actual parameter were PERSON or MUTANT; in the last case the default constraint NEUTER is irrelevant. Remember that the actual parameter must be a type mark and not a subtype indication.

Finally we recall that our use of generic formal parameters within the body is restricted by the rule that they are not static.

---

*Exercise 13.2*

1    Instantiate NEXT to give a function behaving like **not**.

2    Rewrite the specification of the package RATIONAL_NUMBERS so that it is a generic package taking the integer type as a parameter. See Exercise 9.1(**3**).

3    Rewrite the function OUTER of Exercise 7.1(**3**) so that it is a generic function with appropriate parameters. Instantiate it to give the original function.

**4**     Write the body of the package SET_OF.

**5**     Rewrite the private part of SET_OF so that an object of the type
        SET is by default given the initial value EMPTY when declared.

## 13.3  Subprogram parameters

As mentioned earlier a generic parameter can also be a subprogram. There
are a number of distinct characteristic applications of this facility and we
introduce the topic by considering the classical problem of sorting.

Suppose we wish to sort an array into ascending order. There are a
number of general algorithms that can be used but they do not depend on
the type of the values being sorted. All we need is some comparison
operation such as "<" which is defined for the type.

We might start by considering the specification

```
generic
    type INDEX is (<>);
    type ITEM is (<>);
    type COLLECTION is array (INDEX range <>) of ITEM;
procedure SORT(C: in out COLLECTION);
```

Although the body is largely irrelevant it might help to illustrate the
problem to consider the following crude possibility

```
procedure SORT(C: in out COLLECTION) is
    MIN: INDEX;
    TEMP: ITEM;
begin
    for I in C'FIRST .. INDEX'PRED(C'LAST) loop
        MIN:= I;
        for J in INDEX'SUCC(I) .. C'LAST loop
            if C(J) < C(MIN) then MIN:= J; end if;    -- use of <
        end loop;
        TEMP:= C(I); C(I):= C(MIN); C(MIN):= TEMP;
    end loop;
end SORT;
```

This trivial algorithm repeatedly scans the part of the array not
sorted, finds the least component (which because of the previous scans will
be not less than any component of the already sorted part) and then swaps
it so that it is then the last element of the now sorted part. Note that
because of the generality we have imposed upon ourselves, we cannot
write

```
for I in C'FIRST .. C'LAST−1 loop
```

because we cannot rely upon the array index being an integer type. We
only know that it is a discrete type and therefore have to use the attributes

INDEX'PRED and INDEX'SUCC which we know to be available since they are common to all discrete types.

However, the main point to note is the call of "<" in the body of SORT. This calls the predefined function corresponding to the type ITEM. We know that there is such a function because we have specified ITEM to be discrete and all discrete types have such a function. Unfortunately the net result is that our generic sort can only sort arrays of discrete types. It cannot sort arrays of floating types. Of course we could write a version for floating types by replacing the generic parameter for ITEM by

```
type ITEM is digits <>;
```

but then it would not work for discrete types. What we really need to do is specify the comparison function to be used in a general manner. We can do this by adding a fourth parameter which is a formal subprogram so that the specification becomes

```
generic
    type INDEX is (<>);
    type ITEM is private;
    type COLLECTION is array (INDEX range <>) of ITEM;
    with function "<" (X, Y: ITEM) return BOOLEAN;
procedure SORT(C: in out COLLECTION);
```

The formal subprogram parameter is like a subprogram declaration preceded by **with**. (The leading **with** is necessary to avoid a syntactic ambiguity and has no other subtle purpose.)

We have also made the type ITEM private since the only common property now required (other than supplied through the parameters) is that the type ITEM can be assigned. The body remains as before.

We can now sort an array of any (unlimited) type provided that we have an appropriate comparison to supply as parameter. So in order to sort an array of our type VECTOR, we first instantiate thus

```
procedure SORT_VECTOR is
    new SORT(INTEGER, REAL, VECTOR, "<");
```

and we can then apply the procedure to the array concerned

```
AN_ARRAY: VECTOR( ... );
...
SORT_VECTOR(AN_ARRAY);
```

Note carefully that our call of "<" inside SORT is actually a call of the function passed as actual parameter; in this case it is indeed the predefined function "<" anyway.

Passing the comparison rule gives our generic sort procedure amazing flexibility. We can, for example, sort in the reverse direction by

```
procedure REVERSE_SORT_VECTOR is
    new SORT(INTEGER, REAL, VECTOR, ">");
...
REVERSE_SORT_VECTOR(AN_ARRAY);
```

This may come as a slight surprise but it is a natural consequence of the call of the formal "<" in

```
if C(J) < C(MIN) then ...
```

being, after instantiation, a call of the actual ">". No confusion should arise because the internal call is hidden but the use of the named notation for instantiation would look curious

```
procedure REVERSE_SORT_VECTOR is
                   new SORT(INDEX => INTEGER,
                             ITEM => REAL,
                       COLLECTION => VECTOR,
                             "<" => ">");
```

We could also sort our second FARMYARD of Section 6.5 assuming it to be a variable

```
subtype STRING_3 is STRING(1 .. 3);

procedure SORT_STRING_3_ARRAY is
        new SORT(POSITIVE, STRING_3, STRING_3_ARRAY, "<");
...
SORT_STRING_3_ARRAY(FARMYARD);
```

The "<" operator passed as parameter is the predefined operation applicable to one-dimensional arrays described in Section 6.6.

The correspondence between formal and actual subprograms is such that the formal subprogram just renames the actual subprogram. Thus the matching rules regarding parameters, results and so on are as described in Section 8.5. In particular the constraints on the parameters are those of the actual subprogram and any implied by the formal subprogram are ignored. A parameterless formal function can also be matched by an enumeration literal of the result type just as for renaming.

Generic subprogram parameters (like generic object parameters) can have default values. These are given in the generic formal part and take two forms. In the above example we could write

```
with function "<" (X, Y: ITEM) return BOOLEAN is <>;
```

This means that we can omit the corresponding actual parameter if there is visible at the point of *instantiation* a unique subprogram with the same designator and matching specification. With this alteration to SORT we could have omitted the last parameter in the instantiation giving SORT_VECTOR.

The other form of default value is where we give an explicit name for the default parameter. The usual rules for defaults apply; the default name is only evaluated if required by the instantiation but the binding of identifiers in the expression which is the name occurs at the point of *declaration* of the generic unit. In our example

**with function** "<" (X, Y: ITEM) **return** BOOLEAN **is** LESS_THAN;

could never be valid because the specification of LESS_THAN must match that of "<" and yet the parameter ITEM is not known until instantiation. The only valid possibilities are where the formal subprogram has no parameters depending on formal types or the default subprogram is itself another formal parameter or an attribute. Thus we might have

**with function** NEXT(X: T) **return** T **is** T'SUCC;

The same rules for mixing named and positional notation apply to generic instantiation as to subprogram calls. Hence if a parameter is omitted, subsequent parameters must be given using named notation. Of course, a generic unit need have no parameters in which case the instantiation takes the same form as for a subprogram call – the brackets are omitted.

As a final example of the use of our generic SORT (which we will assume now has a default parameter <> for "<"), we show how any type can be sorted provided we supply an appropriate rule.

Thus consider sorting an array of the type DATE from Section 6.7. We write

**type** DATE_ARRAY **is array** (POSITIVE **range** <>) **of** DATE;

**function** "<" (X, Y: DATE) **return** BOOLEAN **is**
**begin**
    **if** X.YEAR /= Y.YEAR **then**
        **return** X.YEAR < Y.YEAR;
    **elsif** X.MONTH /= Y.MONTH **then**
        **return** X.MONTH < Y.MONTH;
    **else**
        **return** X.DAY < Y.DAY;
    **end if**;
**end** "<";

**procedure** SORT_DATE_ARRAY **is**
    **new** SORT(POSITIVE, DATE, DATE_ARRAY);

where the function "<" is passed through the default mechanism.

It might have been nicer to give our comparison rule a more appropriate name such as

**function** EARLIER(X, Y: DATE) **return** BOOLEAN;

but we would then have to pass it as an explicit parameter; this might be considered better style anyway.

Formal subprograms can be used to supply further properties of type parameters in a quite general way. Consider the generic function SUM of the last section. We can generalize this even further by passing the adding operator itself as a generic parameter.

```
generic
    type INDEX is (<>);
    type ITEM is private;
    type VEC is array (INDEX range <>) of ITEM;
    with function "+" (X, Y: ITEM) return ITEM;
function APPLY(A: VEC) return ITEM;

function APPLY(A: VEC) return ITEM is
    RESULT: ITEM:= A(A'FIRST);
begin
    for I in INDEX'SUCC(A'FIRST) .. A'LAST loop
        RESULT:= RESULT+A(I);
    end loop;
    return RESULT;
end APPLY;
```

The operator "+" has been added as a parameter and ITEM is now just private and no longer floating. This means that we can apply the generic function to any binary operation on any type. However, we no longer have a zero value and so have to initialize RESULT with the first component of the array A and then iterate through the remainder. In doing this, remember that we cannot write

```
for I in A'FIRST+1 .. A'LAST loop
```

because the type INDEX may not be an integer type.

Our original function SUM of Section 7.1 is now given by

```
function SUM is new APPLY(INTEGER, REAL, VECTOR, "+");
```

We could equally have

```
function PROD is new APPLY(INTEGER, REAL, VECTOR, "*");
```

A very important use of formal subprograms is in mathematical applications such as integration. In traditional languages such as Algol and Pascal, this is done by passing subprograms as parameters to other subprograms. In Ada, subprograms can only be parameters of generic units and so we use the generic mechanism.

We could have a generic function

```
generic
    with function F(X: REAL) return REAL;
function INTEGRATE(A, B: REAL) return REAL;
```

which evaluates

$$\int_a^b f(x)\ dx$$

In order to integrate a particular function we must instantiate INTEGRATE with our function as actual generic parameter. Thus suppose we needed

$$\int_0^P e^t \sin t\ dt$$

We would write

```
function G(T: REAL) return REAL is
begin
    return EXP(T)*SIN(T);
end;

function INTEGRATE_G is new INTEGRATE(G);
```

and then our result is given by the expression

```
INTEGRATE_G(0.0, P)
```

As we have seen, the specification of the formal function could depend on preceding formal types. Thus we could extend our integration function to apply to any floating point type by writing

```
generic
    type FLOATING is digits <>;
    with function F(X: FLOATING) return FLOATING;
function INTEGRATE(A, B: FLOATING) return FLOATING;
```

and then

```
function INTEGRATE_G is new INTEGRATE(REAL, G);
```

In practice the function INTEGRATE would have other parameters indicating the accuracy required and so on.

Examples such as this are often found confusing at first sight. The key point to remember is that there are two distinct levels of parameterization. First, we fix the function to be integrated at instantiation, and then we fix the bounds when we call the integration function thus declared. The sorting examples were similar; first, we fixed the parameters defining the type of array to be sorted and the rule to be used at instantiation, and then we fixed the actual array to be sorted when we called the procedure.

We conclude this section with an important philosophical remark. Generics provide an extremely powerful mechanism for parameterization.

Moreover, this mechanism does not increase run-time costs because all type and subprogram identification is static. Thus Ada enables us to write reusable software of greater applicability without a penalty on run-time performance.

---

*Exercise 13.3*

1    Instantiate SORT to apply to

        **type** POLY_ARRAY **is**
                **array** (INTEGER **range** <>) **of** POLYNOMIAL;

     See Section 11.1. Define a sensible ordering for polynomials.

2    Instantiate SORT to apply to an array of the type MUTANT of Section 11.3. Put neuter things first, then females, then males and within each class the younger first. Could we sort an array of the type PERSON from the same section?

3    Sort the array PEOPLE of Section 6.7.

4    What happens if we attempt to sort an array of less than two components?

5    Describe how to make a generic sort procedure based on the procedure SORT of Section 11.4. It should have an identical specification to the procedure SORT of this section.

6    Instantiate APPLY to give a function to "and" together all the components of a Boolean array.

7    Rewrite APPLY so that a null array can be a parameter without raising an exception. Use this new version to redo the previous exercise.

8    Write a generic function EQUALS to define the equality of one-dimensional arrays of a limited private type. See Exercise 9.2(**4**). Instantiate it to give the function "=" applying to the type STACK_ARRAY.

9    Given a function

        **generic**
            **with function** F(X: REAL) **return** REAL;
        **function** SOLVE **return** REAL;

     that finds a root of the equation $f(x) = 0$, show how you would find the root of

        $e^x + x = 7$

## 13.4   The mathematical library

The reader will be surprised to learn that the *LRM* says nothing about everyday mathematical functions such as SQRT. This is in strong contrast to most languages such as Algol, Pascal and FORTRAN where the provision of standard mathematical functions is taken for granted.

However, the flexibility and generality of Ada is such that the specification of a suitable package is not immediately obvious. There are a number of conflicting requirements

- ease of casual use for simple calculations,

- ability to provide the ultimate in accuracy for serious numerical work,

- portability across different implementations.

Although numerical applications are in a minority, we will nevertheless consider the topic in some detail because it provides a good illustration of the use of generics and other key features of Ada.

The packages to be described are (at the time of writing) proposed ISO standards and therefore subject to change. They were developed by the Ada-Europe and SigAda working groups on Ada Numerics.

First there is a package containing useful numbers of type universal real and given to immense precision. It has no body.

```
package MATHEMATICAL_CONSTANTS is

    PI            : constant:= 3.14159_26535_89793_23846_26433...;
    TWO_PI        : constant:= 2*PI;
    HALF_PI       : constant:= PI/2;
    ONE_OVER_PI   : constant:= 1.0/PI;
    SQRT_PI       : constant:= 1.77245_38509_05516_02729_81674...;

    NATURAL_E     : constant:= 2.71828_18284_59045_23536_02874...;
    ONE_OVER_E    : constant:= 1.0/NATURAL_E;

    GAMMA         : constant:= 0.57721_56649_01532_86060_65120...;

end MATHEMATICAL_CONSTANTS;
```

Then there is a package containing a single exception which is raised under appropriate circumstances. It also has no body.

```
package MATHEMATICAL_EXCEPTIONS is
    ARGUMENT_ERROR: exception;
end MATHEMATICAL_EXCEPTIONS;
```

Finally there is a generic package containing the mathematical functions themselves. Its specification is as follows

```
with MATHEMATICAL_EXCEPTIONS;
generic
    type FLOAT_TYPE is digits <>;
package GENERIC_ELEMENTARY_FUNCTIONS is

    function SQRT (X:        FLOAT_TYPE) return FLOAT_TYPE;
    function LOG (X:         FLOAT_TYPE) return FLOAT_TYPE;
    function LOG (X, BASE:   FLOAT_TYPE) return FLOAT_TYPE;
    function EXP (X:         FLOAT_TYPE) return FLOAT_TYPE;
    function "**" (X, Y:     FLOAT_TYPE) return FLOAT_TYPE;

    function SIN (X:         FLOAT_TYPE) return FLOAT_TYPE;
    function SIN (X, CYCLE:  FLOAT_TYPE) return FLOAT_TYPE;
    function COS (X:         FLOAT_TYPE) return FLOAT_TYPE;
    function COS (X, CYCLE: FLOAT_TYPE) return FLOAT_TYPE;
    function TAN (X:         FLOAT_TYPE) return FLOAT_TYPE;
    function TAN (X, CYCLE: FLOAT_TYPE) return FLOAT_TYPE;
    function COT (X:         FLOAT_TYPE) return FLOAT_TYPE;
    function COT (X, CYCLE: FLOAT_TYPE) return FLOAT_TYPE;
    function ARCSIN (X:          FLOAT_TYPE) return FLOAT_TYPE;
    function ARCSIN (X, CYCLE:  FLOAT_TYPE) return FLOAT_TYPE;
    function ARCCOS (X:          FLOAT_TYPE) return FLOAT_TYPE;
    function ARCCOS (X, CYCLE:FLOAT_TYPE) return FLOAT_TYPE;
    function ARCTAN (Y: FLOAT_TYPE; X: FLOAT_TYPE:= 1.0)
                                        return FLOAT_TYPE;
    function ARCTAN (Y: FLOAT_TYPE; X: FLOAT_TYPE:= 1.0;
                CYCLE: FLOAT_TYPE) return FLOAT_TYPE;
    function ARCCOT (X: FLOAT_TYPE; Y: FLOAT_TYPE:= 1.0)
                                        return FLOAT_TYPE;
    function ARCCOT (X: FLOAT_TYPE; Y: FLOAT_TYPE:= 1.0;
                CYCLE: FLOAT_TYPE) return FLOAT_TYPE;

    function SINH (X: FLOAT_TYPE) return FLOAT_TYPE;
    function COSH (X: FLOAT_TYPE) return FLOAT_TYPE;
    function TANH (X: FLOAT_TYPE) return FLOAT_TYPE;
    function COTH (X: FLOAT_TYPE) return FLOAT_TYPE;
    function ARCSINH (X: FLOAT_TYPE) return FLOAT_TYPE;
    function ARCCOSH (X: FLOAT_TYPE) return FLOAT_TYPE;
    function ARCTANH (X: FLOAT_TYPE) return FLOAT_TYPE;
    function ARCCOTH (X: FLOAT_TYPE) return FLOAT_TYPE;

    ARGUMENT_ERROR: exception
        renames MATHEMATICAL_ EXCEPTIONS.ARGUMENT_ERROR;

end GENERIC_ELEMENTARY_FUNCTIONS;
```

The single generic parameter is the floating type. The package might be instantiated with a predefined type such as FLOAT or LONG_FLOAT but hopefully more likely with a user's own type such as REAL.

```
package REAL_ELEMENTARY_FUNCTIONS is
    new GENERIC_ELEMENTARY_FUNCTIONS(REAL);
```

The body could then choose an implementation appropriate to the accuracy of the user's type through the attribute FLOAT_TYPE'DIGITS rather than necessarily using the accuracy of the predefined type from which the user's type has been derived. This could have significant timing advantages.

The functions SQRT and EXP need little comment except perhaps concerning exceptions. Calling SQRT with a negative parameter will raise ARGUMENT_ERROR whereas calling EXP with a large parameter will raise NUMERIC_ERROR (CONSTRAINT_ERROR).

The general principle is that intrinsic mathematical restrictions raise ARGUMENT_ERROR whereas implementation range restrictions raise NUMERIC_ERROR.

Observe that the exception ARGUMENT_ERROR is declared in a separate non-generic package. This means that there is only one such exception which applies to all instantiations of the main package. The renaming declaration enables us to refer to the exception without reference to the package MATHEMATICAL_EXCEPTIONS. We will meet this technique again when we discuss input–output in Chapter 15.

There are two overloadings of LOG. That with a single parameter gives the natural logarithm to base $e$, whereas that with two parameters allows us to choose any base at all. Thus to find $\log_{10}2$, we write

```
LOG(2.0, 10.0)           -- 0.3010...
```

The reader may wonder why there is not just a single function with a default parameter thus

```
function LOG(X: FLOAT_TYPE; BASE: FLOAT_TYPE:=
    MATHEMATICAL_CONSTANTS.NATURAL_E) return FLOAT_TYPE;
```

which would seem to give the desired result with less fuss. The reason concerns obtaining the ultimate in precision. Passing a default parameter means that the accuracy of the value of $e$ used can only be that of the FLOAT_TYPE. Using a separate function enables the function body to obtain the benefit of the full accuracy of the universal real named number.

The restrictions on the parameters of LOG are $X > 0.0$, $BASE > 0.0$ and also $BASE \ /= 1.0$. So BASE could be 0.5 which is an amusing thought.

As an aside, we note that we cannot formally rename a named number because renaming requires a type name and the universal types cannot be explicitly named. Consequently we are unable to rename MATHEMATICAL_CONSTANTS.NATURAL_E with a more convenient name such as E. However, there is no need, we can just declare another named number

E: **constant**:= MATHEMATICAL_CONSTANTS.NATURAL_E;

which is no disadvantage because the named numbers are not run-time objects anyway and so there is no duplication.

The function "**" effectively extends the predefined operator to allow non-integral exponents. X must not be negative.

The trigonometric functions SIN, COS, TAN and COT also come in pairs like LOG and for a similar reason. The single parameter versions assume the parameter is in radians whereas the second parameter allows the use of any unit by giving the number of units in a whole cycle. Thus to find the sine of 30 degrees, we write

SIN(30.0, 360.0)　　　　　　　　　-- 0.5

because there are 360 degrees in a cycle.

In these functions the single parameter versions enable the highly accurate number TWO_PI to be used directly rather than being passed with less accuracy as a parameter.

Of the inverse functions, ARCSIN and ARCCOS need no comment. However, ARCTAN has a default value of 1.0 for a second parameter (the CYCLE then being third). This enables us to call ARCTAN with two parameters giving the classical $x$- and $y$-coordinates (thus fully identifying the quadrant). So

ARCTAN(Y => −1.0, X => +1.0)　　　-- −PI/4
ARCTAN(Y => +1.0, X => −1.0)　　　-- +3*PI/4

Note carefully that the first parameter of ARCTAN is Y since it is the $x$-coordinate that is taken to be 1.0 by default. ARCCOT is very similar except that the parameters are naturally in the other order.

There are no obvious comments to make on the hyperbolic functions.

We now turn to an interesting illustration of the use of default subprogram parameters for conveniently passing properties of generic types. Although the example is of a rather mathematical nature it is hoped that the general principles will be appreciated. It follows on from the above elementary functions package and concerns the provision of similar functions but working on complex arguments. Suppose we want to provide the ability to compute SQRT, LOG, EXP, SIN and COS with functions such as

**function** SQRT(X: COMPLEX_TYPE) **return** COMPLEX_TYPE;

Many readers will have forgotten that this can be done or perhaps never knew. It is not necessary to dwell on the details of how such calculations are performed or their use; the main point is to concentrate on the principles involved. These computations use various operations on the real numbers out of which the complex numbers are formed. Our goal is to write a generic package which works however the complex numbers are implemented (cartesian or polar) and also allows any floating point type as the basis for the underlying real numbers.

Here are the formulae which we will need to compute

Taking, $z \equiv x + iy \equiv r(\cos \theta + i \sin \theta)$, as the argument:

sqrt $z\ =\ \sqrt{r}(\cos\ \theta/2\ +\ i\ \sin\ \theta/2)$
log $z\ =\ \log r\ +\ i\ \theta$
exp $z\ =\ e^x(\cos\ y\ +\ i\ \sin\ y)$
sin $z\ =\ \sin x\ \cosh y\ +\ i\ \cos x\ \sinh y$
cos $z\ =\ \cos x\ \cosh y\ -\ i\ \sin x\ \sinh y$

We thus see that we will need functions to decompose the complex number into both cartesian and polar forms plus SQRT, COS, SIN, LOG, EXP, COSH and SINH applying to the underlying floating type. We also need to be able to put the result together from both cartesian and polar forms.

Our generic package COMPLEX_NUMBERS (see Sections 9.1 and 13.2) is a good starting point. However, it only gives a cartesian view of a complex number and so needs augmenting with additional functions to provide a polar view. We will assume that this has been done and that the extra visible functions are

```
function CONS_POLAR (R, THETA: REAL) return COMPLEX;
function "abs" (X: COMPLEX) return REAL;
function ARG (X: COMPLEX) return REAL;
```

The package GENERIC_ELEMENTARY_FUNCTIONS described above provides all the operations we need on the underlying floating type. Now consider

```
generic
    type REAL_TYPE is digits <>;
    type COMPLEX_TYPE is private;

    with function CONS(R, I: REAL_TYPE) return
                                COMPLEX_TYPE is <>;
    with function CONS_POLAR(R, THETA: REAL_TYPE) return
                                COMPLEX_TYPE is <>;
    with function RL_PART(X: COMPLEX_TYPE) return
                                REAL_TYPE is <>;
    with function IM_PART(X: COMPLEX_TYPE) return
                                REAL_TYPE is <>;
    with function "abs" (X: COMPLEX_TYPE) return REAL_TYPE
                                is <>;
    with function ARG (X: COMPLEX_TYPE) return
                                REAL_TYPE is <>;

    with function SQRT (X: REAL_TYPE) return REAL_TYPE is <>;
    with function LOG   (X: REAL_TYPE) return REAL_TYPE is <>;
```

```
with function EXP   (X: REAL_TYPE) return REAL_TYPE is <>;
with function SIN   (X: REAL_TYPE) return REAL_TYPE is <>;
with function COS   (X: REAL_TYPE) return REAL_TYPE is <>;
with function SINH  (X: REAL_TYPE) return REAL_TYPE is <>;
with function COSH (X: REAL_TYPE) return REAL_TYPE is <>;

package GENERIC_COMPLEX_FUNCTIONS is

    function SQRT (X: COMPLEX_TYPE) return COMPLEX_TYPE;
    function LOG  (X: COMPLEX_TYPE) return COMPLEX_TYPE;
    function EXP  (X: COMPLEX_TYPE) return COMPLEX_TYPE;
    function SIN  (X: COMPLEX_TYPE) return COMPLEX_TYPE;
    function COS  (X: COMPLEX_TYPE) return COMPLEX_TYPE;

end GENERIC_COMPLEX_FUNCTIONS;
```

This generic package looks extremely tedious to use. Apart from the obviously necessary parameters REAL_TYPE and COMPLEX_TYPE, it has 13 other functions as parameters. However, we note that they all have the default form <>. So, if at the point of instantiation, by good luck or careful planning, we happen to have all the functions visible with the correct names and matching types then we need not mention them in the instantiation. In other words we can pass all the properties of the types on the sly.

So we could write

```
type MY_REAL is digits 9;

package MY_ELEMENTARY_FUNCTIONS is
    new GENERIC_ELEMENTARY_FUNCTIONS(FLOAT_TYPE =>
                                            MY_REAL);

package MY_COMPLEX_NUMBERS is
    new GENERIC_COMPLEX_NUMBERS(REAL => MY_REAL);

use MY_ELEMENTARY_FUNCTIONS, MY_COMPLEX_NUMBERS;

package MY_COMPLEX_FUNCTIONS is
    new GENERIC_COMPLEX_FUNCTIONS(MY_REAL, COMPLEX);

use MY_COMPLEX_FUNCTIONS;
```

and *Hey presto!* it all works. Note that irritatingly the complex type is just COMPLEX and not MY_COMPLEX. We could remedy this using a subtype or derived type as we did for the type COLOUR and the package SET_OF in Section 13.2. Another point to note is that we have to write the use clause for MY_ELEMENTARY_FUNCTIONS and MY_COMPLEX_NUMBERS before the instantiation of GENERIC_COMPLEX_FUNCTIONS otherwise the various exported functions would not be directly visible.

Of course it was not entirely an accident that the parameters matched. But if one of them had not then it could have been explicitly provided. For example the formal parameter for constructing a complex number from its cartesian form might have had the better name CONS_CARTESIAN rather than the rather abbreviated CONS. If that had been the case then the instantiation could be

```
package MY_COMPLEX_FUNCTIONS is
    new GENERIC_COMPLEX_FUNCTIONS(MY_REAL, COMPLEX,
                                  CONS_CARTESIAN => CONS);
```

where we have used named notation for the extra parameter although by coincidence it comes next anyway.

Another way to overcome the mismatch is to use renaming. This works because, as mentioned earlier, the matching of actual to formal generic subprogram parameters is defined in terms of renaming anyway. This is a bit tedious because the parameters and result type have to be written out in full and so we leave this as an exercise.

It should also be noted that matching would not have been possible at all if only a single (two parameter) function with default parameter had been provided for LOG, SIN and so on in the package GENERIC_ELEMENTARY_FUNCTIONS. Matching requires that the number of parameters be the same irrespective of any defaults.

As a final point, the astute reader may have realized that adding the polar functions to our package GENERIC_COMPLEX_NUMBERS means that its body also needs access to some of the elementary functions applied to the underlying floating type. These can be provided via default parameters in a similar way.

A completely different approach to the whole exercise which applies to both GENERIC_COMPLEX_FUNCTIONS itself as well as to GENERIC_COMPLEX_NUMBERS is to instantiate the elementary functions inside the bodies so that we do not have to pass the functions as parameters. This works but will result in wasteful and unnecessary multiple instantiations, especially since we may well need them at the user level anyway. A possible advantage, however, is that there is then no risk that the wrong function is passed by default which would happen if the user were foolish enough to redeclare perhaps LOG to have a completely different meaning (which might be something to do with logging a result). This would be both unfortunate and unlikely.

It is hoped that the general principles have been understood and that the mathematics has not clouded the issues. The principles are important but not easily illustrated with short examples. It should also be noted that although the package GENERIC_ELEMENTARY_FUNCTIONS described above is exactly as the proposed standard, the complex number packages are just an illustration of how generics can be used.

*Note added during reprinting:* The proposed standard package MATHEMATICAL_EXCEPTIONS is now named ELEMENTARY_FUNCTIONS_EXCEPTIONS and the package MATHEMATICAL_CONSTANTS is no longer a part of the proposed standard (since it is not required for the specification of GENERIC_ELEMENTARY_FUNCTIONS).

*Exercise 13.4*

1    Write a body for the package SIMPLE_MATHS of Exercise 2.2(**1**) using an instantiation of GENERIC_ELEMENTARY_FUNCTIONS. Raise NUMERIC_ERROR for all exceptional circumstances.

2    Write a body for the package GENERIC_COMPLEX_FUNCTIONS using the formulae defined above. Ignore exceptions.

3    Write the renaming of CONS required to overcome the parameter mismatch discussed above.

4    Rewrite the package GENERIC_COMPLEX_NUMBERS adding the extra generic parameters to supply the required elementary functions. Implement the type COMPLEX in cartesian form.

## Checklist 13

The generic mechanism is not text replacement; non-local name binding would be different.

Object **in out** parameters are bound by renaming.

Object **in** parameters are always copied unlike parameters of subprograms.

Subprogram generic parameters are bound by renaming.

Generic subprograms may not overload – only the instantiations can.

Generic subprograms always have a separate specification and body.

Formal parameters (and defaults) may depend upon preceding parameters.

Generic formal parameters and their attributes are not static.

# Chapter 14
# Tasking

The final major topic to be introduced is tasking. This has been left to the end, not because it is unimportant or particularly difficult, but because, apart from the interaction with exceptions, it is a fairly self-contained part of the language.

## 14.1 Parallelism

So far we have only considered sequential programs in which statements are obeyed in order. In many applications it is convenient to write a program as several parallel activities which cooperate as necessary. This is particularly true of programs which interact in real time with physical processes in the real world, simulation programs (which mimic parallel activities in the real world), and programs which wish to exploit multi-processor architectures directly.

In Ada, parallel activities are described by means of tasks. In simple cases a task is lexically described by a form very similar to a package. This consists of a specification describing the interface presented to other tasks and a body describing the dynamic behaviour of the task.

```
task T is                -- specification
   ...
end T;

task body T is           -- body
   ...
end T;
```

In some cases a task presents no interface to other tasks in which case the specification reduces to just

**task** T;

As a simple example of parallelism, consider a family going shopping to buy ingredients for a meal. Suppose they need meat, salad and wine and that the purchase of these items can be done by calling procedures BUY_MEAT, BUY_SALAD and BUY_WINE respectively. The whole expedition could be represented by

```
procedure SHOPPING is
begin
    BUY_MEAT;
    BUY_SALAD;
    BUY_WINE;
end;
```

However, this solution corresponds to the family buying each item in sequence. It would be far more efficient for them to split up so that, for example, mother buys the meat, the children buy the salad and father buys the wine. They agree to meet again perhaps in the car park. This parallel solution can be represented by

```
procedure SHOPPING is
    task GET_SALAD;

    task body GET_SALAD is
    begin
        BUY_SALAD;
    end GET_SALAD;

    task GET_WINE;

    task body GET_WINE is
    begin
        BUY_WINE;
    end GET_WINE;

begin
    BUY_MEAT;
end SHOPPING;
```

In this formulation, mother is represented as the main processor and calls BUY_MEAT directly from the procedure SHOPPING. The children and father are considered as subservient processors and perform the locally declared tasks GET_SALAD and GET_WINE which respectively call the procedures BUY_SALAD and BUY_WINE.

The example illustrates the declaration, activation and termination of tasks. A task is a program component like a package and is declared in a similar way inside a subprogram, block, package or indeed another task body. A task specification can also be declared in a package specification, in which case the task body must be declared in the corresponding package body. However, a task specification cannot be declared in the specification of another task but only in the body.

The activation of a task is automatic. In the above example the local tasks become active when the parent unit reaches the **begin** following the task declaration.

Such a task will terminate when it reaches its final **end**. Thus the task GET_SALAD calls the procedure BUY_SALAD and then promptly terminates.

A task declared in the declarative part of a subprogram, block or task body is said to depend on that unit. It is an important rule that a unit cannot be left until all dependent tasks have terminated. This termination rule ensures that objects declared in the unit, and therefore potentially visible to local tasks, cannot disappear while there exists a task which could access them. (Note that a task cannot depend on a package – we will return to this later.)

It is important to realize that the main program is itself considered to be called by a hypothetical main task. We can now trace the sequence of actions when this main task calls the procedure SHOPPING. First the tasks GET_SALAD and GET_WINE are declared and then when the main task reaches the **begin** these dependent tasks are set active in parallel with the main task. The dependent tasks call their respective procedures and terminate. Meanwhile the main task calls BUY_MEAT and then reaches the **end** of SHOPPING. The main task then waits until the dependent tasks have terminated if they have not already done so. This corresponds to mother waiting for father and children to return with their purchases.

In the general case termination therefore occurs in two stages. We say that a unit is completed when it reaches its final **end**. It will subsequently become terminated only when all dependent tasks, if any, are also terminated. Of course, if a unit has no dependent tasks then it naturally becomes completed and terminated at the same time.

---

*Exercise 14.1*

1    Rewrite procedure SHOPPING to contain three local tasks so that the symmetry of the situation is revealed.

---

## 14.2  The rendezvous

In the SHOPPING example the various tasks did not interact with each other once they had been set active except that their parent unit had to wait for them to terminate. Generally, however, tasks will interact with each other during their lifetime. In Ada this is done by a mechanism known as a rendezvous. This is similar to the human situation where two people meet, perform a transaction and then go on independently.

A rendezvous between two tasks occurs as a consequence of one task calling an entry declared in another. An entry is declared in a task specification in a similar way to a procedure in a package specification.

```
task T is
    entry E( ... );
end;
```

An entry can have **in**, **out** and **in out** parameters in the same way as a procedure. It cannot however have a result like a function. An entry is called in a similar way to a procedure

```
T.E( ... );
```

A task name cannot appear in a use clause and so the dotted notation is necessary to call the entry from outside the task. Of course, a local task could call an entry of its parent directly – the usual scope and visibility rules apply.

The statements to be obeyed during a rendezvous are described by corresponding accept statements in the body of the task containing the declaration of the entry. An accept statement usually takes the form

```
accept E( ... ) do
    -- sequence of statements
end E;
```

The formal parameters of the entry E are repeated in the same way that a procedure body repeats the formal parameters of a corresponding procedure declaration. The **end** is optionally followed by the name of the entry. A significant difference is that the body of the accept statement is just a sequence of statements. Any local declarations or exception handlers must be provided by writing a local block.

The most important difference between an entry call and a procedure call is that in the case of a procedure, the task that calls the procedure also immediately executes the procedure body, whereas in the case of an entry, one task calls the entry but the corresponding accept statement is executed by the task owning the entry. Moreover, the accept statement cannot be executed until a task calls the entry and the task owning the entry reaches the accept statement. Naturally one of these will occur first and the task concerned will then be suspended until the other reaches its corresponding statement. When this occurs the sequence of statements of the accept statement is executed by the called task while the calling task remains suspended. This interaction is called a rendezvous. When the end of the accept statement is reached the rendezvous is completed and both tasks then proceed independently. The parameter mechanism is exactly as for a subprogram call; note that expressions in the actual parameter list are evaluated before the call is issued.

We can elaborate our shopping example by giving the task GET_SALAD two entries, one for mother to hand the children the money for the salad and one to collect the salad from them afterwards. We do the same for GET_WINE (although perhaps father has his own funds in which case he might keep the wine to himself anyway).

We can also replace the procedures BUY_SALAD, BUY_WINE and BUY_MEAT by functions which take money as a parameter and return the appropriate ingredient. Our shopping procedure might now become

```
procedure SHOPPING is
    task GET_SALAD is
        entry PAY(M: in MONEY);
        entry COLLECT(S: out SALAD);
    end GET_SALAD;

    task body GET_SALAD is
        CASH: MONEY;
        FOOD: SALAD;
    begin
        accept PAY(M: in MONEY) do
            CASH:= M;
        end PAY;

        FOOD:= BUY_SALAD(CASH);

        accept COLLECT(S: out SALAD) do
            S:= FOOD;
        end COLLECT;
    end GET_SALAD;

    -- GET_WINE similarly

begin
    GET_SALAD.PAY(50);
    GET_WINE.PAY(100);
    MM:= BUY_MEAT(200);
    GET_SALAD.COLLECT(SS);
    GET_WINE.COLLECT(WW);
end SHOPPING;
```

The final outcome is that the various ingredients end up in the variables MM, SS and WW whose declarations are left to the imagination.

The logical behaviour should be noted. As soon as the tasks GET_SALAD and GET_WINE become active they encounter accept statements and wait until the main task calls the entries PAY in each of them. After calling the function BUY_MEAT, the main task calls the COLLECT entries. Curiously, mother is unable to collect the wine until after she has collected the salad from the children.

As a more abstract example consider the problem of providing a task to act as a single buffer between one or more tasks producing items and one or more tasks consuming them. Our intermediate task can hold just one item.

```
task BUFFERING is
    entry PUT(X: in ITEM);
    entry GET(X: out ITEM);
end;

task body BUFFERING is
    V: ITEM;
begin
    loop
        accept PUT(X: in ITEM) do
            V:= X;
        end PUT;
        accept GET(X: out ITEM) do
            X:= V;
        end GET;
    end loop;
end BUFFERING;
```

Other tasks may then dispose of or acquire items by calling

```
BUFFERING.PUT( ... );
BUFFERING.GET( ... );
```

Intermediate storage for the item is the variable V. The body of the task is an endless loop which contains an accept statement for PUT followed by one for GET. Thus the task alternately accepts calls of PUT and GET which fill and empty the variable V.

Several different tasks may call PUT and GET and consequently may have to be queued. Every entry has a queue of tasks waiting to call the entry – this queue is processed in a first-in-first-out manner and may, of course, be empty at a particular moment. The number of tasks on the queue of entry E is given by E'COUNT but this attribute may only be used inside the body of the task owning the entry.

An entry may have several corresponding accept statements (usually only one). Each execution of an accept statement removes one task from the queue.

Note the asymmetric naming in a rendezvous. The calling task must name the called task but not vice versa. Moreover, several tasks may call an entry and be queued but a task can only be on one queue at a time.

Entries may be overloaded both with each other and with subprograms and obey the same rules. An entry may be renamed as a procedure

```
procedure WRITE(X: in ITEM) renames BUFFERING.PUT;
```

This mechanism may be useful in avoiding excessive use of the dotted notation. An entry, renamed or not, may be an actual or default generic parameter corresponding to a formal subprogram.

An entry may have no parameters, such as

**entry** SIGNAL;

and it could then be called by

T.SIGNAL;

An accept statement need have no body as in

**accept** SIGNAL;

In such a case the purpose of the call is merely to effect a synchronization and not to pass information. However, an entry without parameters can have an accept statement with a body and vice versa. There is nothing to prevent us writing

```
accept SIGNAL do
    FIRE;
end;
```

in which case the task calling SIGNAL is only allowed to continue after the call of FIRE is completed. We could also have

**accept** PUT(X: ITEM);

although clearly the parameter value is not used.

There are few constraints on the statements in an accept statement. They may include entry calls, subprogram calls, blocks and further accept statements (but not for the same entry or one of the same family – see Section 14.8). On the other hand, an accept statement may not appear in a subprogram body but must be in the sequence of statements of the task, although it could be in a block or other accept statement. The execution of a **return** statement in an accept statement corresponds to reaching the final end and therefore terminates the rendezvous. Similarly to a subprogram body, a **goto** or **exit** statement cannot transfer control out of an accept statement.

A task may call one of its own entries but, of course, will promptly deadlock. This may seem foolish but programming languages allow lots of silly things such as endless loops and so on. We could expect a good compiler to warn us of obvious potential deadlocks.

---

*Exercise 14.2*

**1**　　Write the body of a task whose specification is

```
task BUILD_COMPLEX is
    entry PUT_RL(X: in REAL);
    entry PUT_IM(X: in REAL);
```

```
        entry GET_COMP(X: out COMPLEX);
    end;
```

and which alternately puts together a complex number from calls
of PUT_RL and PUT_IM and then delivers the result on a call of
GET_COMP.

2    Write the body of a task whose specification is

```
        task CHAR_TO_LINE is
            entry PUT(C: in CHARACTER);
            entry GET(L: out LINE);
        end;
```

where

```
        type LINE is array (1 .. 80) of CHARACTER;
```

The task acts as a buffer which alternately builds up a line by
accepting successive calls of PUT and then delivers a complete line
on a call of GET.

---

## 14.3  Timing and scheduling

As we have seen, an Ada program may contain several tasks. Conceptually, it is best to think of these tasks as each having its own personal
processor so that, provided a task is not waiting for something to happen, it
will actually be executing.

In practice, of course, most implementations will not be able to
allocate a unique processor to each task and indeed, in many cases, there
will be only one physical processor. It will then be necessary to allocate the
processor(s) to the tasks that are logically able to execute by some
scheduling algorithm. This can be done in many ways.

One of the simplest mechanisms is to use time slicing. This means
giving the processor to each task in turn for some fixed time interval such as
10 milliseconds. Of course, if a task cannot use its turn (perhaps because it
is held up awaiting a partner in a rendezvous), then a sensible scheduler
would allocate its turn to the next task. Similarly, if a task cannot use all of
its turn then the remaining time could be allocated to another task.

Time slicing is somewhat rudimentary since it treats all tasks
equally. It is often the case that some tasks are more urgent than others
and in the face of a shortage of processing power this equality is a bit
wasteful. The idea of a task having a priority is therefore introduced. A
simple scheduling system would be one where each task had a distinct
priority and the processor would then be given to the highest priority task
which could actually run. Combinations of time slicing and priority
scheduling are also possible. A system might permit several tasks to have
the same priority and time slice between them.

Ada allows various scheduling strategies to be used. If an implementation has the concept of priority, then the priority of a task can be indicated by a pragma appearing somewhere in the task specification as for example

```
task BUFFERING is
    pragma PRIORITY(7);
    entry PUT ...
        ...
    end;
```

In the case of the main program, which, as we have seen, is also considered to be a task, the pragma goes in its outermost declarative part.

The priority must be a static expression of the subtype PRIORITY of the type INTEGER but the actual range of the subtype PRIORITY depends upon the implementation. Note that the priority of a task is static and therefore cannot be changed in the course of execution of the program. A larger priority indicates a higher degree of urgency. Several tasks can have the same priority but on the other hand a task need not have an explicit priority at all.

The effect of priorities on the scheduling of Ada tasks is given by the following rule taken from the *LRM*

'If two tasks with different priorities are both eligible for execution and could sensibly be executed using the same physical processors and the same other processing resources, then it cannot be the case that the task with the lower priority is executing while the task with the higher priority is not.'

Basically this says that scheduling must be preemptive – a higher priority task *always* preempts a lower priority task. This rule has been misinterpreted but AI-32 confirms that preemption is mandatory.

However, this rule says nothing about tasks whose priorities are not defined, nor does it say anything about tasks with the same priority. The implementation is therefore free to do whatever seems appropriate in these cases. Moreover, nothing prevents an implementation from having PRIORITY'FIRST = PRIORITY'LAST in which case all tasks could be time sliced equally and the concept of priority disappears. The rule also contains the phrase 'could sensibly be executed using the same ... processing resources'; this is directed towards distributed systems where it may not be at all sensible for a processor in one part of the system to be used to execute a task in a different part of the system.

In the case of a rendezvous (and activation, to be discussed later), a complication arises because two tasks are involved. If both tasks have explicit priorities, the rendezvous is executed with the higher priority. If only one task has an explicit priority, then the rendezvous is executed with at least that priority. If neither task has a defined priority then the priority of the rendezvous is not defined. Of course, if the accept statement contains a further entry call or accept statement, then the rules are applied once more.

The rendezvous rules ensure that a high priority task is not held up just because it is engaged in a rendezvous with a low priority task. On the other hand, the order of accepting the tasks in an entry queue is always first-in-first-out and is not affected by priorities. If a high priority task wishes to guard against being held up because of lower priority tasks in the same entry queue, it can always use timed out or conditional calls as we shall see in the next section.

The use of priorities needs care. They are intended as a means of adjusting relative degrees of urgency and should not be used for synchronization. It should not be assumed that the execution of task A precludes the execution of task B just because task A has a higher priority than task B. There might be several processors or later program maintenance might result in a change of priorities because of different realtime requirements. Synchronization should be done with the rendezvous and priorities should be avoided except for fine tuning of responsiveness.

A task may be held up for various reasons; it might be waiting for a partner in a rendezvous or for a dependent task to terminate. It can also be held up by executing a delay statement such as

**delay** 3.0;

This suspends the task (or main program) executing the statement for three seconds. The expression after the reserved word **delay** is of a predefined fixed point type DURATION and gives the period in seconds. (The *LRM* says the task is suspended for 'at least' the duration specified. This is solely because, after the expiry of the interval, there might not be a processor immediately available to execute the task since in the meantime a higher priority task might have obtained control. It does not mean that the scheduler can leave the suspended task rotting indefinitely. If it has a higher priority than a task running when the interval expires then it will preempt.)

The type DURATION is a fixed point type so that the addition of durations can be done without systematic loss of accuracy. If we add together two fixed point model numbers, we always get another model number; this does not apply to floating point. On the other hand, we need to express fractions of a second in a convenient way and so the use of a real type rather than an integer type is much more satisfactory.

Delays can be more easily expressed by using suitable constant declarations, thus

```
SECONDS: constant DURATION:= 1.0;
MINUTES: constant DURATION:= 60.0;
HOURS: constant DURATION:= 3600.0;
```

We can then write for example

**delay** 2*HOURS+40*MINUTES;

in which the expression uses the rule that a fixed point value can be multiplied by an integer giving a result of the same fixed point type.

A delay statement with a zero or negative argument has no effect.
Although the type DURATION is implementation defined we are
guaranteed that it will allow durations (both positive and negative) of up to
at least one day (86 400 seconds). Delays of more than a day (which are
unusual) would have to be programmed with a loop. At the other end of
the scale, the smallest value of DURATION, that is DURATION'SMALL, is
guaranteed to be not greater than 20 milliseconds. This should not be
confused with SYSTEM'TICK which gives the basic clock cycle and is, for
example, and as confirmed by AI-201, the accuracy with which a delay
statement must be executed (as opposed to being requested).

More sophisticated timing operations can be performed by using the
predefined package CALENDAR whose specification is

```
package CALENDAR is

    type TIME is private;

    subtype YEAR_NUMBER is INTEGER range 1901 .. 2099;
    subtype MONTH_NUMBER is INTEGER range 1 .. 12;
    subtype DAY_NUMBER is INTEGER range 1 .. 31;
    subtype DAY_DURATION is DURATION range 0.0 .. 86_400.0;

    function CLOCK return TIME;

    function YEAR(DATE: TIME) return YEAR_NUMBER;
    function MONTH(DATE: TIME) return MONTH_NUMBER;
    function DAY(DATE: TIME) return DAY_NUMBER;
    function SECONDS(DATE: TIME) return DAY_DURATION;

    procedure SPLIT(DATE: in TIME;
                    YEAR: out YEAR_NUMBER;
                    MONTH: out MONTH_NUMBER;
                    DAY: out DAY_NUMBER;
                    SECONDS: out DAY_DURATION);

    function TIME_OF(YEAR: YEAR_NUMBER;
                    MONTH: MONTH_NUMBER;
                    DAY: DAY_NUMBER;
                    SECONDS: DAY_DURATION:= 0.0)
                                            return TIME;

    function "+" (LEFT: TIME; RIGHT: DURATION) return TIME;
    function "+" (LEFT: DURATION; RIGHT: TIME) return TIME;
    function "−" (LEFT: TIME; RIGHT: DURATION) return TIME;
    function "−" (LEFT: TIME; RIGHT: TIME) return DURATION;
    function "<" (LEFT, RIGHT: TIME) return BOOLEAN;
    function "<=" (LEFT, RIGHT: TIME) return BOOLEAN;
    function ">" (LEFT, RIGHT: TIME) return BOOLEAN;
    function ">=" (LEFT, RIGHT: TIME) return BOOLEAN;
```

```
        TIME_ERROR: exception;
                        -- can be raised by TIME_OF, +, and -

    private
        -- implementation dependent
    end CALENDAR;
```

A value of the private type TIME is a combined time and date; it can be decomposed into the year, month, day and the duration since midnight of the day concerned by the procedure SPLIT. Alternatively the functions YEAR, MONTH, DAY and SECONDS may be used to obtain the individual values. On the other hand, the function TIME_OF can be used to build a value of TIME from the four constituents; the seconds parameter has a default of zero. Note the subtypes YEAR_NUMBER, MONTH_NUMBER and DAY_NUMBER; the range of YEAR_NUMBER is such that the leap year calculation is simplified. The exception TIME_ERROR is raised if the parameters of TIME_OF satisfy the constraints but nevertheless do not form a proper date. A careful distinction must be made between TIME and DURATION. TIME is absolute but DURATION is relative.

The current TIME is returned by a call of the function CLOCK. The result is, of course, returned in an indivisible way and there is no risk of getting the time of day and the date inconsistent around midnight as there would be if there were separate functions delivering the individual components of the current time and date.

The various overloadings of "+", "−" and the relational operators allow us to add, subtract and compare times and durations as appropriate. Attempts to create a time outside the allowed range of years or to create a duration outside the implemented range will result in TIME_ERROR being raised. Note the strange formal parameter names LEFT and RIGHT; these are the normal names for the parameters of the predefined operators in the package STANDARD.

As an example of the use of the package CALENDAR suppose we wish a task to call a procedure ACTION at regular intervals, every five minutes perhaps. Our first attempt might be to write

```
    loop
        delay 5*MINUTES;
        ACTION;
    end loop;
```

However, this is unsatisfactory for various reasons. First, we have not taken account of the time of execution of the procedure ACTION and the overhead of the loop itself, and secondly, we have seen that a delay statement sets a minimum delay only (since a higher priority task may retain the processor on the expiry of the delay). Furthermore, we might get preempted by a higher priority task at any time anyway. So we will inevitably get a cumulative timing drift. This can be overcome by writing for example

```
declare
   use CALENDAR;
   INTERVAL: constant DURATION:= 5*MINUTES;
   NEXT_TIME: TIME:= FIRST_TIME;
begin
   loop
      delay NEXT_TIME - CLOCK;
      ACTION;
      NEXT_TIME:= NEXT_TIME + INTERVAL;
   end loop;
end;
```

In this formulation NEXT_TIME contains the time when ACTION is next to be called; its initial value is in FIRST_TIME and it is updated exactly on each iteration by adding INTERVAL. The delay statement is then used to delay by the difference between NEXT_TIME and the current time obtained by calling CLOCK. This solution will have no cumulative drift provided the mean duration of ACTION plus the overheads of the loop and updating NEXT_TIME and so on do not exceed INTERVAL. Of course, there may be a local drift if a particular call of ACTION takes a long time or other tasks temporarily use the processors. There is one other condition that must be satisfied for the required timing to be obtained: the interval has to be a safe number.

---

*Exercise 14.3*

1    Write a generic procedure to call a procedure regularly. The
     generic parameters should be the procedure to be called, the time
     of the first call, the interval and the number of calls. If the time
     of the first call passed as parameter is in the past use the current
     time as the first time.

2    What is the least number of bits required to implement the type
     DURATION?

---

## 14.4  Simple select statements

The select statement allows a task to select from one of several possible rendezvous.

Consider the problem of protecting a variable V from uncontrolled access. We might consider using a package and two procedures READ and WRITE.

```
package PROTECTED_VARIABLE is
   procedure READ(X: out ITEM);
   procedure WRITE(X: in ITEM);
end;
```

```
package body PROTECTED_VARIABLE is
    V: ITEM;

    procedure READ(X: out ITEM) is
    begin
        X:= V;
    end;

    procedure WRITE(X: in ITEM) is
    begin
        V:= X;
    end;

begin
    V:= initial value;
end PROTECTED_VARIABLE;
```

However this is generally unsatisfactory. For one thing, the initial value is set in a rather arbitrary way. It would be better if somehow we could ensure that a call of WRITE had to be done first. We could, of course, have an internal state marker and raise an exception if READ is called first but this complicates the interface. The major problem, however, is that nothing prevents different tasks in our system from calling READ and WRITE simultaneously and thereby causing interference. As a more specific example, suppose that the type ITEM is a record giving the coordinates of an aircraft or ship

```
type ITEM is
    record
        X_COORD: REAL;
        Y_COORD: REAL;
    end record;
```

Suppose that a task A acquires pairs of values and uses a call of WRITE to store them into V and that another task B calls READ whenever it needs the latest position. Now assume that A is halfway through executing WRITE when it is interrupted by task B which promptly calls READ. It is clear that B could get a value consisting of the new x-coordinate and the old y-coordinate which would no doubt represent a location where the vessel had never been. The use of such inconsistent data for calculating the heading of the vessel from regularly read pairs of readings would obviously lead to inaccuracies.

The reader may wonder how the task A could be interrupted by task B anyway. In a single processor system with time slicing it may merely have been that B's turn came at an unfortunate moment. Alternatively B might have a higher priority than A; if B had been waiting for time to elapse before taking the next reading by obeying a delay statement, then A might be allowed to execute and B's delay might expire just at the wrong moment. In practical realtime situations things are always happening at the wrong moment!

The proper solution is to use a task rather than a package, and entry calls rather than procedure calls. Consider now

```
task PROTECTED_VARIABLE is
    entry READ(X: out ITEM);
    entry WRITE(X: in ITEM);
end;

task body PROTECTED_VARIABLE is
    V: ITEM;
begin
    accept WRITE(X: in ITEM) do
        V:= X;
    end;
    loop
        select
            accept READ(X: out ITEM) do
                X:= V;
            end;
        or
            accept WRITE(X: in ITEM) do
                V:= X;
            end;
        end select;
    end loop;
end PROTECTED_VARIABLE;
```

The body of the task starts with an accept statement for the entry WRITE; this ensures that the first call accepted is for WRITE so that there is no risk of the variable being read before it is assigned a value. Of course, a task could call READ before any task had called WRITE but the calls of READ will be queued until a call of WRITE has been accepted.

Having accepted a call of WRITE, the task enters an endless loop containing a single select statement. A select statement starts with the reserved word **select** and finishes with **end select**; it contains two or more alternatives separated by **or**. In this example each alternative consists of an accept statement – one for READ and one for WRITE.

When we encounter the select statement various possibilities have to be considered according to whether calls of READ or WRITE or both or neither have been made. We consider these in turn.

- If neither READ nor WRITE has been called then the task is suspended until one or the other is called and then the corresponding accept statement is obeyed.

- If one or more calls of READ are queued but there are no queued calls of WRITE then the first call of READ is accepted and vice versa with the roles of READ and WRITE reversed.

- If calls of both READ and WRITE are queued then an arbitrary choice is made.

Thus each execution of the select statement results in one of its branches being obeyed and one call of READ or WRITE being dealt with. We can think of the task as corresponding to a person serving two queues of customers waiting for two different services. If only one queue has customers then the server deals with it; if there are no customers then the server waits for the first irrespective of the service required; if both queues exist, the server rather capriciously serves either and makes an arbitrary choice each time.

So each time round the loop the task PROTECTED_VARIABLE will accept a call of READ or WRITE according to the demands upon it. It thus prevents multiple access to the variable V since it can only deal with one call at a time but does not impose any order upon the calls. Compare this with the task BUFFERING in Section 14.2 where an order was imposed upon the calls of PUT and GET.

Another point to notice is that this example illustrates a case where we have two accept statements for the same entry (WRITE). It so happens that the bodies are identical but they need not be.

The reader may wonder what the phrase 'arbitrary choice' means when deciding which alternative to choose. The intent is that there is no rule and the implementor is free to choose some efficient mechanism that nevertheless introduces an adequate degree of nondeterminism so that the various queues are treated fairly and none gets starved. A random choice with equal probability would be acceptable but hard to implement efficiently. The most important point is that a program must not rely on the selection algorithm used; if it does, it is erroneous.

A more complex form of select statement is illustrated by the classic problem of the bounded buffer. This is similar to the problem in Section 14.2 except that up to N items can be buffered. A solution is

```
task BUFFERING is
    entry PUT(X: in ITEM);
    entry GET(X: out ITEM);
end;

task body BUFFERING is
    N: constant:= 8;          -- for instance
    A: array (1 .. N) of ITEM;
    I, J: INTEGER range 1 .. N:= 1;
    COUNT: INTEGER range 0 .. N:= 0;
begin
    loop
        select
            when COUNT < N =>
            accept PUT(X: in ITEM) do
                A(I):= X;
            end;
            I:= I mod N+1; COUNT:= COUNT+1;
        or
            when COUNT > 0 =>
            accept GET(X: out ITEM) do
```

```
            X:= A(J);
         end;
         J:= J mod N+1; COUNT:= COUNT-1;
      end select;
   end loop;
end BUFFERING;
```

The buffer is the array A of length N which is a number set to 8 in this example. The variables I and J index the next free and last used locations of the buffer respectively and COUNT is the number of locations of the buffer which are full. Not only is it convenient to have COUNT, but it is also necessary in order to distinguish between a completely full and completely empty buffer which both have I = J. The buffer is used cyclically so I need not be greater than J. The situation in Figure 14.1 shows a partly filled buffer with COUNT = 5, I = 3 and J = 6. The portion of the buffer in use is shaded. The variables I and J are both initialized to 1 and COUNT is initialized to 0 so that the buffer is initially empty.

The objective of the task is to allow items to be added to and removed from the buffer in a first-in-first-out manner but to prevent the buffer from being overfilled or under-emptied. This is done with a more general form of select statement which includes the use of guarding conditions.

Each branch of the select statement commences with

**when** condition =>

and is then followed by an accept statement and then some further statements. Each time the select statement is encountered, all the guarding conditions are evaluated. The behaviour is then as for a select statement without guards but containing only those branches for which the conditions were true. So a branch will be taken and the corresponding rendezvous performed. After the accept statement a branch may contain further statements. These are executed by the server task as part of the select statement but outside the rendezvous.

So the guarding conditions are conditions which have to be true before a service can be offered. The accept statement represents the rendezvous with the customer and the giving of the service. The statements after the accept statement represent bookkeeping actions performed as a consequence of giving the service and which can be done after the customer has left but, of course, need to be done before the next customer is served.

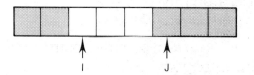

**Figure 14.1**   The bounded buffer.

In our example the condition for being able to accept a call of PUT is simply that the buffer must not be full; this is the condition COUNT < N. Similarly, we can accept a call of GET provided that the buffer is not empty; this is the condition COUNT > 0. The statements in the bodies of the accept statements copy the item to or from the buffer. After the rendezvous is completed, the index I or J as appropriate and COUNT are updated to reflect the change of state. Note the use of **mod** to update I and J in a cyclic manner.

Thus we see that the first time the select statement is executed, the condition COUNT < N is true but COUNT > 0 is false. Hence, only a call of PUT can be accepted. This puts the first item in the buffer. The next time both conditions will be true so either PUT or GET can be accepted, adding a further item or removing the one item. And so it goes on; allowing items to be added or removed with one of the guarding conditions becoming false in the extreme situations and thereby preventing overfilling or under-emptying.

A few points need emphasis. The guards are re-evaluated at the beginning of each execution of the select statement (but their order of evaluation is not defined). An absent guard is taken as true. If all guards turn out to be false then the exception PROGRAM_ERROR is raised. It should be realized that a guard need not still be true when the corresponding rendezvous is performed because it might use global variables and therefore be changed by another task. Later we will discuss an example where guards could change unexpectedly. In the example here, of course, nothing can go wrong. One guard is always true, so PROGRAM_ERROR can never be raised and they both only involve the local variable COUNT and so cannot be changed between their evaluation and the rendezvous.

For our next example consider again the task PROTECTED_VARIABLE. This allowed either read or write access but only one at a time. This is somewhat severe; the usual classical problem is to allow only one writer of course, but to allow several readers together. A simple solution is shown below. It takes the form of a package containing a local task.

```
package READER_WRITER is
    procedure READ(X: out ITEM);
    procedure WRITE(X: in ITEM);
end;

package body READER_WRITER is
    V: ITEM;

    task CONTROL is
        entry START;
        entry STOP:
        entry WRITE(X: in ITEM);
    end;

    task body CONTROL is
        READERS: INTEGER:= 0;
    begin
```

```
        accept WRITE(X: in ITEM) do
           V:= X;
        end;
        loop
           select
              accept START;
              READERS:= READERS+1;
           or
              accept STOP;
              READERS:= READERS-1;
           or
              when READERS = 0 =>
              accept WRITE(X: in ITEM) do
                 V:= X;
              end;
           end select;
        end loop;
     end CONTROL;

     procedure READ(X: out ITEM) is
     begin
        CONTROL.START;
        X:= V;
        CONTROL.STOP;
     end READ;

     procedure WRITE(X: in ITEM) is
     begin
        CONTROL.WRITE(X);
     end WRITE;

  end READER_WRITER;
```

The task CONTROL has three entries: WRITE to do the writing and START and STOP associated with reading. A call of START indicates a wish to start reading and a call of STOP indicates that reading has finished. The task is wrapped up in a package because we wish to provide multiple reading access. This can be done by providing a procedure READ which can then be called reentrantly; it also enforces the protocol of calling START and then STOP.

So the whole thing is a package containing the variable V, the task CONTROL and the access procedures READ and WRITE. As stated, READ enforces the desired calls of START and STOP around the statement X:= V; the procedure WRITE merely calls the entry WRITE.

The task CONTROL declares a variable READERS which indicates how many readers are present. As before it begins with an accept statement for WRITE to ensure that the variable is initialized and then enters a loop containing a select statement. This has three branches, one for each entry. On a call of START or STOP the count of number of readers is incremented or decremented. A call of WRITE can only be accepted if the condition

READERS = 0 is true. Hence writing when readers are present is forbidden. Of course, since the task CONTROL actually does the writing, multiple writing is prevented and, moreover, it cannot at the same time accept calls of START and so reading is not possible when writing is in progress. However, multiple reading is allowed as we have seen.

Although the above solution does fulfil the general conditions, it is not really satisfactory. A steady stream of readers will completely block out a writer. Since writing is probably rather important, this is not acceptable. An obvious improvement would be to disallow further reading if one or more writers are waiting. We can do this by using the attribute WRITE'COUNT in a guard so that the select statement now becomes

```
select
    when WRITE'COUNT = 0 =>
    accept START;
    READERS:= READERS+1;
or
    accept STOP;
    READERS:= READERS-1;
or
    when READERS = 0 =>
    accept WRITE(X: in ITEM) do
        V:= X;
    end;
end select;
```

The attribute WRITE'COUNT is the number of tasks currently on the queue for the entry WRITE. The use of the count attribute in guards needs care. It gives the value when the guard is evaluated and can well change before a rendezvous is accepted. It could increase because another task joins the queue – that would not matter in this example. But, as we shall see later, it could also decrease unexpectedly and this would indeed give problems. We will return to this example in a moment.

---

*Exercise 14.4*

**1**    Rewrite the body of the task BUILD_COMPLEX of Exercise 14.2(**1**) so that the calls of PUT_RL and PUT_IM are accepted in any order.

---

## 14.5  Timed and conditional rendezvous

There are also various other forms of select statement. It is possible for one or more of the branches to start with a delay statement rather than an accept statement. Consider

```
select
    accept READ( ... ) do
        ...
```

```
        end;
    or
        accept WRITE( ... ) do
            ...
        end;
    or
        delay 10*MINUTES;
        -- time out statements
    end select;
```

If neither a call of READ nor WRITE is received within ten minutes, then the
third branch is taken and the statements following the delay are executed.
The task might decide that since its services are no longer apparently
required it can do something else or maybe it can be interpreted as an
emergency. In a process control system we might be awaiting an acknowledgement from the operator that some action has been taken and after a
suitable interval take our own emergency action

```
    OPERATOR.CALL("PUT OUT FIRE");

    select
        accept ACKNOWLEDGE;
    or
        delay 1*MINUTES;
        FIRE_BRIGADE.CALL;
    end select;
```

A delay alternative can be guarded and indeed there could be
several in a select statement although clearly only the shortest one with a
true guard can be taken. It should be realized that if one of the accept
statements is obeyed then any delay is cancelled – we can think of a delay
alternative as waiting for a rendezvous with the clock. A delay is, of
course, set from the start of the select statement and reset each time the
select statement is encountered. Finally, note that it is the start of the
rendezvous that matters rather than its completion as far as the time out is
concerned.
      Another form of select statement is one with an else part. Consider

```
    select
        accept READ( ... ) do
            ...
        end;
    or
        accept WRITE( ... ) do
            ...
        end;
    else
        -- alternative statements
    end select;
```

In this case the final branch is preceded by **else** rather than **or** and consists of just a sequence of statements. The else branch is taken at once if none of the other branches can be immediately accepted. A select statement with an else part is rather like one with a branch starting **delay** 0.0; it times out at once if there are no customers to be dealt with. A select statement cannot have both an else part and delay alternatives.

There is a subtle distinction between an accept statement starting a branch of a select and an accept statement anywhere else. In the first case the accept statement is bound up with the workings of the select statement and is to some extent conditional. In the second case, once encountered, it will be obeyed come what may. The same distinction applies to a delay statement starting a branch of a select statement and one elsewhere. Thus if we change the **or** to **else** in our emergency action to give

```
select
    accept ACKNOWLEDGE;
else
    delay 1*MINUTES;
    FIRE_BRIGADE.CALL;
end select;
```

then the status of the delay is quite different. It just happens to be one of a sequence of statements and will be obeyed in the usual way. So if we cannot accept a call of ACKNOWLEDGE at once, we immediately take the else part. The fact that the first statement is a delay is fortuitous – we immediately delay for one minute and then call the fire brigade. There is no time out. We see therefore that the simple change from **or** to **else** causes a dramatic difference in meaning which may not be immediately obvious; so take care!

If a select statement has an else part then PROGRAM_ERROR can never be raised. The else part cannot be guarded and so will always be taken if all branches have guards and they all turn out to be false.

There are two other forms of select statement which are rather different; they concern a single entry call rather than one or more accept statements. The timed out entry call allows a sequence of statements to be taken as an alternative to an entry call if it is not accepted within the specified duration. Thus

```
select
    OPERATOR.CALL("PUT OUT FIRE");
or
    delay 1*MINUTES;
    FIRE_BRIGADE.CALL;
end select;
```

will call the fire brigade if the operator does not accept the call within one minute. Again, it is the start of the rendezvous that matters rather than its completion. Finally there is the conditional entry call. Thus

```
select
    OPERATOR.CALL("PUT OUT FIRE");
else
    FIRE_BRIGADE.CALL;
end select;
```

will call the fire brigade if the operator cannot immediately accept the call.

The timed out and conditional entry calls are quite different to the general select statement. They concern only a single unguarded call and so these select statements always have exactly two branches – one with the entry call and the other with the alternative sequence of statements. Timed out and conditional calls apply only to entries. They do not apply to procedures or even to entries renamed as procedures.

Timed out and conditional calls are useful if a task does not want to be unduly delayed when a server task is busy. They correspond to a customer in a shop giving up and leaving the queue after waiting for a time or, in the conditional case, a highly impatient customer leaving at once if not immediately served.

Timed out calls, however, need some care particularly if the COUNT attribute is used. A decision based on the value of that attribute may be invalidated because of a timed out call unexpectedly removing a task from an entry queue. Consider for example the package READER_WRITER. As it stands the entry calls cannot be timed out because they are encapsulated in the procedures READ and WRITE. However, we might decide to provide further overloadings of these procedures in order to provide timed out facilities. We might add, for example

```
procedure WRITE(X: in ITEM; T: DURATION; OK: out BOOLEAN) is
begin
    select
        CONTROL.WRITE(X);
        OK:= TRUE;
    or
        delay T;
        OK:= FALSE;
    end select;
end WRITE;
```

Unfortunately this is invalid. Suppose that one writer is waiting (so that WRITE'COUNT = 1) but the call is timed out between the evaluation of the guards and the execution of an accept statement. There are two cases to consider according to the value of READERS. If READERS = 0, then no task can call STOP since there are no current readers; a call of START cannot be accepted because its guard was false and the expected call of WRITE will not occur because it has been timed out; the result is that all new readers will be unnecessarily blocked until a new writer arrives. On the other hand, if READERS > 0, then although further calls of WRITE correctly cannot be accepted, nevertheless further calls of START are unnecessarily delayed until an existing reader calls STOP despite there being no waiting writers. We therefore seek an alternative solution.

The original reason for using WRITE'COUNT was to prevent readers from overtaking waiting writers. One possibility in cases of this sort is to make all the customers call a common entry to start with. This ensures that they are dealt with in order. This entry call can be parameterized to indicate the service required and the callers can then be placed on a secondary queue if necessary. This technique is illustrated by the solution which now follows. The package specification is as before.

```
package body READER_WRITER is
    V: ITEM;
    type SERVICE is (READ, WRITE);

    task CONTROL is
        entry START(S: SERVICE);
        entry STOP_READ;
        entry WRITE;
        entry STOP_WRITE;
    end CONTROL;

    task body CONTROL is
        READERS: INTEGER:= 0;
        WRITERS: INTEGER:= 0;
    begin
        loop
            select
                when WRITERS = 0 =>
                accept START(S: SERVICE) do
                    case S is
                        when READ =>
                            READERS:= READERS+1;
                        when WRITE =>
                            WRITERS:= 1;
                    end case;
                end START;
            or
                accept STOP_READ;
                READERS:= READERS-1;
            or
                when READERS = 0 =>
                accept WRITE;
            or
                accept STOP_WRITE;
                WRITERS:= 0;
            end select;
        end loop;
    end CONTROL;
```

```
procedure READ(X: out ITEM) is
begin
   CONTROL.START(READ);
   X:= V;
   CONTROL.STOP_READ;
end READ;

procedure WRITE(X: in ITEM) is
begin
   CONTROL.START(WRITE);
   CONTROL.WRITE;
   V:= X;
   CONTROL.STOP_WRITE;
end WRITE;

end READER_WRITER;
```

We have introduced a variable WRITERS to indicate how many writers are
in the system; it can only take values of 0 and 1. All requests initially call
the common entry START but have to wait until there are no writers. The
count of readers or writers is then updated as appropriate. In the case of a
reader it can then go ahead as before and finishes by calling STOP_READ.
A writer, on the other hand, must wait until there are no readers; it does
this by calling WRITE and then finally calls STOP_WRITE in order that the
control task can set WRITERS back to zero. Separating STOP_WRITE from
WRITE enables us to cope with time outs as we shall see; we also take the
opportunity to place the actual writing statement in the procedure WRITE
so that it is similar to the read case.

In this solution, the variable WRITERS performs the function of
WRITE'COUNT in the previous but incorrect solution. By counting for
ourselves we can keep the situation under control. The calls of START and
WRITE can now be timed out provided that we always call STOP_READ
or STOP_WRITE once a call of START has been accepted. The details of
suitable overloadings of READ and WRITE to provide timed out calls are left
as an exercise.

Note that the above solution has ignored the problem of ensuring
that the first call is a write. This can be catered for in various ways, by using
a special initial entry, for instance, or by placing the readers on a second
auxiliary queue so that they are forced to wait for the first writer.

We finish this section by showing a rather slick alternative to the above

```
task CONTROL is
   entry START(S: SERVICE);
   entry STOP;
end CONTROL;

task body CONTROL is
   READERS: INTEGER:= 0;
begin
   loop
      select
```

```
            accept START(S: SERVICE) do
              case S is
                when READ =>
                  READERS:= READERS+1;
                when WRITE =>
                  while READERS > 0 loop
                    accept STOP;          -- from readers
                    READERS:= READERS-1
                  end loop;
              end case;
            end START;

            if READERS = 0 then
              accept STOP;                -- from the writer
            end if;
          or
            accept STOP;                  -- from a reader
            READERS:= READERS-1;
          end select;
        end loop;
      end CONTROL;

      procedure READ(X: out ITEM) is
      begin
        CONTROL.START(READ);
        X:= V;
        CONTROL.STOP;
      end READ;

      procedure WRITE(X: in ITEM) is
      begin
        CONTROL.START(WRITE);
        V:= X;
        CONTROL.STOP;
      end WRITE;
```

The essence of this solution is that the writer waits in the rendezvous for any readers to finish and the whole of the writing process is dealt with in the one branch of the select statement. No guards are required at all and the control task only has two entries. A common STOP entry is possible because the structure is such that each accept statement deals with only one category of caller. A minor disadvantage of the solution is that less flexible timed calls are possible. Once the writer has been accepted by the call of START, he is committed to wait for all the readers to finish.

---

*Exercise 14.5*

1    Write additional procedures READ and WRITE for the
     (penultimate) package READER_WRITER in order to provide

timed out calls. Take care with the procedure WRITE so that the calls of the entries START and WRITE are both timed out appropriately.

---

## 14.6 Task types and activation

It is sometimes useful to have several similar but distinct tasks. Moreover, it is often not possible to predict the number of such tasks required. For example, we might wish to create distinct tasks to follow each aircraft within the zone of control of an air traffic control system. Clearly, such tasks need to be created and disposed of in a dynamic way not related to the static structure of the program.

A template for similar tasks is provided by a task type declaration. This is identical to the simple task declarations we have seen so far except that the reserved word **type** follows **task** in the specification. Thus we may write

```
task type T is
    entry E( ... );
end T;
```

```
task body T is
    ...
end T;
```

The task body follows the same rules as before.

To create an actual task we use the normal form of object declaration. So we can write

```
X: T;
```

and this declares a task X of type T. In fact the simple form of task declaration we have been using so far such as

```
task SIMPLE is
    ...
end SIMPLE;
```

is exactly equivalent to writing

```
task type anon is
    ...
end anon;
```

followed by

```
SIMPLE: anon;
```

Task objects can be used in structures in the usual way. Thus we can declare arrays of tasks

```
AOT: array (1 .. 10) of T;
```

records containing tasks

```
type REC is
    record
        CT: T;
        ...
    end record;
R: REC;
```

and so on.

The entries of such tasks are called using the task object name; thus we write

```
X.E( ... );
AOT(I).E( ... );
R.CT.E( ... );
```

A most important consideration is that task objects are not variables but behave as constants. A task object declaration creates a task which is permanently bound to the object. Hence assignment is not allowed for task types and nor are the comparisons for equality and inequality. A task type is therefore another form of limited type and so could be used as the actual type corresponding to a formal generic parameter specified as limited private and as the actual type in a private part corresponding to a limited private type. Although task objects behave as constants, they cannot be declared as such since a constant declaration needs an explicit initial value. Subprogram parameters may be of task types; they are always effectively passed by reference and so the formal and actual parameters always refer to the same task. As in the case of other limited types, outside their defining package, parameters of mode **out** are not allowed; of course there is no defining package in the case of task types anyway.

In Section 14.1 we briefly introduced the idea of dependency. Each task is dependent on some unit and there is a general rule that a unit cannot be left until all tasks dependent upon it have terminated.

A task declared as a task object (or using the abbreviated simple form) is dependent upon the enclosing block, subprogram or task body in which it is declared. Inner packages do not count in this rule – this is because a package is merely a passive scope wall and has no dynamic life. If a task is declared in a package (or nested packages) then the task is dependent upon the block, subprogram or task body in which the package or packages are themselves declared. For completeness, a task declared in a library package is said to depend on that package and we refer to it as a library task. After termination of the main program, the main environment task (which calls the main program) must wait for all library tasks to terminate. Only then does the program as a whole terminate (AI-222).

We saw earlier that a task becomes active only when the declaring unit reaches the **begin** following the declaration. The execution of a task can be thought of as a two-stage process. The first stage, known as activation, consists of the elaboration of the declarations of the task body whereas the second stage consists, of course, of the execution of its statements. During the activation stage the parent unit is not allowed to proceed. If several tasks are declared in a unit, then their activations and the subsequent execution of their statements occur independently and in parallel. But it is only when the activation of all the tasks is complete that the parent unit can continue with the execution of the statements following the **begin** in parallel with the new tasks.

Note that the activation of a task (like the rendezvous) involves two tasks: the parent and itself. Similar priority rules apply as for the rendezvous so that the activation occurs at the higher of the priority of the task and that of its parent (if defined) and so on (AI-288).

The activation process is depicted in Figure 14.2 which illustrates the behaviour of a block containing the declarations of two tasks A and B

```
declare
    ...
    A: T;
    B: T;
    ...
begin
    ...
end;
```

Time flows from left to right and a solid line indicates that a unit is actively doing something whereas a dashed line indicates that it exists but is suspended.

For the sake of illustration, we show task A finishing its activation after task B so that the parent resumes execution when task A enters its execution stage. We also show task A finishing its execution and therefore becoming completed and terminated before task B. The parent is shown reaching its **end** and therefore completing execution of the block after task A has terminated but before task B has terminated. The parent is

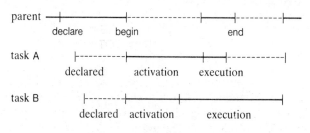

**Figure 14.2**   Task activation.

therefore suspended until task B is terminated when it can then resume execution with the statements following the block.

The reason for treating task activation in this way concerns exceptions. The reader may recall that an exception raised during the elaboration of declarations is not handled at that level but immediately propagated. So an exception raised in the declarations in a new task could not be handled by that task at all. However, since it is clearly desirable that some means be provided for detecting such an exception, it is obvious that an exception has to be raised in the parent unit. In fact the predefined exception TASKING_ERROR is raised irrespective of the original exception. It would clearly make life rather difficult if this exception were raised in the parent unit after it had moved on in parallel and so it is held up until all the new tasks have been activated. The exception TASKING_ERROR is then raised in the parent unit as soon as it attempts to move on from the **begin**. Note that if several of the new tasks raise exceptions during activation then TASKING_ERROR is only raised once. Such tasks become completed (not terminated) and do not affect sibling tasks being simultaneously activated.

The other thing that can go wrong is that an exception can occur in the declarations of the parent unit itself. In this case any new tasks which have been declared (but of course will not have been activated because the parent unit has not yet reached its **begin**) will automatically become terminated and are never activated at all.

Task objects can be declared in a package and although not dependent on the package are nevertheless set active at the **begin** of the package body. If the package body has no initialization statements and therefore no **begin**, then a null initialization statement is assumed. Worse, if a package has no body, then a body with just a null initialization statement is assumed. So the task CONTROL in the package READER_WRITER of the previous section is set active at the end of the declaration of the package body.

Tasks can also be created through access types. We can write

**type** REF_T **is access** T;

and then we can create a task using an allocator in the usual way

RX: REF_T:= **new** T;

The type REF_T is a normal access type and so assignment and equality comparisons of objects of the type are allowed. The entry E of the task accessed by RX can be called as expected by

RX.E( ... );

Tasks created through access types obey slightly different rules for activation and dependency. They commence activation immediately upon evaluation of the allocator whether it occurs in a sequence of statements or in an initial value – we do not wait until the ensuing **begin**. Furthermore, such tasks are not dependent upon the unit where they are created but are dependent upon the block, subprogram body or task body containing the declaration of the access type itself. The strong analogies between tasks declared as objects and those created through an allocator are revealed when we consider tasks which are components of a composite object.

Suppose we have the following somewhat artificial type

```
type R is
    record
        A: T;
        I: INTEGER:= E;
        B: T;
    end record;
```

where A and B are components of some task type T and E is the default initial expression for the component I.

If we declare an object X of type R thus

```
declare
    X: R;
begin
```

then it is much as if we declared the individual objects

```
declare
    XA: T;
    XI: INTEGER:= E;
    XB: T;
begin
```

using the rules explained above.

Now suppose we have an access type

```
type REF_R is access R;
```

and create an object using an allocator

```
RR: REF_R:= new R;
```

The first thing that happens is that the various components are declared and the initial expression is evaluated and assigned to RR.I. It is only when this has been done that activation of the tasks RR.A and RR.B can commence; in a sense we wait until reaching **end record** by analogy with waiting until we reach **begin** in the case of directly declared objects. The component tasks are then activated in parallel but the parent unit is suspended and the access value is not returned until all the activations are complete just as we could not move past the **begin**. Similarly, if an exception is raised by the activation of one or both component tasks, then, on return from the allocator, TASKING_ERROR is raised just once in the parent unit. Such rogue tasks will then become completed but will not interfere with any other sibling component tasks. Finally, if the evaluation of E raises an exception in the parent unit then the component tasks will automatically become terminated without even being activated.

The reader will probably feel that the activation mechanism is somewhat elaborate. However, in practice, the details will rarely need to be considered. They are mentioned in order to show that the mechanism is well defined rather than because of their everyday importance.

Note that entries in a task can be called as soon as it is declared and even before activation commences – the call will just be queued. However, situations in which this is sensibly possible are rare.

An interesting use of task types is for the creation of agents. An agent is a task that does something on behalf of another task. As an example suppose a task SERVER provides some service that is asked for by calling an entry REQUEST. Suppose also that it may take SERVER some time to provide the service so that it is reasonable for the calling task USER to go away and do something else while waiting for the answer to be prepared. There are various ways in which the USER could expect to collect his answer. He could call another entry ENQUIRE; the SERVER task would need some means of recognizing the caller – he could do this by issuing a key on the call of REQUEST and insisting that it be presented again when calling ENQUIRE. This corresponds to taking something to be repaired, being given a ticket and then having to exchange it when the repaired item is collected later. An alternative approach which avoids the issue of keys, is to create an agent. This corresponds to leaving your address and having the repaired item mailed back to you. We will now illustrate this approach.

First of all we declare a task type as follows

```
task type MAILBOX is
    entry DEPOSIT(X: in ITEM);
    entry COLLECT(X: out ITEM);
end;

task body MAILBOX is
    LOCAL: ITEM;
begin
    accept DEPOSIT(X: in ITEM) do
        LOCAL:= X;
    end;
    accept COLLECT(X: out ITEM) do
        X:= LOCAL;
    end;
end MAILBOX;
```

A task of this type acts as a simple mailbox. An item can be deposited and collected later. What we are going to do is to give the identity of the mailbox to the server so that the server can deposit the item in the mailbox from which the user can collect it later. We need an access type

```
type ADDRESS is access MAILBOX;
```

The tasks SERVER and USER now take the following form

```
task SERVER is
   entry REQUEST(A: ADDRESS; X: ITEM);
end;

task body SERVER is
   REPLY: ADDRESS;
   JOB: ITEM;
begin
   loop
      accept REQUEST(A: ADDRESS; X: ITEM) do
         REPLY:= A;
         JOB:= X;
      end;

      -- work on job

      REPLY.DEPOSIT(JOB);
   end loop;
end SERVER;

task USER;

task body USER is
   MY_BOX: ADDRESS:= new MAILBOX;
   MY_ITEM: ITEM;
begin
   SERVER.REQUEST(MY_BOX, MY_ITEM);

   -- do something while waiting

   MY_BOX.COLLECT(MY_ITEM);
end USER;
```

In practice the user might poll the mailbox from time to time to see if the item is ready. This is easily done using a conditional entry call.

```
select
   MY_BOX.COLLECT(MY_ITEM);
   -- item collected successfully
else
   -- not ready yet
end select;
```

It is important to realize that the agent serves several purposes. It enables the deposit and collect to be decoupled so that the server can get on with the next job. Moreover, and perhaps of more importance, it means that the server need know nothing about the user; to call the user directly would mean that the user would have to be of a particular task type and this would be most unreasonable. The agent enables us to factor off the only property required of the user, namely the existence of the entry DEPOSIT.

If the decoupling property were not required then the body of the agent could be written as

```
task body MAILBOX is
begin
    accept DEPOSIT(X: in ITEM) do
        accept COLLECT(X: out ITEM) do
            COLLECT.X:= DEPOSIT.X;
        end;
    end;
end MAILBOX;
```

The agent does not need a local variable in this case since the agent now only exists in order to aid closely coupled communication. Note also the use of the dotted notation in the nested accept statements in order to distinguish the two uses of X; we could equally have written X:= DEPOSIT.X; but the use of COLLECT is more symmetric.

## 14.7   Termination and exceptions

A task can become completed and then terminate in various ways as well as running into its final end. It will have been noticed that in many of our earlier examples, the body of a task was an endless loop and clearly never terminated. This means that it would never be possible to leave the unit on which the task was dependent. Suppose, for example, that we needed to have several protected variables in our program. We could declare a task type

```
task type PROTECTED_VARIABLE is
    entry READ(X: out ITEM);
    entry WRITE(X: in ITEM);
end;
```

so that we can just declare variables such as

```
PV: PROTECTED_VARIABLE;
```

and then access them by

```
PV.READ( ... );
PV.WRITE( ... );
```

However, we could not leave the unit on which PV depends without terminating the task in some way. We could, of course, add a special entry

STOP and call it just before leaving the unit, but this would be inconvenient. Instead it is possible to make a task automatically terminate itself when it is of no further use by a special form of select alternative.

The body of the task can be written as

```
task body PROTECTED_VARIABLE is
    V: ITEM;
begin
    accept WRITE(X: in ITEM) do
        V:= X;
    end;
    loop
        select
            accept READ(X: out ITEM) do
                X:= V;
            end;
        or
            accept WRITE(X: in ITEM) do
                V:= X;
            end;
        or
            terminate;
        end select;
    end loop;
end PROTECTED_VARIABLE;
```

The terminate alternative is taken if the unit on which the task depends has reached its end and so is completed and all sibling tasks and dependent tasks are terminated or are similarly able to select a terminate alternative. In such circumstances all the tasks are of no use since they are the only tasks that could call their entries and they are all dormant. Thus the whole set automatically terminates.

In practice, this merely means that all service tasks should have a terminate alternative and will then quietly terminate themselves without more ado.

Strictly speaking, the initial WRITE should also be in a select statement with a terminate alternative otherwise we are still stuck if the task is never called at all.

A terminate alternative may be guarded. However, it cannot appear in a select statement with a delay alternative or an else part.

Selection of a terminate alternative is classified as normal termination – the task is under control of the situation and terminates voluntarily.

At the other extreme the abort statement unconditionally terminates one or more tasks. It consists of the reserved word **abort** followed by a list of task names as for example

**abort** X, AOT(3), RX.**all**;

If a task is aborted then all tasks dependent upon it or a subprogram or block currently called by it are also aborted. If the task is suspended for some reason, then it immediately becomes completed; any delay is cancelled; if the task is on an entry queue, it is removed; other possibilities are that it has not yet even commenced activation or it is at an accept or select statement awaiting a partner. If the task is not suspended, then completion will occur as soon as convenient and certainly no new communication with the task will be possible. The reason for this somewhat vague statement concerns the rendezvous. If the task is engaged in a rendezvous when it is aborted, then we also have to consider the effect on the partner. This depends on the situation. If the called task is aborted, then the calling task receives the exception TASKING_ERROR. On the other hand, if the calling task is aborted, then the called task is not affected; the rendezvous carries on to completion with the caller in a somewhat abnormal state and it is only when the rendezvous is complete that the caller becomes properly completed. The rationale is simple; if a task asks for a service and the server dies so that it cannot be provided, then the customer should be told. On the other hand, if the customer dies, too bad – but we must avoid upsetting the server who might have the database in a critical state.

Note that the above rules are formulated in terms of completing the tasks rather than terminating them. This is because a parent task cannot be terminated until its dependent tasks are terminated and if one of those is the caller in a rendezvous with a third party, then its termination will be delayed. Thus completion of the tasks is the best that can be individually enforced and their termination will then automatically occur in the usual way.

The abort statement is very disruptive and should only be used in extreme situations. It might be appropriate for a command task to abort a complete subsystem in response to an operator command.

Another possible use for the abort statement might be in an exception handler. Remember that we cannot leave a unit until all dependent tasks are terminated. Hence, if an exception is raised in a unit, then we cannot tidy up that unit and propagate the exception on a layered basis while dependent taks are still alive and so one of the actions of tidying up might be to abort all dependent tasks. Thus the procedure CLEAN_UP of Section 10.2 might do just this.

However, it is probably always best to attempt a controlled shutdown and only resort to the abort statement as a desperate measure. Statements in the command task might be as follows

```
select
    T.CLOSEDOWN;
or
    delay 60*SECONDS;
    abort T;
end select;
```

If the slave task does not accept the CLOSEDOWN call within a minute, then it is ruthlessly aborted. We are assuming, of course, that the slave task polls the CLOSEDOWN entry at least every minute using a conditional accept statement such as

```
select
    accept CLOSEDOWN;
```

```
        -- tidy up and die
    else
        -- carry on normally
    end select;
```

If we cannot trust the slave to close down properly even after accepting the entry call, then the command task can always issue an abort after a due interval just in case. Aborting a task which has already terminated has no effect. So the command task might read

```
    select
        T.CLOSEDOWN;
        delay 10*SECONDS;
    or
        delay 60*SECONDS;
    end select;
    abort T;
```

Of course, even this is not foolproof since the malevolent slave might continue for ever in the rendezvous itself

```
    accept CLOSEDOWN do
        loop
            PUT("CAN'T CATCH ME");
        end loop;
    end;
```

Some minimal degree of cooperation is obviously needed!

The status of task T can be ascertained by the use of two attributes. Thus T'TERMINATED is true if a task is terminated. The other attribute, T'CALLABLE, is true unless the task is completed or terminated or in the abnormal state pending final abortion. The use of these attributes needs care. For example, between discovering that a task has not terminated and taking some action based on that information, the task could become terminated. However, the reverse is not possible since a task cannot be restarted and so it is quite safe to take an action based on the information that a task has terminated.

As an illustration of the impact of abnormal termination and how it can be coped with, we will reconsider the task CONTROL in the package READER_WRITER in Section 14.5 in its final form

```
    task body CONTROL is
        READERS: INTEGER:= 0;
    begin
        loop
            select
                accept START(S: SERVICE) do
                    case S is
                        when READ =>
                            READERS:= READERS+1;
```

```
                    when WRITE =>
                       while READERS > 0 loop
                          accept STOP;      -- from readers
                          READERS:= READERS-1;
                       end loop;
                  end case;
               end START;
               if READERS = 0 then
                  accept STOP;              -- from the writer
               end if;
         or
               accept STOP;                 -- from a reader
               READERS:= READERS-1;
            end select;
         end loop;
      end CONTROL;
```

Suppose that a reading task has called START and is then aborted before it can call STOP. The variable READERS will then be inconsistent and can never be zero again. The next writer will then be locked out for ever. Similarly, if a writing task has called START and is then aborted before it can call STOP, then all other users will be locked out for ever.

The difficulty we have run into is that our task CONTROL assumes certain behaviour on the part of the calling tasks and this behaviour is not guaranteed. (We had a similar difficulty with our elementary solution to this example in Section 14.5 regarding the COUNT attribute and timed out entry calls.) We can overcome our new difficulty by the use of intermediate agent tasks which we can guarantee cannot be aborted.

The following shows the use of agents for the readers; a similar technique can be applied to the writers. The package body now becomes

```
package body READER_WRITER is
   V: ITEM;
   type SERVICE is (READ, WRITE);

   task type READ_AGENT is
      entry READ(X: out ITEM);
   end;

   type RRA is access READ_AGENT;

   task CONTROL is
      entry START(S: SERVICE);
      entry STOP;
   end;

   task body CONTROL is
      -- as before
   end CONTROL;
```

```
task body READ_AGENT is
begin
    select
        accept READ(X: out ITEM) do
            CONTROL.START(READ);
            X:= V;
            CONTROL.STOP;
        end;
    or
        terminate;
    end select;
end READ_AGENT;

procedure READ(X: out ITEM) is
    TASK_007: RRA:= new READ_AGENT;
begin
    TASK_007.READ(X);
end READ;

procedure WRITE(X: in ITEM) is
begin
    ...
end WRITE;

end READER_WRITER;
```

If we now abort the task calling the procedure READ, then either the rendezvous with its agent (TASK_007) will be in progress, in which case it will be completed, or the rendezvous will not be in progress, in which case there will be no interference. The agent therefore either does its job completely or not at all. Note that if we made the agent a direct task object (rather than an access to a task object), then aborting the task calling the procedure READ would also immediately abort the agent because it would be a dependent task. Using an access type makes the agent dependent on the unit in which the READER_WRITER is declared and so it can live on.

The agent task body contains a select statement with a terminate alternative. This ensures that if the user task is aborted between creating the agent and calling the agent then nevertheless the agent can quietly die when the unit on which it depends is left.

It is worth summarizing why the above solution works

- the agent is invisible and so cannot be aborted,
- if the calling task in a rendezvous is abnormally terminated, the called task (the agent) is not affected,
- the agent is an access task and is not dependent on the caller.

The moral is not to use abort without due care; or, as in life, if you cannot trust the calling tasks, use indestructible secret agents.

We finish this section by discussing a few remaining points on exceptions. The exception TASKING_ERROR is concerned with general communication failure. As we have seen, it is raised if a failure occurs during task activation and it is also raised in the caller of a rendezvous if the server is aborted. In addition, no matter how a task is completed, all tasks still queued on its entries receive TASKING_ERROR. Similarly calling an entry of a task that is already completed also raises TASKING_ERROR in the caller.

If an exception is raised during a rendezvous (that is as a consequence of an action by the called task) and is not handled by the accept statement, then it is propagated into both tasks as the same exception on the grounds that both need to know. Of course, if the accept statement handles the exception internally, then that is the end of the matter anyway.

It might be convenient for the called task, the server, to inform the calling task, the user, of some event by the explicit raising of an exception. In such a case it is likely that the server task will not wish to take any action and so a null handler will be required. So in outline we might write

```
begin
  select
    accept E( ... ) do
      ...
      raise ERROR;            -- tell user
      ...
    end E;

  or
    ...
  end select;
exception
  when ERROR =>
    null;                     -- server forgets
end;
```

Finally, if an exception is not handled by a task at all, then, like the main program, the task is abandoned and the exception is lost; it is not propagated to the parent unit because it would be too disruptive to do so. However, we might expect the run time environment to provide a diagnostic message. If it does not, it might be good practice for all significant tasks to have a general handler at the outermost level in order to guard against the loss of exceptions and consequential silent death of the task.

---

*Exercise 14.7*

1    Rewrite the task BUFFERING of Section 14.4 so that it has the following specification

```
task BUFFERING is
  entry PUT(X: in ITEM);
```

```
        entry FINISH;
        entry GET(X: out ITEM);
    end;
```

The writing task calls PUT as before and finally calls FINISH. The reading task calls GET as before; a call of GET when there are no further items raises the global exception DONE.

---

## 14.8   Resource scheduling

When designing tasks in Ada it is important to remember that the only queues over which we have any control are entry queues and that such queues are handled on a strictly first-in-first-out basis. This might be thought to be a problem in situations where requests are of different priorities or where later requests can be serviced even though earlier ones have to wait. (Note that in this section we will assume that calling tasks are not aborted.)

Requests with priorities can be handled by a family of entries. A family is rather like a one-dimensional array. Suppose we have three levels of priority given by

```
    type PRIORITY is (URGENT, NORMAL, LOW);
```

and that we have a task CONTROLLER providing access to some action on a type DATA but with requests for the action on three queues according to their priority. We could do this with three distinct entries but it is neater to use a family of entries. Consider

```
    task CONTROLLER is
        entry REQUEST(PRIORITY) (D: DATA);
    end;

    task body CONTROLLER is
    begin
        loop
            select
                accept REQUEST(URGENT) (D: DATA) do
                    ACTION(D);
                end;
            or
                when REQUEST(URGENT)'COUNT = 0 =>
                accept REQUEST(NORMAL) (D: DATA) do
                    ACTION(D);
                end;
            or
                when REQUEST(URGENT)'COUNT = 0 and
                        REQUEST(NORMAL)'COUNT = 0 =>
                accept REQUEST(LOW) (D: DATA) do
```

```
                ACTION(D);
            end;
        end select;
      end loop;
  end CONTROLLER;
```

REQUEST is a family of entries, indexed by a discrete range which in this case is the type PRIORITY. Clearly this approach is only feasible if the number of priority values is small. If it is large, a more sophisticated technique is necessary. We could try checking each queue in turn thus

```
task body CONTROLLER is
begin
  loop
    for P in PRIORITY loop
      select
        accept REQUEST(P) (D: DATA) do
          ACTION(D);
        end;
        exit;
      else
        null;
      end select;
    end loop;
  end loop;
end CONTROLLER;
```

Unfortunately this is not satisfactory since it results in the task CONTROLLER continuously polling when all the queues are empty. We need a mechanism whereby the task can wait for the first of any request. This can be done by a two-stage process; the calling task must first sign in by calling a common entry and then call the appropriate entry of the family. The details are left as an exercise for the reader.

We now illustrate a quite general technique which effectively allows the requests in a single entry queue to be handled in an arbitrary order. Consider the problem of allocating a group of resources from a set. We do not wish to hold up a later request that can be satisfied just because an earlier request must wait for the release of some of the resources it wants. We suppose that the resources are represented by a discrete type RESOURCE. We can conveniently use the generic package SET_OF from Section 13.2.

```
package RESOURCE_SETS is new SET_OF(RESOURCE);
use RESOURCE_SETS;
```

and then

```
package RESOURCE_ALLOCATOR is
  procedure REQUEST(S: SET);
  procedure RELEASE(S: SET);
end;
```

```
package body RESOURCE_ALLOCATOR is
   task CONTROL is
      entry FIRST(S: SET; OK: out BOOLEAN);
      entry AGAIN(S: SET; OK: out BOOLEAN);
      entry RELEASE(S: SET);
   end;

   task body CONTROL is
      FREE: SET:= FULL;
      WAITERS: INTEGER:= 0;
      procedure TRY(S: SET; OK: out BOOLEAN) is
      begin
         if S <= FREE then
            FREE:= FREE-S;
            OK:= TRUE;          -- allocation successful
         else
            OK:= FALSE;         -- no good, try later
         end if;
      end TRY;

   begin
      loop
         select
            accept FIRST(S: SET; OK: out BOOLEAN) do
               TRY(S, OK);
               if not OK then
                  WAITERS:= WAITERS+1;
               end if;
            end;
         or
            accept RELEASE(S: SET) do
               FREE:= FREE+S;
            end;
            for I in 1 .. WAITERS loop
               accept AGAIN(S: SET; OK: out BOOLEAN) do
                  TRY(S, OK);
                  if OK then
                     WAITERS:= WAITERS-1;
                  end if;
               end;
            end loop;
         end select;
      end loop;
   end CONTROL;

   procedure REQUEST(S: SET) is
      ALLOCATED: BOOLEAN;
   begin
      CONTROL.FIRST(S, ALLOCATED);
```

```
        while not ALLOCATED loop
            CONTROL.AGAIN(S, ALLOCATED);
        end loop;
    end REQUEST;

    procedure RELEASE(S: SET) is
    begin
        CONTROL.RELEASE(S);
    end RELEASE;

end RESOURCE_ALLOCATOR;
```

This is another example of a package containing a control task; the overall structure is similar to that of the package READER_WRITER introduced in Section 14.4. The package RESOURCE_ALLOCATOR contains two procedures REQUEST and RELEASE which have as parameters the set S of resources to be acquired or returned; the type SET is from the instantiation of SET_OF. These procedures call the entries of the task CONTROL as appropriate.

The task CONTROL has three entries: FIRST, AGAIN and RELEASE. The entries FIRST and AGAIN are similar; as well as the parameter S giving the set of resources required, they also have an out parameter OK which indicates whether the attempt to acquire the resources was successful or not. The accept statements for FIRST and AGAIN are identical and call a common procedure TRY. This checks the set S against the set FREE of available resources using the inclusion operator "<=" from (the instantiation of) SET_OF. If all the resources are available, FREE is altered correspondingly using the symmetric difference operator "−" from SET_OF and OK is set TRUE; if they are not all available, OK is set FALSE. The entry RELEASE returns the resources passed as the parameter S by updating FREE using the union operator "+" from SET_OF. Note that the declaration of FREE gives it the initial value FULL which is also from SET_OF.

The entries FIRST and AGAIN are called by the procedure REQUEST. It makes an immediate attempt to acquire the resources by a call of FIRST; if they are not all available, the Boolean ALLOCATED is set FALSE and the request is queued by calling AGAIN. This call is then repeated until successful. The entry RELEASE is merely called by the procedure RELEASE.

The body of CONTROL is the inevitable select statement in a loop. It has two branches, one for FIRST and one for RELEASE. Thus a call of RELEASE is always acceptable and a call of FIRST is also accepted promptly except when the task is dealing with the consequences of RELEASE. After a call of RELEASE, the requests which could not be satisfied on their call of FIRST and were consequently placed on the AGAIN queue are reconsidered since the resources made available by the call of RELEASE may be able to satisfy one or more requests at arbitrary points in the queue. The queue is scanned by doing a rendezvous with each call; a user which cannot be satisfied places itself back on the queue by a further call of AGAIN in the procedure REQUEST. In order that each user should only have one retry the scan is done by a loop controlled by the variable WAITERS. This indicates how many callers have called FIRST unsuccessfully and so are waiting in the system; it is initially zero and is incremented on an unsuccessful call of FIRST and decremented on a successful call of AGAIN. Note that we cannot use AGAIN'COUNT; deadlock might arise if all the resources were released between a task unsuccessfully calling FIRST and actually calling AGAIN. The moral of the readers and writers example is thus echoed; avoid the COUNT attribute – we must count for ourselves.

The above solution is reasonably satisfactory although there is a risk of unfairness. Tasks could overtake each other in the race from the front of the queue to the back; a newcomer could also miss a turn.

It is interesting to modify the above solution so that the requests are always satisfied in order. That is, a later request is always held up for an earlier one even if the resources they require are quite different. The essence of the solution is to allow only one waiting task in the system at a time. The modification is left as an exercise for the reader.

For this modified problem the following alternative solution is perhaps better. It has the merit of avoiding the task scheduling associated with the waiting task repeatedly calling AGAIN. We show just the task CONTROL and the procedure REQUEST.

```
task CONTROL is
    entry SIGN_IN(S: SET);
    entry REQUEST;
    entry RELEASE(S: SET);
end;

task body CONTROL is
    FREE: SET:= FULL;
    WAITERS: INTEGER range 0 .. 1:= 0;
    WANTED: SET;

begin
    loop
        select
            when WAITERS = 0 =>
            accept SIGN_IN(S: SET) do
                WANTED:= S;
            end;
            WAITERS:= WAITERS+1;
        or
            when WAITERS > 0 and then WANTED <= FREE =>
            accept REQUEST do
                FREE:= FREE-WANTED;
            end;
            WAITERS:= WAITERS-1;
        or
            accept RELEASE(S: SET) do
                FREE:= FREE+S;
            end;
```

```
      end select;
    end loop;
  end CONTROL;

  procedure REQUEST(S: SET) is
  begin
      CONTROL.SIGN_IN(S);
      CONTROL.REQUEST;
  end REQUEST;
```

In this solution we use a guarding condition which is true when the request can be honoured. A sign in call is required in order to hand over the parameter first because of course a guarding condition cannot depend upon the parameters of the actual entry call it is guarding. Note the short circuit condition which prevents the evaluation of WANTED when there is no waiting task. The variable WAITERS should perhaps be a Boolean; it can only be zero or one.

---

*Exercise 14.8*

1    Modify the first form of the package RESOURCE_ALLOCATOR so that requests are dealt with strictly in order.

2    Rewrite the task CONTROLLER as a package containing a task in a way which avoids continuous polling. The package specification should be

```
        package CONTROLLER is
          procedure REQUEST(P: PRIORITY; D: DATA);
        end;
```

---

## 14.9  Examples of task types

In this final section on tasking we briefly summarize the main differences between packages and tasks and then give a number of examples which illustrate various ways in which task types can be used.

Tasks and packages have a superficial lexical similarity – they both have specifications and bodies. However, there are many differences

- A task is an active construction whereas a package is passive.
- A task can only have entries in its specification. A package can have anything except entries. A task cannot have a private part.
- A package can be generic but a task cannot. The general effect of a parameterless generic task can be obtained by a task type. Alternatively the task can be encapsulated by a generic package.
- A package can appear in a use clause but a task cannot.

- A package can be a library unit but a task cannot. However, a task body can be a subunit.

The overall distinction is that the package should be considered to be the main tool for structuring purposes whereas the task is intended for synchronization. Thus typical subsystems will consist of a (possibly generic) package containing one or more tasks. This general structure has as we have seen the merit of giving complete control over the facilities provided; internal tasks cannot be unwillingly aborted and entry calls cannot be unwillingly timed out if they are not visible.

Our first example illustrates the use of task types as private types by the following generic package which provides a general type BUFFER.

```
generic
    N: POSITIVE;
    type ITEM is private;
package BUFFERS is
    type BUFFER is limited private;
    procedure PUT(B: in out BUFFER; X: in ITEM);
    procedure GET(B: in out BUFFER; X: out ITEM);
private
    task type CONTROL is
        entry PUT(X: in ITEM);
        entry GET(X: out ITEM);
    end;
    type BUFFER is new CONTROL;
end;

package body BUFFERS is

    task body CONTROL is
        A: array (1 .. N) of ITEM;
        I, J: INTEGER range 1 .. N:= 1;
        COUNT: INTEGER range 0 .. N:= 0;
    begin
        loop
            select
                when COUNT < N =>
                accept PUT(X: in ITEM) do
                    A(I):= X;
                end;
                I:= I mod N+1; COUNT:= COUNT+1;
            or
                when COUNT > 0 =>
                accept GET(X: out ITEM) do
                    X:= A(J);
                end;
                J:= J mod N+1; COUNT:= COUNT-1;
            or
                terminate;
```

```
        end select;
      end loop;
    end CONTROL;

    procedure PUT(B: in out BUFFER; X: in ITEM) is
    begin
        B.PUT(X);
    end PUT;

    procedure GET(B: in out BUFFER; X: out ITEM) is
    begin
        B.GET(X);
    end GET;

end BUFFERS;
```

The buffer is implemented as a task object of a task type derived from CONTROL so that when we declare an object of the type BUFFER a new task is created which in turn declares the storage for the actual buffer. Calls of the procedures PUT and GET access the buffer by calling the corresponding entries of the appropriate task. Note that the select statement contains a terminate alternative so that the task object automatically disappears when we leave the scope of its declaration. Moreover, the system is robust even if the calling task is aborted.

We could have dispensed with the derived type and have written directly

```
    task type BUFFER is
        entry PUT(X: in ITEM);
        entry GET(X: out ITEM);
    end;
```

thus illustrating that a task type declaration can give the full type corresponding to a limited private type – remember that a task type is limited. However, the derived type enables us to use two different names according to whether we are thinking about the buffer or the control aspects of the one concept.

We now come to an interesting demonstration example which illustrates the dynamic creation of task objects. The objective is to find and display the first few prime numbers using the Sieve of Eratosthenes.

This ancient algorithm works using the observation that if we have a list of all the primes below $N$ so far, then $N$ is also prime if none of these divide exactly into it. So we try the existing primes in turn and as soon as one divides $N$ we discard $N$ and try again with $N$ set to $N + 1$. On the other hand, if we get to the end of our list of primes without dividing $N$, then $N$ must be prime, so we add it to our list and also start again with $N + 1$.

Our implementation (reproduced by permission of Alsys) uses a separate task for each prime P which is linked (via an access value) to the previous prime task and next prime task as shown in Figure 14.3. Its duty is to take a trial number N from the previous task and to check whether it is

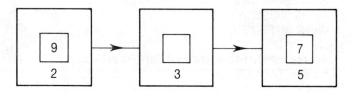

**Figure 14.3**    The Sieve of Eratosthenes.

divisible by its prime P. If it is, the number is discarded; if it is not, the number is passed to the next prime task. If there is no next prime task then P was the largest prime so far and N is a newly found prime; the P task then creates a new task whose duty is to check for divisibility by N and links itself to it. Each task thus acts as a filter removing multiples of its own prime value.

On the screen each task displays a frame containing its own prime and an inner box which displays the trial value currently being tested, if any. Figure 14.3 shows the situation when the primes 2, 3 and 5 have been found. The 5 task is testing 7 (which will prove to be a new prime), the 3 task is resting and waiting to receive another number from the 2 task, the 2 task (having just discarded 8) is testing 9 (which it will pass to the 3 task in a moment).

The program comprises a package FRAME containing subprograms which manipulate the display (the body of this package is not shown), a task type FILTER which describes the activities of the prime tasks and a main program SIEVE.

```
package FRAME is
    type POSITION is private;
    function MAKE_FRAME(DIVISOR: INTEGER) return POSITION;
    procedure WRITE_TO_FRAME(VALUE: INTEGER;
                              WHERE: POSITION);
    procedure CLEAR_FRAME(WHERE: POSITION);
private
    ...
end FRAME;

use FRAME;

task type FILTER is
    entry INPUT(NUMBER: INTEGER);
end FILTER;

type A_FILTER is access FILTER;

function MAKE_FILTER return A_FILTER is
begin
    return new FILTER;
end MAKE_FILTER;

task body FILTER is
    P: INTEGER;              -- prime divisor
```

```
    N: INTEGER;              -- trial number
    HERE: POSITION;
    NEXT: A_FILTER;
begin
  accept INPUT(NUMBER: INTEGER) do
      P:= NUMBER;
  end;
  HERE:= MAKE_FRAME(P);
  loop
    accept INPUT(NUMBER: INTEGER) do
        N:= NUMBER;
    end;
    WRITE_TO_FRAME(N, HERE);
    if N mod P /= 0 then
      if NEXT = null then
        NEXT:= MAKE_FILTER;
      end if;
      NEXT.INPUT(N);
    end if;
    CLEAR_FRAME(HERE);
  end loop;
end FILTER;

procedure SIEVE is
    FIRST: A_FILTER:= new FILTER;
    N: INTEGER:= 2;
begin
  loop
    FIRST.INPUT(N);
    N:= N+1;
  end loop;
end SIEVE;
```

The subprograms in the package FRAME behave as follows. The function MAKE_FRAME draws a new frame on the screen and permanently writes the divisor number (that is P for the task calling it) into the frame; the inner box is left empty. The function returns a value of the private type POSITION which identifies the position of the frame; this value is later passed as a parameter to the two other procedures which manipulate the inner box in order to identify the frame concerned. The procedure WRITE_TO_FRAME has a further parameter giving the value to be written in the inner box; the procedure CLEAR_FRAME wipes the inner box clean.

The task type FILTER is fairly straightforward. It has a single entry INPUT which is called by the preceding task to give it the next trial divisor except that the first call passes the value of P which identifies the task. Hence FILTER has two accept statements, the first collects the value of P and the other is within the main loop. After collecting P it creates its frame (noting the position in HERE) and then enters the loop and awaits a number N to test. Having collected N it displays it in the inner box and then tests for divisibility by P. If it is divisible, it clears the inner box and goes to the beginning of the loop for a new value of N. If N is not divisible by P, it makes a successor task if necessary and in any event passes the value of N to it by calling its entry INPUT. Only after the successor task has taken the value does it clear the inner box and go back to the beginning. (The use of the function MAKE_FILTER is necessary to overcome a rule that in the body of a task type its name refers to the current task and not to the type.)

Note that the task FILTER automatically creates its own storage when it is activated (just as the task CONTROL in the previous example). It should also be noticed that the task does not know who it is until told; this is a characteristic of Ada task types since there is no way of parameterizing them.

The driving procedure SIEVE makes the first task, sets N to 2 and then enters an endless loop giving the task successive integer values until the end of time (or some other limitation is reached).

Our final example illustrates in outline a typical application using several processors. In recent years the cost of processors has fallen dramatically and for many applications it is now more sensible to use several individual processors rather than one very high performance processor. Indeed the finite value of the velocity of light coupled with the nonzero value of Planck's constant places physical limits to the perform-ance that one can get from a single processor. We are then faced with the software organizational problem of how to use several processors effec-tively. For many applications this is hard, but for those where there is a replication of some sort it is often feasible. The processing of algorithms on arrays in graphics, signal processing and so on are good examples.

In Ada the task type gives us a natural means of describing a process which can be run in parallel on several processors simultaneously. For the moment we will suppose that we have a computer comprising several processors with a common address space. Thus when several tasks are active they really will be active and we assume that there are enough processors for all the tasks in the program to truly run in parallel.

Suppose we wish to solve the differential equation

$$\frac{\partial^2 P}{\partial x^2} + \frac{\partial^2 P}{\partial y^2} = F(x, y)$$

over a square region. The value of $P$ is given on the boundary and the value of $F$ is given throughout. The problem is to find the value of $P$ at internal points of the region. This equation arises in many physical situations. One example might concern the flow of heat in a thin sheet of material; $P(x, y)$ would be the temperature of point $(x, y)$ in the sheet and $F(x, y)$ would be the external heat flux applied at that point. However, the physics doesn't really matter.

The standard approach is to consider the region as a grid and to replace the differential equation by a corresponding set of difference equations. For simplicity we consider a square region of side $N$ with unit grid. We end up with something like having to solve

$$4P(i, j) = P(i - 1, j) + P(i + 1, j) + P(i, j - 1)$$
$$+ P(i, j + 1) - F(i, j) \qquad 0 < i, j < N$$

This equation gives a value for each point in terms of its four neighbours. Remember that the values on the boundary are known and fixed. We use an iterative approach (Gauss-Seidel) and allocate a task to each point $(i, j)$. The tasks then repeatedly compute the value of their point from the neighbouring points until the values cease to change. The function $F$ could be of arbitrary complexity. A possible program is as follows

```
procedure GAUSS_SEIDEL is
    N: constant:= 5;
    subtype FULL_GRID is INTEGER range 0 .. N;
    subtype GRID is FULL_GRID range 1 .. N-1;
    type REAL is digits 7;
    type MATRIX is (INTEGER range <>, INTEGER range <>)
                                                      of REAL;
    P: MATRIX(FULL_GRID, FULL_GRID);
    DELTA_P: MATRIX(GRID, GRID);
    TOLERANCE: constant REAL:= 0.0001;
    ERROR_LIMIT: constant REAL:= TOLERANCE * (N-1)**2;
    CONVERGED: BOOLEAN:= FALSE;
    ERROR_SUM: REAL;
    pragma SHARED(CONVERGED);

    function F(I, J: GRID) return REAL is separate;

    task type ITERATOR is
        entry START(I, J: in GRID);
    end;

    PROCESS: array (GRID, GRID) of ITERATOR;

    task body ITERATOR is
        I, J: GRID;
        NEW_P: REAL;
    begin

        accept START(I, J: in GRID) do
            ITERATOR.I:= START.I;
            ITERATOR.J:= START.J;
        end START;

        loop
            NEW_P:= 0.25 * (P(I-1, J) + P(I+1, J) + P(I, J-1)
                                      + P(I, J+1) - F(I, J));
            DELTA_P(I, J):= NEW_P - P(I, J);
            P(I, J):= NEW_P;
            exit when CONVERGED;
        end loop;
```

```
      end ITERATOR;

begin      -- of main program; the ITERATOR tasks are now active

      ...      -- initialize P and DELTA_P

  for I in GRID loop
    for J in GRID loop
      PROCESS(I, J).START(I, J);      -- tell them who they are
    end loop;
  end loop;

  loop
    ERROR_SUM:= 0.0;
    for I in GRID loop
      for J in GRID loop
        ERROR_SUM:= ERROR_SUM + DELTA_P(I, J)**2;
      end loop;
    end loop;

    CONVERGED:= ERROR_SUM < ERROR_LIMIT;
    exit when CONVERGED;
  end loop;

      ...      -- output results

end GAUSS_SEIDEL;
```

The main task starts by telling the ITERATOR tasks who they are through the call of the entry START. Thereafter the individual tasks execute independently and communicate through shared variables. The ITERATOR tasks continue until the Boolean CONVERGED is set by the main task; they then exit their loop and terminate. The main task repeatedly computes the sum of squares of the errors from DELTA_P (set by the ITERATOR tasks) and sets CONVERGED accordingly. When stability is reached the main task outputs the results.

The normal way in which tasks communicate is through the rendezvous but there are occasions as here when this might prove too slow. In this example there are three shared objects: the Boolean CONVERGED and the two arrays P and DELTA_P. Ada discourages the use of shared variables on the grounds that optimization through holding values in registers is impeded. The rules in the *LRM* (to which the reader is referred) guarantee that sharing works only under certain circumstances. One such circumstance is that the pragma SHARED is specified for the variables concerned. We have done this for CONVERGED but the *LRM* appears to forbid this for composite objects. So our program is strictly erroneous but we will assume that our implementation keeps the arrays P and DELTA_P in store so that sharing works.

The program as shown (with $N = 5$) requires 17 tasks and thus 17 processors. This is not unreasonable and of course the program is based on the assumption of one asynchronous processor per task. Nevertheless, the reader will observe a number of flaws. The convergence criterion is a bit suspect. It might be possible for waves of divergence to slurp around the grid in a manner which escapes the attention of the asynchronous main task – but this is unlikely. Another point is that the ITERATOR tasks might still be computing one last iteration while the main task is printing the results. It would be better to add a STOP entry so that the main task can wait until the ITERATOR tasks have finished their loops. Alternatively the array of tasks could be declared in an inner block and the main task could do the printing outside that block where it would know that the other tasks must have terminated. Thus

```
begin      -- main program

    ...    -- initialize arrays

declare
    PROCESS: array (GRID, GRID) of ITERATOR;
begin      -- ITERATOR tasks active
    ...
    ...
end;       -- wait for ITERATOR tasks to terminate

    ...    -- output results

end GAUSS_SEIDEL;
```

Many multiprocessor systems will not have a shared memory in which case a different approach is necessary. A naive first attempt might be to give each ITERATOR an entry which when called delivers the current value of the corresponding point of the grid. Direct *ad hoc* calls from one task to another in a casual design will quickly lead to deadlock. A better approach is to have two tasks per point; one to do the computation and one to provide controlled access to the point (much like the task type PROTECTED_VARIABLE of Section 14.4). We might use one physical processor for each pair of tasks.

It is hoped that our simple example has given the reader some glimpse of how tasking may be distributed over a multiprocessor system. It is a complex subject which is only now being addressed seriously. Of course our example had a ludicrously trivial computation in each task and the system (especially without shared memory) will spend much of its time on communication rather than computation. Nevertheless the principles should be clear. Note that we have not discussed how the different tasks become associated with the different processors; this lies outside the domain of the language itself.

*Exercise 14.9*

1    A boot repair shop has one man taking orders and three others actually repairing the boots. The shop has storage for 100 boots awaiting repair. The person taking the orders notes the address of the owner and this is attached to the boots; he then puts the boots in the store. Each repairman takes boots from the store when he is free, repairs them and then mails them.

   Write a package COBBLERS whose specification is

   **package** COBBLERS **is**
      **procedure** MEND(A: ADDRESS; B: BOOTS);
   **end**;

   The package body should contain four tasks representing the various men. Use an instantiation of the package BUFFERS to provide a store for the boots and agent tasks as mailboxes to deliver them.

2    Sketch a solution of the differential equations using two tasks for each point and no shared variables. Assume one physical processor per point and set the priorities so that the data manager task is of a higher priority than the iterator task. Evaluate and store DELTA_P in the data task. The main program should use the same convergence rule as before. You will not need arrays (other than for the tasks) since the data will be distributed in the data manager tasks.

# Checklist 14

A task is active whereas a package is passive.

A task specification can contain only entries.

A task cannot be generic.

A task name cannot appear in a use clause.

Entries may be overloaded and renamed as procedures.

The COUNT attribute can only be used inside the task owning the entry.

An accept statement must not appear in a subprogram.

Do not attempt to use priorities for synchronization.

Scheduling is preemptive.

The order of evaluation of guards is not defined.

A select statement can have just one of an else part, a single terminate alternative, one or more delay alternatives.

A terminate or delay alternative can be guarded.

Several alternatives can refer to the same entry.

Beware of the COUNT attribute in guards.

Task types are limited.

A task declared as an object is dependent on a block, subprogram or task body but not an inner package.

A task created by an allocator is dependent on the block, subprogram or task body containing the access type definition.

A task declared as an object is made active at the following (possibly notional) **begin**.

A task created by an allocator is made active at once.

Do not use **abort** without good reason.

# Chapter 15
# External Interfaces

In this chapter we consider various aspects of how an Ada program interfaces to the outside world. This includes obvious areas such as input–output, interrupt handling and so on, but we will also consider the mapping of our abstract Ada program onto an implementation. However, the discussion in this chapter cannot be exhaustive because many details of this area will depend upon the implementation. The intent, therefore, is to give the reader a general overview of the facilities available.

## 15.1   Input and output

Unlike many other languages, Ada does not have any intrinsic features for input–output. Instead existing general features such as subprogram overloading and generic instantiation are used. This has the merit of enabling different input–output packages to be developed for different application areas without affecting the language itself. On the other hand this approach can lead to a consequential risk of anarchy in this area; the reader may recall that this was one of the reasons for the downfall of Algol 60. In order to prevent such anarchy the *LRM* defines standard packages for input–output. We discuss the general principles of these packages in this and the next section. For further fine detail the reader should consult the *LRM*.

Two categories of input–output are recognized and we can refer to these as binary and text respectively. As an example consider

```
I: INTEGER:= 75;
```

We can output the binary image of I onto file F by

```
WRITE(F, I);
```

and the pattern transmitted might be (on a 16 bit machine)

    0000 0000 0100 1011

In fact the file can be thought of as essentially an array of the type INTEGER. On the other hand we can output the text form of I by

    PUT(F, I);

and the pattern transmitted might then be

    0011 0111 0011 0101

which is the representation of the characters '7' and '5' without parity bits. In this case the file can be thought of as an array of the type CHARACTER.

Input–output of the binary category is in turn subdivided into sequential and direct access and is provided by distinct generic packages with identifiers SEQUENTIAL_IO and DIRECT_IO respectively. Text input–output (which is always sequential) is provided by the special non-generic package TEXT_IO. There is also a package IO_EXCEPTIONS which contains the declarations of the exceptions used by the three other packages. We will deal here first with SEQUENTIAL_IO and then with DIRECT_IO and consider TEXT_IO in the next section.

The specification of the package SEQUENTIAL_IO is as follows

```
with IO_EXCEPTIONS;
generic
    type ELEMENT_TYPE is private;
package SEQUENTIAL_IO is
    type FILE_TYPE is limited private;
    type FILE_MODE is (IN_FILE, OUT_FILE);

    -- File management

    procedure CREATE(FILE: in out FILE_TYPE;
                     MODE: in FILE_MODE:= OUT_FILE;
                     NAME: in STRING:= "";
                     FORM: in STRING:= "");
    procedure OPEN(FILE: in out FILE_TYPE;
                   MODE: in FILE_MODE;
                   NAME: in STRING;
                   FORM: in STRING:= "");
    procedure CLOSE(FILE: in out FILE_TYPE);
    procedure DELETE(FILE: in out FILE_TYPE);
    procedure RESET(FILE: in out FILE_TYPE;
                               MODE: in FILE_MODE);
    procedure RESET(FILE: in out FILE_TYPE);
    function MODE(FILE: in FILE_TYPE) return FILE_MODE;
    function NAME(FILE: in FILE_TYPE) return STRING;
    function FORM(FILE: in FILE_TYPE) return STRING;
```

```
          function IS_OPEN(FILE: in FILE_TYPE) return BOOLEAN;

          -- Input and output operations

          procedure READ(FILE: in FILE_TYPE;
                                            ITEM: out ELEMENT_TYPE);
          procedure WRITE(FILE: in FILE_TYPE; ITEM: in ELEMENT_TYPE);
          function END_OF_FILE(FILE: in FILE_TYPE) return BOOLEAN;

          -- Exceptions

          STATUS_ERROR: exception renames
                                    IO_EXCEPTIONS.STATUS_ERROR;
          MODE_ERROR: exception renames
                                    IO_EXCEPTIONS.MODE_ERROR;
          NAME_ERROR: exception renames
                                    IO_EXCEPTIONS.NAME_ERROR;
          USE_ERROR: exception renames
                                    IO_EXCEPTIONS.USE_ERROR;
          DEVICE_ERROR: exception renames
                                    IO_EXCEPTIONS.DEVICE_ERROR;
          END_ERROR: exception renames
                                    IO_EXCEPTIONS.END_ERROR;
          DATA_ERROR: exception renames
                                    IO_EXCEPTIONS.DATA_ERROR;

      private
          -- implementation-dependent
      end SEQUENTIAL_IO;
```

The package has a single generic parameter giving the type of element to be manipulated. Note that limited types (and that, thankfully, includes task types) cannot be handled since the generic formal parameter is private rather than limited private.

Externally a file has a name which is a string but internally we refer to a file by using objects of type FILE_TYPE. An open file also has an associated value of the enumeration type FILE_MODE; there are two possible values, IN_FILE or OUT_FILE according to whether read-only or write-only access is required. Read–write access is not allowed for sequential files. The mode of a file is originally set when the file is opened or created but can be changed later by a call of the procedure RESET. Manipulation of sequential files is done using various subprograms whose behaviour is generally as expected.

As an example, suppose we have a file containing measurements of various populations and that we wish to compute the sum of these measurements. The populations are recorded as values of type INTEGER and the name of the file is "CENSUS 47". (The actual conventions for the external file name are dependent upon the implementation.) The

computed sum is to be written onto a new file to be called "TOTAL 47".
This could be done by the following program

```
with SEQUENTIAL_IO;
procedure COMPUTE_TOTAL_POPULATION is
    package INTEGER_IO is new SEQUENTIAL_IO(INTEGER);
    use INTEGER_IO;

    DATA_FILE: FILE_TYPE;
    RESULT_FILE: FILE_TYPE;
    VALUE: INTEGER;
    TOTAL: INTEGER:= 0;
begin
    OPEN(DATA_FILE, IN_FILE, "CENSUS 47");

    while not END_OF_FILE(DATA_FILE) loop
        READ(DATA_FILE, VALUE);
        TOTAL:= TOTAL+VALUE;
    end loop;
    CLOSE(DATA_FILE);

    -- now write the result

    CREATE(RESULT_FILE, NAME => "TOTAL 47");
    WRITE(RESULT_FILE, TOTAL);
    CLOSE(RESULT_FILE);
end COMPUTE_TOTAL_POPULATION;
```

We start by instantiating the generic package SEQUENTIAL_IO with
the actual parameter INTEGER. The use clause enables us to refer to the
entities in the created package directly.

The file with the data to be read is referred to via the object
DATA_FILE and the output file is referred to via the object RESULT_FILE of
the type FILE_TYPE. Note that this type is limited private; this enables the
implementation to use techniques similar to those described in Section 9.3
where we discussed the example of the key manager.

The call of OPEN establishes the object DATA_FILE as referring to
the external file "CENSUS 47" and sets its mode as read-only. The external
file is then opened for reading and positioned at the beginning.

We then obey the loop statement until the function END_OF_FILE
indicates that the end of the file has been reached. On each iteration the
call of READ copies the item into VALUE and positions the file at the next
item. TOTAL is then updated. When all the values on the file have been
read, it is closed by a call of CLOSE.

The call of CREATE creates a new external file named "TOTAL 47"
and establishes RESULT_FILE as referring to it and sets its mode by default
to write-only. We then write our total onto the file and then close it.

The procedures CREATE and OPEN have a further parameter FORM;
this is provided so that auxiliary implementation dependent information
can be specified; the default value is a null string so its use is not

mandatory. Note that the NAME parameter of CREATE also has a default null value; such a value corresponds to a temporary file. The procedures CLOSE and DELETE both close the file and thereby sever the connection between the file variable and the external file. The variable can then be reused for another file. DELETE also destroys the external file if the implementation so allows.

The overloaded procedures RESET cause a file to be repositioned at the beginning as for OPEN. RESET can also change the access mode so that, for example, having written a file, we can now read it.

The functions MODE, NAME and FORM return the corresponding properties of the file. The function IS_OPEN indicates whether the file is open; that is, indicates whether the file variable is associated with an external file or not.

The procedures READ and WRITE automatically reposition the file ready for a subsequent call so that the file is processed sequentially. The function END_OF_FILE only applies to an input file and returns true if there are no more elements to be read.

If we do something wrong then one of the exceptions in the package IO_EXCEPTIONS will be raised. This package is as follows

```
package IO_EXCEPTIONS is
    STATUS_ERROR:    exception;
    MODE_ERROR:      exception;
    NAME_ERROR:      exception;
    USE_ERROR:       exception;
    DEVICE_ERROR:    exception;
    END_ERROR:       exception;
    DATA_ERROR:      exception;
    LAYOUT_ERROR:    exception;
end IO_EXCEPTIONS;
```

This is an example of a package that does not need a body. The various exceptions are declared in this package rather than in SEQUENTIAL_IO so that the same exceptions apply to all instantiations of SEQUENTIAL_IO. If they were inside SEQUENTIAL_IO then each instantiation would create different exceptions and this would be rather more inconvenient in the case of a program manipulating files of various types since general purpose exception handlers would need to refer to all the instances. The renaming declarations on the other hand enable the exceptions to be referred to without use of the name IO_EXCEPTIONS. (A similar technique was used with the mathematical library in Section 13.4.)

The following brief summary gives the general flavour of the circumstances giving rise to each exception

| | |
|---|---|
| STATUS_ERROR | File is open when expected to be closed or vice versa. |
| MODE_ERROR | File of wrong mode, for example, IN_FILE when should be OUT_FILE. |
| NAME_ERROR | Something wrong with NAME parameter of CREATE or OPEN. |

| USE_ERROR | Various such as unacceptable FORM parameter or trying to print on card reader. |
|---|---|
| DEVICE_ERROR | Physical device broken or not switched on. |
| END_ERROR | Malicious attempt to read beyond end of file. |
| DATA_ERROR | READ or GET (see next section) cannot interpret data as value of desired type. |
| LAYOUT_ERROR | Something wrong with layout in TEXT_IO (see next section) or PUT overfills string parameter. |

For fuller details of which exception is actually raised in various circumstances the reader is referred to the *LRM* and to the documentation for the implementation concerned.

We continue by considering the package DIRECT_IO which is very similar to SEQUENTIAL_IO but gives us more flexibility by enabling us to manipulate the file position directly.

As mentioned earlier, a file can be considered as a one-dimensional array. The elements in the file are ordered and each has an associated positive index. This ranges from 1 to an upper value which can change since elements can be added to the end of the file. Not all elements necessarily have a defined value in the case of a direct file as we shall see.

Associated with a direct file is a current index which indicates the position of the next element to be transferred. When a file is opened or created this index is set to 1 so that the program is ready to read or write the first element. The main difference between sequential and direct input–output is that in the sequential case this index is implicit and can only be altered by calls of READ, WRITE and RESET whereas in the direct case, the index is explicit and can be directly manipulated.

The extra facilities of DIRECT_IO are as follows. The enumeration type FILE_MODE has a third value INOUT_FILE so that read-write access is possible; this is also the default mode when a new file is created (thus the MODE parameter of CREATE has a different default for direct and sequential files). The type and subtype

```
type COUNT is range 0 .. implementation_defined;
subtype POSITIVE_COUNT is COUNT range 1 .. COUNT'LAST;
```

are introduced so that the current index can be referred to and finally there are various extra subprograms whose specifications are as follows

```
procedure READ(FILE: in FILE_TYPE; ITEM: out ELEMENT_TYPE;
                    FROM: POSITIVE_COUNT);
procedure WRITE(FILE: in FILE_TYPE; ITEM: in ELEMENT_TYPE;
                    TO: POSITIVE_COUNT);
procedure SET_INDEX(FILE: in FILE_TYPE;
                                    TO: in POSITIVE_ COUNT);
function INDEX(FILE: in FILE_TYPE) return POSITIVE_COUNT;
function SIZE(FILE: in FILE_TYPE) return COUNT;
```

The extra overloadings of READ and WRITE first position the current index to the value given by the third parameter and then behave as before. A call of INDEX returns the current index value; SET_INDEX sets the current index to the given value and a call of SIZE returns the number of elements in the file. Note that a file cannot have holes in it; all elements from 1 to SIZE exist although some may not have defined values.

As an illustration of the manipulation of these positions we can alter our example to use DIRECT_IO and we can then write the total population onto the end of an existing file called "TOTALS". The last few statements then become

```
        -- now write the result

        OPEN(RESULT_FILE, OUT_FILE, "TOTALS");
        SET_INDEX(RESULT_FILE, SIZE(RESULT_FILE)+1);
        WRITE(RESULT_FILE, TOTAL);
        CLOSE(RESULT_FILE);
    end COMPUTE_TOTAL_POPULATION;
```

Note that if we set the current index well beyond the end of the file and then write to it, the result will be to add several undefined elements to the file and then finally the newly written element.

Note also that the language does not define whether it is possible to write a file with SEQUENTIAL_IO and then read it with DIRECT_IO or vice versa. This depends upon the implementation.

---

*Exercise 15.1*

1    Write a generic library procedure to copy a file onto another file but with the elements in reverse order. Pass the external names as parameters.

---

## 15.2   Text input–output

Text input–output, which we first met in Chapter 2, is the more familiar form and provides two overloaded procedures PUT and GET to transmit values as streams of characters as well as various other subprograms such as NEW_LINE for layout control. In addition the concept of current default files is introduced so that every call of the various subprograms need not tiresomely repeat the file name. Thus if F is the current default output file, we can write

```
        PUT("MESSAGE");
```

rather than

```
        PUT(F, "MESSAGE");
```

There are two current default files, one of mode OUT_FILE for output, and one of mode IN_FILE for input. There is no mode INOUT_FILE in the package TEXT_IO.

When we enter our program these two files are set to standard default files which are automatically open; we can assume that these are attached to convenient external files such as an interactive terminal or (in olden days) a card reader and line printer. If we wish to use other files and want to avoid repeating the file names in the calls of PUT and GET then we can change the default files to refer to our other files. We can also set them back to their original values. This is done with subprograms

```
function STANDARD_OUTPUT return FILE_TYPE;
function CURRENT_OUTPUT return FILE_TYPE;
procedure SET_OUTPUT(FILE: FILE_TYPE);
```

with similar subprograms for input. The function STANDARD_OUTPUT returns the initial default output file, CURRENT_OUTPUT returns the current default output file and the procedure SET_OUTPUT enables us to change the current default output file to the file passed as parameter.

Thus we could bracket a fragment of program with

```
F: FILE_TYPE;
...
OPEN(F, ... );
SET_OUTPUT(F);
-- use PUT
SET_OUTPUT(STANDARD_OUTPUT);
```

so that having used the file F, we can reset the default file to its standard value.

The more general case is where we wish to reset the default file to its previous value which may, of course, not be the standard value. The reader may recall that the type FILE_TYPE is limited private and therefore values cannot be assigned; at first sight, therefore, it might not seem possible to make a copy of the original current value. However, with suitable contortion it can be done by using the parameter mechanism. We could write

```
procedure JOB(OLD_FILE, NEW_FILE: FILE_TYPE) is
begin
    SET_OUTPUT(NEW_FILE);
    ACTION;
    SET_OUTPUT(OLD_FILE);
end;
```

and then

```
JOB(CURRENT_OUTPUT, F);
```

When we call JOB, the present current value is preserved in the parameter OLD_FILE from whence it can be retrieved for the restoring call of

SET_OUTPUT. However, although this works, it does feel a bit like standing on one's head!

The full specification of TEXT_IO is rather long and so only the general form is reproduced here.

```
with IO_EXCEPTIONS;
package TEXT_IO is
    type FILE_TYPE is limited private;
    type FILE_MODE is (IN_FILE, OUT_FILE);


    type COUNT is range 0 .. implementation_defined;
    subtype POSITIVE_COUNT is COUNT range 1 .. COUNT'LAST;
    UNBOUNDED: constant COUNT:= 0;      -- line and page length

    subtype FIELD is INTEGER range 0 .. implementation_defined;
    subtype NUMBER_BASE is INTEGER range 2 .. 16;
    type TYPE_SET is (LOWER_CASE, UPPER_CASE);

    -- File management

    -- CREATE, OPEN, CLOSE, DELETE, RESET, MODE, NAME,
    -- FORM and IS_OPEN as for SEQUENTIAL_IO

    -- Control of default input and output files

    procedure SET_OUTPUT(FILE: in FILE_TYPE);
    function STANDARD_OUTPUT return FILE_TYPE;
    function CURRENT_OUTPUT return FILE_TYPE;

    -- Similarly for input

    -- Specification of line and page lengths

    procedure SET_LINE_LENGTH(TO: in COUNT);
    procedure SET_PAGE_LENGTH(TO: in COUNT);
    function LINE_LENGTH return COUNT;
    function PAGE_LENGTH return COUNT;

    -- also with FILE parameter

    -- Column, line and page control

    procedure NEW_LINE(SPACING: in POSITIVE_COUNT:= 1);
    procedure SKIP_LINE(SPACING: in POSITIVE_COUNT:= 1);
    function END_OF_LINE return BOOLEAN:
    procedure NEW_PAGE;
    procedure SKIP_PAGE;
    function END_OF_PAGE return BOOLEAN;
    function END_OF_FILE return BOOLEAN;
```

```
procedure SET_COL(TO: in POSITIVE_COUNT);
procedure SET_LINE(TO: in POSITIVE_COUNT);
function COL return POSITIVE_COUNT;
function LINE return POSITIVE_COUNT;
function PAGE return POSITIVE_COUNT;

-- also with FILE parameter

-- Character input-output

procedure GET(FILE: in FILE_TYPE; ITEM: out CHARACTER);
procedure GET(ITEM: out CHARACTER);
procedure PUT(FILE: in FILE_TYPE; ITEM: in CHARACTER);
procedure PUT(ITEM: in CHARACTER);

-- String input-output

procedure GET(ITEM: out STRING);
procedure PUT(ITEM: in STRING);
procedure GET_LINE(ITEM: out STRING; LAST: out NATURAL);
procedure PUT_LINE(ITEM: in STRING);

-- Generic package for input-output of integer types

generic
    type NUM is range <>;
package INTEGER_IO is
    DEFAULT_WIDTH: FIELD:= NUM'WIDTH;
    DEFAULT_BASE: NUMBER_BASE:= 10;

    procedure GET(ITEM: out NUM; WIDTH: in FIELD:= 0);
    procedure PUT(ITEM: in NUM;
                WIDTH: in FIELD:= DEFAULT_WIDTH;
                BASE: in NUMBER_BASE:= DEFAULT_BASE);
    procedure GET(FROM: in STRING; ITEM: out NUM;
                LAST: out POSITIVE);
    procedure PUT(TO: out STRING;
                ITEM: in NUM;
                BASE: in NUMBER_BASE:= DEFAULT_BASE);
end INTEGER_IO;

-- Generic packages for input-output of real types

generic
    type NUM is digits <>;
package FLOAT_IO is
    DEFAULT_FORE: FIELD:= 2;
    DEFAULT_AFT: FIELD:= NUM'DIGITS-1;
    DEFAULT_EXP: FIELD:= 3;
```

```
    procedure GET(ITEM: out NUM; WIDTH: in FIELD:= 0);
    procedure PUT(ITEM: in NUM;
                  FORE: in FIELD:= DEFAULT_FORE;
                  AFT: in FIELD:= DEFAULT_AFT;
                  EXP: in FIELD:= DEFAULT_EXP);
    procedure GET(FROM: in STRING;
                  ITEM: out NUM;
                  LAST: out POSITIVE);
    procedure PUT(TO: out STRING;
                  ITEM: in NUM;
                  AFT: in FIELD:= DEFAULT_AFT;
                  EXP: in FIELD:= DEFAULT_EXP);
end FLOAT_IO;

generic
    type NUM is delta <>;
package FIXED_IO is
    DEFAULT_FORE: FIELD:= NUM'FORE;
    DEFAULT_AFT: FIELD:= NUM'AFT;
    DEFAULT_EXP: FIELD:= 0;
    -- then as for FLOAT_IO
end FIXED_IO;

-- Generic package for input–output of enumeration types

generic
    type ENUM is (<>);
package ENUMERATION_IO is
    DEFAULT_WIDTH: FIELD:= 0;
    DEFAULT_SETTING: TYPE_SET:= UPPER CASE;

    procedure GET(ITEM: out ENUM);
    procedure PUT(ITEM: in ENUM;
                  WIDTH: in FIELD:= DEFAULT_WIDTH;
                  SET: in TYPE_SET:= DEFAULT_SETTING);
    procedure GET(FROM: in STRING;
                  ITEM: out ENUM;
                  LAST: out POSITIVE);
    procedure PUT(TO: out STRING;
                  ITEM: out ENUM;
                  SET: in TYPE_SET:= DEFAULT_SETTING);
end ENUMERATION_IO;

-- Exceptions

STATUS_ERROR: exception renames
                  IO_EXCEPTIONS.STATUS_ERROR;
...
LAYOUT_ERROR: exception renames
                  IO_EXCEPTIONS.LAYOUT_ERROR;
```

    **private**

       -- implementation-dependent

    **end** TEXT_IO;

The types FILE_TYPE and FILE_MODE and the various file management procedures are similar to those for SEQUENTIAL_IO since text files are of course sequential in nature.

Procedures PUT and GET occur in two forms for characters and strings, one with the file and one without; both are shown only for type CHARACTER.

In the case of type CHARACTER, a call of PUT just outputs that character; for type STRING a call of PUT outputs the characters of the string.

A problem arises in the case of numeric and enumeration types since there is not a fixed number of such types. This is overcome by the use of internal generic packages for each category. Thus for integer input–output we instantiate the package INTEGER_IO with the appropriate type thus

    **type** MY_INTEGER **is range** −1E6 .. +1E6;
    ...
    **package** MY_INTEGER_IO **is new** INTEGER_IO(MY_INTEGER);
    **use** MY_INTEGER_IO;

For integer output, PUT occurs in three forms, one with the file, one without and one with a string as the destination; only the last two are shown.

In the case of PUT to a file, there are two format parameters WIDTH and BASE which have default values provided by the variables DEFAULT_WIDTH and DEFAULT_BASE. The default width is initially NUM' WIDTH which gives the smallest field which is adequate for all values of the type expressed with base 10 (including a leading space or minus). Base 10 also happens to be the initial default base. These default values can be changed by the user by directly assigning new values to the variables DEFAULT_WIDTH and DEFAULT_BASE (they are directly visible); remember that a default parameter is re-evaluated on each call requiring it and so the default obtained is always the current value of these variables. The integer is output as an integer literal without underlines and leading zeros but with a preceding minus sign if negative. It is padded with leading spaces to fill the field width specified; if the field width is too small, it is expanded as necessary. Thus a default width of 0 results in the field being the minimum to contain the literal. If base 10 is specified explicitly or by default, the value is output using the syntax of decimal literal; if the base is not 10, the syntax of based literal is used.

The attribute 'WIDTH deserves attention. It is a property of the subtype of the actual generic type parameter and not that of the base type. Thus the default format is appropriate to the type as the user sees it and not to the predefined type from which it is derived. This is important for portability. So in the case of MY_INTEGER, the attribute has the value 8 (seven digits for one million plus the space or sign).

The general effect is shown by the following sequence of statements where the output is shown in a comment. The quotes delimit the output and s designates a space. We start with the initial default values for the format parameters.

```
X: MY_INTEGER:= 1234;
...
PUT(X);                    -- "ssss1234"
PUT(X, 5);                 -- "s1234"
PUT(X, 0);                 -- "1234"
PUT(X, BASE => 8);         -- "s8#2322#"
PUT(X, 11, 8);             -- "ssss8#2322#"
DEFAULT_BASE:= 8;
PUT(X);                    -- "s8#2322#"
```

In the case of PUT to a string, the field width is taken as the length of the string. If this is too small, then LAYOUT_ERROR is raised. PUT to strings is useful for building up strings containing various bits and pieces and perhaps editing them before actually sending them to a file. It will be found that slices are useful for this sort of manipulation.

Similar techniques are used for real types. A value is output as a decimal literal without underlines and leading zeros but with a preceding minus sign if negative. If EXP is zero, then there is no exponent and the format consists of FORE characters before the decimal point and AFT after the decimal point. If EXP is nonzero, then a signed exponent in a field of EXP characters is output after a letter E with leading zeros if necessary; the exponent value is such that only one significant digit occurs before the decimal point. If the FORE or EXP parts of the field are inadequate, then they are expanded as necessary. Base 10 is always used and the value is rounded to the size of AFT specified.

The initial default format parameters for floating point types are 2, NUM'DIGITS−1 and 3; this gives an exponent form with a space or minus sign plus single digit before the decimal point, NUM'DIGITS−1 digits after the decimal point and a two-digit exponent. The corresponding parameters for fixed point types are NUM'FORE, NUM'AFT and 0; this gives a form without an exponent and the attributes give the smallest field such that all values of the type can be expressed with appropriate precision.

Enumeration types use a similar technique. A default field of zero is used. If the field has to be padded then the extra spaces go after the value and not before as with the numeric types. Upper case is normally used, but lower case may be specified. A value of a character type which is a character literal is output in single quotes.

Note the subtle distinction between PUT defined directly for the type CHARACTER and for enumeration values.

```
TEXT_IO.PUT('X');
```

outputs the single character X, whereas

```
package CHAR_IO is new TEXT_IO.ENUMERATION_IO(CHARACTER);
...
CHAR_IO.PUT('X');
```

outputs the character X between single quotes.

Input using GET works in an analogous way; a call of GET always skips line and page terminators. In the case of the type CHARACTER the next character is read. In the case of the type STRING, the procedure GET reads the exact number of characters as determined by the actual parameter. In the case of enumeration types, leading blanks (spaces or horizontal tabs) are also skipped; input is terminated by a character which is not part of the value or by a line terminator. Numeric types normally have the same behaviour but they also have an additional and optional WIDTH parameter and if this has a value other than zero, then reading stops after this number of characters including skipped blanks. In the case of GET where the source is a string rather than a file, the value of LAST indexes the last character read; the end of the string behaves as the end of a file.

The allowed form of data for reading an enumeration value is an identifer (case of letters being ignored), or a character literal in single quotes. The allowed form for an integer value is first and optionally a plus or minus sign and then according to the syntax of an integer literal which may be a based literal and possibly have an exponent (see Section 3.4). The allowed form for a real value is similarly an optional sign followed by a real literal (one with a radix point in it). If the data item is not of the correct form or not a value of the subtype NUM then DATA_ERROR is raised. The collector of Ada curiosities will note that PUT cannot output integer based forms where the base is 10 such as

```
10#41#
```

although GET can read them. Similarly PUT cannot output real based forms at all although GET can read them. On the other hand GET can read whatever PUT can write.

A text file is considered as a sequence of lines. The characters in a line have a column position starting at 1. The line length on output can be fixed or variable. A fixed line length is appropriate for the output of tables, a variable line length for dialogue. The line length can be changed within a single file. It is initially not fixed. The lines are similarly grouped into pages starting at page 1.

On output a call of PUT will result in all the characters going on the current line starting at the current position in the line. If, however, the line length is fixed and the characters cannot fit in the remainder of the line, a new line is started and all the characters are placed on that line starting at the beginning. If they still will not fit, LAYOUT_ERROR is raised. If the length is not fixed, the characters always go on the end of the current line.

The layout may be controlled by various subprograms. In some cases they apply to both input and output files; in these cases if the file is omitted then it is taken to apply to the output case and the default output file is assumed. In most cases, a subprogram only applies to one direction and then omitting the file naturally gives the default in that direction.

The function COL returns the current position in the line and the procedure SET_COL sets the position to the given value. A call of SET_COL never goes backwards. On output extra spaces are produced and on input characters are skipped. If the parameter of SET_COL equals the current value of COL then there is no effect; if it is less then a call of NEW_LINE or SKIP_LINE is implied.

The procedure NEW_LINE (output only) outputs the given number of newlines (default 1) and resets the current column to 1. Spare positions at the end of a line are filled with spaces. The procedure SKIP_LINE (input only) similarly moves on the given number of lines (default 1) and resets the current column. The function END_OF_LINE (input only) returns TRUE if we have reached the end of a line.

The function LINE_LENGTH (output only) returns the current line length if it is fixed and zero if it is not. The procedure SET_LINE_LENGTH (output only) sets the line length fixed to the given value; a value of zero indicates that it is not to be fixed.

There are also similar subprograms for the control of lines within pages. These are LINE, SET_LINE, NEW_PAGE, SKIP_PAGE, END_OF_PAGE, PAGE_LENGTH and SET_PAGE_LENGTH. Finally the function PAGE returns the current page number from the start of the file. There is no SET_PAGE.

The procedures PUT_LINE and GET_LINE are particularly appropriate for manipulating whole lines. A call of PUT_LINE outputs the string and then moves to the next line (by calling NEW_LINE). A call of GET_LINE reads successive characters into the string until the end of the string or the end of the line is encountered; in the latter case it then moves to the next line (by calling SKIP_LINE); LAST indexes the last character moved into the string. Successive calls of PUT_LINE and GET_LINE therefore manipulate whole lines. However, AI-50 places a curious interpretation on GET_LINE when the string is exactly the right length to accommodate the remaining characters on the line – it does not move to the next line! So, given a series of lines of length 80, successive calls of GET_LINE with a string of length 80 (bounds 1 .. 80) return alternately lines of 80 characters and null strings (or in other words the value of LAST is alternately 80 and 0). This unhelpful behaviour can be overcome by using a string of length 81 or calling SKIP_LINE ourselves after each call of GET_LINE.

It will be found helpful to use slices with GET_LINE and PUT_LINE; thus to copy a text file (with lines of less than 100 characters) and adding the string "--" to each line we could write

```
S: STRING(1 .. 100);
N: NATURAL;
...
while not END_OF_FILE loop
    GET_LINE(S, N);
```

```
        PUT_LINE("--" & S(1 .. N));
    end loop;
```

where we have assumed default files throughout.

The package TEXT_IO may seem somewhat elaborate but for simple output all we need is PUT and NEW_LINE and these are quite straightforward as we have seen.

---

*Exercise 15.2*

1   What do the following calls output? Assume the initial values for the default parameters.

    (a)   PUT("FRED");      (f)   PUT(120, 8, 8);
    (b)   PUT(120);         (g)   PUT(−38.0);
    (c)   PUT(120, 8);      (h)   PUT(0.07, 6, 2, 2);
    (d)   PUT(120, 0);      (i)   PUT(3.14159, 1, 4);
    (e)   PUT(−120, 0);    (j)   PUT(9_999_999_999.9, 1, 1, 1);

Assume that the real values are of a type with **digits** = 6 and the integer values are of a type with 16 bits.

2   Write a body for the package SIMPLE_IO of Section 2.2. Ignore exceptions.

---

## 15.3   Interrupts

An interrupt is another form of input. In Ada this can be achieved through the rendezvous mechanism. From within the program, an interrupt appears as an entry call performed by an external task whose priority is higher than that of any task in the program. The interrupt handler is then naturally represented in the program by a task with accept statements for the corresponding entry. The entry is identified as an interrupt by what is known as a representation clause giving the relevant hardware address.

As an example suppose a program wishes to act upon an interrupt arising from the closing of an electrical contact and the interrupt is associated with the address 8#72#. We could write

```
        task CONTACT_HANDLER is
            entry CONTACT;
            for CONTACT use at 8#72#;
        end;

        task body CONTACT_HANDLER is
        begin
            loop
                accept CONTACT do
```

```
        ...
      end;
    end loop;
  end CONTACT_HANDLER;
```

The body of the accept statement corresponds to the direct response to the interrupt. The rule that the external mythical task has a priority higher than that of any software task ensures that the response takes precedence over ordinary tasks.

An interrupt entry will usually have no parameters but it can have **in** parameters through which control information is passed. An accept statement for an interrupt entry can also occur in a select statement.

The detailed behaviour of interrupt entry calls is somewhat dependent upon the implementation. They could, for example, appear as conditional entry calls and therefore be lost if the response task is not ready to execute the corresponding accept statement. The exact interpretation of the address in the representation clause is also dependent on the implementation.

## 15.4 Representation clauses

In the last section we introduced the representation clause as a means of informing the compiler of additional information about the interrupt entry. Representation clauses take various forms and apply to various entities. Their general purpose is to provide the compiler with directions regarding how the entity is to be implemented. A representation clause must occur in the same declaration list as the declaration of the entity it refers to.

An address clause is of the form used for the entry. It can be used to assign an explicit address to an object, to indicate the start address of the code body of a subprogram, package or task, or as we have seen, to specify an interrupt to which an entry is to be linked.

A length clause allows us to specify the amount of storage to be allocated for objects of a type, for the collection of an access type and for the working storage of a task type. This is done by indicating the value of certain attributes. Thus

```
  type BYTE is range 0 .. 255;
  for BYTE'SIZE use 8;
```

ensures that objects of the type BYTE occupy only 8 bits.

The space for access collections and tasks is indicated using the attribute STORAGE_SIZE. In these cases the unit is not bits but storage units. The number of bits in a storage unit is implementation dependent and is given by the constant STORAGE_UNIT in the package SYSTEM. Thus if we wanted to ensure that the access collection for

```
  type LIST is access CELL;
```

will accommodate 500 cells then we write

> **for** LIST'STORAGE_SIZE **use**
> 500*(CELL'SIZE / SYSTEM.STORAGE_UNIT);

Similarly the data space for each task of a task type can be indicated by

> **for** MAILBOX'STORAGE_SIZE **use** 128;

The value of *small* for a fixed point type can also be indicated by a length clause as was discussed in Section 12.4.

An enumeration representation clause can be used to specify, as an aggregate, the internal integer codes for the literals of an enumeration type. We might have a status value transmitted into our program as single bit settings, thus

> **type** STATUS **is** (OFF, READY, ON);
> **for** STATUS **use** (OFF => 1, READY => 2, ON => 4);

There is a constraint that the ordering of the values must be the same as the logical ordering of the literals. However, despite the holes, the functions SUCC, PRED, POS and VAL always work in logical terms.

If these single bit values were autonomously loaded into our machine at location octal 100 then we could conveniently access them in our program by declaring a variable of type STATUS and placing it at that location using an address clause

> S: STATUS;
> **for** S **use at** 8#100#;

However, if by some hardware mishap a value which is not 1, 2 or 4 turns up then the program will be erroneous and its behaviour quite unpredictable. We will see how to overcome this difficulty in Section 15.6.

The final form of representation clause is used to indicate the layout of a record type. Thus if we have

> **type** REGISTER **is range** 0 .. 15;
> **type** OPCODE **is** ( ... );
>
> **type** RR **is**
>   **record**
>     CODE: OPCODE;
>     R1    : REGISTER;
>     R2    : REGISTER;
>   **end record**;

which represents a machine instruction of the RR format in the IBM System 370, then we can specify the exact mapping by

> **for** RR **use**
>   **record at mod** 2;

```
        CODE  at 0 range 0 .. 7;
        R1    at 1 range 0 .. 3;
        R2    at 1 range 4 .. 7;
    end record;
```

The optional alignment clause

```
    at mod 2;
```

indicates that the record is to be aligned on a double byte boundary; the alignment is given in terms of the number of storage units and in the case of the 370 a storage unit would naturally be one 8 bit byte.

The position and size of the individual components are given relative to the start of the record. The value after **at** gives a storage unit and the range is in terms of bits. The bit number can extend outside the storage unit; we could equally have written

```
    R1 at 0 range 8 .. 11;
```

If we do not specify the location of every component, the compiler is free to juggle the rest as best it can. However, we must allow enough space for those we do specify and they must not overlap unless they are in different alternatives of a variant. There may also be hidden components (array dope information for example) and this may interfere with our freedom.

We conclude this section by noting an important rule that only one representation clause is allowed for (a particular aspect of) any type. Moreover, any type derived from a type after the declaration of a representation clause will inherit that representation. Nevertheless, we can have two types, one derived from the other with different representations by placing the representation clauses after the derivation. So, in essence, derived types allow us to have different representations for essentially the same type and conveniently force us to use explicit type conversions to transfer from one representation to another.

## 15.5   Implementation considerations

It is hard to be specific in this area since so much depends upon the implementation. However, there is a package SYSTEM which includes the values of various machine constants. Its specification is as follows

```
package SYSTEM is
    type ADDRESS     is implementation_defined;
    type NAME        is implementation_defined_enumeration_type;

    SYSTEM_NAME      : constant NAME:= implementation_defined;

    STORAGE_UNIT     : constant:= implementation_defined;
```

```
        MEMORY_SIZE      : constant:= implementation_defined;

        -- system-dependent named numbers

        MIN_INT          : constant:= implementation_defined;
        MAX_INT          : constant:= implementation_defined;
        MAX_DIGITS       : constant:= implementation_defined;
        MAX_MANTISSA     : constant:= implementation_defined;
        FINE_DELTA       : constant:= implementation_defined;
        TICK             : constant:= implementation_defined;

        -- other system-dependent declarations

        subtype PRIORITY is INTEGER range implementation_defined;
        ...
    end SYSTEM;
```

The type ADDRESS is that used in an address clause and given by the corresponding attribute; it might be an integer type or possibly a record type. The numbers STORAGE_UNIT and MEMORY_SIZE give the size of a storage unit in bits and the memory size in storage units; both are of type universal integer. MIN_INT and MAX_INT give the most negative and most positive values of an integer type, MAX_DIGITS is the largest number of decimal digits of a floating type and MAX_MANTISSA is the largest number of binary digits of a fixed type; they are all of type universal integer. FINE_DELTA is a bit redundant since it always has the value $2.0**$ $(-MAX\_MANTISSA)$ and TICK is the clock period in seconds; they are both of type universal real.

Various pragmas enable us to set certain parameters of the implementation, and attributes enable us to read the value of certain parameters. The predefined pragmas and attributes are listed in Appendix 1 although an implementation is free to add others.

Some pragmas enable us to guide the compiler regarding the balance of the implementation between integrity and efficiency and also between space and time.

The pragma SUPPRESS can be used to indicate that the run-time checks associated with detecting conditions which could give rise to exceptions can be omitted if to do so would lead to a more efficient program. However, it should be remembered that a pragma is merely a recommendation and so there is no guarantee that the exception will not be raised. Indeed it could be propagated from another unit compiled with checks.

The checks corresponding to the exception CONSTRAINT_ERROR are ACCESS_CHECK (checking that an access value is not null when attempting to access a component), DISCRIMINANT_CHECK (checking that a discriminant value is consistent with the component being accessed or a constraint), INDEX_CHECK (checking that an index is in range), LENGTH_CHECK (checking that the number of components of an array match) and RANGE_CHECK (checking that various constraints are satisfied).

The checks corresponding to NUMERIC_ERROR are DIVISION_ CHECK (checking the second operand of /, **rem** and **mod**) and OVERFLOW_ CHECK (checking for numeric overflow).

The check corresponding to STORAGE_ERROR is STORAGE_CHECK (checking that space for an access collection or task has not been exceeded).

The check corresponding to PROGRAM_ERROR is ELABORATION_ CHECK (checking that the body of a unit has been elaborated).

The pragma takes the form

**pragma** SUPPRESS(RANGE_CHECK);

in which case it applies to all operations in the unit concerned or it can list the types and objects to which it is to be applied. Thus

**pragma** SUPPRESS(ACCESS_CHECK, LIST);

indicates that no checks are to be applied when accessing objects of the access type LIST.

The other pragmas in this category apply to the balance between speed and time. They are CONTROLLED, INLINE, OPTIMIZE and PACK; they are described in Appendix 1.

Finally, there are various machine dependent attributes defined for real types. For example there is the attribute MACHINE_ROUNDS which indicates whether rounding is performed for the type concerned. Another is the attribute MACHINE_OVERFLOWS which indicates whether NUMERIC_ ERROR is raised for computations which exceed the range of the type. If a program uses these attributes then care is required if portability is to be ensured.

## 15.6   Unchecked programming

Sometimes the strict integrity of a fully typed language is a nuisance. This particularly applies to system programs where, in different parts of a program, an object is thought of in different terms. This difficulty can be overcome by the use of a generic function called UNCHECKED_CONVERSION. Its specification is

```
generic
    type SOURCE is limited private;
    type TARGET is limited private;
function UNCHECKED_CONVERSION(S: SOURCE) return TARGET;
```

As an example, we can overcome our problem with possible erroneous values of the type STATUS of Section 15.4. We can receive the values into our program as values of type BYTE, check their validity in numeric terms and then convert the values to type STATUS for the remainder of the program. In order to perform the conversion we first instantiate the generic function thus

```
function BYTE_TO_STATUS is
    new UNCHECKED_CONVERSION(BYTE, STATUS);
```

and we can then write

```
B: BYTE;
for B use at 8#100#;
S: STATUS;
...
case B is
    when 1 | 2 | 4 =>
        null;
    when others =>
        raise BAD_DATA;
end case;

S:= BYTE_TO_STATUS(B);
```

The effect of the unchecked conversion is nothing; the bit pattern of the source type is merely passed on unchanged and reinterpreted as the bit pattern of the target type. Clearly, certain conditions must be satisfied for this to be possible; an obvious one which may be imposed by the implementation is that the number of bits in the representations of the two types must be the same. We cannot get a quart into a pint pot.

Another area where the programmer can be given extra freedom is in the deallocation of access types. As mentioned in Section 11.4 there may or may not be a garbage collector. In any event we may prefer to do our own garbage collection perhaps on the grounds that this gives us better timing control in a realtime program. We can do this with a generic procedure called UNCHECKED_DEALLOCATION. Its specification is

```
generic
    type OBJECT is limited private;
    type NAME is access OBJECT;
procedure UNCHECKED_DEALLOCATION(X: in out NAME);
```

If we take our old friend

```
type LIST is access CELL;
```

then we can write

```
procedure FREE is
    new UNCHECKED_DEALLOCATION(CELL, LIST);
```

and then

> L: LIST;
>
> ...
>
> FREE(L);

After calling FREE, the value of L will be **null** and the cell will have been returned to free storage. Of course, if we mistakenly still had another variable referring to the cell then we would be in a mess; the program would be erroneous. If we use unchecked deallocation then the onus is on us to get it right. We should also insert

> **pragma** CONTROLLED(LIST);

to tell the compiler that we are looking after ourselves and that any garbage collector should not be used for this access type.

The use of both these forms of unchecked programming needs care and it would be sensible to restrict the use of these generic subprograms to privileged parts of the program. Note that since both generic functions are library functions then any compilation unit using them must refer to them in a with clause. This makes it fairly straightforward for a tool to check for their use. And also for our manager to peer over our shoulders to see whether we are writing naughty programs!

## 15.7    Other languages

Another possible form of communication between an Ada program and the outside world is via other languages. These could be machine languages or other high level languages such as FORTRAN. The *LRM* prescribes general methods but the actual details will obviously depend so much upon the implementation that an outline description seems pointless and the reader is therefore referred to specific documentation for the implementation concerned.

# Chapter 16
# Finale

This final chapter covers various overall aspects of Ada. The first four sections consider in more detail and consolidate some important topics which have of necessity been introduced in stages throughout the book. There is then a section on the important issue of portability. Finally, we discuss the general topic of program design as it relates to Ada.

## 16.1  Names and expressions

The idea of a name should be carefully distinguished from that of an identifier. An identifier is a syntactic form such as FRED which is used for various purposes including introducing entities when they are declared. A name, on the other hand, may be more complex and is the form used to denote entities in general. In the *LRM* and in particular in the syntax rules, the term simple name is used to refer to an identifier other than when it is first introduced; we have not used this term since it seems unnecessarily pedantic.

Syntactically, a name starts with an identifier such as FRED or an operator symbol such as "+" and can then be followed by one or more of the following in an arbitrary order

- one or more index expressions in brackets; this denotes a component of an array,
- a discrete range in brackets; this denotes a slice of an array,
- a dot followed by an identifier, operator or **all**; this denotes a record component, an access value or an entity in a package, task, subprogram, block or loop,

- a prime and then an identifier, possibly indexed; this denotes an atrribute,
- an actual parameter list in brackets; this denotes a function call.

A function call in a name must deliver an array, record or access value and must be followed by indexing, slicing, attribution or component selection. This is not to say that a function call must always be followed by one of these things; it could deliver a value as part of an expression, but as part of a name it must be so followed. This point is clarified by considering the assignment statement. The left-hand side must be a name whereas the right-hand side is an expression. Hence, as we saw in Section 11.6, we can write

```
SPOUSE(P).BIRTH:= NEWDATE;
```

but not

```
SPOUSE(P):= Q;
```

although

```
Q:= SPOUSE(P);
```

is of course perfectly legal. (Ada is somewhat less consistent than Algol 68 in this respect.)

Names are just one of the primary components of an expression. The others are literals (numeric literals, enumeration literals, strings and **null**), aggregates, allocators, function calls (not considered as names), type conversions and qualified expressions as well as expressions in brackets. Expressions involving scalar operators were summarized in Section 4.9.

For convenience, all the operators and their predefined uses are shown in Table 16.1. They are grouped according to precedence level. We have also included the short circuit forms **and then** and **or else** and the membership tests **in** and **not in** although these are not technically classed as operators (they cannot be overloaded).

Note the careful distinction between BOOLEAN which means the predefined type and 'Boolean' which means BOOLEAN or any type derived from it. Similarly INTEGER means the predefined type and 'integer' means any integer type (including universal integer). Also 'floating' means any floating type plus universal real.

Observe that the membership tests apply to any type and not just scalar types which were discussed in Section 4.9. Thus we can check whether an array or record has a particular subtype by using a membership test rather than testing the bounds or discriminant. So we can write

```
V in VECTOR_5        -- true, see Section 6.2
JOHN in WOMAN        -- false, see Section 11.3
```

**Table 16.1**  Predefined operators.

| Operator | Operand(s) | | Result |
|---|---|---|---|
| **and**    **or**    **xor** | Boolean | | same |
| | one dim Boolean array | | same |
| **and then**    **or else** | Boolean | | same |
| =    /= | any, not limited | | BOOLEAN |
| <    <=    >    >= | scalar | | BOOLEAN |
| | one dim discrete array | | BOOLEAN |
| **in**    **not in** | scalar | range | BOOLEAN |
| | any | type mark | BOOLEAN |
| + − (binary) | numeric | | same |
| & | one dim array | component | same array |
| + − (unary) | numeric | | same |
| * | integer | integer | same |
| | fixed | INTEGER | same fixed |
| | INTEGER | fixed | same fixed |
| | fixed | fixed | univ fixed |
| | floating | floating | same |
| | univ real | univ integer | univ real |
| | univ integer | univ real | univ real |
| / | integer | integer | same |
| | fixed | INTEGER | same fixed |
| | fixed | fixed | univ fixed |
| | floating | floating | same |
| | univ real | univ integer | univ real |
| **mod**    **rem** | integer | integer | same |
| ** | integer | NATURAL | same integer |
| | floating | INTEGER | same floating |
| **not** | Boolean | | same |
| | one dim Boolean array | | same |
| **abs** | numeric | | same |

rather than

```
V'FIRST = 1 and V'LAST = 5
JOHN.SEX = FEMALE
```

which are equivalent.

Finally, remember that & can take either an array or a component for both operands so four cases arise.

The observant reader will notice that the syntax in Appendix 4 uses the syntactic form 'simple_expression' in some cases where 'expression' might have been expected. One reason for this is to avoid a potential ambiguity regarding the use of **in** as a membership test with ranges.

From time to time we have referred to the need for certain scalar expressions to be static. As explained in Chapter 2 this means that they can be evaluated at compilation time. An expression is static if all its constituents are one of the following

- a numeric or enumeration literal,
- a named number,
- a constant initialized by a static expression,
- a predefined operator,
- a static attribute or a functional attribute with static parameters,
- a qualified static expression provided that any constraint involved is static.

Note that renaming preserves staticness so a renaming of one of the above (for which renaming is allowed) is also an allowed constituent of a static expression (AI-1 and AI-438). However, membership tests and short circuit forms are not allowed (AI-128). Observe that staticness only applies to scalar expressions and that all intermediate subexpressions must also be scalar (AI-219). This excludes bizarre examples such as `'a'&'b' = 'c'&'d'` where the intermediate expressions are arrays although the result is scalar.

The final point we wish to make about expressions concerns array bounds. If an expression delivers an array value then it will have bounds for each dimension. Such an expression can be used in various contexts which can be divided into categories according to the rules regarding the matching of the bounds.

The first category (sliding semantics) includes assignment and initialization in an object declaration. In these cases the bounds of the expression do not have to match the bounds of the object; all that matters is that the number of components in each dimension is the same. Thus as we saw in Section 6.2 we can write

```
V: VECTOR(1 .. 5);
W: VECTOR(0 .. 4);
...
V:= W;
```

The same sliding rules apply in the case of the predefined equality and relational operators.

The second category (matching semantics) includes using an array as an actual parameter, as a function result, as an initial value in an allocator or in a qualified expression. In all of these cases an array type or subtype is involved but it may or may not be constrained. If it is constrained, then the bounds must exactly match; if it is not constrained, then the 'result' takes the bounds of the expression. Thus if we had a function

```
function F return VECTOR_5 is
    V: VECTOR(1 .. 5);
    W: VECTOR(0 .. 4);
begin
    ...
```

then we could write **return** V but not **return** W. If, however, the specification had been

```
function F return VECTOR
```

then we could write either **return** V or **return** W.

There are complications with array aggregates. In the case of a named aggregate without **others** the bounds are evident; such an aggregate can be used in any of the above contexts. In the case of a positional aggregate without **others** the bounds are not evident although the number of components is; such an aggregate can also be used in any of the above contexts – in all the cases of the first category (sliding) and those of the second category (matching) with a constrained type the bounds are taken to be those required by the constraint – in cases of the second category with an unconstrained type the lower bound is given by S'FIRST where S is the index subtype. Finally, if an aggregate (positional or named) contains **others**, then neither the bounds nor the number of components is evident. Such an aggregate can be used in a situation of the second category with a constrained type; in addition a positional aggregate with **others** (or just **others** on its own) is also allowed in a situation of the first category.

Similar rules apply to nested aggregates; the context of the whole aggregate is applied transitively to its components.

Somewhat surprisingly, array type conversion described in Section 6.2 does not fit neatly into either of the above two categories. If the type is constrained, then the sliding rules of assignment are used; if the type is unconstrained, then the result takes the bounds of the operand as for qualification.

---

*Exercise 16.1*

**1**      Given

```
L: INTEGER:= 6;
M: constant INTEGER:= 7;
N: constant:= 8;
```

then classify the following as static or dynamic expressions and give their type

(a)    L+1
(b)    M+1
(c)    N+1

---

## 16.2    Type equivalence

It is perhaps worth emphasizing the rules for type equivalence. The basic rule is that every type definition introduces a new type. Remember the difference between a type definition and a type declaration. A type definition introduces a type whereas a type declaration also introduces an identifier referring to it. Thus

> **type** T **is** (A, B, C);

is a type declaration whereas

> (A, B, C)

is a type definition.

Most types have names but in a few cases a type may be anonymous. The obvious cases occur with the declarations of arrays and tasks. Thus

> A: **array** (I **range** L .. R) **of** C;

is short for

> **type** anon **is array** (I **range** <>) **of** C;
> A: anon(L .. R);

and

> **task** T **is** ...

is short for

> **task type** anon **is** ...
> T: anon;

More subtle cases occur where an apparent type declaration is actually only a subtype declaration. This occurs with array types, derived types and numeric types and so

> **type** T **is array** (I **range** L .. R) **of** C;

is short for

```
subtype index is I range L .. R;
type anon is array (index range <>) of C;
subtype T is anon(L .. R);
```

and

```
type S is new T constraint;
```

is short for

```
type anon is new T;
subtype S is anon constraint;
```

and

```
type T is range L .. R;
```

is short for

```
type anon is new integer_type;
subtype T is anon range L .. R;
```

where integer_type is one of the predefined integer types. Similar expansions apply to floating and fixed types.

When interpreting the rule that each type definition introduces a new type, remember that generic instantiation is equivalent to text substitution in this respect. Thus each instantiation of a package with a type definition in its specification introduces a distinct type. It will be remembered that a similar rule applies to the identification of different exceptions. Each textually distinct exception declaration introduces a new exception; an exception in a recursive procedure is the same for each incarnation but generic instantiation introduces different exceptions.

Remember also that multiple declarations are equivalent to several single declarations written out explicitly. Thus if we have

```
A, B: array (I range L .. R) of C;
```

then A and B are of different anonymous types.

In summary then, Ada has named equivalence rather than the weaker structural equivalence of some languages such as Algol 68. As a consequence Ada gives greater security in the sense that more errors can be found during compilation. However, the Ada type model requires more care in program design. Overzealous use of lots of different types can lead to trouble and there are stories of programs that could never be got to compile.

An obvious area of caution is with numeric types (a novice programmer often uses lots of numeric types with great glee). Attempts to use different numeric types to separate different units of measurement (for example the lengths and areas of Exercise 11.7(**1**)) can lead to messy situations where either lots of overloadings of operators have to be introduced or so many type conversions are required that the clarity sought is lost by the extra clutter. Another problem is that each different numeric type will require a separate instantiation of the relevant package in TEXT_IO if input–output is required. An example of possible overuse of numeric types is in TEXT_IO itself where the distinct integer type COUNT (used for counting characters, lines and pages) is a frequent irritant.

So too many types can be unwise. However, the use of appropriate constraints (as explicit subtypes or directly) always seems to be a good idea. Remember that subtypes are merely shorthands for a base type plus constraint and as a consequence have structural equivalence. Thus, recalling an example in Section 4.4, we can declare

```
subtype DAY_NUMBER is INTEGER range 1 .. 31;
subtype FEB_DAY is DAY_NUMBER range 1 .. 29;
D1: INTEGER range 1 .. 29;
D2: DAY_NUMBER range 1 .. 29;
D3: FEB_DAY;
```

and then D1, D2 and D3 all have exactly the same subtype.

When to use a subtype and when to use a new type is a matter of careful judgement. The guidelines must be the amount of separation between the abstract concepts. If the abstractions are quite distinct then separate types are justified but if there is much overlap and thus much conversion then subtypes are probably appropriate. Thus we could make a case for DAY_NUMBER being a distinct derived type

```
type DAY_NUMBER is range 1 .. 31;
```

but we would find it hard to justify making FEB_DAY not simply a subtype of DAY_NUMBER.

Another important distinction between types and subtypes is in their representation. The basic rule is that a subtype has the same representation as the base type whereas a derived type can have a different representation. Of course, the compiler can still optimize, but that is another matter.

It should also be remembered that checking subtype properties is strictly a run-time matter. Thus

```
S: STRING(1 .. 4):= "abc";
```

raises CONSTRAINT_ERROR although we can expect that any reasonable compiler would pick this up during compilation.

## 16.3   Structure summary and the main program

Ada has four structural units in which declarations can occur; these are blocks, subprograms, packages and tasks. They can be classified in various ways. First of all, packages and tasks have separate specifications and bodies; for subprograms this separation is optional; for blocks it is not possible or relevant since a block has no specification. We can also consider separate compilation: packages, tasks and subprogram bodies can all be subunits but only packages and subprograms can be library units. Note also that only packages and subprograms can be generic. Finally, tasks, subprograms and blocks can have dependent tasks but packages cannot since they are only passive scope control units. These various properties of units are summarized in Table 16.2.

We can also consider the scope and nesting of these four structural units. (Note that a block is a statement whereas the others are declarations.) Each unit can appear inside any of the other units and this lexical nesting can in principle go on indefinitely, although in practical programs a depth of three will not often be exceeded. The only restrictions to this nesting are that a block, being a statement, cannot appear in a package specification but only in its body (and directly only in the initialization sequence) and of course none of these units can appear in a task specification but again only in its body. In practice, however, some of the combinations will arise rarely. Blocks will usually occur inside subprograms and task bodies and occasionally inside other blocks. Subprograms will occur as library units and inside packages and less frequently inside tasks and other subprograms. Packages will usually be library units or inside other packages. Tasks will probably nearly always be inside packages and occasionally inside other tasks or subprograms.

The *Language Reference Manual* is a little vague about the concept of an Ada program. This is perhaps to be expected since Ada is about software components, and undue concern regarding what constitutes a complete program is probably out of place particularly bearing in mind the growing concern with distributed and parallel systems. However, for simple systems we can regard a program as composed out of the library units in a particular program library. The *LRM* does not prescribe how the program is to be started but as discussed in Sections 2.2 and 8.2 we can imagine that one of the library units which is a subprogram (or an instance of a generic subprogram (AI-513)) is called by some magic outside the language itself. Moreover, we must imagine that this originating flow of control is associated with an anonymous task. The priority of this task can be set by the pragma PRIORITY in the outermost declarative part of this main subprogram.

**Table 16.2** Properties of units.

| Property | Blocks | Subprograms | Packages | Tasks |
|----------|--------|-------------|----------|-------|
| Separation | no | optional | yes | yes |
| Subunits | no | yes | yes | yes |
| Library units | no | yes | yes | no |
| Generic units | no | yes | yes | no |
| Dependent tasks | yes | yes | no | yes |

The main program will almost inevitably use dependent library units such as TEXT_IO. These have to be elaborated before the main program is entered and again we can imagine that this is done by our anonymous task. The order of these elaborations is not precisely specified but it must be consistent with the dependencies between the units. In addition, the pragma ELABORATE can be used to ensure that a body is elaborated before a unit that calls it; this may be necessary to prevent PROGRAM_ERROR. Consider the situation mentioned at the end of Section 8.1 thus

```
package P is
    function A return INTEGER;
end P;

package body P is
    function A return INTEGER is
    begin
        return 0;
    end A;
end P;

with P;
package Q is
    I: INTEGER:= P.A;
end Q;
```

The three units can be compiled separately and the requirements are that the body of P and the specification of Q must both be compiled after the specification of P. But there is no need for the body of P to be compiled before the specification of Q. However, when we come to elaborate the three units it is important that the body of P be elaborated before the specification of Q otherwise PROGRAM_ERROR will be raised. The dependency rules are not enough to ensure this and so we have to use the pragma ELABORATE and write

```
with P;
pragma ELABORATE(P);
package Q is
    I: INTEGER:= P.A;
end Q;
```

The pragma immediately follows the context clause and can refer to one or more of the library units mentioned in the context clause.

If the dependencies and any pragmas ELABORATE are such that no consistent order of elaboration exists then the program is illegal; if there are several possible orders and the behaviour of the program depends on the particular order, then it is also illegal (since it then has an incorrect order dependency).

A further point is that whether a main program can have parameters or not or whether there are restrictions on their types and modes or indeed whether the main program can be a function, is dependent on the implementation. Again this is in line with the view that Ada is about the open world of components rather than the closed world of complete programs. It may indeed be very convenient for a main program to have parameters, and for the calling and parameter passing to be performed by the magic associated with the interpretation of a statement in some non-Ada command language.

The above general description is confirmed by AI-222 which also summarizes a number of issues which have been clarified and then illustrates the effect of various rules by the following model

```
task body ... is
begin
    begin
        declare
            package STANDARD is    –– This is Appendix 2
                ...
            end;

            package body STANDARD is
                –– Library units and secondary units needed by
                ––      the main program and the main program
                ––      (procedure or function), in an order
                ––      consistent with the with clauses and any
                ––      pragmas ELABORATE.
            begin
                –– Get parameters required by the main program,
                –– if any.
                –– Call the main program.
            exception
                –– Handle any exceptions associated with main
                –– program execution.
            end STANDARD;
        begin
            null;
        end;         –– Wait for library tasks to terminate.
    exception
        –– Handle any exceptions associated with library unit
        –– elaboration.
    end;
    –– Close external files (optional).
    –– Communicate main program function result, if any.
end;
```

This model captures the following

- The environment task is expressed as an anonymous task.
- Library units and the main program are contained in the package STANDARD.
- Library units needed by the main program, corresponding library unit bodies and the main program are elaborated in an implemen-

tation defined order consistent with the with clauses and any ELABORATE pragmas. These elaborations occur before the main program is called.

- Delay statements executed by the environment task during the elaboration of a library package delay the environment task.

- Tasks that depend on a library unit (and that are not designated by an access value) are started at the end of the declarative part of STANDARD and before the main program is called.

- After normal termination of the main program the environment task must wait for all library tasks to terminate. If all library tasks terminate, then the program as a whole terminates.

- If the main program terminates abnormally by the propagation of an exception then the exception is handled by the environment task. The environment task then waits for any library tasks to terminate. The effect of the environment task's exception handler on unterminated tasks is not defined. In particular, unterminated tasks can be aborted.

- If any external files are used by statements executed in library package bodies, then such operations are performed before execution of the main program begins. If external files are used by library tasks, then these files are processed in accordance with normal Ada semantics, whether or not execution of the main program has begun or has finished. After the main program and all library tasks have terminated (or if execution of the main program is abandoned because of an unhandled exception), any further effects on the external files are not defined; in particular, any files that have been left open may (but need not) be closed.

The reader is warned not to read more into the model than the points listed (it does not cover every subtlety). Nevertheless the model does help to dispel a certain mystery about the nature of the main program and its environment.

## 16.4    Visibility and program composition

The visibility and scope rules have been introduced by stages. The basic rules applicable to the simple block structure were introduced in Section 4.2 and further discussed in Section 7.6 when we considered the use of the dotted notation to provide visibility of an outer identifier which had been hidden by an inner redeclaration. The overloading rules were discussed in Section 7.2 and we recall that the use of identifiers fell into two categories: overloadable (subprograms) and not overloadable (the rest). We then considered the impact of packages in Section 8.4 and the rules regarding the use clause. We also noted in Section 10.3 that exceptions had some special characteristics. We do not intend to repeat all these rules here but rather to illustrate some of their effects particularly with regard to building programs from components.

We begin by recalling from Section 7.5 that enumeration literals behave much like parameterless functions. We could not therefore declare both an enumeration type and a parameterless function returning that type and with the same identifier as one of the literals in the same declarative region thus

```
type COLOUR is (RED, AMBER, GREEN);
function RED return COLOUR;              -- illegal
```

although we could of course declare the function RED in an inner scope where it would hide the literal RED (AI-330). A more subtle illustration is given by

```
package P is
    type LIGHT is new COLOUR;
    function RED return LIGHT;
end;
```

where (assuming COLOUR as above) the function RED replaces the literal RED of the derived type LIGHT. So if we then declared

```
type MORE_LIGHT is new LIGHT;
```

after the package specification then MORE_LIGHT would inherit the function RED rather than the literal RED.

We will now discuss the visibility rules and similar properties of generic packages in more detail. Reconsider the package SET_OF from Section 13.2

```
generic
    type BASE is (<>);
package SET_OF is
    type SET is private;
    type LIST is array (POSITIVE range <>) of BASE;
    ...
end;
```

It is very important to grasp the difference between the rules for the template (the generic text as written) and an instance (the effective text after instantiation).

The first point is that the generic package is not a genuine package and in particular does not export anything. So no meaning can be attached to SET_OF.LIST outside the generic package and nor can SET_OF appear in a use clause. Of course, inside the generic package we can indeed write SET_OF.LIST if we wished to be pedantic or had hidden LIST by an inner redeclaration.

If we now instantiate the generic package thus

```
package CHARACTER_SET is new SET_OF(CHARACTER);
```

then CHARACTER_SET is a genuine package and so we can refer to CHARACTER_SET.LIST outside the package and CHARACTER_SET can appear in a use clause. In this case there is no question of writing CHARACTER_SET.LIST *inside* the package because the inside text is quite ephemeral.

Another very important point concerns the properties of an identifier such as LIST. Inside the generic template we can only use the properties common to all possible actual parameters as expressed by the formal parameter notation. Outside we can additionally use the properties of the particular instantiation. So, inside we cannot write

```
S: LIST(1 .. 6):= "string";
```

because we do not know that the actual type is going to be a character type – it could be an integer type. However, outside we can indeed write

```
S: CHARACTER_SET.LIST(1 .. 6):= "string";
```

because we know full well that the actual type is, in this instance, a character type (AI-398).

Constructing a total program requires putting together various components whose interfaces match much as we can put together hardware components by the use of various plugs and sockets. In order for an entity from one component to be used by another, its name must be exported from the component declaring it and then imported into the component using it. Our normal component is naturally a library package which will often be generic. We will now summarize the various tools at our disposal.

Entities are exported by being in the visible part of a package.

Entities are imported by being generic parameters and also through with clauses. Direct visibility is given by use clauses.

We have also seen that generic actual parameters can be imported into a package and then used to create entities that are exported (the example LIST above); we also noted that specific properties of the actual parameters were reexported but not visible internally (the fact that the actual type was a character type).

The Ada export and import rules work on groups of entities rather than individual entities as in some languages. The Ada technique avoids clutter and is very appropriate when the entities are highly cohesive (that is are strongly related). However, if they are not cohesive then the coarse grouping is a nuisance; there are various (not altogether satisfactory) techniques that can be used to give finer control.

An obvious technique for giving finer control of entities exported from the visible part of a package is simply to declare a hierarchical set of nested packages.

```
package OUTER is
  package INNER1 is
    ...
  end;
```

```
package INNER2 is
   ...
   end;
end;
```

We could then write

```
with OUTER;
package USER is
   use OUTER.INNER1;
```

and then INNER2 and its internal entities will not be directly visible. Note that we cannot put the use clause immediately after the with clause because a use clause in such a position can only refer to the packages mentioned in the with clause itself.

There is no directly corresponding technique for grouping imported generic parameters. Sometimes we would like to only partially instantiate a generic package. Consider the more general function INTEGRATE of Section 13.3

```
generic
   type FLOATING is digits <>;
   with function F(X: FLOATING) return FLOATING;
function INTEGRATE(A, B: FLOATING) return FLOATING;
```

If we want to do lots of different integrations but all with the same floating type, then it would be rather nice to fix the type parameter once and then only have to bother with the function parameter thereafter. This could be done if our generic function were rewritten as a nested generic thus

```
generic
   type FLOATING is digits <>;
package GENERIC_INTEGRATE is
   generic
      with function F(X: FLOATING) return FLOATING;
   function INTEGRATE(A, B: FLOATING) return FLOATING;
end GENERIC_INTEGRATE;
```

We can then write

```
package REAL_INTEGRATE is new GENERIC_INTEGRATE(REAL);
use REAL_INTEGRATE;
```

and now we can instantiate the inner generic with our actual function G as in Section 13.3. This technique obviously works but we do have to impose a predetermined order on our partial parameterization.

Renaming is a useful (although somewhat heavy) tool for filtering visibility. We can import some entities into a package and then just rename those that we wish to reexport. As an example consider again the package SET_OF. Suppose we wish to instantiate this for type CHARACTER but only want the user to have access to MAKE_SET on single values, "+", "−" and SIZE on the grounds that the other operations are superfluous. (This is only an example!) We write and compile

```
with SET_OF;
package XYZ is new SET_OF(CHARACTER);
```

and then

```
with XYZ;
package CHARACTER_SET is
    subtype SET is XYZ.SET;
    function MAKE_SET(X: CHARACTER) return SET renames
                                            XYZ.MAKE_SET;
    function "+" (X, Y: SET) return SET renames XYZ."+";
    function "−" (X, Y: SET) return SET renames XYZ."−";
    function SIZE(X: SET) return NATURAL renames XYZ.SIZE;
end CHARACTER_SET;
```

The user can now access the reexported facilities from the package CHARACTER_SET without having visibility of the facilities of XYZ. Of course the user could still write **with** XYZ; and this would defeat the object of the exercise. However, it might be that our program library has additional tools which can hide library units without deleting them. Thus we see that the flat library structure of Ada without additional tools is not entirely adequate.

Note also that we had to use a subtype because we cannot rename a type. The subtype declaration also makes available the intrinsic ability to declare objects and perform assignment. However, if we wish to do equality comparisons then we must explicitly rename "=" as well thus

```
function "=" (LEFT, RIGHT: SET) return BOOLEAN renames
                                            XYZ."=";
```

This also makes "/=" available as one would expect. The general rule therefore is that predefined operators can be imported by renaming but intrinsic properties which cannot be dealt with that way are available automatically. In order to properly comprehend the mechanism it must be realized that predefined operators such as "=" are implicitly declared immediately after the declaration of the type to which they refer.

Another example is provided by enumeration types; if we want to have visibility of the literals then they have to be renamed. So writing

```
package C is
    type COLOUR is (RED, AMBER, GREEN);
    -- predefined operators such as = and < applying to the
    -- type COLOUR are implicitly declared here
end;
```

```
with C;
package P is
    subtype LIGHT is C.COLOUR;
    function RED return LIGHT renames C.RED;
    function AMBER return LIGHT renames C.AMBER;
    function "<" (LEFT, RIGHT: LIGHT) return BOOLEAN renames
                                                              C."<";
end;
```

will provide visibility (from P) of the literals RED and AMBER but not GREEN and also of "<" but none of the other relational operators. Further details can be found in the *LRM*.

Rather simpler examples of the renaming technique for controlling visibility are given by the renaming of the exceptions declared in IO_ EXCEPTIONS at the end of the three input–output packages.

We conclude this section by reconsidering the rules for order of compilation and recompilation of the units in a program library. The various different units are categorized as library units or secondary units as summarized in Table 16.3 which also shows their basic inter-relationships.

The reader will recall from Chapter 8 that the compilation order is determined by the dependency relationships. A unit cannot be compiled unless all the units on which it depends have already been compiled. And contrariwise, if a unit is recompiled then all units depending upon it also have to be recompiled. The basic rules for dependency are

- A body is dependent on its specification.

- A subunit is dependent on its parent.

- A unit is also dependent on the specifications of units mentioned in its with clauses.

**Table 16.3**   Compilation units.

| Unit | Category | Depends on |
|------|----------|------------|
| package spec | library | |
| package body | secondary | [generic] package spec |
| subprogram spec | library | |
| subprogram body | library | |
| | secondary | [generic] subprogram spec |
| gen package spec | library | |
| gen subprogram spec | library | |
| subunit | secondary | package body │ subprogram body │ subunit |
| gen package instance | library | |
| gen subprogram instance | library | |

In addition, for implementation reasons, there are also the following auxiliary rules

- If a subprogram call is inlined using the pragma INLINE (see Appendix 1) then the calling unit will be dependent upon the called subprogram body (as well as the specification).

- If several units are compiled together then the compiler may carry out fancy optimizations not otherwise possible and this may result in dependencies between the units.

- An implementation is also allowed to create other dependencies concerning generics; a unit containing an instantiation may be dependent on the generic body (as well as the specification) and on any subunits of that body (AI-408 and AI-506). An implementation may also require that a generic specification and body be compiled together and that a generic body and its stubs be compiled together.

The last rule says in effect that an implementation may require that the whole of a generic unit be compiled before any instantiation. The philosophy of separation of specification and body (and subunits) is difficult in the case of generics and likely to lead to poor implementations.

The basic rules for recompilation are as follows. A newly compiled library unit will replace an existing library unit (of any sort) with the same name. A secondary unit will be rejected unless there already exists a matching unit on which it can depend – a body is rejected unless its specification exists and a subunit is rejected unless its parent body or subunit exists. A successfully compiled secondary unit naturally replaces an existing one. If a unit is replaced then all units dependent on it are also deleted.

These fairly straightforward rules are complicated by the fact that a subprogram need not have a distinct specification and a package may not need a body.

If we start with an empty library and compile a procedure body P, then it will be accepted as a library unit (and not needing a distinct specification). If we subsequently compile a new version of the body then it will replace the previous library unit. If, however, we subsequently compile just the specification of P, then it will make the old body obsolete and we must then compile a new body which will now be classed as a secondary unit. In other words we cannot add the specification as an afterthought and then provide a new body perhaps in the expectation that units dependent just on the specification could avoid recompilation. Moreover, once we have a distinct specification and body we cannot join them up again – if we provide a new body which matches the existing distinct specification, then it will replace the old body, if it does not match the specification then it will be rejected.

The situation is somewhat reversed in the case of a package. We remember that some packages do not need a body but that a body might be useful for initialization. There is a certain risk here since we will not get an error if we mistakenly forget to compile the missing but apparently not necessary body (a good implementation will give a warning). Note that once we have provided such a body, we can only get rid of it by providing a new specification and that will mean that all dependent units have to be recompiled. Of course, we can always provide an explicit null body.

Generics also have to be considered and we need to take care to distinguish between generic units and their instantiations. A generic subprogram always has a distinct specification but a generic package may not need a body. Note carefully that the body of a generic package or subprogram looks just like the body of a plain package or subprogram. It will be classed as one or the other according to the category of the existing specification (a body is rejected if there is no existing specification except in the case of a subprogram which we discussed above (AI-225)). An instantiation however is all in one lump, it is classed as a library unit in its own right and the separation of specification and body does not occur. The notional body of a generic instance cannot be replaced by a newly compiled plain body. For example, suppose we first compile

```
generic
procedure GP;

procedure GP is
begin ... end GP;
```

and then separately compile

```
with GP;
procedure P is new GP;
```

and then submit

```
procedure P is
begin ... end P;
```

The result is that the new unit P will be accepted. However, it will be classed as a library unit and completely replace the existing instantiation. It cannot be taken as a new secondary unit since the instantiation is treated as one lump (AI-199).

We conclude by observing that we have been discussing the Ada language rules regarding the behaviour of the program library. We can expect an implementation to provide utility programs which manipulate the library in additional ways. Any such facilities are outside the scope of this book and we must hence refer the reader to the documentation for the implementation concerned.

---

*Exercise 16.4*

1      Draw a dependency graph for the program PRINT_ROOTS modified to use the package SIMPLE_MATHS as well as SIMPLE_IO as described in Exercise 2.2(**1**). Assume that the bodies of

SIMPLE_MATHS and SIMPLE_IO are as in the answers to Exercises 13.4(**1**) and 15.2(**2**). Assume also that our implementation requires generic units to be compiled as a whole.

---

## 16.5  Portability

An Ada program may or may not be portable. In many cases a program will be intimately concerned with the particular hardware on which it is running; this is particularly true of embedded applications. Such a program cannot be transferred to another machine without significant alteration. On the other hand it is highly desirable to write portable program libraries so that they can be reused in different applications. In some cases a library component will be totally portable; more often it will make certain demands on the implementation or be parameterized so that it can be tailored to its environment in a straightforward manner. This section contains general guidelines on the writing of portable Ada programs.

One thing to avoid is erroneous programs and those with incorrect order dependencies. They can be insidious. A program may work quite satisfactorily on one implementation and may seem superficially to be portable. However, if it happens to depend upon some undefined feature then its behaviour on another implementation cannot be guaranteed. A common example in most programming languages occurs with variables which accidentally are not initialized. It is often the case that the intended value is zero and furthermore many operating systems clear the program area before loading the program. Under such circumstances the program will behave correctly but may give surprising results when transferred to a different implementation. So the concept of erroneous programs is not confined to Ada. In the previous chapters we have mentioned various causes of such illegal programs. For convenience we summarize them here.

An important group of situations concerns the order of evaluation of expressions. Since an expression can include a function call and a function call can have side effects, it follows that different orders of evaluation can sometimes produce different results. The order of evaluation of the following is not defined

- the operands of a binary operator,
- the destination and value in an assignment,
- the components in an aggregate,
- the parameters in a subprogram or entry call,
- the index expressions in a multidimensional name,
- the expressions in a range,
- the guards in a select statement.

There is an important situation where a junk value can arise

- reading an uninitialized variable before assigning to it.

There are two situations where the language mechanism is not defined

- the passing of array, record and private parameters,
- the algorithm for choosing a branch of a select statement.

There are also situations where the programmer is given extra freedom to overcome the stringency of the type model; abuse of this freedom can lead to erroneous programs. Examples are

- suppressing exceptions,
- unchecked deallocation,
- unchecked conversion.

Finally, we recall from Section 16.3 that the order of elaboration of library units is not defined.

Numeric types are another important source of portability problems. The reason is, of course, the compromise necessary between achieving absolutely uniform behaviour on all machines and maximizing efficiency. Ada uses the concept of model numbers as the formalization of this compromise. In principle, if we rely only on the properties of the model numbers then our programs will be portable. In practice this is not easy to do; the reader will recall the problems of overflow in intermediate expressions discussed in Section 12.1.

There are various attributes which, if used correctly, can make our programs more portable. Thus we can use BASE to find out what is really going on and MACHINE_OVERFLOWS to see whether NUMERIC_ERROR (CONSTRAINT_ERROR) will occur or not. But the misuse of these attributes can lead to very non-portable programs.

There is, however, one simple rule that can be followed. We should always declare our own real types and not directly use the predefined types such as FLOAT. Ideally, a similar approach should be taken with integer types, but the language does encourage us to assume that the predefined type INTEGER has a sensible range.

Another area to consider is tasking. Any program that uses tasking is likely to suffer from portability problems because instruction execution times vary from machine to machine. This will affect the relative execution times of tasks as well as their individual execution times. In some cases a program may not be capable of running at all on a particular machine because it does not have adequate processing power. Hard guidelines are almost impossible to give but the following points should be kept in mind.

Take care that the type DURATION is accurate enough for the application. Remember that regular loops cannot easily be achieved if the interval required is not a safe number.

Avoid the unsynchronized use of shared variables as far as possible. Sometimes, timing considerations demand quick and dirty techniques; consult your friendly realtime specialist if tempted. In simple cases the pragma SHARED may be able to prevent interference between tasks.

The use of the abort statement will also give portability problems because of its asynchronous nature.

Avoid also the overuse of priorities. If you need to use priorities to obtain adequate responsiveness then the program is probably stretching the resources of the machine.

The finite speed of the machine leads to our final topic in this section – the finite space available. It is clear that different machines have different sizes and so a program that runs satisfactorily on one machine might raise STORAGE_ERROR on another. Moreover, different implementations may use different storage allocation strategies for access types and task data. We have seen how representation clauses can be used to give control of storage allocation and thereby reduce portability problems. However, the unconsidered use of recursion and access types is best avoided.

---

*Exercise 16.5*

1    The global variable I is of type INTEGER and the function F is

```
function F return INTEGER is
begin
    I:= I+1;
    return I;
end F;
```

Explain why the following fragments of program are illegal. Assume in each case that I is reset to 1.

(a)    I:= I+F;
(b)    A(I):= F;
(c)    AA(I, F):= 0;

---

## 16.6  Program design

This final section considers the question of designing Ada programs. As stated in Section 1.3, this book does not claim to be a treatise on program design. Indeed, program design is still largely an art and the value of different methods of design is often a matter of opinion rather than a matter of fact. We have therefore tried to stick to the facts of Ada and to remain neutral regarding design. Nevertheless much has been learnt about design methods over the last decade and many millions of lines of Ada programs have been designed and written. In particular, Object Oriented Design, which matches Ada well, has gained popularity. So although the general guidelines in this section must be treated with some caution there seems little reason to doubt their general validity. Note also that we are only addressing the question of design issues as they relate to Ada.

There are various low level and stylistic issues which are perhaps obvious. Identifiers should be meaningful. The program should be laid out neatly – the style used in this book is based on that recommended from the syntax in the *LRM*. Useful comments should be added. The block structure should be used to localize declarations to their use. Whenever possible a piece of information should only be written once; thus number and constant declarations should be used rather than explicit literals. And so on.

Programming is really all about abstraction and the mapping of the problem onto constructions in the programming language. We recall from Section 1.2 that the development of programming languages has been concerned with the introduction of various levels of abstraction and that Ada in particular introduces a degree of data abstraction not present in other practically used languages.

An important concept in design and the use of abstractions is information hiding. Information should only be accessible to those parts of a program that need to know. The use of packages and private data types to hide unnecessary detail is the cornerstone of good Ada programming. Indeed as we have stated before Ada is a language which aims to encourage the development of reusable software components; the package is the key component.

Designing an Ada program is therefore largely concerned with designing a group of packages and the interfaces between them. Often we will hope to use one or more existing packages. For this to be possible it is clear that they must have been designed with consistent, clean and sufficiently general interfaces. The difficulties are perhaps in deciding what items are sufficiently related or fundamental to belong together in a package and also how general to make the package. If a package is too general it might be clumsy and inefficient; if not general enough it will not be as useful as it might.

The interface to a package is provided by its specification; at least that provides the syntax of how to use the interface, the semantics must also be defined and that can only be provided by a natural language commentary. Thus consider the package STACK of Section 8.1; its specification (in the Ada sense) guarantees that it will provide subprograms PUSH and POP with certain parameter and result types. However, the specification does not, of itself, guarantee that a call of POP will in fact remove and deliver the top item from the stack. From the point of view of the language it would be quite acceptable for the package body to be

```
package body STACK is
    procedure PUSH(X: INTEGER) is
    begin
        null;
    end;

    function POP return INTEGER is
    begin
        return 0;
    end;
end STACK;
```

However, in our imagined future world of the software components industry, anyone selling such package bodies would soon go out of business.

We will now discuss some categories of related items that might make up useful packages.

A very simple form of package is one which merely consists of a group of related types and constants and has no body. The packages SYSTEM and ASCII are in this category. A further example in Section 8.1 is the package DIURNAL; this does not seem a good example – if it has an array TOMORROW then surely it should also have YESTERDAY. Better examples might be packages of related mathematical constants, conversion constants (metric to imperial say), tables of physical and chemical constants and so on. The last could be

```
package ELEMENTS is
    type ELEMENT is (H, He, Li, ... );
        -- beware of Indium - In is reserved!
    ATOMIC_WEIGHT: array (ELEMENT) of REAL
                := (1.008, 4.003, 6.940, ... );
    ...
end ELEMENTS;
```

Another case is where the package contains functions related by application area. An obvious example is the mathematical library discussed in Section 13.4. The individual functions in such a case are really independent although for efficiency SIN and COS for example are likely to share a common procedure. The package body enables us to hide such a procedure from the user because its existence is merely an implementation detail.

Sometimes a package is needed in order to hide a benevolent side effect – an obvious example is the package RANDOM in Exercise 8.1(1).

Packages such as SEQUENTIAL_IO encapsulate a great deal of hidden information and provide a number of related services. A problem here is deciding whether to provide additional subprograms for convenience or to stick to only those absolutely necessary. The package TEXT_IO contains many convenience subprograms.

Many packages can be classified as a means of providing controlled access to some form of database. The database may consist of just one item as in the package RANDOM or it could be the symbol tables of a compiler or a grand commercial style database and so on. The package BANK in Section 9.3 is another example.

An important use of packages is to provide new data types and associated operations. Obvious examples are the packages COMPLEX_NUMBERS (Section 9.1), RATIONAL_NUMBERS (Exercise 9.1(3)) and QUEUES (Exercise 11.5(3)). In such cases the use of private types enables us to separate the representation of the type from the operations upon it. In a way the new types can be seen as natural extensions to the language.

Packages of this sort raise the question of whether we should use operators rather than functions. Ada is not so flexible as some other languages; new operator forms cannot be introduced and the precedence levels are fixed. This ensures that over-enthusiastic use of operators cannot lead to programs that do not even look like Ada programs as can happen with languages such as POP-2. Even so Ada provides opportunities for surprises. We could write

```
function "−" (X, Y: INTEGER) return INTEGER is
begin
    return STANDARD."+" (X, Y);
end "−";
```

but it would obviously be very foolish to do so. Hence a good general guideline is to minimize surprises.

Operators should be considered for functions with a natural mathematical flavour. As a general rule the normal algebraic properties of the operators should be preserved if this is possible. Thus "+" and "*" should be commutative. Mixed type arithmetic is best avoided but there are situations where it is necessary.

The definitions of the operators in the package COMPLEX_ NUMBERS have the expected properties and do not allow mixed working. It would be nice if type conversion could be done by overloading the type name so that we could write COMPLEX(2.0) rather than CONS(2.0, 0.0). However, Ada does not allow this. Type conversion of this form is restricted to the predefined and derived numeric types.

On the other hand, consider the operators in the predefined package CALENDAR in Section 14.3. Here the very essence of the problem requires mixed type addition but commutivity is preserved by providing two overloadings of "+".

When introducing mathematical types such as COMPLEX and RATIONAL, it is always best to use private types. We will then need to provide constructor and selector functions as well as the natural operations themselves. It will usually be the case that construction and selection are best done with functional notation whereas the natural operations can be done with the operators. However, in the case of rational numbers the division operator "/" provides a natural notation for construction.

There is a general and difficult question of how much to provide in a package for a mathematical type. The bare minimum may be rather spartan and incur all users in unnecessary creation of additional subprograms. To be generous might make the package too cumbersome. For instance should we provide a relational operator and if so should we provide all four? Should input–output be included? Such questions are left for the reader to answer from his or her own experience according to the needs of the application.

Another important issue is storage allocation. This is well illustrated by a type such as POLYNOMIAL introduced in Section 11.1. If this is implemented using a discriminated record thus

```
type POLYNOMIAL(N: INDEX:= 0) is
    record
        A: INTEGER_VECTOR(0 .. N);
    end record;
```

then in the case of unconstrained polynomials the compiler will (unless very clever) allocate the maximum space that could be required. Hence it is important that the range of the discriminant has a sensible upper bound. If we had written

**type** POLYNOMIAL(N: INTEGER:= 0) **is** ...

then each unconstrained polynomial would have had the space for an array of length INTEGER'LAST and we would presumably soon run out of storage.

If all the polynomials are to be fairly small, then using a discriminated record is probably satisfactory. On the other hand, if they are likely to be of greatly varying size then it is probably better to use access types. Indeed a mixed strategy could be used – a fixed array for the first few terms and then the use of an access type for the remainder. In order that such alternative implementation strategies can be properly organized and hidden from the user it is clear that the polynomial should be a private type. The design of a suitable package is left as an informal exercise for the reader.

In designing packages there is the question of what to do when something goes wrong. This brings us to exceptions. Although not new to programming languages they are nevertheless not widely used except in PL/I and the experience with PL/I has not been satisfactory. However, exceptions in Ada are different to those in PL/I in one most important aspect. In Ada one cannot go back to the point where the exception was raised but is forced to consider a proper alternative to the part of the program that went wrong.

Having said that, exceptions nevertheless need care. In Chapter 10 we warned against the unnecessary use of exceptions and in particular the casual raising of the predefined exceptions since we have no guarantee, when handling such an exception, that it was raised for the reason we had in mind.

The first goal should always be to have clean and complete interfaces. As an example consider again the factorial function and the action to be taken when the parameter is illegal. We could consider

- printing a message,
- returning a default value,
- returning a status via a Boolean parameter,
- calling an error procedure,
- raising an exception.

Printing a message is highly unsatisfactory because it raises a host of detailed problems such as the identity of the file, the format of the message and so on. Moreover, it gives the calling program no control over the action it would like to take and some file is cluttered with messages. Furthermore, there is still the question of what to do after having printed the message.

Another possibility is to return a default value such as $-1$ as in Exercise 10.1(**2**). This is not satisfactory since there is no guarantee that the user will check for this default value upon return. If we could rely upon the user doing so then we could equally rely upon the user checking the parameter of the function before calling it in the first place.

If we wish to return an auxiliary status value via another parameter then, as we saw when discussing PUSH and POP in Section 10.2, we can no longer use a function anyway and would have to use a procedure instead. We also have to rely upon the caller again as in the case of the default value.

We could call a global procedure to be supplied by the user. This means agreeing on a standard name which is unsatisfactory. We cannot pass the error procedure as a parameter and to resort to the generic mechanism really is using a steam hammer to crack a nut. In any case we still have the problem, as with printing a message, of what to do afterwards and how to return finally from the function. It is highly naive to suppose that the program can just stop. The manager of the steelworks would not wish the control part of the program to stop just because of a minor error in some other part; there must be a way of carrying on.

There are only two ways out of a subprogram in Ada; back to the point of call or by a propagated exception (the global goto and label parameters of other languages are effectively replaced by the exception). We seem to have eliminated the possibility of returning to the point of call as not reliable and so have to come to the conclusion that the raising of an exception is the appropriate solution.

Another criterion we should consider when deciding whether to use exceptions is whether we expect the condition to arise in the normal course of events or not. If we do then an exception is probably wrong. As an example the end of file condition in the package SEQUENTIAL_IO is tested for by a Boolean function and not an exception. We naturally expect to come to the end of the file and so must test for it – see the answer to Exercise 15.1(**1**).

On the other hand, if we are using the package STACK in say an interpreter for mathematical expressions, then, provided that the interpreter is written correctly, we know that the stack cannot underflow. An exception for this unexpected condition is acceptable. Note also that when using SEQUENTIAL_IO, if we accidentally attempt to read after the end of the file then an exception (END_ERROR) is raised.

The raising of exceptions is, however, not a panacea. We cannot sweep the problem under the carpet in this way. The exception must be handled somewhere otherwise the program will terminate. In fact this is one of their advantages – if the user does nothing then the program will terminate safely, whereas if we return status values and the user does nothing then the program will probably ramble on in a fruitless way.

The indiscriminate use of **others** in an exception handler should be avoided. If we write **others** we are really admitting that anything could have gone wrong and we should take appropriate action; we should not use **others** as shorthand for the exceptions we anticipate.

Another major design area concerns the use of tasks. It is usually fairly clear that a problem needs a solution involving tasks but it is not always clear how the various activities should be allocated to individual tasks.

There are perhaps two major problems to be solved regarding the interactions between tasks. One concerns the transmission of messages between tasks, the other the controlling of access to common data by several tasks.

The rendezvous provides a natural mechanism for the closely coupled transmission of a message; examples are provided by the interaction between mother and the other members of her family in the procedure SHOPPING in Section 14.2 and by the interaction between the server and the customer in the package COBBLERS of Exercise 14.9(1). If the transmission needs to be decoupled so that the sender can carry on before the message is received then some intermediary task is required. Examples are the task BUFFERING in Section 14.4 and the task type MAILBOX in Section 14.6.

Controlled access to common data is, in Ada, also done by an intermediary task whereas in other languages it may use passive constructions such as monitors or low level primitives such as semaphores. The Ada approach usually provides a clearer and safer solution to the problem. An example is the task PROTECTED_VARIABLE in Section 14.4. Quite often the task is encapsulated in a package in order to enforce the required protocol; examples are the package READER_WRITER of Section 14.4 and the package RESOURCE_ALLOCATOR of Section 14.8.

Sometimes the distinction between message passing and controlling data access is blurred; the task BUFFERING at the macro level is passing messages whereas at the micro level it is controlling access to the buffer.

Another categorization of tasks is between users and servers. A pure server task is one with entries but which calls no other tasks whereas a pure user has no entries but calls other tasks. The distinction is emphasized by the asymmetry of the naming in the rendezvous. The server does not know the names of user tasks whereas the user tasks must know the names of the server tasks in order to call their entries. Sometimes a task is part server and part user; an example is the task type READ_AGENT in Section 14.7.

One problem when designing a set of interacting tasks is deciding which way round the entries are to go. Our intuitive model of servers and users should help. The entries belong in the servers. Another criterion is provided by the consideration of alternatives; if a task is to have a choice of rendezvous via a select statement then it must own the entries and therefore be a server. A select statement can be used to accept one of several entry calls but cannot be used to call one of several entries.

It cannot be emphasized too much that aborting tasks must not be done casually. The abort statement is for extreme situations only. One possible use is in a supervisory task where it may be desirable to close down a complete subsystem in response to a command from a human operator.

The reason for wishing to avoid abort is that it makes it very difficult to provide reliable services as we saw with the package READER_WRITER in Section 14.7. If we know that the users cannot be abnormally terminated then the fancy use of secret agents is not necessary; indeed that example should be considered as illustrating what can be done rather than what should be done.

A multitasking Ada program will often be seen as a set of cooperating tasks designed together. In such circumstances we can rely on the calling tasks to obey the necessary protocols and the design of the servers is then simplified.

The use of timed out entry calls also needs some care but is a very natural and common requirement in real time systems. Services should where possible be able to cope with timed out calls.

Finally, there are generics and the whole question of parameterization. Should we write specific packages or very general ones? This is a familiar problem with subprograms and generics merely add a new dimension. Indeed, in the imagined future market for software components it is likely that packages of all sorts of generalities and performance will be available. We conclude by imagining a future conversation in our local software shop

*Customer:*   Could I have a look at the reader-writer package you have in the window?

*Server:*   Certainly. Would you be interested in this robust version – proof against abort? Or we have this slick version for trusty callers. Just arrived this week.

*Customer:*   Well – it's for a cooperating system so the new one sounds good. How much is it?

*Server:*   It's 250 Eurodollars but as it's new there is a special offer with it – a free copy of this random number generator and 10% off your next certification.

*Customer:*   Great. Is it validated?

*Server:*   All our products conform to the highest standards. The parameter mechanism conforms to ES98263 and it has the usual international multitasking certificate.

*Customer:*   OK, I'll take it.

*Server:*   Will you take it as it is or shall I instantiate it for you?

*Customer:*   As it is please. I prefer to do my own instantiation.

   . . .

On this fantasy note we come to the end of this book. It is hoped that the reader will have gained some general understanding of the principles of Ada as well as a lot of the detail. Further understanding will come with use and the author hopes that he has in some small way prepared the reader for the future.

# Appendix 1
# Reserved Words, Attributes and Pragmas

This appendix lists the reserved words and predefined attributes and pragmas. An implementation may define additional attributes and pragmas but not additional reserved words.

The lists of attributes and pragmas are taken from Annexes A and B of the *LRM*. The references have been altered to correspond to appropriate sections of this book.

## A1.1 Reserved words

The following words are reserved, their use is described in the sections indicated.

| | |
|---|---|
| abort | 14.7 |
| abs | 4.5 |
| accept | 14.2 |
| access | 11.4 |
| all | 11.4 |
| and | 4.7, 4.9 |
| array | 6.1 |
| at | 15.4 |
| | |
| begin | 4.2, 7.1, 8.1, 14.1 |
| body | 8.1, 14.1 |
| | |
| case | 5.2, 11.3 |
| constant | 4.1 |
| | |
| declare | 4.2 |
| delay | 14.3 |
| delta | 12.4, 13.2 |
| digits | 12.3, 13.2 |
| do | 14.2 |
| | |
| else | 4.9, 5.1, 14.5 |
| elsif | 5.1 |
| end | 4.2, 7.1, 8.1, 14.1, 14.2 |

| | |
|---|---|
| **entry** | 14.2 |
| **exception** | 10.1 |
| **exit** | 5.3 |
| **for** | 5.3, 15.4 |
| **function** | 7.1 |
| **generic** | 13.1 |
| **goto** | 5.4 |
| **if** | 5.1 |
| **in** | 4.9, 5.3, 7.3 |
| **is** | 4.3, 5.2, 7.1, 8.1, 11.3, 14.1 |
| **limited** | 9.2, 13.2 |
| **loop** | 5.3 |
| **mod** | 4.5, 15.4 |
| **new** | 11.4, 11.7, 13.1 |
| **not** | 4.7, 4.9 |
| **null** | 5.2, 6.7, 11.3, 11.4 |
| **of** | 6.1 |
| **or** | 4.7, 4.9, 14.5 |
| **others** | 5.2, 6.3, 10.1 |
| **out** | 7.3 |
| **package** | 8.1 |
| **pragma** | 2.8 |
| **private** | 9.1, 13.1 |
| **procedure** | 7.3 |
| **raise** | 10.2 |
| **range** | 4.4, 6.1, 6.2, 13.2, 15.4 |
| **record** | 6.7 |
| **rem** | 4.5 |
| **renames** | 8.5 |
| **return** | 7.1, 7.3, 14.2 |
| **reverse** | 5.3 |
| **select** | 14.4, 14.5 |
| **separate** | 8.3 |
| **subtype** | 4.4 |
| **task** | 14.1 |
| **terminate** | 14.7 |
| **then** | 4.9, 5.1 |

| **type** | 4.3 |
|---|---|
| **use** | 8.1, 15.4 |
| **when** | 5.2, 5.3, 10.1, 11.3, 14.4 |
| **while** | 5.3 |
| **with** | 8.2, 13.3 |
| **xor** | 4.7 |

The reserved words **delta**, **digits** and **range** are also used as attributes.

## A1.2  Predefined attributes

The following attributes are predefined in the language

P'ADDRESS   For a prefix P that denotes an object, a program unit, a label, or an entry:
> Yields the address of the first of the storage units allocated to P. For a subprogram, package, task unit or label, this value refers to the machine code associated with the corresponding body or statement. For an entry for which an address clause has been given, the value refers to the corresponding hardware interrupt. The value of this attribute is of the type ADDRESS defined in the package SYSTEM. (See Section 15.4)

P'AFT   For a prefix P that denotes a fixed point subtype:
> Yields the number of decimal digits needed after the point to accommodate the precision of the subtype P, unless the delta of the subtype P is greater than 0.1, in which case the attribute yields the value one. (P'AFT is the smallest positive integer N for which $(10**N)*P$'DELTA is greater than or equal to one.) The value of this attribute is of the type universal integer. (See Section 15.2)

P'BASE   For a prefix P that denotes a type or subtype:
> This attribute denotes the base type of P. It is only allowed as the prefix of the name of another attribute, for example P'BASE'FIRST. (See Section 12.1)

P'CALLABLE   For a prefix P that is appropriate for a task type:
> Yields the value FALSE when the execution of the task P is either completed or terminated, or when the task is abnormal; yields the value TRUE otherwise. The value of this attribute is of the predefined type BOOLEAN. (See Section 14.7)

P'CONSTRAINED   For a prefix P that denotes an object of a type with discriminants:
> Yields the value TRUE if a discriminant constraint applies to the object P, or if the object is a constant (including a formal parameter or generic formal parameter of mode **in**); yields the value FALSE otherwise. If P is a generic formal parameter of mode **in out**, or if P is

a formal parameter of mode **in out** or **out** and the type mark given in the corresponding parameter specification denotes an unconstrained type with discriminants, then the value of this attribute is obtained from that of the corresponding actual parameter. The value of this attribute is of the predefined type BOOLEAN. (See Section 11.2)

P'CONSTRAINED   For a prefix P that denotes a private type or subtype:
   Yields the value FALSE if P denotes an unconstrained nonformal private type with discriminants; also yields the value FALSE if P denotes a generic formal private type and the associated actual subtype is either an unconstrained type with discriminants or an unconstrained array type; yields the value TRUE otherwise. The value of this attribute is of the predefined type BOOLEAN. (See Section 13.2)

P'COUNT   For a prefix P that denotes an entry of a task unit:
   Yields the number of entry calls presently queued on the entry (if the attribute is evaluated within an accept statement for the entry P, the count does not include the calling task). The value of this attribute is of the type universal integer. (See Section 14.4)

P'DELTA   For a prefix P that denotes a fixed point subtype:
   Yields the value of the delta specified in the fixed accuracy definition for the subtype P. The value of this attribute is of the type universal real. (See Section 12.4)

P'DIGITS   For a prefix P that denotes a floating point subtype:
   Yields the number of decimal digits in the decimal mantissa of model numbers of the subtype P. (This attribute yields the number D of Section 12.3.) The value of this attribute is of the type universal integer.

P'EMAX   For a prefix P that denotes a floating point subtype:
   Yields the largest exponent value in the binary canonical form of model numbers of the subtype P. (This attribute yields the product $4*B$ of Section 12.3.) The value of this attribute is of the type universal integer.

P'EPSILON   For a prefix P that denotes a floating point subtype:
   Yields the absolute value of the difference between the model number 1.0 and the next model number above, for the subtype P. The value of this attribute is of the type universal real. (See Section 12.3)

P'FIRST   For a prefix P that denotes a scalar type, or a subtype of a scalar type:
   Yields the lower bound of P. The value of this attribute has the same type as P. (See Section 4.8)

P'FIRST   For a prefix P that is appropriate for an array type, or that denotes a constrained array subtype:
   Yields the lower bound of the first index range. The value of this attribute has the same type as this lower bound. (See Sections 6.1 and 6.2)

P'FIRST(N)   For a prefix P that is appropriate for an array type, or that denotes a constrained array subtype:
   Yields the lower bound of the Nth index range. The value of this attribute has the same type as this lower bound. The argument N

must be a static expression of type universal integer. The value of N must be positive (nonzero) and no greater than the dimensionality of the array. (See Sections 6.1 and 6.2)

P'FIRST_BIT   For a prefix P that denotes a component of a record object:
Yields the offset, from the start of the first of the storage units occupied by the component, of the first bit occupied by the component. This offset is measured in bits. The value of this attribute is of the type universal integer. (See Section 15.4)

P'FORE   For a prefix P that denotes a fixed point subtype:
Yields the minimum number of characters needed for the integer part of the decimal representation of any value of the subtype P, assuming that the representation does not include an exponent, but includes a one character prefix that is either a minus sign or a space. (This minimum number does not include superfluous zeros or underlines; and is at least two.) The value of this attribute is of the type universal integer. (See Section 15.2)

P'IMAGE   For a prefix P that denotes a discrete type or subtype:
This attribute is a function with a single parameter. The actual parameter X must be a value of the base type of P. The result type is the predefined type STRING. The result is the image of the value of X, that is, a sequence of characters representing the value in display form. The image of an integer value is the corresponding decimal literal; without underlines, leading zeros, exponent, or trailing spaces; but with a one character prefix that is either a minus sign or a space.
The image of an enumeration value is either the corresponding identifier in upper case or the corresponding character literal (including the two apostrophes); neither leading nor trailing spaces are included. The image of a character other than a graphic character is implementation-defined.

P'LARGE   For a prefix P that denotes a real subtype:
The attribute yields the largest positive model number of the subtype P. The value of this attribute is of the type universal real. (See Sections 12.3 and 12.4)

P'LAST   For a prefix P that denotes a scalar type or a subtype of a scalar type:
Yields the upper bound of P. The value of this attribute has the same type as P. (See Section 4.8)

P'LAST   For a prefix P that is appropriate for an array type, or that denotes a constrained array subtype:
Yields the upper bound of the first index range. The value of this attribute has the same type as this upper bound. (See Sections 6.1 and 6.2)

P'LAST(N)   For a prefix P that is appropriate for an array type, or that denotes a constrained array subtype:
Yields the upper bound of the Nth index range. The value of this attribute has the same type as this upper bound. The argument N

must be a static expression of type universal integer. The value of N must be positive (nonzero) and no greater than the dimensionality of the array. (See Sections 6.1 and 6.2)

P'LAST_BIT    For a prefix P that denotes a component of a record object:
Yields the offset, from the start of the first of the storage units occupied by the component, of the last bit occupied by the component. This offset is measured in bits. The value of this attribute is of the type universal integer. (See Section 15.4)

P'LENGTH    For a prefix P that is appropriate for an array type, or that denotes a constrained array subtype:
Yields the number of values of the first index range (zero for a null range). The value of this attribute is of the type universal integer. (See Sections 6.1 and 6.2)

P'LENGTH(N)    For a prefix P that is appropriate for an array type, or that denotes a constrained array subtype:
Yields the number of values of the Nth index range (zero for a null range). The value of this attribute is of the type universal integer. The argument N must be a static expression of type universal integer. The value of N must be positive (nonzero) and no greater than the dimensionality of the array. (See Sections 6.1 and 6.2)

P'MACHINE_EMAX    For a prefix P that denotes a floating point type or subtype:
Yields the largest value of *exponent* for the machine representation of the base type of P. The value of this attribute is of the type universal integer. (See Section 15.5)

P'MACHINE_EMIN    For a prefix P that denotes a floating point type or subtype:
Yields the smallest (most negative) value of *exponent* for the machine representation of the base type of P. The value of this attribute is of the type universal integer. (See Section 15.5)

P'MACHINE_MANTISSA    For a prefix P that denotes a floating point type or subtype:
Yields the number of digits in the *mantissa* for the machine representation of the base type of P (the digits are extended digits in the range 0 to P'MACHINE_RADIX−1). The value of this attribute is of the type universal integer. (See Section 15.5)

P'MACHINE_OVERFLOWS    For a prefix P that denotes a real type or subtype:
Yields the value TRUE if every predefined operation on values of the base type of P either provides a correct result or raises the exception NUMERIC_ERROR in overflow situations; yields the value FALSE otherwise. The value of this attribute is of the predefined type BOOLEAN. (See Section 15.5)

P'MACHINE_RADIX    For a prefix P that denotes a floating point type or subtype:
Yields the value of the *radix* used by the machine representation of the base type of P. The value of this attribute is of the type universal integer. (See Section 15.5)

P'MACHINE_ROUNDS   For a prefix P that denotes a real type or subtype:
    Yields the value TRUE if every predefined arithmetic operation on values of the base type of P either returns an exact result or performs rounding; yields the value FALSE otherwise. The value of this attribute is of the predefined type BOOLEAN. (See Section 15.5)

P'MANTISSA   For a prefix P that denotes a real subtype:
    Yields the number of binary digits in the binary mantissa of model numbers of the subtype P. (This attribute yields the number B of Section 12.3 for a floating point type, or of Section 12.4 for a fixed point type). The value of this attribute is of the type universal integer.

P'POS   For a prefix P that denotes a discrete type or subtype:
    This attribute is a function with a single parameter. The actual parameter X must be a value of the base type of P. The result type is the type universal integer. The result is the position number of the value of the actual parameter. (See Section 4.8)

P'POSITION   For a prefix P that denotes a component of a record object:
    Yields the offset, from the start of the first storage unit occupied by the record, of the first of the storage units occupied by the component. This offset is measured in storage units. The value of this attribute is of the type universal integer. (See Section 15.5)

P'PRED   For a prefix P that denotes a discrete type or subtype:
    This attribute is a function with a single parameter. The actual parameter X must be a value of the base type of P. The result is of the base type of P. The result is the value whose position number is one less than that of X. The exception CONSTRAINT_ERROR is raised if X equals P'BASE'FIRST. (See Section 4.8)

P'RANGE   For a prefix P that is appropriate for an array type, or that denotes a constrained array subtype:
    Yields the first index range of P, that is, the range P'FIRST .. P'LAST. (See Sections 6.1 and 6.2)

P'RANGE(N)   For a prefix P that is appropriate for an array type, or that denotes a constrained array subtype:
    Yields the Nth index range of P, that is, the range P'FIRST(N) .. P'LAST(N). (See Sections 6.1 and 6.2)

P'SAFE_EMAX   For a prefix P that denotes a floating point type or subtype:
    Yields the largest exponent value in the binary canonical form of safe numbers of the base type of P. (This attribute yields the number E of Section 12.3.) The value of this attribute is of the type universal integer.

P'SAFE_LARGE   For a prefix P that denotes a real type or subtype:
    Yields the largest positive safe number of the base type of P. The value of this attribute is of the type universal real. (See Sections 12.3 and 12.4)

P'SAFE_SMALL   For a prefix P that denotes a real type or subtype:
    Yields the smallest positive (nonzero) safe number of the base type of P. The value of this attribute is of the type universal real. (See Sections 12.3 and 12.4)

P'SIZE    For a prefix P that denotes an object:
> Yields the number of bits allocated to hold the object. The value of this attribute is of the type universal integer. (See Section 15.4)

P'SIZE    For a prefix P that denotes any type or subtype:
> Yields the minimum number of bits that is needed by the implementation to hold any possible object of the type or subtype P. The value of this attribute is of the type universal integer. (See Section 15.4)

P'SMALL    For a prefix P that denotes a real subtype:
> Yields the smallest positive (nonzero) model number of the subtype P. The value of this attribute is of the type universal real. (See Sections 12.3 and 12.4)

P'STORAGE_SIZE    For a prefix P that denotes an access type or subtype:
> Yields the total number of storage units reserved for the collection associated with the base type P. The value of this attribute is of the type universal integer. (See Section 15.4)

P'STORAGE_SIZE    For a prefix P that denotes a task type or task object:
> Yields the number of storage units reserved for each activation of a task of the type P or for the activation of the task object P. The value of this attribute is of the type universal integer. (See Section 15.4)

P'SUCC    For a prefix P that denotes a discrete type or subtype:
> This attribute is a function with a single parameter. The actual parameter X must be a value of the base type of P. The result type is the base type of P. The result is the value whose position number is one greater than that of X. The exception CONSTRAINT_ERROR is raised if X equals P'BASE'LAST. (See Section 4.8)

P'TERMINATED    For a prefix P that is appropriate for a task type:
> Yields the value TRUE if the task P is terminated; yields the value FALSE otherwise. The value of this attribute is of the predefined type BOOLEAN. (See Section 14.7)

P'VAL    For a prefix P that denotes a discrete type or subtype:
> This attribute is a special function with a single parameter which can be of any integer type. The result type is the base type of P. The result is the value whose position number is the universal integer value corresponding to X. The exception CONSTRAINT_ERROR is raised if the universal integer value corresponding to X is not in the range P'POS(P'BASE'FIRST) .. P'POS(P'BASE'LAST). (See Section 4.8)

P'VALUE    For a prefix P that denotes a discrete type or subtype:
> This attribute is a function with a single parameter. The actual parameter X must be a value of the predefined type STRING. The result type is the base type of P. Any leading and any trailing spaces of the sequence of characters that corresponds to X are ignored.
>
> For an enumeration type, if the sequence of characters has the syntax of an enumeration literal and if this literal exists for the base type of P, the result is the corresponding enumeration value. For an

integer type, if the sequence of characters has the syntax of an integer literal, with an optional single leading character that is a plus or minus sign, and if there is a corresponding value in the base type of P, the result is this value. In any other case, the exception CONSTRAINT_ERROR is raised.

P'WIDTH     For a prefix P that denotes a discrete subtype:
Yields the maximum image length over all values of the subtype P (the image is the sequence of characters returned by the attribute IMAGE). The value of this attribute is of the type universal integer. (See Section 15.2)

## A1.3   Predefined pragmas

The following pragmas are predefined in the language

CONTROLLED     Takes the simple name of an access type as the single argument. This pragma is only allowed immediately within the declarative part or package specification that contains the declaration of the access type; the declaration must occur before the pragma. This pragma is not allowed for a derived type. This pragma specifies that automatic storage reclamation must not be performed for objects designated by values of the access type, except upon leaving the innermost block statement, subprogram body, or task body that encloses the access type declaration, or after leaving the main program. (See Section 11.4)

ELABORATE     Takes one or more simple names denoting library units as arguments. This pragma is only allowed immediately after the context clause of a compilation unit (before the subsequent library unit or secondary unit). Each argument must be the simple name of a library unit mentioned by the context clause. This pragma specifies that the corresponding library unit body must be elaborated before the given compilation unit. If the given compilation unit is a subunit, the library unit body must be elaborated before the body of the ancestor library unit of the subunit. (See Section 16.3)

INLINE     Takes one or more names as arguments; each name is either the name of a subprogram or the name of a generic subprogram. This pragma is only allowed at the place of a declarative item in a declarative part or package specification, or after a library unit in a compilation, but before any subsequent compilation unit. This pragma specifies that the subprogram bodies should be expanded inline at each call whenever possible; in the case of a generic subprogram, the pragma applies to calls of its instantiations. (See Section 15.5)

INTERFACE     Takes a language name and a subprogram name as arguments. This pragma is allowed at the place of a declarative item, and must apply in this case to a subprogram declared by an earlier declarative item of the same declarative part or package specification. This pragma is also allowed for a library unit; in this case the pragma must appear after the subprogram declaration, and before any subsequent compilation unit. This pragma specifies the other language (and thereby the calling conventions) and informs the compiler that an object module will be supplied for the corresponding subprogram. (See Section 15.7)

LIST    Takes one of the identifiers ON or OFF as the single argument. This pragma is allowed anywhere a pragma is allowed. It specifies that listing of the compilation is to be continued or suspended until a LIST pragma with the opposite argument is given within the same compilation. The pragma itself is always listed if the compiler is producing a listing. (See Section 2.8)

MEMORY_SIZE    Takes a numeric literal as the single argument. This pragma is only allowed at the start of a compilation, before the first compilation unit (if any) of the compilation. The effect of this pragma is to use the value of the specified numeric literal for the definition of the named number MEMORY_SIZE. (See Section 15.5)

OPTIMIZE    Takes one of the identifiers TIME or SPACE as the single argument. This pragma is only allowed within a declarative part and it applies to the block or body enclosing the declarative part. It specifies whether time or space is the primary optimization criterion. (See Section 15.5)

PACK    Takes the simple name of a record or array type as the single argument. The allowed positions for this pragma, and the restrictions on the named type, are governed by the same rules as for a representation clause. The pragma specifies that storage minimization should be the main criterion when selecting the representation of the given type. (See Section 15.5)

PAGE    This pragma has no argument, and is allowed anywhere a pragma is allowed. It specifies that the program text which follows the pragma should start on a new page (if the compiler is currently producing a listing). (See Section 2.8)

PRIORITY    Takes a static expression of the predefined integer subtype PRIORITY as the single argument. This pragma is only allowed within the specification of a task unit or immediately within the outermost declarative part of a main program. It specifies the priority of the task (or tasks of the task type) or the priority of the main program. (See Section 14.3)

SHARED    Takes the simple name of a variable as the single argument. This pragma is allowed only for a variable declared by an object declaration and whose type is a scalar or access type; the variable declaration and the pragma must both occur (in this order) immediately within the same declarative part or package specification. This pragma specifies that every read or update of the variable is a synchronization point for that variable. An implementation must restrict the objects for which this pragma is allowed to objects for which each of direct reading and direct updating is implemented as an indivisible operation. (See Section 14.9)

STORAGE_UNIT   Takes a numeric literal as the single argument. This pragma is only allowed at the start of a compilation, before the first compilation unit (if any) of the compilation. The effect of this pragma is to use the value of the specified numeric literal for the definition of the named number STORAGE_UNIT. (See Section 15.5)

SUPPRESS   Takes as arguments the identifier of a check and optionally also the name of either an object, a type or subtype, a subprogram, a task unit, or a generic unit. This pragma is only allowed either immediately within a declarative part or immediately within a package specification. In the latter case, the only allowed form is with a name that denotes an entity (or several overloaded subprograms) declared immediately within the package specification. The permission to omit the given check extends from the place of the pragma to the end of the declarative region associated with the innermost enclosing block statement or program unit. For a pragma given in a package specification, the permission extends to the end of the scope of the named entity.

If the pragma includes a name, the permission to omit the given check is further restricted: it is given only for operations on the named object or on all objects of the base type of a named type or subtype; for calls of a named subprogram; for activations of tasks of the named task type; or for instantiations of the given generic unit. (See Section 15.5)

SYSTEM_NAME   Takes an enumeration literal as the single argument. This pragma is only allowed at the start of a compilation, before the first compilation unit (if any) of the compilation. The effect of this pragma is to use the enumeration literal with the specified identifier for the definition of the constant SYSTEM_NAME. This pragma is only allowed if the specified identifier corresponds to one of the literals of the type NAME declared in the package SYSTEM. (See Section 15.5)

# Appendix 2
# Predefined Language Environment

As mentioned earlier, certain entities are predefined through their declaration in a special package STANDARD. It should not be thought that this package necessarily actually exists; it is just that the compiler behaves as if it does. Indeed, as we shall see, some entities notionally declared in STANDARD cannot be truly declared in Ada at all. The general effect of STANDARD is indicated by the outline specification below which is taken from Annex C of the *LRM*.

The operators that are predefined for the types declared in the package STANDARD are given in comments since they are implicitly declared. Italics are used for identifiers that are not available to users (such as the identifier *universal_real*) and for undefined information (such as *implementation_defined* and *any_fixed_point_type*).

**package** STANDARD **is**

   **type** BOOLEAN **is** (FALSE, TRUE);

   -- The predefined relational operators for this type are as follows:

   -- **function** "="   (LEFT, RIGHT: BOOLEAN) **return** BOOLEAN;
   -- **function** "/="  (LEFT, RIGHT: BOOLEAN) **return** BOOLEAN;
   -- **function** "<"   (LEFT, RIGHT: BOOLEAN) **return** BOOLEAN;
   -- **function** "<=" (LEFT, RIGHT: BOOLEAN) **return** BOOLEAN;
   -- **function** ">"   (LEFT, RIGHT: BOOLEAN) **return** BOOLEAN:
   -- **function** ">=" (LEFT, RIGHT: BOOLEAN) **return** BOOLEAN;

   -- The logical operators and the logical negation operator are as
   -- follows:

   **function** "and"  (LEFT, RIGHT: BOOLEAN) **return** BOOLEAN;
   **function** "or"   (LEFT, RIGHT: BOOLEAN) **return** BOOLEAN;
   **function** "xor"  (LEFT, RIGHT: BOOLEAN) **return** BOOLEAN;
   **function** "not"  (RIGHT: BOOLEAN) **return** BOOLEAN;

   -- The universal type *universal_integer* is predefined

   **type** INTEGER **is** *implementation_defined*;

—— The predefined operators for this type are as follows:

—— **function** "=" (LEFT, RIGHT: INTEGER) **return** BOOLEAN;
—— **function** "/=" (LEFT, RIGHT: INTEGER) **return** BOOLEAN;
—— **function** "<" (LEFT, RIGHT: INTEGER) **return** BOOLEAN;
—— **function** "<=" (LEFT, RIGHT: INTEGER) **return** BOOLEAN;
—— **function** ">" (LEFT, RIGHT: INTEGER) **return** BOOLEAN;
—— **function** ">=" (LEFT, RIGHT: INTEGER) **return** BOOLEAN;

—— **function** "+" (RIGHT: INTEGER) **return** INTEGER;
—— **function** "−" (RIGHT: INTEGER) **return** INTEGER;
—— **function** "abs" (RIGHT: INTEGER) **return** INTEGER;

—— **function** "+" (LEFT, RIGHT: INTEGER) **return** INTEGER;
—— **function** "−" (LEFT, RIGHT: INTEGER) **return** INTEGER;
—— **function** "∗" (LEFT, RIGHT: INTEGER) **return** INTEGER;
—— **function** "/" (LEFT, RIGHT: INTEGER) **return** INTEGER;
—— **function** "rem" (LEFT, RIGHT: INTEGER) **return** INTEGER;
—— **function** "mod" (LEFT, RIGHT: INTEGER) **return** INTEGER;
—— **function** "∗∗" (LEFT: INTEGER; RIGHT: INTEGER)
                                          **return** INTEGER;

—— An implementation may provide additional predefined integer
—— types. It is recommended that the names of such additional
—— types end with INTEGER as in SHORT_INTEGER or
—— LONG_INTEGER.
—— The specification of each operator for the type *universal_integer*,
—— or for any additional predefined integer type, is obtained by
—— replacing INTEGER by the name of the type in the specification of
—— the corresponding operator of the type INTEGER, except for the
—— right operand of the exponentiating operator.

—— The universal type *universal_real* is predefined.

**type** FLOAT **is** *implementation_defined*;

—— The predefined operators for this type are as follows:

—— **function** "=" (LEFT, RIGHT: FLOAT) **return** BOOLEAN;
—— **function** "/=" (LEFT, RIGHT: FLOAT) **return** BOOLEAN;
—— **function** "<" (LEFT, RIGHT: FLOAT) **return** BOOLEAN;
—— **function** "<=" (LEFT, RIGHT: FLOAT) **return** BOOLEAN;
—— **function** ">" (LEFT, RIGHT: FLOAT) **return** BOOLEAN;
—— **function** ">=" (LEFT, RIGHT: FLOAT) **return** BOOLEAN;

—— **function** "+" (RIGHT: FLOAT) **return** FLOAT;
—— **function** "−" (RIGHT: FLOAT) **return** FLOAT;
—— **function** "abs" (RIGHT: FLOAT) **return** FLOAT;

```
-- function "+"   (LEFT, RIGHT: FLOAT) return FLOAT;
-- function "-"   (LEFT, RIGHT: FLOAT) return FLOAT;
-- function "*"   (LEFT, RIGHT: FLOAT) return FLOAT;
-- function "/"   (LEFT, RIGHT: FLOAT) return FLOAT;
-- function "**"  (LEFT: FLOAT; RIGHT: INTEGER) return FLOAT;
```

-- An implementation may provide additional predefined floating
-- point types. It is recommended that the names of such additional
-- types end with FLOAT as in SHORT_FLOAT or LONG_FLOAT.
-- The specification of each operator for the type *universal_real*, or
-- for any additional predefined floating point type, is obtained by
-- replacing FLOAT by the name of the type in the specification of the
-- corresponding operator of the type FLOAT.

-- In addition the following operators are predefined for universal
-- types:

```
-- function "*" (LEFT: universal_integer;
                 RIGHT: universal_real) return universal_real;

-- function "*" (LEFT: universal_real;
                 RIGHT: universal_integer) return universal_real;

-- function "/" (LEFT: universal_real;
                 RIGHT: universal_integer) return universal_real;
```

-- The type *universal_fixed* is predefined. The only operators
-- declared for this type are

```
-- function "*" (LEFT: any_fixed_point_type;
                 RIGHT: any_fixed_point_type)
                 return universal_fixed;

-- function "/" (LEFT: any_fixed_point_type;
                 RIGHT: any_fixed_point_type)
                 return universal_fixed;
```

-- The following characters form the standard ASCII character set.
-- Character literals corresponding to control characters are not
-- identifiers; they are indicated in italics in this definition.

**type** CHARACTER **is**

```
(nul,  soh,  stx,  etx,      eot,  enq,  ack,  bel,
 bs,   ht,   lf,   vt,       ff,   cr,   so,   si,
 dle,  dc1,  dc2,  dc3,      dc4,  nak,  syn,  etb,
 can,  em,   sub,  esc,      fs,   gs,   rs,   us,
 ' ',  '!',  '"',  '#',      '$',  '%',  '&',  ''',
```

```
'(',  ')',  '*',  '+',       ',',  '-',  '.',  '/',
'0',  '1',  '2',  '3',       '4',  '5',  '6',  '7',
'8',  '9',  ':',  ';',       '<',  '=',  '>',  '?',
'@',  'A',  'B',  'C',       'D',  'E',  'F',  'G',
'H',  'I',  'J',  'K',       'L',  'M',  'N',  'O',
'P',  'Q',  'R',  'S',       'T',  'U',  'V',  'W',
'X',  'Y',  'Z',  '[',       '\',  ']',  '^',  '_',
'`',  'a',  'b',  'c',       'd',  'e',  'f',  'g',
'h',  'i',  'j',  'k',       'l',  'm',  'n',  'o',
'p',  'q',  'r',  's',       't',  'u',  'v',  'w',
'x',  'y',  'z',  '{',       '|',  '}',  '~',  del);
```

**for** CHARACTER **use** –– 128 ASCII character set without holes
(0, 1, 2, 3, 4, 5, ..., 125, 126, 127);

–– The predefined operators for the type CHARACTER are the same
–– as for any enumeration type.

**package** ASCII **is**

–– Control characters:

```
NUL: constant CHARACTER:= nul;
SOH: constant CHARACTER:= soh;
STX: constant CHARACTER:= stx;
ETX: constant CHARACTER:= etx;
EOT: constant CHARACTER:= eot;
ENQ: constant CHARACTER:= enq;
ACK: constant CHARACTER:= ack;
BEL: constant CHARACTER:= bel;
BS:  constant CHARACTER:= bs;
HT:  constant CHARACTER:= ht;
LF:  constant CHARACTER:= lf;
VT:  constant CHARACTER:= vt;
FF:  constant CHARACTER:= ff;
CR:  constant CHARACTER:= cr;
SO:  constant CHARACTER:= so;
SI:  constant CHARACTER:= si;
DLE: constant CHARACTER:= dle;
DC1: constant CHARACTER:= dc1;
DC2: constant CHARACTER:= dc2;
DC3: constant CHARACTER:= dc3;
DC4: constant CHARACTER:= dc4;
NAK: constant CHARACTER:= nak;
SYN: constant CHARACTER:= syn;
ETB: constant CHARACTER:= etb;
CAN: constant CHARACTER:= can;
EM:  constant CHARACTER:= em;
SUB: constant CHARACTER:= sub;
ESC: constant CHARACTER:= esc;
```

```
FS:    constant CHARACTER:= fs;
GS:    constant CHARACTER:= gs;
RS:    constant CHARACTER:= rs;
US:    constant CHARACTER:= us;
DEL:   constant CHARACTER:= del;
```

-- Other characters

```
EXCLAM:        constant CHARACTER:= '!';
QUOTATION:     constant CHARACTER:= '"';
SHARP:         constant CHARACTER:= '#';
DOLLAR:        constant CHARACTER:= '$';
PERCENT:       constant CHARACTER:= '%';
AMPERSAND:     constant CHARACTER:= '&';
COLON:         constant CHARACTER:= ':';
SEMICOLON:     constant CHARACTER:= ';';
QUERY:         constant CHARACTER:= '?';
AT_SIGN:       constant CHARACTER:= '@';
L_BRACKET:     constant CHARACTER:= '[';
BACK_SLASH:    constant CHARACTER:= '\';
R_BRACKET:     constant CHARACTER:= ']';
CIRCUMFLEX:    constant CHARACTER:= '^';
UNDERLINE:     constant CHARACTER:= '_';
GRAVE:         constant CHARACTER:= '`';
L_BRACE:       constant CHARACTER:= '{';
BAR:           constant CHARACTER:= '|';
R_BRACE:       constant CHARACTER:= '}';
TILDE:         constant CHARACTER:= '~';
```

-- Lower case letters
```
LC_A: constant CHARACTER:= 'a';
    ...
LC_Z: constant CHARACTER:= 'z';
end ASCII;
```

-- Predefined subtypes:

```
subtype NATURAL is INTEGER range 0 .. INTEGER'LAST;
subtype POSITIVE is INTEGER range 1 .. INTEGER'LAST;
```

-- Predefined string type:

```
type STRING is array (POSITIVE range <>) of CHARACTER;
pragma PACK(STRING);
```

-- The predefined operators for this type are as follows:

```
-- function "=" (LEFT, RIGHT: STRING) return BOOLEAN;
-- function "/=" (LEFT, RIGHT: STRING) return BOOLEAN;
```

```
-- function "<"   (LEFT, RIGHT: STRING) return BOOLEAN;
-- function "<=" (LEFT, RIGHT: STRING) return BOOLEAN;
-- function ">"   (LEFT, RIGHT: STRING) return BOOLEAN;
-- function ">=" (LEFT, RIGHT: STRING) return BOOLEAN;
-- function "&"   (LEFT: STRING; RIGHT: STRING)
                                              return STRING;
-- function "&"   (LEFT: CHARACTER; RIGHT: STRING)
                                              return STRING;
-- function "&"   (LEFT: STRING; RIGHT: CHARACTER)
                                              return STRING;
-- function "&"   (LEFT: CHARACTER; RIGHT: CHARACTER)
                                              return STRING;


type DURATION is delta implementation_defined range
                                  implementation_defined;

-- The predefined operators for the type DURATION are the same
-- as for any fixed point type.

-- The predefined exceptions

CONSTRAINT_ERROR:  exception;
NUMERIC_ERROR:     exception;
PROGRAM_ERROR:     exception;
STORAGE_ERROR:     exception;
TASKING_ERROR:     exception;


end STANDARD;
```

The above specification is not complete. For example, although the type BOOLEAN can be written showing the literals FALSE and TRUE, the short circuit control forms cannot be expressed explicitly. Moreover, each further type definition introduces new overloadings of some operators. All types, except limited types, introduce new overloadings of = and /=. All scalar types and discrete one-dimensional array types introduce new overloadings of & and those with BOOLEAN components also introduce new overloadings of and, or, xor and not. Finally, all fixed point types introduce new overloadings of +, −, *, / and abs.

In addition there are also certain other predefined library units such as CALENDAR (see Section 14.3), SEQUENTIAL_IO and DIRECT_IO (see Section 15.1), TEXT_IO (see Section 15.2), SYSTEM (see Section 15.5) and UNCHECKED_CONVERSION and UNCHECKED_DEALLOCATION (see Section 15.6).

# Appendix 3
# Glossary

The following glossary is reproduced from Appendix D of the *LRM*. Italicized terms in the abbreviated descriptions below either have glossary entries themselves or are described in entries for related terms.

**Access statement**  See *entry*.

**Access type**  A value of an access type (an *access value*) is either a null value, or a value that *designates* an *object* created by an *allocator*. The designated object can be read and updated via the access value. The definition of an access type specifies the type of the objects designated by values of the access type. See also *collection*.

**Actual parameter**  See *parameter*.

**Aggregate**  The evaluation of an aggregate yields a value of a *composite type*. The value is specified by giving the value of each of the *components*. Either *positional association* or *named association* may be used to indicate which value is associated with which component.

**Allocator**  The evaluation of an allocator creates an *object* and returns a new *access value* which *designates* the object.

**Array type**  A value of an array type consists of *components* which are all of the same *subtype* (and hence, of the same type). Each component is uniquely distinguished by an *index* (for a one-dimensional array) or by a sequence of indices (for a multidimensional array). Each index must be a value of a *discrete type* and must lie in the correct index *range*.

**Assignment**  Assignment is the *operation* that replaces the current value of a *variable* by a new value. An *assignment statement* specifies a variable on the left, and on the right, an *expression* whose value is to be the new value of the variable.

**Attribute**  The evaluation of an attribute yields a predefined characteristic of a named entity; some attributes are *functions*.

**Block statement**   A block statement is a single statement that may contain a sequence of statements. It may also include a *declarative part*, and *exception handlers*; their effects are local to the block statement.

**Body**   A body defines the execution of a *subprogram*, *package*, or *task*. A *body stub* is a form of body that indicates that this execution is defined in a separately compiled *subunit*.

**Collection**   A collection is the entire set of *objects* created by evaluation of *allocators* for an *access type*.

**Compilation unit**   A compilation unit is the *declaration* or the *body* of a *program unit*, presented for compilation as an independent test. It is optionally preceded by a *context clause*, naming other compilation units upon which it depends by means of one or more *with clauses*.

**Component**   A component is a value that is a part of a larger value, or an *object* that is part of a larger object.

**Composite type**   A composite type is one whose values have *components*. There are two kinds of composite type: *array types* and *record types*.

**Constant**   See *object*.

**Constraint**   A constraint determines a subset of the values of a *type*. A value in that subset *satisfies* the constraint.

**Context clause**   See *compilation unit*.

**Declaration**   A declaration associates an identifier (or some other notation) with an entity. This association is in effect within a region of text called the *scope* of the declaration. Within the scope of a declaration, there are places where it is possible to use the identifier to refer to the associated declared entity. At such places the identifier is said to be a *simple name* of the entity; the *name* is said to *denote* the associated entity.

**Declarative part**   A declarative part is a sequence of *declarations*. It may also contain related information such as *subprogram bodies* and *representation clauses*.

**Denote**   See *declaration*.

**Derived type**   A derived type is a *type* whose operations and values are replicas of those of an existing type. The existing type is called the *parent type* of the derived type.

**Designate**   See *access type*, *task*.

**Direct visibility**   See *visibility*.

**Discrete type**    A discrete type is a *type* which has an ordered set of distinct values. The discrete types are the *enumeration* and *integer types*. Discrete types are used for indexing and iteration, and for choices in case statements and record *variants*.

**Discriminant**    A discriminant is a distinguished *component* of an *object* or value of a *record type*. The *subtypes* of other components, or even their presence or absence, may depend on the value of the discriminant.

**Discriminant constraint**    A discriminant constraint on a *record type* or *private type* specifies a value for each *discriminant* of the *type*.

**Elaboration**    The elaboration of a *declaration* is the process by which the declaration achieves its effect (such as creating an *object*); this process occurs during program execution.

**Entry**    An entry is used for communication between *tasks*. Externally, an entry is called just as a *subprogram* is called; its internal behavior is specified by one or more *accept statements* specifying the actions to be performed when the entry is called.

**Enumeration type**    An enumeration type is a *discrete type* the values of which are represented by enumeration literals which are given explicitly in the *type declaration*. These enumeration literals are either *identifiers* or *character literals*.

**Evaluation**    The evaluation of an *expression* is the process by which the value of the expression is computed. This process occurs during program execution.

**Exception**    An exception is an error situation which may arise during program execution. To *raise* an exception is to abandon normal program execution so as to signal that the error has taken place. An *exception handler* is a portion of program text specifying a response to the exception. Execution of such a program text is called *handling* the exception.

**Expanded name**    An expanded name *denotes* an entity which is *declared* immediately within some construct. An expanded name has the form of a *selected component*: the *prefix* denotes the construct (a *program unit*; or a *block*, loop, or *accept statement*); the *selector* is the *simple name* of the entity.

**Expression**    An expression defines the computation of a value.

**Fixed point type**    See *real type*.

**Floating point type**    See *real type*.

**Formal parameter**    See *parameter*.

**Function**    See *subprogram*.

**Generic unit**    A generic unit is a template either for a set of *subprograms* or for a set of *packages*. A subprogram or package created using the template is called an *instance* of the generic unit. A *generic instantiation* is the kind of *declaration* that creates an instance. A generic unit is written as a subprogram or package but with the specification prefixed by a *generic formal part* which may declare *generic formal parameters*. A generic formal parameter is either a *type*, a *subprogram*, or an *object*. A generic unit is one of the kinds of *program unit*.

**Handler**    See *exception*.

**Index**    See *array type*.

**Index constraint**    An index constraint for an *array type* specifies the lower and upper bounds for each index *range* of the array type.

**Indexed component**    An indexed component *denotes* a *component* in an *array*. It is a form of *name* containing *expressions* which specify the values of the *indices* of the array component. An indexed component may also denote an *entry* in a family of entries.

**Instance**    See *generic unit*.

**Integer type**    An integer type is a *discrete type* whose values represent all integer numbers within a specific *range*.

**Lexical element**    A lexical element is an identifier, a *literal*, a delimiter, or a comment.

**Limited type**    A limited type is a *type* for which neither assignment nor the predefined comparison for equality is implicitly declared. All *task* types are limited. A *private type* can be defined to be limited. An equality operator can be explicitly declared for a limited type.

**Literal**    A literal represents a value literally, that is, by means of letters and other characters. A literal is either a numeric literal, an enumeration literal, a character literal, or a string literal.

**Mode**    See *parameter*.

**Model number**    A model number is an exactly representable value of a *real type*. *Operations* of a real type are defined in terms of operations on the model numbers of the type. The properties of the model numbers and of their operations are the minimal properties preserved by all implementations of the real type.

**Name**   A name is a construct that stands for an entity: it is said that the name *denotes* the entity, and that the entity is the meaning of the name. See also *declaration*, *prefix*.

**Named association**   A named association specifies the association of an item with one or more positions in a list, by naming the positions.

**Object**   An object contains a value. A program creates an object either by *elaborating* an *object declaration* or by *evaluating* an *allocator*. The declaration or allocator specifies a *type* for the object: the object can only contain values of that type.

**Operation**   An operation is an elementary action associated with one or more *types*. It is either implicitly declared by the *declaration* of the type, or it is a *subprogram* that has a *parameter* or *result* of the type.

**Operator**   An operator is an operation which has one or two operands. A unary operator is written before an operand; a binary operator is written between two operands. This notation is a special kind of *function call*. An operator can be declared as a function. Many operators are implicitly declared by the *declaration* of a *type* (for example, most type declarations imply the declaration of the equality operator for values of the type).

**Overloading**   An identifier can have several alternative meanings at a given point in the program text; this property is called *overloading*. For example, an overloaded enumeration literal can be an identifier that appears in the definitions of two or more *enumeration types*. The effective meaning of an overloaded identifier is determined by the context. *Subprograms*, *aggregates*, *allocators*, and string *literals* can also be overloaded.

**Package**   A package specifies a group of logically related entities, such as *types*, *objects* of those types, and *subprograms* with *parameters* of those types. It is written as a *package declaration* and a *package body*. The package declaration has a *visible part*, containing the *declarations* of all entities that can be explicitly used outside the package. It may also have a *private part* containing structural details that complete the specification of the visible entities, but which are irrelevant to the user of the package. The *package body* contains implementations of *subprograms* (and possibly *tasks* and other *packages*) that have been specified in the package declaration. A package is one of the kinds of *program unit*.

**Parameter**   A parameter is one of the named entities associated with a *subprogram*, *entry*, or *generic unit*, and used to communicate with the corresponding subprogram body, *accept statement* or generic body. A *formal parameter* is a designator used to denote the named entity within the body. An *actual parameter* is the particular entity associated with the corresponding formal parameter by a *subprogram call*, *entry call*, or *generic instantiation*. The *mode* of a formal parameter specifies whether the associated actual parameter supplies a value for the formal parameter, or the formal supplies a value for the actual parameter, or both. The association of actual parameters with formal parameters can be specified by *named associations*, by *positional associations*, or by a combination of these.

**Parent type**   See *derived type*.

**Positional association**   A positional association specifies the association of an item with a position in a list, by using the same position in the text to specify the item.

**Pragma**   A pragma conveys information to the compiler.

**Prefix**   A prefix is used as the first part of certain kinds of name. A prefix is either a *function call* or a *name*.

**Private part**   See *package*.

**Private type**   A private type is a *type* whose structure and set of values are clearly defined, but not directly available to the user of the type. A private type is known only by its *discriminants* (if any) and by the set of *operations* defined for it. A private type and its applicable operations are defined in the *visible part* of a *package*, or in a *generic formal part*. *Assignment*, equality, and inequality are also defined for private types, unless the private type is *limited*.

**Procedure**   See *subprogram*.

**Program**   A program is composed of a number of *compilation units*, one of which is a *subprogram* called the *main program*. Execution of the program consists of execution of the main program, which may invoke subprograms declared in the other compilation units of the program.

**Program unit**   A program unit is any one of a *generic unit*, *package*, *subprogram*, or *task unit*.

**Qualified expression**   A qualified expression is an *expression* preceded by an indication of its *type* or *subtype*. Such qualification is used when, in its absence, the expression might be ambiguous (for example as a consequence of *overloading*).

**Raising an exception**   See *exception*.

**Range**   A range is a contiguous set of values of a *scalar type*. A range is specified by giving the lower and upper bounds for the values. A value in the range is said to *belong* to the range.

**Range constraint**   A range constraint of a *type* specifies a *range*, and thereby determines the subset of the values of the type that *belong* to the range.

**Real type**   A real type is a *type* whose values represent approximations to the real numbers. There are two kinds of real type: *fixed point types* are specified by an absolute error bound; *floating point types* are specified by a relative error bound expressed as a number of significant decimal digits.

**Record type**   A value of a record type consists of *components* which are usually of different *types* or *subtypes*. For each component of a record value or record *object*, the definition of the record type specifies an identifier that uniquely determines the component within the record.

**Renaming declaration**   A renaming declaration declares another *name* for an entity.

**Rendezvous**   A rendezvous is the interaction that occurs between two parallel *tasks* when one task has called an *entry* of the other task, and a corresponding *accept statement* is being executed by the other task on behalf of the calling task.

**Representation clause**   A representation clause directs the compiler in the selection of the mapping of a *type*, an *object*, or a *task* onto features of the underlying machine that executes a program. In some cases, representation clauses completely specify the mapping; in other cases, they provide criteria for choosing a mapping.

**Satisfy**   See *constraint, subtype*.

**Scalar type**   An *object* or value of a scalar *type* does not have *components*. A scalar type is either a *discrete type* or a *real type*. The values of a scalar type are ordered.

**Scope**   See *declaration*.

**Selected component**   A selected component is a *name* consisting of a *prefix* and of an identifier called the *selector*. Selected components are used to denote record components, *entries*, and *objects* designated by access values; they are also used as *expanded names*.

**Selector**   See *selected component*.

**Simple name**   See *declaration, name*.

**Statement**  A statement specifies one or more actions to be performed during the execution of a *program*.

**Subcomponent**  A subcomponent is either a *component*, or a component of another subcomponent.

**Subprogram**  A subprogram is either a *procedure* or a *function*. A procedure specifies a sequence of actions and is invoked by a *procedure call* statement. A function specifies a sequence of actions and also returns a value called the *result*, and so a *function call* is an *expression*. A subprogram is written as a *subprogram declaration*, which specifies its *name*, *formal parameters*, and (for a function) its result; and a *subprogram body* which specifies the sequence of actions. The subprogram call specifies the *actual parameters* that are to be associated with the formal parameters. A subprogram is one of the kinds of *program unit*.

**Subtype**  A subtype of a *type* characterizes a subset of the values of the type. The subset is determined by a *constraint* on the type. Each value in the set of values of a subtype *belongs* to the subtype and *satisfies* the constraint determining the subtype.

**Subunit**  See *body*.

**Task**  A task operates in parallel with other parts of the program. It is written as a *task specification* (which specifies the *name* of the task and the names and *formal parameters* of its entries), and a *task body* which defines its execution. A *task unit* is one of the kinds of *program unit*. A *task type* is a *type* that permits the subsequent *declaration* of any number of similar tasks of the type. A value of a task type is said to *designate* a task.

**Type**  A type characterizes both a set of values, and a set of *operations* applicable to those values. A *type definition* is a language construct that defines a type. A particular type is either an *access type*, an *array type*, a *private type*, a *record type*, a *scalar type*, or a *task type*.

**Use clause**  A use clause achieves *direct visibility* of *declarations* that appear in the *visible parts* of named *packages*.

**Variable**  See *object*.

**Variant part**  A variant part of a *record* specifies alternative record *components*, depending on a *discriminant* of the record. Each value of the discriminant establishes a particular alternative of the variant part.

**Visibility**  At a given point in a program text, the *declaration* of an entity with a certain identifier is said to be *visible* if the entity is an acceptable meaning for an occurrence at that point of the identifier.

The declaration is *visible* by *selection* at the place of the *selector* in a *selected component* or at the place of the name in a *named association*. Otherwise, the declaration is *directly visible*, that is, if the identifier alone has that meaning.

**Visible part**   See *package*.

**With clause**   See *compilation unit*.

# Appendix 4
# Syntax

The following syntax rules are taken from Appendix E of the *LRM*. The rules have been rearranged to correspond to the order of introduction of the topics in this book but individual rules have not been changed.

It should be noted that the rules for the construction of lexical elements, which are under the subheading of Chapter 3, have a slightly different status to the other rules since spaces and newlines may be freely inserted between lexical elements but not within lexical elements.

The rules have been sequentially numbered for ease of reference; an index to them will be found in Section A4.2. Note that in rules 65, 81, 124, 131 and 133 the vertical bar stands for itself and is not a metasymbol.

## A4.1  Syntax rules

*Chapter 2*

1    pragma ::= **pragma** identifier [(argument_association
                                      {, argument_association})];

2    argument_association ::= [*argument*_identifier =>] name
                               | [*argument*_identifier =>] expression

*Chapter 3*

3    graphic_character ::= basic_graphic_character
                            | lower_case_letter
                            | other_special_character

4    basic_graphic_character ::= upper_case_letter | digit
                            | special_character | space_character

5    basic_character ::= basic_graphic_character | format_effector

6    identifier ::= letter {[underline] letter_or_digit}

7    letter_or_digit ::= letter | digit

8    letter ::= upper_case_letter | lower_case_letter

9    numeric_literal ::= decimal_literal | based_literal

10    decimal_literal ::= integer [. integer] [exponent]

11    integer ::= digit {[underline] digit}

12    exponent ::= E [+] integer | E − integer

13    based_literal ::=
               base # based_integer [. based_integer] # [exponent]

14    base ::= integer

15    based_integer ::= extended_digit {[underline] extended_digit}

16    extended_digit ::= digit | letter

17    character_literal ::= 'graphic_character'

18    string_literal ::= "{graphic_character}"

*Chapter 4*

19    basic_declaration ::=
               object_declaration              | number_declaration
               | type_declaration              | subtype_declaration
               | subprogram_declaration        | package_declaration
               | task_declaration              | generic_declaration
               | exception_declaration         | generic_instantiation
               | renaming_declaration          | deferred_constant_declaration

20    object_declaration ::=
               identifier_list : [**constant**] subtype_indication [:= expression];
               | identifier_list : [**constant**] constrained_array_definition
                                                   [:= expression];

21    number_declaration ::=
               identifier_list : **constant** := *universal_static*_expression;

22    identifier_list ::= identifier {, identifier}

23    assignment_statement ::= *variable*_name:= expression;

24    block_statement ::= [*block*_simple_name :]
                                   [**declare**
                                       declarative_part]
                                   **begin**
                                       sequence_of_statements
                                   [**exception**
                                       exception_handler
                                       {exception_handler}
                                   **end** [*block*_simple_name];

25    type_declaration ::= full_type_declaration
                                   | incomplete_type_declaration
                                   | private_type_declaration

26    full_type_declaration ::=
               **type** identifier [discriminant_part] **is** type_definition;

27    type_definition ::=
              enumeration_type_definition | integer_type_definition
              | real_type_definition      | array_type_definition
              | record_type_definition    | access_type_definition
              | derived_type_definition

28    subtype_declaration ::= **subtype** identifier **is** subtype_indication;

29    subtype_indication ::= type_mark [constraint]

30    type_mark ::= *type*_name | *subtype*_name

31    constraint ::= range_constraint | floating_point_constraint
                     | fixed_point_constraint | index_constraint
                     | discriminant_constraint

32    range_constraint ::= **range** range

33    range ::= *range*_attribute | simple_expression .. simple_expression

34    enumeration_type_definition ::=
              (enumeration_literal_specification
                              {, enumeration_literal_specification})

35    enumeration_literal_specification ::= enumeration_literal

36    enumeration_literal ::= identifier | character_literal

37    name ::= simple_name | character_literal | operator_symbol
              | indexed_component | slice | selected_component | attribute

38    simple_name ::= identifier

39    prefix ::= name | function_call

40    attribute ::= prefix ' attribute_designator

41    attribute_designator ::= simple_name
                                         [(*universal_static*_expression)]

42    expression ::= relation {**and** relation}
                     | relation {**and then** relation}
                     | relation {**or** relation}
                     | relation {**or else** relation}
                     | relation {**xor** relation}

43    relation ::=
              simple_expression [relational_operator simple_expression]
              | simple_expression [**not**] **in** range
              | simple_expression [**not**] **in** type_mark

44    simple_expression ::=
              [unary_adding_operator] term {binary_adding_operator term}

45    term ::= factor {multiplying_operator factor}

46    factor ::= primary [** primary] | **abs** primary | **not** primary

47    primary ::= numeric_literal | **null** | aggregate | string_literal | name
      | allocator | function_call | type_conversion
      | qualified_expression | (expression)

48    logical_operator ::= **and** | **or** | **xor**

49    relational_operator ::= = | /= | < | <= | > | >=

50    binary_adding_operator ::= + | − | &

51    unary_adding_operator ::= + | −

52    multiplying_operator ::= * | / | **mod** | **rem**

53    highest_precedence_operator ::= ** | **abs** | **not**

54    type_conversion ::= type_mark (expression)

55    qualified_expression ::= type_mark (expression)
      | type_mark ' aggregate

*Chapter 5*

56    sequence_of_statements ::= statement {statement}

57    statement ::= {label} simple_statement
      | {label} compound_statement

58    simple_statement ::=

| null_statement | assignment_statement |
| procedure_call_statement | exit_statement |
| return_statement | goto_statement |
| entry_call_statement | delay_statement |
| abort_statement | raise_statement |
| code_statement | |

59    compound_statement ::= if_statement | case_statement
      | loop_statement | block_statement
      | accept_statement | select_statement

60    label ::= <<*label*_simple_name>>

61    null_statement ::= **null**;

62    if_statement ::= **if** condition **then**
      sequence_of_statements
      {**elsif** condition **then**
      sequence_of_statements}
      [**else**
      sequence_of_statements]
      **end if**;

63    condition ::= *boolean*_expression

64    case_statement ::= **case** expression **is**
      case_statement_alternative
      {case_statement_alternative}
      **end case**;

65    case_statement_alternative ::=
        **when** choice { | choice} => sequence_of_statements

66    choice ::= simple_expression | discrete_range | **others**
        | *component*_simple_name

67    discrete_range ::= *discrete*_subtype_indication | range

68    loop_statement ::= [*loop*_simple_name :]
                        [iteration_scheme] **loop**
                            sequence_of_statements
                        **end loop** [*loop*_simple_name];

69    iteration_scheme ::= **while** condition
                        | **for** loop_parameter_specification

70    loop_parameter_specification ::=
                        identifier **in** [**reverse**] discrete_range

71    exit_statement ::= **exit** [*loop*_name] [**when** condition];

72    goto_statement ::= **goto** *label*_name;

*Chapter 6*

73    array_type_definition ::=
        unconstrained_array_definition | constrained_array_definition

74    unconstrained_array_definition ::=
        **array** (index_subtype_definition {, index_subtype_definition}) **of**
                        *component*_subtype_indication

75    constrained_array_definition ::=
        **array** index_constraint **of** *component*_subtype_indication

76    index_subtype_definition ::= type_mark **range** <>

77    index_constraint ::= (discrete_range {, discrete_range})

78    indexed_component ::= prefix (expression {, expression})

79    slice ::= prefix (discrete_range)

80    aggregate ::= (component_association {, component_association})

81    component_association ::= [choice { | choice} => ] expression

82    record_type_definition ::= **record**
                            component_list
                        **end record**

83    component_list ::=
                    component_declaration {component_declaration}
                    | {component_declaration} variant_part
                    | **null**;

84    component_declaration ::=
        identifier_list : component_subtype_definition [:= expression];

85    component_subtype_definition ::= subtype_indication

86    selected_component ::= prefix . selector

87    selector ::= simple_name | character_literal | operator_symbol | **all**

*Chapter 7*

88    subprogram_declaration ::= subprogram_specification;

89    subprogram_specification ::=
    **procedure** identifier [formal_part]
    | **function** designator [formal_part] **return** type_mark

90    designator ::= identifier | operator_symbol

91    operator_symbol ::= string_literal

92    formal_part ::=
    (parameter_specification {; parameter_specification})

93    parameter_specification ::=
    identifier_list : mode type_mark [:= expression]

94    mode ::= [**in**] | **in out** | **out**

95    subprogram_body ::= subprogram_specification **is**
    [declarative_part]
    **begin**
        sequence_of_statements
    [**exception**
        exception_handler
        {exception_handler}]
    **end** [designator];

96    procedure_call_statement ::=
    *procedure*_name [actual_parameter_part];

97    function_call ::= *function*_name [actual_parameter_part]

98    actual_parameter_part ::=
    (parameter_association {, parameter_association})

99    parameter_association ::=
    [formal_parameter =>] actual_parameter

100   formal_parameter ::= *parameter*_simple_name

101   actual_parameter ::=
    expression | *variable*_name | type_mark (*variable*_name)

102   return_statement ::= **return** [expression];

*Chapter 8*

103   package_declaration ::= package_specification;

104   package_specification ::= **package** identifier **is**
    {basic_declarative_item}
    [**private**
        {basic_declarative_item}]
    **end** [*package*_simple_name]

105  package_body ::= **package body** *package*_simple_name **is**
                      [declarative_part]
                   [**begin**
                        sequence_of_statements
                   [**exception**
                        exception_handler
                        {exception_handler}]]
                   **end** [*package*_simple_name];

106  declarative_part ::=
        {basic_declarative_item} {later_declarative_item}

107  basic_declarative_item ::= basic_declaration | representation_clause
                           | use_clause

108  later_declarative_item ::= body
                           | subprogram_declaration
                           | package_declaration
                           | task_declaration
                           | generic_declaration
                           | use_clause
                           | generic_instantiation

109  body ::= proper_body | body_stub

110  proper_body ::= subprogram_body | package_body | task_body

111  use_clause ::= **use** *package*_name {, *package*_name};

112  compilation ::= {compilation_unit}

113  compilation_unit ::= context_clause library_unit
                        | context_clause secondary_unit

114  library_unit ::= subprogram_declaration | package_declaration
                     | generic_declaration | generic_instantiation
                     | subprogram_body

115  secondary_unit ::= library_unit_body | subunit

116  library_unit_body ::= subprogram_body | package_body

117  context_clause ::= {with_clause {use_clause}}

118  with_clause ::= **with** *unit*_simple_name {, *unit*_simple_name};

119  body_stub ::= subprogram_specification **is separate**;
                 | **package body** *package*_simple_name **is separate**;
                 | **task body** *task*_simple_name **is separate**;

120  subunit ::= **separate** (*parent_unit*_name) proper_body

121  renaming_declaration ::=
        identifier : type_mark **renames** *object*_name;
      | identifier : **exception renames** *exception*_name;
      | **package** identifier **renames** *package*_name;
      | subprogram_specification **renames** *subprogram_or_entry*_name;

*Chapter 9*

122    private_type_declaration ::=
       **type** identifier [discriminant_part] **is** [**limited**] **private**;

123    deferred_constant_declaration ::=
       identifier_list: **constant** type_mark;

*Chapter 10*

124    exception_handler ::=
       **when** exception_choice { | exception_choice} =>
           sequence_of_statements

125    exception_choice ::= *exception*_name | **others**

126    exception_declaration ::= identifier_list : **exception**;

127    raise_statement ::= **raise** [*exception*_name];

*Chapter 11*

128    discriminant_part ::=
       (discriminant_specification {; discriminant_specification})

129    discriminant_specification ::=
       identifier_list : type_mark [:= expression]

130    discriminant_constraint ::=
       (discriminant_association {, discriminant_association})

131    discriminant_association ::=
       [*discriminant*_simple_name { | *discriminant*_simple_name} =>]
                                                           expression

132    variant_part ::= **case** *discriminant*_simple_name **is**
                       variant
                       {variant}
                       **end case**;

133    variant ::= **when** choice { | choice} => component_list

134    access_type_definition ::= **access** subtype_indication

135    incomplete_type_declaration ::= **type** identifier [discriminant_part];

136    allocator ::= **new** subtype_indication | **new** qualified_expression

137    derived_type_definition ::= **new** subtype_indication

*Chapter 12*

138    integer_type_definition ::= range_constraint

139    real_type_definition ::=
                       floating_point_constraint | fixed_point_constraint

140    floating_point_constraint ::=
                       floating_accuracy_definition [range_constraint]

141    floating_accuracy_definition ::= **digits** *static*_simple_expression

142    fixed_point_constraint ::=
                        fixed_accuracy_definition [range_constraint]

143    fixed_accuracy_definition ::= **delta** *static*_simple_expression

*Chapter 13*

144    generic_declaration ::= generic_specification;

145    generic_specification ::=
                        generic_formal_part subprogram_specification
                      | generic_formal_part package_specification

146    generic_formal_part ::= **generic** {generic_parameter_declaration}

147    generic_parameter_declaration ::=
            identifier_list: [**in** [**out**]] type_mark [:= expression];
          | **type** identifier **is** generic_type_definition;
          | private_type_declaration
          | **with** subprogram_specification [**is** name];
          | **with** subprogram_specification [**is** <>];

148    generic_type_definition ::=
            (<>) | **range** <> | **digits** <> | **delta** <>
          | array_type_definition | access_type_definition

149    generic_instantiation ::=
            **package** identifier **is**
                **new** *generic_package_*name [generic_actual_part];
          | **procedure** identifier **is**
                **new** *generic_procedure_*name [generic_actual_part];
          | **function** designator **is**
                **new** *generic_function_*name [generic_actual_part];

150    generic_actual_part ::=
                        (generic_association {, generic_association})

151    generic_association ::=
                        [generic_formal_parameter =>] generic_actual_parameter

152    generic_formal_parameter ::=
                        *parameter_*simple_name | operator_symbol

153    generic_actual_parameter ::= expression | *variable_*name
          | *subprogram_*name | *entry_*name | type_mark

*Chapter 14*

154    task_declaration ::= task_specification;

155    task_specification ::= **task** [**type**] identifier [**is**
                        {entry_declaration}
                        {representation_clause}
                    **end** [*task_*simple_name]]

156    task_body ::= **task body** *task*_simple_name **is**
                    [declarative_part]
                    **begin**
                        sequence_of_statements
                    [**exception**
                        exception_handler
                        {exception_handler}]
                    **end** [*task*_simple_name];

157    entry_declaration ::=
            **entry** identifier [(discrete_range)] [formal_part];

158    entry_call_statement ::= *entry*_name [actual_parameter_part];

159    accept_statement ::=
            **accept** *entry*_simple_name [(entry_index)] [formal_part] [**do**
                sequence_of_statements
            **end** [*entry*_simple_name]];

160    entry_index ::= expression

161    delay_statement ::= **delay** simple_expression;

162    select_statement ::= selective_wait
            | conditional_entry_call | timed_entry_call

163    selective_wait ::= **select**
                            select_alternative
                        {**or**
                            select_alternative}
                        [**else**
                            sequence_of_statements]
                        **end select**;

164    select_alternative ::=
                        [**when** condition =>] selective_wait_alternative

165    selective_wait_alternative ::= accept_alternative
            | delay_alternative | terminate_alternative

166    accept_alternative ::= accept_statement [sequence_of_statements]

167    delay_alternative ::= delay_statement [sequence_of_statements]

168    terminate_alternative ::= **terminate**;

169    conditional_entry_call ::= **select**
                                entry_call_statement
                                [sequence_of_statements]
                            **else**
                                sequence_of_statements
                            **end_select**;

170    timed_entry_call ::= **select**
                            entry_call_statement
                            [sequence_of_statements]
                        **or**
                            delay_alternative
                        **end select**;

171    abort_statement ::= **abort** *task*_name {, *task*_name};

*Chapter 15*

172    representation_clause ::=

type_representation_clause | address_clause

173    type_representation_clause ::= length_clause
| enumeration_representation_clause
| record_representation_clause

174    length_clause ::= **for** attribute **use** simple_expression;

175    enumeration_representation_clause ::=
**for** *type*_simple_name **use** aggregate;

176    record_representation_clause ::= **for** *type*_simple_name **use**
**record** [alignment_clause]
{component_clause}
**end record**;

177    alignment_clause ::= **at mod** *static*_simple_expression;

178    component_clause ::=
*component*_name **at** *static*_simple_expression **range** *static*_range;

179    address_clause ::= **for** simple_name **use at** simple_expression;

180    code_statement ::= type_mark ' *record*_aggregate;

## A4.2   Syntax index

This index lists the syntactic categories in alphabetical order and gives the number of their definition in the previous section.

| Category | Definition number |
|---|---|
| exception_choice | 125 |
| exception_declaration | 126 |
| exception_handler | 124 |
| exit_statement | 71 |
| exponent | 12 |
| expression | 42 |
| extended_digit | 16 |
| factor | 46 |
| fixed_accuracy_definition | 143 |
| fixed_point_constraint | 142 |
| floating_accuracy_definition | 141 |
| floating_point_constraint | 140 |
| formal_parameter | 100 |
| formal_part | 92 |
| full_type_declaration | 26 |
| function_call | 97 |
| generic_actual_parameter | 153 |
| generic_actual_part | 150 |
| generic_association | 151 |
| generic_declaration | 144 |
| generic_formal_parameter | 152 |
| generic_formal_part | 146 |
| generic_instantiation | 149 |
| generic_parameter_declaration | 147 |
| generic_specification | 145 |
| generic_type_definition | 148 |
| goto_statement | 72 |
| graphic_character | 3 |
| highest_precedence_operator | 53 |
| identifier | 6 |
| identifier_list | 22 |
| if_statement | 62 |
| incomplete_type_declaration | 135 |
| index_constraint | 77 |
| index_subtype_declaration | 76 |
| indexed_component | 78 |
| integer | 11 |
| integer_type_definition | 138 |
| iteration_scheme | 69 |
| label | 60 |
| later_declarative_item | 108 |
| length_clause | 174 |
| letter | 8 |
| letter_or_digit | 7 |
| library_unit | 114 |
| library_unit_body | 116 |
| logical_operator | 48 |

# Answers to Exercises

Specimen answers are given to all the exercises. In some cases they do not necessarily represent the best technique for solving a problem but merely one which uses the material introduced at that point in the discussion.

## Answers 2

*Exercise 2.2*

1
```
package SIMPLE_MATHS is
    function SQRT(F: FLOAT) return FLOAT;
    function LOG(F: FLOAT) return FLOAT;
    function LN(F: FLOAT) return FLOAT;
    function EXP(F: FLOAT) return FLOAT;
    function SIN(F: FLOAT) return FLOAT;
    function COS(F: FLOAT) return FLOAT;
end SIMPLE_MATHS;
```

The first few lines of our program PRINT_ROOTS could now become

```
with SIMPLE_MATHS, SIMPLE_IO;
procedure PRINT_ROOTS is
    use SIMPLE_MATHS, SIMPLE_IO;
```

*Exercise 2.7*

1
```
with TEXT_IO, ETC;
use TEXT_IO, ETC;
procedure TEN_TIMES_TABLE is
    use INT_IO;
    ROW, COLUMN: INTEGER;
begin
    ROW:= 1;
    loop
        COLUMN:= 1;
        loop
            PUT(ROW * COLUMN, 5);
            exit when COLUMN = 10;
            COLUMN:= COLUMN+1;
        end loop;
        NEW_LINE;
```

```
        exit when ROW = 10;
        ROW:= ROW+1;
    end loop;
end TEN_TIMES_TABLE;
```

2    ```
     with TEXT_IO, ETC;
     use TEXT_IO, ETC;
     procedure TABLE_OF_SQUARE_ROOTS is
         use INT_IO, REAL_IO, REAL_MATHS;
         N: INTEGER;
         LAST_N: INTEGER;
         TAB: COUNT;
     begin
         TAB:= 10;
         PUT("What is the largest value please? "); GET(LAST_N);
         NEW_LINE(2);
         PUT("Number"); SET_COL(TAB); PUT("Square root");
         NEW_LINE(2);
         N:= 1;
         loop
             PUT(N, 4); SET_COL(TAB); PUT(SQRT(REAL(N)), 3, 5, 0);
             NEW_LINE;
             exit when N = LAST_N;
             N:= N+1;
         end loop;
     end TABLE_OF_SQUARE_ROOTS;
     ```

# Answers 3

*Exercise 3.3*

1    The following are not legal identifiers

| | |
|---|---|
| (b) | contains & |
| (c) | contains hyphens not underlines |
| (e) | adjacent underlines |
| (f) | does not start with a letter |
| (g) | trailing underline |
| (h) | this is two legal identifiers |
| (i) | this is legal – but it is a reserved word |

*Exercise 3.4*

1    
| | | |
|---|---|---|
| (a) | legal – real |
| (b) | illegal – no digit before point |
| (c) | legal – integer |
| (d) | illegal – integer with negative exponent |
| (e) | illegal – closing # missing |
| (f) | legal – real |
| (g) | illegal – C not a digit of base 12 |
| (h) | illegal – no number before exponent |
| (i) | legal – integer – case of letter immaterial |
| (j) | legal – integer |
| (k) | illegal – underline at start of exponent |
| (l) | illegal – integer with negative exponent |

2    
| | |
|---|---|
| (a) | $224 = 14 \times 16$ |
| (b) | $6144 = 3 \times 2^{11}$ |
     ```

(c)    4095.0
(d)    4095.0

**3**    (a)    32 ways

41, 2#101001#, 3#1112#, ...
        10#41#, ... 16#29#
41E0, 2#101001#E0, ... 16#29#E0

(b)    40 ways. As for example (a) plus, since 150 is not prime but $2 \times 3 \times 5^2 = 150$ also

2#1001011#E1
3#1212#E1
5#110#E1
5#11#E2
6#41#E1
10#15#E1
15#A#E1

and of course

15E1

*Exercise 3.5*

**1**    (a)    7
(b)    1
(c)    1
(d)    12

**2**    (a)    This has 3 units
the identifier             delay
the literal                2.0
the single symbol          ;

(b)    This has 4 units
the identifier             delay2
the single symbol          .
the literal                0
the single symbol          ;

Case (a) is a legal delay statement, (b) is just a mess.


# Answers 4

*Exercise 4.1*

**1**    R: REAL:= 1.0;

**2**    ZERO: **constant** REAL:= 0.0;
ONE: **constant** REAL:= 1.0;

but better to write number declarations

ZERO: **constant**:= 0.0;
ONE: **constant**:= 1.0;

**3**    (a)    **var** is illegal – this is Ada not Pascal
(b)    terminating semicolon is missing
(c)    a constant declaration must have an initial value
(d)    no multiple assignment – this is Ada not Algol
(e)    nothing – assuming M and N are of integer type
(f)    2PI is not a legal identifier

*Exercise 4.2*

**1**    There are four errors

    (1)    semicolon missing after declaration of J, K
    (2)    K used before a value has been assigned to it
    (3)    = instead of := in declaration of P
    (4)    Q not declared and initialized

*Exercise 4.4*

**1**    This analysis assumes that the values of all variables originally satisfy their constraints; this will be the case if the program is not erroneous.

    (a)    the ranges of I and J are identical so no checks are required and consequently CONSTRAINT_ERROR cannot be raised,

    (b)    the range of J is a subset of that of K and again CONSTRAINT_ERROR cannot be raised,

    (c)    in this case a check is required since if K > 10 it cannot be assigned to J in which case CONSTRAINT_ERROR will be raised.

*Exercise 4.5*

**1**    

| | | | | | | | |
|---|---|---|---|---|---|---|---|
| (a) | −105 | (d) | −3 | (g) | −1 |
| (b) | −3 | (e) | −3 | (h) | 2 |
| (c) | 0 | (f) | illegal | | |

**2**    All variables are real

    (a)    M*R**2
    (b)    B**2 − 4.0*A*C
    (c)    (4.0/3.0)*PI*R**3    −− brackets not necessary
    (d)    (P*PI*A**4)/(8.0*L*ETA)    −− brackets are necessary

*Exercise 4.6*

**1**    
    (a)    SAT
    (b)    SAT    note that SUCC applies to the base type
    (c)    2

**2**    
    (a)    **type** RAINBOW **is** (RED, ORANGE, YELLOW, GREEN, BLUE, INDIGO, VIOLET);
    (b)    **type** FRUIT **is** (APPLE, BANANA, ORANGE, PEAR);

**3**    GROOM'VAL ((N−1) **mod** 8)

    or perhaps better

    GROOM'VAL ((N−1) **mod** (GROOM'POS(GROOM'LAST) + 1))

**4**    D:= DAY'VAL((DAY'POS(D) + N−1) **mod** 7);

**5**    If X and Y are both overloaded literals then X < Y will be ambiguous. We would have to use qualification such as T'(X) < T'(Y).

*Exercise 4.7*

**1**    T: **constant** BOOLEAN:= TRUE;
    F: **constant** BOOLEAN:= FALSE;

**2**    The values are TRUE and FALSE, not T or F which are the names of constants.

    (a)    FALSE    (c)    TRUE    (e)    FALSE
    (b)    TRUE    (d)    TRUE

**3**    The expression is always TRUE. The predefined operators **xor** and /= operating on BOOLEAN values are the same.

*Exercise 4.9*

1    All variables are real except for N in example (c) which is integer.

(a)    2.0∗PI∗SQRT(L/G)

(b)    M_0/SQRT(1.0 − (V/C)∗∗2)

(c)    SQRT(2.0∗PI∗REAL(N))∗(REAL(N)/E)∗∗N

2    SQRT(2.0∗PI∗X)∗EXP(X∗LN(X)−X)

# Answers 5

*Exercise 5.1*

1
```
declare
    END_OF_MONTH: INTEGER;
begin
    if MONTH = SEP or MONTH = APR or MONTH = JUN or MONTH = NOV then
        END_OF_MONTH:= 30;
    elsif MONTH = FEB then
        if YEAR mod 4 = 0 then
            END_OF_MONTH:= 29;
        else
            END_OF_MONTH:= 28;
        end if;
    else
        END_OF_MONTH:= 31;
    end if;
    if DAY /= END_OF_MONTH then
        DAY:= DAY+1;
    else
        DAY:= 1;
        if MONTH /= DEC then
            MONTH:= MONTH_NAME'SUCC(MONTH);
        else
            MONTH:= JAN;
            YEAR:= YEAR+1;
        end if;
    end if;
end;
```
If today is 31 DEC 2099 then CONSTRAINT_ERROR will be raised on attempting to assign 2100 to YEAR. Note that the range 1901 .. 2099 simplifies the leap year calculation.

2
```
if X < Y then
    declare
        T: REAL:= X;
    begin
        X:= Y;    Y:= T;
    end;
end if;
```

*Exercise 5.2*

1
```
declare
    END_OF_MONTH: INTEGER;
begin
    case MONTH is
        when SEP | APR | JUN | NOV =>
            END_OF_MONTH:= 30;
```

```
            when FEB =>
                if YEAR mod 4 = 0 then
                    END_OF_MONTH:= 29;
                else
                    END_OF_MONTH:= 28;
                end if;
            when others =>
                END_OF_MONTH:= 31;
        end case;
        -- then as before
        ...
    end;
```

2
```
    subtype WINTER is MONTH_NAME range JAN .. MAR;
    subtype SPRING is MONTH_NAME range APR .. JUN;
    subtype SUMMER is MONTH_NAME range JUL .. SEP;
    subtype AUTUMN is MONTH_NAME range OCT .. DEC;
    ...
    case M is
        when WINTER => DIG;
        when SPRING => SOW;
        when SUMMER => TEND;
        when AUTUMN => HARVEST;
    end case;
```

Note that if we wished to consider winter as December to February then we could not declare a suitable subtype.

3
```
    case D is
        when 1 .. 10 => GORGE;
        when 11 .. 20 => SUBSIST;
        when others => STARVE;
    end case;
```

We cannot write 21 .. END_OF_MONTH because it is not a static range. In fact others covers all values of type INTEGER because although D is constrained, nevertheless the constraints are not static.

*Exercise 5.3*

1
```
    declare
        SUM: INTEGER:= 0;
        I: INTEGER;
    begin
        loop
            GET(I);
            exit when I < 0;
            SUM:= SUM+I;
        end loop;
    end;
```

2
```
    declare
        COPY: INTEGER:= N;
        COUNT: INTEGER:= 0;
    begin
        while COPY mod 2 = 0 loop
            COPY:= COPY/2;
            COUNT:= COUNT+1;
        end loop;
        ...
    end;
```

3 **declare**
   G: REAL:= $-$LN(REAL(N));
 **begin**
   **for** P **in** 1 .. N **loop**
     G:= G+1.0/REAL(P);
   **end loop;**
   ...
 **end;**

*Exercise 5.4*

1 **for** I **in** 1 .. N **loop**
   **for** J **in** 1 .. M **loop**
     **if** condition_OK **then**
       I_VALUE:= I;
       J_VALUE:= J;
       **goto** SEARCH;
     **end if;**
   **end loop;**
 **end loop;**

 <<SEARCH>>

This is not such a good solution because we have no guarantee that there may not be other places in the program from where a goto statement leads to the label. It is also a silly name for the label anyway – it ought to be FOUND!

# Answers 6

*Exercise 6.1*

1 **declare**
   F: **array** (0 .. N) **of** INTEGER;
 **begin**
   F(0):= 0;  F(1):= 1;
   **for** I **in** 2 .. F'LAST **loop**
     F(I):= F(I$-$1)+F(I$-$2);
   **end loop;**
   ...
 **end;**

2 **declare**
   MAXI: INTEGER:= A'FIRST(1);
   MAXJ: INTEGER:= A'FIRST(2);
   MAX: REAL:= A(MAXI, MAXJ);
 **begin**
   **for** I **in** A'RANGE(1) **loop**
     **for** J **in** A'RANGE(2) **loop**
      **if** A(I, J) > MAX **then**
        MAX:= A(I, J);
        MAXI:= I;
        MAXJ:= J;
      **end if;**
     **end loop;**
   **end loop;**
   -- MAXI, MAXJ now contain the result
 **end;**

**3**
```
declare
    DAYS_IN_MONTH: array (MONTH_NAME) of INTEGER
        := (31, 28, 31, 30, 31, 30, 31, 31, 30, 31, 30, 31);
    END_OF_MONTH: INTEGER;
begin
    if YEAR mod 4 = 0 then
        DAYS_IN_MONTH(FEB):= 29;
    end if;
    END_OF_MONTH:= DAYS_IN_MONTH(MONTH);

    -- then as Exercise 5.1(1)

end;
```

**4**
```
YESTERDAY: constant array (DAY) of DAY
    := (SUN, MON, TUE, WED, THU, FRI, SAT);
```

**5**
```
BOR: constant array (BOOLEAN, BOOLEAN) of BOOLEAN
    := ((FALSE, TRUE), (TRUE, TRUE));
```

**6**
```
UNIT: constant array (1 .. 3, 1 .. 3) of REAL
    := ((1.0, 0.0, 0.0),
        (0.0, 1.0, 0.0),
        (0.0, 0.0, 1.0));
```

*Exercise 6.2*

**1**    `type BBB is array (BOOLEAN, BOOLEAN) of BOOLEAN;`

**2**    `type RING5_TABLE is array (RING5, RING5) of RING5;`

```
ADD: constant RING5_TABLE
    := ((0, 1, 2, 3, 4),
        (1, 2, 3, 4, 0),
        (2, 3, 4, 0, 1),
        (3, 4, 0, 1, 2),
        (4, 0, 1, 2, 3));
```

```
MULT: constant RING5_TABLE
    := ((0, 0, 0, 0, 0),
        (0, 1, 2, 3, 4),
        (0, 2, 4, 1, 3),
        (0, 3, 1, 4, 2),
        (0, 4, 3, 2, 1));
```

```
A, B, C, D: RING5;
...
D:= MULT(ADD(A, B), C));
```

*Exercise 6.3*

**1**
```
DAYS_IN_MONTH: array (MONTH_NAME) of INTEGER
    := MONTH_NAME'(SEP | APR | JUN | NOV => 30, FEB => 28, others => 31);
```

**2**    `ZERO: constant MATRIX:= (1 .. N => (1 .. N => 0.0));`

**3**    This cannot be done with the material at our disposal at the moment. See Exercise 7.1(**6**).

**4**
```
type MOLECULE is (METHANOL, ETHANOL, PROPANOL, BUTANOL);
type ATOM is (H, C, O);
```

```
ALCOHOL: constant array (MOLECULE, ATOM) of INTEGER
    := (METHANOL => (H =>4, C =>1, O =>1),
        ETHANOL   => (      6,      2,      1),
        PROPANOL => (       8,      3,      1),
        BUTANOL   => (     10,      4,      1));
```

Note the danger in the above. We have used named notation in the first inner aggregate to act as a sort of heading but omitted it in the others to avoid clutter. However, if we had written H, C and O in other than positional order then it would have been very confusing because the positional aggregates would not have had the meaning suggested by the heading.

*Exercise 6.4*

1    ROMAN_TO_INTEGER: **constant array** (ROMAN_DIGIT) **of** INTEGER
            := (1, 5, 10, 50, 100, 500, 1000);

2    **declare**
        V: INTEGER:= 0;
     **begin**
        **for** I **in** R'RANGE **loop**
            **if** I /= R'LAST **and then**
                ROMAN_TO_INTEGER(R(I)) < ROMAN_TO_INTEGER(R(I+1)) **then**
                V:= V − ROMAN_TO_INTEGER(R(I));
            **else**
                V:= V + ROMAN_TO_INTEGER(R(I));
            **end if**;
        **end loop**;
        ...
     **end**;

Note the use of **and then** to avoid attempting to access R(I+1) when I = R'LAST.

*Exercise 6.5*

1    AOA(1 .. 2):= (AOA(2), AOA(1));

2    FARMYARD: STRING_3_ARRAY(1 .. 6)
            := ("pig", "cat", "dog", "cow", "rat", "ass");
        ...
     FARMYARD(4)(1):= 's';

3    **if** R'LAST >= 2 **and then** R(R'LAST−1 .. R'LAST) = "IV" **then**
        R(R'LAST−1 .. R'LAST):= "VI";
     **end if**;

*Exercise 6.6*

1    WHITE, BLUE, YELLOW, GREEN, RED, PURPLE, ORANGE, BLACK

2    (a)    BLACK    (b)    GREEN    (c)    RED

3    **not** (TRUE **xor** TRUE) = TRUE
     **not** (TRUE **xor** FALSE) = FALSE

     the result follows.

4    An aggregate of length one must be named.

5    "123", "ABC", "Abc", "aBc", "abC", "abc"

6    (a)    1        (b)    5

     We note therefore that & like **and, or** and **xor** is not strictly commutative.

*Exercise 6.7*

**1**    **declare**
    DAYS_IN_MONTH: **array** (MONTH_NAME) **of** INTEGER
      := MONTH_NAME'(SEP | APR | JUN | NOV => 30, FEB => 28, **others** => 31);
    END_OF_MONTH: INTEGER;
**begin**
    **if** D.YEAR **mod** 4 = 0 **then**
      DAYS_IN_MONTH(FEB):= 29;
    **end if**;
    END_OF_MONTH:= DAYS_IN_MONTH(D.MONTH);
    **if** D.DAY /= END_OF_MONTH **then**
      D.DAY:= D.DAY+1;
    **else**
      D.DAY:= 1;
      **if** D.MONTH /= DEC **then**
        D.MONTH:= MONTH_NAME'SUCC(D.MONTH);
      **else**
        D.MONTH:= JAN;
        D.YEAR:= D.YEAR+1;
      **end if**;
    **end if**;
**end**;

**2**    C1, C2, C3: COMPLEX;

(a)    C3:= (C1.RL+C2.RL, C1.IM+C2.IM);
(b)    C3:= (C1.RL*C2.RL – C1.IM*C2.IM, C1.RL*C2.IM + C1.IM*C2.RL);

**3**    **declare**
    INDEX: INTEGER;
**begin**
    **for** I **in** PEOPLE'RANGE **loop**
      **if** PEOPLE(I).BIRTH.YEAR >= 1950 **then**
        INDEX:= I;
        **exit**;
      **end if**;
    **end loop**;
    -- we assume that there is such a person
**end**;

# Answers 7

*Exercise 7.1*

**1**    **function** EVEN(X: INTEGER) **return** BOOLEAN **is**
**begin**
    **return** X **mod** 2 = 0;
**end** EVEN;

**2**    **function** FACTORIAL(N: NATURAL) **return** POSITIVE **is**
**begin**
    **if** N = 0 **then**
      **return** 1;
    **else**
      **return** N*FACTORIAL(N−1);
    **end if**;
**end** FACTORIAL;

**3**    **function** OUTER(A, B: VECTOR) **return** MATRIX **is**
    C: MATRIX(A'RANGE, B'RANGE);

```
begin
    for I in A'RANGE loop
        for J in B'RANGE loop
            C(I, J):= A(I)*B(J);
        end loop;
    end loop;
    return C;
end OUTER;
```

4    
```
type PRIMARY_ARRAY is array (INTEGER range <>) of PRIMARY;
function MAKE_COLOUR(P: PRIMARY_ARRAY) return COLOUR is
    C: COLOUR:= (F, F, F);
begin
    for I in P'RANGE loop
        C(P(I)):= T;
    end loop;
    return C;
end MAKE_COLOUR;
```

Note that multiple values are allowed so that

```
MAKE_COLOUR((R, R, R)) = RED
```

5    
```
function VALUE(R: ROMAN_NUMBER) return INTEGER is
    V: INTEGER:= 0;
begin
    for I in R'RANGE loop
        if I /= R'LAST and then
            ROMAN_TO_INTEGER(R(I)) < ROMAN_TO_INTEGER(R(I+1)) then
            V:= V - ROMAN_TO_INTEGER(R(I));
        else
            V:= V + ROMAN_TO_INTEGER(R(I));
        end if;
    end loop;
    return V;
end VALUE;
```

6    
```
function MAKE_UNIT(N: NATURAL) return MATRIX is
    M: MATRIX(1 .. N, 1 .. N);
begin
    for I in 1 .. N loop
        for J in 1 .. N loop
            if I = J then
                M(I, J):= 1.0;
            else
                M(I, J):= 0.0;
            end if;
        end loop;
    end loop;
    return M;
end MAKE_UNIT;
```

We can then declare

```
UNIT: constant MATRIX:= MAKE_UNIT(N);
```

7    
```
function GCD(X, Y: NATURAL) return NATURAL is
begin
    if Y = 0 then
        return X;
    else
        return GCD(Y, X mod Y);
    end if;
end GCD;
```

or

```
function GCD(X, Y: NATURAL) return NATURAL is
    XX: INTEGER:= X;
    YY: INTEGER:= Y;
    ZZ: INTEGER;
begin
    while YY /= 0 loop
        ZZ:= XX mod YY;
        XX:= YY;
        YY:= ZZ;
    end loop;
    return XX;
end GCD;
```

Note that X and Y have to be copied because formal parameters behave as constants.

8
```
function INNER(A, B: VECTOR) return REAL is
    RESULT: REAL:= 0.0;
begin
    if A'LENGTH /= B'LENGTH then
        raise CONSTRAINT_ERROR;
    end if;
    for I in A'RANGE loop
        RESULT:= RESULT + A(I)*B(I+B'FIRST-A'FIRST);
    end loop;
    return RESULT;
end INNER;
```

*Exercise 7.2*

1
```
function "<" (X, Y: ROMAN_NUMBER) return BOOLEAN is
begin
    return VALUE(X) < VALUE(Y);
end "<";
```

2
```
function "+" (X, Y: COMPLEX) return COMPLEX is
begin
    return (X.RL + Y.RL, X.IM + Y.IM);
end "+";

function "*" (X, Y: COMPLEX) return COMPLEX is
begin
    return (X.RL*Y.RL - X.IM*Y.IM, X.RL*Y.IM + X.IM*Y.RL);
end "*";
```

3
```
function "<" (P: PRIMARY; C: COLOUR) return BOOLEAN is
begin
    return C(P);
end "<";
```

4
```
function "<=" (X, Y: COLOUR) return BOOLEAN is
begin
    return (X and Y) = X;
end "<=";
```

5
```
function "<" (X, Y: DATE) return BOOLEAN is
begin
    if X.YEAR /= Y.YEAR then
        return X.YEAR < Y.YEAR;
    elsif X.MONTH /= Y.MONTH then
```

```
        return X.MONTH < Y.MONTH;
    else
        return X.DAY < Y.DAY;
    end if;
end "<";
```

*Exercise 7.3*

1
```
procedure SWAP(X, Y: in out REAL) is
    T: REAL;
begin
    T:= X;  X:= Y;  Y:= T;
end SWAP;
```

2
```
procedure REV(X: in out VECTOR) is
    R: VECTOR(X'RANGE);
begin
    for I in X'RANGE loop
        R(I):= X(X'FIRST + X'LAST – I);
    end loop;
    X:= R;
end REV;
```

or maybe

```
procedure REV(X: in out VECTOR) is
begin
    for I in X'FIRST .. X'FIRST + X'LENGTH/2 – 1 loop
        SWAP(X(I), X(X'FIRST + X'LAST – I));
    end loop;
end REV;
```

This procedure can be applied to an array R of type ROW by

REV(VECTOR(R));

3    The fragment is erroneous because the outcome depends upon whether the parameter is passed by copy or by reference. If it is copied then A(1) ends up as 2.0; if it is passed by reference then A(1) ends up as 4.0.

4

|  |  | calling mode (actual) | | |
|---|---|---|---|---|
|  |  | in | in out | out |
| called mode (formal) | in | ✓ | ✓ | ✗ |
| | in out | ✗ | ✓ | ✗ |
| | out | ✗ | ✓ | ✓ |

*Exercise 7.4*

1
```
function ADD(X: INTEGER; Y: INTEGER:= 1) return INTEGER is
begin
    return X + Y;
end ADD;
```

The following six calls are equivalent

```
ADD(N)
ADD(N, 1)
ADD(X => N, Y => 1)
```

```
ADD(X => N)
ADD(N, Y => 1)
ADD(Y => 1, X => N)
```

2    **function** FAVOURITE_SPIRIT **return** SPIRIT **is**
     **begin**
          **case** TODAY **is**
               **when** MON .. FRI => **return** GIN;
               **when** SAT | SUN => **return** VODKA;
          **end case**;
     **end** FAVOURITE_SPIRIT;

     **procedure** DRY_MARTINI(BASE: SPIRIT:= FAVOURITE_SPIRIT;
                                 HOW: STYLE:= ON_THE_ROCKS;
                                 PLUS: TRIMMING:= OLIVE);

This example illustrates that defaults are evaluated each time they are required and can therefore be changed from time to time.

*Exercise 7.5*

1    The named form of call

     SELL(C => JERSEY);

     is unambiguous since the formal parameter names are different.

# Answers 8

*Exercise 8.1*

1    **package** RANDOM **is**
          MODULUS: **constant**:= 2**13;
          **subtype** SMALL **is** INTEGER **range** 0 .. MODULUS;
          **procedure** INIT(SEED: SMALL);
          **function** NEXT **return** SMALL;
     **end**;

     **package body** RANDOM **is**
          MULTIPLIER: **constant**:= 5**5;
          X: SMALL;

          **procedure** INIT(SEED: SMALL) **is**
          **begin**
               X:= SEED;
          **end** INIT;

          **function** NEXT **return** SMALL **is**
          **begin**
               X:= X*MULTIPLIER **mod** MODULUS;
               **return** X;
          **end** NEXT;

     **end** RANDOM;

2    **package** COMPLEX_NUMBERS **is**
          **type** COMPLEX **is**
               **record**
                    RL, IM: REAL:= 0.0;
               **end record**;

          I: **constant** COMPLEX:= (0.0, 1.0);

          **function** "+" (X: COMPLEX) **return** COMPLEX; -- unary +
```
```

```
      function "−" (X: COMPLEX) return COMPLEX;  −− unary −

      function "+" (X, Y: COMPLEX) return COMPLEX;
      function "−" (X, Y: COMPLEX) return COMPLEX;
      function "*" (X, Y: COMPLEX) return COMPLEX;
      function "/" (X, Y: COMPLEX) return COMPLEX;
   end;

   package body COMPLEX_NUMBERS is

      function "+" (X: COMPLEX) return COMPLEX is
      begin
         return X;
      end "+";

      function "−" (X: COMPLEX) return COMPLEX is
      begin
         return (−X.RL, −X.IM);
      end "+";

      function "+" (X, Y: COMPLEX) return COMPLEX is
      begin
         return (X.RL + Y.RL, X.IM + Y.IM);
      end "+";

      function "−" (X, Y: COMPLEX) return COMPLEX is
      begin
         return (X.RL − Y.RL, X.IM − Y.IM);
      end "−";

      function "*" (X, Y: COMPLEX) return COMPLEX is
      begin
         return (X.RL*Y.RL − X.IM*Y.IM, X.RL*Y.IM + X.IM*Y.RL);
      end "*";

      function "/" (X, Y: COMPLEX) return COMPLEX is
         D: REAL:= Y.RL**2+Y.IM**2;
      begin
         return ((X.RL*Y.RL + X.IM*Y.IM)/D,
                 (X.IM*Y.RL − X.RL*Y.IM)/D);
      end "/";

   end COMPLEX_NUMBERS;
```

*Exercise 8.2*

**1**

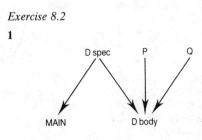

There are 18 different possible orders of compilation.

*Exercise 8.3*

**1**

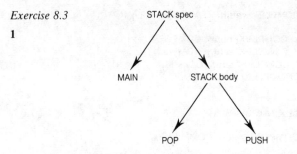

There are 8 different possible orders of compilation.

*Exercise 8.5*

**1**    **function** MONDAY **return** DIURNAL.DAY **renames** DIURNAL.MON;

**2**    This cannot be done because NEXT_WORK_DAY is of an anonymous type.

**3**    PETS: STRING_3_ARRAY **renames** FARMYARD(2 .. 3);

Note that the bounds of PETS are 2 and 3.

# Answers 9

*Exercise 9.1*

**1**    Inside the package body we could write

```
function "*" (X: REAL; Y: COMPLEX) return COMPLEX is
begin
    return (X*Y.RL, X*Y.IM);
end "*";
```

but outside we could only write

```
function "*" (X: REAL; Y: COMPLEX) return COMPLEX is
    use COMPLEX_NUMBERS;
begin
    return CONS(X, 0.0)*Y;
end "*";
```

and similarly with the operands interchanged.

**2**
```
declare
    C, D: COMPLEX_NUMBERS.COMPLEX;
    R, S: REAL;
begin
    C:= COMPLEX_NUMBERS.CONS(1.5, -6.0);
    D:= COMPLEX_NUMBERS."+" (C, COMPLEX_NUMBERS.I);
    R:= COMPLEX_NUMBERS.RL_PART(D) + 6.0;
    ...
end;
```

**3**
```
package RATIONAL_NUMBERS is
    type RATIONAL is private;
    function "+" (X: RATIONAL) return RATIONAL; -- unary +
    function "-" (X: RATIONAL) return RATIONAL; -- unary -
    function "+" (X, Y: RATIONAL) return RATIONAL;
    function "-" (X, Y: RATIONAL) return RATIONAL;
    function "*" (X, Y: RATIONAL) return RATIONAL;
    function "/" (X, Y: RATIONAL) return RATIONAL;
```

```
    function "/" (X: INTEGER; Y: POSITIVE) return RATIONAL;
    function NUMERATOR(R: RATIONAL) return INTEGER;
    function DENOMINATOR(R: RATIONAL) return POSITIVE;
private
    type RATIONAL is
        record
            NUM: INTEGER:= 0;  -- numerator
            DEN: POSITIVE:= 1;  -- denominator
        end record;
end;

package body RATIONAL_NUMBERS is

    function NORMAL(R: RATIONAL) return RATIONAL is
        -- cancel common factors
        G: POSITIVE:= GCD(abs R.NUM, R.DEN);
    begin
        return (R.NUM/G, R.DEN/G);
    end NORMAL;

    function "+" (X: RATIONAL) return RATIONAL is
    begin
        return X;
    end "+";

    function "-" (X: RATIONAL) return RATIONAL is
    begin
        return (-X.NUM, X.DEN);
    end "-";

    function "+" (X, Y: RATIONAL) return RATIONAL is
    begin
        return NORMAL((X.NUM*Y.DEN + Y.NUM*X.DEN, X.DEN*Y.DEN));
    end "+";

    function "-" (X, Y: RATIONAL) return RATIONAL is
    begin
        return NORMAL((X.NUM*Y.DEN - Y.NUM*X.DEN, X.DEN*Y.DEN));
    end "-";

    function "*" (X, Y: RATIONAL) return RATIONAL is
    begin
        return NORMAL((X.NUM*Y.NUM, X.DEN*Y.DEN));
    end "*";

    function "/" (X, Y: RATIONAL) return RATIONAL is
    begin
        return NORMAL((X.NUM*Y.DEN, X.DEN*Y.NUM));
    end "/";

    function "/" (X: INTEGER; Y: POSITIVE) return RATIONAL is
    begin
        return NORMAL((X, Y));
    end "/";

    function NUMERATOR(R: RATIONAL) return INTEGER is
    begin
        return R.NUM;
    end NUMERATOR;

    function DENOMINATOR(R: RATIONAL) return POSITIVE is
    begin
        return R.DEN;
```

```
    end DENOMINATOR;
```

```
end RATIONAL_NUMBERS;
```

4    Although the parameter base types are both INTEGER and therefore the same as for predefined integer division, nevertheless the result types are different. The result types are considered in the hiding rules for functions. See Section 7.5.

*Exercise 9.2*

1
```
package STACKS is
    type STACK is limited private;
    EMPTY: constant STACK;

    ...

private

    ...
    EMPTY: constant STACK:= ((1 .. MAX => 0), 0);
end;
```

Note that EMPTY has to be initialized because it is a **constant** despite the fact that TOP which is the only component whose value is of interest is automatically initialized anyway.

2
```
function EMPTY(S: STACK) return BOOLEAN is
begin
    return S.TOP = 0;
end EMPTY;
```

```
function FULL(S: STACK) return BOOLEAN is
begin
    return S.TOP = MAX;
end FULL;
```

3
```
function "=" (S, T: STACK) return BOOLEAN is
begin
    return S.S(1 .. S.TOP) = T.S(1 .. T.TOP);
end "=";
```

4
```
function "=" (A, B: STACK_ARRAY) return BOOLEAN is
begin
    if A'LENGTH /= B'LENGTH then
        return FALSE;
    end if;
    for I in A'RANGE loop
        if A(I) /= B(I + B'FIRST - A'FIRST) then
            return FALSE;
        end if;
    end loop;
    return TRUE;
end "=";
```

Note that this uses the redefined = (via /=) applying to the type STACK. This pattern of definition of array equality clearly applies to any type. Beware that we cannot use slice comparison (as in the previous answer) because that always uses predefined equality – surprise, surprise!

5
```
procedure ASSIGN(S: in STACK; T: out STACK) is
begin
    T.TOP:= S.TOP;
    for I in 1 .. S.TOP loop
        T.S(I):= S.S(I);
    end loop;
end ASSIGN;
```

The loop could be replaced by the slice assignment

```
T.S(1 .. S.TOP):= S.S(1 .. S.TOP);
```

6    **package** STACKS **is**
    **type** STACK **is private**;
    **procedure** PUSH(S: **in out** STACK; X: **in** INTEGER);
    **procedure** POP(S: **in out** STACK; X: **out** INTEGER);
**private**
    MAX: **constant**:= 100;
    DUMMY: **constant**:= 0;
    **type** INTEGER_VECTOR **is array** (INTEGER **range** <>) **of** INTEGER;
    **type** STACK **is**
      **record**
        S: INTEGER_VECTOR(1 .. MAX):= (1 .. MAX => DUMMY);
        TOP: INTEGER **range** 0 .. MAX:= 0;
      **end record**;
**end**;

**package body** STACKS **is**
    **procedure** PUSH(S: **in out** STACK; X: **in** INTEGER) **is**
    **begin**
      S.TOP:= S.TOP+1;
      S.S(S.TOP):= X;
    **end**;

    **procedure** POP(S: **in out** STACK; X: **out** INTEGER) **is**
    **begin**
      X:= S.S(S.TOP);
      S.S(S.TOP):= DUMMY;
      S.TOP:= S.TOP−1;
    **end**;
**end** STACKS;

Note the use of DUMMY as default value for unused components of the stack.

*Exercise 9.3*

1    **private**
    MAX: **constant**:= 1000; −− no of accounts
    **subtype** KEY_CODE **is** INTEGER **range** 0 .. MAX;
    **type** KEY **is**
      **record**
        CODE: KEY_CODE:= 0;
      **end record**;
**end**;

**package body** BANK **is**
    BALANCE: **array** (KEY_CODE **range** 1 .. KEY_CODE'LAST) **of** MONEY:=
                                  **(others** => 0);
    FREE: **array** (KEY_CODE **range** 1 .. KEY_CODE'LAST) **of** BOOLEAN:=
                                    **(others** => TRUE);

    **function** VALID(K: KEY) **return** BOOLEAN **is**
    **begin**
      **return** K.CODE /= 0;
    **end** VALID;

    **procedure** OPEN_ACCOUNT(K: **in out** KEY; M: **in** MONEY) **is**
    **begin**
      **if** K.CODE = 0 **then**
        **for** I **in** FREE'RANGE **loop**

```
                    if FREE(I) then
                        FREE(I):= FALSE;
                        BALANCE(I):= M;
                        K.CODE:= I;
                        return;
                    end if;
                end loop;
            end if;
        end OPEN_ACCOUNT;

        procedure CLOSE_ACCOUNT(K: in out KEY; M: out MONEY) is
        begin
            if VALID(K) then
                M:= BALANCE(K.CODE);
                FREE(K.CODE):= TRUE;
                K.CODE:= 0;
            end if;
        end CLOSE_ACCOUNT;

        procedure DEPOSIT(K: in KEY; M: in MONEY) is
        begin
            if VALID(K) then
                BALANCE(K.CODE):= BALANCE(K.CODE)+M;
            end if;
        end DEPOSIT;

        procedure WITHDRAW(K: in out KEY; M: in out MONEY) is
        begin
            if VALID(K) then
                if M > BALANCE(K.CODE) then
                    CLOSE_ACCOUNT(K, M);
                else
                    BALANCE(K.CODE):= BALANCE(K.CODE)-M;
                end if;
            end if;
        end WITHDRAW;

        function STATEMENT(K: KEY) return MONEY is
        begin
            if VALID(K) then
                return BALANCE(K.CODE);
            end if;
        end STATEMENT;

    end BANK;
```

Various alternative formulations are possible. It might be neater to declare a record type representing an account containing the two components FREE and BALANCE.

Note that the function STATEMENT will raise PROGRAM_ERROR if the key is not valid. Alternatively we could return a dummy value of zero but it might be better to raise our own exception as described in the next chapter.

2    An alternative formulation which represents the home savings box could be that where the limited private type is given by

```
type BOX is
    record
        CODE: BOX_CODE:= 0;
        BALANCE: MONEY;
    end record;
```

In this case the money is kept in the variable declared by the user. The bank only knows which boxes have been issued but does not know how much is in a particular box. The details are left to the reader.

3   Since the parameter is of a private type, it is not defined whether the parameter is passed by copy or by reference. If it is passed by copy then the call of ACTION will succeed whereas if it is passed by reference it will not. The program is therefore erroneous. However, this does not seem a very satisfactory answer and might be considered a loophole in the design of Ada.

A slight improvement would be for ACTION to check (via VALID say) whether the passed key is free or not by reference to the array FREE but this would not be any protection once the key were reissued. However, a foolproof solution can be devised using access types which will be described in Chapter 11.

4   He is thwarted because of the rule mentioned in the previous section that, outside the defining package, a procedure cannot be declared having an **out** parameter of a limited type. The purpose of this rule is precisely to prevent just this kind of violation of privacy. (As a minor aside note that in any case the parameter may be passed by reference.)

# Answers 10

*Exercise 10.1*

1
```
procedure QUADRATIC(A, B, C: in REAL;
                    ROOT_1, ROOT_2: out REAL; OK: out BOOLEAN) is
    D: constant REAL:= B**2 − 4.0*A*C;
begin
    ROOT_1:= (−B+SQRT(D))/(2.0*A);
    ROOT_2:= (−B−SQRT(D))/(2.0*A);
    OK:= TRUE;
exception
    when NUMERIC_ERROR =>
        OK:= FALSE;
end QUADRATIC;
```

2
```
function FACTORIAL(N: INTEGER) return INTEGER is

    function SLAVE(N: NATURAL) return POSITIVE is
    begin
        if N = 0 then
            return 1;
        else
            return N*SLAVE(N−1);
        end if;
    end SLAVE;

begin
    return SLAVE(N);
exception
    when CONSTRAINT_ERROR | STORAGE_ERROR | NUMERIC_ERROR =>
        return −1;
end FACTORIAL;
```

*Exercise 10.2*

1
```
package RANDOM is
    BAD: exception;
    MODULUS: constant:= 2**13;
```

```
        subtype SMALL is INTEGER range 0 .. MODULUS;
        procedure INIT(SEED: SMALL);
        function NEXT return SMALL;
    end;

    package body RANDOM is
        MULTIPLIER: constant:= 5**5;
        X: SMALL;

        procedure INIT(SEED: SMALL) is
        begin
            if SEED mod 2 = 0 then
                raise BAD;
            end if;
            X:= SEED;
        end INIT;

        function NEXT return SMALL is
        begin
            X:= X*MULTIPLIER mod MODULUS;
            return X;
        end NEXT;

    end RANDOM;
```

2    ```
    function FACTORIAL(N: INTEGER) return INTEGER is

        function SLAVE(N: NATURAL) return POSITIVE is
        begin
            if N = 0 then
                return 1;
            else
                return N*SLAVE(N-1);
            end if;
        end SLAVE;

    begin
        return SLAVE(N);
    exception
        when NUMERIC_ERROR | STORAGE_ERROR =>
            raise CONSTRAINT_ERROR;
    end FACTORIAL;
```

3    ```
    function "+" (X, Y: VECTOR) return VECTOR is
        R: VECTOR(X'RANGE);
    begin
        if X'LENGTH /= Y'LENGTH then
            raise CONSTRAINT_ERROR;
        end if;
        for I in X'RANGE loop
            R(I):= X(I) + Y(I + Y'FIRST - X'FIRST);
        end loop;
        return R;
    end "+";
```

4    No. A malevolent user could write **raise** STACK.ERROR; outside the package. It would be nice if the language provided some sort of 'private' exception that could be handled but not raised explicitly outside its defining package.

*Exercise 10.3*

1       Three checks are required. The one inserted by the user plus the two for the
        assignment to S(TOP) which cannot be avoided since we can say little about the
        value of TOP (except that it is not equal to MAX). So this is the worst of all worlds
        thus emphasizing the need to give appropriate constraints.

*Exercise 10.4*

1       ```
        package BANK is
            ALARM: exception;
            subtype MONEY is NATURAL;
            type KEY is limited private;
            -- as before
        private
            -- as before
        end;

        package body BANK is
            BALANCE: array (KEY_CODE range 1 .. KEY_CODE'LAST) of MONEY:=
                                                                    (others => 0);
            FREE: array (KEY_CODE range 1 .. KEY_CODE'LAST) of BOOLEAN:=
                                                                    (others => TRUE);

            function VALID(K: KEY) return BOOLEAN is
            begin
                return K.CODE /= 0;
            end VALID;

            procedure VALIDATE(K: KEY) is
            begin
                if not VALID(K) then
                    raise ALARM;
                end if;
            end VALIDATE;

            procedure OPEN_ACCOUNT(K: in out KEY; M: in MONEY) is
            begin
                if K.CODE = 0 then
                    for I in FREE'RANGE loop
                        if FREE(I) then
                            FREE(I):= FALSE;
                            BALANCE(I):= M;
                            K.CODE:= I;
                            return;
                        end if;
                    end loop;
                else
                    raise ALARM;
                end if;
            end OPEN_ACCOUNT;

            procedure CLOSE_ACCOUNT(K: in out KEY; M: out MONEY) is
            begin
                VALIDATE(K);
                M:= BALANCE(K.CODE);
                FREE(K.CODE):= TRUE;
                K.CODE:= 0;
            end CLOSE_ACCOUNT;

            procedure DEPOSIT(K: in KEY; M: in MONEY) is
            begin
        ```
        ```

```
        VALIDATE(K);
        BALANCE(K.CODE):= BALANCE(K.CODE)+M;
    end DEPOSIT;

    procedure WITHDRAW(K: in out KEY; M: in out MONEY) is
    begin
        VALIDATE(K);
        if M > BALANCE(K.CODE) then
            raise ALARM;
        else
            BALANCE(K.CODE):= BALANCE(K.CODE)−M;
        end if;
    end WITHDRAW;

    function STATEMENT(K: KEY) return MONEY is
    begin
        VALIDATE(K);
        return BALANCE(K.CODE);
    end STATEMENT;

end BANK;
```

For convenience we have declared a procedure VALIDATE which raises the alarm in most cases. The ALARM is also explicitly raised if we attempt to overdraw but as remarked in the text we cannot also close the account. An attempt to open an account with a key which is in use also causes ALARM to be raised. We do not however raise the ALARM if the bank runs out of accounts but have left it to the user to check with a call of VALID that he was issued a genuine key; the rationale is that it is not the user's fault if the bank runs out of keys.

2      Suppose $N$ is 2. Then on the third call, P is not entered but the exception is raised and handled at the second level. The handler again calls P without success but this time, since an exception raised in a handler is not handled there but propagated up a level, the exception is handled at the first level. The pattern then repeats but the exception is finally propagated out of the first level to the originating call. In all there are three successful calls and four unsuccessful ones. The following diagram may help.

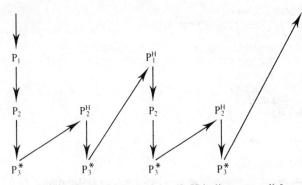

An ∗ indicates an unsuccessful call, H indicates a call from a handler.
       More generally suppose $C_n$ is the total number of calls for the case $N = n$. Then by induction

$$C_{n+1} = 2C_n + 1$$

with the initial condition $C_0 = 1$ since in the case $N = 0$ it is obvious that there is only one call which fails. It follows that the total number of calls $C_N$ is $2^{N+1} - 1$. Of these $2^N$ are unsuccessful and $2^N - 1$ are successful.
       I am grateful to Bob Bishop for this example.

# Answers 11

*Exercise 11.1*

1    TRACE((M'LENGTH, M))

If the two dimensions of M were not equal then CONSTRAINT_ERROR would be raised. Note that the lower bounds of M do not have to be 1; all that matters is that the number of components in each dimension is the same.

2    ```
package STACKS is
    type STACK(MAX: NATURAL) is limited private;
    EMPTY: constant STACK;

    ...

private
    type INTEGER_VECTOR is array (INTEGER range <>) of INTEGER;
    type STACK(MAX: NATURAL) is
        record
            S: INTEGER_VECTOR(1 .. MAX);
            TOP: INTEGER:= 0;
        end record;
    EMPTY: constant STACK(0):= (0, (others => 0), 0);
end;
```

We have naturally chosen to make EMPTY a stack whose value of MAX is zero. Note that the function "=" only compares the parts of the stacks which are in use. Thus we can write S = EMPTY to test whether a stack S is empty irrespective of its value of MAX.

3    ```
function FULL(S: STACK) return BOOLEAN is
begin
    return S.TOP = S.MAX;
end FULL;
```

4    ```
S: constant SQUARE:= (N, MAKE_UNIT(N));
```

*Exercise 11.2*

1    ```
Z: POLYNOMIAL:= (0, (0 => 0));
```

The named notation has to be used because the array has only one component.

2    ```
function "*" (P, Q: POLYNOMIAL) return POLYNOMIAL is
    R: POLYNOMIAL(P.N+Q.N):= (P.N+Q.N, (others => 0));
begin
    for I in P.A'RANGE loop
        for J in Q.A'RANGE loop
            R.A(I+J):= R.A(I+J) + P.A(I)*Q.A(J);
        end loop;
    end loop;
    return R;
end "*";
```

It is largely a matter of taste whether we write P.A'RANGE rather than 0 .. P.N.

3    ```
function "−" (P, Q: POLYNOMIAL) return POLYNOMIAL is
    SIZE: INTEGER;
begin
    if P.N > Q.N then
        SIZE:= P.N;
    else
        SIZE:= Q.N;
    end if;
```

```
declare
    R: POLYNOMIAL(SIZE);
begin
    for I in 0 .. P.N loop
        R.A(I):= P.A(I);
    end loop;
    for I in P.N+1 .. R.N loop
        R.A(I):= 0;
    end loop;
    for I in 0 .. Q.N loop
        R.A(I):= R.A(I)−Q.A(I);
    end loop;
    return NORMAL(R);
end;
end "−";
```

There are various alternative ways of writing this function. We could initialize R.A by using slice assignments

```
R.A(0 .. P.N):= P.A;
R.A(P.N+1 .. R.N):= (P.N+1 .. R.N => 0);
```

or even more succinctly by

```
R.A:= P.A & (P.N+1 .. R.N => 0);
```

4    procedure TRUNCATE(P: in out POLYNOMIAL) is
```
begin
    if P'CONSTRAINED then
        raise TRUNCATE_ERROR;
    else
        P:= (P.N−1, P.A(0 .. P.N−1));
    end if;
end TRUNCATE;
```

5    Any unconstrained POLYNOMIAL could then include an array whose range is 0 .. INTEGER'LAST. This will take a lot of space. Since most implementations are likely to adopt the strategy of setting aside the maximum possible space for an unconstrained record it is thus wise to keep the maximum to a practical limit by the use of a suitable subtype such as INDEX.

6    function "&" (X, Y: V_STRING) return V_STRING is
```
begin
    return (X.N + Y.N, X.S & Y.S);
end "&";
```

7    function "+" (V: V_STRING) return STRING is
```
begin
    return V.S;
end "+";
```

and then PUT(+ZOO(3)); will output the string "camel".

*Exercise 11.3*

1    procedure SHAVE(P: in out PERSON) is
```
begin
    if P.SEX = FEMALE then
        raise SHAVING_ERROR;
    else
        P.BEARDED:= FALSE;
    end if;
end SHAVE;
```

2    
```
procedure STERILIZE(M: in out MUTANT) is
begin
    if M'CONSTRAINED and M.SEX /= NEUTER then
        raise STERILIZE_ERROR;
    else
        M:= (NEUTER, M.BIRTH);
    end if;
end STERILIZE;
```

3    
```
type FIGURE is (CIRCLE, SQUARE, RECTANGLE);

type OBJECT(SHAPE: FIGURE) is
    record
        case SHAPE is
            when CIRCLE =>
                RADIUS: REAL;
            when SQUARE =>
                SIDE: REAL;
            when RECTANGLE =>
                LENGTH, BREADTH: REAL;
        end case;
    end record;
```

4    
```
function AREA(X: OBJECT) return REAL is
begin
    case X.SHAPE is
        when CIRCLE =>
            return PI*X.RADIUS**2;
        when SQUARE =>
            return X.SIDE**2;
        when RECTANGLE =>
            return X.LENGTH*X.BREADTH;
    end case;
end AREA;
```

Note the similarity between the case statement in the function AREA and the variant part of the type OBJECT.

5    
```
function F(N: INTEGER) return INTEGER_VECTOR;

type POLYNOMIAL(N: INDEX:= 0) is
    record
        A: INTEGER_VECTOR(0 .. N):= F(N);
    end record;

function F(N: INTEGER) return INTEGER_VECTOR is
    R: INTEGER_VECTOR(0 .. N);
begin
    for I in 0 .. N−1 loop
        R(I):= 0;
    end loop;
    R(N):= 1;
    return R;
end;
```

In order to declare both the function and the type in the same declarative part we have to give the function specification on its own first. This is because a type declaration may not follow a body as explained in Section 7.6. It does not matter that F is referred to before its body is elaborated provided that it is not actually called. Thus if we declared a polynomial (without an initial value) before the body of F then PROGRAM_ERROR would be raised.

**6**    If the user declared a constrained key with a nonzero discriminant thus

K: KEY(7);

then he will have bypassed GET_KEY and be able to call the procedure ACTION without authority. Note also that if he calls RETURN_KEY then CONSTRAINT_ERROR will be raised on the attempt to set the code to zero because the key is constrained.

Hence forged keys can be recognized since they are constrained and so we could rewrite VALID to check for this

```
function VALID(K: KEY) return BOOLEAN is
begin
    return not K'CONSTRAINED and then K.CODE /= 0;
end VALID;
```

We use the short circuit form so that we only test K.CODE when we are sure it exists. We must also insert calls of VALID into GET_KEY and RETURN_KEY.

**7**
```
package RATIONAL_POLYNOMIALS is
    MAX: constant:= 10;
    subtype INDEX is INTEGER range 0 .. MAX;
    type RATIONAL_POLYNOMIAL(N, D: INDEX:= 0) is private;

    function "+" (X: RATIONAL_POLYNOMIAL) return RATIONAL_POLYNOMIAL;
    function "−" (X: RATIONAL_POLYNOMIAL) return RATIONAL_POLYNOMIAL;

    function "+" (X, Y: RATIONAL_POLYNOMIAL) return RATIONAL_POLYNOMIAL;
    function "−" (X, Y: RATIONAL_POLYNOMIAL) return RATIONAL_POLYNOMIAL;
    function "*" (X, Y: RATIONAL_POLYNOMIAL) return RATIONAL_POLYNOMIAL;
    function "/" (X, Y: RATIONAL_POLYNOMIAL) return RATIONAL_POLYNOMIAL;

    function "/" (X, Y: POLYNOMIAL) return RATIONAL_POLYNOMIAL;
    function NUMERATOR(R: RATIONAL_POLYNOMIAL) return POLYNOMIAL;
    function DENOMINATOR(R: RATIONAL_POLYNOMIAL) return POLYNOMIAL;

private

    function ZERO(N: INDEX) return POLYNOMIAL;
    function ONE(N: INDEX) return POLYNOMIAL;

    type RATIONAL_POLYNOMIAL(N, D: INDEX:= 0) is
        record
            NUM: POLYNOMIAL(N):= ZERO(N);
            DEN: POLYNOMIAL(D):= ONE(D);
        end record;
end;
```

The functions ZERO and ONE are required in order to supply appropriate safe initial values. It is not possible to write a suitable aggregate for ONE although it is for ZERO. Nevertheless the function ZERO is written for symmetry

```
function ZERO(N: INDEX) return POLYNOMIAL is
begin
    return (N, (0 .. N => 0));    -- all coefficients zero
end;

function ONE(N: INDEX) return POLYNOMIAL is
    R: POLYNOMIAL(N):= ZERO(N);
begin
    R.A(0):= 1;              -- coefficient of $x^0$ is one
    return R;
end;
```

We make no attempt to impose any special language constraint on the denominator as we did in the type RATIONAL where the denominator has subtype POSITIVE.

*Exercise 11.4*

1
```
procedure APPEND(FIRST: in out LINK; SECOND: in LINK) is
    L: LINK:= FIRST;
begin
    if FIRST = null then
        FIRST:= SECOND;
    else
        while L.NEXT /= null loop
            L:= L.NEXT;
        end loop;
        L.NEXT:= SECOND;
    end if;
end APPEND;
```

2
```
function SIZE(T: TREE) return INTEGER is
begin
    if T = null then
        return 0;
    else
        return SIZE(T.LEFT)+SIZE(T.RIGHT)+1;
    end if;
end SIZE;
```

3
```
function COPY(T: TREE) return TREE is
begin
    if T = null then
        return null;
    else
        return new NODE'(T.VALUE, COPY(T.LEFT), COPY(T.RIGHT));
    end if;
end COPY;
```

*Exercise 11.5*

1
```
procedure PUSH(S: in out STACK; X: in INTEGER) is
begin
    S:= new CELL'(X, S);
exception
    when STORAGE_ERROR =>
        raise ERROR;
end;
```

```
procedure POP(S: in out STACK; X: out INTEGER) is
begin
    if S = null then
        raise ERROR;
    else
        X:= S.VALUE;
        S:= S.NEXT;
    end if;
end;
```

2
```
procedure PUSH(S: in out STACK; X: in INTEGER) is
begin
    S.LIST:= new CELL'(X, S.LIST);
end;
```

```
procedure POP(S: in out STACK; X: out INTEGER) is
begin
    X:= S.LIST.VALUE;
```

```
            S.LIST:= S.LIST.NEXT;
        end;

        function "=" (S, T: STACK) return BOOLEAN is
            SL: LINK:= S.LIST;
            TL: LINK:= T.LIST;
        begin
            while SL /= null and TL /= null loop
                SL:= SL.NEXT;
                TL:= TL.NEXT;
                if SL.VALUE /= TL.VALUE then
                    return FALSE;
                end if;
            end loop;
            return SL = TL;
        end "=";
```

```
3       package QUEUES is
            EMPTY: exception;
            type QUEUE is limited private;
            procedure JOIN(Q: in out QUEUE; X: in ITEM);
            procedure REMOVE(Q: in out QUEUE; X: out ITEM);
            function LENGTH(Q: QUEUE) return INTEGER;
        private
            type CELL;
            type LINK is access CELL;
            type CELL is
                record
                    DATA: ITEM;
                    NEXT: LINK;
                end record;
            type QUEUE is
                record
                    COUNT: INTEGER:= 0;
                    FIRST, LAST: LINK;
                end record;
        end;

        package body QUEUES is

            procedure JOIN(Q: in out QUEUE; X: in ITEM) is
                L: LINK;
            begin
                L:= new CELL'(DATA => X, NEXT => null);
                Q.LAST.NEXT:= L;
                Q.LAST:= L;
                Q.COUNT:= Q.COUNT+1;
            end JOIN;

            procedure REMOVE(Q: in out QUEUE; X: out ITEM) is
            begin
                if Q.COUNT = 0 then
                    raise EMPTY;
                end if;
                X:= Q.FIRST.DATA;
                Q.FIRST:= Q.FIRST.NEXT;
                Q.COUNT:= Q.COUNT-1;
            end REMOVE;

            function LENGTH(Q: QUEUE) return INTEGER is
            begin
```

```
      return Q.COUNT;
    end LENGTH;

  end QUEUES;
```

*Exercise 11.6*

**1**
```
    function HEIR(P: PERSON_NAME) return PERSON_NAME is
      MOTHER: WOMANS_NAME;
    begin
      if P.SEX = MALE then
        MOTHER:= P.WIFE;
      else
        MOTHER:= P;
      end if;
      if MOTHER = null or else MOTHER.FIRST_CHILD = null then
        return null;
      end if;
      declare
        CHILD: PERSON_NAME:= MOTHER.FIRST_CHILD;
      begin
        while CHILD.SEX = FEMALE loop
          if CHILD.NEXT_SIBLING = null then
            return MOTHER.FIRST_CHILD;
          end if;
          CHILD:= CHILD.NEXT_SIBLING;
        end loop;
        return CHILD;
      end;
    end HEIR;
```

**2**
```
    procedure DIVORCE(W: WOMANS_NAME) is
    begin
      if W.HUSBAND = null or W.FIRST_CHILD /= null then
        return;            -- divorce not possible
      end if;
      W.HUSBAND.WIFE:= null;
      W.HUSBAND:= null;
    end DIVORCE;
```

**3**
```
    procedure MARRY(BRIDE: WOMANS_NAME; GROOM: MANS_NAME) is
    begin
      if BRIDE.FATHER = GROOM.FATHER then
        raise INCEST;
      end if;
      -- then as before
    end MARRY;
```

Note that there is no need to check for marriage to a parent because the check for bigamy will detect this anyway. Our model does not allow remarriage.

**4**
```
    function NO_OF_CHILDREN(P: PERSON_NAME) return INTEGER is
      MOTHER: WOMANS_NAME;
    begin
      if P.SEX = MALE then
        MOTHER:= P.WIFE;
      else
        MOTHER:= P;
      end if;
      if MOTHER = null then
        return 0;
```

```
          end if;
          declare
              CHILD: PERSON_NAME:= MOTHER.FIRST_CHILD;
              COUNT: INTEGER:= 0;
          begin
              while CHILD /= null loop
                  COUNT:= COUNT+1;
                  CHILD:= CHILD.NEXT_SIBLING;
              end loop;
              return COUNT;
          end;
      end NO_OF_CHILDREN;

      function NO_OF_SIBLINGS(P: PERSON_NAME) return INTEGER is
      begin
          return NO_OF_CHILDREN(P.FATHER)−1;
      end NO_OF_SIBLINGS;

      function NO_OF_GRANDCHILDREN(P: PERSON_NAME) return INTEGER is
          MOTHER: WOMANS_NAME;
      begin
          if P.SEX = MALE then
              MOTHER:= P.WIFE;
          else
              MOTHER:= P;
          end if;
          if MOTHER = null then
              return 0;
          end if;
          declare
              CHILD: PERSON_NAME:= MOTHER.FIRST_CHILD;
              COUNT: INTEGER:= 0;
          begin
              while CHILD /= null loop
                  COUNT:= COUNT + NO_OF_CHILDREN(CHILD);
                  CHILD:= CHILD.NEXT_SIBLING;
              end loop;
              return COUNT;
          end;
      end NO_OF_GRANDCHILDREN;

      function NO_OF_COUSINS(P: PERSON_NAME) return INTEGER is
      begin
          return NO_OF_GRANDCHILDREN(P.FATHER.FATHER)
                  + NO_OF_GRANDCHILDREN(P.FATHER.WIFE.FATHER)
                  − 2 * NO_OF_CHILDREN(P.FATHER);
      end NO_OF_COUSINS;
```

We and our siblings get counted twice among the grandchildren and have to be
deducted. We have assumed no intermarriage between our maternal and
paternal aunts and uncles. If there is then some of our cousins may have been
counted twice as well. We leave further contemplation of this complication to
the reader.

*Exercise 11.7*

1    package P is
         type LENGTH is new REAL;
         type AREA is new REAL;
         function "*" (X, Y: LENGTH) return LENGTH;

```
      function "*" (X, Y: LENGTH) return AREA;
      function "*" (X, Y: AREA) return AREA;
   end;

   package body P is

      function "*" (X, Y: LENGTH) return LENGTH is
      begin
         raise NUMERIC_ERROR;
      end "*";

      function "*" (X, Y: LENGTH) return AREA is
      begin
         return AREA(REAL(X)*REAL(Y));
      end "*";

      function "*" (X, Y: AREA) return AREA is
      begin
         raise NUMERIC_ERROR;
      end "*";

   end P;
```

# Answers 12

*Exercise 12.1*

1    P: on A: INTEGER, on B: SHORT_INTEGER
       Q: on A: LONG_INTEGER, on B: INTEGER
       R: on A: cannot be implemented, on B: LONG_INTEGER

2    No, the only critical case is type Q on machine A. Changing to one's complement changes the range of INTEGER to

       −32767 .. +32767

       and so only INTEGER'FIRST is altered.

3    (a)    INTEGER
       (b)    illegal – type conversion must be explicit
       (c)    MY_INTEGER'BASE
       (d)    INTEGER
       (e)    universal integer
       (f)    MY_INTEGER'BASE

4    **type** LONGEST_INTEGER **is range** SYSTEM.MIN_INT .. SYSTEM.MAX_INT;

*Exercise 12.2*

1    (a)    illegal
       (b)    INTEGER
       (c)    universal real
       (d)    INTEGER
       (e)    universal real
       (f)    universal integer

2    R: **constant**:= N*1.0;

*Exercise 12.3*

1    $\frac{1}{16}$

2    REAL has B=18.
       The values of the variables P and Q are model numbers. However, the result

P/Q = ⅔ is not. The nearest model numbers can be determined by considering ⅔ as a binary recurring fraction

0.10101010...

The model number below (L say) is obtained by truncating after 18 digits. The difference between ⅔ and L is clearly ⅔ shifted down by 18 places. So L is ⅔ $(1 - 2^{-18})$. The model number above is obtained by adding $2^{-18}$ to L. Hence P/Q lies in the model interval

⅔$(1 - 2^{-18})$, ⅔$(1 + 2^{-19})$

The mathematical bounds for (P/Q)∗Q are obtained by multiplying the bounds of this interval by 3. The lower bound is then $2(1 - 2^{-18})$ and this is a model number. The upper bound is $2(1 + 2^{-19})$ but this is not a model number; the next model number above is $2(1 + 2^{-17})$. So the final model interval in which R must lie is

$2(1 - 2^{-18})$, $2(1 + 2^{-17})$

**3**    In this example P and Q are numbers of type universal real and since the operators ∗ and / apply to the type universal real we might think that the expression (P/Q)∗Q is always of type universal real and thus evaluated exactly at compilation. However, remember that implicit conversion of the universal types is only performed in the case of single literals, numbers and attributes and that general expressions must be converted explicitly. In the case of the assignment to R the only interpretation is that the individual numbers are implicitly converted to type REAL before the operations ∗ and / are performed. The result is that R is assigned a value in the same model interval as in the previous exercise. In the case of S, however, an explicit conversion is given and the complete expression is thus of type universal real. The result is that S is assigned the model number 2.0.

**4**    1313 = 16 (= possible mantissae)
    ×      41 (= possible exponents)
    ×       2 (= possible signs)
    +       1 (= zero)

**5**    **function** HYPOTENUSE(X, Y: REAL) **return** REAL **is**
        TINY: **constant** REAL:= 2.0∗∗(−REAL'EMAX/2);
    **begin**
        **if abs** X < TINY **and abs** Y < TINY **then**
            **return** SQRT((X/TINY)∗∗2+(Y/TINY)∗∗2)∗TINY;
        **else**
            **return** SQRT(X∗∗2+Y∗∗2);
        **end if**;
    **end** HYPOTENUSE;

Note that REAL'EMAX is always even.

**6**    In the case of type ROUGH we have requested one decimal digit which implies a maximum relative precision of 1 in 10. If we took $B = 4$ then the relative precision would vary from 1 in 8 to 1 in 16. There would therefore be occasional places where the binary numbers are slightly further apart than the decimal ones. In fact, around 10 000 the decimal model numbers for $D = 1$ are

8000,    9000,    10 000,    20 000

whereas the binary model numbers for $B = 4$ are

7680,    8192,    9216,    10 240

and we see that 8192 and 9216 are more than 1000 apart. Hence we have to take $B = 5$ so that the minimum relative precision is 1 in 16. The general result follows.

7    The ratio is $2^{B-1}$ or 1/EPSILON. Thus the hole around zero is relatively more dangerous for higher values of $B$.

8
```
function INNER(A, B: VECTOR) return REAL is
    type LONG_REAL is digits 14;
    RESULT: LONG_REAL:= 0.0;
begin
    for I in A'RANGE loop
        RESULT:= RESULT + LONG_REAL(A(I))*LONG_REAL(B(I));
    end loop;
    return REAL(RESULT);
end INNER;
```

*Exercise 12.4*

1    $\frac{1}{10}(1 - 2^{-12})$, $\frac{1}{10}(1 + 2^{-14})$

2    The operation * cannot be universal real because the general expression 2.0*PI cannot be implicitly converted to type ANGLE before the subtraction. Nor can it be the * applying to two operands of type ANGLE because that delivers a result of the type universal fixed which always has to be explicitly converted and moreover a universal real operand of fixed point multiplication cannot be implicitly converted because of lack of uniqueness. It is fortunate that this is so; otherwise we would have got the wrong answer because 2.0 is not a model number of type ANGLE.

3
```
function "**" (X: COMPLEX; N: INTEGER) return COMPLEX is
    RESULT_THETA: ANGLE:= 0.0;
begin
    for I in 1 .. abs N loop
        RESULT_THETA:= NORMAL(RESULT_THETA+X.THETA);
    end loop;
    if N < 0 then RESULT_THETA:= -RESULT_THETA; end if;
    return (X.R**N, RESULT_THETA);
end "**";
```

We cannot simply write

```
return (X.R**N, NORMAL(X.THETA*N);
```

because if **abs** N is larger than 3 the multiplication is likely to overflow; so we have to repeatedly normalize. A clever solution which is faster for all but the smallest values of **abs** N is

```
function "**" (X: COMPLEX; N: INTEGER) return COMPLEX is
    RESULT_THETA: ANGLE:= 0.0;
    TERM: ANGLE:= X.THETA;
    M: INTEGER:= abs N;
begin
    while M > 0 loop
        if M rem 2 /= 0 then
            RESULT_THETA:= NORMAL(RESULT_THETA + TERM);
        end if;
        M:= M/2;
        TERM:= NORMAL(TERM*2);
    end loop;
    if N < 0 then RESULT_THETA:= -RESULT_THETA; end if;
    return (X.R**N, RESULT_THETA);
end "**";
```

This is a variation of the standard algorithm for computing exponentials by decomposing the exponent into its binary form and doing a minimal number of multiplications. In our case it is the multiplier N which we decompose and then do a minimal number of additions. Note that we cannot write TERM∗2.0 because a universal real operand cannot be implicitly converted in the case of fixed point multiplication. In any event such a product would be of type universal fixed and as mentioned in a previous answer 2.0 is not a model number and so errors would be introduced.

One of the major points about fixed point is the ability to do exact addition; multiplication by integers is treated conceptually as repeated addition which is why it produces a result of the same fixed point type. Multiplication by real values (universal or otherwise) is to be treated with suspicion and hence the concept of universal fixed and compulsory conversion which draws the matter to the programmer's attention. It is hence very appropriate that we are using repeated addition in order to multiply by our integer N. Recognizing that our repeated addition algorithm is essentially the same as for exponentiation, we can in parallel compute X.R∗∗N by the same method. A little manipulation soon makes us realize that we might as well write

```
function "**" (X: COMPLEX; N: INTEGER) return COMPLEX is
    RESULT: COMPLEX= (1.0, 0.0);
    TERM: COMPLEX:= X;
    M: INTEGER:= abs N;
begin
    while M > 0 loop
        if M rem 2 /= 0 then
            RESULT:= RESULT * TERM;      -- COMPLEX *
        end if;
        M:= M/2;
        TERM:= TERM * TERM;              -- COMPLEX *
    end loop;
    if N < 0 then RESULT:= - RESULT; end if;    -- COMPLEX -
    return RESULT;
end "**";
```

This brings us back full circle. This is indeed the standard algorithm for computing exponentials and we are now applying it in the abstract to our type COMPLEX. Note the calls of the functions "∗" and unary "−" applying to the type COMPLEX. This version of "∗∗" can be declared outside the package COMPLEX_NUMBERS and is quite independent of the internal representation (but it will be very inefficient unless the internal representation is polar).

4
```
    private
        type ANGLE is delta 0.05 range -720.0 .. 720.0;
        type COMPLEX is
            record
                R: REAL;
                THETA: ANGLE range 0.0 .. 360.0;
            end record;
        I: constant COMPLEX:= (1.0, 90.0);
    end;
        ...
    function NORMAL(A: ANGLE) return ANGLE is
    begin
        if A >= 360.0 then
            return A - 360.0;
        elsif A < 0.0 then
            return A + 360.0;
        else
            return A;
        end if;
    end NORMAL;
```

The choice of delta is derived as follows. We need 10 bits to cover the range 0 .. 720 plus one bit for the sign thus leaving 5 bits after the binary point. So *small* will be $2^{-5}$ and thus any value of delta greater than that but less than $2^{-4}$ will do. We have chosen 0.05.

# Answers 13

*Exercise 13.1*

1
```
generic
     type ITEM is private;
package STACKS is
     type STACK(MAX: NATURAL) is limited private;
     procedure PUSH(S: in out STACK; X: in ITEM);
     procedure POP(S: in out STACK; X: out ITEM);
     function "=" (S, T: STACK) return BOOLEAN;
private
     type ITEM_ARRAY is array (INTEGER range <>) of ITEM;
     type STACK(MAX: NATURAL) is
          record
               S: ITEM_ARRAY(1 .. MAX);
               TOP: INTEGER:= 0;
          end record;
end;
```

The body is much as before. To declare a stack we must first instantiate the package.

```
package BOOLEAN_STACKS is new STACKS(ITEM => BOOLEAN);
use BOOLEAN_STACKS;
S: STACK(MAX => 30);
```

2
```
generic
     type THING is private;
package P is
     procedure SWAP(A, B: in out THING);
     procedure CAB(A, B, C: in out THING);
end P;

package body P is
     procedure SWAP(A, B: in out THING) is
          T: THING;
     begin
          T:= A;  A:= B;  B:= T;
     end;
     procedure CAB(A, B, C: in out THING) is
     begin
          SWAP(A, B);
          SWAP(A, C);
     end;
end P;
```

*Exercise 13.2*

1
```
function "not" is new NEXT(BOOLEAN);
```

2
```
generic
    type BASE is range <>;
package RATIONAL_NUMBERS is
    type RATIONAL is private;
    function "+" (X: RATIONAL) return RATIONAL;
    function "-" (X: RATIONAL) return RATIONAL;
    function "+" (X, Y: RATIONAL) return RATIONAL;
    function "-" (X, Y: RATIONAL) return RATIONAL;
    function "*" (X, Y: RATIONAL) return RATIONAL;
    function "/" (X, Y: RATIONAL) return RATIONAL;

    subtype POS_BASE is BASE range 1 .. BASE'LAST;
    function "/" (X: BASE; Y: POS_BASE) return RATIONAL;
    function NUMERATOR(R: RATIONAL) return BASE;
    function DENOMINATOR(R: RATIONAL) return POS_BASE;
private
    type RATIONAL is
        record
            NUM: BASE:= 0;
            DEN: POS_BASE:= 1;
        end record;
end;
```

3
```
generic
    type INDEX is (<>);
    type FLOATING is digits <>;
    type VEC is array (INDEX range <>) of FLOATING;
    type MAT is array (INDEX range <>, INDEX range <>) of FLOATING;
function OUTER(A, B: VEC) return MAT;

function OUTER(A, B: VEC) return MAT is
    C: MAT(A'RANGE, B'RANGE);
begin
    for I in A'RANGE loop
        for J in B'RANGE loop
            C(I, J):= A(I)*B(J);
        end loop;
    end loop;
    return C;
end OUTER;

function OUTER_VECTOR is new OUTER(INTEGER, REAL, VECTOR, MATRIX);
```

4
```
package body SET_OF is

    function MAKE_SET(X: LIST) return SET is
        S: SET:= EMPTY;
    begin
        for I in X'RANGE loop
            S(X(I)):= TRUE;
        end loop;
        return S;
    end MAKE_SET;

    function MAKE_SET(X: BASE) return SET is
        S: SET:= EMPTY;
    begin
        S(X):= TRUE;
        return S;
    end MAKE_SET;
```

```
function DECOMPOSE(X: SET) return LIST is
    L: LIST(1 .. SIZE(X));
    I: POSITIVE:= 1;
begin
    for E in SET'RANGE loop
        if X(E) then
            L(I):= E;
            I:= I+1;
        end if;
    end loop;
    return L;
end DECOMPOSE;

function "+" (X, Y: SET) return SET is
begin
    return X or Y;
end "+";

function "*" (X, Y: SET) return SET is
begin
    return X and Y;
end "*";

function "−" (X, Y: SET) return SET is
begin
    return X xor Y;
end "−";

function "<" (X: BASE; Y: SET) return BOOLEAN is
begin
    return Y(X);
end "<";

function "<=" (X, Y: SET) return BOOLEAN is
begin
    return (X and Y) = X;
end "<=";

function SIZE(X: SET) return NATURAL is
    N: NATURAL:= 0;
begin
    for E in SET'RANGE loop
        if X(E) then
            N:= N+1;
        end if;
    end loop;
    return N;
end SIZE;

end SET_OF;

private
    type BASE_ARRAY is array (BASE) of BOOLEAN;
    type SET is
        record
            VALUE: BASE_ARRAY:= (BASE_ARRAY'RANGE => FALSE);
        end record;

    EMPTY: constant SET:= (VALUE => (BASE_ARRAY'RANGE => FALSE));
    FULL: constant SET:= (VALUE => (BASE_ARRAY'RANGE => TRUE));
end;
```

We have to make the full type into a record containing the array as a single component so that we can give it a default initial expression. Unfortunately, this means that the body needs rewriting and moreover the functions become rather untidy. Sadly we cannot write the default expression as EMPTY.VALUE. This is because we cannot use the component name VALUE in its own declaration. In general, however, we can use a deferred constant as a default value before its full declaration. Note also that we have to use the named notation for the single component record aggregates.

*Exercise 13.3*

1    First we have to declare our function "<" which we define as follows: if the polynomials have different degrees, the one with the lower degree is smaller; if the same degree, then we compare coefficients starting at the highest power. So

```
function "<" (X, Y: POLYNOMIAL) return BOOLEAN is
begin
    if X.N /= Y.N then
        return X.N < Y.N;
    end if;
    for I in reverse 0 .. X.N loop    -- or X.A'RANGE
        if X.A(I) /= Y.A(I) then
            return X.A(I) < Y.A(I);
        end if;
    end loop;
    return FALSE;        -- they are identical
end "<";

procedure SORT_POLY is new SORT(INTEGER, POLYNOMIAL, POLY_ARRAY);
```

2    
```
type MUTANT_ARRAY is array (INTEGER range <>) of MUTANT;

function "<" (X, Y: MUTANT) return BOOLEAN is
begin
    if X.SEX /= Y.SEX then
        return X.SEX > Y.SEX;
    else
        return Y.BIRTH < X.BIRTH;
    end if;
end "<";

procedure SORT_MUTANT is new SORT(INTEGER, MUTANT, MUTANT_ARRAY);
```

Note that the order of sexes asked for is precisely the reverse order to that in the type GENDER and so we can directly use ">" applied to that type. Similarly younger first means later birth date first and so we use the function "<" we have already defined for the type DATE but with the arguments reversed.

We could not sort an array of type PERSON because we cannot declare such an array anyway. See the end of Section 11.3.

3    We cannot do this because the array is of an anonymous type.

4    We might get CONSTRAINT_ERROR. If C'FIRST = INDEX'FIRST then the attempt to evaluate INDEX'PRED(C'LAST) will raise CONSTRAINT_ERROR. Considerable care can be required to make such extreme cases foolproof. The easy way out in this case is simply to insert

```
if C'LENGTH < 2 then return; end if;
```

5    The generic body corresponds closely to the procedure SORT in Section 11.4. The type VECTOR is replaced by COLLECTION. I is of type INDEX. The types NODE and TREE are declared inside SORT because they depend on the generic type ITEM. The incrementing of I cannot be done with "+" since the index type may not be an integer and so we have to use INDEX'SUCC. Care is needed not to cause CONSTRAINT_ERROR if the array embraces the full range of values of INDEX. However, the important thing is that the generic specification is completely unchanged and so we see how an alternative body can be sensibly supplied.

**6**     Assuming

**type** BOOL_ARRAY **is array** (INTEGER **range** <>) **of** BOOLEAN;

we have

**function** AND_ALL **is new** APPLY(INTEGER, BOOLEAN, BOOL_ARRAY, **"and"**);

**7**     A further generic parameter is required to supply a value for zero.

**generic**
  **type** INDEX **is** (<>);
  **type** ITEM **is private**;
  ZERO: **in** ITEM;
  **type** VEC **is array** (INDEX **range** <>) **of** ITEM;
  **with function** "+" (X, Y: ITEM) **return** ITEM;
**function** APPLY(A: VEC) **return** ITEM;

**function** APPLY(A: VEC) **return** ITEM **is**
  RESULT: ITEM:= ZERO;
**begin**
  **for** I **in** A'RANGE **loop**
    RESULT:= RESULT+A(I);
  **end loop**;
  **return** RESULT;
**end** APPLY;

and then

**function** AND_ALL **is**
      **new** APPLY(INTEGER, BOOLEAN, TRUE, BOOL_ARRAY, **"and"**);

**8**     **generic**
  **type** ITEM **is limited private**;
  **type** VECTOR **is array** (INTEGER **range** <>) **of** ITEM;
  **with function** "=" (X, Y: ITEM) **return** BOOLEAN **is** <>;
**function** EQUALS(A, B: VECTOR) **return** BOOLEAN;

**function** EQUALS(A, B: VECTOR) **return** BOOLEAN **is**
**begin**
  -- body exactly as for Exercise 9.2(3)
**end** EQUALS;

We can instantiate by

**function** "=" **is new** EQUALS(STACK, STACK_ARRAY, **"="**);

or simply by

**function** "=" **is new** EQUALS(STACK, STACK_ARRAY);

in which case the default parameter is used.

**9**     **function** G(X: REAL) **return** REAL **is**
**begin**
  **return** EXP(X)+X−7.0;
**end**;
  ...
**function** SOLVE_G **is new** SOLVE(G);
  ...
ANSWER: REAL:= SOLVE_G;

*Exercise 13.4*

**1**     **with** GENERIC_ELEMENTARY_FUNCTIONS;
**package body** SIMPLE_MATHS **is**

```
package FLOAT_FUNCTIONS is
   new GENERIC_ELEMENTARY_FUNCTIONS(FLOAT);

function SQRT(F: FLOAT) return FLOAT is
begin
   return FLOAT_FUNCTIONS.SQRT(F);
exception
   when FLOAT_FUNCTIONS.ARGUMENT_ERROR =>
      raise NUMERIC_ERROR;
end SQRT;

function LOG(F: FLOAT) return FLOAT is
begin
   return FLOAT_FUNCTIONS.LOG(F, 10.0);
exception
   when FLOAT_FUNCTIONS.ARGUMENT_ERROR =>
      raise NUMERIC_ERROR;
end LOG;

function LN(F: FLOAT) return FLOAT is
begin
   return FLOAT_FUNCTIONS.LOG(F);
exception
   when FLOAT_FUNCTIONS.ARGUMENT_ERROR =>
      raise NUMERIC_ERROR;
end LN;

function EXP(F: FLOAT) return FLOAT is
begin
   return FLOAT_FUNCTIONS.EXP(F);
end EXP;

function SIN(F: FLOAT) return FLOAT is
begin
   return FLOAT_FUNCTIONS.SIN(F);
end SIN;

function COS(F: FLOAT) return FLOAT is
begin
   return FLOAT_FUNCTIONS.COS(F);
end COS;

end SIMPLE_MATHS;
```

We did not write a use clause for FLOAT_FUNCTIONS largely because it would not have enabled us to write simply

```
return SQRT(F);
```

since this would have resulted in an infinite recursion.

2    ```
package body GENERIC_COMPLEX_FUNCTIONS is

   function SQRT(X: COMPLEX_TYPE) return COMPLEX_TYPE is
   begin
      return CONS_POLAR(SQRT(abs X), 0.5*ARG(X)));
   end SQRT;

   function LOG(X: COMPLEX_TYPE) return COMPLEX_TYPE is
   begin
      return CONS(LOG(abs X), ARG(X));
   end LOG;

   function EXP(X: COMPLEX_TYPE) return COMPLEX_TYPE is
   begin
```
```

```
        return CONS_POLAR(EXP(RL_PART(X)), IM_PART(X));
    end EXP;

    function SIN(X: COMPLEX_TYPE) return COMPLEX_TYPE is
        RL: REAL_TYPE:= RL_PART(X);
        IM: REAL_TYPE:= IM_PART(X);
    begin
        return CONS(SIN(RL)*COSH(IM)), COS(RL)*SINH(IM));
    end SIN;

    function COS(X: COMPLEX_TYPE) return COMPLEX_TYPE is
        RL: REAL_TYPE:= RL_PART(X);
        IM: REAL_TYPE:= IM_PART(X);
    begin
        return CONS(COS(RL)*COSH(IM)), -SIN(RL)*SINH(IM));
    end COS;

end GENERIC_COMPLEX_FUNCTIONS;
```

3
```
    function CONS_CARTESIAN(R, I: MY_REAL) return COMPLEX renames CONS;
```

4
```
    generic
        type REAL is digits <>;
        with function SQRT(X: REAL) return REAL is <>;
        with function SIN(X: REAL) return REAL is <>;
        with function COS(X: REAL) return REAL is <>;
        with function ARCTAN(Y, X: REAL) return REAL is <>;
    package GENERIC_COMPLEX_NUMBERS is
        type COMPLEX is private;

        -- as in Section 9.1 plus

        function CONS_POLAR(R, THETA: REAL) return COMPLEX;
        function "abs" (X: COMPLEX) return REAL;
        function ARG(X: COMPLEX) return REAL;
    private

        -- as before

    end;

    package body GENERIC_COMPLEX_NUMBERS is

        -- as before plus

        function CONS_POLAR(R, THETA: REAL) return COMPLEX is
        begin
            return (R*COS(THETA), R*SIN(THETA));
        end CONS_POLAR;

        function "abs" (X: COMPLEX) return REAL is
        begin
            return SQRT(X.RL**2 + X.IM**2);
        end "abs";

        function ARG(X: COMPLEX) return REAL is
            return ARCTAN(X.IM, X.RL);
        end ARG;

    end GENERIC_COMPLEX_NUMBERS;
```

Numerical analysts will writhe at the poor implementation of **abs** which can unnecessarily overflow in computing the parameter of SQRT. This can be avoided by suitable rescaling.

Note also that if the private type COMPLEX is implemented in polar form then the same set of auxiliary functions will suffice. Thus the formal functions provided do not dictate the internal representation and so the abstraction is not compromised.

# Answers 14

*Exercise 14.1*

1

```
procedure SHOPPING is

    task GET_SALAD;

    task body GET_SALAD is
    begin
        BUY_SALAD;
    end GET_SALAD;

    task GET_WINE;

    task body GET_WINE is
    begin
        BUY_WINE;
    end GET_WINE;

    task GET_MEAT;

    task body GET_MEAT is
    begin
        BUY_MEAT;
    end GET_MEAT;

begin
    null;
end SHOPPING;
```

*Exercise 14.2*

1

```
task body BUILD_COMPLEX is
    C: COMPLEX;
begin
    loop
        accept PUT_RL(X: REAL) do
            C.RL:= X;
        end;
        accept PUT_IM(X: REAL) do
            C.IM:= X;
        end;
        accept GET_COMP(X: out COMPLEX) do
            X:= C;
        end;
    end loop;
end BUILD_COMPLEX;
```

2

```
task body CHAR_TO_LINE is
    BUFFER: LINE;
begin
    loop
        for I in BUFFER'RANGE loop
            accept PUT(C: in CHARACTER) do
                BUFFER(I):= C;
            end;
```

```
            end loop;
            accept GET(L: out LINE) do
                L:= BUFFER;
            end;
        end loop;
    end CHAR_TO_LINE;
```

*Exercise 14.3*

1
```
        generic
            FIRST_TIME: CALENDAR.TIME;
            INTERVAL: DURATION;
            NUMBER: INTEGER;
            with procedure P;
        procedure CALL;

        procedure CALL is
            use CALENDAR;
            NEXT_TIME: TIME:= FIRST_TIME;
        begin
            if NEXT_TIME < CLOCK then
                NEXT_TIME:= CLOCK;
            end if;
            for I in 1 .. NUMBER loop
                delay NEXT_TIME-CLOCK;
                P;
                NEXT_TIME:= NEXT_TIME+INTERVAL;
            end loop;
        end CALL;
```

2       The type DURATION requires at least 24 bits.

*Exercise 14.4*

1
```
        task body BUILD_COMPLEX is
            C: COMPLEX;
            GOT_RL, GOT_IM: BOOLEAN:= FALSE;
        begin
            loop
                select
                    when not GOT_RL =>
                    accept PUT_RL(X: REAL) do
                        C.RL:= X;
                    end;
                    GOT_RL:= TRUE;
                or
                    when not GOT_IM =>
                    accept PUT_IM(X: REAL) do
                        C.IM:= X;
                    end;
                    GOT_IM:= TRUE;
                or
                    when GOT_RL and GOT_IM =>
                    accept GET_COMP(X: out COMPLEX) do
                        X:= C;
                    end;
                    GOT_RL:= FALSE;
                    GOT_IM:= FALSE;
                end select;
```

```
    end loop;
end BUILD_COMPLEX;
```

An alternative solution is

```
task body BUILD_COMPLEX is
    C: COMPLEX;
begin
    loop
        select
            accept PUT_RL(X: REAL) do
                C.RL:= X;
            end;
            accept PUT_IM(X: REAL) do
                C.IM:= X;
            end;
        or
            accept PUT_IM(X: REAL) do
                C.IM:= X;
            end;
            accept PUT_RL(X: REAL) do
                C.RL:= X;
            end;
        end select;
        accept GET_COMP(X: out COMPLEX) do
            X:= C;
        end;
    end loop;
end BUILD_COMPLEX;
```

At first reading this might seem simpler but the technique does not extrapolate easily when a moderate number of components are involved because of the combinatorial explosion.

*Exercise 14.5*

1
```
procedure READ(X: out ITEM; T: DURATION; OK: out BOOLEAN) is
begin
    select
        CONTROL.START(READ);
    or
        delay T;
        OK:= FALSE;
        return;
    end select;
    X:= V;
    CONTROL.STOP_READ;
    OK:= TRUE;
end READ;

procedure WRITE(X: in ITEM; T: DURATION; OK: out BOOLEAN) is
    use CALENDAR;
    START_TIME: TIME:= CLOCK;
begin
    select
        CONTROL.START(WRITE);
    or
        delay T;
        OK:= FALSE;
        return;
```

```
    end select;
    select
        CONTROL.WRITE;
    or
        delay T-(CLOCK-START_TIME);
        CONTROL.STOP_WRITE;
        OK:= FALSE;
        return;
    end select;
    V:= X;
    CONTROL.STOP_WRITE;
    OK:= TRUE;
end WRITE;
```

Note how a shorter time out is imposed on the call of WRITE.

*Exercise 14.7*

1

```
task BUFFERING is
    entry PUT(X: in ITEM);
    entry FINISH;
    entry GET(X: out ITEM);
end;

task body BUFFERING is
    N: constant:= 8;
    A: array (1 .. N) of ITEM;
    I, J: INTEGER range 1 .. N:= 1;
    COUNT: INTEGER range 0 .. N:= 0;
    FINISHED: BOOLEAN:= FALSE;
begin
    loop
        select
            when COUNT < N =>
            accept PUT(X: in ITEM) do
                A(I):= X;
            end;
            I:= I mod N+1; COUNT:= COUNT+1;
        or
            accept FINISH;
            FINISHED:= TRUE;
        or
            when COUNT > 0 =>
            accept GET(X: out ITEM) do
                X:= A(J);
            end;
            J:= J mod N+1; COUNT:= COUNT-1;
        or
            when COUNT = 0 and FINISHED =>
            accept GET(X: out ITEM) do
                raise DONE;
            end;
        end select;
    end loop;
exception
    when DONE =>
        null;
end BUFFERING;
```

This example illustrates that there may be several accept statements for the same entry in the one select statement. The exception DONE is propagated to the caller and also terminates the loop in BUFFERING before being quietly handled. Of course the exception need not be handled by BUFFERING because exceptions propagated out of tasks are lost, but it is cleaner to do so.

*Exercise 14.8*

1    The select statement becomes

```
select
    when WAITERS = 0 =>
    accept FIRST(S: SET; OK: out BOOLEAN) do
        TRY(S, OK);
        if not OK then
            WAITERS:= WAITERS+1;
        end if;
    end;
or
    accept RELEASE(S: SET) do
        FREE:= FREE+S;
    end;
    accept AGAIN(S: SET; OK: out BOOLEAN) do
        TRY(S, OK);
        if OK then
            WAITERS:= WAITERS-1;
        end if;
    end;
end select;
```

2    
```
package CONTROLLER is
    procedure REQUEST(P: PRIORITY; D: DATA);
end;

package body CONTROLLER is

    task CONTROL is
        entry SIGN_IN(P: PRIORITY);
        entry REQUEST(PRIORITY)(D: DATA);
    end;

    task body CONTROL is
        TOTAL: INTEGER:= 0;
        PENDING: array (PRIORITY) of INTEGER:= (PRIORITY => 0);
    begin
        loop
            if TOTAL = 0 then
                accept SIGN_IN(P: PRIORITY) do
                    PENDING(P):= PENDING(P)+1;
                    TOTAL:= 1;
                end;
            end if;
            loop
                select
                    accept SIGN_IN(P: PRIORITY) do
                        PENDING(P):= PENDING(P)+1;
                        TOTAL:= TOTAL+1;
                    end;
                else
                    exit;
```

```
            end select;
        end loop;

    for P in PRIORITY loop
        if PENDING(P) > 0 then
            accept REQUEST(P)(D: DATA) do
                ACTION(D);
            end;
            PENDING(P):= PENDING(P)-1;
            TOTAL:= TOTAL-1;
            exit;
        end if;
    end loop;
end loop;
end CONTROL;

procedure REQUEST(P: PRIORITY; D: DATA) is
begin
    CONTROL.SIGN_IN(P);
    CONTROL.REQUEST(P)(D);
end REQUEST;

end CONTROLLER;
```

The variable TOTAL records the total number of requests outstanding and the array PENDING records the number at each priority. Each time round the outer loop, the task waits for a call of SIGN_IN if no requests are in the system, it then services any outstanding calls of SIGN_IN and finally deals with a request of the highest priority. We could dispense with the array PENDING and scan the queues as before but there is a slight risk of polling if a user has called SIGN_IN but not yet called REQUEST.

Finally, note that the solution will not work if a calling task is aborted; this could be overcome by the use of agents.

*Exercise 14.9*

1
```
package COBBLERS is
    procedure MEND(A: ADDRESS; B: BOOTS);
end;

package body COBBLERS is
    type JOB is
        record
            REPLY: ADDRESS;
            ITEM: BOOTS;
        end record;

    package P is new BUFFERS(100, JOB);
    use P;
    BOOT_STORE: BUFFER;

    task SERVER is
        entry REQUEST(A: ADDRESS; B: BOOTS);
    end;

    task type REPAIRMAN;
    TOM, DICK, HARRY: REPAIRMAN;

    task body SERVER is
        NEXT_JOB: JOB;
    begin
        loop
            accept REQUEST(A: ADDRESS; B: BOOTS) do
```

```
                    NEXT_JOB:= (A, B);
                end;
                PUT(BOOT_STORE, NEXT_JOB);
            end loop;
        end SERVER;

        task body REPAIRMAN is
            MY_JOB: JOB;
        begin
            loop
                GET(BOOT_STORE, MY_JOB);
                REPAIR(MY_JOB.ITEM);
                MY_JOB.REPLY.DEPOSIT(MY_JOB.ITEM);
            end loop;
        end REPAIRMAN;

        procedure MEND(A: ADDRESS; B: BOOTS) is
        begin
            SERVER.REQUEST(A, B);
        end;

    end COBBLERS;
```

We have assumed that the type ADDRESS is an access to a mailbox for handling boots. Note one anomaly; the stupid server accepts boots from the customer before checking the store – if it turns out to be full, he is left holding them. In all, the shop can hold 104 pairs of boots – 100 in store, 1 with the server and 1 with each repairman.

2
```
        procedure GAUSS_SEIDEL is
            N: constant:= 5;
            subtype FULL_GRID is INTEGER range 0 .. N;
            subtype GRID is FULL_GRID range 1 .. N-1;
            type REAL is digits 7;
            DELTA_P: REAL;
            TOLERANCE: constant REAL:= 0.0001;
            ERROR_LIMIT: constant REAL:= TOLERANCE * (N-1)**2;
            CONVERGED: BOOLEAN:= FALSE;
            ERROR_SUM: REAL;

            function F(I, J: GRID) return REAL is separate;

            task type ITERATOR is
                pragma PRIORITY(1);
                entry START(I, J: in GRID);
            end;

            task type POINT is
                pragma PRIORITY(2);
                entry SET_P(X: in REAL);
                entry GET_P(X: out REAL);
                entry GET_DELTA_P(X: out REAL);
                entry SET_CONVERGED(B: in BOOLEAN);
                entry GET_CONVERGED(B: out BOOLEAN);
            end;

            PROCESS: array (GRID, GRID) of ITERATOR;
            DATA: array (GRID, GRID) of POINT;

            task body ITERATOR is
                I, J: GRID;
                P, P1, P2, P3, P4: REAL;
```

```
        CONVERGED: BOOLEAN;
    begin

        accept START(I, J: in GRID) do
            ITERATOR.I:= START.I;
            ITERATOR.J:= START.J;
        end START;

        loop      -- needs modification if adjacent to boundary
            DATA(I-1, J).GET_P(P1);
            DATA(I+1, J).GET_P(P2);
            DATA(I, J-1).GET_P(P3);
            DATA(I, J+1).GET_P(P4);
            P:= 0.25 * (P1+P2+P3+P4-F(I, J));
            DATA(I, J).SET_P(P);
            DATA(I, J).GET_CONVERGED(CONVERGED);
            exit when CONVERGED;
        end loop;

    end ITERATOR;

    task body POINT is
        CONVERGED: BOOLEAN:= FALSE;
        P: REAL;
        DELTA_P: REAL;
    begin

        loop
            select
                accept SET_P(X: in REAL) do
                    DELTA_P:= X-P;
                    P:= X;
                end;
            or
                accept GET_P(X: out REAL) do
                    X:= P;
                end;
            or
                accept GET_DELTA_P(X: out REAL) do
                    X:= DELTA_P;
                end;
            or
                accept SET_CONVERGED(B: in BOOLEAN) do
                    CONVERGED:= B;
                end;
            or
                accept GET_CONVERGED(B: out BOOLEAN) do
                    B:= CONVERGED;
                end;
            or
                terminate;
            end select;
        end loop;

    end POINT;

begin  -- of main program; the tasks are now active

    for I in GRID loop
    for J in GRID loop
        PROCESS(I, J).START(I, J); -- tell them who they are
```

```
            end loop;
        end loop;

        loop
            ERROR_SUM:= 0.0;
            for I in GRID loop
                for J in GRID loop
                    DATA(I, J).GET_DELTA_P(DELTA_P);
                    ERROR_SUM:= ERROR_SUM + DELTA_P**2;
                end loop;
            end loop;

            CONVERGED:= ERROR_SUM < ERROR_LIMIT;
            exit when CONVERGED;
        end loop;

        -- tell the data tasks that it has converged

        for I in GRID loop
            for J in GRID loop
                DATA(I, J).SET_CONVERGED(TRUE);
            end loop;
        end loop;

        -- output results

    end GAUSS_SEIDEL;
```

The main problem with this solution is that we have not taken account of the boundary. Nor have we considered how to initialize the system. However, it must now be clear that using the rendezvous rather than shared variables means that the communication must completely overwhelm the computation unless the function F is extremely complex. Practical applications of distributed tasks of this kind will have much larger computational tasks to perform.

The main loop of the ITERATOR task is a bit painful. It is a pity that we cannot have entry functions. However, it could be made neater by using renaming in order to avoid repeated evaluation of DATA(I, J) and so on; this would also speed things up. Thus we could write

```
procedure GET_P1(X: out REAL) renames DATA(I-1, J).GET_P;
procedure GET_P2(X: out REAL) renames DATA(I+1, J).GET_P;
    ...
procedure SET_P(X: in REAL) renames DATA(I, J).SET_P;
procedure GET_CONVERGED(B: out BOOLEAN) renames
                                DATA(I, J).GET_CONVERGED;
```

and then

```
GET_P1(P1); GET_P2(P2); GET_P3(P3); GET_P4(P4);
SET_P(0.25 * (P1+P2+P3+P4-F(I, J)));
GET_CONVERGED(CONVERGED);
exit when CONVERGED;
```

# Answers 15

*Exercise 15.1*

```
1       with DIRECT_IO;
        generic
            type ELEMENT is private;
        procedure REV(FROM, TO: STRING);
```

```
procedure REV(FROM, TO: STRING) is
    package IO is new DIRECT_IO(ELEMENT);
    use IO;
    INPUT: FILE_TYPE;
    OUTPUT: FILE_TYPE;
    X: ELEMENT;
begin
    OPEN(INPUT, IN_FILE, FROM);
    OPEN(OUTPUT, OUT_FILE, TO);
    SET_INDEX(OUTPUT, SIZE(INPUT));
    loop
        READ(INPUT, X);
        WRITE(OUTPUT, X);
        exit when END_OF_FILE(INPUT);
        SET_INDEX(OUTPUT, INDEX(OUTPUT)-2);
    end loop;
    CLOSE(INPUT);
    CLOSE(OUTPUT);
end REV;
```

Remember that **reverse** is a reserved word. Note also that this does not work if the file is empty (the first call of SET_INDEX will raise CONSTRAINT_ERROR). However, this is an improvement on the solution in earlier editions of this book which always raised CONSTRAINT_ERROR. I am very grateful to Vittorio Frigo of CERN for pointing out this blunder.

*Exercise 15.2*

1    The output is shown in string quotès in order to reveal the layout. Spaces are indicated by s. In reality of course, there are no quotes and spaces are spaces.

(a)    "FRED"
(b)    "sss120"
(c)    "sssss120"
(d)    "120"
(e)    "-120"
(f)    "ss8#170#"
(g)    "-3.80000E+01"
(h)    "sssss7.00E-2"
(i)    "3.1416E+01"
(j)    "1.0E+10"

2    **with** TEXT_IO;
     **package body** SIMPLE_IO **is**

```
    package FLOAT_IO is new TEXT_IO.FLOAT_IO(FLOAT);

    procedure GET(F: out FLOAT) is
    begin
        FLOAT_IO.GET(F);
    end GET;

    procedure PUT(F: in FLOAT) is
    begin
        FLOAT_IO.PUT(F);
    end PUT;

    procedure PUT(S: in STRING) is
    begin
        TEXT_IO.PUT(S);
    end PUT;
```

```
        procedure NEW_LINE(N: in INTEGER:= 1) is
        begin
            TEXT_IO.NEW_LINE(TEXT_IO.COUNT(N));
        end NEW_LINE;

    end SIMPLE_IO;
```

Note that we have chosen to call the instantiated package FLOAT_IO; this causes no confusion (except perhaps for the reader) since the new package merely prevents direct access (via a use clause) to the generic one of the same name. This does not matter since we are using the full dotted notation to access the generic one. In any event we have to use the full notation in the procedures in order to avoid recursion so there is little point in a use clause for TEXT_IO.

The other point of note is the type conversion in NEW_LINE.

# Answers 16

*Exercise 16.1*

**1**  (a)    dynamic – INTEGER
     (b)    static – INTEGER
     (c)    static – universal integer

*Exercise 16.4*

**1**

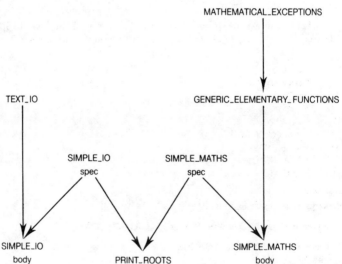

We have assumed that TEXT_IO and GENERIC_ELEMENTARY_FUNCTIONS are self-contained. Note moreover that insisting that generic specifications and bodies are compiled together requires that the specification and body of TEXT_IO are also compiled together; this is because the specifications and bodies of the generic units INTEGER_IO, FLOAT_IO and so on are themselves in the specification and body of TEXT_IO respectively.

*Exercise 16.5*

**1**  (a)    The order of evaluation of the operands I and F of "+" is not defined. As a result the effect could be

```
          I:= 1+2;                          -- I first
   or     I:= 2+2;                          -- F first
```

(b)    The order of evaluation of the destination A(I) and the value F is not defined. The effect could be

```
          A(1):= 2;                         -- I first
   or     A(2):= 2;                         -- F first
```

(c)    The order of evaluation of the two indexes is not defined. The effect could be

```
          AA(1, 2):= 0;                     -- I first
   or     AA(2, 2):= 0;                     -- F first
```

# Bibliography

The following selection for further reading comprises a number of books which the author believes will be found helpful. It is by no means exhaustive and omits many other books which make a valuable contribution to the Ada literature. However, if you are new to Ada and wish to build a library then this list is a good starting point.

Rogers, M. W., ed. (1984). *Ada: Language, Compilers and Bibliography*. Cambridge University Press
   The bulk of this book is a reproduction of the *Language Reference Manual*. However, it is in a smaller format and, provided your eyesight is good, is thus much more convenient. It also includes a checklist on how to select an Ada compiler and an extensive (although somewhat out-of-date) bibliography.

Nissen, J. C. and Wallis, P. J. L., eds. (1984). *Portability and Style in Ada*. Cambridge University Press
   This covers in much more detail some of the topics addressed in Sections 16.5 and 16.6. The section on portability is comprehensive and accurate; that on style is naturally more a matter of opinion. Anyone writing serious portable Ada programs should read this book.

Burns, A. (1986). *Concurrent Programming in Ada*. Cambridge University Press
   This is a very complete account of Ada tasking and contains further examples which complement those in Chapter 14.

Ford, B., Kok, J. and Rogers, M. W., eds. (1986). *Scientific Ada*. Cambridge University Press
   Do not be put off by the apparently specialized topic. This book does indeed deal in depth with the use of Ada for numerical calculations. But it also includes much useful discussion about separate compilation and generics which is relevant to all applications.

Cohen, N. H. (1986). *Ada as a Second Language*. McGraw-Hill
   This is a rather comprehensive account of the Ada language. It is a large book and contains many examples explored in detail. Its coverage of Ada is not quite complete; it omits a number of minor issues which we have addressed in this book but on the other hand it discusses some topics that we have skimped (especially the pragmas and machine-dependent bits). It also has myriads of exercises but no solutions (just as well because otherwise it would be 2000 pages!).

Booch, G. (1986). *Software Engineering with Ada*, 2nd edn. Benjamin Cummings
This well-known classic was one of the first books to discuss how to design programs in Ada; it is especially famed for Object Oriented Programming.

Sommerville, I. and Morrison, R. (1987). *Software Development with Ada*. Addison-Wesley
This book covers a broad number of topics concerning how to develop well structured reliable Ada programs. A good book to dip into. It contains a large bibliography.

Le Verrand, D. (1985). *Evaluating Ada* (English translation). North Oxford Academic
This is a critical review of Ada and gives the reader further insight into the design of Ada and how to get the most out of it.

Hibbard, P., Hisgen, A., Rosenberg, J., Shaw, M. and Sherman, M. (1983). *Studies in Ada Style*, 2nd edn. Springer-Verlag
This excellent book contains a detailed analysis of a small number of intricate programs which explore important issues of structure. A lot can be learnt from really understanding them.

Ausnit, C. N., Cohen, N. H., Goodenough, J. B. and Eanes, R. S. (1985). *Ada in Practice*. Springer-Verlag
This is another book containing a number of examples explored in depth.

Wallis, P. G. L. and Gautier, R. J., eds. (1989). *Ada and Software Reuse*. Peter Peregrinus
This contains a very good discussion on how to design reusable software components in Ada.

Dawes, J. (1988). *Ada*. Pitman
This useful little book is a handy reference guide to Ada. It covers the whole language in 200 pages.

The following books are of a more general nature.

Langley Moore, D. (1977). *Ada, Countess of Lovelace*. John Murray
This is a classical biography of Lord Byron's daughter after whom the language is named.

Stein, D. (1985). *Ada, A Life and a Legacy*. MIT Press
This biography contains more about Ada's relationship and technical work with Charles Babbage.

Nabokov, V. (1969). *Ada*. Weidenfeld and Nicolson
The title of this book is an illustration of overloading. It has nothing to do with either Ada the language or the Countess of Lovelace. However, if you are fed up with programming languages, this novel brings light relief and will provoke interesting comment if placed in your library.

# Index

*Gartside's*

# Model
# Business
# Letters

## & Other Business
## Documents

FIFTH EDITION

### Shirley Taylor
Cert Ed DLCC MIQPS

### Leonard Gartside
Former Chief Examiner in Commercial Subjects
College of Preceptors

**FINANCIAL TIMES**
**PITMAN PUBLISHING**

LONDON · HONG KONG · JOHANNESBURG
MELBOURNE · SINGAPORE · WASHINGTON DC

FINANCIAL TIMES MANAGEMENT
128 Long Acre, London WC2E 9AN
Tel: +44 (0)171 447 2000
Fax:+44 (0)171 240 5771
Website: www.ftmanagement.com

*A Division of Financial Times Professional Limited*

First published in Great Britain 1992
Fifth edition published 1998

© Financial Times Professional Limited 1998

ISBN 0 273 63308 2

*British Library Cataloguing in Publication Data*
A CIP catalogue record for this book can be obtained from the British Library.

10  9  8  7  6  5  4  3  2

Typeset by Northern Phototypesetting Co Ltd, Bolton
Printed and bound in Singapore

*The Publishers' policy is to use paper manufactured from sustainable forests.*

# About the author

**Shirley Taylor** worked as Private Secretary at director level for nine years. She has many advanced secretarial qualifications including the LCCIEB Private Secretary's Diploma and a shorthand speed of 170 wpm.

After obtaining teaching diplomas and the Certficate in Education, Shirley spent several years in Singapore as Training Consultant and Lecturer on LCCIEB Private Secretary's Certificate and Diploma examination courses. She was then Head of Secretarial Department at a college in Bahrain, Arabian Gulf, and has also taught at colleges in the UK.

In recent years Shirley has put her considerable experience into writing. She is the author of *Communication for Business – a Practical Approach* (2nd edition), *The Secretary in Training*, and *Practical Audio Transcription* (workbook and cassette).

In addition to her writing, Shirley works as an examiner in secretarial skills and also as a secretarial training consultant. She enjoys travelling to conduct workshops for teachers and students, most recently in Singapore, Malaysia, Athens and the People's Republic of China.

# Contents

# Preface to the first edition

*by Leonard Gartside*

Few business transactions are carried through successfully without correspondence at some point. Enquiries must be answered, quotations given, orders placed, complaints dealt with, transport and insurance arranged and accounts settled. Letters must be written to customers, salesmen, agents, suppliers, bankers, shipowners and many others; they cover every conceivable phase of business activity. They are the firm's silent salesmen and, often enough, represent its only contact with the outside world. Hence the need to create a good impression, not only of the writer's firm, but also of the writer himself as an efficient person eager to be of service.

In the pages that follow are to be found over five hundred specimen letters dealing with a comprehensive range of transactions of the kind handled in business every day. They are represented, not as models to be copied, for no two business situations are ever quite alike, but rather as examples written in the modern English style to illustrate the accepted principles of good business writing.

Every business letter is written to a purpose; each has its own special aim, and one of the features of this book is its use of explanation to show how the various letters set out to achieve their aims. Basic legal principles relevant to different types of transaction are also touched upon, but only where there is a need to clarify legal relationships. Where the book is used in class, the letters provide material for teachers who may wish to enlarge on these matters and the exercises the means for students to apply in practice what they have been taught.

The many letters included are written in the straightforward and meaningful style of the modern age and should be of special help to the overseas user, and especially to students in schools and colleges where commercial correspondence is taught either as a general business accomplishment or as a preparation for the various examinations.

*November 1971*                                                                                  *L.G.*

# Preface to the fifth edition

*by Shirley Taylor*

With constant technological developments taking place in today's competitive business world, speed is often the key to successful business negotiations. This sense of urgency very often means that many executives and managers regularly compose their own correspondence and other business documents on their desk-top or portable PC.

To meet the exciting challenges of today's fast-paced, ever-changing business world this completely revised fifth edition reflects this modern trend. *Model Business Letters* no longer restricts itself solely to business letters; it now includes many other business documents which are used regularly in business. Hence the book is now called *Model Business Letters and Other Business Documents*. Fax messages are an essential means of communication today; memos are used internally, or email for speed. All these methods of communication are featured in this new edition, as well as many other commonly-used business documents such as job descriptions, itineraries, press releases, invitations, agendas, programmes and reply forms.

While the successful structure of the fourth edition has been retained, all units have been completely revised to bring them right up-to-date especially in terms of modern business language. Many new sections and scenarios have been included and some new features have also been introduced to make this new edition even more user-friendly:

- As each new document is introduced the format is illustrated in a specimen document, with notes highlighting every aspect of document presentation.

- Each section contains full explanations, discussion and theory regarding the various documents concerned.

- Many specimen letters are boxed and marginal notes discuss important features of the text.

- 4-point plans help you to plan and structure your own communications effectively.

- Most chapters end with a checklist to remind you of the key points to remember.

- Instead of the glossary of words being at the end of each chapter (and consequently hard to locate) you will now find definitions of any special terminology or phrases in footnotes on relevant pages.

Improvements have also been made to this fifth edition by a bigger page size, more attractive page design and a much improved overall appearance which should result in it being much more user-friendly.

I could not have revised this book without 'a little help from my friends'. Thanks to Barrie Mort for kindly providing his expertise with Unit 4. Special thanks to Nan Harper for painstakingly going through almost the entire text and making many suggestions about how to make the business language more modern and up-to-date (and for taking out hundreds of commas!) Thanks also to my proofreading chums, especially my dear friend Iris, who went faster than a speeding bullet. I am so grateful for your help.

*Model Business Letters and Other Business Documents* is designed to be a comprehensive, easy-to use reference book which is packed with valuable information, useful techniques, practical tips and useful guidelines. Many people will find this book useful:

- **Executives and managers who regularly compose their own correspondence.** The ready-to-use documents can be copied or adapted to meet your precise needs. They will help you to say what you want to say and achieve the desired result. You will be able to save time and do your job better, more effectively and easily without spending ages thinking about what to say.

- **Students following a business, secretarial or professional examination course which requires composition of business letters and other commonly-used business documents.** You will find the guidelines, theory, specimen documents, 4-point plans, definitions and checklists particularly useful in learning how to compose your own effective communications.

- **Overseas users.** You will appreciate the value of this comprehensive resource book and find it of special help in dealing with global business transactions using modern business language.

I hope this reference book, with its emphasis on high quality presentation, structure, language and tone, helps you to convey your printed messages appropriately and effectively. Remember that in so doing you will not only be helping to create and enhance the corporate image of your organisation; you will also be increasing your value to the company and playing a major part in its success.

*February 1998*                                                                 *Shirley Taylor*

*Please note:* for reasons of consistency and simplicity and to avoid confusion, we have used the UK -ise spelling convention throughout this book. Students/readers should also be familiar with the -ize convention which many countries worldwide prefer to adopt.

# Written communication – an overview

There are many modern communication methods available today but the traditional business letter still remains a very important means of transmitting printed messages. As the business letter acts as an ambassador for the company, it is vital that it gives a good first impression. In this respect, it is good business practice to ensure good quality stationery and printing of the letterheaded paper. The business letter also conveys an impression of the company in many other ways:

### Presentation Structure Language and tone

Constant developments in communications technology mean that on many occasions business letters are being replaced by fax messages and electronic mail; within organisations memos are used for written messages, or email for speed. All these methods will be further discussed later in this unit. However, whatever method is chosen to convey your printed message, the aim should be to ensure a high standard in each of the above three important areas. The main reason for this is because such high standards in your printed communications suggest similarly high standards in business generally.

In this unit these three aspects – presentation, structure, language and tone – will be considered in detail.

# Presentation of the business letter

## PRINTED STATIONERY

The paper used for a company's printed correspondence expresses the personality of that company. A letterhead will comprise:

- The company's name
- The full postal address
- Contact numbers – telephone, telex, fax – and an email address if appropriate
- Registered number and registered office. When the registered office of a company is different to that shown in the address section, it is usual to show the registered address, normally at the foot of the notepaper, along with the registered number.

Experts are often engaged to design a letterhead, especially an eye-catching logo with which the company can be associated.

Many organisations even have printed continuation sheets which are used for the second and subsequent pages of business letters.

✆ **Turner Communications**           Continuation sheet

✆ **Turner Communications**      Mobile Phone specialists

21 Ashton Drive
Sheffield          Tel     +44 114 2871122
S26 2ES         Fax     +44 114 2871123
                   Email   TurnerComm@intl.uk

## LAYOUT

**1.1**  **Fully blocked style with open punctuation**

The fully blocked layout is now the most widely used method of display for all business documents. This style is considered to have a businesslike appearance. With the absence of any indentations for new paragraphs or the closing section it is also true that this layout reduces typing time. Open punctuation is often used with the fully blocked layout. Again this reduces typing time because there is no need for any unnecessary full stops and commas.

Although fully blocked layout is now used by many organisations, some still prefer to adopt their own inhouse style for document layout. Whichever layout you use for your business documents, the most important rule is consistency, ie ensuring that all documents are displayed in the same format.

Fully blocked layout with open punctuation has been used for all the specimen documents in this book. In the business letter shown here, note the consistent spacing (only one single linc space) between all sections of the letter.

| | |
|---|---|
| Letterheaded paper | **FINANCIAL TIMES** |
| | **PITMAN PUBLISHING** |

Financial Times Management
128 Long Acre
London WC2E 9AN
Telephone    +44(0)171 447 2240
Facsimile    +44(0)171 240 5771

Reference (initials of writer/typist, sometimes a filing reference) — ST/PJ

Date (day, month, year) — 12 November 19—

Inside address (name, title, company, full address, postal code) —
Mr Christopher Long
General Manager
Long Printing Co Ltd
34 Wood Lane
London
WC1 8TJ

Salutation — Dear Christopher

Heading (to give an instant idea of the theme) — FULLY BLOCKED LETTER LAYOUT

Body of Letter (one line space between paragraphs) —

This layout has become firmly established as the most popular way of setting out letters, fax messages, memos, reports – in fact all business communications. The main feature of fully blocked style is that all lines begin at the left-hand margin.

Open punctuation is usually used with the fully-blocked layout. This means that no punctuation marks are necessary in the reference, date, inside address, salutation and closing section. Of course essential punctuation must still be used in the text of the message itself. However, remember to use commas minimally today; they should only be used when their omission would make the sense of the message unclear.

Consistency is important in layout and spacing of all documents. It is usual to leave just one clear line space between each section.

I enclose some other examples of fully blocked layout as used in fax messages and memoranda.

Most people agree that this layout is very attractive, easy to produce as well as businesslike.

Complimentary close — Yours sincerely

*Shirley Taylor*

Name of sender — SHIRLEY TAYLOR

Sender's designation or department — Secretarial Consultant

Enc (if anything is enclosed) — Enc

Show if any copies are circulated (if more than one, use alphabetical order) —
Copy    Pradeep Jethi, Publisher
        Amelia Lakin, Publishing Co-ordinator

## 1.2 Continuation pages

Some companies have printed continuation sheets which are used for second or subsequent pages of business letters. Such printed continuation sheets usually show just the company's name and logo. If printed continuation sheets are not available, the second or subsequent page should be typed on plain paper of a similar quality to that of the letterhead.

When a second or subsequent page is necessary, certain details should be shown at the top of the continuation sheet. These details are necessary for reference purposes in case the first and subsequent pages are separated in any way.

When a continuation sheet is necessary remember the following guidelines:

- It is not necessary to include anything at the foot of the previous page to indicate that a further page follows. The fact that there is no closing section or signature should make this quite obvious.

- A continuation page should contain at least three or four lines of typing as well as the usual closing section.

- Do not leave one line of a paragraph either at the bottom of the previous page or at the top of the next page. Try to start a new page with a new paragraph.

❄ *Snowflake Productions plc*                    *Continuation sheet*

Page number — 2

Reference — JL/ST

Date — 19 July 19—

Addressee's name
(or first line of inside — Miss Sophie Bolan
address)

leave 3 or 4 blank lines —
before continuing)

Try to split the text in a — Please sign and return one copy of each of these documents and keep the
suitable place, not in    duplicate copies for your reference.
mid-sentence

You will be expected to attend an induction course on your first day at
Always take at least — Snowflake Productions. A copy of the programme is enclosed.
three or four lines of
typing over to a      I look forward to meeting you again soon and hope that you will be very
continuation page    happy in your new post.

Finish in the usual way — Yours sincerely
with the closing section

*James Leighton*

JAMES LEIGHTON

Personnel Director

Don't forget Enc and — Encs
Copy/ies if necessary

Copy   Michael Lim, Training Manager

# PARTS OF A BUSINESS LETTER

### 1.3 Reference

In the past letterheads used to have 'Our ref' and 'Your ref' printed on them. Today this is rarely the case because with modern word processors and printers it is difficult to line up the printing on such pre-printed stationery. Instead, the typist normally inserts the reference on a line on its own. The reference includes the initials of the writer (usually in upper case) and the typist (in upper or lower case, as preferred). A file or departmental reference may also be included.

**Examples**

GBD/ST          GBD/st/Per1          GBD/ST/134

### 1.4 Date

The date should always be shown in full. In the UK it is usual to show the date in the order day/month/year. No commas are used.

**Example**

12 July 1956

In some other countries the date is typed in the order month/day/year, often with a comma after the month.

**Example**

July 12, 1956

### 1.5 Inside address

The name and address of the recipient should be typed on separate lines as it would appear on an envelope. Care should be taken to address the recipient exactly as they sign their letters. For example, a person signing as 'James Leighton' should be addressed as such in the inside address, preceded with the courtesy title 'Mr'. To address him as 'Mr J Leighton' would be inappropriate.

**Example**

Mr James Leighton
General Manager
Leighton Engineering Co Ltd
12 Bracken Hill
Manchester
M60 8AS

When writing letters overseas, the name of the country should be shown on the final line of this section. As the letter will be sent by airmail, this should be indicated one clear line space above the inside address. Again note that the appropriate courtesy title (Mr/Mrs/Miss/Ms) should always be shown:

**Example**

AIRMAIL

Mr Doug Allen
Eagle Press Inc
24 South Bank
Toronto
Ontario
Canada M4J 7LK

## 1.6  Special markings

If a letter is confidential it is usual to include this as part of the inside address, one clear line space above it. This may be typed in upper case or in initial capitals with underscore.

**Example**

CONFIDENTIAL

Mrs Melanie Jackson
Personnel Director
Soft Toys plc
21 Windsor Road
Birmingham
B2 5JT

It should rarely be necessary to use an attention line in today's business communications where we almost always know the name of the person we are writing to. As shown in the above examples, the name of the recipient is included in the inside address, and a personalised salutation will be used.

In the past, however, an attention line was used when the writer simply wanted to ensure that the letter ended up on a certain person's desk, even though the letter was addressed to the company in general, and always began 'Dear Sirs'.

**Example**

FOR THE ATTENTION OF MR JOHN TYLER, SALES MANAGER

Garden Supplies Ltd
24 Amber Street
Sheffield
S44 9DJ

Dear Sirs

### 1.7 Salutation

If the recipient's name has been used in the inside address, it is usual to use a personal salutation.

**Example**

    Dear Mr Leighton    Dear Douglas    Dear Mrs Jackson

If your letter is addressed generally to an organisation, then the more formal salutation 'Dear Sirs' should be used.

**Example**

    Dear Sirs

If your letter is addressed to a head of department or the head of an organisation whose name is not known, then it would be more appropriate to use a salutation as shown here.

**Example**

    Dear Sir or Madam

### 1.8 Heading

A heading gives a brief indication of the content of the letter. It is usually placed one clear line space after the salutation. Upper case is generally used, although initial capitals with underscore may be used if preferred.

**Example**

    Dear Mrs Jackson

    INTERNATIONAL CONFERENCE – 24 AUGUST 1999

### 1.9 Complimentary close

It is customary to end the letter in a polite way by using a complimentary close. The two most common closes are 'Yours faithfully' (used only with Dear Sir/Sirs/Sir or Madam) and 'Yours sincerely' (used with personalised salutations).

**Examples**

| | |
|---|---|
| Dear Sir | |
| Dear Sirs | Yours faithfully |
| Dear Madam | |
| Dear Sir or Madam | |
| | |
| Dear Mr Leighton | |
| Dear Mrs Jackson | Yours sincerely |
| Dear Melanie | |
| Dear John | |

### 1.10 Name of sender and designation

After the complimentary close 4 or 5 clear spaces should be left so that the letter can be signed. The name of the sender should then be inserted in whatever style is preferred – upper case, or initial capitals only. The sender's designation or department should be shown directly beneath his/her name. In these examples note that the title 'Mr' is never shown when the writer is male. However, it is usual to add a courtesy title for a female; this is shown in brackets after her name.

**Examples**

| Yours faithfully | Yours sincerely |
| --- | --- |
| GEORGE FREEMAN | SOPHIE BOLAN (Mrs) |
| Chairman | General Manager |

When a letter has to be signed on behalf of the sender, it is usual to write 'for' or 'pp' in front of the sender's printed name; 'pp' is an abbreviation for per procurationem, which simply means 'on behalf of'.

**Example**

Yours faithfully

*Shirley Johnson*

for GEORGE FREEMAN
Chairman

### 1.11 Enclosures

There are many different methods of indicating that an enclosure is being sent along with the letter:

- Affix a coloured 'enclosure' sticker usually in the bottom left-hand corner of the letter.
- Type three dots in the left-hand margin on the line where the enclosure is mentioned in the body of the letter.
- Type 'Enc' or 'Encs' at the foot of the letter, leaving one clear line space after the sender's designation. This is the most common form of indicating enclosures.

**Example**

Yours sincerely

SHEILA ROBINSON (Mrs)
Marketing Manager

Enc

### 1.12 Copies

When a copy of a letter is to be sent to a third party (usually someone in the sender's organisation) this may be indicated by typing 'cc' (copy circulated) or 'Copy' followed by the name and designation of the copy recipient. If there are two or more copy recipients, it is usual to show these in alphabetical order.

**Example**

> Copy  Mrs Susan Jones, Accountant
> Mr David Roberts, Company Secretary
> Mr Norman Taylor, General Manager

If the writer does not wish the recipient of the letter to know that a third person is receiving a copy of the letter, then 'bcc' (blind copy circulated) is used. This should not be shown on the top of the letter, only on the file copy and bcc copy/ies.

**Example**

> bcc   Mr Keith Lawson, Chief Executive

# Other methods of communication

It is worth mentioning here that although the telephone or face-to-face discussions are often the key means of communication within an organisation, printed messages are often needed. This is when a memorandum is used. As similar rules can be applied to writing the body of memos as to writing the body of letters, I have included a section here on correct format and structure for this important method of printed communication.

Developments in technology have made it possible for us to have instant communication all over the world. Speed is now becoming the key to successful business communications. As a result fax messages and electronic mail are now taking the place of many business letters. It is also true that instead of a secretary being asked to type documents, many employers are keying in their own text and sending messages straight to recipients. However, that important 'first impression' should still be considered. By setting high standards in the important area of printed communication you will be helping to create and enhance the corporate image of your organisation. So although very often it is time saving for the employer to prepare his/her own communications, it is good business practice to allow a secretary to 'tidy them up' and ensure correct presentation, layout and structure.

Remember that in today's competitive business world, high communication standards are vitally important. Therefore, it is important to ensure that the need for speed does not result in a decline in the standards of communications. Instead, the constant advances in technology should help us to improve and enhance our communications and thereby maximise business potential.

## MEMOS

A memo is a written message from one person to another (or several people) within the same organisation. Memos (or memoranda) serve several purposes:

- To provide information
- To request information
- To inform of actions, decisions
- To request actions, decisions

Some companies have pre-printed forms for internal memos but very often it is now common for templates to be called up on word processing systems. The typist then only has to insert the relevant details alongside the given headings.

### 2.1 Format

The following format is an easy, clear method for displaying internal memos.

Emphasise the word MEMORANDUM

Insert the recipient's name and designation

the sender's name and designation

A reference (initials of sender and typist)

Date of issue

salutation is necessary

bject heading – clearly state the topic of the message

The body of the memo should be separated to paragrphs, reaching a relevant conclusion and close

complimentary close is necessary

ave space for signature The sender's name and ignation are at the top so it is not necessary to peat these details here

Enc (if appropriate)

py/ies (if appropriate)

# MEMORANDUM

*To*      Mandy Lim, Administrative Assistant

*From*   Sally Thomas, PA to Chairman

*Ref*     ST/JJ

*Date*   14 August 19—

INHOUSE DOCUMENT FORMATS

Many congratulations on recently joining the staff in the Chairman's office. I hope you will be very happy here.

I am enclosing a booklet explaining the company's general rules regarding document formats. However, I thought it would be helpful if I summarised the rules for ease of reference.

1    DOCUMENT FORMATS

All documents should be presented in the fully-blocked format using open punctuation. Specimen letters, fax messages, memoranda and other documents are included in the booklet. These examples should guide you in our requirements.

2    SIGNATURE BLOCK (LETTERS)

In outgoing letters it is usual practice to display the sender's name in capitals and the title directly underneath in lower case with initial capitals.

3    NUMBERED ITEMS

In reports and other documents it is often necessary to number items. In such cases the numbers should be displayed alone with no full stops or brackets. Subsequent numbering should be decimal, ie 3.1, 3.2, etc.

I hope these guidelines will be useful and that you will study the layouts shown in your booklet. If you have any questions please do not hesitate to ask me.

*Sally Thomas*

Enc

Copy    Personnel Department

## FAX MESSAGES

A fax machine is a relatively inexpensive essential item of equipment for any business. Fax messages may be sent between branches of the same company or to external business associates. Today many communications which would normally be sent by letter are now in fact sent by fax. When referring to the model letters in this book, therefore, the text of the messages may equally be used in fax communications.

**2.2** **Standard printed form or template**

Many companies have a standard printed form for use when sending fax messages. Very often a template is designed for calling up on computers and word processors. Operators need then just key in the relevant information. Here is an example of how a printed fax form or a template might be designed.

---

# Fax

**To:**                                          **From:**

**Company:**                                     **Date:**

**Fax No:**                                      **No of Pages:**          (including this page)

---

## 2.3 Fully blocked style

When a pre-printed form is not available, the fully blocked style may be used in preparing a fax message, as shown in this example:

Letterheaded paper —

**✆ Turner Communications**          Mobile Phone specialists

21 Ashton Drive
Sheffield                               Tel    +44 114 2871122
S26 2ES                                 Fax    +44 114 2871123
                                        Email  TurnerComm@intl.uk

Include the main heading 'FAX MESSAGE' —

# FAX MESSAGE

These headings are important so that all the essential details can be inserted alongside —

| | |
|---|---|
| To | Janet Benson, General Manager |
| Company | Asia Communication (Singapore) Pte Ltd |
| Fax Number | 65 6767677 |
| From | Sally Turner, Managing Director |
| Ref | ST/DA |
| Date | 6 June 19— |
| Number of Pages (including this page) | 1 |

It is important to state the number of pages being sent —

A salutation may be included if preferred —

The heading should state the main topic of the fax message —

VISIT TO SINGAPORE

Thank you for calling this morning regarding my trip to Singapore next month. I am very grateful to you for offering to meet me at the airport and drive me to my hotel.

The body of the fax message should be composed similarly to a business letter —

I will be arriving on flight SQ101 on Monday 8 July at 1830 hours. Accommodation has been arranged for me at the Supreme International Hotel, Scotts Road.

I will be travelling up to Kuala Lumpur on Sunday 14 July on MH989 which departs from Singapore Changi Airport Terminal 2 at 1545 hours.

A complimentary close is not necessary —

I look forward to meeting you.

*Sally Turner*

# ELECTRONIC MAIL

Most office activities are now being undertaken by electronic and computer-based technology. As a result electronic mail (or email as it is commonly known) is becoming an extremely effective, low-cost and very fast way of communicating with friends and colleagues all over the world.

Email messages may be sent to one individual or simultaneously to several recipients. Email is quick and easy to use and a lot of time and effort is saved in producing formal, printed memos. Of course, a printed copy of email messages can be printed out if required.

Composing an email message should not be an opportunity to forget all the basic rules of good writing (as discussed in Chapters 3 and 4). However, the evolution of email has brought about its own 'netiquette' as discussed here:

1   Check the email address. Correctly addressed email are delivered within seconds. It can take days to receive an error message letting you know that an incorrectly addressed message did not get delivered.

2   Always write a subject heading. This will give the recipient a good idea of the contents of the message and makes for easier handling.

3   Check the time. It is important to keep your computer's internal clock and date settings accurate, otherwise problems may be caused in trying to sort messages chronologically.

4   Keep caps lock off. Capitals indicate shouting and can look threatening.

5   Express yourself. Emoticons can be used to show mood in your email messages. Some of the more common emoticons are:

    :-)   happy
    ;-)   wink
    :-(   sad
    :-I   indifference
    :-/   perplexed
    :-D   shock or surprise

6   Greetings. Formality does not read well in email. Replace formal salutations like 'Dear David' with informal 'Hello David' or even just 'David'. 'Yours sincerely' is not needed in emails, perhaps just 'Best wishes' or 'All the best'.

7   Check your syntax. It is easy to allow sentences to become very long and verbose. Make an effort to keep sentences short and simple, and check your syntax. The more pride you take in your message composition, the more successful you will be in being understood and achieving the desired results.

8   Keep copies. Just as you would keep copies of letters, it is good practice to take a printout of email messages sent and received.

9   Check your message. As soon as you hit the 'send' symbol, your message may

be received in seconds. No calling it back for second thoughts. So check it and get it right first time.

## 2.4 Storage and retrieval

Emails are stored at a communications postal station until the recipient gives a signal to his or her system to receive messages. Although the route taken by emails can seem quite complex, transmission actually takes only seconds. On giving the signal to 'get messages', your emails will be retrieved automatically and shown on the screen.

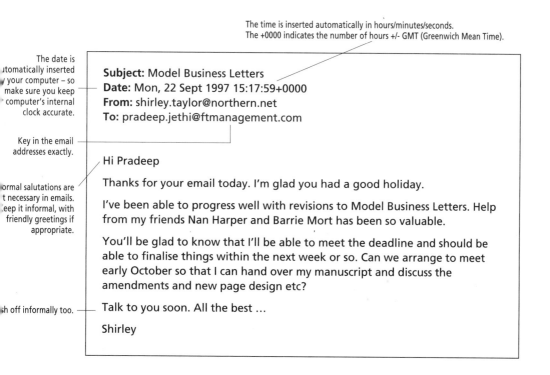

The time is inserted automatically in hours/minutes/seconds.
The +0000 indicates the number of hours +/- GMT (Greenwich Mean Time).

The date is automatically inserted by your computer – so make sure you keep computer's internal clock accurate.

**Subject:** Model Business Letters
**Date:** Mon, 22 Sept 1997 15:17:59+0000
**From:** shirley.taylor@northern.net
**To:** pradeep.jethi@ftmanagement.com

Key in the email addresses exactly.

ormal salutations are t necessary in emails. eep it informal, with friendly greetings if appropriate.

Hi Pradeep

Thanks for your email today. I'm glad you had a good holiday.

I've been able to progress well with revisions to Model Business Letters. Help from my friends Nan Harper and Barrie Mort has been so valuable.

You'll be glad to know that I'll be able to meet the deadline and should be able to finalise things within the next week or so. Can we arrange to meet early October so that I can hand over my manuscript and discuss the amendments and new page design etc?

sh off informally too.

Talk to you soon. All the best ...

Shirley

# Structuring your communications

4 point plan

Whether you are putting together a business letter, a fax message, a memo or even an email, the general rules for structuring the body of the message are the same. The information in this section can be applied equally to structuring any business communication.

## 4 POINT PLAN

Many communications are short and routine. They can be written or dictated without any special preparation. Letters which are not so routine need more thought and careful planning. This 4 point plan was first suggested in *Communication for Business – A Practical Approach*. It provides a useful but simple framework for structuring all business communications and is illustrated simply here:

| | | |
|---|---|---|
| 1 | **Introduction**<br>(Background and Basics) | Why are you writing?<br>Refer to a previous letter, contact or document |
| 2 | **Details**<br>(Facts and Figures) | Give instructions<br>Ask for information<br>Provide all relevant details<br>Separate into paragraphs for separate themes<br>Ensure a logical flow |
| 3 | **Response? Action?** | What action is necessary by the recipient?<br>What action will you take?<br>A conclusion |
| 4 | **Close** | A simple, relevant closing sentence is all that is often necessary |

Let's look at this 4 point plan in more detail:

### 1 Opening or introduction

The first paragraph will state the reason for the communication. It may:

- Acknowledge previous correspondence
- Refer to a meeting or contact
- Provide an introduction to the matter being discussed

**Examples**

Thank you for your letter of ...

It was good to meet you again at last week's conference.

We wish to hold our annual conference at a London hotel In September.

*Caution:* Beware beginning a sentence with 'Further to your letter of ...' This should always be continued as shown:

Further to your letter of 12 July I am sorry for the delay in attending to this matter.

## 2 Central section (details)

This main part of the message gives all the information which the recipient needs to know. Alternatively you may be requesting information, sometimes both. Details should be stated simply and clearly, with separate paragraphs used for individual sections. This section should flow logically to a natural conclusion.

## 3 Conclusion (Action or Response)

This section draws the message to a logical conclusion. It may:

- State the action expected from the recipient
- State the action you will take as a result of the details provided.

### Examples

Please let me have full details of the costs involved together with some sample menus.

If payment is not received within seven days this matter will be placed in the hands of our solicitor.

## 4 Close

A simple one-line closing sentence is usually all that is necessary to conclude a message. This should be relevant to the content of the message.

### Examples

I look forward to meeting you soon.

I look forward to seeing you at next month's conference.

A prompt reply would be appreciated.

Please let me know if you need any further information.

*Caution:* Closes such as the following are incomplete and should not be used:

Hope to hear from you soon.
Looking forward to hearing from you.

This 4 point plan for structuring all written communications is illustrated in this letter.

# Institute of Secretaries
**Wilson House, West Street, London SW1 2AR**

**Telephone 0181 987 2432**
**Fax 0181 987 2556**

LD/ST

12 May 19—

Mrs Lesley Nunn
15 Windsor Road
Manchester
M2 9GJ

Dear Lesley

19— SECRETARIES CONFERENCE, 8/9 OCTOBER 19—

*Opening (give a brief introduction)* — As a valued member of the Institute of Secretaries, I have pleasure in inviting you to attend our special conference to be held at the Clifton Hotel, London on Tuesday/Wednesday 8/9 October 19—.

This intensive, practical conference for professional secretaries aims to:

*Details (separate paragraphs, flowing logically)*

- increase your managerial and office productivity
- improve your communication skills
- bring you up-to-date with the latest technology and techniques
- enable networking with other secretaries

The seminar is power-packed with a distinguished panel of professional speakers who will give expert advice on many useful topics. A programme is enclosed giving full details of this seminar which I know you will not want to miss.

*Conclusion (action expected from the recipient)* — If you would like to join us please complete the enclosed registration form and return it to me before 30 June with your fee of £50 per person.

*Close (a simple closing statement)* — I look forward to seeing you again at this exciting conference.

Yours sincerely

*Louise Dunscombe*

LOUISE DUNSCOMBE (Mrs)
Conference Secretary

Encs

# Language and tone

The secret of composing good business communications is to use plain language, as if you are having a 'conversation in writing'. Simply, it means putting across your message in a natural way, using a courteous style. General business practice is to use an informal style of writing rather than being too formal.

In all communications it is essential to ensure correct grammar, spelling and punctuation. However, more than an ability to structure sentences correctly is needed. Your aim is to transfer thoughts and ideas from one person to another, so you must always remember that you are dealing with a person as well as a situation. The document chosen as well as the approach and the tone used will all be determined by the person who will receive the message.

Put yourself in the place of the recipient and imagine how they will accept what is written in the tone used. Anticipate the recipient's needs, wishes, interests, problems. Consider the best way of dealing with the specific situation.

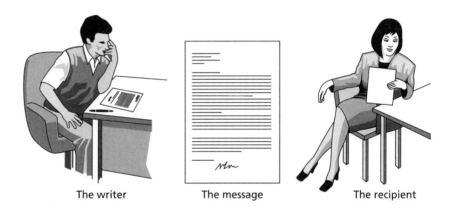

The writer    The message    The recipient

Whether you choose to write a business letter, a fax, a memo or an email, remember the following points:

- Choose the method of communication carefully.
- Create the document with care.
- Present the document so that it looks good and gives an impression of efficiency and reliability.
- Use a format which is neat, easy to read and structured logically.
- Use appropriate tone considering the circumstances, the situation and the recipient.
- Ensure your message is accurate in terms of grammar, spelling and punctuation.

# FOLLOW THE ABC RULE

Good written communication results when you say exactly what you want to say using an appropriate tone. Your message must meet the following essential specifications:

| | |
|---|---|
| Accurate | Check facts carefully |
| | Include all relevant details |
| | Proofread thoroughly |
| Brief | Keep sentences short |
| | Use simple expressions |
| | Use non-technical language |
| Clear | Use plain, simple English |
| | Write in an easy, natural style |
| | Avoid formality or familiarity |

## Be courteous and considerate

Courtesy does not mean using old-fashioned expressions like 'your kind enquiry' or 'your valued custom'. It means show consideration for your correspondent. Writing in a courteous style enables a request to be refused without killing all hope of future business. It allows a refusal to be made without killing a friendship. Courtesy also means:

- Reply promptly to all communications – answer on the same day if possible.
- If you cannot answer immediately, write a brief note and explain why. This will create goodwill.
- Understand and respect the recipient's point of view.
- Resist the temptation to reply as if your correspondent is wrong.
- If you feel some comments are unfair, be tactful and try not to give offence.
- Resist the temptation to reply to an offensive letter in a similar tone. Instead answer courteously without lowering your dignity.

## Use appropriate tone

For your message to achieve its purpose the tone must be appropriate. The tone of your message reflects the spirit in which you put your message across. Even when writing a complaint or replying to one, your message can be conveyed in such a way so as not to be rude or cause offence. Ignoring the need to use an appropriate tone could result in a message that sounds aggressive, tactless, curt, rude, sarcastic or offensive. This will not meet your desired objectives.

| *Instead of* | *Say* |
|---|---|
| We cannot do anything about your problem. | Unfortunately we are unable to help you on this occasion. |
| This problem would not have happened if you had connected the wires properly. | The problem may be resolved by connecting the wires in accordance with the instructions given. |
| Your television's guarantee is up, so you will have to pay for it to be fixed. | The guarantee for your television has expired. Unfortunately you must therefore bear the cost of any repairs. |
| I am writing to complain because I am very unhappy with the way I was treated in your store today. | I was most unhappy with the standard of service I received in your store today. |

## Write naturally and sincerely

Try to show a genuine interest in the recipient and their problems. Your message should sound sincere while written in your own style. Write naturally, as if you were having a conversation.

| *Instead of* | *Say* |
|---|---|
| I have pleasure in informing you … | I am pleased to tell you … |
| We do not anticipate any increase in prices. | We do not expect prices to rise. |
| I should be grateful if you would be good enough to advise us … | Please let us know … |
| Please favour us with a prompt reply. | Please let me have your comments as soon as possible. |

## Come straight to the point

Business people have many documents to read. A message which is direct and straight to the point will be appreciated.

| *Instead of* | *Say* |
|---|---|
| We shall be in a position to … | We shall be able to … |
| In the course of the next few weeks … | During the next few weeks … |
| Would you be so kind as to let me know … | Please let me know … |
| I should be glad if you would … | Please … |
| I would like to remind you that … | Please note that …<br>Please remember that … |
| This is to inform you that I will be on vacation for two weeks from 1 June. | I shall be on vacation for two weeks from 1 June. |

I am sorry to have to point out that we do not have these goods in stock at the present moment in time.

This item is presently out of stock.

## Use modern terminology

Old-fashioned phrases add nothing to the sense of your message. Such unnecessary, long-winded phrases are likely to give a poor impression of the writer and may even lead to confusion. A good business letter will use no more words than are necessary to convey a clear and accurate message.

| Instead of | Say |
| --- | --- |
| We are in receipt of your letter of 12 inst. | Thank you for your letter of 12 June. |
| We acknowledge receipt of your letter of 12 June. | Thank you for your letter of 12 June. |
| I am writing with reference to your letter dated 12 June in which you requested information about the courier services provided by this company. | Thank you for your letter of 12 June enquiring about our courier services. |
| Enclosed herewith you will find ... | I enclose ... |
| Please find enclosed ... | I enclose ... |
| Please be good enough to advise me ... | Please let me know ... |

## Use simple words

Steps should be taken to avoid using long-winded old-fashioned words in modern business communications. Such language adds nothing to the meaning of what is written and very often leads to confusion. Using short simple words will give your writing more meaning, save you time and help you put across your message more efficiently and effectively.

| Instead of | Say |
| --- | --- |
| with reference to, in reference to | about |
| due to the fact that | because |
| purchase | buy |
| take into consideration | consider |
| enclosed herewith | enclosed |
| Please find enclosed | I/We enclose |
| sufficient | enough |
| with the exception of | except |
| for the purpose of | for |
| in the event that | if, when |
| in the meantime | meanwhile |
| at the present time | now, currently, today |
| remittance | payment |

| *Instead of* | *Say* |
|---|---|
| expedite | speed up, hurry |
| under separate cover | separately |
| forward, transmit | send |
| attempt, endeavour | try |
| advise, inform | tell |

*Phrases which should be avoided altogether*

I have noticed that
It has come to my attention that
I am pleased to inform you that
I am writing to let you know that
I must inform you that
Will you (please)
Thanking you in anticipation
Thank you and regards
Kindest regards

## Include essential details

If the recipient of your message must ask a question, then something has been omitted from your message. Do not leave anything to chance. Include all essential information.

| *Instead of* | *Say* |
|---|---|
| My flight arrives at 3.30 on Wednesday. | My flight BA 121 from London Heathrow should arrive at Singapore Changi Airport at 1530 on Wednesday 12 June. |
| I thoroughly enjoyed your article in last month's newsletter. | I thoroughly enjoyed your article on *feng shui* in last month's company newsletter. |
| Our Sales Manager will contact you soon. | Mr John Matthews, our Sales Manager, will contact you soon. |

## Be consistent

Consistency is not only important in the way your message is presented. It is also important to ensure consistency within the message itself.

| Instead of | Say |
|---|---|
| The people attending will be John Wilson, G Turner, Mandy Harrison and Bob from Sales. | The people attending the next committee meeting will be John Wilson, Gloria Turner, Mandy Harrison and Bob Turner. |
| I confirm my reservation of a single room on 16/7 and a double room on 17 Oct. | I confirm my reservation of a single room on 16 July and a double room on 17 October. |

## CHECKLIST

Before signing any communication, ask yourself the following questions:

☐  Will it be understood?

☐  Is the tone appropriate?

☐  Is the language appropriate?

☐  Have I avoided long-winded phrases and old-fashioned terminology?

☐  Are all the essential details included and accurate?

☐  Is it brief, clear and courteous?

☐  Are all the spellings correct?

☐  Is it grammatically correct?

☐  Is it properly punctuated?

☐  Is it structured logically?

☐  Does it look attractive, well-displayed and consistent?

# Routine business letters

# Enquiries and replies

1
2
3
4
**5**
6
7
8
9
10
11
12
13
14
15
16
17
18
19
20
21
22
23
24
25

Enquiries for information about goods or services are sent and received in business all the time. In a routine letter of enquiry follow these guidelines:

1 State clearly and concisely what you want – general information, a catalogue, price list, sample, quotation, etc.

2 If there is a limit to the price at which you are prepared to buy, do not mention this otherwise the supplier may raise the quotation to the limit you state.

3 Most suppliers state their terms of payment when replying so there is no need for you to ask for them unless you are hoping for special rates.

4 Keep your enquiry brief and concise.

Enquiries mean potential business, so they must be acknowledged promptly. If it is from an established customer, say how much you appreciate it; if it is from a prospective customer, say you are glad to receive it and express the hope of a lasting and friendly business relationship.

## REQUESTS FOR CATALOGUES AND PRICE LISTS

### 5.1 Routine requests where formal reply is unnecessary

Suppliers receive many *routine requests*[1] for catalogues and price lists. Unless the writer requests information not already included a written reply is often not necessary, and a *'with compliments' slip*[2] may be sent instead. In the following enquiries, written replies are not necessary. The items requested may be sent under cover of a 'with compliments' slip:

**Example 1**

> Dear Sir/Madam
>
> Please send me a copy of your catalogue and price list of portable disc players, together with copies of any descriptive leaflets that I could pass to prospective customers[3].
>
> Yours faithfully

---

[1] **routine requests** requests of an everyday nature
[2] **with compliments slip** a small printed note containing the company's name, address, contact numbers and the wording 'With compliments'
[3] **prospective customers** people who may be expected to buy

**Example 2**

Dear Sir/Madam

I have seen one of your safes in the office of a local firm, which passed on your address to me.

Please send me a copy of your current catalogue. I am particularly interested in safes suitable for a small office.

Yours faithfully

## 5.2 Potentially large business

Where an enquiry suggests that large or regular orders are possible a 'With Compliments' slip is not enough. Instead write a letter and take the opportunity to promote your products.

### (a) Enquiry

Dear Sir/Madam

I have a large hardware store in Southampton and am interested in the electric heaters you are advertising in the West Country Gazette.

Please send me your illustrated catalogue and a price list.

Yours faithfully

### (b) Reply

Dear Mrs Johnson

*Thank you* — Thank you for your letter enquiring about electric heaters. I am pleased to enclose a copy of our latest illustrated catalogue.

*Provide further information about cific goods and refer to information in catalogue* — You may be particularly interested in our Model FX21 heater, our newest model. Without any increase in fuel consumption, it gives out 15% more heat than earlier models. You will find details of our terms in the price list printed on the inside front cover of the catalogue.

*Suggest action for recipient to take* — Perhaps you would consider placing a trial order to provide you with an opportunity to test its efficiency. At the same time this would enable you to see for yourself the high quality of material and finish put into this model.

If you have any questions please contact me.

*Appropriate close* — Yours sincerely

## 5.3  Requests for advice

A written reply is necessary when the enquiry suggests that the writer would welcome advice or guidance.

### (a) Enquiry

Dear Sir/Madam

Please send me a copy of your current typewriter catalogue and price list. I am particularly interested in purchasing an electronic typewriter with a memory and single-line display.

Yours faithfully

### (b) Reply

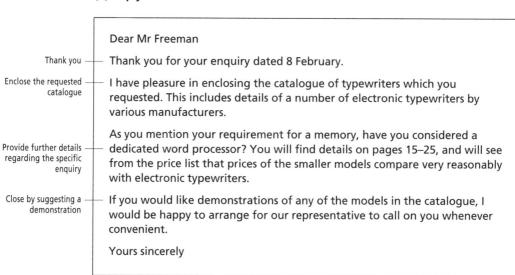

Dear Mr Freeman

*Thank you* — Thank you for your enquiry dated 8 February.

*Enclose the requested catalogue* — I have pleasure in enclosing the catalogue of typewriters which you requested. This includes details of a number of electronic typewriters by various manufacturers.

*Provide further details regarding the specific enquiry* — As you mention your requirement for a memory, have you considered a dedicated word processor? You will find details on pages 15–25, and will see from the price list that prices of the smaller models compare very reasonably with electronic typewriters.

*Close by suggesting a demonstration* — If you would like demonstrations of any of the models in the catalogue, I would be happy to arrange for our representative to call on you whenever convenient.

Yours sincerely

## 5.4 Enquiries through recommendations

When writing to a supplier who has been recommended, it may be to your advantage to mention the fact.

### (a) Enquiry

Dear Sir/Madam

My neighbour, Mr W Stevens of 29 High Street, Derby, recently bought an electric lawnmower from you. He is delighted with the machine and has recommended that I contact you.

I need a similar machine, but smaller, and should be glad if you would send me a copy of your catalogue and any other information that will help me to make the best choice for my purpose.

Yours faithfully

### (b) Reply

Dear Mrs Garson

I enclose a catalogue and price list of our lawnmowers, as requested in your letter of 18 May.

The machine bought by your friend was a 38 cm RANSOME which is an excellent machine. You will find details of the smaller size of 30 cm shown on page 15 of the catalogue. Alternatively, smaller than this is the PANTHER JUNIOR shown on page 17.

We have both these models in stock and should be glad to show them to you if you would care to call at our showroom.

Please contact me if I can provide any further help.

Yours sincerely

## 5.5 Requests for samples

A request for a sample of goods provides the supplier with an excellent opportunity to present products to advantage. A reply should be convincing, giving confidence in the products.

## (a) Enquiry

Dear Sirs

We have received a number of enquiries for floor coverings suitable for use on the rough floors which seem to be a feature of much of the new building taking place in this region.

It would be helpful if you could send us samples showing your range of suitable coverings. A pattern-card of the designs in which they are supplied would also be very useful.

Yours faithfully

## (b) Reply

Dear Mrs King

*Thank you* — Thank you for your enquiry for samples and a pattern-card of our floor coverings.

*Respond to the request in the enquiry* — We have today sent to you separately <u>a range</u>[4] of samples specially selected for their hard-wearing qualities. A pattern-card is enclosed.

*Recommended specific samples and suggest follow-up* — For the purpose you mention we recommend sample number 5 which is specially suitable for rough and uneven surfaces.

We encourage you to test the samples provided. When you have done this if you feel it would help to discuss the matter we will arrange for our technical representative to arrange to come and see you.

*Enclose price list* — Meanwhile, our price list is enclosed which also shows details of our conditions and terms of trading.

Please contact me if I can be of further help.

*Appropriate close* — Yours sincerely

# GENERAL ENQUIRIES AND REPLIES

When writing a general letter of enquiry be sure to be specific in the details required e.g. prices, delivery details, terms of payment. When replying to an enquiry, be sure you have answered every query in the letter of enquiry.

---

[4] **a range** a representative collection

## 5.6 An enquiry for office equipment

### (a) Enquiry

Dear Sir/Madam

We would be pleased to receive details of fax machines which you supply, together with prices.

We need a model suitable for sending complex diagrams and printed messages mostly within the UK.

Yours faithfully

### (b) Reply

Dear Mrs Rawson

In reply to your enquiry I have pleasure in enclosing a leaflet showing our latest fax machines.

All the models illustrated can be supplied from stock at competitive prices as shown on the price list inside the catalogue.

May I suggest a visit to our showrooms where you could see demonstrations of the various machines and at the same time view our wide range of office equipment.

Yours sincerely

### (c) Request for demonstration

Dear Mr Jenkinson

I have studied with interest the literature you sent me with your letter of 28 April.

Our Administration Manager, Mr Gordon Tan, would like to visit your showrooms to see a demonstration and report on which machine would be most suitable for our purposes. Can we arrange this for next Friday 6 May at 3.30 pm. If this is inconvenient please contact Mr Tan direct.

Yours sincerely

## 5.7 An enquiry with numbered points

When you have many points on which information is required, it may be useful to number the various points.

## (a) Enquiry

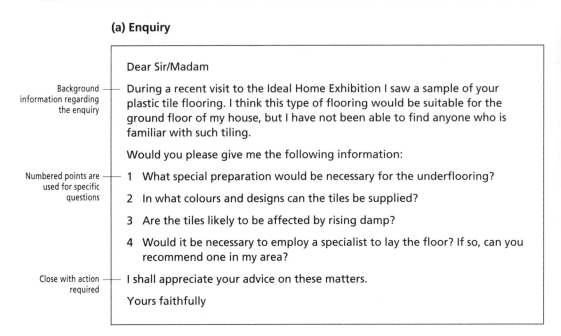

Dear Sir/Madam

*Background information regarding the enquiry* —— During a recent visit to the Ideal Home Exhibition I saw a sample of your plastic tile flooring. I think this type of flooring would be suitable for the ground floor of my house, but I have not been able to find anyone who is familiar with such tiling.

Would you please give me the following information:

*Numbered points are used for specific questions* —— 1  What special preparation would be necessary for the underflooring?

2  In what colours and designs can the tiles be supplied?

3  Are the tiles likely to be affected by rising damp?

4  Would it be necessary to employ a specialist to lay the floor? If so, can you recommend one in my area?

*Close with action required* —— I shall appreciate your advice on these matters.

Yours faithfully

## (b) Reply

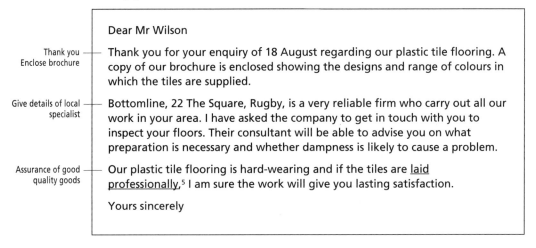

Dear Mr Wilson

*Thank you*
*Enclose brochure* —— Thank you for your enquiry of 18 August regarding our plastic tile flooring. A copy of our brochure is enclosed showing the designs and range of colours in which the tiles are supplied.

*Give details of local specialist* —— Bottomline, 22 The Square, Rugby, is a very reliable firm who carry out all our work in your area. I have asked the company to get in touch with you to inspect your floors. Their consultant will be able to advise you on what preparation is necessary and whether dampness is likely to cause a problem.

*Assurance of good quality goods* —— Our plastic tile flooring is hard-wearing and if the tiles are <u>laid professionally</u>,[5] I am sure the work will give you lasting satisfaction.

Yours sincerely

**5.8  First enquiries**

When your enquiry is to a supplier whom you have not dealt with previously, mention how you obtained their name and give some details about your own business.

A reply to a first enquiry should be given special attention in order to create goodwill.

---

[5] **laid professionally** put down by an expert

## (a) Enquiry

Dear Sir/Madam

Background information about enquiry — Dekkers of Sheffield inform us that you are manufacturers of polyester cotton bedsheets and pillow cases.

We are dealers in textiles and believe there is a promising market in our area for moderately priced goods of this kind.

Request for details — Please let me have details of your various ranges including sizes, colours and prices, together with samples of the different qualities of material used.

Further queries regarding prices for specific quantities of goods — Please state your terms of payment and discounts allowed on purchases of quantities of not less than 500 of specific items. Prices quoted should include delivery to our address shown above.

Your prompt reply would be appreciated.

Yours faithfully

## (b) Reply

Dear Mrs Harrison

Thank you. Enclose relevant publications — I was very pleased to receive your enquiry of 15 January and enclose our illustrated catalogue and price list giving the details requested.

Give further details regarding samples — A full range of samples has also been sent by separate post. When you have had an opportunity to examine them, I feel confident you will agree that the goods are excellent in quality and very reasonably priced.

Reply to specific questions regarding quantities — On regular purchases of quantities of not less than 500 individual items, we would allow a trade discount of 33%. For payment within 10 days from receipt of invoice, an extra discount of 5% of net price would be allowed.

Assurance of quality, demand and delivery — Polyester cotton products are rapidly becoming popular because they are strong, warm and light. After studying our prices you will not be surprised to learn that we are finding it difficult to meet the demand. However, if you place your order not later than the end of this month, we guarantee delivery within 14 days of receipt.

Refer to other products — I am sure you will also be interested to see information on our other products which are shown in our catalogue; if further details are required on any of these please contact me.

I look forward to hearing from you.

Yours sincerely

## 5.9 First enquiry from foreign importers

This letter is from a foreign importer so a friendly and helpful reply is necessary in order to create a good impression.

### (a) Enquiry

Dear Sir/Madam

We learn from Spett, Mancienne Fratelli of Rome that you are producing for export handmade gloves in a variety of natural leathers. There is a steady demand in this country for gloves of high quality, and although sales are not particularly high, good prices are obtained.

Please send me a copy of your catalogue with details of your prices and payment terms. It would also be helpful if you could supply samples of the various skins in which the gloves are supplied.

Yours faithfully

### (b) Reply

Dear Mr Fratelli

Thank you for the interest shown in our products in your letter of 22 August.

A copy of our illustrated catalogue is enclosed with samples of some of the skins we regularly use in our manufactures. Unfortunately we cannot send you immediately a full range of samples, but you may rest assured that such leathers as chamois and doeskin, which are not represented in the parcel, are of the same high quality.

Mr Frank North, our Overseas Director, will be visiting Rome early next month. He will be pleased to visit you and bring with him a wide range of our goods. When you see them I think you will agree that the quality of materials used and the high standard of the craftsmanship[6] will appeal to the most selective buyer.

We also manufacture a wide range of handmade leather handbags in which you may be interested. They are fully illustrated in the catalogue and are of the same high quality as our gloves. Mr North will be able to show you samples when he calls.

Yours sincerely

## REQUESTS FOR GOODS ON APPROVAL

Customers often ask for goods to be sent *on approval*.[7] They must be returned within the time stated, otherwise the customer is presumed to have bought them and cannot return them afterwards.

---

[6] **craftsmanship** expert skill in making something
[7] **on approval** for inspection, and return if not wanted

## 5.10 Customer requests goods on approval

### (a) Request

Dear Sir/Madam

Several of my customers have recently expressed an interest in your waterproof garments, and have enquired about their quality.

If quality and price are satisfactory there are prospects of good sales here. However before placing a firm order I should be glad if you would send me on 14 days' approval a selection of men's and children's waterproof raincoats and leggings. Any of the items unsold at the end of this period and which I decide not to keep as stock would be returned at my expense.

I hope to hear from you soon.

Yours faithfully

### (b) Reply

In this reply the supplier seeks protection by asking for references. Some suppliers request a returnable deposit or a third-party guarantee. While safeguarding oneself, it is important not to offend customers by implying lack of trust.

Dear Mrs Turner

I was very pleased to receive your request of 12 March for waterproof garments on approval.

As we have not previously done business together, you will appreciate that I must request ether the usual <u>trade references</u>,[8] or the name of a bank to which we may refer. As soon as these enquiries are satisfactorily settled we shall be happy to send you a good selection of the items mentioned in your letter.

I sincerely hope that our first transaction together will be the beginning of a long and pleasant business association.

Yours sincerely

### (c) Despatch of goods

Having received satisfactory references, the supplier sends a confident, direct and helpful letter. The reason for the low prices is given in order to *dispel any suspicion*[9] the customer may have that the goods are poor quality.

---

[8] **trade references** names of traders who may be referred to
[9] **dispel any suspicion** remove doubt

Dear Mrs Turner

I have now received satisfactory references and am pleased to be able to send you a generous selection of our waterproof garments as requested in your letter of 12 March.

This selection includes several new and attractive models in which the water-resistant qualities have been improved by a special process. Due to economies in our methods of manufacture, it has also been possible to reduce our prices which are now lower than those for imported waterproof garments of similar quality.

When you have had an opportunity to inspect the garments, please let us know which you have decided to keep and arrange to return the remainder.

I hope this first selection will meet your requirements. If you require a further selection, please do not hesitate to contact me.

Yours sincerely

**(d) Customer returns surplus**

In this letter the customer informs the supplier of the goods to be kept and encloses payment.

Dear Mrs Robinson

A few weeks ago you were good enough to send me a selection of waterproof garments on approval.

Quality and prices are both satisfactory and I have arranged to keep the items shown on the attached statement. My cheque for £1209.55 is enclosed in settlement.

Thank you for the prompt and considerate way in which you have handled this transaction.

Yours sincerely

## VISITS BY TRAVELLERS

Customers often form their opinions of a company from the impressions created by its representatives. This stresses the need for careful selection and proper training of sales staff. Apart from being specialists in the art of persuasion, such travellers must also fulfil the following requirements:

- They should have an excellent knowledge of the goods to be sold and the uses to which they can be put.

- They should be able to anticipate the customer's needs.

- They should be able to give sound advice and guidance to customers.

**5.11** **Request for representative to call**

**(a) Enquiry**

---

Dear Sir/Madam

I read with interest your advertisement for plastic kitchenware in the current issue of the House Furnishing Review.

I should appreciate it if you would arrange for your representative to call when next in this district. It would be helpful if he could bring with him a good selection of items from your product range.

This is a rapidly developing district and if prices are right your goods should find a ready sale.

Yours faithfully

---

**(b) Supplier's offer of visit**

This reply contains a number of good points:

- It is helpful and friendly.
- It presents the case from the buyer's viewpoint.
- It generates interest by referring to successes.
- It gives reasons why an order should be placed without delay.
- It has a personal tone and does not sound like a routine reply.

---

Dear Mr Kennings

Thank you for your enquiry dated 1 November.

Our representative, Ms Jane Whitelaw, will be in your area next week and she will be calling on you. Meanwhile we are enclosing an illustrated catalogue of our plastic goods and details of our terms and conditions of sale.

Plastic kitchenware has long been a popular feature of the modern kitchen. Its bright and attractive colours have strong appeal, and wherever dealers have arranged them in special window displays good sales are reported.

When you have inspected the samples Ms Whitelaw will bring with her, you will understand why we have a large demand for these products. Therefore if you wish to have a stock of these goods before Christmas we advise you to place your order by the end of this month.

Yours sincerely

---

# REQUESTS FOR CONCESSIONS

Customers sometimes ask for goods that are no longer available or special terms which cannot be granted. Such requests need to be handled with care to avoid giving offence or losing business.

## 5.12 Request for <u>sole distribution rights</u>[10]

### (a) Enquiry

| | |
|---|---|
| Background information and specific details | Dear Sir/Madam<br><br>We have recently extended our radio and television department and are thinking of adding new ranges to our present stocks. We are particularly interested in your BELLTONE radio and television models and should be glad if you would send us your trade catalogue and terms of sale and payment. |
| Request for sole distribution rights | Your products are not yet offered by any other dealer in this town, and if we decide to introduce them we should like to request <u>sole distribution rights</u>[10] in this area. |
| Suitable close | I hope to hear from you soon.<br><br>Yours faithfully |

### (b) Request declined

In this reply the supplier tactfully refuses the request. The refusal is not stated in so many words but is implied in the third paragraph.

| | |
|---|---|
| Thank you | Dear Mr Sanderson |
| | Thank you for your letter of 8 April enquiring about our BELLTONE radio and television products. |
| Enclose catalogue and give further details | This range has been discontinued and replaced by the CLAIRTONE. You will see from the enclosed catalogue that the new models are attractively designed and include the latest technical improvements. Although rather more expensive than their predecessors, the CLAIRTONE models have already been well |
| Response to request for sole distribution rights | received and good sales are being reported regularly from many areas. |
| | As part of our efforts to keep down manufacturing costs, I am sure you will understand that we must increase sales by distributing through as many outlets as possible. Dealers in other areas appear to be well satisfied with their sales under this arrangement, and it appears to be working very well. |
| Express a hope for the future | I hope we can look forward to receiving your orders soon, and will be glad to to include your name in our list of approved dealers, with your permission. |
| | Yours sincerely |

[10] **sole distribution rights** the right to be the only distributor in a given area for certain products

## 5.13 Request for special terms

### (a) Enquiry

Dear Sir or Madam

Please send us your current catalogue and price list for bicycles. We are interested in models for both men and women, and also for children.

We are the leading bicycle dealers in this city where cycling is popular, and have branches in five neighbouring towns. If the quality of your products is satisfactory and the prices are reasonable, we expect to place regular orders for fairly large numbers.

In the circumstances please indicate whether you will allow us a special discount. This would enable us to maintain the low selling prices which have been an important reason for the growth of our business. In return we would be prepared to place orders for a guaranteed annual minimum number of bicycles, the figure to be mutually agreed.

If you wish to discuss this please contact me.

Yours faithfully

### (b) Reply

In this reply the manufacturer is cautious, offering allowances on a *sliding scale basis*.[11]

Dear Ms Denning

I was glad to learn from your letter of 18 July of your interest in our products. As requested our catalogue and price list are enclosed, together with details of our conditions of sale and terms of payment.

We have considered your proposal to place orders for a guaranteed minimum number of machines in return for a special allowance. However after careful consideration we feel it would be better to offer you a special allowance on the following sliding scale basis:

On purchases exceeding an annual total of:

| | |
|---|---|
| £1,000 but not exceeding £3,000 | 3% |
| £3,000 but not exceeding £7,500 | 4% |
| £7,500 and above | 5% |

No special allowance could be given on annual total purchases below £1,000.

I feel that an arrangement on these lines would be more satisfactory to both our companies.

Orders will be subject to the usual trade references.

Please let me know if you accept this proposal.

Yours sincerely

[11] **sliding scale basis** varying with the quantity bought

## 5.14 Letter declining special terms

In this letter a supplier tactfully refuses a request to reduce prices. Instead a counter-suggestion is made.

---

Dear Mr Ellis

We have carefully considered your letter of 18 December.

As our firms have done business with each other for many years, we should like to grant your request to lower the prices of our sportswear. However our own overheads[12] have risen sharply in the past 12 months, and to reduce prices by the 15% you mention could not be done without considerably lowering our standards of quality. This is something we are not prepared to do.

Instead of a 15% reduction on sportswear we suggest a reduction of 5% on all our products for orders of £800 or more. On orders of this size we could make such a reduction without lowering our standards.

I hope that you will agree to this suggestion and look forward to continuing to receive regular orders from you.

Yours sincerely

---

[12] **overheads** regular standing charges such as rent, lighting, administration costs, etc.

# USEFUL EXPRESSIONS

## Requests

### Openings

1 We are interested in ... as advertised recently in ...
2 We have received an enquiry for your ...
3 I was interested to see your advertisement for ...
4 I understand you are manufacturers of (dealers in) ... and should like to receive your current catalogue.

### Closes

1 When replying please also include delivery details.
2 Please also state whether you can supply the goods from stock as we need them urgently.
3 If you can supply suitable goods, we may place regular orders for large quantities.

## Replies to requests

### Openings

1 Thank you for your letter of .... As requested we enclose ...
2 In reply to your enquiry of ... we are sending by separate post ...
3 I was pleased to learn ... that you are interested in our ...
4 Thank you for your enquiry dated ... regarding ...

### Closes

1 We look forward to receiving a trial order from you soon.
2 We shall be pleased to send you any further information you may need.
3 Any orders you place with us will have our prompt attention.
4 Please let me know if you need any further details.

# Quotations, estimates and tenders

A quotation is a promise to supply goods on the terms stated. The prospective buyer is under no obligation to buy the goods for which a quotation is requested, and suppliers will not normally risk their reputations by quoting for goods they cannot or do not intend to supply. A satisfactory quotation will include the following:

- An expression of thanks for the enquiry
- Details of prices, discounts and terms of payment
- Clear indication of what the prices cover, eg packing, carriage, insurance
- An undertaking regarding date of delivery
- The period for which the quotation is *valid*[1]
- An expression of hope that the quotation will be accepted.

## TERMINOLOGY

When requesting a quotation the buyer must be careful to establish clearly whether the prices are to include such additional charges as carriage and insurance. Failure to do this may, if not specified in the supplier's quotation, lead to serious disagreement especially where such charges are heavy as in foreign trade dealings. Some terminology associated with quotations is shown here:

- **Carriage paid.** The quoted price includes delivery to the buyer's premises.
- **Carriage forward.** The buyer pays the delivery charges.
- **Loco, ex works, ex factory, ex warehouse.** The buyer pays all expenses of handling from the time the goods leave the factory or warehouse.
- **for (free on rail).** The quotation covers the cost of transport to the nearest railway station and of loading on to truck.
- **fas (free alongside ship).** The quotation covers the cost of using lighters or barges to bring the goods to the ship, but not the expense of lifting the goods on board.
- **fob (free on board).** The quotation covers the cost of loading the goods on to the ship, after which the buyer becomes responsible for all charges.
- **ex ship.** The quoted price includes delivery over the side of the ship, either into lighters or barges or, if the ship is near enough, on to the quay.

## ROUTINE QUOTATIONS

### 6.1 Request for quotations for printing paper

#### (a) Request

This request complies with the requirements of a satisfactory letter of enquiry.

[1] **valid** hold good

- It states clearly and concisely what is required.
- It explains what the paper is for, and thus helps the supplier to quote for paper of the right quality.
- It states the quantity required, which is important because of the effect of quantity upon price.
- It states when delivery is required – an important condition in any contract for the purchase of goods.
- It states what the price is to cover – in this case 'delivery at our works'.

---

Dear Sir,

We will soon be requiring 200 reams of good quality white poster paper suitable for auction bills and poster work generally. We require paper which will retain its white appearance after pasting on walls and hoardings.

Please let us have some samples and a quotation, including delivery at our works within 4 weeks of our order.

Yours faithfully

---

### (b) Quotation

The supplier's reply should be sent promptly and it should be equally businesslike ensuring that all the points from the enquiry are answered.

---

Dear Mr Keenan

Thank you for your enquiry of yesterday. As requested we enclose samples of different qualities of paper suitable for poster work.

We are pleased to quote as follows:
A1 quality Printing Paper white £2.21 per kg
A2 quality Printing Paper white £2.15 per kg
A3 quality Printing Paper white £2.10 per kg

These prices include delivery at your works.

All these papers are of good quality and quite suitable for poster work. We guarantee that they will not discolour when pasted.

We can promise delivery within one week from receiving your order, and hope you will find both samples and prices satisfactory.

Yours sincerely

---

**6.2** ## Request for quotation for crockery

Here is another example of a satisfactory request for a quotation. It states exactly what is wanted and covers the important points of discounts, packing, delivery and terms of payment.

## (a) Request

Dear Sir

You have previously supplied us with crockery and we should be glad if you would now quote for the items named below, manufactured by the the Ridgeway Pottery Company of Hanley. The pattern we require is listed in your 19— catalogue as 'number 59 Conway Spot (Green)'.

300 Teacups and Saucers
300 Tea Plates
 40 1-litre Teapots

Prices quoted should include packing and delivery to the above address.

When replying please state discounts allowable, terms of payment and earliest possible date of delivery.

Yours faithfully

## (b) Quotation

Dear Mr Clarke

CONWAY SPOT (GREEN) GILT RIMS

Thank you for your enquiry of 18 April for a further supply of our crockery. We are pleased to quote as follows:

| Teacups | £83.75 per hundred |
| Tea Saucers | £76.00 per hundred |
| Tea Plates | £76.00 per hundred |
| Teapots, 1-litre | £4.20 each |

These prices include packing and delivery, but a charge is made for crates with an allowance for their return in good condition.

Delivery can be made from stock and we will allow you a discount of 5% on items ordered in quantities of 100 or more. There would be an additional cash discount of 2% on total cost of payment within one month from date of invoice.

We hope that you will find these terms satisfactory.

Yours sincerely

# QUOTATIONS SUBJECT TO CONDITIONS OF ACCEPTANCE

Very often a quotation is made subject to certain conditions of acceptance. These conditions vary according to the circumstances and the type of business.

They may relate to a stated time within which the quotation must be accepted, or to goods of which supplies are limited and cannot be repeated. The supplier must make it clear when quoting for goods in limited supply or subject to their being available when the order is received. Examples of qualifying statements are:

- This offer is made subject to the goods being available when the order is received.
- This offer is subject to acceptance within 7 days.
- The prices quoted will apply only to orders received on or before 31 March.
- Goods ordered from our 19— catalogue can be supplied only while stocks last.
- For acceptance within 14 days.

## 6.3 Foreign buyer's request for quotation

### (a) Enquiry

> Dear Sirs
>
> We have recently received a number of requests for your lightweight raincoats and believe that we could place regular orders with you provided your prices are competitive.
>
> From the description in your catalogue we feel that your AQUATITE range would be most suitable for this region. Please let me have a quotation for men's and women's coats in both small and medium sizes, delivered *cif Alexandria*.[2]
>
> If your prices are right, we shall place a first order for 400 raincoats, namely 100 of each of the 4 qualities. Shipment would be required within 4 weeks of order.
>
> Yours faithfully

### (b) Quotation

The reply by the English manufacturer is a good example of the modern style in business letter writing. The tone is friendly and the language is simple and clear. The writer shows an awareness of the problems of the tropical resident (eg the reference to condensation) and gives information which is likely to bring about a sale (eg mention of 'repeat orders' and 'specially treated').

Another point of interest here is the statement of freight and insurance charges separate from the cost of the goods. This is convenient for calculating the trade

---

[2] **cif Alexandria** price covers charges for insurance and transport to the port named

discount and also tells the buyer exactly what is to be paid for the goods themselves. Note also the statement 'For acceptance within one month'. Here the supplier promises to sell goods at the quoted price within a given period of time.

The supplier's attempt to interest the customer in other products is very good business technique.

---

Dear Mrs Barden

AQUATITE RAINWEAR

*Thank you* — Thank you for your letter of 15 June. I was pleased to learn about the enquiries you have received for our raincoats.

*Discuss popularity of product with particular reference to tropical cimates* — Our AQUATITE range is particularly suitable for warm climates. During the past year we have supplied this range to dealers in several tropical countries. We have already received repeat orders[3] from many of those dealers. This range is popular not only because of its light weight, but also because the material used has been specially treated to prevent excessive condensation on the inside surface.

*Mention of 'repeat orders' gives assurance of quality*

We are pleased to quote as follows:

*Specific details regarding prices*

| | | | | |
|---|---|---|---|---:|
| 100 AQUATITE coats | men's | medium | £17.50 ea | 1750.00 |
| 100 AQUATITE coats | men's | small | £16.80 ea | 1680.00 |
| 100 AQUATITE coats | women's | medium | £16.00 ea | 1600.00 |
| 100 AQUATITE coats | women's | small | £15.40 ea | 1540.00 |
| | | | | 6,570.00 |
| less 33⅓% trade discount | | | | 2187.81 |
| Net price | | | | 4082.19 |
| Freight (London to Alexandria) | | | | 186.00 |
| Insurance | | | | 122.50 |
| TOTAL | | | | 4390.69 |

*Details regarding terms, shipment and acceptance* — Terms: 2½% one month from date of invoice

Shipment: Within 3–4 weeks of receiving order

For acceptance within one month.

*Refer to other products and enclose literature* — We feel you may be interested in some of our other products, and enclose descriptive booklets and a supply of sales literature for issue to your customers.

We hope to receive your order soon.

Yours sincerely

---

## TABULATED QUOTATIONS

Many quotations are either tabulated or prepared on special forms. Such tabulated quotations are:

---

[3] **repeat orders** successive orders for similar goods

- Clear, since information is presented in a form which is readily understood
- Complete, since essential information is unlikely to be omitted

Tabulated quotations are particularly suitable where there are many items. Like quotations on specially prepared forms, they should be sent with a *covering letter*[4] which:

- Expresses thanks for the enquiry
- Makes favourable comments about the goods themselves
- Draws attention to other products likely to interest the buyer
- Expresses hope of receiving an order

Such treatment creates a favourable impression and helps to build goodwill.

### 6.4 Covering letter with quotation on specially prepared form

#### (a) Covering letter

> Dear Mrs Greenway
>
> Thank you for your enquiry of 15 August. Our quotation for leather shoes and handbags is enclosed. All items can be delivered from stock.
>
> These items are made from very best quality leather and can be supplied in a range of designs and colours wide enough to meet the requirements of a fashionable trade such as yours.
>
> Also enclosed is a copy of our catalogue in which you will find details of our other products. These include leather purses and gloves, described and illustrated on pages 18–25.
>
> The catalogue gives all the essential facts about our goods, but if you have any queries please do not hesitate to let us know.
>
> Yours sincerely

#### (b) Quotation

In the quotation shown in Fig. 6.1, note the following points:

- It is given a serial number to assist future reference.
- Use of catalogue numbers identifies items with precision and avoids misunderstandings. Individual shapes and sizes are also given their own serial numbers.
- 'For acceptance within 21 days' protects the supplier should the buyer order goods at a later date when prices may have risen.
- '4% one month' indicates that a discount of 4% will be allowed on quoted prices if payment is made within one month; for payment made after one month but within two months, discount is reduced to 2%.

[4] **covering letter** a brief letter enclosing other documents

**CENTRAL LEATHERCRAFT LTD**
85–87 Cheapside, London EC2V 6AA
Telephone 0171-242-2177/8

Quotation no JBS/234

Date 20 August 19—

Messrs Smith Jenkins & Co
15 Holme Avenue
SHEFFIELD
S6 2LW

| Catalogue Number | Item | Quantity | Unit Price |
|---|---|---|---|
| S 25 | Men's Box Calf Shoes (brown) | 12 pairs | 55.75 |
| | Men's Box Calf Shoes (black) | 36 pairs | 55.50 |
| S 27 | Ladies' Glace Kid Tie Shoes (various colours) | 48 pairs | 54.80 |
| S 42 | Ladies' Calf Colt Court Shoes | 24 pairs | 54.35 |
| H 212 | Ladies' Handbags – Emperor | 36 | 56.50 |
| H 221 | Ladies' Handbags – Paladin | 36 | 58.75 |
| H 229 | Ladies' Handbags – Aristocrat | 12 | 60.00 |
| | FOR ACCEPTANCE WITHIN 21 DAYS | | |

Delivery    ex works

Terms       4% one month 2½% two months

(signed)

for Central Leathercraft Ltd

**Fig. 6.1 A quotation form**

# ESTIMATES AND SPECIFICATIONS

Whereas a quotation is an offer to sell goods at a price and under stated conditions, an estimate is an offer to do certain work for a stated price, usually on the basis of a specification. Like a quotation, an estimate is not legally binding so the person making it is not bound to accept any order that may be placed against it.

## 6.5 Estimate for installation of central heating

### (a) Enquiry

In this enquiry the writer encloses a specification giving a detailed description of the work to be done and materials to be used. This will provide the basis for the contractor's estimate. The plan would consist of a rough sketch (drawn to scale) showing the required positions of the radiators.

---

Dear Sirs

Please let me have an estimate for installing central heating in my bungalow at 1 Margate Road, St Annes-on-Sea. A plan of the bungalow is attached showing required positions and sizes of radiators, together with a specification showing further details and materials to be used.

As you will note from the specification, I am interested only in first-class workmanship and in the use of best quality materials. However, cost is, of course, a matter of some importance. Completion of the work is required by 31 August at the latest.

In your reply please include a firm completion date.

Your prompt reply will be appreciated.

Yours faithfully

---

## (b) Specification

---

SPECIFICATION FOR INSTALLING CENTRAL HEATING at 1 MARGATE ROAD, ST ANNES-ON-SEA

1 Installation[5] of the latest small-bored central heating, to be carried out with best quality copper piping of 15 mm bore, fitted with 'Ryajand' electric pump of fully adequate power and lagged under floor to prevent loss of heat.

2 Existing boiler to be replaced by a Glow-worm No 52 automatic gas fired boiler, rated at 15.2 kW and complete with gas governor, flame failure safety device and boiler water thermostat.

3 Installation of a Randall No 103 clock controller to give automatic operation of the central heating system at predetermined times.

4 Existing hot-water cylinder to be replaced by a *calorifier-type cylinder*[6] suitable for supplying domestic hot water separately from the central heating system.

5 Seven 'Dimplex' or similar flat-type radiators to be fitted under windows of five rooms, and in hall and kitchen, according to plan enclosed; also a towel rail in bathroom. Sizes of radiators and towel rail to be as specified in plan attached to my letter dated 5 July 19— addressed to yourselves.

6 Each radiator to be separately controlled, swivelled for cleaning and painted pale cream with red-lead undercoating.

7 The system to be provided with the necessary fall for emptying and to prevent air-locks.

8 All work to be carried out from under floor to avoid cutting or lifting floor boards, which are tongued and grooved.

9 Insulation[7] of roof with 80 mm fibreglass.

J HARRIS

5 July 19—

---

## (c) Contractor's estimate

The contractor can calculate costs from the information provided, and will send an estimate with a covering letter. The letter should provide the following information:

- A reference regarding satisfactory work carried out elsewhere which will give the customer confidence.

---

[5] **installation** the act of putting equipment in position
[6] **calorifier-type cylinder** a cylinder which keeps water hot
[7] **insulation** a covering used to retain heat

- A promised completion date.
- A market prices and wages adjustment clause to protect the contractor from unforeseen increases that may raise costs and reduce profits.
- A hope that the estimate will be accepted.

In this letter note that the contractor aims to inspire confidence by referring to work done elsewhere and the promise to arrange an inspection if required.

---

Dear Mr Harris

INSTALLATION OF CENTRAL HEATING AT 1 MARGATE ROAD, ST ANNES-ON-SEA

*Thank you* — Thank you for your letter of 6 July enclosing specification and plan for a gas-fired central heating system at the above address.

*Mention price and discount* — We should be glad to carry out the work for a total of £2,062.50 with a 2½% discount for settlement within one month of the date of our account. We can

*Promised completion date* — promise to complete all work by 31 August if we receive your instructions by the end of this month. Please note that the price quoted is based on present

*This clause protects the contractor from unforeseen increases* — costs of materials and labour. Should these costs rise we should have to add the increased costs to our price.

*Mention of satisfactory work carried out elsewhere will give confidence* — We have installed many similar heating systems in your area. Our reputation for high class work is well known; if you would like to inspect one of our recent installations before making a firm decision this can be arranged.

We hope you will be satisfied with the price quoted, and look forward to receiving your instructions soon.

Yours sincerely

---

## TENDERS

A tender is usually made in response to a published advertisement. It is an offer for the supply of specified goods or the performance of specified work at prices and under conditions set out in the tender. A tender becomes legally binding only when it is accepted; up to that time it may be withdrawn. It is usual for tenders to be made on the advertisers' own forms which include a specification where necessary and set out the terms in full detail.

### 6.6 A public invitation to tender

THE COUNTY COUNCIL OF LANCASHIRE
COUNTY HALL, PRESTON PR1 2RL

Tenders are invited for the supply to the Council's power station at Bamford, during the year 19—, of approximately 2,000 tonnes of best quality furnace coke, delivered in quantities as required. Tenders must be submitted on the official form obtainable from County Hall to reach the Clerk of the Council not later than 12.00 noon on Friday 30 June.

The Council does not bind itself to accept the lowest, or any, of the tenders submitted.

B BRADEN

Clerk to the Council

### 6.7 Contractor's letter enclosing tender

After obtaining the official form and completing it accordingly, it should be returned with a formal covering letter.

CONFIDENTIAL

Clerk to the Council
County Hall
PRESTON
PR1 2RL

Dear Mr Braden

TENDER FOR FURNACE COKE

Having read the terms and conditions in the official form supplied by you, I enclose my tender for the supply of coke to the Bamford power station during 19—. I hope to learn that it has been accepted.

Yours sincerely

### 6.8 A closed invitation to tender

An invitation to tender restricted to members of a particular organisation or group is called a 'closed tender'. This example is taken from the *Baghdad Observer*.

STATE ORGANISATION FOR ENGINEERING INDUSTRIES
P O BOX 3093 BAGHDAD IRAQ

TENDER NO 1977
FOR THE SUPPLY OF 16,145 TONNES
OF
ALUMINIUM AND ALUMINIUM ALLOY INGOTS,
BILLETS AND SLABS

1   The SOEI invites tenderers who are registered in the Chamber of Commerce
and hold a Certificate of Income Tax of this year, as well as a certificate
issued by the Registrar of Commercial Agencies confirming that he is
licensed by the Director General of Registration and Supervision of
Companies, to participate in the above tender. General terms and
conditions together with specifications and quantities sheets can be
obtained from the Planning and Financial Control Department at the 3rd
floor of this Organisation against payment of one Iraqi Dinar for each copy.

2   All offers are to be put in the tender box of this Organisation, Commercial
Affairs Department, 4th floor, marked with the name and number of the
tender at or before 1200 hours on Saturday 31 January 19—.

3   Offers should be accompanied by preliminary guarantee issued by the
Rafidain Bank, equal to not less than 5 per cent of the C & F value of the
offer.

4   Any offer submitted after the closing date of the tender, or which does
not comply with the above terms, will not be accepted.

5   This Organisation does not bind itself to accept the lowest or any other
offer.

6   Foreign companies who have no local agents in Iraq shall be exempted
from the conditions stated in item number 1 above.

ALI AL-HAMDANI (ENGINEER)
PRESIDENT

## QUOTATIONS NOT ACCEPTED OR AMENDED

When a buyer rejects a quotation or other offer, it is courteous to write and thank the supplier for their trouble and explain the reason for rejection. The letter of rejection should:

● Thank the supplier for their offer

● Express regret at inability to accept

● State reasons for non-acceptance

● If appropriate, make a *counter-offer*[8]

● Suggest that there may be other opportunities to do business together

[8] **counter-offer** an alternative to another offer

### 6.9 Buyer rejects supplier's quotation

Dear Mr Walton

Thank you for your quotation dated 19 February for strawboards.

I appreciate your trouble in this matter but as your prices are very much higher than those I have been quoted by other dealers, I regret I cannot give you an immediate order.

I shall bear your company in mind when I require other products in the future.

Yours sincerely

### 6.10 Supplier grants request for better terms

**(a) Enquiry**

Dear Ms Hansen

*Thank you* — Thank you for your letter of 18 August and for the samples of cotton underwear you very kindly sent to me.

*Mention good quality but express concern at high prices leaving small profit* — I appreciate the good quality of these garments, but unfortunately your prices appear to be on the high side even for garments of this quality. To accept the prices you quote would leave me with only a small profit on my sales since this is an area in which the principal demand is for articles in the medium price range.

*Repeat feelings regarding quality and desire to do business. Request special allowance* — I like the quality of your goods and would welcome the opportunity to do business with you. May I suggest that perhaps you could make some allowance on your quoted prices which would help to introduce your goods to my customers. If you cannot do so, then I must regretfully decline your offer as it stands.

I hope to hear from you soon.

Yours sincerely

**(b) Reply**

Dear Mr Daniels

Acknowledge letter —— I am sorry to learn from your letter of 23 August that you find our prices too
Respond to query —— high. We do our best to keep prices as low as possible without sacrificing
regarding high prices quality. To this end we are constantly investigating new methods of
manufacture.

Give assurance that —— Considering the quality of the goods offered we do not feel that the prices
prices are reasonable we quoted are at all excessive. However, bearing in mind the special
character of your trade, we are prepared to offer you a special discount of
ecial discount on first —— 4% on a first order for £1000. This allowance is made because we should like
order will be to do business with you if possible, but I must stress that it is the furthest we
appreciated by new can go to help you.
customer

I hope this revised offer will enable you to place an order.

Yours sincerely

## FOLLOW-UP LETTERS

When a buyer has asked for a quotation but does not place an order or even
acknowledge the quotation, it is natural for the supplier to wonder why. A keen
supplier will arrange for a representative to call, or send a follow-up letter if the
enquiry is from a distance.

### 6.11 Supplier's follow-up letter

Here is an effective follow-up letter written in a tone which shows the supplier
genuinely wants to help and in a style which is direct and straight to the point.
It considers the buyer's convenience by offering a choice of action and closes
with a reassuring promise of service.

Dear Mrs Larkin

As we have not heard from you since we sent you our catalogue of filing systems, we wonder whether you require further information before deciding to place an order.

The modern system of lateral filing has important space-saving advantages wherever economy of space is important. However if space is not one of your problems, our flat-top suspended system may suit you better. The neat and tidy appearance it gives to the filing drawers and the ease and speed with which files are located are just two of its features which many users find attractive.

Would you like us to send our representative to call and discuss your needs with you? John Robinson has advised on equipment for many large, modern offices and would be able to recommend the system most suited to your own requirements. There would of course be no obligation of any kind. Perhaps you would prefer to pay a visit to our showroom and see for yourself how the different filing systems work.

You may be sure that whichever of these opportunities you decide to accept, you would receive personal attention and the best possible advice.

Yours sincerely

## 6.12 Letter to save a lost customer

No successful business can afford to lose its regular customers. Periodical checks must be carried out to identify those customers whose orders have tended to fall off, and suitable follow-up letters must be sent.

Dear Sirs

We notice with regret that it is some considerable time since we last received an order from you. We hope this is in no way due to dissatisfaction with our service or with the quality of goods we have supplied. In either of these situations we should be grateful to hear from you. We are most anxious to ensure that customers obtain maximum satisfaction from their dealings with us. If the lack of orders from you is due to changes in the type of goods you handle, we may still be able to meet your needs if you will let us know in what directions your policy has changed.

As we have not heard otherwise, we assume that you are selling the same range of sports goods, so a copy of our latest illustrated catalogue is enclosed. We feel this compares favourably in range, quality and price with the catalogues of other manufacturers. At the same time we take the opportunity to mention that our terms are now much easier than previously, following the withdrawal of exchange control[9] and other official measures since we last did business together.

I hope to hear from you soon.

Yours faithfully

[9] **exchange control** official control in the foreign exchange market

# USEFUL EXPRESSIONS

## Requests for quotations, estimates, etc.

### Openings

1  Please quote for the supply of ...
2  Please send me a quotation for the supply of ...
3  We wish to have the following work carried out and should be glad if you would submit an estimate.

### Closes

1  As the matter is urgent we should like this information by the end of this week.
2  If you can give us a competitive quotation, we expect to place a large order.
3  If your prices compare favourably with those of other suppliers, we shall send you an early order.

## Replies to requests for quotations, etc.

### Openings

1  Thank you for your letter of ...
2  We thank you for your enquiry of ... and are pleased to quote as follows:
3  With reference to your enquiry of ..., we shall be glad to supply ... at the price of ...
4  We are sorry to learn that you find our quotation of ... too high.

### Closes

1  We trust you will find our quotation satisfactory and look forward to receiving your order.
2  We shall be pleased to receive your order, which will have our prompt and careful attention.
3  As the prices quoted are exceptionally low and likely to rise, we would advise you to place your order without delay.
4  As our stocks of these goods are limited, we suggest you place an order immediately.

# Orders and their fulfilment

1
2
3
4
5
6
7
8
9
10
11
12
13
14
15
16
17
18
19
20
21
22
23
24
25

## PLACING ORDERS

### Printed order forms

Most companies have official printed order forms (see Fig. 7.1). The advantages are:

(a)  such forms are pre-numbered and therefore reference is easy;

(b)  printed headings ensure that no information will be omitted.

Printed on the back of some forms are general conditions under which orders are placed. Reference to these conditions must be made on the front, otherwise the supplier is not legally bound by them.

### Letter orders

Smaller companies may not have printed forms but instead place orders in the form of a letter. When sending an order by letter, accuracy and clarity must be ensured by including:

(a)  an accurate and full description of goods required

(b)  catalogue numbers

(c)  quantities

(d)  prices

(e)  delivery requirements (place, date, mode of transport, whether the order will be carriage paid or *carriage forward,*[1] etc) and

(f)  terms of payment agreed in *preliminary negotiations.*[2]

### Legal position of the parties

According to English law the buyer's order is only an offer to buy. The arrangement is not legally binding until the supplier has accepted the offer. After that both parties are legally bound to honour their agreement.

#### (a) The buyer's obligations

When a binding agreement comes into force, the buyer is required by law to:

- Accept the goods supplied as long as they comply with the terms of the order.

- Pay for the goods at the time of delivery or within the period specified by the supplier.

- Check the goods as soon as possible (failure to give prompt notice of faults to the supplier will be taken as acceptance of the goods).

---

[1]  **carriage forward** transportation costs paid by the buyer
[2]  **preliminary negotiations** earlier discussions regarding terms

```
                    J B SIMPSON & CO LTD
              18 Deansgate, Sheffield S11 2BR
                   Telephone 0114 234234
                     Fax: 0114 234235
```

Order no 237                                          Date 7 July 19—

Nylon Fabrics Ltd
18 Brazenose Street
MANCHESTER
M60 8AS

Please supply:

| Quantity | Item(s) | Catalogue Number | Price |
|----------|---------|------------------|-------|
| 25 | Bed Sheets (106 cm) blue | 75 | £5.50 each |
| 25 | Bed Sheets (120 cm) primrose | 82 | £5.00 each |
| 50 | Pillow Cases blue | 117 | £2.90 each |
| 50 | Pillow Cases primrose | 121 | £2.90 each |

(signed)
_____
for J B Simpson & Co Ltd

**Fig. 7.1 An order form**

### (b) The supplier's obligations

The supplier is required by law to:

- Deliver the goods exactly as ordered at the agreed time.
- Guarantee the goods to be free from faults of which the buyer could not be aware at the time of purchase.

If faulty goods are delivered, the buyer can demand either a reduction in price, a replacement of the goods or cancellation of the order. Damages may possibly be claimed.

# ROUTINE ORDERS

Routine orders may be short and formal but they must include essential details describing the goods, as well as delivery and terms of payment. Where two or more items are included on an order, they should be listed separately for ease of reference.

## 7.1 Confirmation of telephone order

Dear

We confirm the order which was placed with you by telephone this morning for the following:

3 'Excelda Studio' electronic typewriters
  each with 12 pitch daisy wheel

Price: £595 each, less 40% trade discount
                    carriage forward

These machines are urgently required. We understand that you are arranging for immediate delivery from stock.

Yours sincerely

## 7.2 Tabulated order

Dear Sirs

Please accept our order for the following books on our usual discount terms of 25% off published prices:

| NUMBER OF COPIES | TITLE | AUTHOR | PUBLISHED PRICE |
|---|---|---|---|
| 50 | Communication for Business | Shirley Taylor | £8.99 |
| 40 | The Secretary in Training | Shirley Taylor | £7.99 |

We look forward to prompt delivery.

Yours faithfully

## `7.3` Order based on quotation

> Dear
>
> Thank you for your quotation of 4 June. Please supply:
>
> 100 reams of A2 quality Printing Paper, white, at £2.16 per kg, including delivery.
>
> Delivery is required not later than the end of this month.
>
> Yours sincerely

## `7.4` Covering letter with order form

When a covering letter is sent with an order form (as shown in Fig. 7.1), all essential details will be shown on the form and any additional explanations in the covering letter.

> Dear
>
> Thank you for your quotation of 5 July. Our order number 237 for 4 of the items is enclosed.
>
> All these items are urgently required by our customer so we hope you will send them immediately.
>
> Yours sincerely

# ACKNOWLEDGING ORDERS

An order should be acknowledged immediately if it cannot be fulfilled straight away. For small routine orders a printed acknowledgement or a postcard may be enough, but a short letter stating when delivery may be expected also helps to create good will. If the goods cannot be supplied at all, you should write explaining why and offer suitable substitutes if they are available.

## `7.5` Formal acknowledgement of routine order (by fax)

> Thank you for your order number 237 for bed coverings.
>
> As all items were in stock, they will be delivered to you tomorrow by our own transport.
>
> We hope you will find these goods satisfactory and that we may have the pleasure of further orders from you.

## 7.6 Acknowledgement of a first order

First orders, ie orders from new customers, should most certainly be acknowledged by letter.

<table>
<tr><td>Thank you</td><td>Dear<br><br>We were very pleased to receive your order of 18 June for cotton prints, and welcome you as one of our customers.</td></tr>
<tr><td>Confirm prices and delivery information<br>Give assurance of satisfaction</td><td>We confirm supply of the prints at the prices stated in your letter. Delivery should be made by our own vehicles early next week. We feel confident that you will be completely satisfied with these goods and that you will find them of exceptional value for money.</td></tr>
<tr><td>Mention other goods and enclose catalogue</td><td>As you may not be aware of the wide range of goods we have available, we are enclosing a copy of our catalogue.</td></tr>
<tr><td>Close with a wish for future business dealings</td><td>We hope that our handling of your first order with us will lead to further business between us and mark the beginning of a happy working relationship.<br><br>Yours sincerely</td></tr>
</table>

## 7.7 Acknowledgement of order pointing out delayed delivery

When goods ordered cannot be delivered immediately, a letter should apologise for the delay and give an explanation. A delivery date should also be given, if possible, and express the hope that the customer is not inconvenienced unduly.

### (a) Reason for delay: breakdown in production

Dear

Thank you for your order of 15 March for electric shavers. We regret that we cannot supply them immediately owing to a fire in our factory.

Every effort is being made to resume production and we fully expect to be able to deliver the shavers by the end of this month.

We apologise for the delay and trust it will not cause you serious inconvenience.

Yours sincerely

### (b) Reason for delay: stocks not available

> Dear
>
> We were pleased to receive your order of 20 January.
>
> Unfortunately we regret that we are at present out of stock of the model you ordered. This is due to the prolonged cold weather which has increased demand considerably. The manufacturers have, however, promised us a further supply by the end of this month and if you could wait until then we would fulfil your order promptly.
>
> We are sorry not to be able to meet your present order immediately, but hope to hear from you soon that delivery at the beginning of next month will not inconvenience you unduly.
>
> Yours sincerely

### (c) Reason for delay: a transport strike

> Dear
>
> YOUR ORDER NUMBER 531
>
> Much to our regret a strike of transport workers in Liverpool is causing some delay in the despatch of a number of our consignments. The goods in your order dated 25 June are among those held up.
>
> To ensure the goods reached you on time we sent them by rail to Liverpool 3 days ahead of schedule. However we now learn that they are still at the station awaiting transport to the docks.
>
> We are making private arrangements to get them to the docks in time for shipment by SS Arabian Prince, which is due to sail for Alexandria on 2 August.
>
> Please accept our apologies for this delay. We hope you will understand that it is due entirely to circumstances outside our control.
>
> Yours sincerely

## DECLINING ORDERS

There may be times when a supplier will not accept a buyer's order:

- He is not satisfied with the buyer's terms and conditions
- The buyer's credit is suspect.
- The goods are not available.

Utmost care should be taken when writing to reject an order so that goodwill and future business are not affected.

### 7.8 Supplier refuses price reduction

When a supplier cannot grant a request for a lower price, reasons should be given.

---

Dear

We have carefully considered your <u>counter-proposal</u>[3] of 15 August to our offer of woollen underwear, but regret that we cannot accept it.

The prices quoted in our letter of 13 August leave us with only the smallest of margins. They are in fact lower than those of our competitors for goods of similar quality.

The wool used in the manufacture of our THERMALINE range undergoes a special patented process which prevents shrinkage and increases durability. The fact that we are the largest suppliers of woollen underwear in this country is in itself evidence of the good value of our products.

We hope you will give further thought to this matter, but if you then still feel you cannot accept our offer we hope it will not prevent you from contacting us on some future occasion.

We will always be happy to consider carefully any proposals likely to lead to business between us.

Yours sincerely

---

### 7.9 Supplier rejects buyer's delivery terms

When delivery terms cannot be met, the supplier should show a genuine desire to help customers in difficulty.

---

Dear Mr Johnson

YOUR ORDER NUMBER R345

*Thank you. Mention that delivery date cannot be met*

We were pleased to receive your order of 2 November for 24 ATLANTIS television sets. However since you state the firm condition of delivery before Christmas, we deeply regret that we cannot supply you on this occasion.

*Further details regarding demand for the goods and how orders are being dealt with*

The manufacturers of these goods are finding it impossible to meet <u>current demand</u>[4] for this popular television set. We placed an order for 100 sets one month ago but were informed that all orders were being met <u>in strict rotation</u>.[5] Our own order will not be met before the end of January.

*This suggestion that the customer should try another supplier is sure to be appreciated and will help to build goodwill*

I understand from our telephone conversation this morning that your customers are unwilling to consider other models. In the circumstances I hope you will be able to meet your requirements from some other source. May I suggest that you try Television Services Ltd of Leicester. They usually carry large stocks and may be able to help you.

Yours sincerely

---

[3] **counter-proposal** an alternative to an earlier proposal
[4] **current demand** requirements at the present time
[5] **in strict rotation** in turn, as received

## 7.10 Supplier refuses to extend credit

If a previous account remains unpaid, the utmost tact is necessary when rejecting another order. Nothing is more likely to offend a customer than the suggestion that they may not be trustworthy. In this letter, the writer tactfully avoids suggestion of mistrust and instead gives internal difficulties as the reason for refusing further credit.

---

Dear Mr Richardson

We were pleased to receive your order of 15 April for a further supply of CD players.

However, owing to current difficult conditions we have had to try and ensure that our many customers keep their accounts within reasonable limits. Only in this way can we meet our own commitments.[6]

At present the balance of your account stands at over £1800. We hope that you will be able to reduce it before we grant credit for further supplies.

In the circumstances we should be grateful if you would send us your cheque for, say, half the amount owed. We could then arrange to supply the goods now requested and charge them to your account.

Yours sincerely

---

## COUNTER-OFFERS FROM SUPPLIERS

When a supplier receives an order which cannot be met for some reason, any of the following options are available:

1 Send a *substitute*.[7] Careful judgement will be required, however, since there is the risk that the customer may be annoyed to receive something different from what was ordered. It is advisable to send a substitute only if a customer is well known or if there is a clear need for urgency. Such substitutes should be sent 'on approval', with the supplier accepting responsibility for carriage charges both ways.

2 Make a counter-offer.

3 Decline the order.

---

[6] **commitments** obligations to be fulfilled
[7] **substitute** goods which take the place of others

### 7.11 Supplier sends a substitute article

Dear

We were pleased to receive your letter of 10 April together with your order for a number of items included in our quotation reference RS980.

All the items ordered are in stock except for the 25 cushion covers in strawberry pink. Stocks of these have been sold out since our quotation, and the manufacturers inform us that it will be another 4 weeks before they can send replacements.

As you state that delivery of all items is a matter of urgency, we have substituted cushion covers in a fuschia pink, identical in design and quality with those ordered. They are attractive and rich-looking, and very popular with our other customers. We hope you will find them satisfactory. If not, please return them at our expense. We shall be glad either to exchange them or to arrange credit.

All items will be on our delivery schedule tomorrow. We hope you will be pleased with them.

Yours sincerely

### 7.12 Supplier makes a counter-offer

In making a counter-offer the supplier must exercise a great deal of skill to bring about a sale. The buyer is, after all, being offered something that has not been asked for. Therefore it is important that the suggested substitute is at least as good as the one ordered.

Dear

**Thank you** — Thank you for your letter of 12 May ordering 800 metres of 100 cm wide watered silk.

**Respond to the enquiry with regret that the material is no longer available** — We regret to say that we can no longer supply this silk. Fashions constantly change and in recent years the demand for watered silks has fallen to such an extent that we no longer produce them.

**Mention a replacement material and give assurance of quality and reliability** — In their place we can offer our new GOSSAMER brand of rayon.[8] This is a finely woven, hard-wearing, non-creasable material with a most attractive lustre.[9] The large number of repeat orders we regularly receive from leading distributors and dress manufacturers is clear evidence of the widespread

**Include price information** — popularity of this brand. At the low price of only £3.20 per metre, this rayon is much cheaper than silk and its appearance is just as attractive.

**Mention other products/ samples sent separately. Give delivery details** — We also manufacture other cloths in which you may be interested and are sending a complete range of patterns by separate post. All these cloths are selling very well in many countries and can be supplied from stock. If you decide to place an order we can meet it within one week.

Please contact me if you have any queries.

Yours sincerely

[8] **rayon** artificial silk
[9] **lustre** a shiny surface

# PACKING AND DESPATCH

When goods are despatched the buyer should be notified either by an advice note or by letter stating what has been sent, when it was sent, and the means of transport used. The customer then knows that the goods are on the way and can make the necessary arrangements to receive them.

## 7.13 Request for forwarding instructions

Dear

We are pleased to confirm that the 12 Olivetti KX R193 word processors which you ordered on 15 October are now ready for despatch.

When placing your order you stressed the importance of prompt delivery, and I am glad to say that by making a special effort we have been able to improve by a few days on the delivery date agreed.

We await your shipping instructions, and immediately we hear from you we will send you our advice of despatch.

Yours sincerely

## 7.14 Advice of goods ready for despatch

Dear

We are pleased to confirm that all the books which you ordered on 3 April are packed and ready for despatch.

The consignment awaits collection at our warehouse and consists of two cases, each weighing about 100 kg.

Arrangements for shipment, cif Singapore, have already been made with W Watson & Co Ltd, our forwarding agents.[10] As soon as we receive their statement of charges, we will arrange for shipping documents to be sent to you through Barclays Bank against our draft for acceptance, as agreed.

We look forward to further business with you.

Yours sincerely

---

[10] **forwarding agents** agents who arrange for transportation of goods

### 7.15 Notification of goods despatched

Dear

ORDER NUMBER S 524

The mohair rugs you ordered on 5 January have been packed in four special waterproof-lined cases. They will be collected tomorrow by British Rail for consignment by passenger train and should reach you by Friday.

We feel sure you will find the consignment supports our claim to sell the best rugs of their kind and hope we may look forward to further orders from you.

Yours sincerely

### 7.16 Report of damage in transit

It is the legal duty of the buyer to collect any purchases from the supplier. Unless the terms of the sale include delivery, the railway or other carrier is considered the agent of the buyer. The buyer is, therefore, responsible for any loss, damage or delay which may affect the goods after the carrier has taken over.

Dear

ORDER NUMBER S 524

We regret to inform you that of the four cases of mohair rugs which were despatched on 28 January, one was delivered damaged. The waterproof lining was badly torn and it will be necessary to send seven of the rugs for cleaning before we can offer them for sale.

Will you therefore please arrange to send replacements immediately and charge them to our account.

We realise that the responsibility for damage is ours and have already taken up the matter of compensation[11] with the railway authorities.

Yours sincerely

### 7.17 Report of non-delivery of goods

When goods do not arrive as promised, avoid the tendency to blame the supplier as it may not be their fault. Your letter should be restricted to a statement of the facts and a request for information.

---

[11] **compensation** payment for loss

Dear

ORDER NUMBER S 524

You wrote to us on 28 January informing us that the mohair rugs supplied to the above order were being despatched.

We expected these goods a week ago and on the faith of your notification of despatch promised immediate delivery to a number of our customers. As the goods have not yet reached us, we naturally feel our customers have been let down.

Delivery of the rugs is now a matter of urgency. Please find out from British Rail what has happened to the consignment and let us know when we may expect delivery.

We are of course making our own enquiries at this end.

Yours sincerely

## 7.18 Complaint to carrier concerning non-delivery

Upon receiving the report of non-delivery the supplier should at once take up the matter with the carriers, by telephone, letter or fax. If a fax is sent it must contain no suggestion of the annoyance that is naturally felt, but should be confined to the facts and ask for an immediate enquiry into the circumstances.

Dear

We regret to report that a consignment of mohair rugs addressed to W Hart & Co, 25–27 Gordon Avenue, Warrington, has not yet reached them.

These cases were collected by your carrier on 28 January for consignment by passenger train and should have been delivered by 1 February. We hold your carrier's receipt number 3542.

As our customer is urgently in need of these goods, we must ask you to make enquiries and let us know the cause of the delay and when delivery will be made.

Please treat this matter as one of extreme urgency.

Yours sincerely

## USEFUL EXPRESSIONS

### Placing orders

#### Openings

1 Thank you for your quotation of …

2 We have received your quotation of … and enclose our official order form.

3 Please supply the following items as quickly as possible and charge to our account:

#### Closes

1 Prompt delivery would be appreciated as the goods are needed urgently.

2 Please acknowledge receipt of this order and confirm that you will be able to deliver by …

3 We hope to receive your advice of delivery by return of post.

### Acknowledging orders

#### Openings

1 Thank you for your order dated …

2 We thank you for your order number … and will despatch the goods by …

3 We are sorry to inform you that the goods ordered on … cannot be supplied.

#### Closes

1 We hope the goods reach you safely and that you will be pleased with them.

2 We hope you will find the goods satisfactory and look forward to receiving your further orders.

3 We are pleased to say that these goods have been despatched today (will be despatched in …/are now awaiting collection at …).

# Invoicing and settlement of accounts

Payment of the amount owing for goods supplied or services rendered is the final stage in a business transaction. In the retail trade transactions are usually for cash whereas in wholesale and foreign trade it is customary to allow credit.

## INVOICES AND ADJUSTMENTS

When goods are supplied on credit the supplier sends an invoice to the buyer to:

- Inform the buyer of the amount due.
- Enable the buyer to check the goods delivered.
- Enable entry in the buyer's purchases day book.

When an invoice is received it should be checked carefully, not only against the goods supplied but also for the accuracy of both prices and calculations.

Invoices are sometimes sent with the goods but they are more usually posted separately. Any buyer who is not a regular customer will be expected to settle the account at once; regular customers will be given credit with invoices being charged to their accounts. Payment will then be made later on the basis of a statement of account sent by the supplier monthly or at other periodic intervals.

An example of an invoice is shown in Fig. 8.1.

## PRO FORMA INVOICES

'Pro forma' means 'for form's sake'. A pro forma invoice is used:

- To cover goods sent 'on approval' or 'on consignment'.
- To serve as a formal quotation.
- To serve as a request for payment in advance for goods ordered by an unknown customer or a doubtful payer.
- Where the value of goods exported is required for customs purposes.

Pro forma invoices are not entered in the books of account and are not charged to the accounts of the persons to whom they are sent.

### Covering letter with invoice

**8.1** It is not normally necessary to send a covering letter with an invoice, particularly when the invoice is sent with the goods. If the invoice is sent separately a short but polite covering letter may be sent with it.

**JOHN G GARTSIDE & CO LTD**
Albion Works, Thomas Street
Manchester M60 2QA
Telephone 0161-980-2132

INVOICE

Johnson Tools & Co Ltd
112 Kingsway
LIVERPOOL
L20 6HJ

Your order no: AW 25

Date: 18 August 19—

Invoice no: B 832

| Quantity | Item(s) | Unit Price | Total £ |
|----------|---------|------------|---------|
| 10 | Polyester shirts, small | 15.00 | 150.00 |
| 21 | Polyester shirts, medium | 16.00 | 336.00 |
| 12 | Polyester shirts, large | 17.25 | 207.00 |
| | | | 693.00 |
| | VAT (@ 17.5%) | | 121.28 |
| | One case (returnable) | | 13.25 |
| | | | 827.53 |
| | Terms 2½% one month | | |

E & OE

Registered in England No 523807

**Fig. 8.1 Invoice**
The invoice informs the buyer of the amount due for goods supplied on credit.

VAT: Value Added Tax. A tax on goods and services, payable to HM Customs and Excise.

E & OE: Errors and omissions excepted. This statement reserves the supplier's right to correct any errors which the document may contain.

### (a) Non-regular customer

Dear Sir/Madam

YOUR ORDER NUMBER AW25

We are pleased to enclose our invoice number B 832 for the polyester shirts ordered on 13 August.

The goods are available from stock and will be sent to you immediately we receive the amount due, namely £312.28.

Yours faithfully

### (b) Regular customer

Dear Sir or Madam

YOUR ORDER NUMBER AW 25

Our invoice number B 832 is enclosed covering the polyester shirts ordered on 13 August.

These shirts have been packed ready for despatch and are being sent to you, <u>carriage paid</u>,[1] by rail. They should reach you within a few days.

Yours faithfully

# DEBIT AND CREDIT NOTES

If the supplier has undercharged the buyer a debit note may be sent for the amount of the undercharge. A debit note is in the nature of a supplementary invoice.

If the supplier has overcharged the buyer then a credit note is sent. Credit notes are also issued to buyers when they return either goods (as where they are unsuitable) or packing materials on which there is a rebate.[2] Credit notes are usually printed in red to distinguish them from invoices and debit notes. Examples of credit and debit notes are shown in Figs 8.2 and 8.3.

[1] **carriage paid** sender pays for transport
[2] **rebate** a refund or allowance

**JOHN G GARTSIDE & CO LTD**
Albion Works, Thomas Street
Manchester M60 2QA
Telephone 0161-980-2132

DEBIT NOTE

Johnson Tools & Co Ltd
112 Kingsway
LIVERPOOL
L20 6HJ

Date 22 August 19—

Debit Note No. D.75

| Date | Details | Price |
|------|---------|-------|
| | | £ |
| 18.8.— | To 21 Polyester Shirts, medium charged on invoice number B 832 @ £16.00 each | |
| | Should be £16.70 each | |
| | Difference | 14.70 |

Registered in England No 523807

**Fig. 8.2 Debit note** A debit note is sent by the supplier to a buyer who has been undercharged in the original invoice.

**JOHN G GARTSIDE & CO LTD**
Albion Works, Thomas Street
Manchester M60 2QA
Telephone 0161-980-2132

CREDIT NOTE

Johnson Tools & Co Ltd
112 Kingsway
LIVERPOOL
L20 6HJ

Date 25 August 19—

Credit Note No. C.521

| Date | Details | Price |
|------|---------|-------|
| | | £ |
| 18.8.— | By One case returned charged to you on invoice number B 832 | 13.25 |

Registered in England No 523807

**Fig. 8.3 Credit note** A credit note is sent by the supplier to a buyer who has been overcharged in the original invoice, or to acknowledge and allow credit for goods returned by the buyer. It is usually printed in red.

### 8.2 Supplier sends debit note

Dear Sir/Madam

I regret to have to inform you that an unfortunate error has been discovered in our invoice number B 832 of 18 August.

The correct charge for polyester shirts, medium, is £16.70 and not £16.00 as stated. We are therefore enclosing a debit note for the amount undercharged, namely £14.70.

This mistake is due to an input error and we are sorry it was not noticed before the invoice was sent.

Yours faithfully

### 8.3 Buyer requests credit note

When notifying of an overcharge it is the practice of some customers to send a debit note to the supplier as a claim for the amount overcharged. If the supplier agrees to the claim, he will then issue a credit note to the customer.

#### (a) Returned packing case

Dear Sirs

We have today returned to you by rail one empty packing case, charged on your invoice number B 832 of 18 August at £13.25.

A debit note for this amount is enclosed and we shall be glad to receive your credit note in return.

Yours faithfully

#### (b) Incorrect trade discount

Dear Sirs

Your invoice number 2370 dated 10 September allows a trade discount of only 33⅓% instead of the 40% to which you agreed in your letter of 5 August because of the unusually large order.

Calculated on the invoice gross total of £1,500 the difference in discount is exactly £100. If you will please adjust your charge we shall be glad to pass the invoice for immediate payment.

Yours faithfully

## 8.4 Supplier refuses request for credit note

### (a) Retailer's request

Dear Sir or Madam

On 1 September we returned to you by parcel post one cassette tape recorder, Model EK76, Serial Number 048617, one of a consignment of 12 delivered on 5 August and charged on your invoice number 5624 dated 2 August.

The customer who bought this recorder complained about its performance. It was for this reason that we returned it to you after satisfying ourselves that the complaint was justified.

We have received no acknowledgement of the returned recorder or of the letter we sent to you on 1 September. It may be that you are trying to obtain a replacement for us. If this is the case and a replacement is not immediately available, please send us a credit note for the invoiced cost of the returned recorder, namely £175.

We hope to hear from you soon.

Yours faithfully

### (b) Wholesaler's reply

Dear

We are sorry to learn from your letter of 16 September of the need to return one of the recorders supplied to you and charged on our invoice number 5624.

We received your letter of 1 September but regret that we have no trace of the returned recorder. It would help if you could describe the kind of container in which it was packed and state exactly how it was addressed and the method of delivery used. As soon as we receive this information we will make a thorough investigation.[3]

Meanwhile I am sure you will understand that we cannot either provide a free replacement or grant the credit you request. If you could wait for about 10 days, we could replace the tape recorder but would have to charge it to your account if our further enquiries should prove unsuccessful.

Yours sincerely

---

[3] **investigation** a detailed enquiry

# STATEMENTS OF ACCOUNT

A statement (see Fig. 8.4) is a demand for payment. It is a summary of the transactions between buyer and supplier during the period it covers, usually one month. It starts with the balance owing at the beginning of the period, if any. Thereafter amounts of invoices and debit notes issued are listed, and amounts of any credit notes issued and payments made by the buyer are deducted. The closing balance shows the amount owing at the date of the statement.

Statements, like invoices, are generally sent without a covering letter. If a covering letter is sent, it need only be very short and formal.

---

**JOHN G GARTSIDE & CO LTD**
Albion Works, Thomas Street
Manchester M60 2QA
Telephone 0161-980-2132

STATEMENT

Johnson Tools & Co Ltd                                     Date 31 August 19—
112 Kingsway
LIVERPOOL
L20 6HJ

| Date | Details | Debit | Credit | Balance |
|------|---------|-------|--------|---------|
| | | £ | £ | £ |
| 1.8.— | Account rendered | | | 115.53 |
| 18.8.— | Invoice B 832 | 827.53 | | 943.06 |
| 20.8.— | Cheque received | | 500.00 | 443.06 |
| 22.8.— | Debit Note D 75 | 14.70 | | 457.76 |
| 25.8.— | Credit Note C 52 | | 13.25 | 444.51 |

E & OE                                          Registered in England No 523807

---

**Fig. 8.4 Statement** A statement is a demand for payment sent at regular periods by the supplier to buyers. It summarises all transactions over the period it covers and enables the buyer to check against the particulars given. Any errors discovered and agreed will be adjusted either by debit or credit note.

## 8.5 Covering letter with statement

Dear Sirs

We enclose our statement of account for all transactions during August. If payment is made within 14 days you may deduct the customary cash discount of 2½%.

Yours faithfully

## 8.6 Supplier reports underpaid statement

### (a) Supplier's letter

Dear Sirs

We are enclosing our September statement totalling £820.57.

The opening balance brought forward is the amount left uncovered by the cheque received from you against our August statement which totalled £560.27. The cheque received from you, however, was drawn for £500.27 only, leaving the unpaid balance of £60 brought forward.

We should appreciate early settlement of the total amount now due.

Yours faithfully

### (b) Buyer's reply

Dear Sirs

We have received your letter of 15 October enclosing September's statement.

We apologise for the underpayment of £60 on your August statement. This was due to a misreading of the amount due. The final figure was not very clearly printed and we mistakenly read it as £500.27 instead of £560.27.

Our cheque for £820.57, the total amount on the September statement, is enclosed.

Yours faithfully

### 8.7 Supplier reports errors in statement

#### (a) Buyer's notification

Dear Sirs

On checking your statement for July we notice the following errors:

1  The sum of £14.10 for the return of empty packing cases, covered by your credit note number 621 dated 5 July, has not been entered.

2  Invoice Number W825 for £127.32 has been debited twice – once on 11 July and again on 21 July.

We are, therefore, deducting the sum of £141.42 from the balance shown on your statement, and enclose our cheque for £354.50 in full settlement.

Yours faithfully

#### (b) Supplier's acknowledgement

Dear Sirs

Thank you for your letter of 10 August enclosing your cheque for £354.50 in full settlement of the amount due against our July statement.

We confirm your deduction of £141.42 and apologise for the errors in the statement. Please accept our apologies for the inconvenience caused.

Yours faithfully

## VARYING THE TERMS OF PAYMENT

When a customer is required to pay for goods when, or before, they are delivered, he is said to pay 'on invoice'. Customers known to be *creditworthy*[4] may be granted 'open account' terms, under which invoices arc charged to their accounts. Settlement is then made on the basis of statements of account sent by the supplier.

When a customer finds it necessary to ask for time to pay, the reasons given must be strong enough to convince the supplier that the difficulties are purely temporary and that payment will be made later.

---

[4] **creditworthy** believed to be financially sound

## 8.8 Customer requests time to pay (granted)

### (a) Customer's request

Dear Sirs

Acknowledge supplier's letter — We have received your letter of 6 August reminding us that payment of the amount owing on your June statement is overdue.

Explain why payment has not been made — We were under the impression that payment was not due until the end of August when we would have had no difficulty in settling your account. However it seems that we misunderstood your terms of payment.

Request deferred payment and give assurance — In the circumstances we should be grateful if you could allow us to <u>defer payment</u>[5] for a further 3 weeks. Our present difficulty is purely temporary. Before the end of the month payments are due to us from a number of our regular customers who are notably prompt payers.

Express regret — We very much regret having to make this request and hope you will be able to grant it.

Yours faithfully

### (b) Supplier's reply

Dear Mr Jensen

Respond to request for deferred payment — Having carefully considered your letter of 8 August, we have decided to allow you to defer payment of your account to the end of August.

Explain reason for granting request — This request is granted as an exceptional measure only because of the promptness with which you have settled your accounts in the past. We sincerely hope that in future dealings you will be able to keep to our terms of payment. We take this opportunity to remind you that they are as follows:

Reminder about future terms — 2½% discount for payment within 10 days
Net cash for payment within one month

Yours sincerely

---

[5] **defer payment** pay at a later date

## 8.9  Customer requests time to pay (not granted)

### (a) Customer's request

Dear Mr Wilson

Thank you for your letter of 23 July asking for immediate payment of the £687 due on your invoice number AV54.

When we wrote promising to pay you in full by 16 July, we fully expected to be able to do so. However we were unfortunately called upon to meet an unforeseen and unusually heavy demand earlier this month.

We are therefore enclosing a cheque for £200 on account,[6] and ask you to be good enough to allow us a further few weeks in which to settle the balance. We fully expect to be able to settle your account in full by the end of August. If you would grant this deferment, we should be most grateful.

Yours sincerely

### (b) Supplier's reply

In refusing requests of this kind it is better for suppliers to stress the benefits the customer is likely to gain from making payments promptly rather than to stress their own difficulties in seeking prompt payment. The customer is, after all, more interested in problems closer to home.

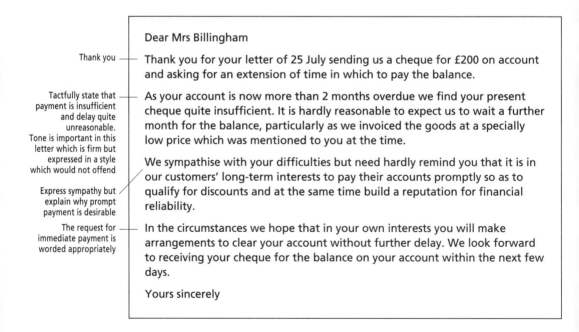

Dear Mrs Billingham

*Thank you* —— Thank you for your letter of 25 July sending us a cheque for £200 on account and asking for an extension of time in which to pay the balance.

*Tactfully state that payment is insufficient and delay quite unreasonable. Tone is important in this letter which is firm but expressed in a style which would not offend* —— As your account is now more than 2 months overdue we find your present cheque quite insufficient. It is hardly reasonable to expect us to wait a further month for the balance, particularly as we invoiced the goods at a specially low price which was mentioned to you at the time.

*Express sympathy but explain why prompt payment is desirable* —— We sympathise with your difficulties but need hardly remind you that it is in our customers' long-term interests to pay their accounts promptly so as to qualify for discounts and at the same time build a reputation for financial reliability.

*The request for immediate payment is worded appropriately* —— In the circumstances we hope that in your own interests you will make arrangements to clear your account without further delay. We look forward to receiving your cheque for the balance on your account within the next few days.

Yours sincerely

[6] **on account** in part payment

### 8.10 Supplier questions partial payment

When making payment on a statement, the debtor should always state whether the payment is 'on account' or 'in full settlement' otherwise it may give rise to letters such as the following.

---

Dear

We thank you for your letter of 10 October enclosing your cheque for £58.67. Our official receipt is enclosed as requested.

As you do not say that the cheque is on account, we are wondering whether the amount of £58.67 was intended to be £88.67 – the balance on your account as shown in our September statement.

In any case we look forward to receiving the uncleared balance of £30 within the next few days.

Yours sincerely

---

### 8.11 Supplier disallows discount deduction

---

Dear

Thank you for your letter 15 October enclosing your cheque for £292.50 in full settlement of our May statement.

We regret that we cannot accept this payment as a full discharge of the £300 due on our statement. The terms of payment allow the 2½% cash discount only on accounts paid within 10 days of statement whereas your present payment is more than a month overdue.

The balance still owing is £7.50 and to save you the trouble of making a separate payment we will include this amount in your next payment and will prepare our July statement accordingly.

Yours sincerely

---

## METHODS OF PAYMENT

Various methods of payment may be used in settling accounts. The form of payment to be used is a matter for arrangement between the parties concerned.

**1 Cash (coins and notes).**

**2 Payments through the Post Office**

(a) *Postal orders and money orders* (the latter for foreign payments only). British postal orders and money orders are issued and paid in many countries abroad. Payment is made in the currency of the country of payment at the current rate of exchange. Postal orders are used for small sums (up to £20 in the United Kingdom).

Money orders (other than telegraph money orders) are no longer issued for payment in the United Kingdom but are issued for amounts up to £50 for payment abroad. This method is used by senders who have no bank or giro (postal cheque) account. A person sending a money order should ask the payee for a receipt since there is no other evidence of payment.

(b) *Giro transfers.* 'Giro' is a term commonly applied to the postal cheque system run by post offices in most Western European countries and Japan. Apart from cash transactions, giro transfer or postal cheque is the chief means of payment. Anyone can make a deposit or receive a payment, whether or not a giro account is held.

(c) *The COD system.* In the COD (cash on delivery) system the buyer pays for the goods at the time they are handed over by the carrier (this includes the postal system). In this way the supplier makes certain of receiving payment for goods supplied to unknown customers.

### 3 Payments through banks

(a) Home trade relies on cheques, credit transfers (bank giro), banker's drafts and letters of credit.

- *Cheques:* A bank cheque is always payable on demand. It is by far the most common form of payment used to settle credit transactions in the home trade of countries where the bank cheque system has been developed. It may also be used to pay debts abroad. A receipt is the best, but not the only, evidence of payment and cheques which have been paid by a banker and later returned to customers may be produced as receipts. When payment is made by cheque a separate receipt is therefore unnecessary but the payer may legally demand a receipt if required.

- *Credit transfers:* The system of credit transfers operated by banks is in many ways similar to the postal cheque (giro) system and is now commonly referred to as a bank giro. The payer completes a credit transfer or giro transfer slip for each separate payment and enters it on a list, which is passed (in duplicate) to the banker together with the slips and a cheque for the total amount. The banker then distributes the slips to the banks of the payees concerned and their accounts are then credited. Payees receive the transfer slips from their bankers. A separate advice of payment by the payer is therefore unnecessary but some payers make it their practice to send one.

- *Banker's drafts:* A banker's draft is a document bought from a bank. It orders the branch bank, or the agent on whom it is drawn, to pay the stated sum of money on demand to the person named in the draft (the payee). In foreign transactions the payee receives payment in the local currency at the current rate of exchange. Banker's drafts are convenient for paying large sums of money in circumstances where a creditor would hesitate to take a cheque in payment. Like cheques, they may be crossed for added safety.

(b) Foreign trade may use bank transfers (mail, telegraphic and telex); bills of exchange and promissory notes; bank commercial credits (documentary credits if a documentary bill is used); banker's drafts; and letters of credit.

## 8.12 Supplier asks customer to select terms of payment

> Dear
>
> Thank you for your letter of 3 April, but you do not say whether you wish this transaction to be for cash or on credit.
>
> When we wrote to you on 20 March we explained our willingness to offer easy credit terms to customers who do not wish to pay cash, and also that we allow generous discounts to cash customers.
>
> We may not have made it clear that when placing orders customers should state whether cash or credit terms are required.
>
> Please let me know which you prefer so that we can arrange your account accordingly.
>
> Yours sincerely

## 8.13 Form letter enclosing payment (and acknowledgement)

Every business has a good deal of purely routine correspondence. Letters enclosing or acknowledging payments are of this kind. They often take a standard form suitable for all occasions and are therefore known as 'form letters'. In such cases a supply of preprinted letters is prepared with blank spaces for the insertion of variable types of information (reference numbers, names and addresses, dates, sums of money, etc).

Of course the personal touch which personalised letters provide is lost with such form letters. However many companies now use mail merge facilities on word processors to produce personalised form letters which look like originals.

### (a) Sender's form letter

> Dear Sir or Madam
>
> We have pleasure in enclosing our cheque (bill/draft/etc.) for £... in full settlement (part settlement) of your statement (invoice) dated ...
>
> Please send us your official receipt.
>
> Yours faithfully

**(b) Form letter acknowledging payment**

> Dear
>
> Thank you for your letter of ... enclosing cheque (bill/draft/etc.) for £... in full settlement (part payment) of our statement of account (invoice) dated ...
>
> We enclose our official receipt.
>
> Yours sincerely

## 8.14 Letter informing supplier of payment by credit transfer (bank giro)

> Dear Sirs
>
> A credit transfer has been made to your account at the Barminster Bank, Church Street, Dover, in payment of the amount due for the goods supplied on 2 May and charged on your invoice number 1524.
>
> Yours faithfully

## 8.15 Letter informing supplier of payment by banker's draft

> Dear Sirs
>
> Our banker's draft is enclosed, drawn on the Midminster Bank, Benghazi, for £672.72 and crossed 'Account Payee only'.
>
> The draft is sent in full settlement of your account dated 31 May.
>
> Please acknowledge its safe receipt.
>
> Yours faithfully

## 8.16 Supplier sends goods COD (cash on delivery)

> Dear Sir or Madam
>
> Thank you for your order for one of our Model X50 cameras. This model is an improved version of our famous Model X40, which has already established itself firmly in public favour. We feel sure you will be delighted with it. At the price of £89.25 we believe it represents the best value on the market for cameras of this type.
>
> Your camera will be sent to you today by compensation-fee parcel post, for delivery against payment of our trade charge of £90. This charge includes packing and postal registration and COD charges.
>
> Under our guarantee you are entitled to a refund of your payment in full if you are not completely satisfied, but you must return the camera by compensation-fee parcel post within 7 days.
>
> Yours faithfully

# USEFUL EXPRESSIONS

## Payments Due

### Openings

1 Enclosed is our statement for the quarter ended ...

2 We enclose our statement to 31... showing a balance of £...

3 We are sorry it was necessary to return our invoice number ... for correction.

4 We very much regret having to ask for an extension of credit on your January statement.

### Closes

1 Please let us have your credit note for the amount of this overcharge.

2 Please make the necessary adjustment and we will settle the account immediately.

3 We apologise again for this error and enclose our credit note for the overcharge.

## Payments made

### Openings

1 We enclose our cheque for £... in payment for goods supplied on ...

2 We enclose our cheque for ... in payment of your invoice number ...

3 We acknowledge with thanks your cheque for £...

4 We thank you for your cheque for £... in part payment of your account.

### Closes

1 We hope to receive the amount due by the end of this month.

2 We should be obliged if you would send us your cheque immediately.

3 As the amount owing is considerably overdue, we must ask you to send us your cheque by return.

# Letters requesting payment

## TONE

When a customer fails to pay promptly it is always annoying to the supplier, but no suggestion of annoyance must be allowed to creep into the correspondence. It may be better not to write at all and instead call on the customer if possible, or telephone tactfully to persuade at least part payment to be made on account. In difficult cases it may even be good policy to accept a part payment rather than resort to legal action which would be both expensive and time-consuming.

There may be several good reasons why a customer fails to pay on time, some of them deserving sympathy. There is, however, always the customer who is only too ready to invent excuses and who needs to be watched. Each case must be treated on its merits.

The style and tone of any letters should depend on such factors as the age of the debt, whether later payment is *habitual*,[1] and how important the customer is. However no letter must ever be less than polite, and even the final letter threatening legal action must be written 'with regret'.

## LATE PAYMENTS

When there is a need to write explaining difficulties in paying an account by the due date and to ask to defer payment, the following plan is useful:

1 Refer to the account which cannot be paid immediately.
2 Regret inability to pay and give reasons.
3 Suggest an extension of period for payment.
4 Hope that the suggestion will be accepted.

### 9.1 Customer explains inability to pay

This letter is from a regular and reliable customer. It makes a reasonable request and a supplier refusing it would run the risk of driving away that customer. If the supplier refuses, the customer might pay the outstanding amount, but could then start buying from a competitor. In the process the supplier could lose many valuable future orders.

[1] **habitual** customary, usual

Dear Sirs

Your invoice number 527 dated 20 July for £1516 is due for payment at the end of this month.

Most unfortunately a fire broke out in our Despatch Department last week and destroyed a large part of a valuable consignment due for delivery to a cash customer. Our claim is now with the insurance company but it is unlikely to be met for another 3 or 4 weeks. Until then we are faced with a difficult financial problem.

I am therefore writing for permission to defer payment[2] of your invoice until the end of September.

As you are aware my accounts with you have always been settled promptly, and it is with regret that I am now forced to make this request. I hope that you will find it possible to grant it.

Yours faithfully

## 9.2 Customer explains late payment

Dear

Further to your letter of 4 July I enclose a cheque for £1182.57 in full settlement of your invoice number W 563, with my apologies for late payment.

This is due to my absence from the office through illness and my failure to leave instructions for your account to be paid. I did not discover the oversight[3] until I returned to the office yesterday.

I would not like you to think that failure to settle your account on time was in any way intentional. My apologies once again for this delay.

Yours sincerely

## COLLECTION LETTERS

The preliminary steps in debt collection are as follows:

1  A first end-of-month statement of account.

2  A second end-of-month statement of account with added comment.

3  A first letter worded formally.

4  Second and third letters.

5  A final letter notifying that legal action will be taken unless the amount is paid within a stipulated period of time.

---

[2] **defer payment** pay later
[3] **oversight** unintentional omission

A customer whose account is only slightly *overdue*[4] would understandably be offended to receive a personal letter concerning this. This is why the first 2 reminders usually take the form of end-of-the-month statements of account. Even where the second of these statements is marked with such comments as 'Second application', 'Account overdue – please pay' or 'Immediate attention is requested', this is unlikely to give offence.

## 1 FIRST APPLICATIONS FOR PAYMENT

It is not wise to write a letter until a customer has been given the opportunity to pay on these impersonal statements. Letters requesting payment of overdue accounts are termed 'collection letters'. They aim to:

(a) persuade the customer to settle the account;

(b) retain custom and goodwill.

It would be easy to give offence so any letters must be written with tact and restraint. It may also be the case that the supplier is at fault, as in the case where a payment received has not been recorded, or goods sent or service given is not satisfactory.

### 9.3 A printed collection letter

A first collection letter may be printed as a 'form letter' as in this example where the individual details are keyed in appropriately. Alternatively the details may be stored on a word processor so that the letter may be personalised.

---

Dear Sir/Madam

ACCOUNT NUMBER ...

According to our records the above account dated ... has not been settled.

The enclosed statement shows the amount owing to be £...

We hope to receive an early settlement[5] of this account.

Yours faithfully

---

### 9.4 Personalised collection letters

There may be circumstances when an individual letter rather than a form letter is more appropriate. It should then be addressed to a named senior official and marked 'Confidential'.

---

[4] **overdue** remaining unpaid
[5] **settlement** completion by payment

### (a) To a regular payee

---

Dear

ACCOUNT NUMBER 6251

As you are usually very prompt in settling your accounts, we wonder whether there is any special reason why we have not received payment of this account, which is already a month overdue.

In case you may not have received the statement of account sent on 31 May showing a balance owing of £105.67, a copy is enclosed. We hope this will receive your early attention.

Yours sincerely

---

### (b) To a new customer

---

Dear Sir/Madam

ACCOUNT NUMBER 5768

We regret having to remind you that we have not received payment of the balance of £105.67 due on our statement for December. This was sent to you on 2 January and a copy is enclosed.

We must remind you that unusually low prices were quoted to you on the understanding of an early settlement.

It may well be that non-payment is due to an oversight, and so we ask you to be good enough to send us your cheque within the next few days.

Yours faithfully

---

### (c) To a customer who has sent a part-payment

---

Dear

Thank you for your letter of 8 March enclosing a cheque for £500 in part-payment of the balance due on our February statement.

Your payment leaves an unpaid balance of £825.62. As our policy is to work on small profit margins, we regret that we cannot grant long term credit facilities.

We are sure that you will not think it is unreasonable for us to ask for immediate payment of this balance.

Yours sincerely

---

## 9.5  Reminder to customer who has already paid

The need for a cautious approach is always necessary since the customer may not be at fault, as where the payment has *gone astray*,[6] or where the supplier has received it but failed to record it.

---

[6] **gone astray** been lost in transit

### (a) Request for payment

Dear Sir/Madam

ACCOUNT NUMBER S542

According to our records our account for cutlery supplied to you on 21 October has not been paid.

We enclose a detailed statement showing the amount owing to be £310.62 and hope you will make an early settlement.

Yours faithfully

### (b) Customer's reply

Dear

YOUR ACCOUNT NUMBER S542

I was surprised to receive your letter of 8 December stating that you had not received payment of the above account.

In fact our cheque (number 065821, drawn on Barclays Bank, Blackpool) for £310.62 was posted to you on 3 November. As this cheque appears to have gone astray, I have instructed the bank not to pay on it. A replacement cheque for the same amount is enclosed.

Yours sincerely

## 2 SECOND APPLICATION LETTERS

If a reply to the first application is not received a second application should be sent after about 10 days. This should be firmer in tone but still polite. Nothing must be said to cause annoyance or ill will. Co-operation is required and this will not be achieved by annoying the customer.

Such letters should be addressed to a senior official under 'Confidential' cover and planned as follows:

1  refer to previous application
2  assume that something unusual accounts for the delay in payment
3  suggest tactfully that an explanation would be welcome
4  ask for payment to be sent

## 9.6 Specimen second application letters

### (a) Second letter, following 9.4(a)

Dear Sir/Madam

ACCOUNT NUMBER 6251

As we have not received a reply to our letter of 5 July requesting settlement of the above account, we are writing again to remind you that the amount still owing is £105.67.

No doubt there is some special reason for the delay in payment, and we should welcome an explanation together with your remittance.

Yours faithfully

### (b) Second letter, following 9.4(b)

Dear Sir/Madam

On 18 February we wrote to remind you that our December statement sent on 2 January showed a balance of £105.67 outstanding and due for payment by 31 January.

Settlement of this account is now more than a month overdue. Therefore we must ask you either to send us your remittance within the next few days or at least to offer an explanation of the delay in payment.

Your prompt reply will be appreciated.

Yours faithfully

### (c) Second letter, following 9.4(c)

Dear Sir/Madam

We have not heard from you since we wrote on 10 March about the unpaid balance of £825.62 on your account. In view of your past good record we have not previously pressed for a settlement.

To regular customers such as yourself our terms of payment are 3% one month,[7] and we hope you will not withhold payment any longer, otherwise it will be necessary for us to revise these terms.

In the circumstances we look forward to receiving your cheque for the outstanding amount within the next few days.

Yours faithfully

---

[7] **3% one month** subject to a 3 per cent discount if paid within one month

## 3 THIRD APPLICATION LETTERS

If payment is still not made and if no explanation has been received, a third letter becomes necessary. Such a letter should show that steps will be taken to enforce payment if necessary, such steps depending on individual circumstances. Third letters should follow this plan:

1 Review earlier efforts to collect payment.

2 Give a final opportunity to pay by stating a reasonable *deadline date*.[8]

3 State that you wish to be fair and reasonable.

4 State action to be taken if this third request is ignored.

5 Regret the necessity for the letter.

### 9.7 Specimen third application letters

**(a) Third letter, following 9.6(a)**

---

Dear Sir/Madam

ACCOUNT NUMBER 6251

We do not appear to have received replies to our two previous requests of 5 and 16 July for payment of the sum of £105.67 still owing on this account.

It is with the utmost regret that we have reached the stage when we must press for immediate payment. We have no wish to be unreasonable, but failing payment by 7 August you will leave us no choice but to place the matter in other hands.

We sincerely hope this will not become necessary.

Yours faithfully

---

**(b) Third letter, following 9.6(b)**

---

Dear Sir/Madam

*Even in this third letter restraint is shown in the wording rather than directly attacking the customer* — It is very difficult to understand why we have not heard from you in reply to our two letters of 18 February and 2 March about the sum of £105.67 due on our December statement. We had hoped that you would at least explain why the account continues to remain unpaid.

*Terms like 'every consideration' and 'no choice...' somewhat soften the blow* — I am sure you will agree that we have shown every consideration in the circumstances. Failing any reply to our earlier requests for payment, I am afraid we shall have no choice but to take other steps to recover the amount due.

*This paragraph gives the customer a final chance to clear the account* — We are most anxious to avoid doing anything through which your credit and reputation might suffer. Therefore even at this late stage we are prepared to give you a further opportunity to put matters right.

*A specific timeframe is given* — In the circumstances, we propose to give you until the end of this month to clear your account.[9]

Yours faithfully

---

[8] **deadline date** final date for payment
[9] **clear your account** pay the total balance owing

### (c) Third letter, following 9.6(c)

---

Dear Sir/Madam

We are surprised and disappointed not to have heard from you in response to our two letters of 10 and 23 March reminding you of the balance of £825.62 still owing on our February statement.

This failure either to clear your account or even to offer an explanation is all the more disappointing because of our past satisfactory dealings over many years.

In the circumstances we must say that unless we hear from you within 10 days we shall have to consider seriously the further steps we should take to obtain payment.

Yours faithfully

---

## 4 FINAL COLLECTION LETTERS

If all three applications are ignored, it is reasonable to assume that the customer either cannot, or will not, settle the account. A brief notification of the action that is to be taken must then be sent as a final warning.

## 9.8 Specimen final collection letters

### (a) Final letter, following 9.7(a)

---

Dear Sir/Madam

We are surprised and very much regret that we have received no reply to the further letter we sent to you on 28 July regarding the long overdue payment of £105.67 on your account.

Our relations in the past have always been good. Even so we cannot allow the amount to remain unpaid indefinitely. Unless the amount due is paid or a satisfactory explanation received by the end of this month, we shall be reluctantly compelled to put this matter in the hands of our solicitors.

Yours faithfully

---

### (b) Final letter, following 9.7(b)

Dear Sir/Madam

We are disappointed not to have received any response from you in answer to our letter of 16 March concerning non-payment of the balance of £105.67 outstanding on our December statement.

As our business relations in the past have always been pleasant and friendly, we are now making a final request for payment in the hope that it will not be necessary to hand the matter over to an agent for collection.

We have decided to defer this step for 7 days to give you the opportunity either to pay or at least to send us an explanation.

Yours faithfully

### (c) Final letter, following 9.7(c)

Dear Sir/Madam

We are quite unable to understand why we have received no reply to our letter of 7 April, our third attempt to secure payment of the balance of £826.62 still owing on your account with us.

We feel that we have shown reasonable patience and treated you with every consideration. However we must now regretfully take steps to recover payment at law, and the matter will be placed in the hands of our solicitors.

Yours faithfully

## CHECKLIST

- ☐ Use a tone which is firm but understanding
- ☐ Mention when the payment was originally due
- ☐ State the amount owed
- ☐ State the penalties if any
- ☐ Mention the grace period
- ☐ Give a new deadline
- ☐ Indicate the consequences

# USEFUL EXPRESSIONS

## First applications

### Openings

1 We notice that your account which was due for payment on ..., is still outstanding.

2 We wish to draw your attention to our invoice number ... for £... which remains unpaid.

3 We must remind you that we have not yet received the balance of our ... statement amounting to £..., payment of which is now more than a month overdue.

### Closes

1 We hope to receive your cheque by return.

2 We look forward to your payment within the next few days.

3 As our statement may have gone astray, we enclose a copy and shall be glad if you will pass it for payment immediately.

## Second applications

### Openings

1 We do not appear to have had any reply to our request of ... for settlement of £... due on our invoice ... dated ...

2 We regret not having received a reply to our letter of ...

3 We are at a loss to understand why we have received no reply to our letter of ... requesting settlement of our ... statement in the sum of £...

### Closes

1 We trust you will attend to this matter without further delay.

2 We must ask you to settle this account by return.

3 We regret that we must ask for immediate payment of the amount outstanding.

## Third applications

### Openings

1 We wrote to you on ... and again on ... concerning the amount owing on our invoice number ...

2 We have had no reply to our previous requests for payment of our ... statement ...

3 We note with surprise and disappointment that we have had no replies to our two previous applications for payment of your outstanding account.

### Closes

1 Unless we receive your cheque in full settlement by ... we shall have no alternative but to instruct our solicitors to recover the amount due.

2 Unless we receive your cheque in full settlement by the end of this month, we shall be compelled to take further steps to enforce payment.

3 We still hope you will settle this account without further delay and thus save yourself the inconvenience and considerable costs of legal action.

# Complaints and adjustments

1
2
3
4
5
6
7
8
9
10
11
12
13
14
15
16
17
18
19
20
21
22
23
24
25

## HANDLING COMPLAINTS

No matter how good our intentions and efforts there are bound to be occasions when it is necessary to deal with a complaint, or even make one. Complaints may be necessary for many reasons such as:

- wrong goods received
- poor service
- unsatisfactory quality of goods
- late delivery
- damaged goods
- prices not as agreed

### Making a complaint

When you have a genuine complaint you will feel angry, but you must show *restraint*[1] in your letter, if only because the supplier may not be to blame. The following points need to be considered:

(a) Do not delay as this will weaken your position and the supplier may have difficulty in investigating the cause.

(b) Do not assume that the supplier is automatically to blame; they may have a perfectly good defence.

(c) Confine your complaint to a statement of the facts, followed by either an enquiry as to what the supplier proposes to do about it, or a suggestion of how the matter can be rectified.

(d) Avoid rudeness; this would create ill-feeling and cause the supplier to be unwilling to resolve matters.

### Dealing with a complaint

Most suppliers naturally wish to hear if customers have cause to complain. This is better than custom being lost and trade taken elsewhere. It also provides an opportunity to investigate, to explain, and to put things right. In this way good-will may be preserved. Receiving such complaints may also suggest ways in which the supplier's products or services could be improved. When dealing with dissatisfied customers remember the following rules:

(a) It is often said that the customer *is always right*. This may not always be the case but it is sound practice to assume that the customer *may be right*.

(b) Acknowledge a complaint promptly. If you are unable to reply fully, explain that it is being investigated and a full reply will be sent later.

[1] **restraint** an effort to hold back an emotion

(c) If the complaint is unreasonable, point this out politely and in a way that will not offend.

(d) If you are to blame, admit it readily, express regret and promise to put matters right.

(e) Never blame any of your staff; in the end you are responsible for their actions.

(f) Thank the customer for informing you about the matter.

## COMPLAINTS CONCERNING GOODS

### 10.1 Complaint concerning wrong goods

If goods are received which are not of the kind or quality ordered then you are entitled to return them at the supplier's expense.

**(a) Complaint**

| | |
|---|---|
| der number and date | Dear Sirs<br><br>On 12 August I ordered 12 copies of <u>Background Music</u> by H Lowery under my order number FT567. |
| Reasons for dissatisfaction | On opening the parcel received this morning I found that it contained 12 copies of <u>History of Music</u> by the same author. I regret that I cannot keep these books as I have an adequate stock already. I am therefore returning the books by parcel post for immediate replacement, as I have several customers waiting for them. |
| Action requested | I trust you will credit my account with the invoiced value of the returned copies including <u>reimbursement</u>[2] for the postage cost of £17.90.<br><br>Yours faithfully |

**(b) Reply**

| | |
|---|---|
| Express regret | Dear Mr Ramsay<br><br>I was sorry to learn from your letter of 18 August that a mistake occurred in dealing with your order. |
| lain how the mistake occurred | This mistake is entirely our own and we apologise for the inconvenience it is causing you. This occurred because of staff shortage during this unusually busy season and also the fact that these 2 books by Lowery have identical bindings. |
| ction taken to rectify the matter | 12 copies of the correct title have been despatched by parcel post today.<br><br>Your account will be credited with the invoiced value of the books and cost of return postage. Our credit note is enclosed. |
| A closing apology | We apologise again for this mistake.<br><br>Yours sincerely |

[2] **reimbursement** a refund of money

## 10.2 Complaint concerning quality

A buyer is entitled to *reject*[3] goods which are not of the quality or description ordered. However, later deliveries may also not be accepted, even if the goods are correct.

### (a) Complaint

Dear Sirs

*Reasons for complaint* — We have recently received several complaints from customers about your fountain pens. The pens are clearly not giving satisfaction and in some cases we have had to refund the purchase price.

*Further details* — The pens are part of the batch of 500 supplied against our order number 8562 dated 28 March. This order was placed on the basis of a sample pen left by your representative. We have ourselves compared the performance of this sample with that of a number of the pens from this batch, and there is little doubt that many of them are faulty – some of them leak and others blot when writing.

The complaints we have received relate only to pens from the batch mentioned. Pens supplied before these have always been satisfactory.

*Action required* — We therefore wish to return the unsold balance, amounting to 377 pens. Please replace them with pens of the quality which our earlier dealings with you have led us to expect.

*Close* — Please let us know what arrangements you wish us to make for the return of these unsuitable pens.

Yours faithfully

### (b) Reply (accepting complaint)

Dear

Thank you for your letter dated 10 May pointing out faults in the pens supplied to your order number 8562. This has caused us a good deal of concern and we are glad that you brought this matter to our notice.

We have tested a number of pens from the production batch you mention, and agree that they are not perfect. The defects have been traced to a fault in one of the machines which has now been rectified.

Please arrange to return to us your unsold balance of 377 pens; the cost of postage will be reimbursed in due course. We have already arranged for 400 pens to be sent to replace this unsold balance. The extra 23 pens are sent without charge, and will enable you to provide free replacement of any further pens about which you may receive complaints.

We apologise for the inconvenience this has caused you.

Yours sincerely

[3] **reject** refuse

## (c) Alternative reply (rejecting complaint)

If circumstances show that a complaint must be rejected, you must show an understanding of the customer's position and carefully explain why a rejection is necessary.

---

Dear

We are sorry to learn from your letter of 10 May of the difficulties you are having with the pens supplied to your order number 8562.

All our pens are manufactured to be identical in design and performance and we cannot understand why some of them should have given trouble to your customers. It is normal practice for each pen to be individually examined by our Inspection Department before being passed into store. However, from what you say, it would seem that a number of the pens included in the latest batch escaped the usual examination.

We sympathise with your problem but regret that we cannot accept your suggestion to take back all the unsold stock from the batch concerned. Indeed there should be no need for this since it is unlikely that the number of faulty pens can be very large. We will gladly replace any pen found to be unsatisfactory, and on this particular batch are prepared to allow you a special discount of 5% to compensate for your inconvenience.

We trust you will accept this as being a fair and reasonable solution of this matter.

Yours sincerely

---

## 10.3 Complaint concerning quantity

### (a) Surplus goods delivered

When a supplier delivers more than the quantity ordered, the buyer is legally entitled to reject either all the goods or only the excess quantity. Alternatively all the goods may be accepted and the excess paid for at the same rate. In this letter the buyer rejects the surplus goods but is not obliged to return them; it is the supplier's responsibility to arrange for their collection.

---

Dear Sirs

Thank you for your promptness in delivering the coffee we ordered on 30 July. However 160 bags were delivered this morning instead of 120 as stated on our order.

Our present needs are completely covered and we cannot make use of the 40 bags sent in excess of our order. These bags will therefore be held in our warehouse until we receive your instructions.

Yours faithfully

---

## (b) Shortage in delivery

When a supplier delivers less than the quantity ordered the customer cannot be compelled to accept delivery by instalments. Immediate delivery of the balance may be requested.

---

Dear Sir/Madam

OUR ORDER NUMBER 861

We thank you for so promptly delivering the gas coke ordered on 20 March. Although we ordered 5 tonnes in 50-kg bags, only 80 bags were delivered. Your carrier was unable to explain the shortage and we have not received any explanation from you.

We still need the full quantity ordered and shall be glad if you will arrange to deliver the remaining 20 bags as soon as possible.

Yours faithfully

---

## 10.4 Complaint to manufacturer

### (a) Customer's complaint

In this letter the buyer was informed by the supplier to write directly to the manufacturer regarding faulty goods.

---

Dear Sirs

On 15 September I bought one of your 'Big Ben' alarm clocks (mains operated) from Stansfield Jewellers in Leeds. Unfortunately I have been unable to get the alarm system to work and am very disappointed with my purchase.

The manager of Stansfield's has advised me to return the clock to you for correction of the fault. This is enclosed.

Please arrange for the clock to be put in full working order and return it to me as soon as possible.

Yours faithfully

---

### (b) Manufacturer's reply

In this reply the manufacturer shows genuine interest in the complaint and does everything possible to ensure customer satisfaction. The considerate manner in which the complaint is treated helps to build a reputation for reliability and fair dealing.

Dear Mrs Wood

Thank you for your letter of 20 September enclosing the defective 'Big Ben' alarm clock.

Your comments on the performance of the clock are very interesting and I have passed it to our engineers for inspection.

Meanwhile we are arranging to replace your clock with a new one which has been tested thoroughly to ensure that it is in perfect working order. This will be sent to you within the next few days.

I am sorry for the trouble and inconvenience this matter has caused you, but am confident that the replacement clock will prove satisfactory and give you the service you are entitled to expect from our products.

Yours sincerely

## COMPLAINTS CONCERNING DELIVERY

No supplier likes to be accused of negligence or carelessness which is often what a complaint about packaging amounts to. Such complaints must be carefully worded so as not to give offence. Nothing is to be gained by being sarcastic or insulting – you are much more likely to get what you want by being courteous. Show that you regret having to complain, but explain that the trouble is too serious not to be reported.

### 10.5 Complaint concerning damaged goods

#### (a) Complaint

The writer of this letter points out damage which was discovered after checking the consignment. Any suggestion that the damage to the goods is due to faulty packing is tactfully avoided.

Dear Sirs

OUR ORDER NUMBER R569

*Introduction and background details*

We ordered 160 compact discs on 3 January and they were delivered yesterday. I regret that 18 of them were badly scratched.

*Explain details which [appear]ed after receipt of goods*

The package containing these goods appeared to be in perfect condition and I accepted and signed for it without question.[4] It was on unpacking the compact discs when the damage was discovered; I can only assume that this was due to careless handling at some stage prior to packing.

*Enclose full list of [d]amaged goods and [re]quest replacement*

I am enclosing a list of the damaged goods and shall be glad if you will replace them. They have been kept aside in case you need them to support a claim on your suppliers for compensation.

Yours faithfully

---

[4] **without question** without raising any objection

## (b) Reply

The supplier's reply promptly complies with the customer's request and shows a desire to improve the service to customers.

---

Dear

YOUR ORDER NUMBER R569

*Acknowledge letter and show regret about damages* — I was sorry to learn from your letter of 10 January that some of the compact discs supplied to this order were damaged when they reached you.

*Give details about replacements* — Replacements for the damaged goods have been sent by parcel post this morning. It will not be necessary for you to return the damaged goods; they may be destroyed.

*Give further information about follow-up action* — Despite the care we take in packing goods there have recently been several reports of damage. To avoid further inconvenience and annoyance to customers, as well as expense to ourselves, we are now seeking the advice of a packaging consultant in the hope of improving our methods of handling.

*Assurance about future orders* — We regret the need for you to write to us and hope the steps we are taking will ensure the safe arrival of all your orders in future.

Yours sincerely

---

## 10.6 Complaint regarding bad packing

### (a) Complaint

---

Dear Sirs

*Introduction about reason for writing* — The carpet supplied to our order number C395 of 3 July was delivered by your carriers this morning.

*Details about complaint* — We noticed that one of the outer edges of the wrapping has been worn through, presumably as a result of friction in transit. When we took off the wrapping it was not surprising to find that the carpet itself was soiled and slightly frayed at the edge.

*Further details and questions about precautions* — This is the second time in 3 weeks that we have had cause to write to you about the same matter. We find it hard to understand why precautions could not be taken to prevent a repetition of the earlier damage.

*Suggestions about future handling of orders* — Although other carpets have been delivered in good condition, this second experience within such a short time suggests the need for special precautions against friction when carpets are packed onto your delivery vehicles. We hope that you will bear this in mind in handling our future orders.

*Requests for special concession* — In view of the condition of the present carpet we cannot offer it for sale at the normal price and propose to reduce our selling price by 10%. We suggest that you make us an allowance of 10% on the invoice cost. If you cannot do this, we shall have to return the carpet for replacement.

Yours faithfully

---

## (b) Reply

Express regret at customer's dissatisfaction

Explain circumstances surrounding the complaint

Follow-up action taken

Confirm special discount to customer

> Dear
>
> I was very sorry to learn from your letter of 15 August that the carpet supplied to your order number C395 was damaged on delivery.
>
> Our head packer informs us that the carpet was first wrapped in heavy oiled waterproof paper and then in a double thickness of jute canvas. Under normal conditions this should have been enough protection. However on this occasion our delivery van contained a full load of carpets for delivery to other customers on the same day, and it is obvious that special packing precautions are necessary in such cases.
>
> In all future consignments, we are arranging for specially reinforced end-packings which should prevent any future damage.
>
> We realise the need to reduce your selling price for the damaged carpet and readily agree to the special allowance of 10% which you suggest.
>
> Yours sincerely

## 10.7 Complaint regarding non-delivery

### (a) Complaint

> Dear Sirs
>
> On 25 September we placed our order number RT56 for printed headed notepaper and invoice forms. You acknowledged the order on 30 September. As that is some 3 weeks ago and we have not yet received advice of delivery, we are wondering whether the order has since been overlooked.
>
> Your representative promised an early delivery and this was an important factor in persuading us to place this order with you.
>
> The delay in delivery is causing considerable inconvenience. We must ask you to complete the order immediately, otherwise we shall have no option but to cancel it and obtain the stationery elsewhere.
>
> Yours faithfully

### (b) Reply

Only a very *diplomatic*[5] reply can keep the goodwill of this customer, who is obviously feeling very let down. With an understanding and helpful reply from the printer as shown here, the customer cannot continue to feel annoyed.

---

[5] **diplomatic** tactful and considerate

Dear Mr Sargeant

Thank you for your letter of 18 October. I quite understand your annoyance at not yet having received the stationery ordered on 25 September.

Orders for printed stationery are at present taking from 3 to 4 weeks for delivery, and our representatives have been instructed to make this clear to customers. Apparently you were not told that it would take so long, and I apologise for this oversight.

On receiving your letter we put your order in hand at once. The stationery will be sent from here tomorrow by express parcel post, and it should reach you within 24 hours of your receiving this letter.

It is very unfortunate that there should have been this misunderstanding but we hope you will forgive the delay which has been caused.

Yours sincerely

## 10.8 Complaint regarding frequent late deliveries

This correspondence shows how important it is when sending letters of complaint to write with restraint and not to assume that the supplier is at fault.

### (a) Complaint

Dear Sirs

We ordered 6 filing cabinets from you on 2 July on the understanding that they would be delivered within one week. However these were not received until this morning.

Unfortunately there have been similar delays on several previous occasions, and their increasing frequency in recent months compels us to say that business between us cannot continue in conditions such as these.

We have felt it necessary to make our feelings known since we cannot give reliable delivery dates to our customers unless we can count on undertakings given by our suppliers.

We hope you will understand our position in this matter, and trust that from now on we can rely on punctual delivery of our orders.

Yours faithfully

### (b) Reply

In this reply the supplier carefully explains that the fault is not on their part, and goodwill with the customer should be retained.

Dear

Your letter of 18 July regarding delays in delivery came as a surprise as the absence of any earlier complaints led us to believe that goods supplied to your orders were reaching you promptly.

It is our usual practice to deliver goods well in advance of the promised delivery dates; the filing cabinets to which you refer left here on 5 July. We are very concerned that our efforts to ensure punctual delivery should be frustrated by delays in transit. It is possible that other customers are also affected and we are taking up this whole question with our carriers.

We thank you for drawing our attention to a situation of which we had been quite unaware until you wrote to us. Please accept our apologies for the inconvenience you have been caused.

Yours sincerely

## 10.9 Complaint regarding uncompleted work

This correspondence relates to a builder's failure to complete work on a new bungalow within the agreed contract time. The buyer's letter is firm but reasonably worded. The builder's reply shows understanding and is convincing, businesslike and helpful.

### (a) Complaint

Dear Sirs

BUNGALOW AT 1 CRESCENT ROAD, CHINGFORD

When I signed the contract for the building of this property you estimated that the work would be completed and the bungalow ready for occupation 'in about 6 months'. That was 8 months ago and the work is still only half finished.

The delay is causing inconvenience not only to me but also to the buyer of my present home which I cannot transfer until this bungalow is finished.

I urge you to press forward with this work without any further delay. Please let me know when you expect it to be completed.

Yours faithfully

**(b) Reply**

Dear Mr Watson

BUNGALOW AT 1 CRESCENT ROAD, CHINGFORD

Thank you for your letter of 18 June. We are of course aware that the estimated period for completion of your bungalow has already been exceeded and wish to say at once that we realise what inconvenience the delay must be causing you.

We would ask you, however, to remember first that we have had an exceptionally severe winter, work on the site has been quite impossible during several prolonged periods of heavy snow. Secondly, there has been a nationwide shortage of building materials, especially bricks and timber, from which the trade is only just recovering. Without these 2 difficulties, which could not be foreseen, the estimated completion period of 6 months would have been observed.

In the improved weather conditions work on the bungalow is now proceeding satisfactorily. Unless we have other unforeseen hold-ups[6] we can safely promise that the bungalow will be ready for you by the end of August.

Yours sincerely

## 10.10 Complaint regarding delivery charges

Some customers are only too ready to complain if things do not suit them. Others who are dissatisfied do not complain, but instead they quietly withdraw their custom and transfer it to some other supplier. This correspondence relates to such a case.

**(a) Supplier's enquiry**

Dear Sirs

We are sorry to notice that we have had no orders from you since last April. As you have at no time notified us of defects in our products or about the quality of our service, we can only assume that we have given you no cause to be dissatisfied. If we have, then we should be glad to know of it.

If the cause of your discontinued orders is the present depressed state of the market, you may be interested in our latest price list showing a reduction of 7½% on all grocery items. A copy of this is enclosed.

Should there be any matter in which we have given you cause to be dissatisfied, we hope you will give us the opportunity to put it right so that our custom can be renewed.

Yours faithfully

---

[6] **hold-ups** delays

### (b) Customer's reply (complaint)

Dear

Thank you for your letter of 5 July. As you wish to know why we have placed no orders with you recently, I will point out a matter which caused us some annoyance.

On 21 April last year we sent you two orders, one for £274 and one for £142. Your terms at the time provided for free delivery of all orders for £300 or more, but although you delivered these two orders together we were charged with the cost of carriage.

As the orders were submitted on different forms, we grant that you had a perfect right to treat them as separate orders. However for all practical purposes they could very well have been treated as one, as they were placed on the same day and delivered at the same time. The fact that you did not do this seemed to us to be a particularly ungenerous[7] way of treating a regular long-standing customer.

Having given you our explanation, we should welcome you comments.

Yours sincerely

### (c) Supplier's reply

Dear

*Suitable introduction* — Thank you for your letter of 8 July. Your explanation gives us the opportunity to explain a most regrettable misunderstanding.

*Circumstances surrounding the situation are explained in detail* — Our charge for carriage on your last two orders arose because they were for goods dealt with by two separate departments, neither of which was aware that a separate order was being handled by another.

*Further details given to assure the customer that this situation will not be repeated* — At that time these departments were each responsible for their own packing and despatch arrangements. Since then this work has been taken over by a centralised packing and despatch department so a repetition of the same kind of misunderstanding is now unlikely.

*This tactful close expresses a hope for renewed business dealings* — I hope you will understand that the charge we made was quite unintentional.[8] In the circumstances I hope you will feel able to renew your former custom.

Yours sincerely

### 10.11 Complaint regarding poor service

This correspondence relates to circumstances where a customer does not receive proper attention. In answer to their telephone enquiry regarding a damaged tape recorder the supplier suggests that the goods be sent for inspection in order to obtain a quotation for its repair. The customer does so but then hears no more.

[7] **ungenerous** mean, selfish
[8] **unintentional** not done purposely

### (a) Customer's initial letter

The customer writes to the supplier on 28 June after a telephone conversation with Mr Jackson.

---

Dear Mr Jackson

STEREO CASSETTE RECORDER, MODEL NUMBER 660

Further to our telephone conversation this morning, I am sending my faulty tape recorder. I understand that arrangements can be made for it to be inspected and also a quotation given for its repair.

The following faults will be found:

1 The recorder does not reproduce clearly on the right-hand speaker.
2 Distortion suggests that the recording head may need replacing.
3 The winding mechanism appears to be faulty.

It is possible that an inspection may reveal other faults.

It would help to speed matters if you would let me have the quotation by telephone as I want this work to be carried out and the recorder returned as quickly as possible.

Yours faithfully

*Introduction refers to telephone conversation and details discussed*

*The faults are listed and numbered for clarity*

*Closing section requests an immediate quotation*

---

### (b) Supplier's acknowledgement

On 5 July the supplier sent a printed form number WE69376 acknowledging receipt of both the recorder and the customer's letter of 2 June, but did not quote as promised. Two weeks later, on 18 July, the customer wrote to the supplier again. Note that rather than suggest that the quotation has not been sent, the letter states more tactfully that it has not yet been received.

---

Dear Mr Jackson

STEREO CASSETTE RECORDER, MODEL NUMBER 660

On 28 June I sent the above recorder to you for inspection and a quotation for servicing. As the matter was of some urgency I requested a quotation by telephone.

On 5 July your form number WE69376 acknowledged receipt of the recorder and my letter, but to date I have not received a quotation.

If a quotation has not already been sent I should be grateful if you would send it immediately to enable work on the recorder to be put in hand without further delay.

A prompt reply will be appreciated.

Yours sincerely

---

### (c) Quotation is received and customer sends remittance

On 25 July a service card headed 'Job Reference WE69376' was received by the customer requesting payment of £60.85 before the service could be carried out. On 28 July the customer sends a cheque for this amount with a covering letter.

---

Dear Mr Jackson

STEREO CASSETTE RECORDER, MODEL NUMBER 660

I am returning your service card WE69376 with a cheque for £60.86 to cover the cost of servicing the above recorder.

This recorder has been with you for over 4 weeks and I am greatly inconvenienced without it. I hope you can arrange for its immediate repair and that it can be returned within the next few days.

Yours sincerely

---

### (d) Customer receives a further payment request

No acknowledgement of receipt of the customer's cheque was received. On 14 August the customer received a printed note stating that work on the recorder had been completed and requesting payment of the amount due.

### (e) Customer writes to the Manager

Delay in returning the recorder and a request for payment of an amount already paid understandably angered the customer. The immediate reaction was to write a strong letter to the Manager. Instead the result was in terms more likely to gain co-operation in rectifying what was probably quite an innocent mistake.

---

Dear Mrs Stansfield

STEREO CASSETTE RECORDER, MODEL NUMBER 660

I am sorry to have to write to you personally regarding delay in the return of the above recorder sent in for repair on 28 June. The facts are as follows:

1   On 28 June I spoke to your Mr Keith Jackson regarding my faulty tape recorder. As a result I sent my letter dated 28 June with the recorder requesting a quotation.

2   On 5 July your Service Department acknowledged receipt of the recorder and my letter.

3   Not having received the quotation I sent a reminder on 18 July, and on 25 July I received a service card (reference WE69376) quoting a charge of £60.85 for servicing.

4   This card was returned on 28 July with my cheque for that amount and my letter asking for the service to be carried out and the recorder returned as a matter of urgency.

---

I heard nothing more until this morning when I was surprised to receive a printed form stating that the work had been completed and asking for payment of the amount due.

I am sure you will appreciate my concern at the length of time involved in this matter. As it is 2 full months since I sent the recorder to you, I hope you will arrange to return it immediately.

Yours faithfully

## (f) Manager's apology

In the reply the Manager admits fault. Sincerity in this matter will help to restore customer confidence and goodwill.

Dear Mr Richards

STEREO CASSETTE RECORDER, MODEL NUMBER 660

I was very sorry to learn from your letter of 14 August of the problems experienced in the repair and return of your tape recorder.

I have investigated this matter personally, and regret that the delay is due to the absence through illness of the assistant who was dealing with your order initially.

Please accept my apologies for the inconvenience which has been caused. The recorder has been sent to you today by express parcel post, and I hope it will reach you quickly and in good condition.

Please do not hesitate to contact me if I can be of further assistance.

Yours sincerely

## (g) Customer thanks Manager

The correspondence could have ended with the Manager's letter, but the customer rightly felt that it would be a matter of courtesy to thank the manager for such prompt intervention.

Dear Mrs Stansfield

STEREO CASSETTE RECORDER, MODEL NUMBER 660

Thank you for your letter of 3 September and for dealing so promptly with this matter. I can appreciate the circumstances which led to the delay which was experienced.

My tape recorder has been delivered and appears to be in good working order.

Yours sincerely

# CANCELLING ORDERS

A buyer is legally entitled to cancel his order at any time before it has been accepted by the supplier, or if:

- the goods delivered are of the wrong type or quality (if they do not conform to sample).
- the goods are not delivered by the stated time (or within a reasonable time if no delivery date has been fixed).
- more or less than the quantity ordered is delivered.
- the goods arrive damaged (but only where transportation is the supplier's responsibility).

Unless the contract provides otherwise, it is the buyer's legal duty to collect and transport the goods from the supplier's premises. This would be so where the goods are sold *loco*, ex works or similar terms. The buyer is then liable for any loss or damage occurring during transport. Similarly under an fob or a cif contract, the customer is liable from the time the goods are loaded onto the ship.

## 10.12 Buyer seeks to cancel order due to adequate stocks

### (a) Customer's letter

> Dear Sirs
>
> On 2 March I ordered 100 tennis rackets to be delivered at the end of this month.
>
> Persistent bad weather has seriously affected sales so I find that my present stock will probably satisfy demand in the present season. I am therefore writing to ask you to cancel part of my order and to deliver only 50 of these rackets instead of the 100 ordered.
>
> I am sorry to make this request so late but hope that you will be able to agree to it in view of our long-standing business association. Should sales improve I will get in touch with you again and take a further delivery.
>
> Yours faithfully

### (b) Supplier agrees to cancel order

A supplier will often agree to cancel or modify the buyer's order for a number of reasons:

- A wish to oblige a good customer.
- The loss of profit involved may be minimal.
- It helps to create customer good will.
- There may be a ready market for the goods elsewhere.

- The customer's financial position may be doubtful.
- Legal proceedings are costly.

---

Dear

We have received your letter of 2 May asking us to cancel part of the order you placed on 2 March for tennis rackets.

We are naturally disappointed that there should be any need for this request. However we always like to oblige our regular customers and in the circumstances are prepared to reduce the number of rackets from 100 to 50 as requested.

We do hope that your sales will improve sufficiently to enable you to take up the balance of your order at a later date.

In this respect we hope to hear from you again soon.

Yours sincerely

---

**(c) Supplier refuses to cancel order**

The supplier will sometimes refuse to cancel an order for various reasons:

- A wish to retain a sale.
- The manufacture of goods that cannot easily be sold elsewhere may have begun.
- A keen entrepreneur may be unwilling to forgo their legal rights.

The letter refusing a request for cancellation must be worded carefully and considerately if it is not to cause offence and drive a customer away for good. Such a letter must show that you understand the buyer's problems, and tactfully explain the difficulties that cancellation would create for the supplier. The reasons given must be convincing, otherwise the supplier is liable to lose the customer's goodwill.

---

Dear

We have received your letter of 2 May asking us to cancel part of your order of 2 March for tennis rackets.

We are sorry you find it necessary to make this request especially at this late stage. To be able to meet our customers' needs promptly we have to place our orders with manufacturers well in advance of the season. In estimating quantities we rely very largely upon the orders we have received.

We do not like to refuse requests of any kind from regular customers. However, on this occasion we have no choice but to do so. All orders, including your own, have already been made up and are awaiting delivery.

I hope you will understand why we must hold you to your order. If we had received your request earlier we should have been glad to help you.

Yours sincerely

---

## 10.13 Cancellation of order through delay in delivery

Dear

In our order number 8546 dated 18 August we stressed the importance of delivery by 4 October at the very latest.

We have already written to you twice reminding you of the importance of prompt delivery. However as you have failed to make delivery on time we are left with no choice but to cancel the order.

We take this action with regret but as the goods were required for shipment abroad, and as the boat by which they were to be sent sails tomorrow, we have no means of getting them to our client in time for the exhibition for which they were required.

We have informed our client of the action we have taken and should be glad if you would acknowledge the cancellation.

Yours sincerely

## CHECKLIST

**Making a complaint**

- ☐ Act promptly
- ☐ Show restraint in your wording – the supplier may have a good defence
- ☐ State the facts briefly, exactly and clearly
- ☐ Avoid rudeness
- ☐ Suggest desired results/action

**Dealing with a complaint**

- ☐ Investigate the complaint promptly
- ☐ If unreasonable: be firm but polite and try not to offend
- ☐ If you are at fault: express regret and admit it
- ☐ Explain how the matter will be put right
- ☐ Never blame staff
- ☐ Reassure the customer of future good service

## USEFUL EXPRESSIONS

### Letters of complaint

#### Openings

1 The goods we ordered from you on ... have not yet been delivered.

2 Delivery of the goods ordered on ... is now considerably overdue.

3 We regret having to report that we have not yet received the goods ordered on ...

4 We regret to report that one of the cases of your consignment was badly damaged when delivered on ...

5 When we examined the goods despatched by you on ... we found that ...

6 We have received a number of complaints from several customers regarding the ... supplied by you on ...

#### Closes

1 Please look into this matter at once and let us know the reason for this delay.

2 We hope to hear from you soon that the goods will be sent immediately.

3 We feel there must be some explanation for this delay and await your prompt reply.

4 We hope to learn that you are prepared to make some allowance in these circumstances.

### Replies to complaints

#### Openings

1 We are concerned to learn from your letter of ... that the goods sent under your order number ... did not reach you until ...

2 We are sorry that you have experienced delays in the delivery of...

3 We note with regret that you are not satisfied with the goods supplied to your order of ...

4 Thank you for your letter of ... which has given us the opportunity to rectify a most unfortunate mistake.

5 We wish to apologise for the unfortunate mistake pointed out in your letter of ...

#### Closes

1 We assure you that we are doing all we can to speed delivery and offer our apologies for the inconvenience this delay is causing you.

2 We hope you will be satisfied with the arrangements we have made.

3 We trust these arrangements will be satisfactory and look forward to receiving your future orders.

4 We regret the inconvenience which has been caused in this matter.

5 We apologise once again for the unfortunate mistake and can assure you that a similar incident will not occur again.

# Credit and status enquiries

## REASONS FOR CREDIT

The main reason for buying on credit is for convenience. Basically it allows us to 'buy now, pay later'.

1 Credit enables a retailer to hold stocks and to pay for them out of the proceeds of later sales. This increases the working capital and thus helps to finance the business.

2 Credit enables the buying public to enjoy the use of goods before they have saved the money needed to buy them.

3 Credit avoids the inconvenience of separate payments each time a purchase is made.

The main reason for selling on credit is to increase profits. Credit sales not only attract new customers but also keep old customers, since people who run accounts tend to shop at the place where the account is kept, whereas cash customers are free to shop anywhere.

## DISADVANTAGES OF CREDIT

There are a number of disadvantages in dealing on credit both for the supplier and for the customer:

1 It increases the cost of doing business since it involves extra work in keeping records and collecting payments.

2 It exposes the supplier to the risk of bad debts.

3 The buyer pays more for the goods since the supplier must raise prices to cover the higher costs.

## REQUESTS FOR CREDIT

A buyer who makes regular purchases from the same supplier will usually wish to avoid the inconvenience of paying for each transaction separately, and will ask for '*open account*'[1] terms under which purchases will be paid for monthly or quarterly or at some other agreed period. In other words the goods are to be supplied on credit.

---

[1] **open account** credit terms with periodic settlements

## 11.1 Customer requests open-account terms

### (a) Request

Dear

We have been well satisfied with your handling of our past orders and as our business is growing expect to place even larger orders with you in the future.

As our dealings have extended over a period of nearly 2 years, we should be glad if you would grant us open-account facilities with, say, quarterly settlements. This arrangement would save us the inconvenience of making separate payments on invoice.[2]

Banker's and trade references can be provided on request.

We hope to receive your favourable reply soon.

Yours sincerely

### (b) Reply

Dear

Thank you for your letter of 18 November requesting the transfer of your business from payment on invoice to open-account terms.

As our business relations with you over the past 2 years have been entirely satisfactory, we are quite willing to make the transfer, based on a 90-day settlement period. In your case it will not be necessary to supply references.

We are pleased that you have been satisfied with our past service and that expansion of your business is likely to lead to increased orders. You may rely upon our continued efforts to give you the same high standard of service as in the past.

Yours sincerely

## 11.2 Customer requests extension of credit

### (a) Cash flow problem

Dear

We regret you have had to remind us that we have not settled your account due for payment on 30 October.

We had intended to settle this account before now, but because of the present depressed state of business our own customers have not been meeting their obligations as promptly as usual. This has adversely affected[3] our cash flow.

Investment income due in less than a month's time will enable us to clear your account by the end of next month. We should therefore be grateful if you would accept the enclosed cheque for £200 as a payment on account.[4] The balance will be cleared as soon as possible.

Yours sincerely

---

[2] **payments on invoice** payment due on presentation of invoice
[3] **adversely affected** made worse
[4] **payment on account** part payment

### (b) Lending restrictions and bad trade

Dear

STATEMENT OF ACCOUNT FOR AUGUST 19—

We have just received your letter of 8 October requesting settlement of our outstanding balance of £1686.00.

We are sorry not to have been able to clear this balance with our usual promptness but the present depressed state of business and the current restrictions on bank lending have created difficulties for us. These difficulties are purely temporary as payments from customers are due to us early in the New Year on a number of recently completed contracts.

Our <u>resources</u>[5] are quite sufficient to meet all our obligations, but as you will appreciate we have no wish to <u>realise on our assets</u>[6] at the moment. We should therefore be grateful if you would grant us a 3 month extension of credit, when we will be able to settle your account in full.

Yours sincerely

##  Customer requests credit extension due to bankruptcy

### (a) Letter to supplier

Dear

*Introduction gives background details*
We have received and checked your statement for the quarter ended 30 September and agree with the balance of £785.72 shown to be due.

*History of prompt payment is explained and details of current situation mentioned*
Until now we have had no difficulty in meeting our commitments and have always settled our accounts with you promptly. We could have done so at this time but for the <u>bankruptcy</u>[7] of an important customer whose affairs are not likely to be settled for some time.

*Tactful request to defer payment*
We should be most grateful if you would allow us to defer payment of your present account to the end of next month. This would enable us to meet a temporarily difficult situation forced upon us by events that could not be foreseen.

*Final assurance of early settlement*
During the next few weeks we will be receiving payments under a number of large contracts. If you grant our request we shall have no difficulty in settling with you in full in due course.

If you wish to discuss this please do not hesitate to contact me.

Yours sincerely

---

[5] **resources** financial position
[6] **realise on our assets** sell assets in order to raise cash
[7] **bankruptcy** inability to pay one's debts

## (b) Request granted

Refer to customer's letter and request

State reason for agreeing to extension

Give a final date for full settlement

> Dear
>
> Thank you for your letter of 10 October requesting an extension of time for payment of the amount due on our 30 September statement.
>
> In view of the promptness with which you have always settled with us in the past, we are willing to grant this extension in these special circumstances.
>
> Please let us have your cheque in full settlement by 30 November.
>
> Yours sincerely

## (c) Request refused

Refer to customer's letter and request

Tactful wording is necessary when a request is refused

Explain regret at requesting immediate payment

> Dear
>
> I am sorry to learn from your letter of 10 October of the difficulty in which the bankruptcy of an important customer has placed you.
>
> I should like to say at once that we fully understand your wish for an extension of time and would like to be able to help you. Unfortunately this is impossible because of commitments which we must meet by the end of this month.
>
> Your request is not at all unreasonable and if it had been possible we would have been pleased to grant it. In the circumstances, however, we must ask you to settle with us on the terms of payment originally agreed.
>
> Yours sincerely

# BUSINESS REFERENCES

When goods are sold for cash there is no need for the supplier to enquire into the financial standing of the buyer. Where they are sold on credit, however, the ability to pay will be important.

For credit to be allowed the supplier will want to know what the buyer's reputation is like, the extent of their business, and in particular whether accounts are paid promptly. It is on this information that the supplier will decide whether to allow credit and, if so, how much.

This information can be obtained from:

- trade references supplied by the customer
- the customer's banker
- various trade associations
- credit enquiry agencies

When a customer places an order with a new supplier it is customary to supply trade references, that is the names of persons or firms to whom the supplier may refer for information. Alternatively or additionally the customer may give the name and address of the banker. References of this kind, supplied as they are by customers themselves, must be accepted with caution since naturally only those who are likely to report favourably will be named as referees. Even a bank reference can be misleading – a customer may have a satisfactory banking account and yet have business dealings which would not bear looking into.

## 11.4 Supplier requests references

When a new customer places an order but fails to provide references the supplier will naturally want some evidence of the customer's creditworthiness, especially if the order is a large one. The supplier's letter asking for references must avoid any suggestion that the customer is not to be trusted.

---

Dear

We were pleased to receive your first order with us dated 19 May.

When opening new accounts it is our practice to ask customers for trade references. Please be good enough to send us the names and addresses of two other suppliers with whom you have dealings.

We hope to receive this information by return, and meanwhile your order has been put in hand for despatch immediately we hear further from you.

Yours sincerely

---

## 11.5 Supplier asks for completion of credit application form

### (a) Letter from supplier

---

Dear

Thank you for your order number 526 of 15 June for polyester bedspreads and pillow cases.

As your name does not appear on our books and as we should like you to take advantage of our usual credit terms, we enclose our usual credit application form for your completion and return as soon as possible.

We should be able to deliver your present order in about 2 weeks, and look forward to receiving your further orders.

We hope that this first transaction will mark the beginning of a pleasant business connection.

Yours sincerely

---

**(b) Customer returns completed credit application form**

> Dear
>
> Thank you for your letter of 18 June. As we fully expect to place further orders, we should obviously like to take advantage of your offer of credit facilities.
>
> We quite understand the need for references and have completed your credit application form giving the relevant information. This is enclosed.
>
> We look forward to receiving delivery of our first order by the end of this month and to our future business dealings with you.
>
> Yours sincerely

## 11.6 Customer supplies trade references

> Dear Sirs
>
> Thank you for the catalogue and price list received earlier this month.
>
> We have pleasure in sending you our first order, number ST6868, for 6 Olivetti portable electronic typewriters, elite type, at your list price of £255 less 25% on your usual monthly terms.
>
> These machines are needed for early delivery to customers and as we understand you have the machines in stock we should be glad if you would arrange for them to reach us by the end of next week. We hope this will leave enough time for you to take up references with the following firms with which we have had dealings over many years:
>
> B Kisby & Co Ltd, 28–30 Lythan Square, Liverpool
> The Atlas Manufacturing Co Ltd, Century House, Bristol
>
> We look forward to doing further business with you in the future.
>
> Yours faithfully

## 11.7 Customer supplies a banker's reference

> Dear Sirs
>
> Our cheque for £2513 is enclosed in full settlement of your invoice number 826 for the stereo tape recorders supplied earlier this month.
>
> My directors have good reason to believe that these particular products will be a popular selling line in this part of the country. As we expect to place further orders with you from time to time, we should be glad if you would arrange to provide open-account facilities on a quarterly basis.
>
> For information concerning our credit standing[8] we refer you to Barclays Bank Ltd, 25–27 The Arcade, Southampton.
>
> Yours faithfully

---

[8] **credit standing** financial position

## STATUS ENQUIRIES

Letters taking up trade references are written in formal polite terms. They usually conform to the following 4 point plan:

- Give background information about the customer's situation
- Request information about the prospective customer's *standing*[9] and an opinion on the wisdom of granting credit within a stated limit
- Give an assurance that the information will be treated confidentially
- Enclose a stamped addressed envelope or an international postal reply coupon if the correspondent lives abroad

Some large firms make their enquiries on a specially printed form containing the questions they would like answering. Use of such forms makes it easier for the companies approached, and helps to ensure prompt replies.

When the supplier receives the information requested, it is courteous to send a suitable letter of acknowledgement and thanks.

Letters taking up references should be addressed to a senior official and marked 'Confidential'.

### 11.8 Supplier takes up trade references

(a) Example 1

---

Dear Sirs

Watson & Jones of Newcastle wish to open an account with us and have given your name as a reference.

We should be grateful for your view about the firm's general standing and your opinion on whether they are likely to be reliable for credit up to £1,000 and to settle their accounts promptly.

Any information provided will of course be treated in strict confidence.

We enclose a stamped, addressed envelope for your reply.

Yours faithfully

---

[9] **standing** status, reputation

**(b) Example 2**

Dear Sirs

We have received a request from Shamlan & Shamlan & Co of Bahrain for supplies of our products on open-account terms. They state that they have regularly traded with you over the past 2 years and have given your name as a reference.

We should be obliged if you would tell us in confidence whether you have found this company to be thoroughly reliable in their dealings with you and prompt in settling their accounts.

We understand their requirements with us may amount to approximately £2,000 a quarter, and should be glad to know if you feel they will be able to meet commitments of this size. Any other information you can provide would be very welcome.

Your reply, for which we enclose an international postal reply coupon, will of course be treated in strict confidence.

Yours faithfully

## 11.9 Supplier requests his banker to take up bank reference

In view of the highly confidential relationship between bankers and their customers, a banker will not normally reply direct to private enquiries about the standing of a client. This information is usually given willingly to fellow bankers. When taking up a bank reference, the supplier must do so through their own banker.

Dear Sir/Madam

The Colston Engineering Co Ltd in Oyo have asked for a standing credit of £5,000 but as our knowledge of this company is limited to a few months trading on a cash-on-invoice basis, we should like some information about their financial standing before dealing with their request.

The only reference they give us is that of their bankers – the National Bank of Nigeria, Ibadan. We shall be most grateful for any information you can let us have.

Yours faithfully

### 11.10 Supplier refers to credit enquiry agency

A supplier who wants an independent reference concerning a customer's business standing may refer either to a trade association or to one of the numerous credit enquiry agencies. These agencies make it their business to supply information on the financial standing of both trading firms and professional and private individuals. They have a remarkable store of information which is kept up-to-date from a variety of sources including their own local agents. If the information requested is not immediately available from their records, they will set up enquiries and can usually supply it within a few days.

---

Dear Sirs

We have been asked by A Griffiths & Co, Cardiff to supply goods to the value of £1,750 on open-account terms against their first order.

We have no information about this company but as there are prospects of further large orders from them, we should like to meet the present order on the terms requested if it is safe to do so.

Please let us have a report on the reputation and financial standing of the company and in particular your advice on whether it would be advisable to grant credit for this first order. Your advice on the maximum amount for which it would be safe to grant credit on a quarterly account would also be appreciated.

Yours faithfully

---

## REPLIES TO STATUS ENQUIRIES

Where a company's credit has been found to be satisfactory, the reply to the enquiry presents no problem. However, if the firm's credit is uncertain, the reply calls for the utmost care. It is usual to phrase such replies in a manner that leaves the enquirer to 'read between the lines', ie to gather for themselves the true meaning, rather than bluntly state disparaging facts.

Replies to letters taking up references should be marked 'Confidential' and follow the following 4 point plan:

- Acknowledge the request and give background information.
- Statement of the facts and an honest expression of opinion.
- Hope that the information supplied will be useful.
- Tactfully remind that the information is confidential and that no responsibility for it can be accepted.

## 11.11 Trader's replies to credit information enquiry

### (a) Favourable reply to 11.8(a)

Dear

Thank you for your letter of 25 May.

We are pleased to inform you that this company is a small but well-known and highly respectable firm which has been established in this town for more than 25 years.

We have been doing business with this company for over 7 years on quarterly-account terms. Although they have not usually taken advantage of cash discounts they have always paid their account promptly on the net dates. The credit we have allowed this company has at times been well over the £5,000 you mention.

We hope this information will be helpful and that it will be treated as confidential.

Yours

### (b) Discouraging reply to 11.8(b)

Dear

The company mentioned in your letter of 25 May has placed regular orders with us for several years. We believe the company to be trustworthy and reliable, but we have to say that they have not always settled their accounts by the due date.

Their account with us is on quarterly settlement terms but we have never allowed it to reach the sum mentioned in your letter. This to us seems to be a case in which caution is necessary.

We are glad to be of help but ask you to ensure that the information provided is treated as strictly confidential.

Yours

### 11.12 Banker's replies to credit information enquiry

**(a) Favourable reply to 11.9**

> Dear
>
> We have received from the National Bank of Nigeria the information requested in your letter of 18 September.
>
> The company you mention is a private company which was founded 15 years ago and is run as a family concern by three brothers. It enjoys a good reputation. Our information shows that the company punctually meets its commitments and a credit in the sum you mention would seem to be safe.
>
> This information is strictly confidential and is given without any responsibility on our part.
>
> Yours sincerely

**(b) Unfavourable reply to 11.9**

> Dear
>
> We have received information from the National Bank of Nigeria concerning the company mentioned in your letter of 18 September.
>
> This is a private company run as a family concern and operating on a small scale.
>
> More detailed information we have received suggests that this is a case in which we would advise caution. You will of course treat this advice as strictly confidential.
>
> Yours sincerely

### 11.13 Agency's replies to credit information enquiry

**(a) Favourable reply to 11.10**

> Dear
>
> *Introduction acknowledges letter and gives initial details* — Thank you for your letter of 10 February.
>
> We have completed our enquiries relating to A Griffiths & Co and are pleased to report favourably.
>
> *Details regarding the firm's standing are given with a personal opinion* — This is a well-founded and highly reputable firm. There are four partners and their capital is estimated to be at least £100,000. They do an excellent trade and are regarded as one of the safest accounts in Cardiff.
>
> *Recommendation about credit which could be allowed* — From the information we have obtained we believe that you need not hesitate to allow the initial credit of £1,750 requested. On a quarterly account you could safely allow at least £5,000.
>
> Yours sincerely

**(b) Unfavourable reply to 11.10**

Dear

Introduction — acknowledges letter and advises caution

We have completed our enquiries concerning A Griffiths & Co following your letter of 10 February. We regret that we must advise caution in their request for credit.

Details are given regarding knowledge of the firm in question

About a year ago an action was brought against this company by one of its suppliers for recovery of sums due, though payment was later recovered in full.

The facts as known are stated

Our enquiries reveal nothing to suggest that the firm is not straightforward. On the contrary the firm's difficulties would seem to be due to bad management and in particular to <u>overtrading</u>.[10] Consequently most of the firm's suppliers either give only very short credit for limited sums or make deliveries on a cash basis.

A reminder that the information should be kept confidential

This information is of course supplied in the strictest confidence.

Yours sincerely

[10] **overtrading** trading beyond one's means

## USEFUL EXPRESSIONS

### Suppliers' requests for references

**Openings**

1 Thank you for your letter of ... Subject to satisfactory references we shall be glad to provide the open account facilities requested.

2 We were pleased to receive your order dated ... If you will kindly supply the usual trade references, we will be glad to consider open-account terms.

**Closes**

1 We will be in touch with you as soon as references are received.

2 It is our usual practice to request references from new customers, and we hope to receive these soon.

### Customers supply references

**Openings**

1 Thank you for your letter of ... in reply to our request for open-account terms.

2 We have completed and return your credit application form.

**Closes**

1 The following firms will be pleased to answer your enquiries ...

2 For the information required please refer to our bankers, who are ...

### Suppliers take up references

**Openings**

1 ... of ... has supplied your name as a reference in connection with his (her, their) application for open-account terms.

2 We have received a large order from ... and should be grateful for any information you can provide regarding their reliability.

3 We should be grateful if you would obtain reliable information for us concerning ...

**Closes**

1 Any information you can provide will be appreciated.

2 Any information provided will be treated in strictest confidence.

3 Please accept our thanks in advance for any help you can give us.

## Replies to references taken up

### Openings

1 We welcome the opportunity to report favourably on ...

2 In reply to your letter of ... we can thoroughly recommend the firm you mention.

3 The firm mentioned in your letter of ... is not well known to us.

### Closes

1 This information is given on the clear understanding that it will be treated confidentially.

2 We would not hesitate granting this company credit up to £...

3 This information is given to you in confidence and without any responsibility on our part.

# A typical business transaction
## (correspondence and documents)

Letters of the kind considered in this unit are handled in business every day. This chapter illustrates their use in a typical transaction in the home trade.

G Wood & Sons have recently opened an electrical goods store in Bristol and place an order with Electrical Supplies Ltd, Birmingham, for the supply of goods on credit. The transaction opens with a request by G Wood & Sons for information regarding prices and terms for credit.

### 12.1 Request for quotation

---

**G WOOD & SONS**
36 Castle Street
Bristol BSl 2BQ
Telephone 0117 9354967

GW/ST

15 November 19—
Mr Henry Thomas
Electrical Supplies Ltd
29–31 Broad Street
Birmingham
Bl 2HE

Dear Mr Thomas

We have recently opened an electrical goods store at the above address and have received a number of enquiries for the following domestic appliances of which at present we do not hold stocks:

Swanson Electric Kettles, 2 litre
Cosiwarm Electric Blankets, single-bed size
Regency Electric Toasters
Marlborough Kitchen Wall Clocks

When I phoned you this morning you informed me that all these items are available in stock for immediate delivery.

Please let me have your prices and terms for payment 2 months from date of invoicing. If prices and terms are satisfactory, we would place with you a first order for 10 of each of these items.

The matter is of some urgency and I would appreciate an early reply.

Yours faithfully

GORDON WOOD
Manager

---

**12.2** **Supplier's quotation**

---

ELECTRICAL SUPPLIES LTD
29–31 Broad Street
Birmingham B1 2HE
Tel: 0121–542 6614

HT/JH

17 November 19—
Mr Gordon Wood
Messrs G Wood & Sons
36 Castle Street
Bristol
BS1 2BQ

Dear Mr Wood

QUOTATION NUMBER E542

Thank you for your enquiry of 15 November. I am pleased to quote as follows:

| | £ |
|---|---|
| Swanson Electric Kettles, 2 litre | 25.00 each |
| Cosiwarm Electric Blankets, single-bed size | 24.50 each |
| Regency Electric Toasters | 25.50 each |
| Marlborough Kitchen Wall Clocks | 27.50 each |

The above are current catalogue prices from which we would allow you a trade discount of 33⅓%. Prices include packing and delivery to your premises.

It is our usual practice to ask all new customers for trade references. Please let us have the names and addresses of two suppliers with whom you have had regular dealings. Subject to satisfactory replies, we shall be glad to supply the goods and to allow you the 2 months credit requested.

As there may be other items in which you are interested, I enclose copies of our current catalogue and price list.

I look forward to the opportunity of doing business with you.

Yours sincerely

HENRY THOMAS
Sales Manager

Enc

---

### 12.3 Request for permission to quote company as reference

A buyer should obtain permission from the suppliers whose names are to be submitted as references. Consent may be obtained verbally if there is urgency, but otherwise the buyer should make this request in writing. In this case, a letter was sent to J Williamson & Co, Southey House, Coventry, CVl 5RU, as well as the addressee of the following letter.

---

**G WOOD & SONS**
36 Castle Street
Bristol BS1 2BQ
Telephone 0117 954967

GW/ST

19 November 19—

Mr Robert Johnson
Johnson Traders Ltd
The Hayes
Cardiff
CF1 IJW

Dear Robert

I wish to place an order with Electrical Supplies Ltd, Birmingham, with facilities on credit. As this will be is a first order they have asked me to supply trade references.

I have been a regular customer of yours for the past 4 years and should be grateful if you would allow me to submit your company's name as one of my references.

I shall very much appreciate your consent to stand as referee and hope to hear from you soon.

GORDON WOOD
Manager

---

**12.4** **Permission granted**

JOHNSON TRADERS LTD
The Hayes
Cardiff CFI IJW
Telephone 01222 572382

RH/KI

22 November 19—

Mr Gordon Wood
G Wood & Sons
36 Castle Street
Bristol
BS1 2BQ

Dear Mr Wood

Thank you for your letter of 19 November requesting permission to use our name as a reference in your transaction with Electrical Supplies Ltd.

During the time we have done business together you have been a very reliable customer. If your suppliers decide to approach us for a reference we shall be very happy to support your request for credit facilities.

Yours sincerely

ROBERT JOHNSON
Financial Controller

## 12.5 Order

### (a) Covering letter

G WOOD & SONS
36 Castle Street
Bristol BS1 2BQ
Telephone 0117 954967

GW/ST

24 November 19—

Mr Henry Thomas
Electrical Supplies Ltd
29–31 Broad Street
Birmingham
B1 2HE

Dear Mr Thomas

ORDER NUMBER 3241

Thank you for your letter of 17 November quoting for domestic appliances and enclosing copies of your current catalogue and price list.

We have had regular dealings with the following suppliers for the past 4 or 5 years. They will be happy to provide the necessary references.

Johnson Traders Ltd, The Hayes, Cardiff CF1 IJW
J Williamson & Co, Southey House, Coventry CV1 5RU

Our order number 3241 is enclosed for the goods mentioned in our original enquiry. They are urgently needed and as they are available from stock we hope you will arrange prompt delivery.

I appreciate your agreement to allow 2 months credit on receipt of satisfactory references.

Yours sincerely

GORDON WOOD
Manager

Enc

**(b) Order form**

G WOOD & SONS
36 Castle Street
Bristol BS1 2BQ
Telephone 0117 954967

ORDER NO 3241                                  Date 24 November 19—

Electrical Supplies Ltd
29–31 Broad Street
BIRMINGHAM
B1 2HE

Please supply

| Quantity | Item(s) | Price |
|---|---|---|
| | | £ |
| 10 | Swanson Electric Kettles (2 litre) | 25.00 each |
| 10 | Cosiwarm Electric Blankets (single-bed size) | 24.50 each |
| 10 | Regency Electric Toasters | 25.50 each |
| 10 | Marlborough Kitchen Wall Clocks | 27.50 each |

Terms                     33⅓% trade discount

_____
for G Wood & Sons

### 12.6 Supplier's acknowledgement

It is good business practice to acknowledge and thank buyers particularly for a first order and trade reference information. The supplier will then take up the references and put the order in hand when favourable replies are received.

---

ELECTRICAL SUPPLIES LTD
29–31 Broad Street
Birmingham B1 2HE
Telephone 0121–542–6614

HT/JH

1 December 19—

Mr G Wood
G Wood & Sons
36 Castle Street
Bristol
BS1 2BQ

Dear Mr Wood

YOUR ORDER NUMBER 3241

Thank you for your letter of 24 November. We were very pleased to receive your order and confirm that the goods will be supplied at the prices and on the terms stated.

Your order has been passed to our warehouse for immediate despatch of the goods from stock. We hope you will be pleased with them.

Please do not hesitate to contact me if I can be of any further help.

Yours sincerely


HENRY THOMAS
Sales Manager

---

## 12.7 Advice note

Documents dealing with the despatch and delivery of goods include packing notes, advice of despatch notes, consignment notes and delivery notes. These documents are really copies of the invoice and are often prepared in sets, with the use of NCR (no carbon required) paper, at the same time as the invoice. The copy which acts as the advice note will not contain information regarding pricing.

The advice or despatch note informs the buyer that the goods are on the way and enables a check to be made when they arrive. Very often, however, an advice note is replaced either by an invoice sent on or before the day the goods are despatched or sometimes by a letter notifying despatch.

For small items sent by post a packing note, which is simply a copy of the advice note, would be the only document used. Some suppliers, especially those using their own transport, dispense with the advice note and instead use either a packing note or a delivery note.

## 12.8 Consignment note

When goods are sent by rail the supplier is required to complete a consignment note which represents the contract of carriage with the railway. It gives particulars of the quantity, weight, type and destination of the goods and states whether they are being sent carriage paid (ie paid by the sender) or carriage forward (ie paid by the buyer). In most cases the printed forms supplied by the railway are used but a trader will sometimes prefer to use their own.

The completed consignment note is handed to the carrier when the goods are collected and it travels with them. When the goods are delivered to the buyer the note must be signed as proof of delivery.

## 12.9 Delivery note

Sometimes two copies of the delivery note are prepared, one to be retained by the buyer, the other to be given back to the carrier signed as evidence that the goods have been delivered. Alternatively the carrier may ask the buyer to sign a Delivery Book or a Delivery Sheet recording the calls a carrier has made.

Where it is not possible for the buyer to inspect the goods before signing for them, the signature should be qualified with some such comment as 'not examined' or 'goods unexamined' as a precaution.

## 12.10 Invoice

Invoice practice varies. Sometimes the invoice is enclosed with the goods and sometimes it is sent separately, either in advance of the goods (in which case it also serves as an advice note) or after the goods. The invoice will be sent separately where the goods are baled or supplied loose or in bulk.

### (a) Covering letter

It is not always necessary to send a covering letter with an invoice, but if a letter is sent it need only be very short and formal.

---

**ELECTRICAL SUPPLIES LTD**
29–31 Broad Street
Birmingham B1 2HE
Telephone 0121–542–6614

HT/JH

3 December 19—

G Wood & Sons
36 Castle Street
Bristol
BS1 2BQ

Dear Sirs

YOUR ORDER NUMBER 3241

We enclose our invoice number 6740 for the domestic electrical appliances supplied to your order dated 24 November.

The goods have been packed in three cases, numbers 78, 79 and 80, and sent to you today by rail, carriage paid. We hope they will reach you promptly and in good condition.

If you settle the account within 2 months we will allow you to deduct from the amount due a special cash discount of 1½%.

Yours faithfully



MICHELLE SMITH (Mrs)
Credit Control Manager

Enc

---

### (b) Invoice

When G Wood & Sons receive the invoice they will check it with the packing note or delivery note received with the goods to ensure all goods invoiced have been received. They will check the invoice for trade discounts and arithmetical accuracy before recording it in their books of account.

As a rule the invoice is not used as a demand for payment, but as a record of the transaction and statement of the indebtedness to which it gives rise. The supplier will then later send a statement of account to the buyer.

ELECTRICAL SUPPLIES LTD
29–31 Broad Street
Birmingham B1 2HE
Telephone 0121–542–6614

INVOICE

G Wood & Sons
36 Castle Street
BRISTOL
BS1 2BQ

Date 3 December 19—

Your order no 3241

Invoice No 6740

r reference purposes
the invoice is given a
al number. The order
umber is also quoted.

| Quantity | Item(s) | Unit Price | Total Price |
|---|---|---|---|
| | | £ | £ |
| 10 | Swanson Electric Kettles (2 litre) | 25.00 | 250.00 |
| 10 | Cosiwarm Electric Blankets (single-bed size) | 24.50 | 245.00 |
| 10 | Regency Electric Toasters | 25.50 | 255.00 |
| 10 | Marlborough Kitchen Wall Clocks | 27.50 | 275.00 |
| | | | 1025.00 |
| | Less 33⅓% trade discount | | 341.66 |
| | | | 683.34 |
| | VAT @ 17.5% | | 119.58 |
| | | | 802.92 |
| | 3 packing cases (returnable) | | 15.00 |
| | | | 817.92 |
| | Terms: 1½% two months | | |

e agreed 33⅓% trade
count has been given

he terms of payment
ndicate an allowable
cash discount for
payment within 2
months from date of
voice. This discount is
ducted at the time of
payment.

& O E' means 'errors
omissions excepted'.
reserves the right for
e seller to correct any
error in or omissions
from the invoice.

E & OE

Registered in England No 726549

## 12.11 Debit and credit notes

For the purposes served by these two documents, refer to pages 90–1.

### (a) Buyer requests credit note

In our specimen transaction, G Wood & Sons will return the three packing cases charged on the invoice. They will then write to the suppliers asking for a credit note for the invoiced value of the cases. Depending on their usual practice G Wood & Sons may or may not prepare and send a debit note when making the request.

---

**G WOOD & SONS**
36 Castle Street, Bristol BS1 2BQ
Telephone 0117 954967

GW/ST

10 December 19—

Mrs Michelle Smith
Credit Control Manager
Electrical Supplies Ltd
29–31 Broad Street
Birmingham
B1 2HE

Dear Mrs Smith

INVOICE NUMBER 6740

We have today returned to you by rail the three packing cases charged on this invoice at a cost of £15.00.

We enclose a debit note for this amount and shall be glad to receive your credit note by return.

All the goods supplied and invoiced reached us in good condition. Thank you for the promptness with which you dealt with our first order.

Yours sincerely


GORDON WOOD
Manager

Enc

---

```
                    G WOOD & SONS
                    36 Castle Street
                    Bristol BSI 2BQ
                 Telephone 0117 954967

                      DEBIT NOTE

Electrical Supplies Ltd                Date 10 December 19—
29–31 Broad Street
BIRMINGHAM
B1 2HE                                 Debit Note No D 841
```

| Date | Details | Total |
|------|---------|-------|
|  |  | £ |
| 10.12.— | To  3 packing cases charged on your invoice number 6740 and returned | 15.00 |
|  |  |  |

**Debit Note**

### (b) Seller issues credit note

When Electrical Supplies Ltd receive the debit note they will check return of the cases. They will then prepare the credit note requested and send it to G Wood & Sons, with or without a covering letter. Any letter sent need only be short and formal, but as this is the buyer's first transaction the supplier would be wise to add a short note to encourage future business.

ELECTRICAL SUPPLIES LTD
29–31 Broad Street
Birmingham B1 2HE
Telephone 0121–542–6614

HT/JH

14 December 19—

Mr Gordon Wood
Manager
G Wood & Sons
36 Castle Street
Bristol
BS1 2BQ

Dear Mr Wood

Thank you for your letter of 10 December enclosing debit note number D841.
I confirm receipt of the three packing cases returned. Our credit note number
C672 for the sum of £15.00 is enclosed.

Yours sincerely

MICHELLE SMITH (Mrs)
Credit Control Manager

Enc

---

ELECTRICAL SUPPLIES LTD
29–31 Broad Street
Birmingham BI 2HE
Telephone 0121–524–6614

CREDIT NOTE

G Wood & Sons                                    Date 14 December 19—
36 Castle Street
BRISTOL
BS1 2BQ                                          Credit Note No C 672

| Date | Details | Total |
|------|---------|-------|
|      |         | £ |
| 10.12.— | To  3 packing cases charged on your invoice number 6740 and returned | 15.00 |
|      |         |   |

**Credit note**

## 12.12 Statement of account

Statements of accounts are sent to customers at periodic intervals, normally monthly. As well as serving as a request for payment the statement enables the buyer to compare the account kept by the supplier with that kept in the buyer's own books. Statements are usually sent without a covering letter (see page 94).

---

**ELECTRICAL SUPPLIES LTD**
29–31 Broad Street
Birmingham Bl 2HE
Telephone 0121–524–6614

**STATEMENT**

G Wood & Sons                                             Date 31 January 19—
36 Castle Street
BRISTOL
BS1 2BQ

| Date | Details | Debit | Credit | Balance |
|------|---------|-------|--------|---------|
|      |         | £     | £      | £       |
| 3.12.— | Invoice 6740 | 817.92 |        | 817.92 |
| 14.12.— | Credit note C 672 |        | 15.00 | 802.92 |
|      | (2½% seven days) |        |        |        |

E & OE                                        Registered in England No 726549

---

Statement

### 12.13 Payment

Invoices and statements usually indicate the terms of payment. For example:

*Prompt Cash:*    A somewhat elastic term but generally taken to mean payment within 15 days from date of invoice or statement.

*2½% 30 days:*    This means that the debtor is entitled to deduct 2½% from the amount due if payment is made within 30 days of the invoice or statement, otherwise the full amount becomes payable.

*Net 30 days:*    This means that the debtor must pay in full within 30 days.

Payments in business are usually made by cheque or, if they are numerous, by credit transfer (bank giro). In this transaction the buyer settles the account by sending a cheque to the supplier.

---

**G WOOD & SONS**
36 Castle Street, Bristol B51 2BQ
Telephone 0117 954967

GW/ST

4 February 19—

Mrs Michelle Smith
Credit Control Manager
Electrical Supplies Ltd
29–31 Broad Street
Birmingham
B1 2HE

Dear Mrs Smith

We are in receipt of your statement of account dated 31 January 19—.

From the total amount due on the statement I have deducted the allowable cash discount of 2½% and enclose a cheque for £810.89 in full settlement.

Yours sincerely


GORDON WOOD
Manager

Enc

---

## 12.14 Receipt

A cheque usually supplies all the evidence of payment necessary. Consequently it is not usual practice for formal receipts to be issued. This does not affect the payer's legal right to request a receipt if one is required.

In this transaction evidence of payment could be obtained by the supplier's formal receipt or the buyer's cheque after being paid by the bank.

# Special business documents

# Goodwill
# letters

1
2
3
4
5
6
7
8
9
10
11
12
**13**
14
15
16
17
18
19
20
21
22
23
24
25

One of the most important functions of communications is to create good business relations. Many managers and executives take the opportunity to send goodwill letters on many different occasions such as:

| | | | |
|---|---|---|---|
| apologies | unwelcome news | sympathy | welcome |
| promotion | congratulations | death | special award |
| thanks | condolence | appreciation | wedding |

Every opportunity should be taken to write goodwill letters. They are appreciated by customers and colleagues and are very good for business. For very little cost and effort they not only strengthen existing relationships but they may also create new business opportunities.

Goodwill letters should be written and sent promptly. They should be brief and to the point, always sincere and informal. Handwritten notes will give an added touch of sincerity and intimacy where appropriate.

## GENERAL GOODWILL LETTERS

The following letters are examples of ways in which goodwill can be built into the everyday business letter. The tone of the letters is courteous and friendly, and the added touches of personal interest are certain to make a good impression.

### 13.1 Letter with short personal greeting

A personal touch may sometimes take the form of a short final paragraph conveying a personal greeting.

---

Dear Mr Ellis

I am sorry not to have replied sooner to your letter of 25 October regarding the book <u>English and Commercial Correspondence</u>. My Export Director is in Lebanon and Syria on business; as I am dealing with his work as well as my own I am afraid my correspondence has fallen behind.

Whether this book should be published in hardback or paperback is a decision I must leave to my Editorial Director, Tracie James, to whom I have passed on your letter. No doubt she will be writing to you very soon.

I hope you are keeping well.

With best wishes

Yours sincerely

---

## 13.2 Letter with extended personal greeting

An even more personal note may be introduced in the final paragraph.

---

Dear Mrs Jenner

<u>Importing Made Easy</u>

I have had an opportunity to review the book you sent to me recently.

This book presents a concise and clear account of the new import regulations with good examples of how they are likely to be applied.

More detailed comments are made on my written review which is attached.

I remember you mentioned that you will be spending your summer holiday in the south of France. I hope you have good weather and an enjoyable time.

Yours sincerely

---

## 13.3 Letter explaining delayed reply

A favourable impression is created when a letter is answered on the day it is received. If this is not possible the letter should be acknowledged as soon as possible with an explanation of the delay.

---

Dear Mrs Jones

I am sorry we cannot send you immediately the catalogue and price list requested in your letter of 13 March as we are presently out of stock.

Supplies are expected from our printers in 2 weeks time; as soon as they are received, we will send a copy to you.

Yours sincerely

---

## 13.4 Supplier's letter with friendly tone

Customers always look for a spirit of friendliness in those with whom they seek to do business. In this letter the writer is both helpful and friendly. The aim is to interest the prospective customer, to create a feeling of confidence and to win their consideration, friendship – and ultimately their custom.

Dear Mr Jackson

I am pleased to enclose our catalogue and price list as requested in your letter of 12 October.

In this latest catalogue we have taken trouble to ensure it is both attractive and informative; particulars of our trade discounts are shown inside the front cover.

May I suggest that next time you are in Bristol you should allow us to show you our factory where you could see for yourself the high quality of materials and workmanship put into our products. This would also enable you to see at first hand the latest fancy leather goods, and to return home with interesting and useful information for your customers.

If I can be of service in any way please do not hesitate to let me know.

Yours sincerely

## 13.5 Letter welcoming a visitor from abroad

When customers from overseas visit your country it is sound business practice to extend hospitality and to give any help and advice you can. The tone of such letters must sound sincere and friendly, giving the impression that the writer is genuinely anxious to be of service.

Dear Mr Brandon

I was pleased to receive your letter of 24 April and to learn that your colleague, Mr John Gelling, is making plans to visit England in July. We shall be very pleased to welcome him and to do all we can to make his visit enjoyable and successful.

I understand this will be Mr Gelling's first visit to England, and am sure he will wish to see some of our principal places of interest. A suitable programme is something we can discuss when he arrives. I would be pleased to introduce him to several firms with whom he may like to do business.

When the date of Mr Gelling's visit is settled please let me know his arrival details. I will arrange to meet him at the airport and drive him to his hotel. He may be assured of a warm welcome.

Yours sincerely

## LETTERS OF APOLOGY

When it is necessary to apologise for something, it is important to get the tone right. Sometimes you may have to swallow your pride and say you are sorry even if you're not. Legal pressure may mean an apology is necessary if you have caused injury or offence to someone.

## 13.6 Apology for poor service

Dear Mrs Taylor

*Background details regarding complaint* — Thank you for your letter of 12 June regarding the poor service you received when you visited our store recently.

*State action taken and express regret* — The incident was most unlike our usual high standards of service and courtesy. The member of staff who was rude to you has been reprimanded; he also expresses his regret.

*Follow-up action* — I am enclosing a gift voucher for £20 which you may use at any Omega store. If I can be of any further assistance to you please do not hesitate to contact me.

*Apologise again* — With my apologies once again.

Yours sincerely

## 13.7 Apology for cancelling an appointment

Dear Mr James

I am so sorry that I had to cancel our meeting yesterday at such short notice. As my secretary explained to you I am afraid an urgent matter came up which I had to deal with immediately.

I understand our appointment has been rearranged for next Tuesday 12 May at 11.30.

Perhaps we can extend our meeting over lunch.

Yours sincerely

# LETTERS IN WHICH TONE IS PARTICULARLY IMPORTANT

In business it is sometimes necessary to refuse requests, to increase prices, explain an unfortunate oversight, apologise for mistakes, etc. In such letters tone has to be the writer's main concern. Without due consideration, offence could be caused, bad feeling created and business may be lost.

### 13.8 Letter conveying unwelcome news

It is sometimes necessary to refuse a request or to convey unwelcome news. When this is necessary think of the reader – prepare the way for their disappointment by a suitable opening paragraph, and use an appropriate tone.

---

Dear Mr Foster

It was good of you to let me see your manuscript on <u>English for Business Studies</u>. I read it with interest and was impressed by the careful and thorough way in which you have treated the subject. I particularly like the clear and concise style of writing.

Had we not recently published <u>Practical English</u> by Freda Leonard, a book that covers very similar ground, I would have been happy to accept your manuscript for publication. In the circumstances, I am unable to do so and am returning your manuscript with this letter.

I am sorry to have to disappoint you.

Yours sincerely

---

### 13.9 Letter disclaiming liability for loss

Here is another letter in which the opening paragraph is used to prepare the recipient for the rejection of his insurance claim.

---

Dear Mr Burn

When we received your letter of 23 November we sent a representative to inspect and report on the damage caused by the recent fire in your warehouse.

This report has now been submitted and it confirms your claim that the damage is extensive. However, it states that a large proportion of the stock damaged or destroyed was very old and some of it obsolete.

Unfortunately, therefore, we cannot accept your figure of £45,000 as a fair estimate of the loss as it appears to be based on the original cost of the goods.

Yours sincerely

---

### 13.10 Letter refusing a request for credit

A letter refusing a request for credit without causing offence is one of the most difficult to write. Refusal will be prompted by doubts about the would-be creditor's standing but the letter must contain no suggestion of this. Other reasons for the refusal must be given and tactfully explained.

This letter is a wholesaler's reply to a trader who has started a new business which appears to be doing well. However, the business has not been established long enough to inspire confidence in the owner's financial standing.

---

Dear Miss Wardle

We were glad you approached us with a view to placing an order, and to learn of the good start of your new business.

The question of granting credit for newly-established businesses is never an easy one. Many owners get into difficulties because they overcommit themselves before they are thoroughly established. Although we believe that your own business promises very well, we feel it would be better for you to make your purchases on a cash basis at present. If this is not possible for the full amount, we suggest that you cut the size of your order, say by half.

If you are willing to do this we will allow you a special cash discount of 4% in addition to our usual trade terms. If this suggestion is acceptable to you the goods could be delivered to you within 3 days.

We hope that you will look upon this letter as a mark of our genuine wish to enter into business with you on terms that will bring lasting satisfaction to us both. When your business is firmly established we will be very happy to welcome you as one of our credit customers.

Yours sincerely

---

## 13.11 Letter regretting an oversight

If you have made a mistake or are in any way at fault, it should be admitted freely and without excuses. A letter written in an apologetic tone is likely to create goodwill, and it will be difficult for the recipient to continue to feel a grudge against you.

---

Dear Mrs Wright

I was very concerned when I received your letter of yesterday stating that the central heating system in your home has not been completed by the date promised.

On referring to our earlier correspondence I find that I had mistaken the date for completion. The fault is entirely mine and I deeply regret that it should have occurred.

I realise the inconvenience which my oversight must be causing you and will do everything possible to avoid any further delay.

I have already given instructions for this work to take first priority; our engineers will be placed on overtime to complete the work. These arrangements should ensure that the work is completed by next weekend.

My apologies once again for the inconvenience caused.

Yours sincerely

---

### 13.12 Letter regretting price increase

Customers will naturally resent increases in prices of goods especially if they feel the increases are not justified. Goodwill can be preserved by explaining clearly and convincingly the reasons for the increases.

---

Dear

Many businesses have been experiencing steadily rising prices over the past few years and it will come as no surprise to you that our own costs have continued to rise with this general trend.

Increasing world demand has been an important factor in raising the prices of our imported raw materials. A recent national wage award has added to our labour costs which have been increased still further by constantly increasing overheads.

Until now we have been able to absorb rising costs by economies in other areas. We find that we can no longer do so, and therefore increases in our prices are unavoidable. The new prices will take effect from I October, and revised price lists are being prepared. These should be ready within the next 2 weeks and copies will be sent to you.

We are sorry that these increases have been necessary but can assure you that they will not amount to an average of more than about 5%. As general prices have risen by nearly 10% since our previous price list, we hope you will not feel that our own increases are unreasonable.

Yours sincerely

---

## LETTERS OF THANKS

Business executives have many opportunities for writing letters expressing appreciation and creating goodwill. Such letters of thanks can be as brief and as simple as you like, but they must express your appreciation with warmth and sincerity, making the reader feel that you really mean what you say – and that you enjoy saying it.

In letters of appreciation do not include specific sales matters or it may be thought that your thanks are merely an excuse for promoting business.

## 13.13 Letter of thanks for a first order

Dear Mr Martin

You will have already received our formal acknowledgement of your order number 456 dated 12 July. However as this is your first order with us I felt I must write to say how pleased we were to receive it and to thank you for the opportunity given to us to supply the goods you need.

I hope our handling of your order will lead to further business between us, and to a happy and mutually beneficial association.

Yours sincerely

## 13.14 Letter of thanks for a large order

Dear Mrs Usher

I understand that you placed an unusually large order with us yesterday, and I want to say how very much your continued confidence in us is appreciated.

The happy working relationship between us for many years has always been valued and we shall do our best to maintain it.

Yours sincerely

## 13.15 Letter of thanks for prompt settlement of accounts

Dear Mr Watts

I am writing to say how much we appreciate the promptness with which you have settled your accounts with us during the past year, especially as a number of them have been for very large amounts.

This has been of great help to us at a time when we have been faced with heavy commitments connected with the expansion of our business.

I hope our business relationship will continue in the future.

Yours sincerely

### 13.16 Letter of thanks for a service performed

> Dear Miss Armstrong
>
> Thank you for your letter of 30 March returning the draft of the catalogue we propose to send to our customers.
>
> I am very grateful for the trouble you have taken to examine the draft and comment on it in such detail. Your suggestions will be very helpful.
>
> I realise the value of time to a busy person like you and this makes me all the more appreciative of the time you have so generously given.
>
> Yours sincerely

### 13.17 Letter of thanks for information received

> Dear Mrs Webster
>
> Thank you for your letter enclosing an article explaining the organisation and work of your local trade association.
>
> I am very grateful for the interest you have shown in our proposal to include details of your association in the next issue of the <u>Trade Association Year Book</u>, and for your trouble in providing such an interesting account of your activities. This feature is sure to inspire and encourage associations in other areas.
>
> Yours sincerely

## LETTERS OF CONGRATULATION

One of the best ways to promote goodwill is to write a letter of congratulation. The occasion may be a promotion, a new appointment, the award of an honour, the establishment of a new business, success in an examination, even a marriage or a birthday. Your letter may be short and formal, or conversational and informal, depending on the circumstances and the relationship between you and the recipient.

### 13.18 Formal letter of congratulation on the award of a public honour

Letters of congratulation sent to mark the award of a public honour need only be short and formal. To show a sign of personal interest the salutation and complimentary close should be handwritten.

I was delighted to learn that your work at the South Down College of Commerce has been recognised in the New Year Honours List.

At a time when commercial education is so much in the public eye, it gives us all at the Ministry great pleasure to learn of your OBE.

## 13.19 Informal letter of congratulation on the award of a public honour

On looking through the <u>Camford Times</u> this morning I came across your name in the New Years Honours List. I would like to add my congratulations to the many you will be receiving.

The award will give much pleasure to a wide circle of people who know you and your work. Your services to local industry and commerce over many years have been quite outstanding and it is very gratifying to know that they have been so suitably rewarded.

With very best wishes

## 13.20 Formal letter of congratulation on a promotion

Dear Dr Roberts

I would like to convey my warm congratulations on your appointment to the Board of Electrical Industries Ltd.

My fellow directors and I are delighted that the many years of service you have given to your company should at last have been rewarded in this way.

We all join in sending you our very best wishes for the future.

Yours sincerely

## 13.21 Letter acknowledging congratulations

Courtesy requires that letters of congratulation should be acknowledged. In most cases a short formal acknowledgement is all that is necessary.

This letter would be a suitable reply to the letter of congratulation in 13.18. The writer very properly takes the opportunity to acknowledge her debt to colleagues who have supported her in her work.

> Dear Mrs Fleming
>
> Thank you for your letter conveying congratulations on the award of my OBE.
>
> I am very happy that anything I may have been able to do for commercial education in my limited field should have been rewarded by a public honour. At the same time I regard the award as being less of a tribute to me personally than to the work of my college as a whole – work in which I have always enjoyed the willing help and support of many colleagues.
>
> Thank you again for your good wishes.
>
> Yours sincerely

## LETTERS OF CONDOLENCE AND SYMPATHY

Letters of condolence are not easy to write. There can be no set pattern to such letters since a lot depends on what kind of relationship the writer has with the recipient. As a general rule such letters should usually be short and written with sincerity. To show special consideration letters of this kind should be hand-written.

Your letter should be written as soon as you learn the news. Express your sympathy in simple words which are warm and convincing and say what you feel sincerely.

### 13.22 Letter of condolence to a neighbour

> Dear Mrs McDermott
>
> It was not until late last night that my wife and I learned of your husband's tragic death. Coming as it did without warning, it must have been a great shock to you. I want you to know how very sorry we both are, and to send our sincere sympathy.
>
> If there is any way in which we can be of any help, either now or later, do please let us know. We shall be only too glad to do anything we can.
>
> Yours sincerely
>
> Peter Brand

## 13.23 Letter of condolence to a customer

Dear Mr Kerr

I have just learned with deep regret of the death of your wife.

There is not much one can say at a time like this, but all of us at Simpsons who have dealt with you would like to extend our sincere sympathy in your loss.

Please include us among those who share your sorrow at this sad time.

Yours sincerely

## 13.24 Letter of condolence to a business associate

Dear Mrs Anderson

We were distressed to read in <u>The Times</u> this morning that your Chairman had died and I am writing at once to express our deep sympathy.

I had the privilege of knowing Sir James for many years and always regarded him as a personal friend. By his untimely passing our industry has lost one of its best leaders. He will be greatly missed by all who knew him.

Please convey our sympathy to Lady Langley and her family.

Yours sincerely

## 13.25 Letter of condolence to an employee

Dear Maxine

I was very sorry to learn of your father's death. I remember your father very well from the years he served in our Company's Accounts Department until his retirement 2 years ago. I well recall his love for his family and the great sense of pride with which he always spoke of his daughters. He has been greatly missed at Wilson's since his retirement. We all join in expressing our sympathy to you and your family at this very sad time.

Yours sincerely

### 13.26 Letter of condolence to a friend

> *Dear Henry*
>
> *I felt I must write to say how deeply sorry we were at the news of Margaret's passing.*
>
> *She was a very dear friend and we shall greatly miss her cheerful outlook on life, her generous nature and her warmth of feeling for anyone in need of help. Above all we will miss her for her wonderful sense of fun.*
>
> *Tom and I send you our love and our assurance of continued friendship, now and always. If there is any help we can provide at any time, just let us know.*
>
> *Yours*
>
> *Alice*

### 13.27 Letter of sympathy to a business associate

> Dear Bill
>
> When I called at your office yesterday I was very sorry to learn that you had been in a car accident on your way home from work recently. However I was equally relieved to learn that you are making good progress and are likely to be back at work again in a few weeks.
>
> I had a long talk with Susan Carson and was glad to learn of your rising export orders. I expect to be in Leicester again at the end of next month and shall take the opportunity to call on you.
>
> Meanwhile I wish you a speedy recovery.
>
> Yours sincerely

### 13.28 Acknowledgements of sympathy or condolence

You will naturally wish to acknowledge letters of the kind illustrated in this section. Such acknowledgements need only be short but they show that you are genuinely moved by the warm expressions of sympathy you have received.

## (a) Personal acknowledgement

Individual personalised acknowledgements should be made to relatives and close friends.

---

Dear Mrs Hughes

My mother and family join me in thanking you for your very kind letter on the occasion of my father's death.

We have all been greatly comforted by the kindness and sympathy of our relatives and friends. Both at home and in the hospital, where my father spent 2 weeks prior to his passing, the kindness and sympathy shown by everyone has been almost overwhelming.

Yours sincerely

Laura Darabi

---

## (b) Printed acknowledgement

When many letters of condolence have been received it will be sufficient to prepare a printed general acknowledgement.

---

Mr and Mrs Ashton and family thank you most sincerely for your kind expression of sympathy in their sad loss.

The kindness of so many friends and the many expressions of affection and esteem in which Margaret was held will always remain a proud and cherished memory.

97 Lake Rise
Romford
Essex
RMl 4EF

---

## CHECKLIST

- ☐ Write and send them promptly
- ☐ Use an appropriate tone
- ☐ Be sincere
- ☐ Use an informal style
- ☐ Use a personalised approach (handwritten if appropriate)
- ☐ Keep them short and to the point
- ☐ Ask yourself how you would feel on receiving such a letter

# Circular letters

Circular letters are used to send the same information to a number of people. They are extensively used in sales campaigns (see Chapter 15) and for announcing important developments in business, such as extensions, reorganisations, changes of address, etc.

A circular letter is prepared once only and it may then be duplicated for distribution to the various recipients. Names, addresses and individual salutations may be inserted after duplication in order to personalise the letter.

Word processing with its mail-merge facilities makes it possible for each letter to be an original, with the 'variable' details (eg inside address, salutation, etc) being merged with the letter during printing.

Although circulars are being sent to many people, it is important to suggest an interest in the recipient by giving them a personal touch. Remember the following rules:

1  Be brief – people will not read a long-winded circular.

2  Make the letter as personal as possible by addressing each letter to a particular person, by name if you know it. Use *Dear Mr Smith* instead of *Dear Reader, Dear Subscriber* or *Dear Customer* instead of *Dear Sir or Madam*. Never use the plural form for the salutation – remember, one recipient will read each individual letter.

3  Create the impression of personal interest by using *you*, never *our customers, all customers, our clients, everyone*.

| *Instead of* | *Say* |
| --- | --- |
| Our customers will appreciate ... | You will appreciate |
| We are pleased to inform all our clients ... | We are pleased to inform you ... |
| Everyone will be interested to learn .. | You will be interested to learn ... |
| Anyone visiting our new showroom will see ... | If you visit our new showroom you will see ... |

## CIRCULARS ANNOUNCING CHANGES IN BUSINESS ORGANISATION

Changes in a firm's business arrangements may be announced by circular letters such as those which follow. Where the salutation has been left blank, it has been presumed that the letter would be word processed and individual names, addresses and salutations would be merged to add a personal touch.

## 14.1 Expansion of existing business

Dear Customer

To meet the growing demand for a hardware and general store in this area we have decided to extend our business by opening a new department.

Our new department will carry an extensive range of hardware and other domestic goods at prices which compare very favourably with those charged by other suppliers.

We would like the opportunity to demonstrate our new merchandise to you and so are arranging a special window display during the week beginning 24 June. The official opening of our new department will take place on the following Monday 1 July.

We hope you will visit our new department during opening week and give us the opportunity to show you that the reputation enjoyed by our other departments for giving sound value for money will apply equally to this new department.

Yours sincerely

## 14.2 Opening of a new business

Dear Householder

We are pleased to announce the opening of our new retail grocery store on Monday 1 September.

Mrs Victoria Chadwick has been appointed Manager. She has 15 years experience of the trade and we are sure that the goods supplied will be of sound[1] quality and reasonably priced.

Our new store will open at 0800 hours on Monday 1 September. As a special celebration offer a discount of 10% will be allowed on all purchases made by the first 50 customers. We hope we can look forward to your being one of them.

Yours sincerely

---

[1] **sound** reliable

**14.3** ## Establishment of a new branch

Dear

Owing to the large increase in the volume of our trade with the Kingdom of Jordan, we have decided to open a branch in Amman. Mr Faisal Shamlan has been appointed as Manager.

Although we hope we have provided you with an efficient service in the past, this new branch in your country will result in your orders and enquiries being dealt with more promptly.

This new branch will open on 1 May and from that date all orders and enquiries should be sent to

Mr Faisal Shamlan
Manager
Tyler & Co Ltd
18 Hussein Avenue
Amman
Tel: (00962)6–212421
Fax: (00962)6–212422

We take this opportunity to express our thanks for your custom in the past. We hope these new arrangements will lead to even higher standards in the service we provide.

Yours sincerely

**14.4** ## Removal to new premises

Dear

The steady growth of our business has made necessary an early move to new and larger premises. We have been fortunate in acquiring[2] a particularly good site on the new industrial estate at Chorley, and from 1 July our new address will be as follows:

Unit 15
Chorley Industrial Estate
Grange Road
Chorley
Lincs CH2 4TH
Telephone 456453 Fax 456324

This new site is served by excellent transport facilities, both by road and rail, enabling deliveries to be made promptly. It also provides scope[3] for better methods of production which will increase output and also improve the quality of our goods even further.

We have very much appreciated your custom in the past and confidently expect to be able to offer you improvements in service when the new factory moves into full production.

Yours sincerely

[2] **acquiring** obtaining
[3] **scope** opportunity

## 14.5 Reorganisation of a store's departments

Dear

In order to provide you with even better service, we have recently extended and relocated[4] a number of departments in our store.

- On the ground floor we have a wide selection of greetings cards, including both boxed and single Christmas cards.
- In the Children's and Babywear Department on the first floor there is a new 'Ladybird' section.
- Our Fashion Fabrics and Soft Furnishings Departments are together on the second floor. Light Fittings and Electrical Goods are relocated on the third floor.
- The basement displays a good collection of wallpapers, most of which we are able to supply within 24 hours.

We thank you for your past custom and hope we may continue to be of service to you.

Yours sincerely

## 14.6 Death of a colleague

Dear

It is with much sadness that I have to tell you of the sudden death of our Marketing Director, Michael Spencer. Michael had been with this company for 10 years and he made an enormous contribution to the development of the business. He will be greatly missed by all his colleagues.

I am anxious to ensure continuing service to you. Please contact me directly with any matters which Michael would normally deal with.

Yours sincerely

# CIRCULARS ANNOUNCING CHANGES IN BUSINESS PARTNERSHIPS

When a change takes place in the membership of a partnership, suppliers and customers should be informed by letter. For retiring partners this is particularly important since they remain liable not only for debts contracted by the firm during membership but also for debts contracted with old creditors in retirement.

[4] **relocated** moved to a different place

The correct signature on such letters is that of the name of the firm without the addition of any partner's name.

## 14.7  Retirement of a partner

Dear

We regret to inform you that our senior partner, Mr Harold West, has decided to retire on 31 May due to recent extended ill-health.

The withdrawal of Mr West's capital will be made good by contributions from the remaining partners, and the value of the firm's capital will therefore remain unchanged. We will continue to trade under the name of West, Webb & Co, and there will be no change in policy.

We trust that the confidence you have shown in our company in the past will continue and that we may rely on your continued custom. We shall certainly do everything possible to ensure that our present standards of service are maintained.

Yours sincerely

## 14.8  Appointment of a new partner

Dear

A large increase in the volume of our business has made necessary an increase in the membership of this company. It is with pleasure that we announce the appointment of Mrs Briony Kisby as partner.

Mrs Kisby has been our Head Buyer for the past 10 years and is well acquainted with every aspect of our policy. Her expertise and experience will continue to be of great value to the company.

There will be no change to our firm's name of Taylor, Hyde & Co.

We look forward to continuing our mutually beneficial business relationship with you.

Yours sincerely

## 14.9 Conversion of partnership to private company

Dear

The need for additional capital to finance the considerable growth in the volume of our trade has made it necessary to reorganise our business as a private company. The new company has been registered with limited liability in the name Barlow & Hoole Limited.

We wish to stress that this change is in name only and that the nature of our business will remain exactly as before. There will be no change in business policy.

The personal relationship which has been built up with all customers in the past will be maintained; we shall continue to do our utmost to ensure that you are completely satisfied with the way in which we handle your future orders.

Yours sincerely

# LETTERS ANNOUNCING CHANGE OF REPRESENTATIVES

## 14.10 Dismissal of firm's representative

Dear

We wish to inform you that Miss Rona Smart who has been our representative in North-West England for the past 7 years has left our service. Therefore she no longer has authority to take orders or to collect accounts on our behalf.

In her place we have appointed Mrs Tracie Coole. Mrs Coole has for many years had control of our sales section and is thoroughly familiar with the needs of customers in your area. She intends to call on you some time this month to introduce herself and to bring samples of our new spring fabrics.

We look forward to continuing our business relationship with you

Yours faithfully

NB If the representative left of her own free will and was a valued member of staff the first paragraph of the above letter would be more suitably expressed as follows:

It is with regret that we inform you that Miss Rona Smart who has been our representative for the past 7 years has decided to leave us to take up another appointment.

### 14.11 Appointment of new representative

Dear

Mr Samuel Goodier who has been calling on you regularly for the past 6 years, has now joined our firm as junior partner. His many friends will doubtless be sorry that they will see him much less frequently and we can assure you that he shares their regret.

Mr Goodier hopes to keep in touch with you and other customers by occasional visits to his former territory.

Mr Lionel Tufnell has been appointed to represent us in the South West and Mr Goodier will introduce him to you when he makes his last regular call on you next week. Mr Tufnell has worked closely with Mr Goodier in the past and he will continue to do so in the future. Mr Goodier will continue to offer help and advice in matters affecting you and other customers in the South West, and his intimate knowledge of your requirements will be of great benefit to Mr Tufnell in his new responsibilities.

Our business relations with you have always been very good, and we believe we have succeeded in serving you well. It is therefore with confidence that we ask you to extend to our new representative the courtesy and friendliness you have always shown to Mr Goodier.

Yours faithfully

## INTERNAL CIRCULARS TO STAFF

Many circulars are written to staff regarding various matters concerning the general running of the business, safety and security, administrative matters and many other things. A memo is sometimes used for more day-to-day matters, but for some matters a formal letter may be printed on the company's letterheaded paper.

### 14.12 Announcement about new working hours

NEW WORKING HOURS

With effect from 1 September 19— working hours will be amended to 0930 to 1730 Monday to Friday instead of the present working hours of 0900 to 1700.

I hope you will find these new hours convenient. If you anticipate experiencing any difficulties please let me know before 14 August.

## 14.13 Notice about new car park

NEW CAR PARK

You may be aware that some old buildings on our site have been demolished. A piece of land in this area has been cleared so that it may be used as a car park.

The new car park should be ready for use by 28 October. It will be available between 0730 and 1830 hours Monday to Friday. The company takes no responsibility for loss or damage to vehicles or contents while in the car park.

If you wish to use the car park please obtain an agreement form from Mr John Smithson, Security Officer. This form must be completed and returned to him before using the car park.

Copy    John Smithson, Security Officer

## 14.14 Information about store discount

DISCOUNT AT QUANTUM STORES

An agreement has been reached which will allow all our employees to take advantage of the special discount scheme operated by Quantum Stores.

As an employee of Omega International you will receive 10% discount on any goods which are not already reduced in price. A discount of 2½% will be given on reduced price or sale goods. If you wish to claim the discount you must show your Omega identification badge.

These discounts will take effect from 1 September 19—.

## 14.15 Security information to Heads of Department

SECURITY

Reason for writing — In view of recent bomb threats received by several competitors, please brief your staff on the following points of security.

1  All employees must wear a name badge at all times.
Number points for ease — 2  All areas must be kept as clean and tidy as possible. This will reduce of reference     potential areas where bombs may be hidden.
3  Do not tamper with or move any suspicious object. The manager should be informed and the police notified.
4  Evacuation should follow established fire drills.

Follow-up action — All incidents must be taken seriously and a detailed report must be submitted to me.

Final emphasis — Please stress to all your staff that they have an important part to play in maintaining a high level of security in all areas at all times.

# CIRCULARS WITH REPLY FORMS

A tear-off slip is often used when a reply is required from people to whom a circular is sent. Alternatively a separate reply form may be used. The important points to remember with such reply sections are:

- Always begin with ' Please return by ... to ...' . This is a safeguard in case someone separates the tear-off portion or reply form from the main letter.
- Use double spacing for the portion which will be completed.
- Leave sufficient space for completion after each question/heading.
- Use continuous dots where answers are required.

## 14.16 Invitation to function (with tear-off slip)

10TH ANNIVERSARY CELEBRATION

Omega International is celebrating its 10th year of providing quality communications equipment. Approximately 50 representatives from Omega clients are expected to attend a special 10th Anniversary Celebration on Friday 29 October 19—.

The directors have decided to invite all employees who have been with Omega for at least 5 years to attend this special function. I am pleased to extend to you an invitation to join us at Omega's 10th Anniversary Celebration. Cocktails and a buffet supper will be provided.

This special function will take place from 1800 to 2300 hours at The Mandarin Suite, Oriental Hotel, West Street, London.

Please let me know whether you will be attending by returning the tear-off portion before 31 August.

I hope you will be able to join us.

..................................................................................................................

*For use internally, just include name/title; the full address is not required*

Please return to Mrs Judy Brown, Administration Manager, before 31 August.

I shall/shall not* be attending the 10th Anniversary Celebration on Friday 29 October.

*Keep it simple and precise*

Name ..........................................................................................................

*Use double spacing*

Designation/Department ......................................................................

Signature ...............................................................Date ........................

*Remember footnote where appropriate*

* Please delete as applicable.

**14.17** **Reply form**

(reproduced with permission from *Communication for Business* by Shirley Taylor)

Here is a reply form to accompany a letter sent to clients of a training organisation. Clients were asked to specify whether or not they would like to attend a one-day management conference, when accommodation will be required, and enclose a cheque to cover the cost.

---

REPLY FORM

Give full address when used externally; don't forget reply date ———— Please complete and return by 15 February 19— to

Mr F J Fredericks
Personnel Manager
Professional Training Pte Ltd
126 Buona Vista Boulevard
KUALA LUMPUR
Malaysia

Use same heading as on covering document ———— ONE-DAY MANAGEMENT CONFERENCE
SATURDAY 3 APRIL 199—

Use numbered points if appropriate ———— 1   I wish/do not wish* to attend this conference.

Use the personal term 'I wish..., require...', etc ———— 2   I require accommodation on

☐ Friday 2 April

Use option/boxes where appropriate ———— ☐ Saturday 3 April    (Please tick)

3   My cheque for M$400 is attached (made payable to Professional Training Pte Ltd)

Signature ........................................................ Date....................................

Name (in caps)  ...............................................................................................

Choose appropriate details at the foot ———— Title  ...............................................................................................................

Company  ........................................................................................................

Address  ..........................................................................................................

Leave sufficient space ———— ..........................................................................................................................

........................................................... Post code...............................

Telephone ....................................... Fax ...........................................

Don't forget footnote ———— * Please delete as necessary.

---

## CHECKLIST FOR CIRCULAR LETTERS

☐ Personalise circular letters by merging individual inside address

☐ Address the recipient by name if you know it, otherwise use singular form 'Dear Customer', 'Dear Reader' – NOT 'Customers', 'Readers'

☐ Insert a handwritten salutation if appropriate

☐ Show a personal interest – use 'you' instead of 'all customers', 'everyone'.

## CHECKLIST FOR TEAR-OFF SLIP/REPLY FORM

☐ State reply date

☐ Mention to whom the form should be returned:

Internal forms – name/title only

External forms – name/title/company name and address

☐ Use same heading as covering document

☐ Use double spacing

☐ Use personal terms – I wish, I shall/shall not

☐ Use options/boxes where appropriate

☐ Leave sufficient space for completion

☐ Ensure the form contains everything you need to know

# Sales letters and voluntary offers

# SALES LETTERS

A sales letter is the most selective of all forms of advertising. Unlike press and poster advertising a sales letter aims to sell particular kinds of goods or services to selected types of customers. The purpose of the sales letter is to persuade readers that they need what you are trying to sell and persuade them to buy it.

You take something attractive and make it seem necessary, or you take something necessary and make it seem attractive.

The same rules discussed for circular letters in Chapter 14 also apply to sales letters, so when composing sales letters be careful to follow the rules listed on page 192.

## Elements of the sales letter

A good sales letter must be structured to follow a general 4-point plan as follows:

- arouse interest
- create desire
- carry conviction
- induce action

Each of these elements will now be considered in detail.

## Arouse interest

Your opening paragraph must arouse interest and encourage the reader to take notice of what you have to say. If care is not taken in this opening paragraph your letter could end up in the waste-paper bin without being read. Your letter may begin with a question, an instruction or a quotation. Here are some examples:

**(a) An appeal to self-esteem**

> Are you nervous when asked to propose a vote of thanks, to take the Chair at a meeting, or to make a speech? If so this letter has been written specially for you!

**(b) An appeal to economy**

> Would you like to cut your domestic fuel costs by 20 per cent? If your answer is 'yes', read on …

**(c) An appeal to health**

> 'The common cold', says Dr James Carter, 'probably causes more lost time at work in a year than all other illnesses put together.'

**(d) An appeal to fear**

> More than 50 per cent of people have eye trouble and in the past year no fewer than 16,000 people in Britain have lost their sight. Are your eyes in danger?

## Create desire

Having aroused interest in the opening paragraph, you must now create a desire for the product or service you are selling. To do this it must point out the benefits to the readers and how it will affect them.

If the letter is sent to a person who knows nothing about the product, you must describe it and give a clear picture of what it is and what it can do. Study the product and then select those features which make it superior to others of its kind. Stress the features from the reader's point of view.

To claim that a particular hi-fi system is 'the best on the market' or 'the latest in electronic technology' is of little use. Instead stress such points as quality of the materials used and the special features that make the equipment more convenient or efficient than its rivals. The following description stresses such points:

description, note the final statement 'as hed as a Rolls-Royce' tes the product with which is well known recognised as a high oduct. This creates a cture of a reasonably yet superb product.

> This hi-fi system is carefully designed and incorporates the latest technological developments to give high quality sound including full stereo recording and playback on the twin-cassette deck. Its clearly arranged controls make for very simple operation. It is supplied with two detachable loudspeakers separately mounted in solid, polished teak cabinets, as finely finished as a Rolls-Royce.

## Carry conviction

You must somehow convince your reader that the product is what you claim it to be. You must support your claims by evidence – facts, opinions. You can do this in a number of ways, eg:

- invite the reader to your factory or showroom
- offer to send goods on approval
- provide a guarantee
- quote your 100 years of experience in the field.

In this extract from a r from a cotton-shirt nufacturer, note how convincing it sounds. manufacturer would o make such an offer out the firm belief in at is claimed. All the of is supplied to give the reader complete nce and to persuade them to buy.

> Remember, we have manufactured cotton shirts for 50 years and are quite confident that you will be more than satisfied with their quality.
>
> This offer is made on the clear understanding that if the goods are not completely to your satisfaction you can return them to us without any obligation whatever and at our own expense. The full amount you paid will be refunded immediately.

As a caution, however, remember that it is against the law to make false or exaggerated claims. Remember also that the good name and standing of your business – as well as its success – depends upon honest dealing.

## Induce action

Your closing paragraph must persuade the reader to take the action that you want – to visit your showrooms, to receive your representative, to send for a sample or to place an order.

The final paragraph must also provide readers with a sound reason why they should reply

> If you will <u>return the enclosed request card</u> we will show <u>you how you can have all the advantages of cold storage and at the same time save money</u>.

Sometimes the closing paragraph will give special reasons why the reader should act immediately

> The special discount now offered can be allowed only on orders placed by 30 June. So hurry and take advantage of this limited offer while there is still time.

You must make it easy for the reader to do these things, such as by providing a tear-off slip to complete and return or by enclosing a prepaid card.

When composing sales letters remember: your readers will not be anywhere near as interested in the product, service or idea you have to sell as they are in how it will benefit them. You must persuade your readers of the benefits of what you are selling and tell them what it can do for them.

# SPECIMEN SALES LETTERS

Here are some examples of effective sales letters which follow the four-point plan of *interest*, *desire*, *conviction* and *action*.

## 15.1 Sales appeal to economy

Dear Mr Reading

Interest —— Have you ever thought how much time your typist wastes in taking down your dictation? It can be as much as a third of the time spent on correspondence. Why not record your dictation – on our <u>Stenogram</u> – and she can be doing other jobs while you dictate?

Desire —— You will be surprised at how little it costs. For 52 weeks in the year your <u>Stenogram</u> works hard for you, and you can never give it too much to do – all for less than an average month's salary for a secretary! It will take dictation anywhere at any time – during lunch-hour, in the evening, at home – you can even dictate while you are travelling or away on business. Simply post the recorded messages back to your secretary for typing.

Conviction —— The <u>Stenogram</u> is efficient, reliable, time-saving and economical. Backed by our international reputation for reliability, it is in regular use in thousands of offices all over the country. It gives superb reproduction quality with every syllable as clear as a bell. It is unbelievably simple to use – just slip in a preloaded cassette, press a button, and it is ready to record your dictation, interviews, telephone conversations, reports, instructions or whatever. Nothing could be simpler! And with our unique after-sales service contract you are assured lasting operation at the peak of efficiency.

Action —— Some of your business friends are sure to be using our <u>Stenogram</u>. Ask them about it before you place an order and we are sure they will back up our claims. If you prefer, return the enclosed prepaid card and we will arrange for our representative to call and arrange a demonstration for you. Just state the day and time which will be most convenient for you.

Yours sincerely

## 15.2 Sales appeal to efficiency

Dear Mr Wood

Interest — Reports from all over the world confirm what we have always known – that the RELIANCE solid tyre is the fulfilment of every car owner's dream.

Desire — You will naturally be well aware of the weaknesses of the ordinary air-filled tyre – punctures, outer covers which split under sudden stress, and a tendency to skid on wet road surfaces, to mention only a few of motorists' main complaints. Our RELIANCE tyre enables you to offer your customers a tyre which is beyond criticism in those vital[1] qualities of road-holding and reliability.

Conviction — We could tell you a lot more about RELIANCE tyres but would prefer you to read the enclosed copies of reports from racing car drivers, test drivers, motor dealers and manufacturers. These reports really speak for themselves.

Action — To encourage you to hold a stock of the new solid RELIANCE, we are pleased to offer you a special discount of 3% on any order received by 31 July.

Yours sincerely

## 15.3 Sales appeal to security

Dear Mr Goodwin

Interest — A client of mine is happier today than he has been for a long time – and with good reason. For the first time since he married 10 years ago he says he feels really comfortable about the future. Should he die within the next 20 years, his wife and family will now be provided for. For less than £2 a week paid now, his wife would receive £50 per month for a full 20 years, and then a lump sum of £10,000.

Desire — Such protection would have been beyond his reach a short time ago, but a new and novel scheme has enabled him to ensure this security for his family. The scheme does not have to be for 20 years. It can be for 15 or 10 or any other number of years. And it need not be for £10,000. It could be for much more or much less so that you arrange the protection you want.

Conviction — For just a few pounds each month you can buy peace of mind for your wife, your children and for yourself. You cannot – you dare not – leave them unprotected.

Action — I would appreciate an opportunity to call on you to tell you more about this scheme which so many families are finding so attractive. I shall not press you to join; I shall just give you all the details and leave the rest to you. Please return the enclosed prepaid reply card and I will call at any time convenient to you.

Yours sincerely

[1] **vital** essential

## 15.4 Sales appeal to comfort

Dear Mrs Walker

Interest —— What would you say to a gift that gave you a warmer and more comfortable home, free from draughts, and a saving of over 20% in fuel costs?

Desire —— You can enjoy these advantages, not just this year but every year, simply by installing our SEALTITE panel system of <u>double glazing</u>.[2] Can you think of a better gift for your entire family? The enclosed brochure will outline some of the benefits which make SEALTITE the most completely satisfactory double-glazing system on the market thanks to a number of features not provided in any other system.

Conviction —— Remember that the panels are precision-made[3] by experienced craftsmen to fit your own particular windows. Remember too that you will be dealing with a well established company which owes its success to the satisfaction given to scores of thousands of customers.

Action —— There is no need for you to make up your mind right now. First why not let us give you a free demonstration in your own home without any obligation whatsoever? If you are looking for an investment with an annual average return of over 20%, then here is your opportunity. If you post the enclosed card to reach us by the end of August, we can complete the installation for you in good time before winter sets in.

Secure your home with SEALTITE!

Yours sincerely

## 15.5 Sales appeal to leisure

Dear Mrs Hudson

Interest —— 'Modern scientific invention is a curse to the human race and will one day destroy it', said one of my customers recently. Rather a <u>rash statement</u>,[4] and quite untrue for there are modern inventions which, far from being a curse, are real blessings.

Desire —— Our new AQUAMASTER washer is just one of them. It takes all the hard work out of the weekly wash and makes washing a pleasure. All you have to do is put your soiled clothes in, press a button and sit back while the machine does the work. It does everything – washing, rinsing and drying – and we feel it does it quicker and better than any washing machine on the market today.

Conviction —— Come along and see the AQUAMASTER at work in our showroom. A demonstration will take up only a few minutes of your time, but it may rid you of your dread of washing day and make life much more pleasant.

Action —— I hope you will accept this invitation and come along soon to see what this latest of domestic time-savers can do for you.

Yours sincerely

[2] **double glazing** double-glass window panels
[3] **precision-made** manufactured to a high degree of accuracy
[4] **rash statement** a statement made recklessly, without thought

SALES LETTERS AND VOLUNTARY OFFERS **209**

### 15.6 Sales appeal to sympathy

This letter was sent together with a leaflet containing a form for readers to return with a donation.

---

Dear Reader

You can walk about the house, at work, in the streets, in the country. You take this ability for granted, yet it is denied to thousands of others – those who are born crippled, or crippled in childhood by accident or illness.

It is estimated that every 5 minutes in Britain a deformed child is born or a child is crippled by accident or illness. This means that every day there could be 288 more crippled children.

Does this not strike you as unfair? Most of what is unfair in life is something we can do little about but here is one very important inequality which everyone can help with. The enclosed leaflet explains how you can help. Please read it carefully while remembering again just how lucky you are.

Yours faithfully

---

### 15.7 Sales appeal to comfort

---

Dear Sir

At half the actual cost you can now have SOLAR HEATING installed in your home.

As part of our research and development scheme introduced two years ago we are about to make our selection of a number of properties throughout the country as 'Research Homes' – yours could be one of them.

The information received from selected 'Research Homes' in the past two years has proved that SOLAR HEATING is successful even in the most northern parts of the United Kingdom. This information has also enabled us to modify[5] and improve our designs, which we will continue to do.

If your home is selected as one of the properties to be included in our research scheme, we will bear half the actual cost of installation.

If you are interested in helping our research programme in return for a half-price solar heating system, please complete the enclosed form and return it by the end of May. Within three weeks we will inform you if your home has been selected for the scheme.

Yours faithfully

---

[5] **modify** alter, rearrange

## 15.8  Sales appeal to health

Dear Madam

Thousands of people who normally suffer from the miseries of cold, damp, changeable weather wear THERMOTEX. Why? The answer is simple – tests conducted at the leading Textile Industries Department at Leeds University have shown that of all the traditional underwear fabrics THERMOTEX has the highest warmth insulating properties.

THERMOTEX has been relieving aches and pains for many years, particularly those caused by rheumatism. It not only brings extra warmth but also soothes those aches caused by icy winds cutting into your bones and chilling you to the marrow. THERMOTEX absorbs much less moisture than conventional underwear fabrics, so perspiration passes straight through the material. It leaves your skin dry but very, very warm.

Don't just take our word for it – take a good look at some of the testimonials shown in the enclosed catalogue. The demand for THERMOTEX garments has grown so much in recent years that we often have to deal with over 20,000 garments in a single day.

The enclosed catalogue is packed with lots of ways in which THERMOTEX can keep you warm and healthy this winter. Just browse through it, choose the garment you would like, and send us your completed order form – our FREEPOST address means there is no need even for a postage stamp!

Warmth and health will soon be on their way to you. If you are not completely satisfied with your purchase, return it to us within 14 days and we will refund your money without question and with the least possible delay.

Let THERMOTEX keep you warm this winter!

Yours faithfully

# VOLUNTARY OFFERS

An offer which is not asked for and which is sent to an individual or a small number of individuals is a form of sales letter. It serves the same purpose and follows the same general principles.

Such offers take a variety of forms. They may be:

- offers of free samples
- goods on approval
- special discounts on orders received within a stated period
- offers to send brochures, catalogues, price lists, patterns, etc., upon return of a form or card which is usually prepaid.

### 15.9 Offer to a newly established trader

Dear Sir

We would like to send our best wishes for the success of your new shop specialising in the sale of toys. Naturally you will wish to offer your customers the latest toys – toys which are attractive, hard wearing and reasonably priced. Your stock will not be complete without the mechanical toys for which we have a national reputation.

We are sole importers of VALIFACT toys and as you will see from the enclosed price list our terms are very generous. In addition to the trade discount stated, we would allow you a special first-order discount of 5%.

We hope that these terms will encourage you to place an order with us and feel sure you would be well satisfied with your first transaction.

We will be happy to arrange for one of our representatives to call on you to ensure that you are fully briefed on the wide assortment of toys we can offer. Please complete and return the enclosed card to say when it would be convenient.

Yours faithfully

### 15.10 Offer to a regular customer

Dear Mr Welling

We have just bought a large quantity of high quality rugs and carpets from the bankrupt stock of one of our competitors.

As you are one of our most regular and long-standing customers, we should like you to share in the excellent opportunities which our purchase provides. We can offer you mohair rugs in a variety of colours at prices ranging from £55 to £1500; also premier quality Wilton and Axminster carpeting in a wide range of patterns at 20% below current wholesale prices.

This is an exceptional opportunity for you to buy a stock of high quality products at prices we cannot repeat. We hope you will take full advantage of it.

If you are interested please call at our warehouse to see the stock for yourself not later than next Friday, 14 October. Or alternatively call our Sales Department on 0114-453 2567 to place an immediate order.

Yours sincerely

## 15.11 Offer to new home owners

Dear Newcomers

Welcome to your new home! We have no wish to disturb you as you settle in but we would like to tell you why people in this town and the surrounding areas are very familiar with the name BAXENDALE.

Our store is situated at the corner of Grafton Street and Dorset Road and we invite you to visit us to see for yourself the exciting range of goods which have made us a household name.

Our well-known shopping guide is enclosed for you to browse through at your leisure. You will see practically everything you need to add to the comfort and beauty of your home.

As a special attraction to newcomers into the area we are offering a free gift worth £2 for every £20 spent in our store. The enclosed card is valid for one calendar month and it will entitle you to select goods of your own choice as your free gift.

We sincerely hope that you enjoy living in your new home.

Yours faithfully

## 15.12 Offer of a demonstration

Dear Mrs Thornton

The Ideal Home Exhibition opens at Earls Court on Monday 21 June and you are certain to find attractive new designs in furniture as well as many new ideas.

The exhibition has much to offer which you will find useful, but we would like to extend our special invitation to our own display on Stand 26 where we shall be revealing our new WINDSOR range of unit furniture.[6]

WINDSOR represents an entirely new concept in luxury unit furniture at very modest prices and we hope you will not miss the opportunity to see it for yourself. The inbuilt charm of this range comes from the use of solid elm and beech, combined with expert craftsmanship to give a perfect finish to each piece of furniture.

I enclose two admission tickets to the Ideal Home Exhibition. I am sure you will not want to miss this opportunity to see the variety of ways in which WINDSOR unit furniture can be arranged to suit any requirements.

I look forward to seeing you there.

Yours sincerely

---

[6] **unit furniture** furniture made in standard sections

## CHECKLIST

- ☐ Arouse interest in first paragraph
- ☐ Create a desire for the product or service
- ☐ Describe the product if appropriate
- ☐ Point out the benefits
- ☐ Stress quality and special features
- ☐ Convince the reader that what you claim is correct
- ☐ Give evidence to support your claim
- ☐ Persuade the reader to take appropriate action

## USEFUL EXPRESSIONS

### Openings

1 We are enclosing a copy of our latest catalogue and price list.

2 As you have placed many orders with us in the past, we would like to extend our special offer to you.

3 We are able to offer you very favourable prices on some goods we have recently been able to purchase.

4 We are pleased to introduce our new ... and feel sure that you will find it very interesting.

5 I am sorry to note that we have not received an order from you for over ...

### Closes

1 We hope you will take full advantage of this exceptional offer.

2 We feel sure you will find a ready sale for this excellent material and that your customers will be well satisfied with it.

3 We should be pleased to provide a demonstration if you would let us know when this would be convenient.

4 We feel sure you will agree that this product is not only of the highest quality but also very reasonably priced.

# Personnel

# LETTERS OF APPLICATION

A letter of application for a job is essentially a sales letter. In such a letter you are trying to sell yourself. The general principles of writing sale letters (Chapter 15) will therefore apply: Your letter must

- arouse *interest* in your qualifications
- carry *conviction* by your past record and testimonials
- bring about the *action* you want the prospective employer to take – to grant an interview and eventually give you the job.

## Style of application

Unless an advertisement specifies that you must apply in your own handwriting, or the post is purely clerical or bookkeeping, your application should be typed. A well-displayed, easy-to-read letter will attract attention at once and create a favourable first impression.

Some applicants write a long letter containing lots of information about education, qualifications and experience – this is not advisable as the information is not easy to locate and it can sound rather boastful.

Your curriculum vitae should give full details of your personal background, education, qualifications and experience.

It is preferable to write a short letter applying for the post and stating that your curriculum vitae (or résumé) is enclosed.

Do not duplicate such information in your covering letter.

## Points of guidance

- Remember the purpose of your application is not to get the job, but to get an interview.
- Ensure your application looks attractive and neatly presented; make it stand out from the rest.
- Be brief; give all the relevant information in as few words as possible.
- Write sincerely, in a friendly tone, but without being familiar.
- Do not make exaggerated claims or sound boastful; simply show a proper appreciation of your abilities.
- Do not imply that you are applying for the job because you are bored with your present one.
- If your main interest is the salary, do not state the figure you expect. Instead mention what you are earning now.
- Do not enclose originals of your testimonials; send copies with your application but take your originals along to the interview.

## Checklist

A busy employer has little time for long rambling correspondence. Avoid the temptation to include details in which the recipient is unlikely to be interested, no matter how important they may be to you. You should also avoid generalising, and instead be quite specific in the information provided. For example instead of saying 'I have had several years' of relevant experience in a well-known firm of engineers', state the number of years, state the experience and give the name of the firm.

When you have written your letter, read it carefully and ask yourself these questions:

(a)  Does it read like a good business letter?

(b)  Will the opening paragraph interest the employer enough to prompt the rest to be read?

(c)  Does it suggest that you are genuinely interested in the post and the kind of work to be done?

(d)  Is your letter neatly presented and logically structured?

If your answer to these questions is 'Yes', then you may safely send your letter.

## 16.1 Application for an advertised post

### (a) Application letter

When your application is in response to an advertisement in a newspaper or journal, this should always be mentioned in the opening paragraph or in the subject heading.

26 Windsor Road
CHINGFORD
CH4 6PY

> The writer's address is placed at the top right-hand corner of the letter

15 May 19—

> All other details begin at the left margin in fully blocked style. (It would be satisfactory to place the date at the right if preferred.)

Mrs W R Jenkinson
Personnel Manager
Leyland & Bailey Ltd
Nelson Works
CLAPTON
CH5 8HA

Dear Mrs Jenkinson

PRIVATE SECRETARY TO MANAGING DIRECTOR

> Mention the post and where you saw the advertisement

I was interested to see your advertisement in today's Daily Telegraph and would like to be considered for this post.

> Give an outline of your present post and briefly discuss your duties

I am presently working as Private Secretary to the General Manager at a manufacturing company and have a wide range of responsibilities. These include attending and taking minutes of meetings and interviews, dealing with callers and correspondence in my employer's absence, and supervising junior staff, as well as the usual secretarial duties.

> An indication of why you are interested in the advertised post would be useful

The kind of work in which your company is engaged particularly interests me, and I would welcome the opportunity it would afford to use my language abilities which are not utilised in my present post.

> Enclose your CV and copies of testimonials if available

A copy of my curriculum vitae is enclosed with copies of previous testimonials.

> Suitable close

I hope to hear from you soon and to be given the opportunity to present myself at an interview.

Yours sincerely

*Jean Carson*

JEAN CARSON (Miss)

Encs

### (b) Curriculum vitae

Your curriculum vitae (sometimes called a résumé) should set out all your personal details, together with your education, qualifications and working experience. It should be displayed attractively so that all the information can be seen at a glance. It should not extend to more than 2 pages. Wherever possible, the information should be categorised under headings and columns.

# CURRICULUM VITAE

| | |
|---|---|
| NAME | Jean Carson |
| ADDRESS | 26 Gordon Road<br>Chingford<br>Essex CH4 6PY |
| TELEPHONE | 0181 529 3456 |
| DATE OF BIRTH | 26 May 1965 |
| NATIONALITY | British |
| MARITAL STATUS | Single |

*sonal details should be shown at the beginning*

## EDUCATION

*te full and part time educational courses*

| | |
|---|---|
| 19— to 19— | Woodford High School |
| 19— to 19— | Bedford Secretarial College<br>(Secretarial Course) |

## QUALIFICATIONS

*qualifications in full (don't just say '4 A levels')*

| | | |
|---|---|---|
| GCE A Level | English Language | 19— |
| | Mathematics | 19— |
| | Spanish | 19— |
| | French | 19— |
| GCE O Level | Biology | 19— |
| | Philosophy | 19— |
| | Commerce | 19— |
| | History | 19— |
| LCCI | Private Secretary's Diploma | 19— |
| LCCI 3rd level | Text Production | 19— |
| | Audio | 19— |
| | Shorthand | 19— |
| | English for Business | 19— |
| RSA | 140 wpm Shorthand | 19— |
| PITMAN | 160 wpm Shorthand | 19— |

*Mention any special achievements*

## SPECIAL AWARDS

RSA Silver medal for shorthand 140 wpm
Governors' prize for first place in college examinations

*ention your present job first and work backwards*

## WORKING EXPERIENCE

| | | |
|---|---|---|
| April 19—<br>to present | Personal Secretary to<br>General Manager | Reliance Cables<br>Vicarage Road<br>Leyton<br>LONDON E10 5RG |
| Sept 19— to<br>March 19— | Shorthand Typist | Bains, Hoyle & Co<br>Solicitors<br>60 Kingsway<br>LONDON WC2B 6AB |

Hobbies, interests or other relevant information

**INTERESTS**

Music; Languages; Hockey; Golf; Swimming

**REFEREES**

Give at least 2 referees – a former employer? a teacher?

1  Dr R G Davies
Principal
Bedford Secretarial College
Righton Road
Bedford MH2 2BS

2  Ms W Harris
Partner
Bains, Hoyle & Co
60 Kingsway
London WC2B 6AB

3  Mr W J Godfrey OBE
Managing Director
Reliance Cables
Vicarage Road
Leyton
London E10 5RG

Date your CV with month/year

June 19—

## 16.2  Application using an introduction

Sometimes your application will result from an introduction by a friend or colleague. In this case such an introduction should be mentioned in the opening paragraph as a useful way of attracting attention.

Dear Mr Barker

Mrs Phyllis Naish, your Personnel Officer, has told me that you have a vacancy for a Marketing Assistant. I should like to be considered for this post.

As you will see from my enclosed Curriculum Vitae I have several A levels as well as secretarial qualifications gained during an intensive one-year course at Walthamstow College of Commerce.

I have been Shorthand Typist in the Marketing Department of Enterprise Cables Ltd for 2 years and have been very happy there gaining a lot of valuable experience. However the office is quite small and I now wish to widen my experience and hopefully improve my prospects.

My former headmistress has written the enclosed testimonial and has kindly agreed to give further details should they be needed. If you are interested in my application my present employer has agreed to provide further information.

I am able to attend an interview at any time and hope to hear from you soon.

Yours sincerely

## 16.3 Application for post of Sales Manager

Dear Sir

Mention the post and advertisement — I was very interested to see your advertisement for a Sales Manager in yesterday's <u>Daily Telegraph</u> and should like to be considered for this post.

Enclose CV and briefly discuss working experience — My full particulars are shown on my enclosed curriculum vitae, from which you will see that I have had 10 years' experience in the sales departments of two well-known companies. My special duties at Oral Plastics Ltd include the training of sales personnel, dealing with the company's foreign correspondence and organising market research and sales promotion

Mention why you are applying — programmes. I thoroughly enjoy my work and am very happy here but feel that the time has come when my experience in marketing has prepared me for the responsibility of full sales management.

Refer to referees — Mr James Watkinson, my Managing Director, and Ms Harriet Webb, Sales Manager of my former company, have both consented to provide references for me: their details can be found on my curriculum vitae.

Suitable close — I shall be pleased to provide any further information you may need and hope I may be given the opportunity of an interview.

Yours faithfully

## 16.4 Application for a teaching post

This letter of application is sent by a trainee teacher to the Chief Education Officer of her local authority enquiring about suitable teaching posts.

Dear Sir

At the end of the present term I shall complete my one-year teacher training course at Garnett College of Education. For domestic reasons, I would like to obtain a post at a school or college in the area administered by your authority.

From my curriculum vitae which is attached you will see that I have 6 0 level and 2 A level passes, as well as advanced qualifications in many secretarial subjects. I have held secretarial positions in the London area for a total of 8 years, during which time I studied for my RSA Shorthand and Typewriting Teachers' Diplomas. Having enjoyed the opportunity to teach these subjects in evening classes at the Chingford Evening Institute for 2 years, I was prompted to take up a full-time Certificate in Education at Garnett.

I like young people and get on well with them, and I am looking forward to helping them in the very practical way which teaching makes possible. If there is a suitable vacancy in your area, I hope you will consider me for it.

Yours faithfully

### 16.5  Application for post of Data Processing Trainee

In this letter the writer gives details of his education and qualifications in his letter instead of in a separate curriculum vitae. This style is useful when the applicant does not have a lot of previous working experience to warrant a CV.

---

Dear Sir

I would like to apply for the post of Management Trainee in your Data Processing Department advertised today in <u>The Guardian.</u>

I obtained A level passes in Mathematics, Physics and German at Marlborough College, Wiltshire. The College awarded me an open scholarship to Queens College, Cambridge, where I obtained a first in Mathematics and a second in Physics. After leaving University last year I accepted a temporary post with Firma Hollander & Schmidt in order to improve my German and gain some practical experience in their laboratories at Bremen. This work comes to an end in 6 weeks time.

My special interest for many years has been computer work and I should like to make it my career. I believe my qualifications in Mathematics and Physics would enable me to do so successfully.

I am unmarried and would be willing to undertake the training courses away from home to which you refer in your advertisement.

My former Housemaster at Marlborough, Mr T Gartside, has consented to act as my referee (telephone 0117 234575) as has Dr W White, Dean of Queens College, Cambridge (telephone 01246 453453). I hope that you will take up these references and grant me the opportunity of an interview.

Yours faithfully

---

### 16.6  An unsolicited application

An *unsolicited*[1] application is the most difficult to write since there is no advertisement or introduction to tell you anything about the work or indeed whether there is a vacancy. In such a situation you must try to find out something about the company's activities and then show how your qualifications and experience could be used.

[1] **unsolicited** not asked for

Dear Sir

For the past 8 years I have been a Statistician in the Research Unit of Baron & Smallwood Ltd, Glasgow. I am now looking for a change of employment which would widen my experience and at the same time improve my prospects. It has occurred to me that a large and well known organisation such as yours might be able to use my services.

I am 31 years of age and in excellent health. At the University of London I specialised in merchandising and advertising, and was awarded a PhD degree for my thesis on 'Statistical Investigation in Research'. I thoroughly enjoy working on investigations particularly where the work involves statistics.

Although I have had no experience in consumer research, I am familiar with the methods employed and fully understand their importance in the recording of buying habits and trends. I should like to feel that there is an opportunity to use my services in this type of research and that you will invite me to attend an interview. I could then give you further information and bring testimonials.

I hope to hear from you soon.

Yours faithfully

## TESTIMONIALS

As well as sending a copy of your curriculum vitae with an application letter, it is useful to send copies of any testimonials you may have from previous employers. The originals of such open testimonials are addressed TO WHOM IT MAY CONCERN. They are generally given by your previous employers if requested; you should always retain the originals and send photocopies only to prospective employers.

There is no legal obligation for anyone to give a testimonial, but if one is written it must state only what is true otherwise the writer may become legally liable, either to the applicant for *libel*[2], or to the employer if the testimonial is at all misleading.

Any testimonial should follow the following 4-Point Plan:

1  state duration of employment and post(s) held
2  give details of the duties carried out
3  mention work attitude and personal qualities
4  finish with a recommendation

---

[2] **libel** a statement damaging a person's reputation

## 16.7 Formal testimonial for Secretary

This testimonial was requested by an employee who worked at a company for a period of 8 years until she took up teacher training.

TO WHOM IT MAY CONCERN

*Duration of employment/ Position* — Miss Sharon Tan was employed as Shorthand Typist in this Company's Sales Department when she left secretarial college in July 19—. She was promoted to my Personal Secretary in 19—.

*Duties* — Her responsibilities included the usual secretarial duties involved in such a post as well as attending meetings, transcribing minutes and supervising and advising junior secretaries.

*Working attitude* — Sharon used her best endeavours at all times to perform her work conscientiously and expeditiously. She was an excellent secretary, an extremely quick and accurate shorthand typist and meticulous in the layout, presentation and accuracy of her work. I cannot overstress her exceptional work rate which did not in any way detract from the very high standards she set for herself.

*Personal qualities* — Sharon enjoyed good health and was a good time-keeper. She was very personable, friendly, sociable and quick to share in a joke. It was a great loss to both myself and the Company when Sharon took up teacher-training.

*Recommendation* — In my opinion, Sharon has the necessary character, dedication and approach to be suitable for the position of personal secretary or to enter the teaching profession. I can recommend her highly and may be contacted for further information.

IAN HENLEY
Deputy Chairman

## 16.8 Testimonial for Head of Department

Here is another very favourable testimonial which was issued to someone who left a private college after completing a 2-year contract as Head of Department.

---

TO WHOM IT MAY CONCERN

Norman Tyler has been employed by this College as Head of Business Studies from August 19— to 9 March 19—.

As well as capably handling the responsibilities for the overall administration of his department Norman ably taught Economics, Commerce and Management Appreciation to students of a wide range of ability and age groups on courses leading to Advanced LCCI examinations.

Norman is a highly competent and professional teacher whose class preparation is always thorough and meticulous. His committed approach to teaching is matched by his administrative abilities. He has made a substantial contribution to course planning, student counselling, curriculum development and program marketing.

Norman possesses an outgoing personality and he mixes well. He makes his full contribution to a team and is popular with his students and colleagues alike.

In view of his his dedication and ability I am confident that Norman will prove to be a valuable asset to any organization fortunate enough to employ him. It is with pleasure that I recommend him highly and without hesitation.

FAISAL SHAMLAN
Principal

---

# FAVOURABLE REFERENCES

Even if testimonials are provided at the time of sending an application letter, it is usual to state (either on your CV or covering letter) the names of one or two people who have consented to act as referees. Prospective employers may contact such referees either by telephone or letter to obtain further information about an applicant's work performance and character.

### 16.9 Letter taking up a reference

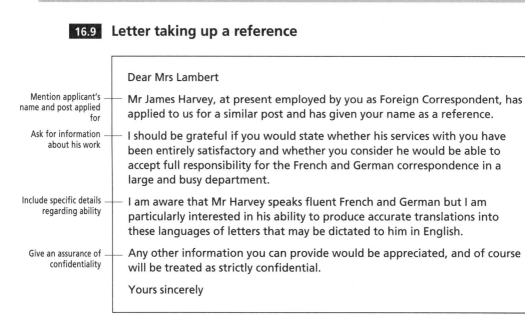

Dear Mrs Lambert

*Mention applicant's name and post applied for* —— Mr James Harvey, at present employed by you as Foreign Correspondent, has applied to us for a similar post and has given your name as a reference.

*Ask for information about his work* —— I should be grateful if you would state whether his services with you have been entirely satisfactory and whether you consider he would be able to accept full responsibility for the French and German correspondence in a large and busy department.

*Include specific details regarding ability* —— I am aware that Mr Harvey speaks fluent French and German but I am particularly interested in his ability to produce accurate translations into these languages of letters that may be dictated to him in English.

*Give an assurance of confidentiality* —— Any other information you can provide would be appreciated, and of course will be treated as strictly confidential.

Yours sincerely

### 16.10 Favourable reply

In this reply, the writer recommends the employee very highly and without hesitation, feeling confident that he can carry out the duties required in the post stated.

Dear Mr Brodie

I am pleased to be able to reply favourably to your enquiry of 6 April concerning Mr James Harvey.

Mr Harvey is an excellent linguist and for the past 5 years has been in sole charge of our foreign correspondence, most of which is with European companies especially in France and Germany.

We have been extremely pleased with the services provided by Mr Harvey. Should you engage him you may rely upon him to produce well-written and accurate transcripts of letters into French and German. He is a very reliable and steady worker and has an excellent character.

We wish him success, but at the same time shall be very sorry to lose him.

Yours sincerely

### 16.11 Cautious reply

In this reply the writer is very cautious, implying that the applicant lacks the experience needed for control of a department. However the writer is very careful not to come straight out and say this in so many words.

Dear Mr Brodie

Thank you for your letter of 6 April concerning Mr James Harvey.

Mr Harvey is a competent linguist and for the past 5 years has been employed as senior assistant in our foreign correspondence section. He has always been conscientious[3] and hard-working. Whether he would be capable of taking full responsibility for a large and busy department is difficult to say; his work with us has always been carried out under supervision.

Should you require any further information please do not hesitate to contact me.

Yours sincerely

## 16.12 Enquiry letter requesting a reference

In this letter another prospective employer requests information about the work and character of an applicant.

Dear Mr Jones

Mr Lionel Picton has applied to us for an appointment as Manager of our factory in Nairobi. We are leading manufacturers of engineered components used in the petrochemical industry and are looking for a qualified engineer with works manager's experience in medium or large batch production.

Mr Picton informs us that he is employed by you as Assistant Manager of your factory in Sheffield. We should be grateful for any information you can give us about his competence, reliability and general character.

Any information provided will be treated in strictest confidence.

Yours sincerely

## 16.13 Favourable reply

Dear Mr Gandah

*knowledge letter and give background information*

Thank you for your letter of 6 August regarding Mr Lionel Picton, who has been employed by this Company for the past 10 years.

*Give details about the applicant's work, qualifications and attitude*

Mr Picton served his apprenticeship with Vickers Tools Ltd in Manchester, followed by a three-year course for the Engineering and Work Study Diploma of the Institution of Production Engineers. He is technically well-qualified and for the past five years has been our Assistant Works Manager responsible for production and associated activities in our Sheffield factory. In all aspects of his work he has shown himself to be hard-working, conscientious and in every way a very dependable employee.

*Finish with a recommendation and rsonal word about the applicant*

I can recommend Mr Picton without the slightest hesitation. I feel sure that if he was appointed to manage your factory in Nairobi he would bring to his work a genuine spirit of service, which would be found stimulating and helpful by all who worked with him.

Yours sincerely

[3] **conscientious** careful to do what is right

## 16.14  Applicant's thank you letter

Those who have provided references will naturally be pleased to know how the applicant has fared and whether successful or not. Applicants should therefore always inform and thank those who supported them.

---

Dear Mr Freeman

I would like to thank you for supporting my application for the post as Manager of the Barker Petrochemical Company in Nairobi.

I know that the generous terms in which you wrote about me had much to do with my being offered the post and I am very grateful to you for the reference you provided for me.

Your help and encouragement has always been much appreciated and this will always be remembered.

Yours sincerely

---

## 16.15  Enquiry using numbered points

In this enquiry the writer is looking for certain qualities. To make sure that each one is covered in a reply, numbered points are used.

---

Dear Miss French

*Introduction states name of applicant and post applied for* — Miss Jean Parker has applied for a post as Administrator in our Sales Department. She states that she is presently employed by you and has given your name as a referee.

*Specific questions regarding the applicant are numbered and listed* — I should be grateful if you would answer the following questions regarding her abilities and character:

1  Is she conscientious, intelligent and trustworthy?

2  Is she capable of dealing with any difficult situations?

3  Are her keyboarding and administrative skills satisfactory?

4  Is she capable of dealing accurately with figure work?

5  Is her output satisfactory?

6  Does she get on well with her colleagues?

7  Is her health and time-keeping satisfactory?

*Give an assurance of confidentiality* — Any information you are kind enough to provide will be treated in strict confidence.

Yours sincerely

---

## 16.16 Reply

Dear Mr Kingston

In reply to your letter of 15 April I have nothing to say but good about Miss Jean Parker. She has been employed as Assistant Sales Administrator in our general office for the past 2 years and I feel sure that you will find her in every way satisfactory.

In reply to each of the questions in your letter, I have no hesitation in saying that Miss Parker meets all these requirements.

We will be sorry to lose Miss Parker, but realise that her abilities demand wider scope than is possible at this Company.

Yours sincerely

## 16.17 Favourable reference – Former Student

Dear Mrs Thompson

MISS CAROLINE BRADLEY

In reply to your enquiry of 3 June I welcome the opportunity to support Miss Bradley's application for the post of your Marketing Assistant.

Miss Bradley was a student at this College during the year 19— to 19—. Admission to this intensive one-year course is restricted to students with good school-leaving qualifications. The fact that Miss Bradley was admitted to the course is in itself evidence of excellent academic ability. Upon completing her course she was awarded the title 'Student of the Year', being the student gaining highest qualifications over the one-year course.

In all other respects Miss Bradley's work and attitude were entirely satisfactory, and I can recommend her to you with every confidence. I feel sure that if she was appointed she would perform her duties diligently and reliably.

Yours sincerely

## 16.18 Favourable reference – Department Manager

Dear Mr Lee

In reply to your letter of yesterday Mr Leonard Burns is both capable and reliable. He came to us 5 years ago to take charge of our Hardware Department.

Leonard knows the trade thoroughly and does all the buying for his department with notable success. I know that for some time he has been looking for a similar post with a larger store. While we would be sorry to lose his services, we would not wish to stand in the way of the advancement which could be offered by a store such as yours.

Yours sincerely

# UNFAVOURABLE REFERENCES

If an employer is asked for a testimonial by an employee whose services have not been entirely satisfactory, the safest course of action is to tell the employee that their name may be given as a referee.

There is always a danger that unfavourable reports may be seen by unauthorised people so it is safer to make such comments either over the telephone or in person instead of in writing. If an unfavourable reference is put in writing, it should be worded with caution and restraint and with as little detail as possible.

## 16.19 Unfavourable reference

A reference such as this would almost certainly prevent this prospective employee from getting a good post anywhere, but if the writer sincerely believes in what is said then they should not fear to send it.

Dear Ms Samson

I am replying to your letter of 18 January in which you enquire about Mr Ian Bell.

Mr Bell was employed as Clerk in this Company from February to October last year. We released him because his work fell below the standards we normally require. His punctuality also left a lot to be desired and he had a disturbing influence on other members of our staff.

Mr Bell is an intelligent young man and with the exercise of a little self-discipline he could do well. However, from my personal experience I am afraid that I cannot conscientiously recommend him.

Yours sincerely

## 16.20 Alternative unfavourable reference

The letter in 16.19 is quite specific about the applicant's unsuitability. Perhaps a safer and wiser course would be to write in more general terms and to be less specific in criticism, as in this letter.

Dear Ms Samson

I am replying to your letter of 18 January in which you enquire about Mr Ian Bell.

This young man was a member of our clerical staff from February to October last year but I am sorry to say that we did not find him suitable. It is quite possible that he may do better in another office.

Yours sincerely

# INTERVIEW LETTERS

If a lot of applications are received for a post it is unlikely that all applicants can be interviewed. In such cases a shortlist will be drawn up of those applicants thought to be most suitable for interview. Letters should also be sent to the unsuccessful applicants.

## 16.21 Invitation to attend for interview

A letter inviting an applicant for interview should first acknowledge receipt of the application, and then go on to give a day, date and time for the interview. The name of the person the applicant should ask for should also be stated. Confirmation is often requested.

---

Dear Miss Wildman

SENIOR SECRETARY TO TRAINING MANAGER

Thank you for your application for this post.

You are invited to attend for an interview with me and Mrs Angela Howard, Training Manager, on Friday 29 May at 3.30 pm.

Please let me know either by letter or telephone whether this appointment will be convenient for you.

Yours sincerely

---

## 16.22 Confirmation of attendance

---

Dear Mrs Graham

SENIOR SECRETARY TO TRAINING MANAGER

Thank you for your letter inviting me to attend for interview on Friday 29 May at 3.30 pm.

I shall be pleased to attend and look forward to meeting you and Mrs Howard.

Yours sincerely

---

### 16.23 Letter of rejection before interview

It is courteous to write to the applicants who have not been included on the shortlist. It can be worded in such a way so that it does not cause offence or negative feelings.

---

Dear

Thank you for your application for the post of Senior Secretary to the Training Manager.

We have received many applications for this post. I am afraid that your experience and qualifications do not match all our requirements closely enough so we cannot include you on our shortlist for this post.

I realise you will be disappointed but would like to thank you for the considerable time and effort you put into preparing your application. You have a lot of useful experience and I am sure that you will soon find suitable employment.

Yours sincerely

---

## OFFERS OF APPOINTMENT

Letters appointing staff should state clearly the salary and any other conditions of appointment. If the duties of the post are described in detail on a Job Description and enclosed with the letter, it will not be necessary to duplicate such details in the letter itself.

### 16.24 Letter confirming offer of employment

If an appointment is made verbally at the interview, it should be confirmed by letter immediately afterwards.

---

Dear Miss Wildman

**Offer the job and include a commencement date** — I am pleased to confirm the offer we made to you yesterday of the post of Senior Secretary to the Training Manager, commencing on 1 August 19—.

**Specify the duties or enclose Job Description** — Your duties will be as outlined at the interview and as described on the attached Job Description.

**Include details of salary and holidays** — This appointment carries a commencing salary of £15,000 per annum, rising to £16,500 after one year's service and thereafter by annual review. You will be entitled to 4 weeks annual holiday.

**Mention termination information** — The appointment may be terminated at any time by either side giving 2 months notice in writing.

**Ask for confirmation** — Please confirm that you accept this appointment on the terms stated and that you will be able to commence your duties on 1 August.

Yours sincerely

---

## 16.25 Job Description

A job description gives details of the duties and responsibilities involved in a post, including any supervisory duties, specific authority and any special features of the post.

| | |
|---|---|
| If plain paper is used include the company's name. Sometimes letterheaded paper is used | **© Turner Communications** |
| | **JOB DESCRIPTION** |
| Use appropriate headings relevant to the post | JOB TITLE — Senior Secretary<br>REPORTS TO — Training Manager<br>LOCATION — Head Office, Sheffield<br>MAIN PURPOSE — To provide a confidential secretarial and support service to the Training Manager |
| | **REQUIREMENTS** |
| Sometimes specific requirements of the post holder are included | 1 Abilities: use initiative, decide priorities, work without supervision<br><br>2 Previous experience at senior level<br><br>3 Skills: Microsoft Office, notetaking skills, minute-taking skills, good organiser, good interpersonal skills<br><br>4 High standard of education with appropriate secretarial/administration qualifications |
| | **MAIN DUTIES AND RESPONSIBILITIES** |
| List the main duties and responsibilities | 1 To provide secretarial support to the Training Manager.<br><br>2 To deal with mail, answer telephone enquiries, take messages and compose correspondence.<br><br>3 To take shorthand dictation and deal with instructions from manuscript, audio or disk and to transcribe documents accurately and consistently. |
| Make sure all points are expressed in a consistent style (eg 'To...') | 4 To maintain the diary of the Training Manager.<br><br>5 To arrange meetings and produce accurate minutes.<br><br>6 To arrange training courses and seminars.<br><br>7 To make travel and accommodation arrangements as may be required.<br><br>8 To ensure the security of the office and confidential documents. |
| Finish with this standard clause | 9 To carry out any other duties as may be expected in a post of this level.<br><br>ST/BT<br><br>June 19— |

## 16.26 Letter offering appointment

When the appointment is not made at the interview, the offer will be made by letter to the selected applicant as soon as possible.

> Dear Miss Jennings
>
> Thank you for attending the interview yesterday. I am pleased to offer you the post of Secretary in our Sales Department at a starting salary of S$1200 (Singapore dollars) per month. Your commencement date will be Monday 1 October.
>
> As discussed, office hours are 0900 to 1730 with one hour for lunch. You will be entitled to 3 weeks annual paid holiday.
>
> Please confirm in writing by return that you accept this appointment on these terms and that you can take up your duties on 1 October.
>
> Yours sincerely

## 16.27 Acceptance of offer of employment

Any offer letter should be accepted in writing immediately.

> Dear Miss Tan
>
> Thank you for your letter of 24 August offering me the post of Secretary in your Sales Department.
>
> I am pleased to accept this post on the terms stated in your letter and confirm that I can commence work on 1 October.
>
> I can assure you that I shall do everything I can to make a success of my work.
>
> Yours sincerely

## 16.28 Declining an offer of employment

If you do not wish to take up the offer of employment you should put this in writing immediately and it is courteous to give a reason for declining the offer. In this way the employer may make a second choice as soon as possible.

> Dear Miss Tan
>
> Thank you for your letter of 24 August offering me the post of Secretary to the Sales Department.
>
> I am sorry that I will be unable to take up this position. My present company has discussed with me their plans for expansion and I have been offered the new post of Office Manager. You will appreciate that this post will offer me a challenge which I feel I must accept.
>
> I wish you every success in appointing a suitable candidate.
>
> Yours sincerely

## 16.29 Letter to unsuitable applicants

As soon as an offer of employment has been accepted by the selected applicant, it is courteous to write letters to the remaining applicants who were interviewed telling them that their application was unsuccessful.

---

Thank – mention post

Explain tactfully, not abruptly

Wish applicant well in future career

Dear

Thank you for attending the interview for the post of Senior Secretary to the Training Manager.

I am sorry to have to inform you that we are unable to offer you this position. Although you have excellent qualifications we have decided to appoint someone with more experience.

I feel sure that you will soon be successful in finding suitable employment.

With best wishes

Yours sincerely

---

## TERMINATION OF EMPLOYMENT

## 16.30 Employee's letter of resignation

A Contract of Employment made for a stated period comes to an end when the period is completed unless both parties agree to an extension. If the contract is for an unstated period it may be ended at any time by either of the parties giving the agreed period of notice.

---

Dear Miss Ward

I regret to inform you that I wish to give 2 weeks notice of my resignation from the Company. My last day of work will be 30 June 19—.

I have been very happy working here for the past 2 years and found my work challenging and enjoyable. However I have obtained a post in which I will have more responsibilities and greater career prospects.

Thank you for your help and guidance during my employment.

Yours sincerely

---

## 16.31 Employer's letter terminating employment (services unsatisfactory)

By the Employment Rights Act 1996 employees who feel they have been unfairly dismissed have the right to appeal to an Industrial Tribunal. An employer must be able to show that the dismissal was justified by referring to the employee's conduct or inability/failure to do the job satisfactorily.

Where it is decided to terminate the employment of a person whose services have been unsatisfactory, it is advisable to do so verbally in the first place. The confirmatory letter should be worded carefully and tactfully.

---

Dear Miss Anderson

Express regret and give a termination date — Following our discussion earlier this week I regret to inform you that your services with the Company will not be required with effect from 31 August 19—.

Give details of employee's unsatisfactory conduct — As you know there have been a number of occasions recently when I have had to point out the unsatisfactory quality of your work. Together with your persistent unpunctuality in spite of several warnings, this has led me to believe

Tactful wording is necessary — that you will perhaps be more successful in a different kind of work.

A carefully worded close is appropriate — I hope you will be successful in finding suitable employment elsewhere. If another employer should wish you to start work before the end of the month, arrangements can be made for you to be released immediately.

Yours sincerely

---

## 16.32 Employer's letter terminating employment (services redundant[3])

The Employment Rights Act 1996 states that employees are entitled to *compensation*[4] for loss of employment due to redundancy as in the case of the employer ceasing to carry on business or having no further need of the employee's services. The amount of compensation payable is calculated on the basis of the employee's age, length of service and weekly earnings.

---

Dear Mr White

As you are aware the reorganisation of our office has been the subject of an investigation by a firm of management consultants. They have made a number of recommendations which will result in a decrease in staff.

I very much regret having to inform you that your position as Ledger Clerk is one which will become redundant on 30 June. I am giving you as much notice as possible so that you can immediately begin looking for alternative employment.

You will be entitled to a redundancy payment which will amount to 2 weeks salary for each of your 5 years service, at the rate prevailing when your services end. This is calculated as follows:

£200 x 2 x 5 = £2,000

I would like to take this opportunity to say that your work has always been entirely satisfactory and I shall be pleased to provide any prospective employer with a reference if required.

I do hope you will soon find another suitable post and wish you all the best for the future.

Yours sincerely

---

[4] **compensation** payment for loss

## 16.33 Warning letter

As a general rule an employee must have received a warning before he or she may be dismissed. The company's rules regarding warnings and dismissal should be laid down in the Conditions of Employment or in the Employment Contract.

In the first place it is good business practice to speak to the employee personally to discuss unsatisfactory work or attitude. A letter should follow as confirmation of what was discussed.

Grounds for dismissal must be specific and if possible measured against the company's general conditions and terms of employment or against the job description. The period of notice served on an employee will depend on the contract of employment. Legal minimum periods of notice for long-serving staff will vary from country to country. These formal requirements should be investigated and considered.

| | |
|---|---|
| | Dear Mark |
| Background details | Further to our meeting today I am sorry to say that your conduct has been found to be unsatisfactory recently. |
| Be specific about incidents/dates | There have been two occasions during the past month in which you were found to be breaching our company rules. On 12 March you were found smoking in a prohibited area, and on 24 March you were rude to a customer. On both occasions you received a verbal warning from your supervisor. |
| Express a hope that conduct will improve | I hope there will be no repeat of either of these incidents, or indeed any other breach of the company's rules or standards of conduct. |
| State follow-up action | I will review the situation again in one month's time. |
| | Yours sincerely |

## 16.34 Second warning

Dear Mark

At our meeting today I gave you a second warning for unsatisfactory conduct. This occurred after your supervisor informed me that you had been caught taking money from the petty cash till this morning. This follows the two previous incidents mentioned in my letter of 12 June.

The sum involved was very small but I stressed to you that integrity and trust are vital in any business. You have appealed to me to give you another chance and against my better judgement I have agreed to do so. However any further unsatisfactory conduct will result in immediate dismissal.

Yours sincerely

## 16.35 Summary dismissal

> Dear Mark
>
> I confirm that you are dismissed from the company with immediate effect following the discovery that you were caught stealing money from a colleague's drawer. This action follows my warning letters dated 25 March and 5 April about unsatisfactory conduct.
>
> Our cheque for one week's salary in lieu of notice is enclosed.
>
> Yours sincerely

## 16.36 Letter giving an employee one month's notice

> Dear Mark
>
> I confirm that you have agreed to leave the company at the end of this month, ie 30 June. This follows my warning letters to you dated 25 March and 5 April and further instances of breaching company rules, smoking in prohibited areas and rudeness to customers. All these incidents have been discussed with you and officially reported under the company's general conditions of employment.
>
> If you find another position before the end of the month we will be happy to release you.
>
> Yours sincerely

## SUNDRY PERSONNEL MATTERS

### 16.37 Transfer of employee to other work

Where it is necessary to transfer an employee from work which has been enjoyed, the reasons for the transfer must be clearly explained and any advantages must be emphasised. Perhaps there will be the prospect of more interesting and responsible work, more experience, better pay, improved prospects. With tact it should be possible to convey what may be unwelcome or disappointing news to an employee without causing hurt feelings or offence. In this way what might otherwise be received as unwelcome news may almost be turned into good news.

In this case a long-standing employee is happily settled into a routine with no wish to change, but this has been made necessary due to technological changes within the company.

Dear Mr Turner

As Mrs Williamson has already discussed with you, we have arranged to appoint you as Section Supervisor in the Stores Department with effect from Monday 1 July. Your salary will be £19,200 per annum.

In your new post you will report directly to Mr James Freeman, Storekeeper, and you will be responsible for the work of the clerical staff employed in the department.

Your 30 years of loyal service in the Invoice Department have been greatly appreciated by the management, and we are sorry that it is necessary to move you from a department with which you are so familiar. Our only reason for doing so is that invoicing will be completely changed by the introduction of computerised methods. We feel sure that you will understand that it is uneconomic for us to retrain our long-standing employees who might find difficulty in adjusting to new ways of working.

In your new post you will find ample scope for your experience. I know you will do a good job and hope you will find it enjoyable.

Yours sincerely

## 16.38 Recruitment of staff through an agency

Employers in need of office staff frequently make their requirements known to employment agencies. Such agencies will introduce either full-time, part time or temporary staff in return for a commission related to the amount of wage or salary paid.

Dear Sir/Madam

I hope you will be able to help me to fill a vacancy which has just arisen in my department.

My Secretary needs secretarial help on a part-time basis. This will be an interesting post and ideal for someone who wishes to work for only a few hours each week. Applicants should be able to undertake normal secretarial duties and have shorthand and typewriting speeds of about 100 and 45 wpm respectively. Applicants of any age would be considered, but willingness and reliability are preferable to someone with high qualifications.

The successful applicant will be required to work for 3 hours on 5 mornings each week. We would be willing to consider an alternative arrangement if necessary.

I propose payment based on an hourly rate of £5.00 to £6.00 according to age and experience.

Please let me know whether you have anyone on your register who would be suitable.

Yours faithfully

### 16.39 Request for an increase in salary

Any letter requesting an increase in salary should be worded very carefully. You should explain tactfully the reason why you feel a salary increase is justified.

---

Dear Mr Browning

My present appointment carries an annual salary of £18,500; this was reviewed in March last year.

During my 5 years with this Company I feel I have carried out my duties conscientiously and have recently acquired additional responsibilities.

I feel that my qualifications and the nature of my work justify a higher salary and have already been offered a similar position with another company at a salary of £20,000 per annum.

My present duties are interesting and I thoroughly enjoy my work. Although I have no wish to leave the Company, I cannot afford to turn down the present offer unless some improvement in my salary can be arranged.

I hope a salary increase will be possible otherwise my only course will be to accept the offer made to me.

Yours sincerely

---

### 16.40 Letter of resignation

When you decide to leave a company you must hand in your notice. It is usual to do so with a formal letter of resignation in accordance with the company's conditions of employment.

---

Dear Mr McKewan

Please accept notice of my intention to leave the company in one month's time, ie 28 July.

As I have discussed with you I have accepted a position with another company which will allow me greater responsibilities and improved opportunities for advancement.

Thank you for your support during my 2 years with Turner Communications. I have gained a lot of valuable experience which will be very useful.

Yours sincerely

---

# USEFUL EXPRESSIONS

## Application letters

### Openings

1 I wish to apply for the post ... advertised in the ... on ... .

2 I was interested to see your advertisement in ... and wish to apply for this post.

3 I am writing to enquire whether you have a suitable vacancy for me in your organisation.

4 I understand from Mr ..., one of your suppliers, that there is an opening in your company for ... .

5 Mrs ... informs me that she will be leaving your company on ... and if her position has not been filled, I should like to be considered.

### Closes

1 I look forward to hearing from you and to being granted the opportunity of an interview.

2 I hope you will consider my application favourably and grant me an interview.

3 I look forward to the opportunity of attending an interview when I can provide further details.

## Favourable references

### Openings

1 Mr ... has applied to us for the above post/position of ... We should be grateful if you would give us your opinion of his character and abilities.

2 We have received an application from Miss ... who has given your name as a reference.

3 I am very glad of this opportunity to speak in support of Miss ...'s application for a position in your company.

4 In reply to your recent enquiry Ms ... has been employed as ... for the past 2 years.

### Closes

1 Any information you can provide will be much appreciated.

2 Any information you are kind enough to provide will be treated in strictest confidence.

3 I am sure you will be more than satisfied with the work of Mr ... .

4 I shall be sorry to lose ... but realise that her abilities demand wider scope than are possible at this company.

## Unfavourable references

1 I find it difficult to answer your enquiry about Mr ... He is a very likeable person but I cannot conscientiously recommend him for the vacancy you mention.

2 The work produced by ... was below the standards expected and we found it necessary to release him.

3 Her poor time-keeping was very disturbing and caused some disruption to the work of the department.

4 We found her attitude quite a bad influence on other staff within the department.

5 Although ... possesses the qualifications to perform such work, I have seen no evidence that she has the necessary self-discipline or reliability.

## Offers of employment

### Openings

1 Thank you for attending the interview last ..., I am pleased to offer you the position of ... .

2 I am pleased to confirm the offer we made to you when you came for interview on ... .

3 Following your interview with ..., I am pleased to offer you the position of ... commencing on ... .

### Closes

1 Written confirmation of your acceptance of this post would be appreciated as soon as possible.

2 Please confirm in writing that you accept this appointment on the terms stated and that you can commence your duties on ... .

3 We look forward to welcoming you to our staff and hope you will be very happy in your work here.

## Termination of employment

### Openings

1 I regret that I wish to terminate my services with this Company with effect from ... .

2 I am writing to confirm that I wish to tender my resignation. My last date of employment will be ... .

3 As my family have decided to emigrate I am sorry to have to tender my resignation.

4  It is with regret that I have to inform you that your position with this Company will become redundant on … .

5  There has been no improvement in your work performance and attitude despite our letters dated … and … . As a result we have no option but to terminate your services with effect from … .

### Closes

1  I have been very happy working here and am grateful for your guidance during my employment.

2  I am sorry that these circumstances make it necessary for me to leave the Company.

3  We have been extremely satisfied with your services and hope that you will soon find another suitable post.

4  I hope you will soon find alternative employment, and extend my best wishes for your future.

## Testimonials

### Openings

1  Mr … has been employed by this Company from … to … .

2  Miss … worked for this company from leaving college in 19— until she emigrated to Canada in March 19—.

### Central section

1  Miss … enjoys good health and is a good time-keeper.

2  She uses her best endeavours at all times to perform her work expeditiously and has always been a hard-working and conscientious employee.

3  Miss … made a substantial contribution to the work of the … department, and always performed her work in a businesslike and reliable manner.

4  Mr … gave considerable help to his colleagues in improvements of teaching methods and materials and also produced many booklets of guidance which are proving valuable to other teachers.

### Closes

1  I have pleasure in recommending … highly and without hesitation.

2  We hope that … meets with the success we feel he deserves.

3  I shall be sorry to lose his services but realise that his abilities demand wider scope than are possible at this company.

4  I can recommend Miss … to you with every confidence.

# Travel and hotels

1
2
3
4
5
6
7
8
9
10
11
12
13
14
15
16
**17**
18
19
20
21
22
23
24
25

In dealing with business travel it may be necessary to arrange for passports to be supplied or renewed, obtain visas when necessary, book travel by air or sea, and make accommodation reservations. Itineraries will also be necessary for business people who travel. Enquiries about such matters are usually made in the first instance by telephone to a travel agent who will deal with most travel requirements on your behalf. Such arrangements need then only be confirmed in writing. This chapter looks at a variety of letters in connection with travel arrangements, including the essential document for business travellers, the itinerary.

## PASSPORTS

A passport is a document of identification issued by the government of a country to ensure protection of its subjects who travel overseas. British subjects of the United Kingdom should obtain a passport application form from any main post office or large travel agent. The completed application form, together with relevant documentary evidence and fee, should be sent to any of the regional offices of the Passport Division of the Foreign Office: London, Liverpool, Peterborough, Glasgow, Newport or Belfast. Postal applications are normally processed within 3–5 weeks of receipt. If a passport is required urgently, a personal visit to a passport office can ensure processing within about 5 days. Standard passports are *valid*[1] for 10 years. New regulations mean that husband and wife passports are no longer issued; any children should be included on the passports of both parties. Full particulars regarding passports are issued with application forms.

### 17.1 Request for passport application form

> Dear Sir
>
> Early next year I intend to visit a number of countries in the Far East and Australasia. Please send me a passport application form and a list of the addresses to which applications for visas for the various countries should be sent.
>
> I have not previously held or applied for a passport of any description.
>
> Yours faithfully

### 17.2 Formal application for passport

> Dear Sir
>
> I have completed and enclose my application form for issue of a United Kingdom passport. Also enclosed are two passport photographs (one certified at the back), my birth certificate and a cheque for the passport fee.
>
> I propose to leave England on 15 January. Please ensure that my passport is prepared and sent to me in good time to enable me to obtain the necessary visas.
>
> Yours faithfully

[1] **valid** legally in order

# VISAS

Visas are required for travel to many countries. Travel arrangements may be made through a travel agent, who will usually obtain any visa which is necessary. Alternatively, visas may be obtained upon application to the visa department of the high commissioners (for British Commonwealth countries) or consuls (in foreign countries) of the countries concerned. A list of their addresses can be obtained from any passport office.

Applications for visas must be returned with the appropriate fee and any documents requested. These may include the applicant's passport, photograph, vaccination or other health certificate, travel ticket and perhaps a statement from an employer or other sponsor guaranteeing the applicant's financial security during overseas visits.

## 17.3 Request for visa application form

> Dear Sir
>
> Our Sales Director, Mr Robert Dickson, proposes to visit Australia in 2 months time on Company business.
>
> As I understand a visa is necessary, please send me the appropriate application form, together with details of your visa requirements.
>
> Yours faithfully

## 17.4 Formal application for visa

> Dear Sir/Madam
>
> I enclose the completed application form for an entry visa to enable Mr Robert Dickson, Sales Director of this Company, to visit Australia.
>
> Mr Dickson will be leaving London on 5 August for a business tour of Singapore and Hong Kong. Subject to issue of the necessary visa, he proposes to fly to Perth, Western Australia, on 7 August. Thereafter he will be visiting Melbourne, Sydney and Cairns.
>
> The purpose of Mr Dickson's visit to Australia is to gain information about recent developments in education there, with special reference to the use of our publications. He intends to visit departments of education, universities, commercial and technical colleges and other educational organisations as well as leading booksellers. This Company guarantees Mr Dickson's financial security during his stay as well as payment of all expenses incurred.
>
> The following supporting documents are enclosed:
>
> 1  Mr Dickson's passport.
>
> 2  A cheque for the visa fee.
>
> 3  A registered stamped addressed envelope for return of the passport.
>
> 4  A copy of the Company's publications catalogue for your reference.
>
> If you require any further information please do not hesitate to let me know.
>
> Yours faithfully

# TRAVEL BY AIR/SEA

There are two main types of airline customer – the business traveller and the holidaymaker. Business travellers usually make their arrangements at very short notice and as a rule make their *reservations*[2] direct with the airline, often by telephone. Holidaymakers usually employ travel agents to make their arrangements well in advance.

## 17.5 Enquiry concerning flights

### (a) Request

In this fax the writer enquires with the Reservations Officer of British Airways regarding flights between London and New York.

> My Company will be arranging a number of business trips to New York during the next 3 months.
>
> Please send me information concerning flights (outward and return) including departure times and cost of single and return fares.
>
> We are particularly interested in information relating to reduced fares.

### (b) Reply

This reply is both courteous and helpful, giving confidence.

> Many thanks for your enquiry of 5 September.
>
> I enclose a timetable giving details of outward and return flights between London and New York together with a price list in which you will find details of both ordinary and discounted fares. As you will see from this list discounted fares can be as little as one-third of the normal fare.
>
> A visa is necessary for all visitors to the United States.
>
> If I can be of any further assistance please do not hesitate to contact me.

[2] **reservation** booking

## 17.6 Enquiry concerning car ferry

Car ferries are an alternative to flying to Europe. In this letter the writer requests details of car ferries from a well-known operator.

### (a) Enquiry

Dear Sir/Madam

Later this year I propose to tour Western Europe with friends and I wish to take a car with me.

Please send me details of your car ferry service including your terms and conditions for transporting a Mercedes-Benz and three passengers from Dover to Calais.

As this would be my first use of the car ferry service I am not familiar with Customs and other formalities involved. I should be grateful for any information you can provide.

Yours faithfully

### (b) Reply

Dear Mr Hanley

Thank you for your letter of 4 August requesting details of our car ferry service.

A brochure is enclosed giving all the information you require together with prices and a timetable.

Formalities for touring Europe by car are now simpler than ever before. All that is necessary is for you to check in at our Dover office one hour before departure time and to produce the following documents:

1   Your travel ticket

2   Your passport

3   Your car registration papers

4   A valid British driving licence

5   An international insurance 'green card'

Your car must carry a GB nationality plate.

If you require further details please contact me. Meanwhile I hope you enjoy travelling with British Car Ferries Ltd.

Yours sincerely

## 17.7 Enquiry concerning sea journey

In this letter the writer makes enquiries about travel on ocean liners.

### (a) Enquiry

Dear Sir/Madam

I am interested in your sailings to New York during August or September this year. Please let me have any available literature giving information about the ships scheduled to sail during this period.

Please also let me have details of fares (single and return) for both first and second-class travel.

I look forward to hearing from you soon.

Yours faithfully

### (b) Reply

Dear Mrs Morrison

Thank you for your letter of 11 June enquiring about sailings to New York.

In the enclosed copy of our Queen Elizabeth 2 sailing list you will find details of sailings and of first-class and tourist fares including excursion fares in both classes.

A valid passport is necessary for all passengers, but an international certificate of vaccination is no longer necessary. All passengers other than United States citizens and holders of re-entry permits will also require a visa issued by a United States consul.

As the Company's liability for baggage is limited under the terms of the passenger ticket, we strongly urge passengers to insure against all risks for the full period of their journey. I shall be glad to supply details on request.

Please let me know if I can be of further assistance.

Yours sincerely

### (c) Reservation of berths

Dear Sir

Thank you for sending me information about the sailings of Queen Elizabeth 2.

Please make a reservation in my name for a first-class single cabin on 3 August sailing to New York. Full payment is enclosed.

I look forward to receiving confirmation of my reservation, together with travel ticket.

Yours faithfully

### **17.8** Enquiry concerning holiday cruises

In this letter the writer enquires about holiday cruises.

**(a) Enquiry**

> Dear Sir
>
> I am interested in learning more about 10–14 day holiday cruises offered by your organisation for this summer.
>
> Please let me have the relevant brochure as well as costs for tourist class travel.
>
> Yours faithfully

**(b) Reply**

> Dear Mrs Tonks
>
> Thank you for your enquiry of 10 February.
>
> I have pleasure in enclosing our illustrated brochure which contains full details of our summer cruises, as well as tourist-class fares. Also enclosed is a leaflet showing the accommodation available for the coming summer; as the booking position is constantly changing this leaflet can serve only as a broad guide to what we can offer.
>
> Please let me know if you require further information or assistance.
>
> Yours sincerely

# HOTEL ACCOMMODATION

Most large hotels are organised as companies and enquiries should be addressed to The Manager. Private hotels are much smaller and enquiries should be addressed to The Proprietor, by whom they are usually owned and managed.

When requesting information about a prospective booking be sure to observe the following rules:

- Keep your letter short and to the point.
- State your requirements clearly and concisely. To avoid misunderstanding mention days as well as dates for which accommodation is required, as well as the exact period of your stay if it is known (eg 'from Monday 6 to Friday 10 July inclusive').
- State times of arrival and departure if known.
- Request confirmation of the booking if there is time.

### 17.9 Booking company accommodation at a hotel

In this enquiry a company writes to the Manager of a London hotel requesting information about accommodation.

#### (a) Enquiry

> Dear Sir/Madam
>
> My company will be displaying products at the forthcoming British Industrial Fair at Earls Court and we shall require hotel accommodation for several members of staff.
>
> Please send me a copy of your current brochure and details of terms for <u>half board</u>.[3] Please also indicate if you have one double and three single rooms available from Monday 13 to Friday 17 May inclusive.
>
> I hope to hear from you soon.
>
> Yours faithfully

#### (b) Reply

Thank you —— > Dear Miss Johnson
>
> Thank you for your letter of 15 March.

Enclose brochure —— > As requested I enclose a copy of our brochure in which you will find all the necessary details required.

Repeat details of rooms and dates to avoid misunderstanding —— > We presently have one double and three single rooms available from Monday 13 to Friday 17 May inclusive. However as we are now entering the busy season and bookings for this period are likely to be heavy, we recommend that you make your reservation without delay.

Refer to advantages offered by the hotel – this will build up a cordial relationship and could lead to further business —— > You will see from our brochure that this is a modern hotel and I am sure your staff would be very comfortable here. We are well served by public transport to Earls Court, and it should be possible to reach there within 15 minutes.
>
> I hope to receive confirmation of your reservation soon.

#### (c) Confirmation of reservation

In the first instance you would normally telephone the hotel to make your reservation. This would be confirmed in writing immediately.

> Dear Mr Nelson
>
> Thank you for your letter of 17 March and our telephone conversation today.
>
> I confirm reservation of one double and three single <u>en suite</u>[4] rooms from 13–17 May inclusive, with half-board. Names of guests are:
>
> Mr & Mrs Philip Andersen
> Mr Geoffrey Richardson
> Miss Lesley Nunn
> Mr Jonathan Denby
>
> The account will be settled by Mr Philip Andersen, our Company's General Manager.
>
> Yours sincerely

[3] **half board** breakfast and evening meal only
[4] **en suite** with attached bathroom

### 17.10 Booking private accommodation

#### (a) Enquiry

> Dear Sir/Madam
>
> I shall be passing through London next week and would like to reserve a single room for Wednesday and Thursday 18 and 19 October.
>
> My previous stays at the Norfolk Hotel have always been very enjoyable; I particularly like the rooms overlooking the gardens. If one of these rooms is available I hope you will reserve it for me.
>
> I expect to arrive at the hotel in time for lunch on the 18th and shall be leaving immediately after breakfast on the 20th.
>
> Yours faithfully

#### (b) Reply

> Dear Mr Robinson
>
> Thank you for your letter of 10 October.
>
> I was glad to learn that you have enjoyed your previous visits to the Norfolk Hotel. Unfortunately a room overlooking the garden is not available for the dates you requested. However I have several pleasant rooms on the south side of the hotel, away from traffic noise and with an open view of the nearby park and lake.
>
> The charge for these rooms is £85 per night. You will find all details in the enclosed brochure.
>
> I have provisionally reserved for you one of the rooms mentioned for the two nights of Wednesday and Thursday 18 and 19 October.
>
> Please let me have your confirmation as soon as possible.
>
> Yours sincerely

### 17.11 Booking private accommodation overseas

The writer here writes to a hotel overseas mentioning that the hotel has been recommended by a friend.

#### (a) Enquiry

> Dear Sir/Madam
>
> Your hotel has been highly recommended by a friend who stayed there last year.
>
> I will be arriving in Singapore at 1730 hours on Monday 15 April on flight SQ24, accompanied by three friends. We wish to stay in Singapore for 4 nights, ie 15–18 April inclusive before arranging independent travel by land in Malaysia.
>
> Please let me know if 2 twin-bedded rooms are available for this period, and what the charges would be. I also understand that your hotel arranges local tours; full details would be appreciated.
>
> I hope to hear from you soon.
>
> Yours faithfully

## (b) Reply

In this reply, the Reservations Officer takes the trouble to point out the benefits in the hotel's position and additions since the enquirer's friend visited.

---

Dear Mr Hill

I am pleased to learn from your letter of 2 February that The Lion Hotel was recommended to you.

A copy of our illustrated brochure is enclosed showing the hotel's many facilities. You will note the recent improvements made to our pool area, with adjoining gym and leisure facilities.

Our hotel's tour operator is Century Tours and a brochure is attached giving details of their half and full-day tours. There would be no problem in reserving places on any of these tours when you arrive in Singapore.

I have taken the liberty of making a provisional reservation of 2 twin bedded rooms from 15–18 April at a cost of S$120 per night. This reservation will be held until 1 March and your confirmation would be appreciated before that date.

Arrangements can be made for our courtesy pick-up service to meet your flight SQ24 at 1730 on 15 April if you mention this at the time of confirming your reservation.

You will find The Lion Hotel very convenient for transport both by MRT (Mass Rapid Transport) and bus. It is also within 5 minutes walking distance of Orchard Road.

I look forward to extending the hospitality of The Lion Hotel to your party and hope to receive confirmation of your reservation before 1 March.

Yours sincerely

---

# HOLIDAY ACCOMMODATION AND ITINERARIES

Information about hotels, guest houses and holiday flats may be obtained from the annual holiday guides prepared by the publicity departments of the holiday resorts. These guides contain details of the resort's attractions – places of interest, entertainments, sport, museums, art galleries and cultural activities. Copies are sent on request usually free of charge.

## 17.12 Request for holiday guide

Requests for guides need only be very short and formal and unless a payment is required may be made on a postcard. Copies of the guide are usually sent out with a compliments slip instead of a formal letter.

Dear Sirs

Please send me a copy of your official holiday guide and a list of hotels and guest houses.

I enclose a large stamped addressed envelope.

Yours faithfully

## 17.13  Enquiry for hotel accommodation

### (a) Enquiry

Dear Sir/Madam

*Introduction mentions background details* — I found the name of your private hotel in the holiday guide received from the Bridlington Information Centre.

*Mention rooms and dates, and mention specific requirements* — Please let me know if you have accommodation for a family of 5 for 2 weeks commencing Saturday 10 August. We shall require 2 twin-bedded rooms and 1 single room – the single room should be on the ground floor or near to the lift as it is for my elderly mother.

*Ask for confirmation and further details* — If you can provide this accommodation please send me a copy of your brochure and also your terms for full board.[5]

Yours faithfully

### (b) Reply

Dear Mr Leeson

*Thank you* — Thank you for your enquiry dated 15 April.

*Confirm rooms are available and repeat dates. Respond to special request* — I am pleased to say that the accommodation you require is available for the 2 weeks commencing Saturday 10 August. We can offer you two adjacent[6] twin-bedded rooms on the first floor, with a single room on the same floor conveniently located about 10 metres from the lift. Should this distance present a problem we can place a wheelchair at your disposal.

*State why early confirmation is necessary* — Early confirmation of this accommodation is necessary as bookings for August are always heavy and I should not wish you to be disappointed.

*Enclose brochure and close with a personal touch* — A brochure containing details of our charges is enclosed. We hope you will give us the opportunity to welcome your family to the Northcliffe.

Yours sincerely

---

[5] **full board** including all meals
[6] **adjacent** adjoining

### 17.14 Enquiry to a small private hotel

#### (a) Enquiry

Dear Sir/Madam

Your hotel has been recommended to me by Mr & Mrs John Windsor who tell me they spent a very happy fortnight with you last summer.

I am planning to bring my family to St Annes for 2 weeks between mid-July and the end of August, and hope you will be able to accommodate us. We need one double and one twin-bedded room fo my wife and myself and our two young children.

Our holiday arrangements are fairly flexible and any 2 consecutive[7] weeks within the period mentioned would be suitable.

An early reply would be appreciated so that our holiday arrangements can be completed as soon as possible.

Yours faithfully

#### (b) Reply

Dear Mr Wilkinson

Thank you for your letter of 10 April. I remember Mr & Mrs Windsor very well; please pass on my thanks for their recommendation.

We are already fully booked for the month of August but the flexibility of your arrangements enables us to offer you one double and one twin bedded room for 2 full weeks from Saturday 18 July.

We are provisionally[8] reserving this accommodation for you, but would appreciate your written confirmation within one week.

Our current brochure is enclosed for your information.

We look forward to welcoming you to St Annes and assure you that everything possible will be done to make your stay here a very happy one.

Yours sincerely

### 17.14 Enquiry to the proprietor of holiday flats

#### (a) Enquiry

Dear Sir/Madam

We wish to arrange a family holiday for 2 weeks from Saturday 14 August. Please let me know whether you have accommodation available which would be suitable for my husband and myself, as well as our two teenage children. We also wish to bring our dog, a clean and well-trained Irish Setter.

If you are able to accommodate us during this period, please let me know the facilities available in your holiday flats, together with your charges.

Yours faithfully

[7] **consecutive** running together
[8] **provisionally** subject to confirmation

**(b) Reply**

Dear Mrs Turner

Thank you for your recent enquiry regarding holiday accommodation for your family for 2 weeks from Saturday 14 August.

I am pleased to say that we have a holiday flat available which would be suitable for your family. This flat is on the first floor and comprises one double and two bunk beds, as well as cooker, fridge, sink, wardrobes and bedside drawers.

We do allow dogs in our holiday flats and refer you to the rules contained in our enclosed brochure. Schedules of prices are also shown on the separate leaflet.

We hope to welcome you to Thornton Holiday Flats and advise you to make an early reservation.

Yours sincerely

**17.16** **Itineraries**

An itinerary gives full details of a journey in order of date. It shows all travel arrangements, accommodation and appointments. It is usual to use sub-headings and columns so that the information is displayed attractively and is easy to refer to.

Use plain paper but show the company's name

Include traveller's name, places being visited and duration of trip

Display all dates as shoulder headings

Use a 2 or 3 column format for ease of reference

Use 24 hour clock for all times

## ✆ Turner Communications

**ITINERARY FOR MRS SALLY TURNER**

TOUR OF SINGAPORE AND MALAYSIA
7–19 JULY 19—

SUNDAY 7 JULY

| 1530 | Depart London Heathrow (flight SQ101) |

MONDAY 8 JULY

| 1830 | Arrive Singapore Changi Airport |
| | (Met by Janet Benson, Asia Communications) |
| | Accommodation: Supreme International Hotel, Scotts Road. |

TUESDAY 9 JULY

| 1030 | Miss Sally Tan, Communications Asia, Funan Centre |
| 1430 | Mr Mark Lim, TalkTime, Bugis Junction |

WEDNESDAY 10 JULY

| 0930–1730 | 5th International Telecommunications Conference |

SUNDAY 14 JULY

| 1545 | Depart Singapore Changi Airport Terminal 2 (flight MH989) |
| 1700 | Arrive Kuala Lumpur |
| | Accommodation: Royal Hotel, Petaling Jaya |

MONDAY 15 JULY

| 1030 | Mr Richard Foo, KL Talk |
| 1530 | Mrs Ong Lee Fong, Malaysia Communications |

TUESDAY 16 JULY

| 1130 | Miss Sylvia Koh, Talklines |

FRIDAY 19 JULY

| 2330 | Depart Kuala Lumpur (BA 012) |

SATURDAY 20 JULY

| 0830 | Arrive London Heathrow |

ST/BT
15 June 19—

# USEFUL EXPRESSIONS

## Openings

1  I wish to visit ... and would be pleased to know if you have a single room available on ... .

2  I should be grateful if you would forward a copy of your current brochure.

3  Please let me know if you have available a first-class single cabin on the ... leaving for ... on ... .

4  I was pleased to hear that our hotel was recommended by ... after his visit in ... .

## Closes

1  When replying please include a copy of your current brochure.

2  I hope to receive an early reply.

3  I look forward to hearing that you can provide this accommodation.

4  As we wish to make arrangements in good time I should appreciate an early reply.

# Publicity material

Press release

Invitations

Replies to invitations

*Checklist*

# PRESS RELEASE

Very often it is necessary to write an article or feature for publication in the press or other media. In this case it is not a letter which is written but a press release. A press release is a good way of publicising many things such as:

- relocation of offices
- expansion of business
- introduction of new products
- changes in top personnel

When writing a press release always follow this 4-point plan:

1 A snappy headline is essential. Then grasp the editor's attention with a good opening which includes the most important details.
2 Keep central paragraphs short and self-contained. The editor may cut them out if necessary.
3 Write in an interesting, punchy style. Even a seemingly uninteresting event can be made into an effective story by clever wording.
4 Close by repeating the main message again. A quotation is useful in the final section.

When writing a press release try not to make it sound like an invitation or advertisement. It should be worded as if you are the newspaper editor, ie use third person. Flat, vague, dull and boring writing will get no further than the editor's waste-paper bin. Write in short sentences using a crisp, punchy style and ensure no essential details are omitted.

**© Turner Communications**      Mobile Phone specialists

21 Ashton Drive
Sheffield                        Tel    +44 114 2871122
S26 2ES                          Fax    +44 114 2871123
                                 Email  TurnerComm@intl.uk

ST/BT

15 June 19—

PUBLICATION DATE: Immediate

NEW JOBS IN TURNER SUPERSTORE

Mobile phone specialists, Turner Communications, have today announced the
opening of their new store Turner's Office Supplies. More than 50 new jobs
have been created.

Turner Communications have established themselves as leaders in the field of
mobile communications in the UK. Roaming agreements have been set up
with many countries throughout the world.

The company has now announced that it is diversifying. Their new Office
Supplies superstore will sell everything from stationery and office sundries to
computers and other office equipment. It will be situated in a prime location
at Meadowhall Retail Park on the outskirts of Sheffield, very close to the M1
motorway.

A grand opening ceremony is planned to take place on Monday 1 July with
special offers to the first 100 customers and a grand draw at 5.00 pm.

Sally Turner, Managing Director, said 'We are very excited about this new
office superstore and feel confident that it will prove to be an overwhelming
success.'

Contact:    Diana Wilson, Marketing Manager, Turner Communications
            Telephone: 0114 2871122

# INVITATIONS

Many companies organise special functions to publicise certain events, for example

- the opening of a new branch office
- the introduction of new products or services
- the retirement of a senior executive
- a special anniversary

Formal invitations are usually printed on A5 or A6 high quality paper or card.

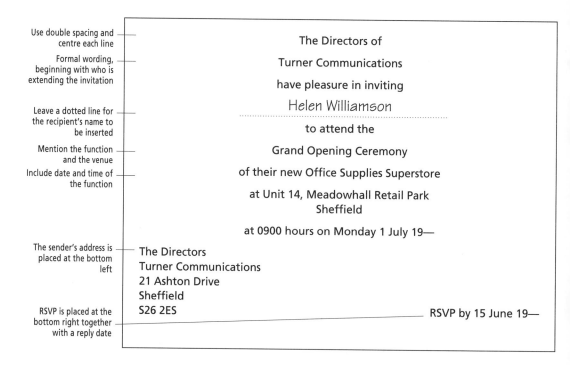

Use double spacing and centre each line ————

Formal wording, beginning with who is extending the invitation ————

Leave a dotted line for the recipient's name to be inserted ————

Mention the function and the venue ————

Include date and time of the function ————

The sender's address is placed at the bottom left ————

RSVP is placed at the bottom right together with a reply date ————

The Directors of

Turner Communications

have pleasure in inviting

Helen Williamson

to attend the

Grand Opening Ceremony

of their new Office Supplies Superstore

at Unit 14, Meadowhall Retail Park
Sheffield

at 0900 hours on Monday 1 July 19—

The Directors
Turner Communications
21 Ashton Drive
Sheffield
S26 2ES
RSVP by 15 June 19—

# REPLIES TO INVITATIONS

When accepting or refusing an invitation it is usual to do so in a similar style to the invitation which was received. If the invitation is refused it is courteous to give a reason.

Use a similar formal style, in double spacing

Use third person and formal wording

Include all relevant details from original invitation

Miss Helen Williamson

of Johnson Electrical Supplies

thanks the Directors of Turner Communications

for their kind invitation to the

Grand Opening Ceremony

of their new Office Supplies Superstore

at Unit 14, Meadowhall Retail Park
Sheffield

at 0900 hours on Monday 1 July 19—

A formal acceptance

he sender's address is cluded at the bottom ft and the date at the right

and has much pleasure in accepting

2 Chamber Road
Aston
Sheffield S26 2ES

2 June 19—

## CHECKLIST FOR A PRESS RELEASE

☐ Include an embargo (publication) date

☐ Make your headline snappy and punchy

☐ The first paragraph should mention the main points and really grasp the editor's attention

☐ Use double line spacing for central section

☐ Keep paragraphs short and self-contained

☐ Write in an interesting, crisp style, no matter how uninteresting the story

☐ Round it off with a conclusion or a quotation

☐ Include contact name and telephone number

# Arranging appointments, meetings and other functions

1
2
3
4
5
6
7
8
9
10
11
12
13
14
15
16
17
18
19
20
21
22
23
24
25

Every day in the business world appointments and meetings are being arranged, and conferences and other special functions are being organised. As a result numerous letters, faxes and other documents are written by secretaries, administrators and organisers. This chapter looks at the various communications and other associated documents which are connected with this very important aspect of day-to-day business life.

## 19.1 Letter requesting appointment

### (a) Request 1

Dear Mr Harrison

Our Mr Chapman has informed me that you have returned home from your visit to the Middle East. There are a number of points which have arisen on the book I am writing on <u>Modern Business Organisation</u> I should like the opportunity to discuss these with you.

I shall be in London from 16 to 19 September and will telephone you on Monday 15 September to arrange a day and time which would be convenient for us to meet.

I look forward to the opportunity of meeting you again.

Yours sincerely

### (b) Reply

Dear Mr Alexander

Thank you for your letter regarding <u>Modern Business Organisation</u>.

I will look forward to meeting you again to discuss this. I note you will be telephoning me on Monday morning and hope that it will be possible to arrange to meet on either Tuesday or Wednesday afternoon.

I look forward to meeting you again.

Yours sincerely

### (c) Request 2

Dear Mr Jones

I am very concerned about the difficulties you are having with the goods we supplied earlier this year.

I should very much like the opportunity to discuss this matter with you personally and wonder if it would be convenient to see you while I am in your area next month. My secretary will telephone you soon to make a convenient appointment.

Yours sincerely

## (d) Request 3

Dear Mrs Graham

I should very much like to see you to discuss various matters of mutual interest. As I shall be in Bradford next week, I wonder if it will be convenient to meet you on Thursday 12 September.

My secretary will call you within the next few days to confirm this appointment or if necessary arrange an alternative appointment.

I look forward to seeing you.

Yours sincerely

## 19.2 Letter inviting speaker to conference

### (a) Invitation

Mention function, location, dates, number of delegates expected

Dear Miss Forrester

Our Society will be holding a conference at the Moat House Hotel, Swansea from 4 to 6 October the theme of which will be 'Changes in the Role of the Secretary'. Approximately 100 delegates are expected, comprising mostly practising secretaries as well as some lecturer members.

Include title of talk and timing. Mention any payments which will be made

We would be delighted if, once again, you would accept our invitation to speak on the subject of 'Effective Communication' on 5 October from 1030 to 1130. We would of course be prepared to pay you the usual fee of £50 and your travel expenses.

Enclose detailed programme. Mention overnight accommodation

A copy of the detailed draft programme is enclosed. You will of course, be welcome to attend other sessions of the conference on that day. Overnight accommodation will be provided for you on 4 October.

Request confirmation and details of any equipment needed

We look forward to hearing that you can accept our invitation. At the same time please let us know if you will need any visual aids or other equipment.

Yours sincerely

### (b) Reply

Dear Ms Bolan

Thank you

Thank you for your letter inviting me to speak at your conference on 5 October on the subject of 'Effective Communication'.

Acceptance and confirmation

I am delighted to accept your invitation, and confirm that I shall require overnight accommodation on 4 October.

Mention any equipment needed

I will require use of an overhead projector for my presentation and hope this can be made available.

The close includes a personal touch

I look forward to meeting you and other members of your Society again at your conference and wish you every success.

Yours sincerely

### (c) Letter declining invitation

Dear Mr Woodhead

I was very pleased to receive your letter of 2 July.

Much as I should like to be able to speak at your conference in October, I am sorry to say that I will be unable to do so as I shall be abroad at the time. I must therefore regretfully decline your kind invitation.

I do hope that the day will be a great success.

Yours sincerely

## 19.3 Letter regarding conference accommodation

Dear Sir

*Mention function, date, timing and reason for writing*

Our Company will be holding a one-day conference on Saturday 18 May from 1000 to 1730, and we are looking for suitable accommodation.

*Include number of delegates expected*

About 200 delegates are expected to attend and our requirements are as follows:

1    A suitable conference room with theatre-style seating

2    A small adjacent room for the display of equipment and accessories

*Number and list the specific requirements*

3    A reception area for welcoming and registering delegates

4    Morning coffee at 1130 and afternoon tea at 1530

5    A buffet luncheon to be served from 1300 to 1400

*Ask for information about facilities and costs*

If you have suitable facilities available please let us know the costs involved. At the same time please send specimen menus for a buffet-style luncheon.

We hope to hear from you soon.

Yours faithfully

**19.4** ## Conference programme

Company's name —— ✆ **Turner Communications**

Main heading —— **5TH ANNIVERSARY CELEBRATIONS**

Date and venue —— to be held on Wednesday 17 September 19—
at Supreme Hotel, Aston, Sheffield

Sub-heading states
whether programme is —— PROVISIONAL PROGRAMME
provisional or final

|  |  |
|---|---|
| 1800 | Arrival of Directors and staff |

Use 24 hour clock, with
or without the word —— 1830 Arrival of guests
'hours'

5th Anniversary folders will be issued to guests on arrival

Cocktails will be served

List each item in turn —— 1900 Introduction by Suzanne Sutcliffe, Marketing Manager
with any extra details who will act as Master of Ceremonies

1915 Opening address (Sally Turner, Managing Director)

Include names of —— 1930 Slide presentation (Mandy Lim, Administration Manager)
presenters in brackets

2000 Buffet supper

2130 Toastmaster (John Stevens, Public Relations Manager)

2145 Closing address (Suzanne Sutcliffe, Marketing Manager)
Clarify the time at which —— Drinks will be served until 2300
the event will finish

SS/ST

5 July 19—

## 19.5 • Memo requesting agenda items

Display memo headings in the usual way

**MEMORANDUM**

To    Departmental Heads

From  Steven Broom, Administration Manager

Ref    SB/ST

Date  2 July 19—

Heading states name and date of meeting

OPERATIONS MEETING – 14 JULY

Clarify meeting, venue, time and date of meeting

Please note that the next Operations Meeting will be held in the Conference Room at 1000 hours on Monday 14 July.

Follow-up items from our last meeting which will be included under Matters Arising are:

Mention any items already included on the agenda

● New brochure (Suzanne Sutcliffe)
● Annual Dinner and Dance (Mandy Lim)

Give a deadline for submission of extra items

If you wish to add any further items to the agenda please let me know before 8 July.

## 19.6 • Memo including agenda

Display memo headings in the usual way

**MEMORANDUM**

To    Departmental Managers

From  Steven Broom, Administration Manager

Ref    SB/ST

Date  2 July 19—

OPERATIONS MEETING

Confirm details regarding venue, date and time

The next monthly Operations Meeting will be held in the Conference Room at 1000 hours on Monday 14 July 19—.

State the word AGENDA

AGENDA

These first 3 items of 'ordinary business' should be included on every agenda

1  Apologies for absence

2  Minutes of last meeting

3  Matters arising from the Minutes

     3.1  New brochure (Suzanne Sutcliffe)

     3.2  Annual Dinner and Dance (Mandy Lim)

4  New branches (Suzanne Sutcliffe)

These are items of 'special' business, specific to this meeting only

5  Far East Trip (Sally Turner)

6  European Telecommunications Conference (John Stevens)

7  5th Anniversary Celebrations (Suzanne Sutcliffe)

These final 2 items are again 'ordinary business'

8  Any other business

9  Date of next meeting

## 19.7 Notice and agenda

| | |
|---|---|
| Company's name | $\mathcal{C}$ **Turner Communications** |
| Title of meeting | **OPERATIONS MEETING** |
| Notice section: state venue, time and date | The monthly Operations Meeting will be held in the Conference Room at 1000 hours on Monday 14 July 19— |

A G E N D A

1  Apologies for absence

*Opening ordinary business* —— 2  Minutes of last meeting

3  Matters arising from the Minutes

     3.1  New brochure (Suzanne Sutliffe)

     3.2  Annual Dinner and Dance (Mandy Lim)

*Special business (note all names in brackets)* —— 4  New branches (Suzanne Sutcliffe)

5  Far East Trip (Sally Turner)

6  European Telecommunications Conference (John Stevens)

7  5th Anniversary Celebrations (Suzanne Sutcliffe)

*Final ordinary business* —— 8  Any other business

9  Date of next meeting

ST/BT

# Classified business letters

# Agencies

1
2
3
4
5
6
7
8
9
10
11
12
13
14
15
16
17
18
19
**20**
21
22
23
24
25

Many businesses with a large volume of foreign trade do their own buying and selling. A large manufacturing business, for instance, will often have its own export department and if the volume of trade is sufficient may establish branches abroad. However there are many smaller firms who find it more economical to buy and sell through commission agents or commission houses, factors, brokers and other types of agent.

Any company considering appointing an agent should make a thorough investigation into such prospective agent's qualifications, experience and personal qualities beforehand, for example:

- Their reliability and financial soundness.
- Their technical ability to handle the goods to be marketed.
- Their market connections and the effectiveness of their sales organisation.
- The nature and extent of other agencies they hold and in particular whether these are connected with the sale of competing products.

These matters are especially important when foreign agents are appointed, since they will be working without local supervision or control. It is advisable to make a formal appointment of an agent in writing, setting out in detail the terms of the agency.

## FINDING AN AGENT

There are useful sources of information for those who want help in finding suitable agents. A British supplier, for instance, wishing to develop trade in an overseas country could make use of one or more of the following:

- The Export Services Division or the appropriate Regional Office of the Department of Trade.
- The Consular Section of the appropriate Embassy.
- HM Trade Commissioner in the country concerned.
- The Chamber of Commerce.
- Banks.
- An advertisement in selected journals in the country concerned.

## APPLICATIONS FOR AGENCIES

When seeking an agency the applicant will stress two things:

- The opportunities in the market waiting to be developed.
- The particular advantages that may be offered.

The applicant will mention such selling points as knowledge of the market, numerous connections, long-established position and wide experience, the efficiency of their sales organisation, the facilities for display offered by their showrooms and so on. The agent may also give the names of persons or firms who may be referred to and mention the rate of commission expected.

## 20.1 Application for home agency

### (a) Application

Dear Sir/Madam

Introduction — We understand from Knowles Hardware Ltd of Glasgow that you are looking for a reliable firm with good connections in the textile trade to represent you in Scotland.

Background details about why you are writing — For some years we have acted as Scottish agents for one of your competitors, Jarvis & Sons of Preston. They have recently registered as a limited company and in the reorganisation decided to establish their own branch in Edinburgh. As they no longer need our services we are now free to offer them to you.

Details of experience, staff, facilities — As we have had experience in marketing products similar to your own, we are familiar with customers' needs and are confident that we could develop a good market for you in Scotland. We have spacious and well equipped showrooms not only at our Glasgow headquarters but also in Edinburgh and Perth, plus many experienced sales representatives who would energetically promote your business.

letter leads logically a statement of what you want. Suggest a meeting — We hope you will be interested in our proposal and will let us know on what terms you would be willing to conclude an agreement. I will be visiting your town in 2 weeks' time and hope it will be possible to discuss details with you then.

The close offers references — We can provide first-class references if required, but for general information concerning our standing in the trade we suggest you refer to Knowles Hardware Ltd.

We hope to hear from you soon.

Yours faithfully

### (b) Reply

Dear Mrs Matthews

Thank you for your letter of 10 September. We are very interested to discuss further your proposal for an agency in Scotland.

Your work with Jarvis & Co is well-known to us and in view of your connections throughout the trade in Scotland we feel there is much you could do to extend our business there.

Our final decision would depend upon the terms and conditions. As you will be visiting our town soon it would be better to discuss these in person rather than to enter upon what may become lengthy correspondence.

Please let me know when we may expect you to call.

Yours sincerely

## (c) Agency appointed

Dear Mrs Matthews

Refer to meeting and offer the appointment on the terms discussed — It was a pleasure to meet you yesterday. We are now pleased to offer you an appointment as our sole agents for Scotland on the terms and conditions agreed verbally with you.

Give full details of period and commission — This appointment will be for a trial period of 12 months initially. We will pay you a commission of 7% on the net value of all sales against orders received through you, to which would be added a del credere[1] commission of 2½%.

Further details regarding stocks or samples — As we are able to facilitate quick delivery there will be no need for you to maintain stocks of our goods, but we will send you full ranges of samples for display in your showrooms.

Refer to the need for a formal agreement — Please confirm these terms in writing as soon as possible, after which we will arrange for a formal agreement to be drawn up. When this is signed a circular will be prepared for distribution to our customers in Scotland announcing your appointment as our agents.

An encouraging close — We look forward to a successful business relationship.

Yours sincerely

## 20.2 Application for overseas agency

### (a) Electrical engineering

Dear Sir/Madam

Introduction stating why you are writing — I was interested to see your advertisement in *The Daily Telegraph* and wish to offer my services as representative of your company in Morocco.

Background details about your company — I am 35 years old, a chartered electrical engineer, and have a good working knowledge of Spanish and German. For the past 5 years I have acted in Egypt as agent for Moxon & Parkinson, electrical engineers in Warrington, Lancashire. This company has recently been taken over by Digital Equipment Ltd and is now being represented in Egypt by its own representative.

Further details of your experience and abilities — I have been concerned with work in the electronic field[2] since I graduated in physics at Manchester University at the age of 22. During my agency with Moxons I also had first-hand experience of marketing electronic and microprocessing equipment.[3] I feel I am well able to promote the sale of your products in the expanding economies of the African countries.

References — For references I suggest you contact Moxon & Parkinson, as well as the two companies named below, both of which I have had close business connections for several years:

Fylde Electronic Laboratories Ltd, 4 Blackpool Road, Preston, Lancs

Sexton Electronic Laboratories Ltd, 25 Deansgate, Manchester

Suggest a personal interview to discuss further — I look forward to being able to give you more information at a personal interview.

Yours faithfully

---

[1] **del credere commission** amount paid to an agent who guarantees payment (a *del credere* agent)
[2] **electronic field** the area of electronics
[3] **microprocessing equipment** electronic equipment such as computers which have been greatly

### (b) Textiles (from an agent abroad)

Dear Sir/Madam

We would like to offer our services as agents for the sale of your products in New Zealand.

Our company was established in 1906 and we are known throughout the trade as agents of the highest standing. We are already represented in several West European countries including France, Germany and Italy.

There is a growing demand in New Zealand for British textiles especially for fancy worsted suitings and printed cotton and lycra fabrics. The prospects for good quality fabrics at competitive prices are very good. According to a recent Chamber of Commerce survey the demand for British textiles is likely to grow considerably during the next 2 or 3 years.

If you would send us details of your ranges with samples and prices, we could inform you of their suitability for the New Zealand market and also indicate the patterns and qualities for which sales are likely to be good. We would then arrange to call on our customers with your collection.

You will naturally wish to have references and may write to Barclays Bank Ltd, 99 Piccadilly, Manchester, or to any of our customers, whose names we will be glad to send you on request.

We feel sure we should have no difficulty in arranging terms to suit us both, and look forward to hearing from you soon.

Yours faithfully

## 20.3 Application for sole agency

### (a) Importer's application

Dear Sir/Madam

We recently attended the International Photographic Exhibition in Cairo and were impressed by the high quality, attractive design and reasonable prices of your cameras. Having since seen your full catalogue, we are convinced that there is a promising market for your products here in Jordan.

If you are not already represented here we should be interested in acting as your sole agents.

As leading importers and distributors of more than 20 years' standing in the photographic trade, we have a good knowledge of the Jordanian market. Through our sales organisation we have good contacts with the leading retailers.

We handle several other agencies in non-competing lines and if our proposal interests you we can supply first-class references from manufacturers in Britain.

We firmly believe that an agency for marketing your products in Jordan would be of considerable benefit to both of us and we look forward to learning that you are interested in our proposal.

Mr Semir Haddad, our Purchasing Director, will be in England during May and will be pleased to call on you if we hear from you positively.

Yours faithfully

## (b) Manufacturer's reply

Dear Mr Jamal

Thank you for your letter of 18 March and for your comments on our cameras.

We are still a young company but are expanding rapidly. At present our overseas representation is confined to countries in Western Europe where our cameras are selling well. However we are interested in the chance of developing our trade further afield.

When your Mr Semir Haddad is in England we should certainly like to meet him to discuss your proposal further. If Mr Haddad will get in touch with me to arrange a meeting, I can also arrange for him to look around our factory and see for himself the quality of the materials and workmanship put into our cameras.

Yours sincerely

## 20.4 Offer to act as del credere agent

In addition to the normal duties sometimes an agent will be held personally liable for goods sold for the principal should the buyer fail to pay. Such agents are known as *del credere* agents and are entitled to an extra commission for undertaking this additional risk.

### (a) Offer

Dear Sir/Madam

The demand for toiletries in the United Arab Emirates has shown a marked increase in recent years. We are convinced that there is a considerable market here for your products.

There is every sign that an advertising campaign, even on a modest scale, would produce very good results if backed by an efficient system of distribution.

We are well-known distributors of over 15 years standing with branches in most of the principal towns. With knowledge of the local conditions we feel we have the experience and the resources necessary to bring about a market development of your trade in this country. Reference to the Embassy of the United Arab Emirates and to Middle East Services and Sales Limited would enable you to verify our statements.

If you were to appoint us as your agents we should be prepared to discuss the rate of commission. However, as the early work on development would be heavy we feel that 10 per cent on orders placed during the first 12 months would be a reasonable figure. As the market would be new to you and customers largely unknown we would be quite willing to act on a *del credere* basis in return for an extra commission of 2½ per cent to cover the additional risk.

We hope you will see a worthwhile opportunity in our proposal, and look forward to your early decision.

Yours faithfully

## (b) Reply

We are interested in your proposals of 8 July and are favourably impressed by your views. However, we are concerned that even a modest advertising campaign may not be worthwhile. We therefore suggest that we first test the market by sending you a representative selection of our products for sale on our account.

In the absence of advertising we realise that you would not have an easy task, but the experience gained would provide a valuable guide to future prospects. If the arrangement was successful we would consider your suggestion for a continuing agency.

If you are willing to receive a trial consignment we will allow commission at 12½ per cent, with an additional 2½ per cent del credere commission, expenses and commission to be set against your monthly payments.

Please let us know as soon as possible if this arrangement is satisfactory to you.

Yours sincerely

## 20.5 Offer to act as buying agents for importer

Dear Sir/Madam

*Introduction gives background details* — We understand from our neighbours, Firma Karl Brandt, that you have conducted your past buying of hardware in the German market through Firma Neymeyer and Schmidt of Bremen, and that in view of the collapse of their business you now require a reliable agent to take their place.

*Introduce yourself and offer your services* — We are well known to manufacturers of hardware in this country and believe we have the experience and connections necessary to meet your needs. We therefore would like to offer our services as your buying agents in Germany.

*Give further details of your experience and service* — Before transferring our business to Germany we had many years in the English trade. Knowing the particular needs of the English market, we can promise you unrivalled service[4] in matters of prices, discounts and freights.

As Firma Brandt have promised to write to you with a recommendation, we would like to summarise the terms we should be willing to accept if we acted for you:

*Separate numbered points ensure clarity* —
1  We would have complete freedom in placing your orders.

2  All purchases would be made on your behalf and in your name.

3  All accounts would be passed to you for settlement direct with suppliers.

4  Commission at 5 per cent payable quarterly would be allowed us on cif values[5] of all shipments.

5  You would have full benefit of the very favourable terms we have arranged with the shipping companies and of any special rates we may obtain for insurance.

*An encouraging close* — We hope you will accept our offer and look forward to receiving your decision very soon.

Yours faithfully

4 **unrivalled service** service which cannot be equalled
5 **cif values** values covering cost, insurance and freight

### 20.6 Manufacturer's confirmation of agency terms

Drafting a formal agreement is a matter which calls for great care. It can be very time-consuming especially if any terms are disputed when drafting is completed. The terms and conditions to be included must, therefore, be clearly agreed by the parties before the agreement is drafted. A precaution similar to that illustrated in the following letter is one to be recommended. The legal touches can be added at the time of drafting.

---

Dear Sirs

*Refer to fax and meeting with the representative* —— We were pleased to learn from your fax of 14 November that you are willing to accept an agency for marketing our goods in Saudi Arabia. Set out below are the terms discussed and agreed with your Mr Williams when he called here earlier this month, but before drafting the formal agreement we should like you to confirm them.

1  The agency will operate as from I January 19— for a period of 3 years, subject to renewal.

2  The agency will be a sole agency for marketing our goods in Saudi Arabia.

*List the terms clearly and simply* —— 3  No sales of competing products will be made in Saudi Arabia either on your own account or on account of any other firm or company.

4  All customers' orders will be transmitted to us immediately for supply direct.

5  Credit terms will not be given or promised to any customer without our <u>express consent</u>.[6]

6  All goods supplied will be invoiced by us direct to customers with copies to you.

7  A commission of 5% based on <u>fob values</u>[7] of all goods shipped to Saudi Arabia, whether on orders placed through you or not, will be payable at the end of each quarter.

8  A special <u>del credere</u> commission of 2½% will be added.

9  Customers will be required to settle their accounts with us direct. A statement will be sent to you at the end of each month of all payments received by us.

10  All questions of difference arising under our agreement will be referred to arbitration.

*Request confirmation* —— I shall be glad if you will please confirm these terms. A formal agreement will then be drafted and copies sent for your signature.

Yours faithfully

---

[6] **express consent** permission clearly stated
[7] **fob values** values cover cost of placing goods on board ship

# OFFERS OF AGENCIES

Sometimes a person seeking an agent will take the first step and make an offer to some person already known or recommended. Like the applicant seeking an agency, reference will be made to the market waiting to be developed but concentration will rest on the special merits of the product in the efforts to persuade a correspondent to handle it. It is important to convince the prospective agent that the product is bound to sell well because of its exceptional quality, its particular uses, its novelty, its moderate price, etc, and because of the publicity with which it will be supported.

When offering an agency it is not possible to include all the details but enough information must be given to enable the correspondent to assess the worth of the offer. Failure to include essential basic information would result in unnecessary correspondence.

### 20.7 Offer of a provincial agency

#### (a) Offer

> Dear Sirs
>
> We have recently received a number of enquiries from dealers in the North of England for information about our range of haberdashery.[8] This leads us to believe there is a promising market waiting to be developed in that part of the country. Sales of our goods in other parts of the United Kingdom have greatly exceeded our expectations, but the absence of an agency in the North has meant poor sales in that region to date.
>
> From our experience elsewhere we believe that an active agent would have little difficulty in expanding sales of our goods in the North of England. As we understand you are well experienced and have good connections in this area we would like to know if you are interested in accepting a sole agency. We are prepared to offer you a 2-year agreement with a commission of 7½% on net invoice values.
>
> As we wish to reach a quick decision I hope you can let me know if this offer interests you. If so then I suggest an early meeting at which details of an arrangement agreeable to both of us could be discussed.
>
> Yours faithfully

---

[8] **haberdashery** ribbons, lace and other small articles of dress

**(b) Reply**

Dear Mr Thompson

Thank you for your letter of 5 April offering us the sole agency for your haberdashery products in the North of England.

We are very interested in your proposal and are confident that we should be able to develop a good demand for your goods.

Your basic terms are agreeable so please let me know when it will be convenient for me to call on you. It would be helpful if you could offer a choice of dates.

I look forward to meeting you.

Yours sincerely

 **20.8** ## Offer of an overseas agency

**(a) Offer**

Dear Sir/Madam

We understand that you deal in stationery and related products, and would like to know if you are interested in marketing our products in your country on a commission basis.

We are a large and well-established firm specialising in the manufacture of stationery of all kinds. Our products sell well in many parts of the world. The enclosed catalogue will show you the wide range of our products, for which enquiries suggest a promising market for many of them waiting for development in your country.

If you are interested in our proposal please let us know which of our products are most likely to appeal to your customers, and also terms for commission and other charges on which you would be willing to represent us. We should be grateful if you could give us some idea of the market prospects for our products and suggest ways in which we could help you to develop the market.

We hope to hear favourably from you soon.

Yours faithfully

**(b) Acceptance**

Dear

I read with interest your letter of 15 May enclosing a copy of your catalogue and inviting me to undertake the marketing of your products in Zambia.

Provided we can agree on terms and conditions I shall be pleased to accept your offer.

I already represent Batson & Sons of Manchester in office equipment. As my customers include many of the principal dealers in Zambia I am sure they would provide a promising outlet for stationery and related products of the kind described in your catalogue.

I shall be in London in July and would like to take the opportunity to discuss arrangements with you in detail. Meanwhile I suggest the following terms and conditions as the basis for a formal agreement:

1   All goods supplied to be invoiced direct to buyers with copies sent to me.

2   Accounts to be made up and statements sent to me monthly, in duplicate, for distribution to buyers.

3   An agency commission of 5% to be payable on net amounts invoiced.

4   A del credere commission of 2½% in return for my guarantee of payments due on all accounts.

As initial expenses of introducing your products are likely to be heavy, I feel it reasonable to suggest an agreement extending over at least 3 years, but this is a matter we can discuss when we meet.

I shall be glad to learn that you are in general agreement with these suggestions.

Yours sincerely

### 20.9 Offer of a del credere agency

Where the agent acts on a *del credere* basis the principal must be satisfied as to the agent's financial standing. Sometimes references from, for example, the agent's banker may be sufficient. In other cases the agent may have to either provide a guarantor or deposit security, as in the following letter:

---

Dear

We thank you for your letter of 20 June and are pleased to hear that you think a good market can be found for our goods in your country. We must confess, however, that credit on the scale you mention opens up a far from attractive prospect.

Nevertheless, we are willing to offer you an appointment on a del credere basis of 12% commission on the net value of all orders received through you, provided you are willing to lodge adequate security with our bankers here.

If security is deposited we shall be willing to protect your interests by entering into a formal agreement giving you the sole agency for a period of 5 years.

Please let me know if you are willing to accept the agency on these terms.

Yours sincerely

---

## FORMAL AGENCY AGREEMENTS

The terms of agency are sometimes set out in correspondence between the parties but where dealings are on a large scale a formal agreement may be desirable. This should be drafted by a solicitor or by one of the parties in consultation with the other. Matters to be covered in such an agreement may include all, or some, of the following:

- The nature and duration of the agency (ie sole agency, *del credere* agency for merely transmitting orders).
- The territory to be covered.
- The duties of agent and principal.
- The method of purchase and sale (eg whether the agent is to buy for their own account or '*on consignment*'[9]).
- Details of commission and expenses to be allowed.
- The law of the country by which the agreement is governed.
- The sending of reports, accounts and payments.
- The arrangements of *arbitration*[10] in the event of disputes.

The following illustrates the construction of a typical agency agreement, and is reproduced from *Specimen Agency Agreements for Exporters* by kind permission of the Institute of Export.

[9] **on consignment** for sale on exporters behalf
[10] **arbitration** settlement of disputes by an independent person or body

## 20.10 Specimen Agency Agreement suitable for exclusive and sole agents representing manufacturers overseas

SPECIMEN AGREEMENT 1

Suitable for exclusive and sole agents representing manufacturers overseas

AN AGREEMENT made this                              day of
19   BETWEEN
whose Registered office is situate at
(hereinafter

called 'the Principal') of the one part and
(hereinafter

called 'the Agent') of the other part

WHEREBY IT IS AGREED as follows:

I.   The Principal appoints the Agent as and from the
     to be its sole Agent in
     (hereinafter called 'the area') for the sale of manufactured by the
Principal and such other goods and merchandise (all of which are hereinafter
referred to as 'the goods') as may hereafter be mutually agreed between
them.
   2.  The Agent will during the term of          years (and thereafter until
determined by either party giving three months' previous notice in writing)
diligently and faithfully serve the Principal as its Agent and will endeavour to
extend the sale of the goods of the Principal within the area and will not do
anything that may prevent such sale or interfere with the development of the
Principal's trade in the area.
   3.  The Principal will from time to time furnish the Agent with a statement
of the minimum prices at which the goods are respectively to be sold and the
Agent shall not sell below such minimum price but shall endeavour in each
case to obtain the best price obtainable.
   4.  The Agent shall not sell any of the goods to any person, company, or firm
residing outside the area, nor shall he knowingly sell any of the goods to any
person, company, or firm residing within the area with a view to their
exportation to any other country or area without the consent in writing of
the Principal.
   5.  The Agent shall not during the continuance of the Agency hereby
constituted sell goods of a similar class or such as would or might compete or
interfere with the sale of the Principal's goods either on his own account or
on behalf of any other person, company, or firm whomsoever.
   6.  Upon receipt by the Agent of any order for the goods the Agent will
immediately transmit such order to the Principal who (if such order is
accepted by the Principal) will execute the same by supplying the goods direct
to the customer.
   7.  Upon the execution of any such order the Principal shall forward to the
Agent a duplicate copy of the invoice sent with the goods to the customer
and in like manner shall from time to time inform the Agent when payment
is made by the customer to the Principal.
   8.  The Agent shall duly keep an account of all orders obtained by him and
shall every three months send in a copy of such account to the Principal.
   9.  The Principal shall allow the Agent the following commissions (based on
fob United Kingdom values) in respect of all orders obtained direct by the
Agent in the area which have been accepted and executed by the Principal.
The said commission shall be payable every three months on the amounts
actually received by the Principal from the customers.

▶

10. The Agent shall be entitled to commission on the terms and conditions mentioned in the last preceding clause on all export orders for the goods received by the Principal through Export Merchants Indent Houses, Branch Buying offices of customers, and Head Offices of customers situate in the United Kingdom of Great Britain, Northern Ireland and Eire for export into the area. Export orders in this clause mentioned shall not include orders for the goods received by the Principals from and sold delivered to customers' principal place of business outside the area although such goods may subsequently be exported by such customers into the area, excepting where there is conclusive evidence that such orders which may actually be transmitted via the Head Office in England are resultant from work done by the Agent with the customers.

11. Should any dispute arise as to the amount of commission payable by the Principal to the Agent the same shall be settled by the Auditors for the time being of the Principal whose certificate shall be final and binding on both the Principal and the Agent.

12. The Agent shall not in any way pledge the credit of the Principal.

13. The Agent shall not give any warranty in respect of the goods without the authority in writing of the Principal.

14. The Agent shall not without the authority of the Principal collect any moneys from customers.

15. The Agent shall not give credit to or deal with any person, company or firm which the Principal shall from time to time direct him not to give credit to or deal with.

16. The Principal shall have the right to refuse to execute or accept any order obtained by the Agent or any part thereof and the Agent shall not be entitled to any commission in respect of any such refused order or part thereof so refused.

17. All questions of difference whatsoever which may at any time hereafter arise between the parties hereto or their respective representatives touching these presents or the subject matter thereof or arising out of or in relation thereto respectively and whether as to construction or otherwise shall be referred to arbitration in England in accordance with the provision of the Arbitration Act 1950 or any re enactment or statutory modification thereof for the time being in force.

18. This Agreement shall in all respects be interpreted in accordance with the Laws of England.

AS WITNESS the hands of the parties hereto the day and year first hereinbefore written.

(Signatures)

## APPOINTING AN AGENT – TYPICAL PROCEDURE

In this section we will look at a series of correspondence which evolves through a publishing company's desire to find a suitable agent to market its publications in Lebanon.

The publishing company decides to approach its bank in order to obtain the relevant information. The various letters shown can be adapted in order to apply to enquiries through other sources.

## 20.11 Publisher's letter to bank (addressed to the Manager)

Dear Sir

At a meeting of our Directors yesterday it was decided to try to develop our trade with the Lebanon. We hope to appoint an agent with an efficient sales organisation in that country to help us to market our publications.

I wonder if your correspondents in Beirut would be able to put us in touch with a suitable and reliable firm. Any help you can provide will be appreciated.

I hope to hear from you soon.

Yours faithfully

## 20.12 Bank's reply to publishers

Dear Miss Southern

Thank you for your letter of 24 August regarding the possibility of appointing a local agent in the Lebanon.

Our correspondents in Beirut are the Banque Nationale whose postal address is:

Banque Nationale
PO Box 25643
Beirut

I have today sent a fax to their Manager explaining that you intend to appoint an agent in the Lebanon and asking him to provide you with any assistance possible.

No doubt you will now write to them direct and I have told them to expect to hear from you.

Yours sincerely

## 20.13 Publisher's thanks to the bank

Dear Mr Johnson

Thank you for your letter of 26 August and for introducing our name to your correspondents in Beirut.

I have today written to the Banque Nationale, and would like to thank you very much for your help.

Yours sincerely

## 20.14 Publisher's fax message to Beirut bank (addressed to the Manager)

The Manager of Midminster Bank Ltd, London, has kindly given us your name. We are interested in appointing an agent to represent our interests in the Lebanon and wonder if you can recommend a reliable person or company.

We specialise in publishing educational books, including students' text books and workbooks. If you could put us in touch with a distributor who has good connections with booksellers, libraries and educational institutions, we would be very grateful.

Thank you in advance for any help you can provide.

## 20.15 Reply from Beirut bank

Dear Miss Southern

Thank you for your fax of 28 August. The Manager of Midminster Bank, London, has already faxed me to explain your proposal to appoint a representative to further your trading interests in the Lebanon.

We are pleased to introduce you to Habib Suleiman Ghanem & Co of Beirut. This company has been our customer for many years. They are a well-known, old-established and highly reputable firm with some 20 years experience of the book trade in this part of the world. We can recommend them to you with the certain knowledge that they would serve you well.

We have taken the opportunity to contact Mr Faisal Ghanem, General Manager, who has expressed interest in your proposal. I believe he will be writing to you soon.

May I wish you success in your venture, and if I can be of further assistance please do not hesitate to contact me.

Yours sincerely

**20.16** Publisher's acknowledgement to Beirut bank

Dear Mr Jenkins

Thank you for your fax of 30 August giving us the name of Habib Suleiman Ghanem & Co. I wish to express my company's sincere thanks for your recommendation and the trouble you have so kindly taken to help us.

This company appears to be well equipped to provide the kind of service we need in the Lebanon, and we shall now look forward to hearing from them.

Yours sincerely

**20.17** Fax from prospective agents

Dear Miss Southern

*Introduction giving background details* — Our bankers, the Banque Nationale, inform us that you require an agent to assist in marketing your publications in the Lebanon. Subject to satisfactory arrangements as to terms and conditions we should be pleased to represent you.

*Details of your experience and knowledge* — As publishers and distributors in Syria and the Lebanon for over 20 years we have a thorough knowledge of the market. We are proud to boast an extensive sales organisation and well-established connections with booksellers, libraries and educational institutions in these two countries.

*Associated interests are stated, and prospects for future business* — We must mention that we are already acting as sole representatives[11] of several other publishers, including two American companies. However, as the preference in the educational field here is for books by British publishers, the prospects for your own publications are excellent, especially those intended for the student market. Adequate publicity would of course be necessary.

*Request details of commission and terms* — Before making any commitment we shall require details of your proposals for commission and terms of payment, and also some idea of the amount you are prepared to invest in initial publicity.[12]

We look forward to receiving this information from you very soon.

Yours sincerely

[11] **sole representatives** the only representatives
[12] **initial publicity** advertising in the early stages

### 20.18 Publisher's fax reply to prospective agents

Dear Mr Ghanem

*Refer to fax* — I was pleased to learn from your fax of 3 September that you will consider an appointment as our agent.

*Background information about previous trading in the area* — Although we transact a moderate amount of business in the Middle East we have so far not had much success in the Lebanon and are now hoping to develop our interests there.

*Send catalogue and prices* — I am sending by Swiftair today a copy of our complete catalogue of publications. The published prices quoted are subject to the usual trade discounts.

I would reply to your various points as follows:

*Numbered points with subheadings ensure clarity* —
1   COMMISSION
    The commission at present allowed to our other agents is 10% on the invoice value of all orders, payable quarterly, and we offer you the same terms. We presume your customers would be able to settle their accounts direct with us on the basis of <u>cash against documents</u>,[13] except of course for supplies from your own stocks.

2   PUBLICITY
    We feel that perhaps an initial expenditure of approximately £4,000 to cover the first 3 months' publicity would be reasonable. However as we are not familiar with conditions in your country this is a matter on which we would welcome your views.

*State next step if terms are accepted* — If you accept these proposals we will send by courier 2 copies our standard agency contract. I am enclosing a copy for your reference and comments.

*Encouraging close* — We look forward to the prospect of welcoming you as our agents.

Yours sincerely

### 20.19 Fax accepting agency

*Refer to fax and thank for documents received* — Thank you for your fax of 10 September enclosing a copy of your standard form of agency agreement and for the copy of your catalogue which arrived very promptly. The catalogue covers an extensive range of interesting titles which appear to be very reasonably priced.

*Comment on information provided* — With the proposed initial expenditure of £4,000 on advertising, backed by active support from our own sales staff, we feel that the prospects for many of your titles are very good, particularly where they are suitable for use in schools and colleges. We take it that you are prepared to leave the choice of <u>advertising media</u>[14] to us.

*State if terms are acceptable and ask for agreement to be sent* — We are grateful for this opportunity to take up your agency here. As your proposed terms are satisfactory we shall be pleased to accept the conditions in the agreement. I presume you will forward this to me without delay.

Yours sincerely

[13] **cash against documents** payment made upon delivery of shipping documents
[14] **advertising media** forms of publicity

## 20.20 Publisher acknowledges acceptance of agreement

Dear Mr Ghanem

Thank you for returning a signed copy of the agency contract with your letter of 26 September.

It is important that you carry stocks of those titles for which there is likely to be a steady demand. When you have had an opportunity to assess the market please let us know the titles and quantities you feel will be needed to enable you to meet small orders quickly.

We will follow the development of our trade with keen interest and look forward to a happy and lasting working relationship with you.

Yours sincerely

# CORRESPONDENCE WITH AGENTS

## 20.21 Agent requests increased commission

To ask for more money is never easy and to get it is often more difficult, especially when the amount payable has been fixed and included in an agreement freely entered into. Any request for increased commission must, therefore, be well founded and tactfully presented.

In the letter which follows the agent presents the case convincingly and with restraint. This ensures that it will have a fair hearing. No one receiving such a letter would wish to lose the goodwill clearly shown.

### (a) Agent's request

Dear Sir/Madam

*tactfully introduce the subject and explain* — We would like to request your consideration of some revision in our present rate of commission. This may strike you as unusual since the increase in sales last year resulted in a corresponding increase in our total commission.

*give further details and fully explain the situation* — Marketing your goods has proved to be more difficult than could have been expected when we undertook to represent you. Since then German and American competitors have entered the market and firmly established themselves. Consequently we have been able to maintain our position in the market only by enlarging our force of sales staff and increasing our expenditure on advertising.

*Tact is required. Clear justification must be given* — We are quite willing to incur[15] the additional expense and even to increase it still further because we firmly believe that the required effort will result in increased business. However we feel we should not be expected to bear the whole of the additional cost without some form of compensation. After carefully calculating the increase in our selling costs we suggest an increase in the rate of commission by say, 2%.

*An encouraging close requesting consideration* — You have always been considerate in your dealings with us and we know we can rely on you to consider our present request with understanding.

Yours faithfully

[15] **incur** be responsible for

## (b) Principal's reply

Dear

**Refer to fax and show an appreciation of problems being experienced** — Thank you for your fax of 28 August.

We note the unexpected problems presented by our competitors and appreciate the extra efforts you have made with such satisfactory results.

**Comment on facts provided in agent's letter** — We feel sure that, <u>in the long run</u>,[16] the high quality of our goods and the very competitive prices at which they are offered will ensure steadily increasing sales despite the competition from other manufacturers. At the same time we realise that, in the short term, this competition must be met by more active advertising and agree that it would not be reasonable to expect you to bear the full cost.

**Suggest how the matter can be rectfied** — To increase commission would be difficult as our prices leave us with only a very small profit. Instead we propose to allow you an advertising credit of £4000 in the current year towards your additional costs. This amount will be reviewed in 6 months time and adjusted according to circumstances.

**Request confirmation** — We hope you will be happy with this arrangement and look forward to your confirmation.

Yours sincerely

## 20.22 Principal proposes reduced rate of commission

Any proposal by a principal to reduce an agent's commission must be well founded and carefully presented, otherwise it would create ill-feeling and strain business relations. If the rate of commission is included in a legally-binding agreement it cannot be varied without the agent's consent, and even that consent is not binding unless the principal gives the agent some concession in return.

Dear

It is with regret that I must ask you to accept a temporary reduction in the agreed rate of commission. I make this request because of an increase in manufacturing costs due to additional duties on our imported raw materials, and to our inability either to <u>absorb these higher costs</u>[17] or to pass them on to consumers. In the event, our profits have been reduced to a level which no longer justifies continued production.

This situation is disturbing but we feel sure it will be purely temporary. In the circumstances we hope you will accept a small reduction of, say, 1½% in the agreed rate of commission. You have our promise that as soon as trade improves sufficiently we shall return to the rate originally agreed.

Yours sincerely

---

[16] **in the long run** eventually
[17] **absorb these higher costs** accept without raising prices

## 20.23 Agent complains of slow delivery

When a buyer is thinking of placing an order the three things which are of interest are quality, price and delivery. Often more importance is attached to the certainty of prompt delivery than to low price, but both are important. Therefore, in an increasingly competitive world, a manufacturer who regularly falls down on delivery dates is placed at a disadvantage and runs the risk of being forced out of business.

---

Dear

We enclose our statement showing sales made on your account during March and commission and expenses payable. If you will confirm our figures we will credit you with the amount due.

These sales are most disappointing but this is due entirely to late arrival of goods we ordered from you last January. Not having received the goods by mid-February, we faxed you on the 18th but found on enquiry that the goods were not shipped until 3 March and consequently did not reach us until 20 March.

This delay in delivery is most unfortunate as the local agents of several of our competitors have been particularly active during the past few weeks and have taken a good deal of the trade that would normally have come our way had the goods been here. What is more disturbing is that these rival firms have now gained a good hold on the market which until now has been largely our own.

We have reminded you on a previous occasion of the competition from Japanese manufacturers, whose low prices and quick deliveries are having a striking effect on local buyers. If you wish to keep your hold on this market prompt delivery of orders we place with you is essential.

Yours sincerely

---

## 20.24 Agent recommends lower price policy

An important reason for appointing a foreign agent is the gain in knowledge of local conditions and of the market for operation. Your agent will know what goods are best suited to the area and what prices the market will bear. Only an unwise exporter would ignore the advice of an agent on these and other matters of which they have special knowledge.

Dear

We are enclosing our customer's order number 252 for card-index and filing equipment.

To secure this order has not been easy because your quoted prices were higher than those which our customer had been prepared for. The quotation was eventually accepted on the grounds of your reputation for quality, but I think we should warn you of the growing competition in the office-equipment market here.

Agents of German and Japanese manufacturers are now active in the market, and as their products are of good quality and in some cases cheaper than yours we shall find it very difficult to maintain our past volume of sales unless you can reduce your prices. For your guidance we are sending you copies of the price lists of competing firms.

Concerning the present shipment please send a draft bill of exchange for acceptance at 2 months for the net value of your invoice after allowing for commission and expenses.

Yours

## 20.25 Agent recommends credit dealings

### (a) Agent's recommendation

Dear

We have studied the catalogue and price list received with your letter of 31 March, and have no doubt that we could obtain good orders for many of the items. However, we feel that it would not be advantageous to either of our companies to adopt a cash settlement basis.

Nearly all business here is done on credit, the period varying from 3 to 6 months. Your prices are reasonable and your products sound in both design and quality. We therefore believe that you could afford to raise your prices sufficiently to cover the cost and fall into line with your competitors in the matter of credit.

In our experience this would be sound policy and would greatly strengthen your hold on the market. With the best will in the world to serve you, we are afraid it would be neither worth your while nor ours to continue business on a cash basis.

If it would help you at all we should be quite willing to assume full responsibility for unsettled accounts and to act as del credere agents for an additional commission of 2½%.

We hope to hear from you soon.

Yours

## (b) Manufacturer's reply

Dear

Thank you for your letter of 10 April. We are glad that you think a satisfactory market could be found for our goods but are not altogether happy at the prospect of transacting all our business on a credit basis.

To some extent your offer to act in a <u>del credere</u> capacity meets our objectives, and for a trial period we are prepared to accept on the terms stated, namely an extra commission of 2½%. We make the condition, however, that you are willing either to provide a guarantor acceptable to us or to lodge adequate security with our bankers.

Please let us know your decision on this matter.

Yours sincerely

## 20.26 Principal complaints to agent

It is always unpleasant to have to make complaints but if a criticism is necessary it must be written with care and restraint. Never assume that the agent, or whoever the other party may be, is at fault. A letter written with courtesy and understanding will usually bring a considerate reply and obtain the co-operation needed to put matters right.

### (a) Poor sales

Dear Sirs

We are very concerned that your sales in recent months have fallen considerably. At first we thought this might be due to the disturbed political situation in your country. However, on looking into the matter more closely we find that the general trend of trade during this period has been upwards.

Of course, it is possible that you are facing difficulties of which we are not aware. If so, we should like to know of them since it may be possible for us to help. Please let us have a detailed report on the situation and also any suggestions of ways in which you feel we may be of some help in restoring our sales to at least their former level.

Yours faithfully

### (b) High expenses

Dear Sirs

We have received your October statement of sales and are concerned at the high figure included for expenses. This figure seems much too high for the volume of business done.

It is of course possible that there are special reasons for these high charges. If so we feel it is reasonable to ask you to explain them. We are particularly concerned because, under pressure of competition, the prices at which we offered the goods was cut to a level which left us with only a very small profit.

We shall be glad to receive your explanation and your assurance that expenses on future sales can be reduced. If for any reason this is not possible we should be left with no choice but to discontinue our business with you, for which we sincerely hope there will be no need.

Yours faithfully

# USEFUL EXPRESSIONS

## Agency applications

### Openings

1  We should be glad if you would consider our application to act as agents for the sale of your ....

2  Thank you for your letter of ... asking if we are represented ... .

3  We have received your letter of ... and should be glad to offer you a sole agency for the sale of our products in ... .

### Closes

1  We hope to hear favourably from you and feel sure we should have no difficulty in arranging terms.

2  If you give us this agency we should spare no effort to further your interests.

3  If required, we can provide first-class references.

## Agency appointments

### Openings

1  Thank you for your letter of ... offering us the sole agency for your products in ... .

2  We thank you for your letter of ... and are favourably impressed by your proposal for a sole agency.

3  Thank you for offering us the agency in ... we appreciate the confidence you have placed in us.

### Closes

1  We hope to receive a favourable response and can assure you of our very best service.

2  We look forward to a happy and successful working relationship with you.

# International trade

Some exporters will deal direct with overseas buyers, but it is more usual for transactions to take place in any of the following ways:

1  The overseas buyer employs a commission agent in the exporter's country.

2  The exporter employs an agent living in the buyer's country.

3  The exporter sends the goods to a *factor*[1] in the importing country for sale 'on consignment'.

The exporter is known as the consignor and the importer is known as the consignee.

Correspondence concerned with buying and selling overseas is generally carried out through fax for obvious reasons of speed. New technology has now given us EDI (Electronic Data Interchange) which substantially reduces the amount of paperwork which needs to be sent between the parties concerned. If both exporter and importer have compatible systems EDI results in huge savings in time, documentation and paperwork.

## IMPORT/EXPORT FLOW CHART

This flow chart in Fig. 21.1 shows the traditional documentation and procedures involved in purchasing goods from abroad.

[1] **factor** any agent who deals in their own name and has possession of the goods they are required to sell

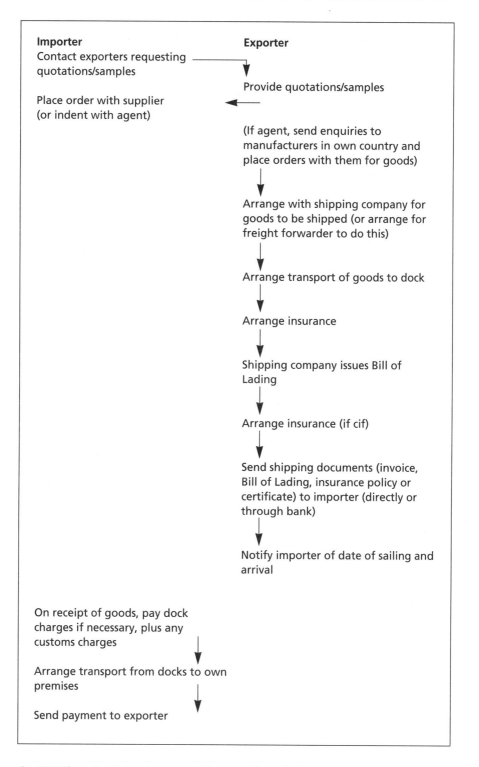

**Importer**
Contact exporters requesting quotations/samples

Place order with supplier (or indent with agent)

**Exporter**

Provide quotations/samples

(If agent, send enquiries to manufacturers in own country and place orders with them for goods)

Arrange with shipping company for goods to be shipped (or arrange for freight forwarder to do this)

Arrange transport of goods to dock

Arrange insurance

Shipping company issues Bill of Lading

Arrange insurance (if cif)

Send shipping documents (invoice, Bill of Lading, insurance policy or certificate) to importer (directly or through bank)

Notify importer of date of sailing and arrival

On receipt of goods, pay dock charges if necessary, plus any customs charges

Arrange transport from docks to own premises

Send payment to exporter

**Fig. 21.1 Flow chart showing a typical transaction relating to purchase of goods from abroad.**

# COMMISSION AGENTS

A commission agent may be either an individual or a firm employed to buy or to sell for a principal. In foreign trade, agents buy and sell in their own names for the accounts of the principals. Their tasks include obtaining quotations, placing orders, supervising their fulfilment and arranging for the despatch of the goods. Agents also collect payments for the principal and sometimes hold themselves personally liable for payment should the buyer fail to pay.

## 21.1 Bahraini buyer deals with commission agent in London

### (a) Agent acknowledges order

> Your order number C75 of 10 February for 1500 fibreglass wash basins in assorted colours will be placed without delay. We have already written to a manufacturer in North London and will do everything we can to ensure early shipment.
>
> We note your request for the basins to be arranged in tens and packed in cartons rather than wooden containers in order to save freight.
>
> We shall arrange insurance on the usual terms and the certificate of insurance will be sent to you through our bankers along with our draft bill and other shipping documents.

### (b) Agent requests quotation from manufacturers

> We have received an order for 1500 (fifteen hundred) 40 cm circular fibreglass wash basins in assorted colours for shipment to Bahrain. Please quote your lowest price fob London and state the earliest possible date by which you can have the consignment ready for collection at your factory.
>
> Your price should include arrangement of the basins in tens and packing in cartons of a size convenient for manual handling.

### (c) Agent sends advice of shipment

When the manufacturer's quotation is accepted and the date of delivery is known the agent will telephone a freight forwarder to find out details of ships sailing to Bahrain and the closing date for accepting cargo. The freight forwarder will need to know the measurements concerned as well as weight and price of the consignment. When the required information is received, the agent will write to the client giving particulars of shipment.

> YOUR ORDER NUMBER C75
>
> The 1500 fibreglass wash basins which you ordered on 10 February will be shipped to you by the SS <u>Tigris</u> sailing from London on 25 March and due to arrive in Bahrain on 15 April.
>
> The bill of lading, commercial invoice, <u>consular invoice</u>[2] and certificate of insurance, together with our <u>draft</u>[3] drawn at <u>sixty (60) days sight</u>,[4] have been passed to the Barminster Bank Ltd, London, and should reach you within a few days. The enclosed copy of the invoice will give you advance information of the consignment.
>
> We hope the goods will prove to be satisfactory.

### (d) Agent passes documents to banker

Payment for the transaction is to be made by bill of exchange drawn at 60 days and sent through the agent's bank to the foreign buyer. The banker's correspondent in Bahrain will not hand over the shipping documents until the buyer accepts the bill as a sign of willingness to meet it when it is presented for payment in 60 days.

On receipt of the letter in Fig. 21.1 the client's bank in Bahrain would present the documents to the client and obtain a signature on the back of the bill of exchange saying that the payment terms are accepted. The documents will then be released and the goods may be collected.

> Enclosed is a bill of lading, consular invoice, certificate of insurance and our invoice relating to a consignment of fibreglass wash basins for shipment by SS <u>Tigris</u> to Mr Ahmed Ashkar of Bahrain.
>
> Please forward these documents to your correspondent in Bahrain with instructions to hand them to the consignee against acceptance of our 60 days draft, also enclosed.

## GOODS ON CONSIGNMENT

Goods on consignment are goods which an exporter sends to an importer, but an invoice will not immediately be issued. The importer will hold the goods in stock until they are sold, at which point the exporter will draw up an invoice for whatever stock has been sold.

---

[2] **consular invoice** an invoice signed by the consul of the country to which goods are exported
[3] **draft** a bill of exchange requiring acceptance
[4] **sixty (60) days sight** for payment within 60 days of acceptance

## 21.2 Company in Nairobi requests goods on consignment

### (a) Buyer's request

Introduce yourself and give background details — We are the largest department store in Nairobi and have recently received a number of enquiries for your stainless steel cutlery. There are very good prospects for the sale of this cutlery, but as it is presently unknown here we do not feel able to make purchases on our own account.

Prpose how an agreement would work — We would like to suggest that you send us a trial delivery for sale on consignment terms. When the market is established we would hope to place firm orders.

Further details regarding payment, expenses, commission and references — If you agree we would render monthly accounts of sales and send you the payments due after deducting expenses and commission at a rate to be agreed. Our bankers are the Nairobi branch of Midminster Bank Ltd, with whom you may check our standing.[5]

An encouraging close — We believe our proposal offers good prospects and hope you will be willing to agree to a trial.

### (b) Seller's acceptance

Thank agent for letter — Thank you for your letter proposing to receive a trial delivery of our cutlery on consignment which we have carefully considered.

Enclose sample goods. State whether agent's proposal is acceptable. Mention commission — We are sending you a representative selection[6] of our most popular lines and hope you will find a ready sale for them. Your suggestion to submit accounts and to make payments monthly is quite satisfactory, and we will allow you commission at 10% calculated on gross profits.

Details of consignment and documents — The consignment is being shipped by SS Eastern Prince, leaving Southampton for Mombasa on 25 January. We will send the bill of lading and other shipping documents as soon as we receive them. Meanwhile a pro forma invoice is enclosed showing prices at which the goods should be offered for sale.

An encouraging close — We are confident that this cutlery will prove popular in your country and look forward to trading with you.

### (c) Agent submits account sales

When the agent has sold the goods an account sales (Fig. 21.2) will be sent to the exporter showing the goods sold and the prices realised, together with the net amount due to the exporter after deducting commission and any charges or expenses incurred. The net amount may be placed to the credit of the exporter in the importing country, or it may be forwarded by means of a banker's draft (unless other means of payment, discussed in Chapter 12 are adopted) .

[5] **check our standing** enquire as to our position in business
[6] **representative selection** a selection covering all types of goods

We enclose our account sales for the month ending 31 March showing a balance of £379.20 due to you after deducting commission and charges. If you will draw on us for this amount at two months we will add our acceptance and return the draft immediately.

---

ACCOUNT SALES
by U Patel & Co
15–17 Rhodes Avenue, Nairobi

25 October 19..

In the matter of stainless steel cutlery ex SS <u>Eastern Prince</u> sold for account of E Hughes & Co Ltd, Victoria Works, Kingsway, Sheffield.

| Quantity | Description | @ per 100 £ | £ |
|---|---|---|---|
| 100 | Knives | 170.00 | 170.00 |
| 100 | Forks | 170.00 | 170.00 |
| 50 | Table Spoons | 150.00 | 75.00 |
| 200 | Tea Spoons | 105.00 | 210.00 |
| | | | 625.00 |

Charges:

| | | |
|---|---|---|
| Ocean Freight | 92.55 | |
| Dock Dues and Cartage | 37.40 | |
| Marine Insurance | 20.50 | |
| Customs Dues | 32.85 | |
| Commission | 62.50 | |
| | | 245.80 |
| Net proceeds, as per banker's draft enclosed | | 379.20 |

E & OE

Nairobi, 28 October 19..
(signed) U Patel & Co

**Fig. 21.2 Account sales.** The account sales is a statement of goods sold by an agent for the consignor. It shows the amount due to the consignor after deduction of charges and agency commission.

### (d) Principal sends payment

Thank you for sending your account sales for March. Our draft for the balance shown of £379.20 is enclosed.

## INDENTS

When foreign buyers place orders through commission agents or *commission houses*[7] in the supplier's country their orders are known as indents (see Fig. 21.3). They give details of the goods required, their prices, packing and shipping instructions and method of payment. An indent is not an order for goods; it is an order to an agent to buy goods on behalf of the foreign buyer.

If the indent names the manufacturer who is to supply the goods it is known as a 'closed' or 'specific' indent. If selection is left to the agent the indent is said to be 'open' and the agent will then obtain quotations from a number of manufacturers before placing an order.

### 21.3 Foreign buyer deals with commission house

#### (a) Buyer (in Egypt) sends Indent to commission house (in England)

We have received the manufacturer's price list and samples you sent us last month and now enclose our indent number 762 for goods to be shipped by the SS *Merchant Prince* due to leave Liverpool for Alexandria on 25 July. The indent contains full instructions as to packing, insurance and shipping documents.

It is important for the goods to be shipped either by the vessel named, or by an earlier vessel; if there are any items which cannot be supplied in time for this shipment they should be cancelled. When we receive the goods we shall pay you the agreed agency commission of 5%. The account for the goods will be settled direct with the manufacturers.

This is a trial order and if it is met satisfactorily we shall probably place further orders.

---

[7] **commission houses** a commission agency organised as a firm or company

**INDENT**
No 64

N WHARFE & CO LTD
19–21 Victoria Street
CAIRO, EGYPT

10 February 19..

H Hopkinson & Co
Commission Agents and Shippers
41 King Street
MANCHESTER
M60 2HB

Dear Sirs

Please purchase and ship on our account for delivery not later than 31 March the following goods or as many of them as possible. Insurance should be arranged for the amount of your invoice plus 10% to cover estimated profit and your charges.

Yours faithfully
for N WHARFE & C0 LTD

J G Gartside
Director

| Identification Marks etc | Quantity | Description of Goods | Remarks |
|---|---|---|---|
| NW 64 Nos 1–12 | 48 | HMV Stereo Model 1636 Walnut finish | Pack 4 per case |
| NW 64 Nos 13–37 | 25 bales | Grey Shirting Medium weight About 1,000 metres per bale | Pack in oil bags |
| NW 64 Nos 38–39 | 500 pairs | Assorted House Slippers Men's (200) Women's (200) Children's (100) | Pack in plain wooden cases |

Ship: By Manchester Liners Ltd
Delivery: cif Alexandria
Payment: Draw at 60 days from sight of documents through Royal Bank, London

**Fig. 21.3 Indent.** An indent is an order sent to a commission agent to arrange for the purchase of goods for the principal.

**(b) Agent places order with a firm in Manchester**

> We have just received an order from Jean Riachi & Co of Mansura, Egypt. Particulars are shown in the enclosed official order form together with details of packing and forwarding, case marks, etc.
>
> The goods are to be ready for collection at your warehouse in time to be shipped to Alexandria by SS <u>Merchant Prince</u> due to sail from Liverpool on 25 July or by an earlier vessel if possible. Prompt delivery is essential and if there are any items which cannot be included in the consignment they should be cancelled.
>
> Invoices priced ex warehouse should be in triplicate and sent to us for forwarding to our customers with the shipping documents. The account will be settled by our customers direct with you. As <u>del credere</u> agents, we undertake to be responsible should the buyer fail to pay.
>
> This is a trial order and if it is completed satisfactorily it is likely to lead to further business. Your special care would therefore be appreciated.
>
> Please confirm by return that you can accept this order, and arrange to inform us when the goods are ready for collection.

## BILLS OF LADING

The bill of lading, prepared by the shipping company, sets out the terms of the contract of carriage with the shipping company. It serves as the consignor's receipt for the goods taken on board ship. The bill of lading is also a document of title so that when it is transferred to the consignee it also gives the right to claim the goods to which it refers.

A bill of lading is usually prepared in a set of 3 originals and 3 copies. It will state the name of the vessel, the time of sailing, marks and identification on the cargo, the delivery address and also the statement 'clean shipped on board', meaning the goods are not damaged and they are actually on board ship.

On issue of the bill of lading the consignor must check that all details are correct and that it has been signed by the ship's captain. The bill of lading then goes, with other documents, to the bank to be forwarded to the consignee.

## IMPORT DOCUMENTATION AND PROCEDURE

Whether goods are imported on consignment or against orders, import procedure is much the same. Before the ship arrives the importer (who will be either a merchant dealing on their own account or an agent) will usually have received the shipping documents. The original documents would go through the bank, but it is normal practice for photocopies to be despatched by a courier service so that the importer can, in advance, go through the import procedures before the goods actually arrive. This makes things easier for the importer and saves a lot of time.

Shipping documents include:

1 An advice of shipment specifying the goods and stating the name of the carrying ship, its date of sailing and probable date of arrival.

2 A bill of lading.

3 An invoice (pro forma if the goods are imported on consignment).

When the ship arrives the importer must obtain release for the bill of lading and proceed as follows:

1 The importer must *endorse*[8] the bill of lading and present it to the shipping company, or their representative, at the port.

2 The freight must be paid (if not already prepaid by the exporter) and any other charges due to the shipping company.

3 The importer must prepare and submit the necessary import entries on official forms provided by the appropriate Customs authorities.

Import duties may either be specific (ie charged on quantity, as on wines and tobacco) or *ad valorem* (ie charged on invoice value, as on television sets and other manufactured goods). If the goods, or any of them, are required for immediate use, duty must be paid before they may be taken away.

Some goods imported into the United Kingdom are liable to VAT (value added tax) and this should generally be paid when the goods are cleared through customs.

## 21.4 An import transaction

### (a) Importer (London) places order (Japan)

> Our order for 20 Super Hitachi Hi-Fi Systems (SDT 400) is enclosed at the cif price of £550 each, as quoted in your letter of 10 June.
>
> Through the Midminster Bank Ltd, 65 Aldwych, London WC2, we have arranged with the Bank of Japan, Tokyo, to open a credit in your favour for £6,000 (six thousand pounds) to be available until 30 September next.
>
> Please let us know when the consignment is shipped.

### (b) Importer opens credit

The importer writes to the Midminster Bank in London opening credit.

> I have completed and enclose your form for an irrevocable credit of £6,000 to be opened with the Bank of Japan, Tokyo, in favour of Kikuki, Shiki & Co, Tokyo, for a consignment of music systems, the credit to be valid until 30 September next.
>
> When the consignment is shipped the company will draw on the Bank of Japan at 30 days after sight; the draft will be accompanied by bills of lading (3/3), invoice and certificate or policy of insurance.
>
> Please confirm that the credit will be arranged.

[8] **endorse** sign on the back

### (c) Supplier in Japan presents documents to Bank of Japan, Tokyo

We enclose a 30 days sight draft together with bill of lading (3/3), invoice, letter of credit and certificate of insurance relating to a consignment of music centres for shipment by SS Yamagata to Videohire Ltd, London.

Please send draft and documents to the Midminster Bank Ltd, 65 Aldwych, London WC2 4LS, with instructions to hand over the documents to Videohire Ltd against their acceptance of the draft.

### (d) Supplier sends advice of shipment

YOUR ORDER NO 825

We thank you for your order for 20 Super Hitachi Music Centres. I am glad to say we can supply these immediately from stock. We have arranged to ship them to your London warehouse at St Katharine Docks, London by SS Yamagata sailing from Tokyo on 3 August and due to arrive in London on or about the 25th.

The shipping documents will be delivered to you through the Aldwych Branch of the Midminster Bank Ltd against your acceptance of the 30 days sight draft as agreed in our earlier correspondence.

We hope you will find everything to your satisfaction.

### (e) Importer acknowledges consignment

ORDER NO 825

Your consignment of Music Centres reached London on 27 August.

Thank you for the care and promptness with which you have fulfilled our first order. We expect to place further orders soon.

# BONDED WAREHOUSES

If imported goods on which duty is payable are not wanted immediately they may be placed in a bonded warehouse, that is a warehouse whose owners have entered into a bond with the customs authorities as a guarantee that the goods will not be removed until duty on them has been paid.

This system enables payment of duty to be *deferred*[9] until the goods, which may be withdrawn by *instalments*,[10] are needed. The main commodities dealt with in this way are tea, tobacco, beer, wines and spirits.

[9] **deferred** delayed
[10] **instalments** in separate lots

When goods are placed in a warehouse, bonded or free, the owner of the goods is given either a warehouse warrant or a warehousekeeper's receipt. A delivery order, signed by the owner of the goods, must be completed when goods are withdrawn.

## 21.5 Clearance of goods from warehouse

This letter is from a tea blender to their broker, who has bought a quantity of tea and holds the delivery order issued by the importer.

> We refer to the 12 chests of Assam, ex City of Bombay, which you bought for us at the auctions yesterday and for which we understand you hold the delivery order.
>
> Please clear all 12 chests at once and arrange with Williams Transport Ltd to deliver them to our Leman Street warehouse.

# USEFUL EXPRESSIONS

## Enquiries and orders

### Openings

1 Thank you for your quotation of ... and for the samples you sent me.

2 One of our best customers has asked us to arrange to purchase ... .

3 Your letter of ... enclosing indent for ... arrived yesterday.

### Closes

1 Please deal with this order as one of special urgency.

2 We look forward to receiving further indents from you.

3 We thank you for giving us this trial order and promise that we will give it our careful attention.

## Consignments

### Openings

1 We regret that we cannot handle your goods on our own account, but would be willing to take them on a consignment basis.

2 We have today sent a consignment of ... by SS *Empress Victoria*, and enclose the shipping documents.

3 The consignment you sent us has been sold at very good prices.

### Closes

1 Please of course credit our account with the amount due.

2 We look forward to hearing that you have been able to obtain satisfactory prices.

3 We will send you our account sales, with banker's draft, in a few days.

4 We enclose our account sales and shall be glad if you will draw on us at 2 months for the amount due.

# Banking
# (home business)

1
2
3
4
5
6
7
8
9
10
11
12
13
14
15
16
17
18
19
20
21
22
23
24
25

Commercial banks offer four main services:

1 They accept customers' deposits.

2 They pay cheques drawn on them by their customers.

3 They grant advances to customers.

4 They provide a payments mechanism for the transfer of funds between its own customers and those of other banks.

# KINDS OF BANK ACCOUNT

**Current accounts** are the most usual type of bank account. Deposits in the account can be withdrawn on demand. This is the main method by which customers may utilise the full money transfer facilities of the bank, involving the use of cheques, credit transfers, *standing orders*[1] and *direct debits.*[2] Traditionally the current account holder did not receive interest on funds but some banks now pay a small rate of credit interest. Besides their main services banks offers customers a wide range of miscellaneous services including safe custody and night safe facilities, the provision of references, executor and trustee, and pension and insurance services plus advice on how to start up a business.

**Deposit accounts** have been used in recent years by banks to attract customers. A range of deposit accounts are offered paying various rates of interest as well as the ordinary deposit account. On ordinary deposit accounts withdrawals are subject to 7 days' notice. Generally the amount of interest depends on the amount of money deposited and to some extent on the length of notice of withdrawal required.

## Opening accounts

Anyone wishing to open an account should legally provide satisfactory references or be introduced by an established customer of the bank. In practice, however, some banks do not necessarily take personal references in respect of customers but may rely on proof of identity and some form of credit referencing.

## Statements

Periodic loose-leaf statements are provided to customers. These statements record all transactions affecting the customer's current account and the balance after each day's transactions.

---

[1] **standing order** an order to make certain payments at stated times
[2] **direct debit** similar to standing orders but instead of the customer stating the amounts and when to pay them the company tells the bank what to pay and when

## Cheques

A cheque is a widely accepted form of payment today. Their acceptability has increased since the introduction of the cheque guarantee card in 1965, which guaranteed the payment of a cheque up to a stated amount (often £50).

A banker is entitled to refuse payment of a cheque in any of the following circumstances:

- When the drawer has countermanded payment.
- When the balance on the drawer's account is insufficient to meet the cheque.
- When the cheque is post-dated, ie dated ahead of time.
- When the cheque has become 'stale', ie over 6 months old.
- When the cheque contains some irregularity, eg a forgery or an unsigned alteration.
- When the banker is aware that the drawer has died or committed an act of bankruptcy.

In any of these circumstances the cheque would be returned to the payee or other holder marked with the reason for its non-payment.

## Bank charges

As long as personal customers keep their accounts in credit they are not liable to any bank charges.

Business customers will normally negotiate their charges with their bankers. Such charges are generally applied quarterly.

## CORRESPONDENCE WITH BANKS

Correspondence between the bank and its customers tends to be standardised and quite formal as shown in the range of correspondence in this chapter.

## CURRENT ACCOUNTS

### 22.1 Notification of signatures to bank

Only officers authorised by a company's board of directors may sign cheques for the company. The bank will want to see a copy of the board's resolution authorising the opening of an account and stating the manner in which cheques are to be signed and by whom, with specimens of their signatures.

Dear Sir

At a meeting of the Board yesterday it was decided that cheques drawn on the Company's account must bear two signatures instead of one as formerly.

One of the signatures must be that of the Chairman or Secretary; the other may be any member of the Board. This change takes place as of today's date.

There have been no changes in membership of the Board since specimen signatures were issued to you in July.

A certified copy of the Board's resolution is attached.

Yours faithfully

## 22.2 Account overdrawn – correspondence with bank

The following is the kind of letter a bank manager would send to a customer who has overdrawn on their account. While being polite, courteous and helpful the letter conveys to the customer the seriousness of an unauthorised overdraft.

### (a) Letter from bank

Dear Mrs Wilson

On a number of occasions recently your account has been overdrawn. The amount overdrawn at close of business yesterday was £150.72. Please arrange for the credits necessary to clear this balance to be paid in as soon as possible.

Overdrafts are allowed to customers only by previous arrangement and as I notice that your account has recently been running on a very small balance, it occurs to me that you may wish to come to some arrangement for overdraft facilities. If so perhaps you will call to discuss the matter. In the absence of such an arrangement I am afraid it will not be possible to honour future cheques drawn against insufficient balances.

Yours sincerely

### (b) Customer's reply

Dear

Thank you for your letter of yesterday. I have today paid into my account cheques totalling £80.42. I realise that this leaves only a small balance to my credit and as I am likely to be faced with fairly heavy payments in the coming months I should like to discuss arrangements for overdraft facilities.

I have recently entered into a number of very favourable contracts, which involve the early purchase of raw materials. As payments under the contracts will not be made until the work is completed I am really in need of overdraft facilities up to about £1500 for 6 months or so.

I will call your secretary in the next few days to arrange a convenient time for me to call on you.

Yours sincerely

### 22.3 Drawer stops payment of cheque

When a payment of a cheque is stopped, as for example where the cheque has been lost in the post, payment is said to be *countermanded*.[3] Only the drawer of the cheque can countermand payment. This is done by notifying the bank in writing. An *oral notification*,[4] even when made by the drawer in person, is not by itself enough and, as with a notification by telephone, it should be immediately confirmed in writing.

---

Dear Sir

I am writing to confirm my telephone call of this morning to ask you to stop payment of cheque number 67582 for the sum of £96.25 payable to the St Annes Electrical Co Ltd.

This cheque appears to have been lost in the post and a further cheque has now been drawn to replace it.

Please confirm receipt of this authority to stop the payment.

Yours faithfully

---

### 22.4 Complaint concerning dishonoured cheque

#### (a) Customer's letter to bank

---

Dear Sir

The Alexandria Radio & Television Co Ltd inform me that you have refused payment of my cheque number 527610 of 15 August for £285.75. The returned cheque is marked 'Effects not cleared'. I believe this refers to the cheques I paid in on 11 August, the amount of which was more than enough to cover the dishonoured cheque.

As there appears to have been ample time for you to collect and credit the sums due on the cheques paid in, please let me know why payment of cheque number 527610 was refused.

Yours faithfully

---

[3] **countermanded** cancelled
[4] **oral notification** a verbal message

**(b) Reply from bank**

Dear

In reply to your letter of yesterday, I regret that we were not able to allow payment against your cheque number 527610. One of the cheques paid in on 11 August – the cheque drawn in your favour by M Tippett & Co – was post-dated to 25 August and that the amount cannot be credited to your account before that date.

To honour your cheque would have created an overdraft of more than £100 and in the absence of previous arrangement I am afraid we could not grant credit for such a sum.

I trust this explanation clarifies this matter.

Yours sincerely

## 22.5 Request for bank reference

Bankers will not give information to private enquirers about their customers. When a buyer, in seeking credit from a supplier, gives the bank as a reference the suppliers must approach their own bank, not the buyer's bank, and ask them to make the necessary enquiries. As a rule the information supplied in answer to such requests is brief, formal and much less personal than that obtainable through a trade reference.

### (a) Supplier's request to bank

Dear Sir

We have received an order for £1,200 from Messrs Joynson and Hicks of 18 Drake Street, Sheffield. They ask for credit and have given the Commonwealth Bank, 10 Albert Street, Sheffield S14 5QP, as a reference.

Would you be good enough to make enquiries and let us know whether the reputation and financial standing of this firm justify a credit of the above amount.

Yours faithfully

### (b) Reply from bank

Dear Sir

As requested in your letter of 18 April we have made enquiries as to the reputation and standing of the Sheffield firm mentioned.

The firm was established in 1942 and its commitments have been met regularly. The directors are reported to be efficient and reliable and a credit of £1,200 is considered sound.

This information is supplied free from all responsibility on our part.

Yours faithfully

# BANK LOANS AND OVERDRAFTS

When granting an advance to a personal customer, especially an overdraft, the bank may require some form of acceptable security. The security should be easy to value, easy for the bank to obtain a good legal title, and it should be readily marketable or realisable. The most common types of security accepted are life policies, shares, mortgages of land and guarantees.

Normally a bank will not require security from a customer to support a personal loan.

Interest on an overdraft is charged on a daily basis, while interest on a personal loan is calculated on the full amount borrowed.

## 22.6 Request for overdraft facilities

### (a) Customer's request

Dear Sir

With the approach of Christmas I am expecting a big increase in turnover,[5] but unfortunately my present stocks are not nearly enough for this. Because my business is fairly new wholesalers are unwilling to give me anything but short-term credit.

I hope you will be able to help me by making me an advance on overdraft until the end of this year.

As security I am willing to offer a life policy, and of course will allow you to inspect my accounts, from which you will see that I have promptly met all my obligations.

Perhaps you will be good enough to let me know when it will be convenient to discuss this matter personally with you.

Yours faithfully

### (b) Banker's reply

Dear Mr Wilson

Thank you for your recent letter requesting overdraft facilities.

We are prepared to consider an overdraft over the period you mention, and have made an appointment for you to see me next Friday 11 November at 2.30 pm. Please bring with you the life policy mentioned together with your company's accounts.

Yours sincerely

[5] **turnover** total sales

### 22.7 Request for loan without security

Dear Sir

In April 19— you were good enough to grant me a credit of £5,000, which was repaid within the agreed period. I now require a further loan to enable me to proceed with work under a contract with the Waterfoot Borough Council for building an extension to their King's Road School.

I need the loan to purchase building materials at a cost of about £6,000. The contract price is £20,000, payable immediately upon satisfactory completion of the work on or before 30 September next.

I hope you will be able to grant me a loan of £5,000 for a period of 9 months.

I enclose a copy of my latest audited balance sheet and shall be glad to call at the bank at your convenience to discuss the matter.

Yours faithfully

### 22.8 Request for loan with security

Dear Sir

I am considering a large extension of business with several firms in Japan and as the terms of dealings will involve additional working capital,[6] I should be glad if you would arrange to grant me a loan of, say, £6,000 for a period of 6 months.

You already hold for safe keeping on my behalf £5,000 Australian 3% stock and £4,500 4% consols.[7] I am willing to pledge these as security. At current market prices I believe they would provide sufficient cover for the loan.

You would be able to rely upon repayment of the loan at maturity[8] as, apart from other income, I have arranged to take into the business a partner who, under the terms of the partnership agreement, will introduce £5,000 capital at or before the end of the present year.

If you will arrange a day and time when I may call on you to discuss my request, I will bring with me evidence supporting the above statements.

Yours faithfully

---

[6] **working capital** the capital needed to keep a business running
[7] **consols** short for 'consolidated annuities' – a form of British Government stock
[8] **at maturity** when it becomes due

## 22.9 Request for extension of loan

Dear Sir

On 1 August you granted me a loan of £2,500 which is due for repayment at the end of this month.

I have already taken steps to prepare for this repayment but due to a fire at my warehouse 2 weeks ago I have been faced with heavy unexpected payments. Damage from the fire is thought to be about £4,000 and is fully covered by insurance. However, as my claim is unlikely to be settled before the end of next month, I hope the period of the loan can be extended until then.

I am sure you will realise that the fire has presented me with serious problems and that repayment of the loan before settlement of my claim could be made only with the greatest difficulty.

Yours faithfully

## 22.10 Request to clear unauthorised overdraft

### (a) Request by bank

Dear Mr Hendon

I notice that since the beginning of last September there have been a number of occasions on which your current account has been overdrawn.[9] As you know it is not the custom of the bank to allow overdrafts except by special arrangement and usually against security.[10]

Two cheques drawn by you have been presented for payment today, one by Insurance Brokers Ltd for £27.50 and one by John Musgrave & Sons for £87.10. As you are one of our oldest customers I gave instructions for the cheques to be paid although the balance on your current account, namely £56.40, was insufficient to meet them.

I am well aware that there is a substantial credit balance on your deposit account. If overdraft facilities on your current account are likely to be needed in future, I suggest that you give the bank the necessary authority to hold the balance on deposit as overdrawn security.

Yours sincerely

---

[9] **overdrawn** withdrawn in excess of balance available
[10] **security** bonds, certificates, or other property pledged to cover a debt

## (b) Customer's reply

Dear Mr Stannard

Thank you for your letter of 2 December.

I am sorry to have given you cause to write to me concerning recent overdrafts on my current account. Although the amounts involved are not large I agree that overdraft facilities should have been discussed with you in advance and regret that this was not done. I am afraid I had overlooked the fact that the balance carried on my current account in recent months had been smaller than usual.

Later this month I expect to receive payment for several large contracts now nearing completion. No question of overdraft facilities will then arise. Meanwhile I am pleased to authorise you to treat the balance on my deposit account as security for any overdraft incurred on my current account. Once again my apologies for the inconvenience caused.

Yours sincerely

# USEFUL EXPRESSIONS

## Openings

1 I have entered into partnership with Mr ... and we wish to open a current account in the name of ... .

2 I enclose a standing order for payment of £15 on the first day of each month to ... .

3 I shall be moving to ... at the end of this month and should be glad if you would transfer my account to your branch in that town.

4 According to the statement received from you yesterday ...

5 The statement you sent me recently shows that my account was overdrawn ... during July

6 On referring to the statement just received I notice that ...

7 This is to confirm my telephone message this morning asking you to stop payment of cheque number ... .

8 I am writing to ask you to consider a loan of £ ... for a period of ... months.

9 Please arrange to buy for me the following securities within the price ranges shown:

## Closes

1 If you require further information please let me know.

2 I shall be glad to call on you should you need any further information.

3 I feel that the charges are excessive and should be glad of your explanation.

4 I should be most grateful if you could grant the credit asked for.

5 If you require a guarantor Mr ... of ... has kindly consented to act.

# Banking
# (international business)

1
2
3
4
5
6
7
8
9
10
11
12
13
14
15
16
17
18
19
20
21
22
23
24
25

Cheques are the main means of settling business debts in the home trade. They are not suitable for payments in international trade since a cheque is payable only in the drawer's country. Settlement of overseas debts may be made in a number of ways:

- by banker's draft, banker's transfer (mail, telex and telegraphic)
- letters of credit
- bill of exchange and promissory note.

The method of payment used by the importer will depend upon the arrangement made with the exporter when the order is placed. This will depend on the exporter's knowledge of the importer and the extent of trust existing between them.

In recent years SWIFT has come into operation (Society for Worldwide Inter Bank Financial Telecommunication). All major banks throughout the world are members of SWIFT. This is an electronic mechanism which enables bankers all over the world to communicate with each other, thus speeding up the fund transfer mechanism and cutting down on paperwork. However, the traditional methods of payment mentioned above still exist and will be dealt with in this chapter.

## BANKER'S DRAFTS

Like cheques, banker's drafts are payable on demand but unlike cheques they carry little or no risk since they are backed by the assets of the bank issuing them. An importer wishing to pay by draft would buy it at a local bank and send it to the exporter who would simply pay it into their own bank account.

### 23.1 Payment by banker's draft

#### (a) Exporter's request for payment

> We enclose your statement for the month of November showing an outstanding balance of £580.50.
>
> We assume you will settle this outstanding amount by banker's draft in UK Pounds Sterling and hope to receive payment soon.

#### (b) Importer's reply

> Thank you for your letter together with our November statement.
>
> Our banker's draft for UK Pounds five hundred and eighty and 50 pence (UK£580.50) is enclosed.

# BANKER'S TRANSFERS (MAIL TELEX AND TELEGRAPHIC TRANSFERS)

The banker's transfer is a simple transfer of funds from the bank account of a debtor in their own country to the creditor's bank account in the creditor's country. This is one of the safest methods of sending money abroad. All the debtor has to do is to instruct their bank, either by letter or on a special form, to make the transfer. The debtor's bank then arranges for the creditor's bank to be credited with an amount in local currency equal to the sum transferred. The calculation is made at the current rate of exchange.

As these transfers are arranged direct between the two banks losses are impossible. However, as delays may occur when the transfers are made by mail, it is now customary for the banks to communicate either by telegram, telex, or more conveniently fax thus giving rise to what are commonly known as the *telegraphic transfer* and *telex transfer*. Exchange rates for these transfers are quoted in the daily press.

## 23.2 Payment by telegraphic transfer

> Dear Sir
>
> We have received your statement for the quarter ended 30 September and find that it agrees with our books. As requested we have instructed our bankers, the Midland Bank Ltd, 2 Deansgate, Manchester, to telegraph the sum of £2,182.89 for the credit of your account at the Bank Nationalé, Sweden.
>
> This payment clears your account up to 31 August. The unpaid balance of £623.42 for goods supplied during September will be telegraphed by our bankers on or before 15 November.
>
> Yours faithfully

# BILLS OF EXCHANGE

A bill of exchange is a written order by a creditor (the drawer) to the debtor (the drawee) requiring payment of the sum of money stated in the order to a named person or firm (the payee), usually on a stated future date. Dealings in bills of exchange are now almost entirely confined to international trade, though even here they have now been largely replaced by other forms of payment, especially by the system of bank credits.

A drawee who agrees to the terms of the bill 'accepts' (ie undertakes to pay) and signs it; they then become liable to meet the bill when it falls due for payment.

In this example:
the *drawer* is: Trevor Gartside,
the *drawee* is: C. Mazzawi,
the *payee* is: E. Hughes & Co.

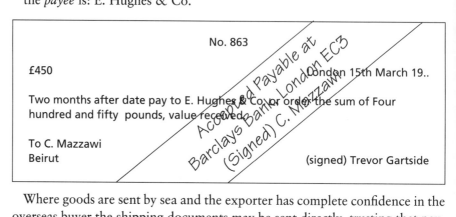

No. 863

£450                                                    London 15th March 19..

Two months after date pay to E. Hughes & Co. or order the sum of Four
hundred and fifty pounds, value received.

To C. Mazzawi
Beirut                                                    (signed) Trevor Gartside

*Accepted Payable at
Barclays Bank London EC3
(Signed) C. Mazzawi*

Where goods are sent by sea and the exporter has complete confidence in the
overseas buyer the shipping documents may be sent directly, trusting that payment will be made for them according to the terms of the contract. Where these
provide for the buyer's acceptance of the exporter's draft bill of exchange, the
buyer is entitled to retain the documents when the goods have been accepted
and returns the draft.

The exporter frequently requires the importer to arrange for the bill to be
accepted by a bank or other financial house. This gives greater security to the
person who holds the bill. Even when the importer accepts the bill, the exporter
may require that it be marked payable at a named bank as in the above illustration. The holder must then present it to that bank for payment. This is called
'domiciling' a bill. Bills *domiciled in London*[1] are readily taken by the Bank of
England for *rediscounting*.[2]

## 23.3   Payment by bill of exchange

### (a) Direct transaction with a trusted customer

Dear Sir

We thank you for your order of 25 June for 1,000 metres of poplin shirting at
the quoted price of £0.86 per metre.

The shirting is now ready for despatch and will be shipped by the SS *Tripoli*
sailing from Liverpool on 18 July.

We are pleased to enclose shipping documents. Also enclosed is our <u>sight</u>
<u>draft</u>[3] drawn at 30 days as agreed. Please accept and return it immediately.

Yours faithfully

---

[1] **domiciled in London** marked as payable in London
[2] **rediscounting** to discount a bill is to obtain payment for it before the due date, at a figure below
face value
[3] **sight draft** a bill of exchange payable immediately upon acceptance

## (b) Direct transaction with unknown customer

Dear Sirs

We are pleased to inform you that we can supply the fancy leather goods included in your order number 582 of 6 August and in accordance with our draft at 30 days for acceptance by your bankers.

Immediately we receive the accepted draft we will arrange to ship the goods. Meanwhile we are holding them for you.

Yours faithfully

## 23.4 Buyer requests extension of time

### (a) Buyer's request

Dear Sirs

You informed me on 25 November that you intended to draw on me at 2 months for the amount due on your invoice number S 256, namely £961.54.

Until now I have had no difficulty in meeting my obligations and have always settled my accounts promptly. I could have done so now had it not been for the bankruptcy of one of my most important customers. I should therefore be most grateful if you could draw your bill at 3 months instead of the proposed 2. This would enable me to meet a temporarily difficult situation which has been forced upon me by circumstances that could not be foreseen.

Yours faithfully

### (b) Seller's reply granting request

Dear Sir

I am replying to your letter of 30 November in which you ask for an extension of the tenor[4] of my draft from 2 to 3 months.

In the special circumstances you mention and because of the promptness with which you have settled your accounts in the past, we are willing to grant the request. Our draft, drawn at 3 months, is enclosed. Please add your acceptance and return it to me.

Yours faithfully

---

[4] **tenor** the period for which a bill of exchange is drawn

### (c) Seller's reply refusing request

When refusing a request it is easy to give offence and lose a customer. This example is a tactful and understanding letter and while it will give rise to disappointment it is unlikely to cause offence.

---

Dear Sir

I am sorry to learn from your letter of 30 November of the difficulty in which the bankruptcy of an important customer has placed you. I should like to say at once that I fully appreciate your wish for an extension of my draft and would very much like to help you. Unfortunately, I cannot do so because of commitments which I have to meet in 2 months time.

In the circumstances you mention your request is not at all unreasonable. If it had been at all possible I would gladly have done so. As matters stand I am left with no choice but to ask you to accept the draft, as drawn at 2 months. This is enclosed for your signature and return.

Yours faithfully

---

## 23.5 Bill dishonoured at maturity

When a buyer who has accepted a bill fails to meet it *at maturity*[5] the bill is said to be 'dishonoured' and the debt for which it was drawn is immediately revived. Dishonour entitles the drawer or other holder of the bill to take legal action against the acceptor either (a) on the bill or (b) on the debt for which it was drawn.

### (a) Drawer requests explanation

---

Dear Sirs

We were very surprised this morning when our bankers returned the bill we drew on you for £325 on 5 August marked 'Refer to drawer'.

Since we are aware from personal knowledge that your firm is financially sound, we presume that failure to honour the bill was due to some mistake. We shall therefore be glad if you will explain the reason. At the same time we must ask you to send by return the sum due on the bill.

Yours faithfully

---

[5] **at maturity** when payment becomes due

## (b) Drawer threatens legal action

> Dear Sir
>
> I regret to say that our bill number 670 for £162.72 of 15 December was not met when we presented it to the bank today.
>
> In view of your earlier promise to meet your obligations on the bill, we are both surprised and disappointed that payment has not been made. We should like to feel that there has been some misunderstanding and ask you to explain why the bill was not <u>honoured</u>.[6]
>
> At the same time we are making a formal request for payment of the sum due and shall be glad to receive your remittance. Should payment not be made I am afraid we shall have no choice but to start proceedings for dishonour.
>
> Yours faithfully

## 23.6 Dishonoured bill protested

When a foreign bill (but not an inland bill) is dishonoured it must be 'protested' as a preliminary to legal action. A 'protest' is a formal declaration by a *notary public*[7] that the terms of the bill have not been fulfilled. Its purpose is to prevent the drawee (the acceptor) from denying that the bill was presented for payment (or for acceptance if it is dishonoured by non-acceptance).

In the following letter the supplier gives the buyer a further opportunity to pay, even after protest.

> Dear Sir
>
> Although you gave your <u>unqualified acceptance</u>[8] to our bill number 670 of 15 December for £462.72, this was not met when presented for payment yesterday.
>
> Non-payment has obliged us to make formal protest of the bill. We now offer you this final opportunity to meet your obligations by payment of the sum of £465.22 to cover the amount for which the bill was accepted and the expenses of protest as follows:
>
> | | |
> |---|---|
> | Nominal value of the bill | £462.72 |
> | Expenses of protest | 2.50 |
>
> We hope to receive payment within the next few days so as to avoid our having to take further proceedings.
>
> Yours faithfully

[6] **honoured** paid when due
[7] **notary public** usually a solicitor specially authorised to witness deeds and other important documents
[8] **unqualified acceptance** a full and complete acceptance

# DOCUMENTARY BILLS

The above examples refer to transactions conducted between importer and exporter direct, but it is more usual for the exporter to gain protection by using the services of the banks. There are three main methods, each requiring the exporter to prepare a documentary bill (ie a draft bill of exchange with shipping documents attached) and to leave it with the bank, which passes it to its foreign branch or correspondent, who then deals with the importer.

1 The importer is ordered to pay the draft either to the exporter, to their order, or to the bank.

2 The exporter again draws on the importer, but asks the bank to discount the draft against the security of the shipping documents, which are passed to the banker.

3 The exporter requires the importer to arrange for a letter of credit, the purpose of which is to enable the exporter to draw on a named bank when the shipping documents are presented. The letter of credit against which the bill is drawn must state the maximum amount and the duration of the credit, the usance (ie the term) of the bill and the shipping documents that are to be sent with the bill.

Where the draft on the importer is drawn for a term, say 60 days, the banker presenting it will hand over the shipping documents only against acceptance (*D/A terms*[9]), but where it is drawn payable on demand, this will be done only against payment (*D/P terms*[10]).

In practice, instructions to the banks are usually given on special forms provided by the banks themselves, thus making certain that all important points are covered. In the correspondence that follows instructions to the banks are given in letters of the kind that would be sent where special forms are not provided.

[9] **D/A terms** documents against acceptance
[10] **D/P terms** documents against payment

## 23.7 Documentary bill presented through bank

### (a) Exporter's letter to Importer, D/P terms

> Dear Sirs
>
> We were pleased to receive your faxed order of 29 June and have arranged to ship the electric shavers by SS Tyrania leaving London on 6 July and due to arrive at Sidon on the 24th.
>
> As the urgency of your order left no time to make the usual enquiries, we are compelled to place this transaction on a cash basis and have drawn on you through Midminster Bank Ltd for the amount of the enclosed invoice. The bank will instruct their correspondent in Sidon to pass the bill of lading to you against payment of the draft.
>
> Special care has been taken to select items suited to your local conditions. We hope you will find them satisfactory and that your present order will be the first of many.
>
> Yours faithfully

### (b) Exporter's letter to importer, D/A terms

> Dear Sirs
>
> YOU ORDER NO B 614
>
> We are pleased to inform you that arrangements have now been made to ship the dress goods you ordered on 15 October. The consignment will leave London on 1 November by SS Manchester Trader and is due to arrive at Quebec on the 22nd.
>
> In keeping with our usual terms of payment we have drawn on you at 60 days and passed the draft and shipping documents to our bankers. The documents will be presented to you by the National Bank of Canada against your acceptance of the draft in the usual way.
>
> Yours faithfully

## 23.8 Exporter's instructions to bank (D/P terms) (to be read with 23.7(a))

> Dear Sirs
>
> On 6 July we are shipping a consignment of 2,000 electric shavers to the Sidon Electrical Co of whom we have little knowledge and whose standing we have been unable to check. We therefore think it would be unwise to surrender the enclosed documents on a D/A basis and enclose a sight draft on the consignees, with bill of lading and insurance certificate attached.
>
> Will you please arrange for your correspondent in Sidon to obtain payment of the amount due before handing over the documents, and let us know when payment has been made.
>
> Yours faithfully

## 23.9 Documentary bill sent through exporter's bank

Exporters sometimes send the documentary bill direct to a bank in the importer's country but they more usually deal with their own bank, who arrange for the bill to be presented to the foreign buyer by their branch or correspondent abroad.

### (a) Exporter's letter to bank

---

Dear Sirs

We have today shipped by SS Seafarer a consignment of haberdashery to the Nigerian Trading Co, Lagos. Since the standing of this company is unknown to us we do not wish to hand over the shipping documents against their mere acceptance of a bill of exchange. Therefore we enclose a sight draft on them, together with bill of lading and the other shipping documents. In the circumstances we shall require payment of the draft in full before the documents are handed over. Please instruct your correspondent in Lagos to arrange for this.

Yours faithfully

---

### (b) Exporters advice of shipment to Nigerian Trading Co.

When sending the above letter to their bankers, the exporters will send advice of shipment to the Nigerian Trading Co and explain the arrangements made for payment.

---

Dear Sirs

The goods which you ordered on 2 October have been shipped to you today by SS Seafarer, due at Lagos on 2 December.

We have taken special care to include in the consignment only items suited to conditions in Nigeria. We hope you will be pleased with our selection and that your first order will lead to further business between us.

From the enclosed copy invoice you will see that the price of £865.75 is well within the maximum figure you stated. We have drawn on you for this amount at sight through the Barminster Bank, who have been instructed to hand over documents against payment of the draft. We hope you will understand that the urgency of your order left us with insufficient time to make the usual enquiries. Therefore we had no choice but to follow our standard practice with new customers of placing the transaction on a cash basis.

We look forward to your further orders. Subject to satisfactory references and regular dealings, we would be prepared to consider open-account terms[11] with quarterly settlements.

Yours faithfully

---

[11] **open-account terms** credit terms with periodic settlement

## 23.10 Documentary bill sent direct to importer's bank

Dear Sir

We enclose shipping documents for 10,000 bags of rice shipped by SS
<u>Thailand</u> which left Bangkok for London on 15 October.

Please hand the documents to Messrs B Stephenson & Co of London
EC2P 2AA, as soon as they are ready to take them up against payment of
£4,260 (four thousand two hundred and sixty pounds) less interest at 2½%
from date of payment to 31 December next. Our account should be credited
with the proceeds after deducting your charges.

Yours faithfully

An exporter in need of immediate funds will sometimes ask their bank to
advance money on a documentary bill. The bank will in return require their
execution of a letter of hypothecation. This is a letter authorising the bank to
sell the goods should the bill be dishonoured by the importer. An exporter who
regularly obtains such advances often signs a general letter of hypothecation
which covers all future transactions.

## BANKERS' COMMERCIAL CREDITS

From the exporter's point of view the documentary bill suffers from the defect
that the foreign buyer may fail to honour the bill. To avoid this risk a system of
*banker's commercial credits* or *documentary credits* has been developed. The
system is now widely used and works in the following manner.

1 Importers ask their own bank to open a credit in favour of the exporter,
usually on a specially printed application form.

2 The importer's bank then sends a letter of credit to the exporter or, more
usually, arranges for one of its branches or correspondents in the exporter's
country to do so.

3 From this point the exporter deals with the correspondent bank and when
the goods are shipped prepares the shipping documents and presents them
(more often than not with a bill of exchange drawn on the correspondent
bank) to the correspondent bank, which 'pays' for them within the limits of
the authorised credit and sends them to the importer's bank.

4 The importer's bank in turn passes the documents to the importer either
against payment or against an acceptance of a bill of exchange, if one accom-
panies the documents.

In effect, the importer's bank is temporarily providing the funds from which
the exporter is paid, though it will usually require the importer to maintain a
sufficient balance in their account to cover the credit.

The credit can be either *revocable*[12] or *irrevocable*.[13] Under a revocable letter of credit the importer is free to modify or even cancel the credit without so much as giving notice to the exporter, but an irrevocable credit can be neither amended nor withdrawn without the permission of the exporter to whom it is granted; the exporter can therefore rely on being paid.

Within the broad pattern illustrated above there may sometimes be slight differences, but they do not affect the general principles on which the system works. Correspondence connected with these credits is very technical; this is evident from the complicated nature of the printed forms used by the banks, and should be handled by someone who is thoroughly familiar with the practice.

## 23.11 A documentary credit – stages in transactions

Perhaps the best way to study the system of bank commercial or documentary credits is to follow a transaction through. In this transaction, Messrs A H Brooks & Son are a firm of London fur dealers. They have agreed to take monthly deliveries of furs from the North American Trading Company over a period of 6 months and to open a credit on which the company can draw as shipments are made. Correspondence would take place on the following lines:

### (a) Buyer approaches bank

Dear Sirs

We have just concluded an agreement to purchase monthly shipments of furs from Canada over the next 3 months and would like to make use of foreign-payment facilities by opening a series of monthly credits for £2,000 each in favour of the North American Trading Company. It has been agreed that we provide credits with a bank in Quebec against which our suppliers would draw for the value of shipments as they are made.

Please let us know on what terms your bank would be prepared to arrange necessary credits and to handle the shipping documents for us.

Yours faithfully

---

[12] **revocable** can be altered or cancelled
[13] **irrevocable** cannot be altered or cancelled

## (b) Bank offers to provide credits

Dear

Thank you for your enquiry of 15 March. We shall be pleased to handle the shipments and to arrange for the necessary documentary credits with our Quebec branch against deposit of bill of lading and other shipping documents. Please complete and return the enclosed form so that we can make the arrangements.

Our commission charges for revocable documentary credits would be ⅛ to ¼% on each of the monthly credits, to which must be added ¼% for irrevocable credits and also our charges for such items as telegrams and postages. In return for these charges you have our assurance that your interests would be carefully protected.

Yours sincerely

## (c) Buyer instructs bank

Dear

Thank you for your letter of 17 March. I have completed and enclose the form of application for a documentary credit. Please arrange to open for our account with your office in Quebec irrevocable credits for £2,000 a month in favour of the North American Trading Company, the credits to be valid until 30 September next.

To enable them to use the credits the company must present the following documents: bills of lading in triplicate, one copy of the invoice, the certificate or policy of insurance and certificate of origin, and draw on your Quebec office at 60 days after sight for each consignment. The documents relate to five cases of mixed furs in each consignment at the value of about £350 per case, cif London.

Yours sincerely

## (d) Bank agrees to open credit

If the bank agrees to open a credit they will usually notify the buyer on one of their own standard printed forms. If this is done by letter instead, they would write in some such terms as the following.

---

Dear

As instructed in your letter of 20 March we are arranging to open a documentary credit with our branch in Quebec in favour of the North American Trading Company, valid until 30 September. Enclosed is a copy of our instruction opening the credit. Please check it to ensure that it agrees with your instructions. As soon as the credits are used we shall debit your account with the amount notified to us as having been drawn against them.

We shall take all necessary steps to make sure that your instructions are carefully carried out. Please note, however, that we cannot assume any responsibility for the safety of the goods or for delays in delivery since these are matters beyond our control.

Yours sincerely

---

### (e) Buyer notifies exporter

The bank in London now sends to its Quebec office a copy of the form completed by Brooks & Son to authorise the opening of the credit.

---

Dear

We have opened irrevocable credits in your favour for £2,000 a month with the Royal Bank of Canada, Quebec, valid until 30 September next.

The terms of the credit authorize you to draw at 60 days on the bank in Quebec for the amount of your invoices after each shipment of five cases. Before accepting the draft, which should include all charges to London, the bank will require you to produce the following documents: bills of lading in triplicate, one copy of the invoice covering cif London, a certificate or policy of insurance and certificate of origin. We will expect your first consignment around the middle of next month.

Yours sincerely

---

### (f) Bank issues letter of credit

The next step is for the Quebec office of the bank to notify the North American Trading Company that the credit is available. They may use a printed form for the purpose. If they were to send the advice by letter or fax and if the London office had requested them to confirm the credit, the message would be something like the following.

Dear

On instructions from Messrs A H Brooks & Son received through our London office, we have opened monthly irrevocable credits for £2,000 in your favour valid until 30 September next. You have authority to draw on us at 60 days against these credits for the amount of your invoices upon shipment of furs to Messrs A H Brooks & Son.

Your draws must be accompanied by the following documents which are to be delivered to us against our acceptance of the drafts: bills of lading in triplicate, commercial invoice, insurance certificate or policy and certificate of origin.

Provided you fulfil the terms of the credit we will accept and pay at maturity the drafts presented to us under these credits and, if required, provide discounting facilities at current rates.

Yours sincerely

In this letter the irrevocable credit is issued by the London Branch of the Royal Bank of Canada and is 'confirmed' by the Quebec branch of the same bank in the final paragraph of its letter to the exporter. Where the bank issuing the credit does not have a branch of its own in the exporter's country it will arrange for the credit to be notified to the exporter through a correspondent bank. Unless the issuing bank has authorised or requested its correspondent to confirm the credit, and it does so, the correspondent is under no obligation to accept the exporter's drafts. If it does confirm the credit, it enters into a definite undertaking with the exporter to accept drafts drawn under the credit, provided they conform to its terms. This undertaking is independent of, and in addition to, that of the bank issuing the irrevocable credit, thus providing the exporter with a twofold assurance of payment.

### (g) Exporter presents documents

Dear

Referring to your advice of 30 March, we enclose shipping documents for the first of the monthly consignments to Messrs A H Brooks & Son.

As required by them we have included all charges in our invoice, which amounts to £1,725.71 and enclose our draft at 60 days for this sum. We shall be glad if, after acceptance, you will discount it at the current rate and send the net amount to our account with the Banque de France, Quebec.

We thank you for your help in this matter.

Yours sincerely

**Note:** The Quebec office now sends the shipping documents to its London office with a statement of the amount of the draft charged against the credit.

### (h) Bank debits buyers

Dear Mr Jones

As instructed by your letter of 20 March, our Quebec office has just accepted for your account a bill for £1,728.71 drawn by the North American Trading Company for a first consignment of furs to you by SS <u>Columbia</u>. We have debited your account with this amount and our charges amounting to £15.30.

The ship left Quebec on 22 April and is due to arrive in London on 2 May. The shipping documents for this consignment are now with us and we shall be glad if you will arrange to collect them.

Yours sincerely

# USEFUL EXPRESSIONS

## Buyer to exporter
### Openings

1  We have received your invoice number ... and agree to accept your draft at 60 days after sight for the amount due.

2  As requested in your letter of ... we have instructed the ... Bank to open a credit for £... in your favour.

3  We are sorry to have to ask for the term of your bill dated ... to be extended for one month.

4  I regret that at the moment I cannot meet in full my acceptance, which is due for payment on ... .

### Closes

1  Please let us know whether you are prepared to give us open-account terms.

2  Please draw on us for the amount due and attach the shipping documents to your draft.

3  We should like to pay by bill of exchange at 60 days after sight and should be glad if you would agree to this.

4  As requested we will arrange to open an irrevocable credit in your favour.

5  Our acceptance will be honoured upon presentation of the bill at the ... branch of the ... Bank.

## Exporter to buyer
### Openings

1  We have considered your letter of ... and are pleased to grant the open-account terms asked for.

2  As requested in your letter of ... we have drawn on you for the amount of our April account at 3 months from ... .

3  As agreed in our earlier correspondence we have drawn on you for the amount of the invoice enclosed.

### Closes

1  Please accept the draft and return it as soon as you can.

2  We are quite willing to put your account on a documents-against-acceptance basis.

3  We have instructed our bank to hand over the shipping documents against acceptance (payment) of our draft.

4 Shipping documents, and our draft for acceptance, have been passed to the ... Bank.

5 As arranged, we have instructed our bank to surrender (hand over) the documents against payment (acceptance) of our draft.

6 As soon as the credit is confirmed, we will ship the goods.

## Buyer to bank

### Openings

1 I enclose accepted bill, drawn on me by ..., and should now be glad to receive the shipping documents.

2 Please accept and pay the following drafts for me and, at maturity, debit them to my account.

3 Please arrange with your correspondents in ... to open a credit in favour of ... .

### Closes

1 Please accept the above draft for me and debit your charges to my account.

2 Please state the amount of your charges for arranging the necessary credits.

## Exporter to bank

### Openings

1 We enclose our sight draft on ... of ... and also the shipping documents.

2 Please surrender the enclosed documents to ... of ... when they accept our draft, also enclosed.

3 Please instruct your correspondent in ... to release the documents only on payment of our sight draft for £... .

### Closes

1 Please obtain acceptance of this draft before surrendering the shipping documents.

2 Please present the bill for acceptance and then discount it for the credit of our account.

3 Please present this acceptance for payment at maturity and credit us with the proceeds.

# Transport

1
2
3
4
5
6
7
8
9
10
11
12
13
14
15
16
17
18
19
20
21
22
23
24
25

# CARRIAGE BY SEA

Transporting goods by sea is still attractive in view of the increase in size and speed of ships and the greatly increased use of the container. Ships are now built specifically to carry particular types of bulk cargoes such as oil, mineral ores, meat and fruit.

## Liners and tramps

It is usual to classify ships into liners (ships which sail at regular times on set routes) and tramps (ships which have no set times or routes, but go wherever they can find suitable cargoes). Hardly any tramps are used these days for long distance hauls except within the United Kingdom. Tramps are essentially cargo boats, ready at any time to make any particular voyage.

Liners may be either passenger liners or cargo liners. Passenger liners usually take a certain amount of miscellaneous cargo, while cargo liners often provide a limited amount of accommodation for passengers.

The contracts entered into between shipowner and shipper (ie the consignor) may take the form of *either*

a charter party (where a complete ship is hired)

*or*

a bill of lading (where the ship carries cargoes belonging to various different shippers).

## Chartering of ships

When goods are shipped in large consignments, and this applies especially to *bulk cargoes*,[1] it may be an advantage to hire or charter a complete ship either for a particular voyage (a voyage charter) or for an agreed period of time (a time charter). The documents setting out the terms and conditions of the contract between the shipowner who provides the ship and the merchant (the charterer) who hires it is called a charter party. Standard forms of charter party have been drawn up but many shipowners prefer to draw up their own forms.

Ship chartering is usually arranged through shipbrokers; in London the Baltic Exchange acts as a special centre where these brokers conduct business.

## The shipping conference system

A shipping conference is an association formed by British and foreign shipping lines, serving a particular sea route. There are some 300 of these conferences,

---

[1] **bulk cargoes** those not packed but loaded loose

each serving its own particular route or area, eg North Atlantic, South African and Australian. The purpose of the conference is to fix and maintain *freight rates*[2] at a profitable level, and to ensure that a sufficient minimum of cargo is always forthcoming to feed the regular sailings they undertake to provide. They do this by establishing 'ties' between shippers and themselves. The 'tie' may take the form of a *deferred rebate*[3] to shippers who confine their shipment to vessels owned by members of the conference; but the rebate system has now been largely replaced by a *preferential rate system.*[4]

The conference system has advantages for both shipper and shipowner. For the shipper it provides the certainty of regular sailings and reliable delivery dates; for the shipowner it ensures that, in return for undertaking to maintain regular sailings, shippers will place their cargoes with him rather than elsewhere. This helps the conference shipowner to keep ships employed.

## The container service

The use of containers provides a highly efficient form of transport by road, rail and air. Its fullest benefits are felt in shipping where costs may be considerably reduced. Containers are constructed in metal and are of standard lengths ranging from 10 to 40 feet (approximately 3–12 metres).

The container service has the following advantages:

- Containers can be loaded and locked at factory premises at nearby container bases making *pilferage*[5] more difficult.
- There is reduced risk of goods getting lost or mislaid in transit.
- Handling is greatly reduced with lower costs and less risk of danger.
- Mechanical handling enables cargoes to be loaded in a matter of hours rather than days, thus reducing the time ships spend in port and greatly increasing the number of sailings.
- Temperature-controlled containers are provided for types of cargo which need them.

[2] **freight rates** transport charges
[3] **deferred rebate** a discount to be allowed later
[4] **preferential rate system** a system offering lower freight rates to Conference members
[5] **pilferage** small thefts

### 24.1 Enquiry for sailings and freight rates

Enquiries of this nature will normally be conducted by telephone or fax. The consignor (or agent) will need to know freight rates and dates of sailings.

> We shall shortly have ready for shipment from Liverpool to Alexandria, four cases of crockery. The cases measure 1¼ x 1¼ x l m, each weighing 70 kg.
>
> Please quote your rate for freight and send us details of your sailings and the time usually taken for the voyage.

### 24.2 Shipping company's reply to enquiry in 24.1

> The SS Princess Victoria will be loading at number 2 dock from 8 to 13 July inclusive. Following her is the SS Merchant Prince, loading at number 5 dock from 20 to 24 July inclusive.
>
> The voyage to Alexandria normally takes 14 days. The freight rate for crockery packed in wooden cases is £97.00 per tonne.
>
> We shall be glad to book your four cases for either of these vessels and enclose our shipping form. Please complete it and return it as soon as possible.

### 24.3 Agent issues forwarding instructions

When notified by the supplier that the goods are ready, the agent either arranges to collect them and despatch them to the docks or will ask the supplier to do so. The shipping form is then returned to the shipping company making arrangements for the goods to be received at the docks.

**(a) Agent's advice to supplier**

> Thank you for informing us that the items ordered on 16 June are now ready for collection.
>
> Please arrange to send the consignment by road to Liverpool for shipment by SS Merchant Prince due to sail for Alexandria on 25 July and to load at number 5 dock from 20 to 24 July inclusive. All cases should be clearly marked and numbered as shown in our official order. Invoices, in triplicate, and your account for transport charges should be sent to us.
>
> All the necessary arrangements have been made with the shipping company.

## (b) Agent's instruction to shipping company

> We have today arranged for H J Cooper & Co. Ltd, Manchester, to forward to you by road the following cases to be shipped to Alexandria by SS <u>Merchant Prince</u> on 25 July.
>
> 4 cases of crockery, marked ◇JR◇ numbers 1–4
>
> The completed shipping form is enclosed together with 4 copies of the bill of lading. Please sign and return 3 copies of the bill and charge the amount to our account.

## Shipping and forwarding agents

A shipping and forwarding agent carries out all the duties connected with collecting and delivering the client's goods. These services are particularly valuable in foreign trade because of the complicated arrangements which have to be made. For exporters, the shipping company collects the goods, makes all the arrangements for shipping them, and notifies their despatch to the forwarding agent in the importing country. The latter takes delivery of the goods and either forwards them to the buyer or arranges for them to be warehoused if the buyer does not want them immediately.

Packing, shipping and forwarding agents are specialists; they know the best methods of packing particular types of goods and the most suitable form of packing to use for the country to which the goods are being sent.

By assembling and repacking in larger lots, small consignments intended for the same destination, the forwarding agent can obtain lower freight rates. It is therefore often cheaper, and certainly much simpler, for suppliers to employ a forwarding agent than to deal directly with the shipping and road transport organisations. Many importers and exporters, however, prefer to reduce their costs by dealing direct with clearing or forwarding agents in the countries of their suppliers (if they are importers) or of their customers (if they are exporters).

### 24.4 Advice of shipment to forwarding agent in buyer's country (Alexandria)

Please note that we have shipped the following goods to you by SS <u>Merchant Prince</u> which left Liverpool yesterday and is due to arrive at Alexandria on 9 August.

| Mark and Numbers | Goods | Gross Weight | Value |
|---|---|---|---|
| JR 1–4 | 4 cases crockery | 280 kg | £3,250 |

Insurance in the sum of £2,200 is provided as far as Alexandria only.

A copy of the bill of lading and the invoice are enclosed. Please arrange to handle the consignment and deliver it to Messrs Jean Riachi & Co, Mansura, who will be responsible for all charges.

The consignment is urgently required so your prompt attention will be appreciated.

### 24.5 Advice of shipment to buyer

When the consignment has been shipped and the buyer's forwarding agent notified, the agent will write to inform the buyer of receipt of the consignment. The letter takes the form of an advice of despatch.

YOUR INDENT N0 762

We are pleased to inform you that all goods ordered on your above indent have now been shipped by SS *Merchant Prince* which sailed from Liverpool yesterday and is due to arrive in Alexandria on 9 August.

The consignment will be handled on arrival by Messrs Behren & Co who will make all the arrangements for delivery.

The bill of lading, invoice, and our account for commission and charges are enclosed. The suppliers have been informed that you will settle their account direct.

We hope to hear from you soon that the goods have arrived safely.

### Forwarding agents

Where exporters arrange shipment through a forwarding agent in their own country, the agent handles the whole transaction. This includes arranging for the goods to be collected and transported to the docks and paying the charges, making the arrangements with the shipping company, paying the freight, insuring the goods, preparing the bill of lading and dealing with any other documents which may be necessary (eg consular invoice, *certificate of origin*,[6] certificate of value and weight, export licence, etc.). When the goods have been shipped the exporter's agent advises the shipping and forwarding agent in the buyer's country, who deals with them when they arrive at the port. In short, a forwarding agent does everything and, as a specialist in the business, does it well.

## 24.6  Supplier seeks forwarding agent's services

We have a consignment of tape recorders now waiting to be shipped to Messrs Tan & Co of Kuala Lumpur. Will you please arrange for the consignment to be collected from the above address and arrange shipment to Klang by the first possible sailing. When it arrives at Klang the consignment will be handled for our customers by Mr J Collins with whom you should make the necessary arrangements.

The recorders are packed in three cases and the enclosed copy of the invoice shows quantities and a total value of £2,800. Insurance should be taken out for £2,900 to include cover for expenses.

When the goods are shipped please send the original bill of lading and one copy to us, together with the certificate or policy of insurance and any other necessary documents.

## CARRIAGE BY AIR

Bills of lading are used for consignments by sea. They are not used for consignments by air because the goods usually reach their destination before a bill of lading could be prepared. Instead the consignor is required to prepare an airway bill giving particulars of the consignment. This normally consists of a number of copies, some of which are treated as originals, one for the issuing air carrier, one for the consignee and one for the consignor. The remaining copies serve for other possible carriers and for customs and record purposes.

It is common practice for the airline or its agent to prepare the airway bill from details supplied by the consignor on a special form – an Instructions for Despatch of Goods form – provided by the airline or by the forwarding agents.

Like the bill of lading, the airway bill serves as a receipt for the goods taken on board and is evidence of the contract of carriage, the terms of which are set out in detail on the back. Unlike the bill of lading, however, the airway bill is not a document of title.

With carriage by air, the consignor may also use the services of a forwarding agent or may deal with the airline direct through its cargo-booking section. The more usual practice is to use an agent.

[6] **certificate of origin** a document entitling importer to preferential customs duties

Air cargo is charged by weight except for bulky commodities which are charged by volume. To encourage movement of traffic by air, special rates are charged for a wide range of enumerated articles. Valuables are subject to a surcharge to cover extra handling costs.

### 24.7 Enquiry for air freight rates (through agent)

> We shall shortly have a consignment of electric shavers, weighing about 20 kg, for a customer in Damascus. We wish to send this by air from London.
>
> Please let us have details of the cost and any formalities to be observed. The invoice value of the consignment is £1,550 and we should require insurance cover for this amount plus the costs of sending the consignment.

### 24.8 Forwarding agent's reply

> Thank you for your enquiry regarding your consignment to Damascus. All our charges including freight, airway bill fee, insurance and our own commission are shown on the attached schedule.
>
> To enable us to prepare your airway bill we shall need the information requested in the enclosed form. Three copies of a certified commercial invoice and a certificate of origin will also be necessary.
>
> Your consignment should be in our hands by 10 am on the morning of departure day. Please telephone me when you are ready to deliver the consignment to our officer at the airport so that we can prepare to receive it and deal with it promptly. Alternatively we can make arrangements to collect the goods.
>
> We hope to receive instructions from you soon.

## CARRIAGE BY ROAD

Road transport is generally cheaper than rail for both passengers and goods, although rail is cheaper for such bulk commodities as oil, sand and timber.

The most important features of road transport are:

- The ease with which it adapts itself to different situations and the fact that a direct delivery service is provided
- Routes are easily varied according to traffic flow
- It is safer for fragile goods and calls for simpler packing than for goods sent by rail
- It is particularly suitable for short distance traffic, mainly because small truck loads can be dealt with easily and quickly.

## Documents used

When goods are handed to a carrier the contract of carriage takes the form of a consignment note or waybill (if transport is by road, rail or air). The originals of these documents are handed to the *consignors*[7] and serve as their receipts. The carrier keeps a copy for himself and a further copy is passed on to the *consignee*[8] with the goods.

## 24.9 Enquiry for freight rates

> Early next month we shall have a consignment of motor-car spares for delivery from our warehouse to a company in Aberdeen.
>
> These spares will be packed in two wooden cases, each measuring 1 x 1 x 0·75 m and weighing about 80 kg.
>
> Please let us know as soon as possible:
>
> 1  Your charge for collecting and delivering these cases.
>
> 2  If you can collect them on the 3rd of next month.
>
> 3  When delivery would be made to the consignee.
>
> An early reply would be appreciated.

## 24.10 Supplier notifies despatch of goods

> Your Order No 825
>
> We have today despatched by Williams Transport Ltd two wooden cases containing the motor-car spares which you ordered recently.
>
> Would you please unpack and examine them as soon as possible after delivery and in the event of any damage notify us and also the carriers at once.
>
> We understand the goods will be delivered to you in 3 days time.

## 24.11 Buyer notifies receipt of goods

> Our Order No 825
>
> The two cases of motor-car spares despatched by Williams Transport Ltd were delivered yesterday in good condition.
>
> The case is being returned to you by Williams Transport. Please credit us with the amount charged for it on your invoice.

[7] **consignor** the one who sends the goods
[8] **consignee** the one to whom the goods are sent

**24.12** **Removal of household furniture**

### (a) Request for quotation

Early next month we will be moving from the above address to 110 Normanshire Drive, Chingford. I would like a quotation on the cost of your removal services.

Our present house has six rooms, all of which are fully furnished. You will no doubt wish to inspect our furniture so please arrange for one of your representatives to call as soon as possible.

I hope to hear from you soon.

### (b) Quotation

We are writing to confirm the removal of your furniture from St Annes to Chingford on 3 May.

Our charge for the removal will be £950, including insurance cover in the sum of £45,000. We enclose an agreement form setting out the terms and conditions and shall be glad if you will sign and return it.

Our van with three workmen will arrive at your house at 7.30 am on 3 May. The loading should be completed in about three hours. We should be able to deliver to your Chingford address and complete unloading by 4.30 pm on the following day.

Please let me know if you have any queries.

### (c) Claim for damage to property during removal

When your workmen removed the furniture from my house in St Annes on 3 May the staircase was badly damaged. The new owner of this house has obtained an estimate for the repair in the sum of £220 and he is now claiming this amount from me.

I realise the insurance policy you provided only covered damage to furniture. However, as the damage now reported is claimed to have been caused by your workmen I have advised the new owner to contact you directly.

## CARRIAGE BY RAIL

Over long distances and for bulk commodities such as oil, sand and timber rail is cheaper than road. However, unlike road transport, it cannot collect and deliver without the help of some other form of transport. This sometimes causes delay, involves double handling, calls for more complicated packing, increases the risk of theft and damage, and consequently increases costs. The railways are increasingly meeting these problems by using 'containers'.

Goods may be carried either at owner's risk or at company's risk, rates for the former being lower. Rates also vary with the class of goods.

Unless otherwise agreed between buyer and seller, responsibility for collecting and transporting the purchases lies with the buyer. If a carrier is engaged, then the carrier becomes the buyer's agent. Once the goods have been taken over by the agent, the seller's responsibility for them ceases and the buyer becomes liable for any loss or damage which may be suffered.

## 24.13 Claim for losses due to pilferage

### (a) Buyer's complaint

> OUR ORDER NO 328
>
> The consignment of cotton shirts despatched on 21 June was delivered yesterday in a very unsatisfactory condition.
>
> It was clear that two of the cases (numbers 4 and 7) had been <u>tampered with</u>.[9] Upon checking the contents we found that case number 4 contained only 372 shirts and case number 7 contained only 375 shirts instead of the 400 invoiced for each case.
>
> Before reporting the matter to the railway please confirm that each of these cases contained the invoiced quantity when they left your warehouse. At the same time please replace the 53 missing shirts with others of the same quality.
>
> You will no doubt be claiming <u>compensation</u>[10] from the railway, in which case we shall be glad to assist you with any information we can provide. Meanwhile, the cases are being held for inspection, together with the contents.

### (b) Supplier's reply

> We were sorry to learn from your letter of 27 June that two of the cases sent to you on 21 June had been tampered with. We confirm that when they left our warehouse each of these cases contained the full quantity of 400 shirts. The cases were in good order when they left our premises; in support of this we hold the carrier's clean receipt.
>
> As we sent the goods by rail at your request, the railway company must be regarded as your agents. We cannot, therefore, accept any responsibility for the losses and can only suggest that you make the claim for compensation directly with the railway company. We are quite willing to support your claim in whatever way we can.
>
> The 53 missing shirts will be replaced but we will have to charge them to your account. In the circumstances we will allow you an extra discount of 10%.
>
> Please let us know in what way we can help in your claim for compensation.

[9] **tampered with** improperly interfered with
[10] **compensation** an amount of money that makes good the loss

### (c) Buyer's claim on railway

We regret to report that two of the cases covered by your consignment receipt number S5321 were delivered to us in a condition that left no doubt of their having been broken into during transit. The cases in question are numbers 4 and 7.

This was noticed when the cases were delivered by your carrier and accordingly we added to our receipt 'Cases 4 and 7 damaged; contents not examined'. A later check of the contents revealed a shortage of 53 shirts.

The consignment was sent by our suppliers on carrier's risk terms. Therefore we must hold you responsible for the loss. Our claim is enclosed for the invoiced value of the missing shirts (at £4.00 each) which is £212.00. In support of our claim we enclose a certified copy of our supplier's invoice.

The two cases and their contents have been put aside to await your inspection.

# USEFUL EXPRESSIONS

## Openings

### Enquiries

1 Thank you for your enquiry of ... we are pleased to quote as follows for the shipment of ... to ... .

2 Thank you for your enquiry regarding sailings to Johannesburg in August.

3 We are due to ship a large quantity of ... to ... and need you to obtain a ship of about ... tons capacity.

4 Please let us know the current rates of freight for the following:

5 Please quote an inclusive rate for collection and delivery of ... from ...

### Goods despatched

1 We have today sent to you a consignment of ... by SS ... .

2 We have given instructions to ... to forward the following consignment to you by rail:

## Closes

1 Please inform us of the date on which the ship closes for cargo.

2 Please complete and return the enclosed instructions form with a signed copy of the invoice.

3 We hope to receive your shipping instructions by return.

# Insurance

1
2
3
4
5
6
7
8
9
10
11
12
13
14
15
16
17
18
19
20
21
22
23
24
25

Insurance is provided as a kind of security to cover almost any kind of occurrence which may result in loss. Its purpose is to make compensation available for those who suffer from loss or damage, in other words a contract to restore to their original position a person who suffers loss.

An insurance claim cannot pay out more than the value of what is lost, and nothing is to be gained from insuring a sum greater than the value of the good(s) insured. If, for example, a ship worth £50,000 is insured for £60,000, the owner would receive only £50,000 if the ship is lost and a claim put forward.

A different kind of insurance is that which provides for payment of a fixed sum in advance to a person when they reach a given age, or to any dependants upon their death. In Britain, this type of insurance is called assurance. Unlike insurance, which is concerned with compensation for loss that may or may not occur, assurance is concerned with providing security for events that are certain to occur.

## THE INSURANCE CONTRACT

A contract of insurance is taken out between two parties:

(i)   The *insurer* is the party who agrees to accept the risk; and

(ii)  The *insured* is the party who seeks protection from the risk.

In return for payment of a *premium*[1] the insurer agrees to pay the insured a stated sum (or a proportion of it) should the event insured against occur. Premiums are quoted as a percentage of the sum insured – in Britain, at so many pence per £100 (eg 25p%).

A person wishing to take out life assurance or accident insurance must usually submit a *proposal form*[2] containing questions which must be answered truthfully. The insured must also make known any other information that is likely to influence the insurer's judgement regarding the risk. If this is not done, the insurer may void the contract. In marine insurance it is not the practice to use proposal forms. They are only rarely used in fire insurance. However, as with other forms of insurance, all information affecting the risk must be disclosed.

If the proposal is accepted the insurer is required by law to issue a policy. This policy sets out the terms of the contract including the risk to be covered, the sum insured and the premium to be paid. If at a later date it is decided to alter the terms of the insurance, this is usually done by *endorsing*[3] the existing policy rather than by issuing a new one.

A person cannot legally insure a risk for which there is no legal interest. Anyone may insure their own property but not that of a neighbour. Anyone may insure the life of a person who owes them money but only up to the amount owing. Ship owners may insure their ships but not the cargo carried, except for the value of the *freight*[4] lost if the cargo were lost.

[1] **premium** the payment made for insurance
[2] **proposal form** a written request for insurance cover
[3] **endorsing** writing on the back of a document – varying the cover stated in the policy by an additional clause
[4] **freight** the charge for carriage of goods

## **25.1** Enquiries for insurance rates

### (a) Cash in transit

Background details about business and banking

Use numbered points for clarity

Request a reply regarding terms

---

Dear Sirs

We normally pay into the bank each morning our takings for the preceding business day. The sums involved are sometimes considerable especially at the weekends: takings on a Saturday may amount to as much as £6,000.

We bank with the local branch of the Barminster Bank on West Street, Milton – about half a mile from our premises.

We therefore wish to take out insurance cover for the following:

1   Against loss of cash on the premises, by fire, theft, or burglary.

2   Against loss of cash in transit between our premises and the bank.

3   Against accident or injury to staff while engaged in taking money to the bank, or bringing it from the bank.

Please let us know on what terms you can provide cover for the risks mentioned.

Yours faithfully

---

### (b) Goods sent by sea

Dear Sirs

We will shortly have a consignment of tape recorders, valued at £50,000 cif Quebec, to be shipped from Manchester by a vessel of Manchester Liners Ltd.

We wish to cover the consignment against all risks from our warehouse at the above address to the port of Quebec. Will you please quote your rate for the cover.

Yours faithfully

---

### (c) Request for special rate

Dear Sirs

We regularly ship consignments of bottled sherry to Australia by both passenger and cargo liners of the Enterprise Shipping Line. We are interested to know if you can issue an all-risks policy for these shipments and, if so, on what terms. In particular we wish to know whether you can give a special rate in return for the promise of regular monthly shipments.

I hope to hear from you soon.

Yours faithfully

---

## 25.2 Applications for insurance cover

### (a) Continuation of 25.1(c)

Dear Mr Johnson

We thank you for your reply to our enquiry of 6 June. The terms you quote, namely 35p%, less 5% special discount for regular shipments, are acceptable. We understand that these terms will apply to all our shipments of bottled sherry by regular liners to Australian ports and cover all risks, including breakages and pilferage.[5]

Our first shipment will be on 2 July for 20 cases of sherry valued at £6,000. Please arrange open-account terms[6] with quarterly settlements.

I look forward to receiving the policy within the next few days.

Yours sincerely

### (b) Insurance of warehouse stock

*(i) Application*

Dear Mr Wilson

Thank you for your letter of 15 April quoting rates for insurance cover for stock stored in our warehouse at the above address.

The value of the stock held varies with the season but does not normally exceed £100,000 at any time.

Please arrange cover in this sum for all the risks mentioned in your letter and on the terms quoted, namely 50p% per annum. Cover should take effect from 1 May next.

Yours sincerely

*(ii) Acknowledgement*

Dear Mr Smith

Thank you for your recent letter. We shall be glad to provide cover in the sum of £50,000 at 50p% per annum on stock in your warehouse at 25 Topping Street, Lusaka. This will take effect from 1 May.

The policy is now being prepared and it should reach you in about a week's time.

Please let me know if I can provide any further help.

Yours sincerely

---

[5] **pilferage** small thefts
[6] **open-account terms** credit terms with periodic statements

### (c) Cargo insurance

> Dear Sirs
>
> Please arrange full a.a.r.[7] cover in the sum of £5,000 for shipment of 20 Hi-fi music centres to Quebec by MV Merchant Shipper, scheduled to sail from Manchester on 2 July. The goods are packed in 5 cases marked AHB 1–5, now lying in our warehouse at 25 Manchester Road, Salford.
>
> Please let us have the policy, and one certified copy, not later than 30 June. The charge should be billed to our account.
>
> Yours faithfully

# INSURANCE BROKERS

Insurance of business risks, and especially of *maritime*[8] risks, calls for special knowledge. The advice and help of a qualified insurance broker is often of great advantage. A broker advises clients on the risks they should cover, recommends the kinds of insurance best suited to their particular needs and places the risks with the most suitable insurers.

## 25.3  Requests to brokers to arrange insurance

### (a) Example 1

> Dear Sir
>
> Will you please arrange to take out an all-risks insurance for us on the following consignment of cameras from our warehouse at the above address to Valletta:
>
> 6 c/s Cameras due to leave Liverpool on 18 August by SS Endeavour.
>
> The invoiced value of the consignment, including freight and insurance, is £11,460.
>
> Please contact me if you have any queries.
>
> Yours faithfully

[7] **a.a.r.** against all risks
[8] **maritime** relating to the sea

## (b) Example 2

Dear Miss Taylor

Thank you for calling me this morning. I confirm that we have decided to accept the quotation of 60p% by the Britannia Insurance Co for insurance to cover the transit by road of two 1¼ tonne boilers on 15 July. The consignment will be taken from our works in Birmingham to the Acme Engineering Co, Bristol.

Please arrange the necessary cover and send us the policy as soon as possible.

Yours faithfully

# INSURANCE PREMIUMS

Statistics enable insurers to assess the extent of particular risks with considerable accuracy. This helps them to fix their premiums at levels that are fair both to themselves and to the insured. Since premiums vary with the degree of risk, lower rates are charged when protective measures such as fire alarms, *automatic sprinklers*,[9] *fire extinguishers*[10] and fire-resistant materials are used.

## 25.4 Request for reduction in premium

Dear Mr Maxwell

POLICY NO F 623104

*Refer to telephone conversation. Request a review – give full details of the premium concerned*

Further to our telephone conversation I should be obliged if you would review the rate of premium charged under the above fire policy for goods in our transit shed[11] at No 4 Dock. As you know, the shed is also used as a bonded store[12] and storage warehouse.

*State main reason for request*

As we discussed I feel that not enough weight may have been given to the following conditions when the present rate of premium was fixed:

1 The shed is not artificially heated.

*Numbered points ensure clarity and ease of reference*

2 No power of any kind is used.

3 All rooms are provided with automatic sprinklers, fireproof doors and fire extinguishers of the latest type.

4 A water main runs round the entire dockside and can be tapped[13] at several points within easy distance of the shed.

*Tactfully request a reduction*

When these conditions are taken into account I believe the present rate of premium seems to be unreasonably high. I hope you will agree to reduce it sufficiently to bring it more into line with the extent of the risk insured under the policy.

I look forward to hearing from you soon.

Yours

[9] **automatic sprinklers** a system which, when overheated, releases water
[10] **extinguisher** an appliance for putting out fires
[11] **transit shed** a shed through which goods pass
[12] **bonded store** a warehouse for goods liable to customs duty
[13] **tapped** used for drawing water

# HOUSEHOLDERS' POLICIES

Most fire insurance companies offer a wide range of cover on the buildings and contents of private dwellings under what are known as 'Householders' or 'All-risk' policies. These are designed to give protection in one document from a variety of risks besides those usually covered by a fire policy, including storms, riots, burst pipes, burglary, theft, accidents to servants, liability to third parties, accidental breakage of mirrors, etc, but not losses due to war. It is a condition of such cover that both buildings and contents are insured for their full value.

## 25.5 Application for householder's insurance

### (a) Application

> Dear Sirs
>
> I have recently bought the property at the above address with possession as from 1 July and wish to take out comprehensive cover on both building and contents in the sums of £120,000 and £30,000 respectively.[14] The former figure represents the estimated rebuilding cost of the property and the latter the full value of the contents.
>
> Please send me particulars of your terms and conditions for the policy and a proposal form if required.
>
> Yours faithfully

### (b) Reply

> Dear Mrs Turner
>
> HOUSEHOLDERS' COMPREHENSIVE INSURANCE
>
> Thank you for your enquiry of 19 June. A copy of our prospectus containing particulars of our policies for householders is enclosed.
>
> You will see that we offer two types of cover for buildings. Cover 'B' (premium rate 21p%) is similar to cover 'A' (premium rate 24p%) but excludes cover for accidental damage. For contents we provide only one type of cover at a rate of 70p% per annum. As you will see from the prospectus, our comprehensive policies provide a very wide range of cover.
>
> I enclose a proposal form. Please complete and return it not later than 7 days before the date from which the policy is to run.
>
> Please give me a call if you have any queries.
>
> Yours sincerely

[14] **respectively** relating to each in turn

## 25.6 Request for increase in cover

Dear Sirs

HOUSE CONTENTS POLICY NO H 96154

On 2 June I sent you a cheque for £175.00 as the premium due for renewal of the above policy.

I now wish to increase the amount of cover from its current figure of £25,000 to £30,000 (thirty thousand pounds) with immediate effect. Please confirm that you have arranged for this and send me the customary endorsement indicating the charge for inclusion in the policy schedule .

From the conditions that apply to your householders' policies I understand that no charge for this increased cover will be made before my next renewal date.

I look forward to receiving your confirmation soon.

Yours faithfully

## 25.7 Notice of increase in premiums

Some insurance companies encourage household policy-holders to increase the amount of cover for buildings and contents by deferring payment of the higher rate of premium until the next renewal of the policy, as in the above letter. Under this arrangement it is possible for the insured to obtain extra cover free of charge for a period of up to twelve months under a policy that is renewable annually.

The following is a circular letter from an insurance company to its household policy holders referring to under-insurance due to inflation.

Dear

Unfortunately, our efforts to encourage household policy-holders to revise the sums insured to take account of inflation[15] have been poorly supported. In the past 5 years the monetary value of property[16] and contents has more than doubled, but most householders have failed to provide for this and as a result are grossly[17] underinsured. The problem of underinsurance has often been made worse because the initial cover[18] was inadequate[19]. On some recent claims research shows that the amount of underinsurance has been well over 50%.

In this situation we have been reluctantly compelled[20] to introduce in all household insurance a provision[21] automatically increasing the amount of cover at each renewal of the policy. The increase, currently[22] 6%, will be reflected[23] in the amount of premium payable. Allowance for this will be made in your next renewal notice.

If you have any queries please contact me.

Yours sincerely

---

[15] **inflation** a rise in the general level of prices
[16] **property** premises
[17] **grossly** very much; considerably
[18] **initial cover** the value insured at the beginning
[19] **inadequate** insufficient
[20] **reluctantly** compelled; forced unwillingly
[21] **provision** a term or condition in an agreement
[22] **currently** at the present time
[23] **reflected** included; covered by

**25.8** **Request for information concerning cover**

Dear

POLICY NO MH 816/89068

Upon receiving your renewal notice on 21 July I sent you a cheque for £250.75 to extend cover of my premises under the above policy. Unfortunately, I have no record of the amount of cover provided by the premium paid and should be obliged if you would let me have this information as soon as possible.

Should the amount of the cover be less than £50,000 I should like to increase it to this amount with immediate effect. Please arrange for this if necessary and send me your account for the amount of additional premium payable. I will then send you a cheque in payment.

Yours sincerely

# HOLIDAY INSURANCE

When a holiday is to be taken abroad it is a wise precaution to insure not only against loss of baggage and other personal property but also against personal accident and illness while away from home.

The costs of medical and hospital care when on holiday must be borne privately and can be very high. In return for a small premium many insurance companies now provide cover for this. Travel agencies are usually willing to make the necessary arrangements.

**25.9** **Holiday insurance – application and claim**

**(a) Application**

Dear Sirs

I shall be touring Italy and Sicily in a 1996 Peugeot 405 GL for 4 weeks commencing 3 July.

Please let me know the terms and conditions on which you could issue a policy to cover loss of and damage to baggage and other personal property. I should also like to consider cover against personal accident and illness, and should be glad if you would send me particulars. The car is already separately insured.

I hope to hear from you soon.

Yours faithfully

**(b) Insurer's reply**

Dear Mr Sanderson

Thank you for your letter of 8 June regarding insurance to cover your tour of Italy and Sicily.

I enclose a leaflet setting out the terms and conditions of the insurance for both personal property and injury and illness, and also a proposal form. The cover for injury and illness extends to the full cost of medical and hospital treatment and of any special arrangements that may be necessary for your return home.

Please complete and return the proposal form by 26 June at the latest, so that we can be sure of issuing the policy in time.

Yours sincerely

# FIDELITY INSURANCE

An employer often seeks protection from the dishonesty of persons employed in positions of trust by taking out a 'Fidelity Guarantee' policy. Employees may be insured either individually or on a group basis under a collective policy guaranteeing a separate amount for each employee. Alternatively, a floating policy may be taken out in which the names of the various employees appear but with one amount of guarantee for the whole.

## 25.10 Enquiry for a Fidelity Guarantee policy

Dear Sirs

We have recently appointed Mrs Tessa Campbell as our chief accountant. She came to us with excellent references, but as a purely precautionary measure we wish to cover her by a fidelity bond for £100,000.

Please let me know what terms you can provide this cover and send me a proposal form if required.

Yours faithfully

# TEMPORARY COVER

No contract comes into effect until the proposal made is accepted by the insurer. However, where a person wants immediate cover while the proposal is being considered, the insurer is usually willing to grant temporary protection and to issue a *cover note*[24] upon request. The note is usually expressed to provide cover up to a stated date.

In the following correspondence the insurer does not issue a cover note, but nevertheless makes it clear that in fact the property is covered.

## 25.11 Request for cover pending issue of policy

### (a) Householder's request

Dear Sirs

1 MARGATE ROAD, ST ANNES-ON-SEA, LANCS

I have recently bought the property at the above address. A covenant[25] in the deeds requires the property to be insured with your company against fire. In a letter to me dated 30 October the solicitors handling the transfer for me stated that you would be getting in touch with me about this.

As I have not yet heard from you, I am writing as a matter of urgency to ask you to insure the property under your usual full-cover householder's policy in the sum of £100,000 as from 7 December inclusive. This is the date fixed for the legal transfer of the property to me. This sum covers the purchase price of £80,000 and estimated rebuilding costs.

In view of the urgency I hope to receive your assurance that you will hold the property covered as from and including next Thursday 7 December. I ask this because I am in no position to accept the risks of non-insurance while the policy is being prepared.

Yours faithfully

### (b) Insurer's reply

Dear Mr Brown

COMPREHENSIVE INSURANCE
1 MARGATE ROAD, ST ANNES-ON-SEA, LANCS

Thank you for your letter of 3rd November. I am pleased to inform you that we will hold this property covered for £100,000 as from 7 December on the terms and conditions of the company's comprehensive policy.

A proposal form is enclosed. Please complete it and return it to me immediately.

Yours sincerely

---

[24] **cover note** a document giving temporary insurance cover pending issue of policy
[25] **covenant** a clause in a deed (a sealed contract)

## CLAIMS

Claims for loss or damage should always be made promptly by letter and supported by whatever information or evidence can be offered at the time. If a claim relates to goods delivered it should be made immediately the loss or damage is discovered:

1  To the insurer, if the goods have been insured by the buyer.

2  To the seller, where the insurance has been taken out by them.

### 25.12  Claim for damage to house property

When a claim is made it is usually necessary for a claim form to be completed, as in this correspondence.

#### (a) Householder's claim

State policy number
Give details of the incident

State cost involved in repair

Tactfully request permission to proceed with the work

> Dear Sirs
>
> POLICY NO PK 850046
>
> I am sorry to have to report a slight accident to the work surface of the sink-unit work-table. This was burnt and cracked when an electric iron was accidentally knocked over on it.
>
> I have made enquiries and am informed that replacement cost of the damaged work surface will be about £80 (eighty pounds). There will also be an additional charge for fixing.
>
> I hope to receive your permission to arrange for the work to be carried out. Should you wish to inspect the damage I am at home on most days, but it would be helpful to know when to expect your representative.
>
> Yours faithfully

#### (b) Insurer's reply

> Dear Mrs Crowther
>
> POLICY NO PK 850046
>
> I refer to your letter of 14 September and our representative's recent call on you. Our claim form is enclosed. Please complete and return this to me as soon as possible with the contractor's estimate for replacement of the damaged work surface. I will then deal with the matter immediately.
>
> Yours sincerely

## 25.13 Insurer requests further information

Sometimes a person suffering a loss gives incomplete or even inaccurate information, hoping that by doing so excessive compensation may be recovered. In such cases the insurer will either ask for further information, as in the following letter, or will *dispute*[26] the claim. Such cases are fairly numerous and varied, and the following is only one of the many kinds of letter the insurer may send. It relates to a claim by a contractor for loss of business suffered as a result of damage to a lorry in a road accident.

A person who suffers loss must do whatever possible to limit the loss, otherwise they may fail to get full compensation.

---

Dear

I refer to your claim of 17 February for £1,500 as compensation for loss of business due to damage to your lorry.

Before I can deal with your claim I shall need the following further information from you:

1   What is the actual financial loss suffered as a result of the accident, and how is it calculated?

2   What steps, if any, were taken to hire a suitable lorry until the damaged lorry could be replaced?

3   If no steps to hire were taken, please give the reason.

As soon as I receive this information asked for I will deal with your claim immediately.

Yours sincerely

---

## 25.14 Buyer requests seller to make claim

Where, on behalf of the buyer, the seller insures goods in transit, the buyer will report the loss or damage to the seller and ask him to make the claim, as in the following letter.

[26] **dispute** to contest; oppose

Dear

OUR ORDER NO C 541

When the SS <u>Lancastria</u> arrived at Famagusta on 10 November, it was noticed that one side of case number 12 containing radio receivers was split. Therefore the case was opened and the contents were examined by a local insurance surveyor in the presence of the shipping company's agents. The case was invoiced as containing 24 Hacker 'Mayflower' radio receivers, 8 of which were badly damaged.

The surveyor's report is enclosed with statement from the shipping agent.

As you hold the insurance policy I should be grateful if you would take up this matter with the insurers.

Eight replacement receivers will be required. Please arrange to supply these as soon as possible and charge them to our account.

Thank you in advance for your trouble on our behalf. If there are any queries please do not hesitate to call me.

Yours faithfully

## 25.15 Claim for damage by fire

### (a) Claim

Dear Sirs

POLICY NO AR 3854

I regret to report that a fire broke out in our factory stores last night. The cause is not yet known but we estimate the damage to stock to be about £100,000. Fortunately no records were destroyed so there should be no difficulty in assessing the value of the loss.

Please arrange for your representative to call and let me have your instructions regarding <u>salvage</u>.[27]

Yours faithfully

---

[27] **salvage** items that can be recovered

**(b) Insurer's reply**

> Dear
>
> FIRE POLICY NO AR 3854
>
> Thank you for your letter of 21 May. I was sorry to hear about the fire in your factory stores.
>
> As a first step will you please make your claim on the enclosed form. Meanwhile, I am arranging for Mr John Watson, a loss adjuster, to call and assess the damage. He will be in touch with you soon.
>
> If you need help in completing the claim form Mr Watson will be able to assist you.
>
> Yours sincerely

## 25.16 Insurer declines to meet claim in full (continuation of 25.15)

Sometimes it is necessary for a letter to convey disappointing or unwelcome news, as when a claim is rejected, or in any other circumstances likely to cause disappointment. In such a letter the opening paragraph should be in terms that prepare the receiver for what is coming and soften the blow when it does come. This indirect approach to unwelcome news is used in the following letter.

> Dear
>
> POLICY NO AR 3854
>
> When we received your letter of 5 June we sent Mr John Watson to inspect and report on the damage caused by the fire. He has now submitted his report, which confirms your claim that the damage is extensive. He reports, however, that much of the stock damaged or destroyed was either obsolete[28] or obsolescent.[29]
>
> We therefore regret that we cannot accept as a fair estimate of the loss the figure of £100,000 mentioned in your letter – a figure which we understand is based on the actual cost of the goods.
>
> Our own estimate of the stock damaged or destroyed, based on present market values, does not exceed £60,000. We feel that this valuation is a very generous one, but are prepared to pay on the basis of it under the policy. Please let me know if you will accept this in full settlement of your claim for the value of the stock lost.
>
> Yours sincerely

---

[28] **obsolete** out of date
[29] **obsolescent** becoming out of date

**25.17** **Claim for injury to worker**

**(a) Claim**

Dear Sirs

POLICY NO 56241

Our foreman, Mr James MacDonald, met with an accident on 2 March. He crushed his thumb when operating a machine. At the time we did not think the accident was serious enough to report: However, after an absence of 3 weeks Mr MacDonald has returned to his work and is still unable to carry on his normal duties.

We therefore wish to make a claim under the above policy. Please send the necessary claim form to me as soon as possible.

Yours faithfully

**(b) Insurer's reply**

Dear

POLICY NO 56341

Refer to claim received — Thank you for your letter of 27 March regarding your claim for the accident to Mr J MacDonald.

Tactfully comment on details provided — Under the terms of the policy his claim should have been submitted within 3 days of the accident. As more than 3 weeks have now passed, your claim for compensation under the policy has been forfeited.

The insurer does not have to meet the claim, but he does so as a gesture of goodwill. This is tactfully explained here — Nevertheless, as a gesture of goodwill we have decided to overlook this late submission. However we feel it should have been clear from Mr MacDonald's prolonged absence from work that his accident was more serious than you had thought and that there seems to be no good reason why the claim should not have been made earlier.

Enclose claim form. Clearly state position in the future — I enclose a claim form as requested but must emphasise that future claims cannot be entertained where the terms of the policy are not complied with.

Yours sincerely

**25.18** **Request to support illness claim**

Claims arising from accident, sickness or similar causes must be supported by medical evidence either from the attendant doctor or from the institution treating the patient.

A patient recovering from an operation is required by their insurance company to provide evidence of any stay in hospital. In the following letter a doctor is asked to complete the form received from the company. By providing the details and enclosing an addressed envelope the patient tries to help a busy doctor.

Dear Dr Edwards

The London Life Insurance Co Ltd, of which I am a policy holder, have asked for completion of the enclosed claim form for benefits for the period I was in your hospital and later the Avala Nursing Home.

I have pencilled in the details requested on the side of the form which the company wish you to complete; this may assist you.

I have attached 4 accounts covering both hospital and nursing home accommodation for 6 weeks as follows:

Hospital (23 April to 7 May 19—)
Nursing Home (7 May to 2 June 19—)

The company would like you to return the completed claim form to them. I enclose an addressed envelope for this purpose.

Please give me a call if you have any queries.

Yours sincerely

## MARINE INSURANCE

Most of the world's business in marine insurance is centred in London though there are other important markets. At the heart of these activities is Lloyd's, a London corporation of insurers who issue most kinds of policy but are especially active in marine insurance. Lloyd's membership comprises insurers (or underwriters as they are called) and brokers. The underwriters work in *syndicates*[30] specialising in different types of risk. All insurance business with underwriter members must be placed through Lloyd's brokers, but anyone who chooses to place business with insurance companies rather than with Lloyd's may employ any broker, or may deal with the matter directly.

Under the Marine Insurance Act of 1906 all marine insurance contracts must be in the form of a policy. Marine policies may be either *valued* or *unvalued*, both classes being further subdivided into *voyage policies*, *time policies*, *mixed policies* and *floating* or *open policies*. A *valued policy* is one based on values agreed in advance and stated in the policy. With an *unvalued policy* the value of any loss (within the limit of the sum insured) is left to be assessed at the time of the loss.

A *voyage policy*, like a voyage charter, covers a particular ship for a stated voyage (eg London to Melbourne). A *time policy*, like a time charter, covers a particular ship for an agreed period of time not exceeding 12 months (eg from noon 5 April 1997 to noon 5 April 1998). A *mixed policy* combines the features of both time and voyage policies.

Policies may be issued to cover 'All risks', or they may contain clauses relieving the underwriter of certain risks. The premium for an all-risks policy is naturally higher than that for a policy with exemptions.

[30] **syndicates** groups formed for a common purpose

### 25.19 Request for an all-risks policy

**(a) Request**

Dear Sir/Madam

We wish to insure the following consignment against all risks for the sum of £10,000.

4 c/s Fancy Leather Goods, marked
1–4

These goods are now held at Number 2 Dock, Liverpool, waiting to be shipped by SS Rajputana due to leave for Bombay on Friday 23 June.

We require immediate cover as far as Bombay. Please let us have the policy as soon as it is ready. In the meantime please confirm that you hold the consignment covered.

Yours faithfully

**(b) Reply**

Dear

Thank you for your letter of 16 June asking us to cover the consignment of 4 cases of fancy leather goods from Liverpool to Bombay.

The premium for this cover is at the rate of £2.30% of the declared value of £10,000. The policy is being prepared and will be sent to you within a few days. Meanwhile, I confirm that we hold the consignment covered as from today.

Yours sincerely

### 25.20 Request to insure goods at docks

Dear Sir

Please arrange to insure for one calendar month from today the following consignment ex SS Ansdell from Hamburg:

2 cases Cameras, marked ⟨AR⟩ value £30,000 and now held at Royal Victoria Dock.

Please confirm that you hold the consignment covered and, when send the policy as soon as possible, together with your account for the premium.

Yours faithfully

# FLOATING AND OPEN-COVER POLICIES

Floating policies are sometimes used by merchants engaged in regular oversea trade. A policy of this kind covers a number of shipments by any ship to any port or ports that may be agreed. The merchant takes out a policy for a round sum, say £100,000. As each consignment is shipped it is 'declared' on a special form provided by the underwriter who records the value on a duplicate copy of the policy and issues a *certificate of insurance* stating that the consignment is covered. When the sum insured has been fully declared, (or, used up), a new policy is taken out.

Floating policies are sometimes referred to as 'Open' or 'Declaration' policies; but they are not greatly used today, being largely replaced by long-term policies issued on open cover. These open-cover policies extend the floating policy principle and cover all shipments for certain voyages or trades for an extended period, usually a year, *irrespective of their aggregate value*,[31] which may not be known, but with a specified limit for each shipment. The arrangement avoids any risk that a shipment will be left uninsured through oversight.

## 25.21 Enquiry for open-policy terms

### (a) Enquiry

> Dear Sirs
>
> Please quote your rate for an all-risks open policy for £100,000 to cover shipments of general merchandise[32] by Manchester Liners Ltd, from Manchester and Liverpool to Atlantic ports in Canada and the United States.
>
> As shipments are due to begin on 30 June, please let us have your quotation by return.
>
> Yours faithfully

### (b) Reply

> Dear Mr Yates
>
> Thank you for your enquiry of yesterday. Our rate for a £100,000 A R open policy on general merchandise by Manchester Liners from Manchester and Liverpool to Atlantic ports in Canada and the United States is £2.10% of declared value.
>
> This is an exceptionally low rate and we trust you will give us the opportunity to handle your insurance business.
>
> Yours sincerely

[31] **irrespective of their aggregate value** apart from their total worth
[32] **merchandise** articles of commerce

**(c) Acceptance**

> Dear Mr Summers
>
> Thank you for your letter of 19 June quoting your rate for an open policy of £100,000 covering consignments on the routes named.
>
> The rate of £2.10% is satisfactory. Please prepare and send us the policy as soon as possible. Meanwhile please let us have your cover note and statement of charges for our first shipment under the policy, which is:
>
> 3 c/s General Merchandise (Textiles), marked ⟨G⟩ Value £2,500.
>
> I hope to hear from you soon.
>
> Yours sincerely

## 25.22 Application for an open policy

> Dear Sirs
>
> We will shortly be making regular shipments of fancy leather goods to South America by approved ships. I should be glad if you would issue an a/r open policy for, say, £75,000 to cover these shipments from our warehouse at the above address to port of destination.
>
> All goods will be packed in wooden cases and despatched by road to Southampton and, less frequently, to Liverpool.
>
> Yours faithfully

## 25.23 Declaration of shipment of open policy

When accepting the application in 25.22 the underwriter will send the original policy to the merchant and also a supply of declaration forms, one of which the merchant will complete and send to the underwriter each time goods are shipped.

> Dear Sirs
>
> POLICY NO 18752
>
> Please note that under the above open policy, dated 18 March 19—, we have today shipped a third consignment, valued at £1,620, by SS Durham Castle, due to sail from Southampton tomorrow. The necessary declaration form is enclosed.
>
> This leaves an undeclared value on the policy of £48,380. Please confirm this figure as soon as possible.
>
> Yours faithfully

## 25.24 Renewal of an open policy (continuation of 25.23)

Dear Sir

POLICY NO 18752

We enclose a completed form declaring a further consignment, valued £2,325.

This will be the last full declaration under the above policy as the undeclared balance now stands at only £825, which will not be sufficient to cover our next consignment in December. Therefore please issue a new policy on the same terms and for the same amount, namely £75,000, as the current policy.

When we make the next shipment, we shall declare it against the present policy for £825 and against the new policy for the amount by which the value of the shipment exceeds this amount.

Yours faithfully

## AVERAGE

*Average* is a term used in marine insurance to refer to partial losses. *Particular average* means partial loss or damage caused by accident to the ship or to some particular cargo. Such losses are borne by the owner of the particular property suffering the damage. *General average* on the other hand refers to loss or damage carried out intentionally for the common good at a time when a ship and its cargo are in danger, as when cargo is thrown overboard to save the ship in a storm. Losses of this kind are shared by all who have a financial interest in the *venture*[33] in *proportion to*[34] the value of their interests.

As a rule, the manufacturer or merchant insures goods 'against all risks' and receives a WA policy containing a 'with average' clause. This means that the underwriters pay for partial losses. Under an FPA policy, which contains a 'free from particular average' clause, the underwriters pay only for total losses. An FPA policy will therefore be issued for a lower premium than a WA policy.

## MOTOR INSURANCE

The owner of a motor vehicle must possess a current road licence and is also required by law to insure against accidents to third parties, against death and bodily injury, and up to £250,000 for damages to property (1988 Road Traffic Act). It is customary, but not compulsory, to insure against loss or damage to the vehicle. All these risks may be covered by what is termed a 'comprehensive' policy, ie a single policy providing all-inclusive cover.

---

[33] **venture** the voyage and its risks
[34] **in proportion to** as relative share of the whole

## 25.25 Renewal of policy

Dear Mr Wrenshall

POLICY NO M 346871

Your policy and certificate of insurance as required by the Road Traffic Acts will expire at noon on 3 April next.

To maintain the insurance in force instructions should be given to your broker not later than, but preferably 6 days before, the date on which the policy expires so that you may receive the new certificate of insurance in time. You will realise that it is an offence under the Road Traffic Acts to use a vehicle on the road without a current certificate of insurance.

As a protection to you against any failure to observe the Acts I am enclosing a temporary cover note and certificate of insurance. However, please remember that this extension of cover applies only to that part of the policy which is necessary to comply with[35] the requirements of the Road Traffic Acts, namely third party personal injury liability and damage to third party property.

The temporary cover note should be kept carefully until the certificate of insurance reaches you.

Yours sincerely

---

[35] **comply with** carry out; observe

# USEFUL EXPRESSIONS

## Requests for cover

### Openings

1 Please quote your lowest All Risks rates for shipments of ... to ... .

2 Please hold us covered for the consignment referred to below (on the attached sheet).

3 We should be glad if you would provide cover of £. . . on . . ., in transit from ... to... .

4 We wish to renew this policy for the same amount and on the same terms as before.

### Closes

1 Please inform us on what terms this insurance can be arranged.

2 Please send us the necessary proposal form.

3 We leave the details to you, but wish to have the consignment covered against All Risks.

4 I shall be glad to receive your certificate of insurance as soon as possible.

## Replies to requests for cover

### Openings

1 Thank you for your letter of . . . . We quote below our terms for arranging cover for ... .

2. Your letter regarding renewal of open policy number ... covering ...

### Closes

1 The policy is being prepared and should reach you by ... . Meanwhile I confirm that we are holding you covered.

2 We undertake all classes of insurance and would welcome the opportunity to transact further business with you.

## Claims

### Openings

1 I regret to report the loss of . . . which is insured with you under the above policy.

2 I regret to report a fire in one of the bedrooms at this address.

3 I have completed and enclose the form of claim for loss of ... .

**Closes**

1 Please let me know any details you need from me when I submit my claim.

2 If you will make out your claim on the enclosed form we will attend to it immediately.

3 Your claim will be carefully considered when we receive the information requested.

# Index